CONSTITUTIONAL ENGAGEMENT IN A TRANSNATIONAL ERA

CONSTITUTIONAL ENGAGEMENT IN A TRANSNATIONAL ERA

VICKI C. JACKSON

OXFORD
UNIVERSITY PRESS

OXFORD
UNIVERSITY PRESS

Oxford University Press, Inc., publishes works that further Oxford University's objective of excellence in research, scholarship, and education.

Oxford New York
Auckland Cape Town Dar es Salaam Hong Kong Karachi Kuala Lumpur Madrid Melbourne Mexico City Nairobi New Delhi Shanghai Taipei Toronto

With offices in
Argentina Austria Brazil Chile Czech Republic France Greece Guatemala Hungary Italy Japan Poland Portugal Singapore South Korea Switzerland Thailand Turkey Ukraine Vietnam

Published by Oxford University Press, Inc.
198 Madison Avenue, New York, New York 10016

Library of Congress Cataloging-in-Publication Data

Jackson, Vicki C.
Constitutional engagement in a transnational era / Vicki C. Jackson.
p. cm.
Includes bibliographical references and index.
ISBN 978-0-19-533344-2 (hardback. : alk. paper)
1. Constitutional law--Foreign influences. 2. Law and globalization. I. Title.
K3165.J3253 2009
342--dc22 2008053011

1 2 3 4 5 6 7 8 9

Printed in the United States of America on acid-free paper

Note to Readers
This publication is designed to provide accurate and authoritative information in regard to the subject matter covered. It is based upon sources believed to be accurate and reliable and is intended to be current as of the time it was written. It is sold with the understanding that the publisher is not engaged in rendering legal, accounting, or other professional services. If legal advice or other expert assistance is required, the services of a competent professional person should be sought. Also, to confirm that the information has not been affected or changed by recent developments, traditional legal research techniques should be used, including checking primary sources where appropriate.

(Based on the Declaration of Principles jointly adopted by a Committee of the American Bar Association and a Committee of Publishers and Associations.)

CONTENTS

ACKNOWLEDGMENTS AND PERMISSIONS

This book has benefitted from the input and reactions of more colleagues and friends than I can possibly thank here. I want to single out Mark Tushnet, my intellectual companion in comparative constitutional law for more than a decade, for years of conversation that have influenced my own thinking. Although we often see things differently, I benefit greatly from his insights and reactions.

Many colleagues have read and commented on chapters of this book, or have provided feedback in response to my presentation of its ideas, or were willing to talk through ideas or concerns in ways that benefitted the work. Robert Ahdieh, Roger Alford, Susan Low Bloch, Richard Briffault, Sarah Cleveland, David Fontana, Gillian Metzger, Julie O'Sullivan, Judith Resnik, David Schneiderman, Jane Stromseth, Dan Tarullo, Bob Taylor, Mark Tushnet and Carlos Vázquez read all or substantial portions of the book, and I have benefitted greatly from their valuable advice and intellectual generosity. Other colleagues at Georgetown who have provided significant assistance include Alex Aleinikoff, Judy Areen, Winfried Brugger, Peter Byrne, Richard Diamond, Jim Feinerman, Steve Goldberg, Mike Gottesman, Lisa Heinzerling, John Jackson, Neal Katyal, Patricia King, David Luban, Marty Lederman, Carrie Menkel-Meadow, Gary Peller, Wendy Collins Perdue, Susan Deller Ross, Mike Seidman, Gerry Spann, Bob Stumberg, Jay Thomas, and Robin West. Colleagues from elsewhere and jurists who have likewise been helpful include Bruce Ackerman, Aharon Barak, Daphne Barak-Erez, George Bermann, Christina Duffy Burnett, Paolo Carozza, Wen-Chen Chang, Margit Cohen, Rosalind Dixon, Jeff Dunoff, Richard Fallon, Victor Ferreres Comella, Martha Field, George Fletcher, Barry Friedman, Lech Garlicki, Ruth Bader Ginsberg, Richard Goldstone, Jamal Greene, Tania Groppi, Tara Grove, Lani Guinier, Daniel Halberstam, Sarah Harding, Elon Harel, Karen Knop, Donald Kommers, Daryl Levinson, Tokujin Matsudaira, Dan Meltzer, Frank Michelman, Martha Minow, Henry Monaghan, Trevor Morrison, Christina Murray, Gerry Neuman, Noah Novogrodsky, Kate O'Regan, Cesare Pinelli, Mark Rahdert, Balakrishnan Rajagopal, Neomi Ro, Theunis Roux, Kim Rubenstein, Cheryl Saunders, Yuval Shany, Andrea Simoncini, Larry Solum, Peter Spiro, Adrienne Stone, David Super, Adrian Vermeule, Ann Wallwork, and Ben Zipursky.

I want to express appreciation for the opportunities to present ideas or chapters, as they were developing, in the Geoffrey Sawer Lecture at Australia National University and at faculty workshops or seminars at the law schools at George Washington, Georgetown, Columbia, Harvard, Hebrew University, UCLA and William & Mary. I thank the organizers of and faculty and in some cases student participants in those workshops and seminars for their helpful comments.

I am very grateful to Dean Alex Aleinikoff and to the Georgetown Law Center for generous support of my research for this book. The professional and support staffs at Georgetown are unexcelled in their commitment to helping faculty with their scholarship. I am especially indebted to the excellent librarians at Georgetown, who provided invaluable aid, including especially Barbara Monroe, Marylin Raisch and Mabel Shaw, to whom I turned on countless occasions.

A number of able and cheerful Research Assistants have checked and rechecked sources, including Tom Davies, Nancy Dinsmore, Christopher Dryer, William Durkin, Meredith Esser, Lauren Grugan, Cindy Heidelberg, Sonam (Sandy) Henderson, Jennifer Hojaiban, Hayley Horowitz, Pablo Kapusta, Nazneen Mehta, Devin Mills, Peng Wu, Julian Perez, Jeff Poulin, Sushila Rao, Dan Taylor, and Loretta Wiatr. Faculty assistants and administrative staff, at Georgetown (and at Columbia and Harvard, where I was a visiting professor in the Fall and Spring of 2008, respectively) including Terican Gross, Sylvia Johnson, Kate Minette, Nicole Patton, Toni Steadman, and Steven Wagner, have helped me in many ways.

Any errors that remain after all this help are solely my responsibility.

* * *

I am grateful to all of the following publications listed in this paragraph for their publishing my earlier essays or articles relating to the topics of this book and for permission (where relevant) to draw from those earlier works, in which some ideas in or some parts of this work first appeared, including: *Book Review, Being Proportional About Proportionality*, 21 Const. Commentary 803 (2004) (reviewing David M. Beatty, The Ultimate Rule of Law (2004)); *Narratives of Federalism: Of Continuities and Comparative Constitutional Experience*, 51 Duke L. J. 223 (2001); *Transnational Challenges to Constitutional Law: Convergence, Resistance, Engagement*, 35 Fed'l L. Rev. 161 (2007) (Austral.); *Constitutions as "Living Trees?' Comparative Constitutional Law and Interpretive Metaphors*, 75 Fordham L. Rev. 921 (2006); *Constitutional Law and Transnational Comparisons: The Youngstown Decision and American Exceptionalism*, 30 Harv. J. L. & Pub. Pol'y 191 (2006); *The Supreme Court, 2004 Term—Comment: Constitutional Comparisons: Convergence, Resistance, Engagement*, 119 Harv. L. Rev. 109 (2005); *Comparative Constitutional Federalism and Transnational Judicial Discourse*, 2 Int'l J. Const. L. 91 (2004); *Comparative Constitutional Federalism: its Strengths and Limits*, Chapter 2 in Le Fédéralisme dans tous ses états: The States and Moods of Federalism; (English title:) The States and Moods of Federalism: Governance, Identity and Methodology (Jean-François Gaudreault-DesBiens & Fabien Gélinas eds., Bruylant Bruxelles, 2005); *Transnational Discourse, Relational Authority and the U.S. Court; Gender Equality*, 37 Loyola of Los Angeles L. Rev. 271 (2003); *Multi-Valenced Constitutional Interpretation and Constitutional Comparisons: An Essay in Honor of Mark Tushnet*, 26 Quinnipiac L. Rev. 599 (2008); *Holistic Constitutional Interpretation: Fitzpatrick v. Bitzer and Our Bifurcated Constitution*, 53 Stan. L. Rev. 1259 (2001); *Holistic Interpretation, Comparative Constitutionalism and Fiss-ian*

Freedoms, 58 U. MIAMI L. REV. 265 (2003); and *What's In a Name? Reflections on Timing, Naming and Constitution-Making*, 49 WM & MARY L. REV. 1249 (2008). I also thank the University of Pennsylvania Journal of Constitutional Law for their permission concerning Vicki C. Jackson, *Ambivalent Resistance and Comparative Constitutionalism: Opening Up the Conversation on "Proportionality," Rights and Federalism*, 1 U. PA. J. CONST. L. 583 (1999), and I thank the Notre Dame Law Review for its permission concerning *Principle and Compromise in Constitutional Adjudication: The Eleventh Amendment and State Sovereign Immunity*,

Vol. 75 NOTRE DAME LAW REVIEW, Page 953 (2000).
Reprinted with permission © by Notre Dame Law Review, University of Notre Dame.[1]

I thank my colleagues Julie O'Sullivan and Carlos Vázquez for permission to draw from materials that we collectively prepared for a course at Georgetown Law Center, called "Law in a Global Context: Week One," concerning the *Soering* case and related case law from the European Court of Human Rights.

* * *

Most of all, I want to thank my spouse, whose loving support across all areas of my life has been a blessing to me for over thirty years, and my three children, each of whose very existence is a joy to me and who, like their father, have been more than patient with my work habits. I am grateful to have so wonderful a family to love.

Vicki C. Jackson
December 2008

1. The publisher bears responsibility for any errors which may have occurred in reprinting or editing of material from this work. [Notice required by Notre Dame Law Review].

A NOTE TO READERS ON CITATIONS AND ABBREVIATIONS

Although Blue Book legal citation form is generally followed, shorter forms are on occasion used, for example, to refer to the two major acts that, with others, make up the Canadian constitution,[*] or to the conventions or treaties set forth below. Citations are sometimes consolidated in single footnotes.

References, quotations, and citations to foreign constitutions are generally to whatever English translation is available from official government sources for the country involved.[†] If no official source is available, references or quotations are checked against multiple sources. If multiple sources are not available, or disagree, or if a government source is difficult to find, the specific source of the translation is noted.

Research for this book was largely completed by academic year 2007–08; materials published thereafter are for the most part not included.

The following abbreviations will be used from time to time:

ACHR—American Convention on Human Rights[‡]

CEDAW—Convention on the Elimination of All Forms of Discrimination against Women[§]

---

[*]*See* Constitution Act, 1867, 30-31 Vict., ch. 3, § 22 (U.K.), *as reprinted in* R.S.C., No. 5 (Appendix 1985); Constitution Act, 1982, being Schedule B to the Canada Act 1982, ch. 11 (U.K.). The Canadian Charter of Rights and Freedoms is Part I of the Constitution Act, 1982, and will hereafter be referred to simply as the Charter of Rights and Freedoms, 1982.

[†]For example, except as otherwise noted, references to the English translations of the German Basic Law would be to the Basic Law for the Federal Republic of Germany (as amended to June 2008), *transl. by* Christian Tomuschat and Professor David P. Currie, *available at* the German Bundestag's website, http://www.bundestag.de/htdocs_e/info/infomat/basic_english/basiclaw_artikel.html; references to the English translations of the Constitution of Spain are from the Spanish Senate's website, http://www.senado.es/constitu_i/index.html; references to English translations of the French Constitution of 4 October 1958 are to the French National Assembly's website, http://www.assemblee-nationale.fr/english/8ab.asp; and references to English translations of the Federal Constitution of the Swiss Confederation of April 18, 1999 are from the Federal Authorities of the Swiss Confederation webpage, http://www.admin.ch/org/polit/00083/index.html?lang=en.

[‡]American Convention on Human Rights, Nov. 22, 1969, O.A.S.T.S. No. 36, 1144 U.N.T.S. 123.

[§]Convention on the Elimination of All Forms of Discrimination against Women, Dec. 18, 1979, 1249 U.N.T.S. 13.

ECHR—European Convention for the Protection of Human Rights and Fundamental Freedoms[¶]

ECJ—European Court of Justice

ECtHR—European Court of Human Rights

EU—European Union

IACtHR—Inter-American Court of Human Rights

IACHR—Inter-American Commission on Human Rights

ICCPR—International Covenant on Civil and Political Rights[**]

ICESCR—International Covenant on Economic, Social and Cultural Rights[††]

ICJ—International Court of Justice

NAFTA—North American Free Trade Agreement[‡‡]

UDHR—Universal Declaration of Human Rights[§§]

UK—United Kingdom

UN—United Nations

UNHRC—United Nations Human Rights Committee

WTO—World Trade Organization

[¶]European Convention for the Protection of Human Rights and Fundamental Freedoms, Nov. 4, 1950, 213 U.N.T.S. 221. This treaty will sometimes be referred to as the European Convention on Human Rights or the ECHR. References are generally to the Convention as Amended by Protocol 11, European Treaty Series 155, entered into force Nov. 1, 1998.

[**]International Covenant on Civil and Political Rights, Dec. 16, 1966, 999 U.N.T.S. 171.

[††]International Covenant on Economic, Social and Cultural Rights, Dec. 16, 1966, 993 U.N.T.S. 3.

[‡‡]North American Free Trade Agreement, U.S.-Can.-Mex., Dec. 17, 1992, 32 I.L.M. 289, 605 (1993).

[§§]Universal Declaration of Human Rights, G.A. Res. 217A, U.N. GAOR, 3d Sess., 1st plen. mtg., U.N. Doc. A/810 (Dec. 12, 1948).

INTRODUCTION

Constitutional Cosmology—Convergence, Resistance, and Engagement

A committee of the House of Representatives of the U.S. Congress holds hearings on a bill providing that U.S. courts "may not rely upon" laws, rules, or judicial decisions of foreign countries or international organizations in deciding constitutional cases.[1] The Lord Chief Justice of England and Wales issues a "practice direction" regulating the citation to foreign law in briefs before the courts.[2] The Constitution of South Africa requires judges to consider international law in interpreting that constitution's Bill of Rights, and specifically authorizes the consideration of foreign law.[3] Argentina's constitution incorporates several named human rights instruments as of constitutional stature.[4] Colombia's Constitutional Court interprets its constitution to preclude certain bilateral investment treaties; in partial response, the constitution is amended.[5] France amends its constitution to permit judicial review of laws after they are enacted, moving away from its longstanding constitutional opposition to judges having such power.[6]

These and other events are manifestations of the new universe in which domestic constitutions operate—an increasingly transnational legal environment of international treaties, customary international law, multilateral and bilateral agreements, and supranational infrastructures of trade law and human rights law. This new universe also includes pressures and influences from transnational business firms, human rights groups, and social movements (in the global North and South) that seek to reconstruct and use law at local, national, and global levels. It includes, as well, increased comparative judicial awareness reflected in cross-national references in constitutional court decisions around the world, and some degree of transnational convergence towards judicial enforcement of constitutions. How do these multiple transnational phenomena affect our understanding of the role of constitutions and of courts in deciding constitutional cases? How do constitutions and constitutional courts affect these transnational legal phenomena? Is there an emerging phenomenon of "transnational constitutionalism" and, if so, how should it be conceptualized? How should the U.S. Supreme Court respond? This book will explore these questions.

Transnationalism and Constitutional Review Recent U.S. debate over the role of transnational law (that is, both foreign and international law) in constitutional interpretation reflects both the gravitational pull of transnational legal sources and resistance to their influence.[7] It has been clear since the early 1990s that something transnational is reflected in the spread of constitutional review and in the discourse of constitutional courts around the world. Transnational regional legal arrangements, especially in Europe, have assumed increasing legal significance, and European scholars have begun to focus on the role of national constitutions and constitutionalism under "a plurality of legal orders."[8] The global economy has developed an increasingly legalized infrastructure in the World Trade Organization (WTO). The development of transnational common markets, both in the EU and elsewhere, may have diminished the importance of national states in conferring economic benefits, thereby providing fertile conditions for the strengthening of subnational ethnic nationalisms and/or regionalisms and demands for devolution. Moreover, economic globalization, the rise of multinational businesses and nongovernmental organizations, and privatization of government functions have arguably drawn power away from national states, while at the same time occasioning social justice movements that resist or seek to reconstruct relationships of law and society.[9] Both new technologies and new threats cut across national boundaries, challenging the functions of traditional national states and calling forth transnational responses, sometimes produced under the auspices of international organizations.[10]

Yet, in the same period, constitutional review at the national level is becoming increasingly prominent. We have seen "super-activist" courts in India and Israel; the sometimes activist, sometimes deferential American and German courts; and the self-consciously internationalist South African and Canadian courts. Constitutional law and constitutional rights are spreading even to some of the regimes most deeply committed to parliamentary sovereignty, with both New Zealand and the United Kingdom incorporating—through quasi-constitutional statutes—legal norms drawn from transnational or international sources. Nascent (though even that may be too strong an adjective) constitutional review may even be emerging in China.[11]

These two sets of developments may at first seem contradictory. If transnational legal, economic, and social forces are becoming more significant, why would there be so much development of law—and constitutional law, no less—at the national level? There are many reasons: some sociological, some political, and some distinctly legal. Some of the growth in national constitutions and constitutional law is a continuing consequence of decolonization and foreign withdrawal, not only in Africa but in Eastern Europe and the states of the former Soviet Union; adopting or amending constitutions is a legal signal of regime change. The growth of transnational regimes and the possibilities of external support they provide may have encouraged smaller areas that formerly might have remained as dependencies or semi-autonomous regions within one country to seek independent status as their own countries. Though neither of these factors account for the robust embrace of constitutional review in countries such as South Africa and Israel, or the UK's constitutional changes, changes in the global sociology of law—as well as political factors internal to the polities—may do so. Having a national constitution, enforced by a court, has become part of the "'script' of modernity."[12] Part of the story also includes a changing legal consciousness, in both elite and popular opinion, about the benefits of law as enforced by courts, changes arising from subtle (at times acknowledged, at times invisible) influences of other constitutional regimes, and the new face of international law in the post–World War II period. Indeed, the growth of the transnational may elicit reactive resort to specifically national constitutions to demarcate a now more contested sphere of national identity and decision-making. Thus, part of the story has to do with the more specific roles, functions, and attractions of national constitutions.

The Distinctiveness of Constitutions as Law Constitutions are a distinctive form of law. First, they are bearers of particular conceptions of national identity. The U.S. Constitution is said to provide a form of secular religion, in a sense constituting a basis of national self-identity. But even where a constitution is not *constitutive* of national identity, it is likely to reflect and express distinctive markers of national identity—from flags, to territorial boundaries, to values.

Second, constitutions are typically entrenched to a greater degree than statutes. Formal mechanisms for their amendment or replacement require greater legislative majorities, multiple readings, agreements by some number of constituent units, referenda, or some combination thereof, in contrast to those for ordinary lawmaking. Although in practice statutory frameworks in the rest of the legal order may have greater longevity than constitutions in some countries,[13] aspirations for longevity and for constitutions to function as foundational law are widely associated with national constitutions.

Third, national constitutions typically address a broad array of subjects, internal and external: They provide a framework for governance (establishing offices and procedures to fill them, allocating governance responsibilities, and addressing relationships among different parts of the government); they specify rights held by citizens or residents of the country; and they identify responsibilities for national defense and for legal relationships with other countries and the international community. Finally, constitutions typically provide some mechanism for their own enforcement, and many authorize one or more courts to apply, enforce, or protect the constitution through their adjudicatory (or in some cases advisory) capacities. Constitutions, and the interpretive evolution that their formal entrenchment may encourage, are thus concerned with a complex mix of values, goals, and functions.

The Functions of Judicial Review If constitutions serve complex, and at times conflicting, purposes, so, too, may this be said of judicial review. Political scientists might focus on judicial review as a signal of a credible commitment to enforce the constitution; or they may understand constitutional review as an effort by elites to entrench existing privilege or power. Constitutions and constitutional review may be viewed as devices to protect existing rights holders from the adverse effects on their standing and interests of increased democratic mobilizations; Ran Hirschl, for example, has argued that where judicial constitutional review begins without any obvious regime change or emergency, it is often in response to "growing influence on the part of historically disenfranchised or underrepresented groups" that threaten existing elites.[14] On other accounts, strong judicial review (or judicial "activism," measured by a court's propensity to find government acts unconstitutional) is related to the degree of political competition; systems characterized by a very dominant single party are unlikely to see strong judicial review.[15] If political competition is a precondition for strong judicial review, then, it might be inferred, one function of judicial review is to sustain the conditions for its own institutional efficacy—to wit, a system of political competition. Still another account offered by political scientists is that constitutional review is related to vertical divisions of powers, or federalism; here, as in the political competition model, it is in the mutual interest of existing power holders to enforce an agreed-on balance of power through a more neutral arbiter that forms a foundation for judicial review.[16] On all of these accounts, it would seem, judicially enforced constitutional law functions both to deter potential "bad acting" by powerful political forces and to provide opportunities for losers in the political arena to continue their contest in the courts, under the banner of the constitution.

But these functions—including that of providing some reassurance to those who might lose on issues in political forums that constitutional lines can be enforced elsewhere, and thus providing added stability to the overall system—do not exhaust the possibilities. Constitutions that are difficult to amend may represent "precommitment" strategies, whose purposes include at once providing a check on government abuse by separating powers so as to preserve liberty and promote deliberation and good decisions, and establishing a framework for elections, political institutions, and relationships that enable and provide for effective governance. Precommitment in these terms may also help preserve the conditions of democracy and political competition—not only (as political scientists might suggest) for institutionally self-interested but also for public-regarding reasons.[17] Constitutions may also "precommit" a polity to protect inalienable or "prepolitical" human rights, especially from majority action, as well as to enforce agreements designed to overcome collective action problems and maximize longterm benefit within the country, for example, by foreclosing internal trade barriers or barriers to free movement.[18] Judicial review is a key mechanism (though not necessarily the only one) for enforcing these precommitments, and to the extent that rights are conceived as "prepolitical," inalienable rights of all persons, international or comparative law on point may be relevant.

Additionally, constitutions may have the purposes of protecting very particular rights or powers that, for historic reasons, are important within a polity, or of enforcing foundational compromises, without which the initial agreement to function as a polity would not have been possible and which remain of continuing importance. It is perhaps only in this latter sense of protecting foundational compromises that constitutions, enforced through judicial review, may function, at least for a period of time, to take highly contentious issues "off the ordinary political agenda."[19] In contrast to the view of a constitution "as a philosophical work in which everything is deduced from a principle,"[20] working constitutions combine commitment to high principles with hard-fought political compromises—as Federalist No. 43 noted, "theoretic reasoning in this, as in most other cases, must be qualified by the lessons of practice."[21] Courts' enforcement of these compromises may permit them to be made in the first place and allow a union to be sustained over time. Moreover, some argue, judicial review performs a validating function, as well as a checking or enforcement function, providing an added form of public legitimacy to those laws that are upheld.[22]

Another important function of a national constitution is the expressive, representing national values and particularities—a function that might lend itself to resort to comparative law in resolving constitutional controversies as courts identify aversive and affiliative examples.[23] In some legal cultures constitutions might function less as precommitment strategies than as "power maps," designed more to describe than to constrain power, or as proclaimers of national sovereignty to the rest of the world—expressing national identity, and constituting the nation as a player in the world community, with capacities to conduct relations with other nations and to be regarded as exercising the powers of a territorial state in international law.[24] In this setting, judicial review (if it exists at all) would be expected not to constrain government but to facilitate its instrumental goals. But other countries might adopt constitutions as legal and aspirational frameworks designed to help effectuate dramatic political transformations—and for similar reasons may commit themselves to some international legal regimes, or to judicial interpretation to assure compliance with some transnational norms.[25]

National constitutions, and their interpretation by courts, thus may be said to perform both internal and external functions, at once clarifying the legal foundation for a state to function as a national state in the world community, providing for its internal allocations of powers and governance, expressing a particular national identity, checking that governance remains within the limits of the constitution as law, and promoting the legitimacy of governance under the constitution. While some national constitutions may be designed primarily as a show of sovereignty and modernity, and expected to function (if at all) primarily as instruments of government policy or entrenched elites, this book is concerned mainly with those constitutions intended to constrain their governments, and enforced (at least in part) by courts. Such constitutions may be designed to effectuate high principles and political compromises; to sustain a system of checks on arbitrary power, promoting order and stability while at the same time providing the flexibility needed for effective governance; to provide a forum for political losers and small minorities apart from the forum of politics; to provide for the conditions of politically competitive democracy and of material well-being; and to protect the capacity of the nation to deal with external threats and with other nations.

An Expanding Universe of Law It is much harder today than in the past for constitutional courts to avoid taking positions on the role of international or foreign law. Debate and discussion reflect increased awareness of and access to such law. The Internet and its search engines have created enormous accessibility of resources. Increasing numbers of foreign courts provide translations of their decisions into English.[26] The valuable reference tool, *Constitutions of the Countries of the World*, has developed an online edition, expanding readers' ability to access knowledge about foreign constitutional texts, as have many governments' decisions to post translations of their constitutions online.[27] Due to the work of the Venice Commission, developments in the constitutional jurisprudence of the countries of Europe (and several non-European members) are identified and made available in regular summary bulletins.[28] Decisions of the International Court of Justice and other international tribunals are available online, as are UN human rights conventions and decisions of the UN committees that interpret these instruments; the World Trade Organization's website includes a repository of appellate body reports, available in English, French, and Spanish.

Not only is foreign and international law more accessible, but there is simply more of it in the world today—more constitutional law, and more international law, touching on topics historically viewed as belonging to the realm of constitutional law. The decisions of the European Court of Justice (ECJ) and of the European Court of Human Rights (ECtHR) provide a rich jurisprudence. Both courts were created after World War II; their decisions are available online, in English and in other languages. The number of countries in the world has almost "quadrupled since 1900,"[29] and the number having written constitutions has also increased dramatically.[30] In 1948, forty-eight member states of the UN General Assembly voted to adopt the Universal Declaration of Human Rights (UDHR), with eight member states abstaining;[31] by mid-2008 the two major human rights covenants designed to implement the UDHR's principles had 162 and 159 parties, respectively.[32] So it is not simply a matter of increased awareness and accessibility but also an increase in transnational sources that are arguably relevant to a broad range of legal questions.

Historic Relationships of Constitutions to a Global Audience Yet the interface between constitutional interpretation and the transnational is not entirely new. National constitutions and constitutional law have been entailed in a set of transnational relationships from their modern beginnings.[33] "We the People of the United States," as the Preamble to the U.S. Constitution says, were addressing themselves not just to a domestic audience but to a broader world stage. In ideological terms, the U.S. Constitution was seen as a test case for a more democratic political philosophy, an "experiment in self-rule" whose success or failure "might well determine the fate of republican government for all humanity."[34] A copy of the Constitution was reportedly sent to Britain by ship on September 18, 1787, the day after it was signed by its drafters.[35] Functionally, the Constitution written in 1787 was motivated in important part by concerns that the existing government under the Articles of Confederation was too weak in its ability to deal with foreign governments and foreign pressure, unable to secure compliance with treaty obligations, and suffering disadvantage in foreign trade and commerce and from threat of war.[36] Indeed, George Washington, as president of the

Constitutional Convention, began the substance of his transmittal letter sending the proposed Constitution to the Congress by noting that "The friends of our country have long seen and desired, that the power of making war, peace and treaties, that of levying money and regulating commerce, and the correspondent executive and judicial authorities should be fully and effectually vested in the general government of the Union."[37]

An important goal of the U.S. Constitution was to help build a united nation strong enough to earn the respect of European nations, in order to avoid foreign wars and be able to engage in foreign commerce;[38] the audience for the constitution-making project was at once domestic and foreign. Each of the three branches of the federal government—Congress, the President, and the judiciary—was given jurisdictional competence over matters relating to the external affairs of the nation: the Congress in its legislative powers to declare war, to define and punish piracies and "Offenses against the Law of Nations," to regulate foreign commerce, and to issue letters of marque and reprisal; the President in his competence to "receive Ambassadors and other public Ministers," and to make treaties and nominate ambassadors subject to Senate approval; and the federal courts in their jurisdiction over "all Cases affecting Ambassadors, other public Ministers and Consuls" and over cases "arising under" U.S. treaties.[39]

A number of the earliest cases before the U.S. Supreme Court involved claims of right by foreign governments or foreign citizens; in one very early decision the Supreme Court concluded that a foreign nation could not establish a court within the United States without positive authority by treaty, thus affirming the importance of the national territorial boundary.[40] In 1796, the Court in *Ware v. Hylton* articulated and applied the principle of the supremacy of federal law found in Article VI of the Constitution; in a case involving claims brought by British creditors under the Treaty of 1783, it held that a state law in violation of a federal treaty was invalid.[41] In other cases in its early years the U.S. Constitution was interpreted and cases were decided with evident awareness of the law of nations and the respects in which the Constitution was intended to facilitate compliance with that law (or of how it represented a departure from international law principles with respect to the legal status and authority of the American states).[42]

In other countries, as well, the promulgation of national constitutions has had as one important goal establishing the status of the country on the international scene and establishing a form of government that could use that status to the benefit of the inhabitants. As H.W.O. Okoth-Ogendo has written, "The idea of and the necessity for a constitution appear fully established in the minds of state elites in Africa. . . . [T]he constitution is an act without which the polity can have no legitimate or sovereign existence; it is of no small significance, for example, that the very first article of most African constitutions *declare[s]* that each respective country is *sovereign*."[43] This pattern is by no means limited to African nations. The first "title" of the French Constitution of 1958 is on "Sovereignty," and addresses the sovereign status and nature of France in several articles; the first article, which precedes title I, declares France an "indivisible... Republic." Section one of the Spanish Constitution speaks of its "national sovereignty." Article I of the 1999 Swiss constitution begins by defining the Swiss Confederation. Section 1 of the 1996 South African constitution declares South Africa to be "one, sovereign, democratic state." Each of these constitutions, moreover, addresses various "foreign affairs" powers. It is a distinctive function of constitutions as a form of law that they address both internal and external relationships of their polity, allocating competences to engage in a range of functions associated with national governments acting in a world community.

Three Postures toward the Transnational These multiple purposes complicate any effort to define or defend an appropriate attitude toward transnational law for all constitutions and all their purposes, and with respect to the many different forms and sources of international and comparative law. Indeed, there are a number of postures that domestic national constitutions and their judicial interpreters could take vis-à-vis the transnational legal environment, described in more detail in the first three chapters of this book.

One is a posture of *resistance*, differentiation, or indifference, which is often associated with a particular kind of nationalist, expressive use of constitutionalism. On this view, only those legal norms that have been adopted in accordance with the controlling procedural rules within the particular national legal community (and thus reflect the presumed will or identity of that particular community), should be considered in interpreting law, and both foreign and international law are regarded with some skepticism or suspicion as sources of constitutional understandings. In the United States, Justice Antonin Scalia has been a leading proponent of this posture, though resistance to treating foreign or international law as persuasive authority has also been advanced by a leading pragmatist, Richard Posner.[44] Postures of resistance to the foreign are found not only in interpretive debates in the United States, but also in some other countries' constitutional provisions themselves—for example, those that purport to preclude foreign investment in or control of certain sectors of national life.

At the opposite end of the spectrum of postures lies one of national identification with transnational and international legal norms—a posture that might view domestic constitutional law as a site for the implementation of international legal norms, or, alternatively, as a participant in a decentralized but normatively progressive process of transnational norm convergence. As discussed in Chapter 2, such a posture of *convergence* might be based on a universalist view of rights or on a positivist commitment to universalist values or international law set forth in founding national documents; alternatively, instrumental, institutionalist concerns that "checks" on government from outside the polity are necessary to subserve domestic legal values may support a posture of convergence. Convergence might have weaker and stronger versions, entailing different forms of presumption. Scholars have made arguments for cosmopolitan approaches to the interpretation of basic rights, and some national constitutions manifest this posture by incorporating specific international human rights instruments into their constitutions or treating them as of constitutional stature.

Still a third posture—one that occupies a large middle ground on what might be conceived as a continuum of postures—is one of *engagement* with the transnational, founded on commitments to judicial deliberation and open to the possibilities of either harmony or dissonance between national self-understandings and transnational norms. As discussed in Chapter 3, a posture of engagement might assume simply that interpretation of national fundamental law can be improved by engagement with transnational norms, on those occasions where lawyers or jurists have some relevant knowledge and where issues are relatively "open" within the domestic discourse. Alternatively, an engagement posture might proceed on the idea that the concept of domestic constitutional law itself must now be understood in relation to transnational norms, an assumption that might argue for engagement with the transnational across a wider range of cases and issues. Both aspects of this posture are reflected in the constitutional decisions of a number of countries, and by constitutional provisions, as in South Africa, which specifically authorize courts to consider foreign law and require consideration of international law in interpreting the national bill of rights. Engagement models of considering foreign or international law, without a presumption that it necessarily be followed, fit comfortably within both "purposive" and "common law" forms of constitutional interpretation.

This schematic is necessarily overdrawn. These postures can best be understood as arrayed along a continuum, so that stronger forms of engagement may be very similar to milder forms of convergence. Moreover, one can see different postures being exhibited by members of the same court in the same country; there may be other postures, including a process-oriented posture that views constitutions as a guide to choice of law in conflicts-of-law settings. Further, within each of these three major postures there are important differences in jurisdictional assumptions and doctrinal implications; different postures may coexist, for example, as where a country internalizes supranational legal norms but does not entirely reject instances of "resistance" as courts seek to maintain the possibility of national distinctiveness in the interpretation of such norms.

The schematic's application may also be limited by the countries whose opinions I have studied, which include only those countries with courts authorized to interpret and give effect to a domestic constitution—thus excluding such large and important countries as China.[45] Within this limited set, furthermore, I have focused primarily on opinions and decisions of courts in countries with established political freedoms and rule of law traditions,[46] with well-developed jurisprudence, and whose opinions are available in English or in English translations (including the courts of Australia, Canada, France, Germany, India, Israel, South Africa, the United Kingdom, the United States, and the two major

European courts).[47] I do, however, discuss some opinions from courts in other countries whose jurisprudence is less well known.

With all its limitations and caveats, the argument in the first three chapters is that these postures—of convergence, resistance, and engagement—provide important insights into the relationships between domestic constitutions and the transnational, and capture a significant range of the reactions and relationships one sees looking at constitutional courts' opinions. Each of the first three chapters of the book seeks to provide a richer description of these postures, and will explore the jurisprudential assumptions, doctrinal characteristics, and related tendencies associated with each. The effort is one of positive analysis, to elucidate both the obvious and the less visible sets of relationships and influences—of attraction or resistance—among national constitutions and between national constitutions and transnational legal regimes, and in so doing to describe the challenges of the more complex new universe of legal orders in which constitutions now operate. These opening chapters will show how domestic constitutional interpretation proceeds, implicitly or explicitly, within a transnational framework of differentiation, harmonization, or engagement.

Transnational Sources, Foreign and International As readers will see, both international law and foreign law are viewed in this book as potential "transnational" sources of insight or influence, positive or negative, on the interpretation of constitutions. At times I will distinguish between them, as one must. International law may impose international legal obligations on countries; and international law plays a more prominent role in convergence postures than in postures of engagement. Distinctions and comparisons between the role of international and foreign law in constitutional interpretation—including the actual or potential binding force of the source of law, the differential dangers of selectivity in the use of these sources, and the different degrees of what I call "legal seriousness" entailed in the diverse mechanisms for formation, interpretation, application and enforcement of law—are discussed in Chapter 6.

Although there are important debates about the nature of international law, about the relationship between its legitimacy and binding force and the processes by which it is made or determined, about the degree to which international obligations are internally binding in different nations, and about the authority of different organs of national government to give effect to customary international law or to treaty law,[48] these questions are *not* the primary focus of this work. This book is concerned less with defining those situations in which international law, as such, is internally binding than with exploring the possibilities of international law serving as a reflective or persuasive resource in the interpretation of domestic constitutions themselves (and, to a lesser degree, the impact of domestic constitutional interpretation on international law). Full understanding of the emerging cosmology of constitutionalism in the twenty-first century should encompass all of these (and many other) issues about international law, including the degree to which aspects of international law should be regarded as in a sense constitutional. But while this last topic is addressed briefly in the final chapter, the focus of most of this book is on national constitutions and their interpretation.

Engagement and Constitutional Law in the United States The second part of the book, beginning with Chapter 4, takes a more normative stance, asking what the posture of the United States Supreme Court *should* be toward the role of transnational law in constitutional adjudication. Resistance, I argue, is neither plausible nor normatively attractive as an across-the-board posture, though it may be appropriate on some issues. The complete autonomy of law is no longer a part of legal self-consciousness, so an approach to interpretation that requires indifference or resistance to widely available knowledge about other legal systems is unlikely to be effective and, if relied upon, will do more to conceal than to constrain intuitive comparative views. Resistance or indifference, to the extent that it is rooted in theories of originalism,[49] may be internally conflicted, since originalism may well support transnational interpretive strategies with respect to at least some terms and provisions. Moreover, most constitutional interpretation is dominated not by specific forms of originalism but by more purposive and multi-valenced approaches, under which transnational sources may appropriately be considered.[50] Although concerns for the democratic legitimacy of constitutional interpretation, along with the challenges of fair and accurate comparisons, raise important questions and cautions, some constitutional purposes require or would be well-served by looking outward as well as inward. The real debate is between engagement and convergence as general interpretive postures.

The most powerful arguments for convergence, often made implicitly, or only about discrete issues, are based on some or all of the following: natural law theories of universal human rights or "common law" ius commune approaches,[51] cosmopolitan theories of democratic self-governance founded on recognition of the transnational effects of domestic laws and actions (especially of major powers),[52] the interests of maintaining an international legal system,[53] and the self-interests of the United States as a leading power.[54] As an aspiration, convergence has both appeal and drawbacks. The appeal is that of a transnational moral-legal universe that operates to constrain the worst temptations of ongoing governments and to inspire humane approaches. But the arena of genuinely broad and deep agreement on the content of "universal" human rights or values is likely to be too small to serve as a reasonable guide for interpretation across the full range of issues that arise. Further, the nontrivial possibilities of error in transnational consensus cannot be assumed away by mere presumptions. And there are risks to the judiciary's self-conception, and hence its capacity to maintain the independence and impartiality that is its hallmark, from interpretive approaches that place undue weight on the diplomatic interests of the judges' country. More importantly, convergence approaches ignore the human need to belong to particular and distinctive groupings and the related functions of constitutions to give expression to national particularity and historically important compromises. Finally, convergence is not a fully attainable goal; transnational norms themselves evolve, and change, and are contested in different fora, national and transnational.

As Chapter 4 argues, the most appropriate posture for the U.S. Court to take toward transnational legal sources is one of engagement, rather than convergence or resistance.[55] Deliberative engagement implies a willingness in appropriate cases to *consider* transnational sources of law. Considering foreign or international law, however, does not imply following (or resisting) its force, nor does engaging on some constitutional issues imply doing so on all. Engagement may be particularly appropriate when, for example, a constitutional provision requires some degree of reciprocity with transnational understandings, or refers to a widespread human value on which illumination may come from transnational sources, or when a constitutional issue involves understanding the consequences of particular applications or doctrinal approaches to common constitutional problems. In other arenas for engagement, judges may benefit from considering how members of other high national courts reflect on the role of a judge interpreting the constitution of a liberal democracy, or on the characteristic analytics of constitutional decision-making. The Supreme Court's surprisingly long record of considering foreign and international law suggests that deliberative engagement contributes to the project of U.S. constitutional self-expression and self-understanding, provides a potential self-monitoring device to prevent serious constitutional errors, and may increase judges' capacity for informed impartiality through considering multiple perspectives. Moreover, some degree of comparison is inevitable and can be better managed through transparent consideration than through covert (and potentially erroneous) assumptions. Chapter 4 also examines arguments for stronger, more relational forms of engagement—those contemplating an *obligation* to *consider* some transnational sources of law on at least some issues, and to justify divergences from broad and deep transnational consensus.

Chapter 5 analyzes engagement as a posture in comparison to resistance and convergence, and situates engagement within the framework of leading approaches to U.S. constitutional interpretation. Engagement with the transnational has potential relevance across interpretive approaches, though for some more than others, and most notably for the multi-sourced forms of interpretation most common in the United States. Arguments for resistance relating to expertise and competence, the risk of error, and opportunity costs, are considered, as are more substantive objections drawn from democratic theories of judicial review or concerns for national sovereignty. The engagement model does not treat foreign and international law as binding sources, or as presumptively to be followed in constitutional interpretation, but rather as interpretive aids to the Court's decision about what the best interpretation of the U.S. Constitution is, a point that diminishes the force of arguments from democratic theory or national sovereignty. As between engagement and resistance, there is too long a tradition of usage and too many potential benefits of considering transnational law for constitutional adjudication to resist as a general matter.

As between engagement and convergence, Chapter 5 argues that the multiple functions of a constitution (at least in the United States) militate against convergence as a goal. These functions include not only the protection of rights but also the implementation of a federal system and recognition of founding compromises; not only the framework for democratic governance but also the recognition of national self-identity. Engagement as a posture keeps open the possibilities of improved understanding through comparison, including arguments for and against convergence with or resistance to particular transnational norms, in a manner that can take into account the variety of relationships those transnational norms may have with our specifically national constitution.

Elaboration of what "engagement" means in practice will be explored in Chapter 6. Different categories of use—such as to inform the meaning of reciprocal terms like "treaty," or to implement constitutional norms by illuminating the range and consequences of doctrinal choices, or to provide a "mirror" for value checking or clarification—have different implications for what and how to consider or compare. Courts must consider whether the domestic issue is one likely to benefit from comparison; what the nature of the transnational source is (for example, whether it is foreign constitutional law or customary international law); and how comparable the source's legal environment is to the domestic context. Questions of fairness and accuracy of usage are considered, as is the possible need to improve existing practice and procedure to avoid errors or misunderstandings of transnational sources of laws.

In later chapters I show how other, more particular features of the U.S. Constitution bear on the choice of appropriate posture. For one thing, it is a very old constitution, a point developed in Chapters 7 and 8. Relatively newer constitutional orders, those that came into being after the development of modern human rights law in the latter part of the twentieth century, may be better positioned or may have more reason to adopt convergence as a general interpretive strategy than do older constitutional orders. Engagement, rather than convergence, is a better fit for the older and historically distinct U.S. Constitution to be able to fulfill its multiple functions, including national self-expression. Engagement permits older constitutional orders to learn from newer constitutional orders—for example, about how to reconcile eighteenth century commitments to liberty with nineteenth and twentieth century commitments to equality—while at the same time recognizing that established institutional structures and doctrines may be so integral a part of an existing and well-functioning constitutional order that, whatever would be the case if one were drafting a new constitution, change would destabilize and present risks not worth taking.[56]

Analysis of equality-related constitutional law in Chapter 7 will consider how "engagement" could be applied in the United States across several issues, including gender discrimination, reproductive choice, and affirmative action.

Transnational sources, both those rejecting and those upholding gender distinctions, may illuminate the permissibility, under intermediate scrutiny, of certain gender distinctions in U.S. law. Considering how other liberal constitutional orders have regulated abortion suggests both that a diversity of approaches coexist with commitments to gender equality and that absent the positive governmental commitments of a "social state," a greater degree of protection for autonomous decision-making may be necessary to protect women's equality. On affirmative action, reflecting on India's experience with a modern transformational constitution and its approach to past group injustices may cast a different light on "societal" discrimination and "compelling interests" in U.S. equal protection law, while at the same time providing support for the idea that affirmative action programs should be carefully tailored and require individualized consideration.

The presence of federal as opposed to unitary structures of constitutional government may affect the relationship of constitutional claims to transnational law in complex and diverse ways. As Chapter 8 will show, the historically contingent nature of federal systems and the necessarily interdependent aspects of the many constitutional provisions that relate to any federal "balance" impose limitations on the relevance of transnational sources of law on domestic constitutional issues of federalism. A comparative study of Canadian and U.S. federalism in the chapter will illustrate how particular federal allocations of power, as well as the "paradigm cases" for each country's basic federal bargain, may influence each country's receptivity to explicit engagement with transnational legal sources on a range of constitutional questions, including issues of individual rights.

Engagement in a Pluralist Global Context: Transnational Constitutionalism? In the concluding chapter, I explore the relationship between postures of engagement and broader questions about transnational constitutionalism. After showing how constitutions and international law have been to some extent interdependent from their modern beginnings, I examine the intensification of those relationships in recent decades as the subjects of international law have increasingly come to overlap with the subjects of domestic constitutions. In a setting of such legal pluralism, engaging with foreign and international legal sources in constitutional interpretation will not by itself cause convergences; likewise, refraining from such consideration will not prevent convergences. More powerful forces of ideas, of economics, of technology, and of various forms of identity-based social movements, will have much larger effects on the possibilities for both convergence and social fragmentation. At the same time it would be a mistake to assume that transnational judicial dialogue is not one part of these broader processes, and a part that is likely to continue for reasons that transcend the particular position of the United States.

Legitimate national governance is becoming contingent on compliance with supranational law or values, as is shown most powerfully in Europe, where European human rights law may be enforced domestically even by those national courts that cannot review national laws for noncompliance with national constitutions. International law may promote domestic constitutional change, but national constitutional interpretations may in turn influence understandings of supranational norms. At present, the emergence of a form of transnational constitutionalism can most clearly be seen at moments of national constitutional disjuncture, involving, for example, redefinition of national boundaries, or major constitutional amendment or regime change. Although thin, a set of transnational constitutional norms—favoring representative democracy, human rights, and some separation of powers (notably including independent courts for enforcement of individual rights)—both influence and are constructed by national constitutional law and international law. Caution is needed, however, in moving from transnational legal values to concrete constitutional rules in particular polities.

Postures of engagement recognize the importance of these emerging transnational constitutional norms in a legal universe that at the same time is quite plural and diverse. The diversity of legal orders—including subnational or regional orders—calls for national constitutions to play a mediating role between global and local legal demands, considering both similarities and differences in approach and relying on public reason-giving to account for choices made. Engagement takes account of the multiple functions of domestic constitutions and is built on a recognition that justice will not reside uniquely at only one locus (e.g., transnational, national, local) of lawmaking. Engagement is respectful of the need for balance between democratic and universalist elements characteristic of many constitutions. It is responsive to the *inevitability* of comparison in an increasingly transnational legal environment. And it is a jurisprudential manifestation of how national constitutions and international law have been coconstituted from their modern beginnings, in relationships that have grown stronger in recent decades. Finally, in an era in which transnational nonstate actors threaten the physical and economic security, and capacities for social trust and tolerance, on which constitutional governance in the long run rests (and which it in turn promotes), engaging with transnational sources of constitutional law in a serious way may help legitimize and strengthen constitutional democracies in their efforts to sustain effective constitutional governance.

1. RESISTING THE TRANSNATIONAL

Justice Antonin Scalia is a leading proponent of the idea that interpreters of national constitutions ought to "resist" foreign or international influences. There is a difference, he famously wrote, between writing a new constitution—when comparison is appropriate—and interpreting it. He has written in his opinions, and argued extrajudicially, both in the United States and abroad, that foreign or international law is irrelevant to the interpretation of a written constitution. In 2005, Justices Scalia and Stephen Breyer took their debate over foreign law "on the road," in Melbourne, Australia, where, a journalist wrote, Australian High Court Justice John Dyson Heydon may have shared some of Justice Scalia's concerns over the countermajoritarian implications of resort to foreign law; in the reporter's words, instead of being ruled democratically, this practice would open the door to members of each polity being ruled by laws made by "a new political elite of international lawyers."[1]

In confirmation hearings for positions on the U.S. Supreme Court held in 2005 and 2006, Chief Justice John Roberts and Justice Samuel Alito were questioned about their views, and each affirmed a general opposition to considering transnational sources in constitutional interpretation. For Roberts, foreign law posed two problems: first, it compounded the countermajoritarian problem in judicial review, and second, it offered too much opportunity for judicial "cherry-picking" of precedents, simply finding foreign precedents that support a judge's own preferences and then using them to "cloak" that preference in apparent authority.[2] Alito drew a distinction between the relevance of foreign constitutional decisions in law and in political science, a distinction perhaps reflecting his own earlier interest in comparative constitutional law in his Princeton senior thesis about the Italian Constitutional Court. Because of the distinctiveness of U.S. governance and constitutional institutions, however, he saw little to be gained from such an examination by judges.

Opposition to the use of foreign or international law in constitutional interpretation is not limited to conservative justices on constitutional courts in older Western democracies. The courts of Singapore, for example, have been at times inhospitable to efforts based on foreign constitutional law (or international law) to promote a less statist (or communitarian) approach to the interpretation of rights, insisting that the specificity of its constitutional provisions resist comparison.[3] An influential Argentine constitutionalist, Carlos Rosenkrantz, has argued that it was a mistake for Argentina to rely on foreign (U.S.) constitutional law in the past, and that such reliance should be avoided by countries that have yet to develop a constitutional culture, in order to promote development of a more autochthonous form of interpretation.[4] Rosenkrantz would treat differently references to foreign law used to distinguish a country from those relied on as positive examples, a differentiating use being consistent with such autochthonous development. This is a somewhat different distinction than that raised by Professor Mary Ann Glendon, who has suggested that foreign law could legitimately be considered to uphold the validity of a statute but not to strike it down.[5]

Given the purposes of domestic constitutions to express and perhaps even to constitute a particular group of people and provide the terms for their governance in a bounded territory, this kind of resistance is not surprising. Resistance to embracing foreign and international forces in interpreting constitutions is born of many sources, and may apply to a wide range of uses—from "decorative" citations of foreign or international sources amidst domestic sources, to the considered discussion of foreign law as a relevant source of information in analysis, to the treatment of some forms of international law as either binding or highly authoritative on a constitutional issue. The remainder of this chapter will try to explain the different sources of resistance, their jurisprudential concomitants, and how resistance is expressed in case law and doctrine.

A. SOURCES OF RESISTANCE

In explaining the sources of resistance, I will begin with some ideas about the purposes of constitutions and approaches to constitutional interpretation, then take up concerns about the rationality and capacity of judging, and finally turn to political and cultural factors.

Constitutions as Self-Constituting and Self-Expressive

The idea of a constitution is itself one that may seem to invite resistance or indifference to foreign or international law. National constitutions are often documents of both self-constitution and self-expression. They may be written to describe, or inscribe, a particular set of self-conceptions of the dominant groups in their society (those with the power to be at the constitutional table). They may be highly aspirational, seeking to return to a former, better time, or to transform the society into something new and better. Constitutions may serve what Mark Tushnet has called an "expressivist" role, embodying a particular national identity and self-understanding.[6]

Preambles are a particular location of these kinds of national specificities. In an almost poetic narrative, Iraq's constitution asserts, "We are the people of the land between two rivers, the homeland of the apostles and prophets,. . . pioneers of civilization. . . . Upon our land the first law made by man was passed. . . ."

The French Constitution of 1958 proclaims France's commitment to the Declaration of the Rights of Man, and to liberty, equality, and fraternity; the constitution also proclaims France an "indivisible, secular, democratic and social Republic," and defines its national language, its national anthem, and its national flag. Its commitment to secularism may be contrasted with the Preamble to the German Basic Law, which begins "Conscious of their responsibility before God and man," or the Irish Constitution's invocation of "the Name of the Most Holy Trinity, from Whom is all authority and to Whom, as our final end, all actions both of men and States must be referred. . . ." The French constitution emphasizes the role of "citizens" in its early articles; the German Basic Law's preamble emphasizes that "Germans" have achieved "unity and freedom," echoing important differences in conceptions of national citizenship in these two countries. The Germans are moved "by the determination to promote world peace as an equal partner in a united Europe." Ireland refers to its "heroic and unremitting struggle to regain [its] rightful independence." The preamble to the Constitution of China reads like a tract on national history and the accomplishments of the collective people since 1949, noting "[m]ajor successes . . . in economic development . . . [and] marked increase in agricultural production," and asserting that Taiwan is part of China.[7] In these preambular provisions much of what historians and sociologists might describe as dominant national tropes are evident. The preamble to the U.S. Constitution speaks in the name of "We the People," but it does not say who "We the People" are; rather, it sets forth what "the People's" objectives are, for example, to "establish Justice" and "promote the general Welfare"—a goal-oriented (if very general) call for purposive understanding of what follows.

The point for these purposes is the degree to which expressive components of constitutions function as differentiators. If each national constitution is primarily a self-constituting document, designed at least in part to differentiate, then resistance might seem naturally to follow. As Justice Scalia has written, "We must never forget that it is a Constitution for the United States of America that we are expounding."[8] If constitutions are understood as intimately connected to distinctive social or cultural groups—if part of their very purpose is to help constitute and express how one national group differs from all others—then resistance or indifference to what other groups say or think might logically seem to follow: what others say is irrelevant or, if relevant, relevant only insofar as it helps establish the boundaries between "us" and "them." The sociocultural force of this understanding of constitutions is reinforced, moreover, by the focus of much constitutional theory, described by Robert Post as "centrally concerned with authorship" and with how constitutional legitimacy is rooted in a particular polity.[9]

Given these purposes of national constitutions and their correspondence to what seem to be fairly universal social needs for differentiation, it is not surprising that in many constitutional cultures, there is episodic resistance to arguments based on what foreign jurisdictions have concluded. If a constitution is fundamentally an inward-looking legal instrument, whose purpose is to express the commitments, constraints, and uniqueness of a particular people, the views of foreign courts or international tribunals are of less interest or may even be harmful. As will be discussed in later chapters, this understanding of constitutional purpose and even of the source of its legitimacy is incomplete. A more complete understanding will open the door far wider to transnational influence; indeed, engaging with foreign materials can be a helpful way of better understanding one's own particularities. But the purpose of this chapter is to understand resistance, and it is supported by far more than this expressivist understanding of a constitution's purposes.

Interpretive Theory: Originalism, Contractarianism, and Popular Sovereignty

Resistance to the foreign in the interpretation of domestic law may be associated with particular interpretive commitments, such as originalism or intentionalism, or to certain understandings of the inherent nature of a constitution (for example, as a social "contract"). There are, of course, multiple versions of originalism and intentionalism; and some may overlap with other theories hospitable to considering comparative experience (for example, if original understandings embraced supranational or natural law conceptions of justice or good government).[10] And although originalism is a particularly important trope in U.S. constitutional discourse, originalism (in the sense of original meaning) and a related concern for popular sovereignty play an important role in Australia as well. For example, Justice Ian Callinan has argued that it would be "an anachronistic error to believe that the Constitution, which was drafted and adopted by the people of the colonies well before international bodies such as the United Nations came into existence, should be regarded as speaking to the international community. The Constitution is *our* fundamental law, not a collection of principles amounting to the rights of man, to be read and approved by people and institutions elsewhere."[11]

An influential argument for originalism has been made by Professor Randy Barnett, who argues that the original public meaning of the text must control later interpretation. Analogizing a constitution to a contract, Barnett argues that the purpose of embodying basic constitutional commitments in a written document would be undermined if the words agreed to could be interpreted in ways that depart from that public meaning.[12] Current foreign or international law would be irrelevant, on Barnett's theory, to understand original meaning; the question, as he describes it, is what, in the common language of the time of ratification—and presumably, within the polity adopting the constitution—the words of the constitution's text were generally understood to mean. The key period of inquiry is the moment in the past when the constitutional text was adopted—that is the moment at which the original meaning must be determined.

Although this theory provides a coherent account of why contemporary foreign or international law is not relevant to determining the starting point ("original meaning") of constitutional interpretation, Barnett acknowledges that some interpretive questions will arise that cannot be resolved by reference to original meaning, both because the application of a provision to future problems may not have been contemplated and because some constitutional texts are vague (contracts, after all, may include deliberately indefinite terms) or the constitution is otherwise underdetermined. Barnett also seems to accept the important distinction, made by Ronald Dworkin and others, between "semantic originalism" and "expectations originalism,"[13] or, as Australian legal scholar Jeffrey Goldsworthy puts it, between "enactment intentions" and "application intentions."[14] On this account, the original *meaning* of an enactment is controlling, but not (necessarily) the intentions or expectations of the ratifiers as to how it would be applied. A broader range of authority, possibly including contemporary foreign or international law, might be relevant in those areas of interpretive discretion or in constitutional "construction."[15]

Originalist interpretive theories are sometimes justified by reference to theories of democracy or popular sovereignty, although Barnett does not so argue. Rather, he suggests, it is the character of the constitution as a written legal instrument, designed to constrain governments and to provide a clear and formal embodiment of a legal agreement that, he says, requires interpretive commitment to original meaning. If words do not mean the same thing as when they were ratified, he suggests, the purpose of formalizing a constitution in writing is defeated.[16] This "purpose of written law" argument is closely linked to the conception of a constitution as a form of "precommitment." A widespread view of constitutions is that they are designed to constrain the future, to make decisions that are not merely default provisions pending later legislation but which limit future decisions—how and when legislators and members of governments are elected, what form the government takes, what powers and responsibilities the governments have, and what rights are secured to the people. Although constitutions do function as a constraint (and perform a valuable function in so doing), the argument that, absent an interpretive theory that treats original meaning as an invariable constraint, the words of the constitution cannot serve this function of written law, does not necessarily follow. Texts can constrain and empower in more complex ways, as other forms of exegesis illustrate.[17]

Although Barnett's defense of original meaning does not rest on popular sovereignty or democracy, many theorists and jurists do argue that the legitimacy of the constitution derives from its having been more or less democratically consented to and that constitutions so adopted must be interpreted only in accord with what was consented to (at more or less specific levels of generality). "Importing" foreign norms or understandings into the project of constitutional interpretation is seen as inconsistent with the self-governing (and thus legitimating) origins and ambitions of the constitution, and as a threat to the capacity of the polity for continued self-government, constrained only by that polity's "own" prior self-restraining choices. Doing so may imply a form of "natural law," inconsistent with the assumptions of a written constitution and of self-governing democracy.[18]

To the extent that popular sovereignty arguments treat the idea of a constitution as legitimate only insofar as it is accepted, consensually, by the people it governs, consideration of sources other than the consensual acts of that people may be seen as inconsistent with the basis of constitutional legitimacy—at least in the absence of a clear authorization for such use, consented to by the people.[19] On this view, foreign or international law may be considered only insofar as it bears on the original understandings agreed to in founding acts of popular sovereignty or insofar as the constitution itself embodies consent to such interpretation, but not otherwise. Without very explicit constitutional license, any interpretive method that looks beyond the polity in which democratic decisions can be made about constitutional amendment is suspect. Concerns for both democracy and sovereignty are raised with respect to uses of foreign or international law to provide information related to "values"—in the United States, values implicit in constitutional commitments to equality and due process, as applied to highly controversial social issues.[20] These concerns fit within a larger set of questions about the balance between constitutional empowerment and constitutional constraint and the appropriate role of judicial interpreters in identifying and enforcing those constraints. Although an originalist who sought to constrain discretion by specific original meanings would have fewer occasions to resort to external sources, there would inevitably be some; a "popular sovereigntist" might be more inclined to distinguish between domestic and foreign sources. And, as will be discussed in Chapter 4, interpretive theories based on original moments of constitution-making from which large portions of the population were excluded, and conceptions of popular sovereignty that ignore the permeability and complexity of U.S. legal culture in its relations to others, raise legitimacy questions of their own.

Interpretive Theory: Representation-Reinforcement and "Majoritarianism"

Arguments from the democratically given, popular sovereignty view of a constitution might preclude a resort to any interpretive source not present at the founding. But there are also what Roger Alford has called "majoritarian" approaches to constitutional interpretation, which do not insist on seeing the constitution's text, or the moment of constitution-making, as the only moment worthy of influencing constitutional meaning. But these approaches also might be thought to preclude or limit resort to foreign or international law as a basis of determining constitutional meaning or application.

According to Professor Alford's description, in "majoritarian" constitutional theory, key moments of democratic decision-making and popular sovereignty are contemporary; they lie in the products of daily politics, in legislation, and in contemporary opinion. Thus, he writes:

> Majoritarianism is a constitutional theory that embraces sovereign expressions of ordered society. The conservative version of majoritarianism seeks a limited role for the Constitution, recognizing that any declaration of unconstitutionality thwarts the will of the majority reflected in legislative and executive action. The activist version of majoritarianism seeks to embody in the text of the Constitution current contemporary standards, on the view that the founding document is a living instrument embracing the broadest ideals of our evolving national experience.[21]

"Majoritarian" forms of interpretation do not insist on "original meanings" but contemplate, in what Alford calls their "conservative" structural form, positions of deference to the current output of legislative or executive decision makers who are elected by popular majorities. John Hart Ely's work is treated as theorizing grounds for such deference in most areas, and Alford points to the failure of the U.S. Court in *McConnell v. FEC*[22] to address arguments made by amici concerning the practice in other countries. For Alford, "activist" or "interpretive" majoritarianism means that constitutional meanings may evolve depending on the views of contemporary majorities, and through means short of formal amendment. He cites as examples the constitutional "community standards" doctrine in First Amendment obscenity cases, in which comparative materials have played little role, and argues that in Eighth Amendment case law comparative material has played only a subsidiary role.

The empirical foundations of some of these claims may be questioned.[23] As a normative matter, "conservative" majoritarianism might well find foreign experience helpful on its basic questions. If other Western democracies share a commitment to both majoritarianism and the judicial protection of rights, understanding how their constitutional courts resolve contemporary challenges to legislation might bear on more generally understanding the role of constitutional courts. That is, apart from the result, the analytical process of weighing, categorizing, or analyzing the limited role of the court in a democracy might benefit from the comparative experience of other, similarly situated judges.[24] Moreover, on Ely's account,[25] courts must determine what kinds of laws are obstructions of the representative process or result from prejudice or exclusions that corrupt those processes; these questions might well benefit from comparative illumination. With respect to what Alford calls "interpretive majoritarianism," it seems correct that foreign or international experience would not be of direct relevance, although to the extent that evolving views within the polity have themselves been influenced by transnational developments, they may be of some value.[26]

Coming from the Argentine context, Carlos Rosenkrantz has suggested a different but related problem in "authoritative" uses of foreign law in domestic constitutional interpretation—what he calls the "difficulties in . . . democratic validation."[27] For him and many others, what validates the binding force of law in particular democratic societies is that law is made through the collective and procedurally fair choices of those who are bound by it; that being so, treating foreign law as binding authority cannot be democratically validated. Thus far Rosenkrantz' argument tracks arguments raised, for example, by Professors Nelson Lund and John McGinnis, and familiar in the U.S. literature,[28] though the contexts differ significantly: the U.S. courts have never treated another nation's constitutional law as binding, as the Argentine Supreme Court did with respect to U.S. constitutional law for many decades.

But, Rosenkrantz suggests, courts are distinguished not only from constitutional conventions and ratifiers, but also from legislatures in their capacity to license borrowing, because when a court borrows or refers to foreign law, it is not "we the people" who do so. "Because it is difficult for us to identify with a court it is therefore also difficult to validate the coercion implicit in the implementation of the legal norm borrowed by a court."[29] By highlighting the issue of whether to treat this objection as based on popular sovereignty and democratic self-determination or on the particular limitations of courts as embodying that popular sovereignty, Rosenkrantz advances a distinctive argument. In so doing he also raises a question of where national self-identification rests, as well as bringing attention to different conceptions of "sovereignty." If in some societies there is greater popular identification with the work of legislatures than courts, in other societies, popular understanding of what the law is may be expressed through some form of identification with, or trust in, the constitutional court; indeed, on some theoretical accounts constitutional courts may speak for the people, in their constitution-making mode, to a greater extent than does the legislature in the realm of ordinary politics.[30]

This critique from "democratic validation" is limited to uses of foreign law that depend on its being treated as binding authority within the domestic jurisdiction. Readers should understand that the U.S. Constitution functioned as something of a model for the drafting of the mid-nineteenth century Argentine constitution, and that some influential participants in the Argentine process argued that U.S. constitutional law should bind those charged with interpreting the new Argentine constitution to what the drafters saw as a better system.[31] In the *De la Torre* case and others, the Argentina Supreme Court treated U.S. law as controlling authority, a "wholesale adoption" of foreign constitutional law, Rosenkrantz argues, that prevented development of a distinctively Argentine constitutional tradition.[32] Absent authorization in the constitution's text or ratification process for reliance on foreign law as a form of binding authority the objection from democracy has considerable force. But, as we shall see later, few contemporary uses are of this form.

Law as Autochthonous Identity

These arguments from democratic theory differ from another form of objection to the use of foreign law, which proceeds from a conception of law as organically related to a historically specific people and their development over time. Formal authorization to consider foreign law may not be sufficient from the perspective that views law anthropologically, culturally, or sociologically as an expression or outgrowth of a particular culture, and thus resistant to use as a positive instrument of transformation or of ideals inconsistent with that society's overarching culture. Notwithstanding the heterogeneous and dynamic nature of many legal cultures, some studies of constitutional failures have blamed the borrowing, or imposition, of institutions that were either discredited by their colonial origin or were otherwise not an outgrowth and expression of a particular culture.[33]

That constitutions may fail in part because the constitutions were modeled inappropriately on foreign structures does not necessarily speak to the appropriateness of *considering* foreign legal sources in constitutional design or interpretation. It provides even less of a foundation for objecting to the consideration of general principles of international law, which by definition emerge from a transnational consensus capable of application across many cultures. Some argue, however, that successful constitutionalism requires a constitutional culture and that even nonauthoritative references to foreign law—as persuasive or informational authority—may prevent the development of such a culture. Thus, nonauthoritative uses of foreign law as evidence of "constitutional facts," in the sense of understanding the consequences of different constitutional regimes or rules, or "as a source of innovation and knowledge," should be avoided; so, too, Rosenkrantz argues, should "dialog[ical]" uses of foreign constitutional law, as, for example, to emphasize the importance of certain facts to resolution of a legal controversy, or to show a developing consensus on a point. Such discussions of foreign law add to the complexity of judicial decisions, which makes them harder to read and follow, and are thus antithetical to the goal of developing an understandable and autochthonous tradition.[34] While Rosenkrantz writes from a perspective that seeks to build a constitutional culture, related concerns have been expressed by some U.S. scholars—that if the Court begins to cite foreign law in its opinions, it may cause Americans to lose their "affection" for the Constitution as something that is "theirs."[35]

Interestingly, Rosenkrantz makes an exception for use of foreign law as a negative authority, which he sees as not inconsistent with, but helpful toward, development of autochthonous constitutional law by "fixing the essential constitutional character of a national polity." Foreign laws generally, though, should be understood as scaffolding, which can assist in the work of constitution building but are never seen at the end and are removed—they are "never components of the final work and are never determinants of the shape of what is constructed."[36] As this passage suggests, this form of objection is not so much to judges' knowledge of comparative law, nor even to their consideration of it in the course of interpreting domestic law; rather, it is in important part an objection to the public acknowledgment of this consideration.

Judging under Constraints: Sources and Discretion, Expertise, Opportunity Costs, and Comparison

A posture of resistance or indifference to the external might also be seen to flow from insistence on the constraints on, and autonomy of, law and/or judging. This concern has two faces: on the one hand, a concern that judging under law must be seen as a constrained activity, distinct from the realm of politics and preference, in order to maintain its legitimacy; and on the other hand, a concern that judges must be constrained in order to limit the opportunity for their own discretion, attitudes, or preferences to intervene. Charles Fried raised concern about "expand[ing] the canon" of legitimate legal sources for constitutional interpretation when Justice Breyer in a dissent referred to comparative federalism; Fried argued that the limitation of sources helps distinguish the activity of law and judging from that of scholarship.[37] Richard Posner recently wrote that "If foreign decisions are freely citable, any judge wanting a supporting citation has only to troll deeply enough in the world's *corpora juris* to find it."[38] The concern about judges "cherry-picking" among foreign precedents, noted above, reflects the second half of the concern about the need for constraint, and has been raised by jurists and scholars in the United States and elsewhere.[39] Whether resort to foreign precedents will provide broader discretion on contested issues than the domestic precedents generated in a decentralized system of constitutional adjudication like that of the United States, though, is a question whose answer is at best uncertain and may well be no.[40]

Concerns for bounded rationality, and limited time and competence raise related sets of issues. Paradigms of bounded rationality caution about the difficult challenges of mastering multiple bodies of law. The possibility of error and misunderstanding in relying on foreign law is not merely hypothetical, as Christopher McCrudden's description of European litigation over affirmative action for women suggests.[41] Not only are there limitations raised by lack of training and expertise, but there may also be important opportunity costs to learning enough international or foreign law for judges to be competent at using it.[42] Expanding the field of research to international and foreign law in constitutional cases imposes potential burdens of research and analysis on the lawyers for the parties, arguably raising the costs of litigation and increasing advocacy advantages for wealthier litigants.

Further, there are epistemological objections to the consideration of foreign law, which grow out of the challenges of comparison. Some argue that while international law may constitute a field with some coherence and clarity, the constitutions and constitutional law of any particular foreign state should not be considered because of inevitable and insurmountable difficulties of comparison. Mark Tushnet has explained the challenges of comparison in functional terms as involving the inevitable "omitted variable"; when all potential variables are filled in, each country looks quite distinctive, and its constitutional system can be examined comparatively for expressive purposes but not for functional comparison.[43]

Professor Rosenkrantz has gone so far as to suggest that the "heterogeneity of constitutional law" simply precludes reliance on foreign law for information or dialogical purposes: contexts are never sufficiently similar, and this is a confounding factor even if the law of other countries is adopted in a procedural way that supports its authority in its own context.[44]

Finally, if the epistemological challenge in the use of foreign law is that of comparability, that of international law may have to do with its increasing breadth and scope. International human rights law alone arguably embraces both individual and collective rights, both "negative" rights and positive rights, and these rights may conflict (in much the same way that domestic constitutional rights may come into conflict). In addition, other aspects of international law, imposing duties on states to, inter alia, fight crime, battle terrorism, combat environmental harms, and so forth, may further expand or complicate analysis. Some critics are thus concerned that international law has become so pervasive, but at the same time so indeterminate, that it offers simply too broad a range of discretion to be a genuinely helpful source of constitutional interpretation.

Political Resistance: Nation-Building, Western Dominance, and Cultural Exceptionalism

Apart from resistance grounded in conceptions of a constitution and authorized constitutional interpretation, in commitments to democratic self-governance, in concerns for constraint in judgment, and in cognitive challenges of comparison, factors of history and politics may underlie resistance to foreign influence in constitutional interpretation. Proponents in the U.S. debate may be unaware that in a number of other countries resistance to the influence of foreign constitutional law is often resistance to U.S. conceptions of constitutional rights. The economic and military hegemony of the United States, its past interventions in other nations' political choices (including constitution-making), and the widespread dislike of some contemporary U.S. interventions in other countries underlie some of this foreign resistance. Resistance to former colonial powers and to past exploitation and dominance by those powers may underlie resistance elsewhere.[45]

In the United States, resistance to the foreign is not grounded as much in fear of foreign hegemony as it is in the idea of popular and legal "exceptionalism"—the belief in the uniqueness, and, more important, the superiority of the United States and its legal system. Cultural and political anxieties over the position of the United States (perhaps heightened by increased awareness of the relative decline in the status of the U.S. constitutional system as the preeminent model for other nations) may contribute to more aggressive assertions of the autonomy of U.S. constitutional law. Professor Steven Calabresi has recently argued that the idea of the United States as a "City on a Hill," means that courts should avoid influence by foreign law.[46] Whatever the logic of this position,[47] there is no question that xenophobia exists in law as in popular culture. When a witness before a congressional committee hearing (on a proposed resolution that courts generally not consider foreign law in interpreting the U.S. Constitution or laws) feels comfortable using a national slur to describe the French,[48] it would be foolish to deny xenophobia's force.

Indeed, to the extent that prudence is a legitimate part of judicial decision-making, it may at times dictate that foreign or international influences, or other factors influencing decisions, be suppressed from public statement. Although a default rule of candor has many virtues, constitutional decisions must work not in an abstract universe, but in a real and practical one. Domestic audiences must be persuaded to comply with and respect decisions. At the level of everyday acceptance and compliance, there may well be occasions when ensuring public acceptance of the local authenticity of a decision might caution against overt reference to foreign or international sources, even if the judges have found them helpful.

Yet, nation-building and political aspects of constitutions and constitutional law may point in different directions. To the extent that a constitution's purpose is viewed not as a constraint on government but as what H.W.O. Okoth-Ogendo calls a "power map," the relationship of such a constitution to the transnational may be primarily oriented toward communicating outward about the status of the state as sovereign and/or about the legitimate holders of power within the state.[49] This outward communication may take the form of resistance to outside interference, a kind of resistance to the transnational. As will be illustrated further, some constitutions have provisions designed to discriminate against noncitizens for nation-building or natural-resource conserving purposes. These provisions provide a textual foundation for resistance—not only to international or foreign norms of free trade and nondiscrimination in law, but also to foreign investment, purchase, or activity. Other constitutions, however, have identified their nation-building efforts with an identification with foreign or, increasingly, with international law, incorporating international human rights regimes into their constitutional structure or as super-statutory norms.[50] Nation-building can work in many ways, but certainly resistance to the foreign, or to forms of foreign or international control, is one manifestation.

Political Resistance and Principled Substantive Disagreement

Some resistance to considering international or foreign law is based on a combination of principle and political concerns, informed by a substantive view of the overall valence between a particular domestic constitution and transnational norms. Thus, some critics of international human rights argue that both the Universal Declaration of Human Rights and the International Covenant on Civil and Political Rights embody Western conceptions that place undue emphasis on individuals and ignore group and collective forms of rights assertion and identity.[51] From a different vantage, some critics in the United States argue that, on the whole, transnational norms protect liberty and freedom to a lesser extent than does the U.S. Constitution. It is argued that freedoms of expression, of the press, and of religion, in addition to reproductive freedoms and freedoms from searches and seizures, are likely to be less well-protected if the U.S. Constitution came to be interpreted in accordance with dominant transnational norms. Resistance to a posture of openness to considering the transnational might be based on the fear that such a posture—if followed in a principled way—might lead to the rejection of valuable, substantively worthy aspects of a nation's own constitutional tradition.[52]

The Political Economy of Transnationalism and Constitutional Interpretation

Professor John McGinnis has added to the arguments for resistance to authoritative uses of foreign or international law in two ways. (McGinnis addresses these arguments only to those uses of foreign or international law that affect the outcome—a category that may be difficult to define, particularly in jurisdictions that rely on multifactor, common law forms of reasoning and interpretation.) First, he suggests, to the extent that references to foreign or international law tend to move national constitutional laws toward a common position, it would "decreas[e] the diversity of global rules and undermin[e] American experimentation that has in the past paid dividends to the entire world."[53] In the nonhierarchical system in which national courts have considered foreign or international authority, however, it is uncertain whether diversity would be reduced, or whether common positions would be identified within distinctive communities of nations and only with respect to some issues that have long been vetted; it is also unclear whether some reduction in diversity is, on balance, a good or bad thing.[54] Moreover, far more powerful forces than judges' consideration of foreign or international law as forms of persuasive authority exist, which will tend to promote convergence of legal regulation in a number of areas.

Second, McGinnis argues, the practice of referring to foreign or international law could "undermin[e] self-governance by giving incentives to interest groups, domestic and foreign, to frame international and foreign law with a view toward influencing our domestic law."[55] The idea that foreign nations would adopt domestic laws that they would not otherwise adopt in order to influence another country seems farfetched. But the possibility of norm entrepreneurs using international fora to influence the development of forms of "soft law", or treaties, or judicial interpretations, is a real one, and both progressive and conservative groups have made their presence and their interests known in these fora.[56] Whether such activity should be understood to promote or to detract from democratic decision-making at the national level, however, is complicated, and may depend on the particular contexts of action—including, at the international level, the transparency, inclusiveness, duration, and quality of the processes by which norms emerged. Under U.S. practice, the binding character of international norms (with the possible and limited exception of jus cogens norms) depends on national political action (for example, ratifying a treaty, or deciding whether to dissent from a rule of customary international law) and any influence on domestic constitutional interpretation depends on decisions by U.S. judges, thus further complicating the argument from self-governance.[57]

Cultural Elites, Self-Interested Judges, and the Politics of Citation

Arguments based on popular sovereignty and the authenticity of constitutional interpretation are concerned not with the motivations of those who rely on or consider foreign or international law, but on the effects of doing so in domestic interpretation. But another source of resistance to considering foreign or international law is more concerned with the presumed motive and institutional interests of those seen to favor such consideration. Some versions of this resistance have an almost Manichaean tone: resort to foreign and international law is seen as the product of elite cooperation to change popularly supported views of law and good policy.[58] Resort to foreign or international law is seen as a way for self-interested cultural elites to remake national polities in their own image by undermining or avoiding democratic politics, through unjustified new rulings and overrulings of rightly decided cases.[59] Alternatively, an institutionalist focus considers the position of judges, their situational interests in aligning themselves with judges in other countries, and the possibility that what Anne-Marie Slaughter has called "trans-judicial networks" will influence judges to care more about what their counterparts in other countries think than they do about the meaning of their own domestic legal instruments.[60] Finally, some might worry that citation of foreign authority would place courts in positions of engaging in diplomacy on behalf of their countries, choosing what to cite as a way of expressing alignment or disagreement,[61] in ways that would undermine or be incompatible with norms separating judging from other aspects of governance.

B. JURISPRUDENTIAL ASSUMPTIONS

As this discussion has suggested, the posture of resistance cannot be ascribed to only a single, or even dominant, jurisprudential approach to law. Indeed, resistance may be associated with quite different conceptions of law, and may resist certain kinds of uses of foreign or international law more than others.[62]

Positivism

Some forms of resistance might be supported by those versions of positivism that associate law with the product of an authorized, and specifically national, lawmaker.[63] Criticisms of judges using foreign law as a "cloak" for their own preferences may assume that what the judges ought to be doing is interpreting a particular legal instrument, authorized by the legitimate lawgiver (the people as a whole or whatever body enacts or amends the constitution), that governs their decisional task in a relatively determinate way.

Yet, on this account, if the authorized lawgiver were to license consideration of transnational legal sources (foreign or international), it would presumably be permissible for the authorized interpreter (here, the courts) to do so. Such resistance must turn on a substantive view of what the constitution's makers contemplated for its own interpretation. Since constitutions are often silent on their own interpretation, positivist defenses of resistance must rest on implicit interpretive norms; such norms might reasonably be thought to vary for different parts of an instrument depending on their character. Moreover, if a constitution has authorized judicial interpretation without specifying interpretive methods, it might follow that the authorized interpreter is to decide on the appropriate interpretive sources. Since very few constitutions of which I am aware specify their own interpretive norms, and because in the absence of such specification there is considerable room for interpretive disagreement, positivism standing alone is, in most jurisdictions, not a very firm foundation for resistance to nonbinding uses of foreign or international sources, not as "precedent" but as persuasive authority.[64]

Organic Conceptions of Law

Other sources of resistance rest, instead, on a more organic conception of law, indeed, on a conception that law's legitimacy or power or efficacy depends on its being, and being seen as, organically developed from within the polity it binds. Law, in this view, must never lose its connection with the historical consciousness of the specific people whom it governs. This view is less concerned with the authority of the lawgiver than with the authenticity of law's cultural connections to its society, an authenticity that, it is claimed, depends on being seen as uncomplicated by comparative references. The expressive and self-constituting character of some of the provisions quoted earlier in this chapter might be understood to capture the importance, for constitutional law, of its close association with particular national histories and traditions. This view of law is prominently associated with the nineteenth-century German scholar, Friedrich Karl von Savigny, who "professed a historicist conception of law, according to which the true law is found and not made, it is found in the spirit of the people and in social customs."[65] For this reason, "legislation and institutional design should be extremely cautious and follow, not promote social development."[66]

Written constitutions are themselves in some tension with at least some of the premises of organicity. First, it might be thought, truly organic culture and law need not proclaim their identity in a written instrument, but this is probably not so in any complex modern polity. Modern historicist views insist that while complex states do require written laws, the law "must never become merely a body of ideal propositions or a mere system of rules promulgated by the state; it must always remain a particular expression of the social and historical consciousness of a people at a given time and place."[67] Constitutions, though, insofar as they represent precommitments (that is, more entrenched codifications), are arguably more deeply in tension with organic, historicist concepts of law.

They are efforts to embody with some rigidity what the basic precommitments of the society are, thereby constraining "organic" transformations in the society's culture which may later arise,[68] as some historicists contemplate,[69] and which may, in particular, arise from the presence of very different groups with very different experiences and senses of culture (that is, from more pluralist cultures). Moreover, constitutions are in further tension with more organic conceptions of law when those constitutions are designedly transformational or seek to constrain their society's own worst tendencies.[70]

Attitudes toward law are influenced, but not necessarily constrained in an entirely logical manner, by jurisprudential assumptions. If, as Holmes said, "[t]he life of the law has not been logic; it has been experience,"[71] this may imply not only a historical approach to understanding law, but also a need to tolerate shifting jurisprudential modalities in the justification of law's validity and legitimacy. It is thus not surprising to find both positivist and organic conceptions of law underlying postures of resistance.[72] Indeed, these postures may reinforce each other, as evinced in Jed Rubenfeld and Kenneth Anderson's arguments about the nature of the American constitutional tradition.

Will, Organicity, and Exceptionalism

Professor Rubenfeld argues that the American historicist conception of constitutionalism is one in which will and consent by the people (as authorized lawgivers) play dominant roles in justifying restraint by law. In contrast to other countries whose views of themselves and their relationship to law is based on concepts of universal "reason," the historical focus on popular sovereignty in the United States, he argues, leads to a kind of constitutional, as well as international, "unilateralism," making even brief reference to other countries' laws in constitutional interpretation a matter of controversy.[73] Professor Anderson adopts this historicist account of the role of democratic decision-making about constitutional values as normatively fundamental: the United States has "a vision of democratic constitutional self-government founded on democracy and popular sovereignty—everything that international constitutionalism and the European tradition most rejects." Thus, "if there is a conflict between fidelity to the inside political community and the desires of outsiders, . . . judges *cannot* satisfy the desires of outsiders . . ." by giving weight to legal decisions with foreign "provenance."[74]

In the next section, I explore some discrete settings in which postures of resistance play out in constitutional decision-making.

C. MANIFESTATIONS OF RESISTANCE: SILENCE, INDIFFERENCE, AND ACTIVE RESISTANCE

One of the difficulties in identifying doctrinal manifestations of postures of resistance is that the resistance often takes the form of indifference. To illustrate indifference, one must point to absences of discussion or acknowledgment, and show that they result not from unawareness but from lack of interest or unwillingness to engage with foreign or transnational sources. Identifying absences is always difficult; assertions of indifference or resistance are also, in a sense, self-contradictory, insofar as they manifest awareness of the foreign or transnational, if only to reject their relevance. Nevertheless, it is possible to identify some active positions of resistance or deliberate indifference.

Systems with thoroughgoing and clearly expressed commitments to resist or maintain indifference to foreign and international law are rare if not unheard of.[75] To the extent that explanations of "resistance" involve some specific comparative effort at differentiation one has in a certain sense engaged; resistance based on internal theories of legitimate (and constrained) sources may be more wholly "disengaged" from any particular transnational sources. As shall be seen, a common form of expressed "resistance"—one in which another country's constitutional design, experience, or jurisprudence is viewed as a negative or "aversive" precedent[76]—may represent not so much a general resistance to transnational influence but a particular and important mode of engagement with the transnational to aid in making better choices for one's own polity. Of course, there may well be constitutional courts that pay no attention to the jurisprudence of other regimes, but if they do not proclaim themselves as such, or if academic literature does not comment on it (in a language others can access), their existence goes unnoticed.[77] With these caveats, let us consider in more detail some possible examples.

Both originalism (or intentionalism) and a form of national historicism (exceptionalism) are tropes doctrinally associated with postures of resistance to finding foreign or international law relevant to domestic constitutional interpretation. Formalism in constitutional interpretation, if understood as a restraint on judicial discretion by limiting the sources considered and questions to be answered to resolve cases, might also tend to exclude nonbinding forms of transnational law. With respect to international treaties and conventions, this model of resistance might also be associated with functionally "dualist" approaches under which international treaties require further legislation to have domestic legal effect. Examples of each are discussed below.

Articulated Resistance Inside the United States

Although much attention has been paid to sharply critical dissents in cases dealing with the death penalty and criminalization of homosexual acts, "resistance" also emerged in 1997 when, in *Printz v United States*,[78] Justice Scalia distinguished between the consideration of foreign models in constitutional design and the consideration of how foreign models worked in interpretation: Consistent with his broader argument about the appropriate focus of constitutional interpretation, Justice Scalia argued that foreign or comparative law was irrelevant to determining the correct meaning of a national constitution once made. This approach is both originalist and formalist, in that it excludes many legal sources as irrelevant. For Justice Breyer, in dissent, original intentions or original meaning were at best opaque on whether "commandeering" of state executive officials was permitted; different sources looked in different directions; and determining how a rule that would have upheld the national statute worked in other federal systems was an appropriate source. Had the "original meaning" of the Constitution on the permissibility of executive commandeering been more clear, Justice Breyer might not have considered foreign law relevant. In holding the federal statute unconstitutional, Justice Scalia drew on a range of sources (including constitutional structure, legislative practice under the Constitution and recent precedent), rejecting—in this case[79]—the weaker form of resistance that would permit consideration of foreign law to uphold, but not to invalidate, a statute.

Silent Resistance or Indifference

As noted, another doctrinal manifestation of resistance, apart from originalist tropes, might be reluctance to permit international agreements to affect constitutional interpretation. A striking silence is found in another U.S. case, *United States v. Morrison.*[80] In *Printz* the issue of foreign law was raised in a dissenting opinion, but not in the briefs before the Court; in *Morrison,* however, an amicus brief argued a basis in treaty law to sustain the challenged federal law, eliciting responses from two other amici briefs.[81] Yet no member of the Court addressed even the possibility that the scope of Congress's powers had been affected by the country's ratified international obligations. Although the availability of treaty law as a basis for implementing legislation was far from clear (as discussed further in Chapter 8 below), the Court's failure even to consider the argument, which might have avoided the need to strike down a statute enacted by Congress, is, perhaps, a form of silent resistance to claims about international law affecting constitutional interpretation.

Articulated Resistance Outside the United States

Reliance on a specifically national constitution to resist change emanating from international agreements to which the nation is a party is by no means unique to the United States. Justice Michael McHugh of the Australian High Court, though willing to make deliberative use of foreign law in resolving Australian constitutional cases, resisted arguments to construe the constitution in light of international legal rules because doing so would enable the executive to change the constitution, without resort to amendment, by entering treaties.[82] The Constitutional Court of Turkey has been criticized for its disinclination to cite or refer to decisions of the European Court of Human Rights (although it has not entirely failed to do so), as has the French Conseil Constitutionnel.[83] Moreover, the German Constitutional Court, the Italian Constitutional Court, and others have resisted agreement with the proposition that the European Court of Justice has final "competence-competence" in the event of a conflict.[84]

An "exceptionalist" narrative trope is found in a number of constitutional courts that either generally, or on occasion, resists considering foreign law. The resistance of the United States to considering comparative legal sources in interpreting constitutional rights has recently been compared to that of Malaysia and Singapore (which, like the United States, seem to have ambivalent strains of both resistance and willingness to consider foreign law in their constitutional jurisprudence).[85] These countries have developed the so-called "four walls" doctrine, asserted in 1963 by the Chief Justice of the Federation of Malaysia. The doctrine holds that its constitution is "primarily to be interpreted within its own four walls and not in light of the analogies drawn from other countries, such as Great Britain, the United States of America, or Australia."[86] The spirit of resisting the influence of foreign authority in cases interpreting Singapore's constitution was seen in decisions upholding a rebuttable presumption in a narcotics statute against a challenge that it was inconsistent with the presumption of innocence, rejecting freedom of speech defenses (in actions for contempt and in defamation actions), and upholding a ban on Jehovah's Witness publications as not inconsistent with freedom of religion.[87]

Ambivalent Resistance

Although resistance to foreign authority is notable in cases adopting a more statist (or communitarian) understanding of claims of rights, some judges in Malaysia and Singapore do refer to foreign cases to support arguments as well as to distinguish or reject their applicability.[88] One scholar suggests that the "appeal to local conditions to dismiss the relevance of foreign case law," and the questioning of international consensus on rights issues reflects an attitude both "dismissive and receptive of foreign case law," which in some instances are used to help normatively reason about the content of rights.[89] Such ambivalence about considering foreign law is found as well in the United States Court's decisions over time.[90] In the late 19th century, Justice Stephen Field (with no less passion than Justice Scalia in more recent years), asserted that the United States, being a government "of limited and delegated powers. . . . *takes nothing*" from European legal practices,[91] while on other occasions the Court or its members looked to foreign practices to confirm the "reasonableness" of statutes challenged under the Due Process Clause,[92] or to support interpretations of the scope of national power to regulate economic matters or of the limited scope of presidential power to act against private interests without legislative authority.[93]

Resistance in Specific Settings—Foreign Investment, Control of Natural Resources, and Supranational Regimes

So far this chapter has considered resistance to the interpretation of domestic norms in light of foreign legal norms, in contexts that involve primarily domestic parties and in which the foreign norm is being considered for its informational or normative value about law and the effects of different interpretive possibilities.

But constitutions and their interpreters may resist the transnational in other settings: for example, where foreign business interests seek to make investments or acquire control of resources under terms that differ from those provided in national constitutions. Here, the arguments by proponents of a transnational (free trade or investor protection) norm are primarily economic, and resistance may be primarily focused on the intrusion of foreign economic activity in violation of domestic norms. The source of resistance may be less about general questions of interpretation by courts and more about whether protections for domestic control of resources or economic activity, extant in many constitutions into the late 20th century, will be modified—either through interpretation or amendment—in response to transnational economic pressures.

In Colombia, the Philippines, and Mexico constitutional provisions for the protection of national resources and control over resources have come under challenge when they are seen to obstruct economic globalization. Courts in some of these countries have relied on particular provisions of national constitutions to resist certain foreign investment, privatization, or foreign or transnational standards of compensation that differ from the domestic rule. Each of these countries staked out in their constitutional design a distinctive position from the emerging consensus in transnational law on particular issues. But these "resisters" may find the posture of resistance difficult to sustain, in part because of the long-term commitments of international investment treaties, and in part because of the economic force of global capital. That, at least, is the narrative Professor David Schneiderman offers with respect to those countries which, in reliance on domestic constitutional norms, resist emerging transnational legal norms in favor of free trade and foreign investment.[94]

For example, the "Calvo Clause" and other aspects of Article 27 of the Mexican constitution were important outcomes of the Mexican Revolution and represented a distinctive (though widely followed in Latin America) approach to takings and expropriation of foreign property.[95] The clause limited foreign investors who claimed their property had been taken to the remedies made available under local law to citizens of the same state. However, as a result of the economic incentives and pressures of the NAFTA regime, "informal constitutional edicts" were issued "in order to neutralize the full effect of Article 27" to allow investors covered by NAFTA to receive the greater benefits of that regime.[96] In much of Latin America, Schneiderman has argued, countries have cooperated in or facilitated transnational economic engagement and changed their own law in order to comply with the requirements of the new international trade regime.[97] Although some scholars suggest that the "new constitutionalism" limits the power of domestic states to insist on constitutional norms that differ from prevailing free trade and investor protection norms,[98] Schneiderman points out that states have helped engineer this transformation. For present purposes, it is important to note that some of these transformations were adopted through "positive" constitutional amendment, using at least the forms of democratic decision within sovereign national states. Whether to see these moves as failed "resistance" or successful and self-interested convergence, then, is no easy matter, and highlights the forces for both that may exist within domestic polities.

National constitutional courts, interpreting national constitutions, have been sources of resistance in explicating constitutional norms that have stood in the way of foreign investment contracts or other international economic pressures for change. Where the courts are interpreting explicit clauses designed to protect national patrimony, or to limit the economic power of foreign nationals or companies, they may be seen not as resisting the influence of foreign law but as enforcing their particular national constitutions' commitments in a way that obstructs economic change. Exclusionary interpretations of these provisions have in some states, like Colombia, led to constitutional amendments. Given the interpretive malleability of even these constitutional texts, courts have not always adhered to exclusionary interpretations. For example, the Philippines Supreme Court in December 2004, on rehearing, reversed its decision of January 2004 on whether a proposed service contract with a foreign company violated a constitutional provision concerning national control of natural resources.[99] In these kinds of cases, resistance is primarily a resistance to transnational economic pressures or interventions, but it is also a resistance to outsider understandings of the role of law and the relationship of state power to state resources, capital development, and social welfare.

Although, on one level, these cases are quite distinct from those in which the issue is understood as the legitimacy of resort to foreign law in interpreting a national constitution, at another level these two kinds of cases are related. For one thing, they illustrate the degree to which convergences in legal regimes may be driven far less by courts and far more by economic actors and governments than some of the literature on the effects of foreign citation would suggest. Second, to the extent that domestic constitutional norms permit foreign businesses to enter markets and provide services (and in some cases to manage major sectors of both economic and governmental functions), the increased interchange between nationals of the domestic country and foreign nationals employed by or in the foreign businesses may increase the pressures for assimilation of other legal ideas.

As later chapters will discuss in more detail, there may be other areas of constitutional law in which the nature of the issue invites a form of resistance or indifference to other countries' experiences. Thus, for example, constitutional issues of federalism that come before courts—though they have been the subject of some amount of transnational citation and discussion at least in cases among the common law federal jurisdictions—may be peculiarly unsuited to benefitting from detailed comparisons with other federal polities, given the interdependent and highly contingent nature of most federal bargains.[100] Issues of national security and protection of the state might be thought to invite a kind of insular insistence on peculiarly national needs,[101] though, at the same time, these issues are ones that might well benefit from consulting the experience of similarly situated nations.[102] National courts in Europe have been described as, at times, "stand[ing] at the gate and defend[ing] national constitutions against illicit encroachment from Brussels."[103] When the nature of the resistance is related to the peculiarities of particular issues, however, it is more helpful to see these cases as involving not a general posture of resistance, but a more nuanced approach that treats foreign law as helpful on some—but not all—issues of interpretation, or that treats supranational law as valid and controlling on some issues but not others.

D. RESISTANCE, DIFFERENTIATION, AND THE EXPRESSIVE FUNCTION OF CONSTITUTIONS

This chapter has shown that there are multiple sources and types of resistance to the transnational as an element in constitutional interpretation. Their jurisprudential underpinnings and doctrinal manifestations may vary; whether they condemn all references or only some kinds of references to contemporary foreign and international law also varies. For some, *considering* foreign or international law in constitutional interpretation is permissible but *referring* to it is not; for others, the judge should attempt to ignore beliefs, assumptions, and knowledge about foreign law and focus only on domestic legal sources. For some resisters, "decorative" references to foreign law are relatively unproblematic, and for others, references to foreign law to *uphold* the validity of legislation is more acceptable than references in cases striking down domestic legislation. Exceptionalist impulses may support the use of foreign legal experience to *differentiate* the polity, but not as a positive normative example. Originalism may prohibit most consideration of contemporary transnational law, but might permit consideration of, for example, current understandings of international law in interpreting provisions relating to foreign affairs.

Although arguments from positivist understandings of constitutional texts turn out to be surprisingly hard to make in justifying a general posture of resistance, the arguments from democracy support resistance to the treatment of transnational norms as binding on constitutional interpretation—at least absent their adoption through appropriately democratic national processes. Arguments from the limits of judging surely raise cautions about the capacities of judges to determine what is truly comparable, and to do so while remaining rooted in their own national legal context (and perceived as such). Perhaps the strongest arguments that support some forms of resistance, however, are those based on the expressive and self-constituting functions of constitutions—functions that in some countries and for some periods of time provide significant support for resistance to reliance on transnational legal sources for interpretive purposes.

2. CONVERGENCE WITH THE TRANSNATIONAL

At the opposite pole from resistance, some constitutions and some constitutional court judges embrace a posture of national identification with transnational legal norms. Justice Scalia accused his colleagues in a 2005 juvenile death penalty case of holding as a "basic premise . . . that American law should conform to the laws of the rest of the world,"[1] a characterization that aptly captures this posture. While Justice Scalia erred in attributing this view to his colleagues on the U.S. Supreme Court, there are constitutions that require an interpretive posture of convergence with international law, and judges and scholars who would favor transnational convergences in the interpretation of constitutions.

Part A describes some contemporary influences that help produce such postures. Part B identifies specific national constitutions that require postures of convergence with respect to rights and discusses jurisprudential justifications offered for such postures, including a universalist view of rights, commitments to developing an international legal system, and the epistemic value of transnational consensus. Postures of convergence might also be motivated by institutional concerns to have "checks" on government from outside the polity, or by instrumental desires to be seen as part of a particular community of nations with associated benefits in status and economic opportunity.

Part C explores some of the doctrinal manifestations of convergence, a posture that has weaker and stronger versions. Proportionality analysis emerges as a possible point of methodological convergence, and a willingness to impose norms extraterritorially as a possibly associated doctrine. Convergence postures may require a "margin of appreciation" doctrine, or its equivalent, to accommodate the claim of universalism with the inevitable pluralism of approaches that will arise even among like-minded democratic countries. Relationships between formal constitutional rules concerning the priority of international law and convergence postures are considered.

Part D explores the grounding for and the limits of convergence as an interpretive posture. While explicit constitutional incorporation of international human rights instruments is growing, it is less common to find incorporation of international economic treaties (although some constitutions authorize participation in international organizations or legal systems involving commercial or economic relations).[2] Constitutional law as a field spans a wide range of rights, negative or positive, individual or group, as well as issues of governance; there are many constitutional issues on which a strong transnational consensus is difficult to identify, including, for example, rights of private property. Arguments about convergence in such areas face important challenges, which may also have more general implications suggestive of the limitations of convergence postures.

A. INFLUENCES TOWARD POSTURES OF CONVERGENCE

In the independence-seeking metanarratives that permeate U.S. constitutionalism, the distinctiveness of the Constitution and its nation is in a sense almost assumed. The framers, or some of them, were conscious of the novelty of their exercise: while they drew on what they could learn of comparative experience, and on experience with colonial charters and then state constitutions, they were aware at the time of embarking on a distinctive form of republican, constitutional government in a large and complex political entity. In the post–World War II era of global constitutionalism, a different set of assumptions—strongly influenced by existing constitutional systems and by the development of international human rights norms—has come into existence.

Of Archetypes, Incentives, and Supranational Courts and Organizations

There are at least three important influences, on which there is wide agreement in the literature, that help account both for the development of some convergences in constitutional expression of rights and for the normative posture favoring convergence expressed by some courts and constitutional judges.

First, many foreign constitutions drafted since World War II rely on international human rights instruments (or on other constitutions that relied on these instruments) as archetypes, leading to parallel rights-protecting provisions. Similarities in coverage are often accompanied by similarities in language in modern constitutional rights provisions. New constitutions and further development of international human rights declarations and instruments have mutually influenced one another's production, in ways sometimes difficult to disentangle.[3] And in recent years, embrace of international human rights within domestic legal orders has increasingly been deployed as a marker for regime shift from authoritarianism or military rule to democracy.[4]

Second, membership—or sought-for membership—in the EU and the Council of Europe, and participation in the British Commonwealth, are significant both legally and culturally in promoting exchange, and to some degree convergence, of constitutional ideas; other regional courts or organizations, including those in Latin America and Africa, may come to have similar influence.[5] The importance of human rights in the development of a modern European legal identity emerged from the shared historic experience of the horrors of World War II, as well as from the challenges of constructing a political union for multiple national peoples. The sense that a legal commitment to certain human rights norms—opposition to the death penalty being a prominent example—is a necessary concomitant of being a full member of European legal institutions is strikingly illustrated by the decision of the Hungarian Constitutional Court, in its first year of existence, holding unconstitutional that country's death penalty.[6] For those states that have entered the EU and those additional states that are parties to the European Convention on Human Rights (ECHR), the judgments and the jurisprudence of the European Court of Justice (ECJ) and of the European Court of Human Rights (ECtHR) exert significant pressures toward legal convergences.[7]

Third, the policies of many international bodies—including non-governmental organizations (NGOs), UN-related bodies involved in monitoring, conflict resolution, and peacemaking, and other intergovernmental bodies, like the World Bank or International Monetary Fund, that offer financial assistance to developing countries—seek to promote the "rule of law" and the protection of certain individual rights, and may offer financial and other incentives to induce compliance.[8] The very act of constitution-making has been, to some extent, internationalized; as one scholar has observed, "[c]onstitution-making has become an international and comparative exercise in a way that it rarely was in the century before 1989 . . . a new democracy that excluded foreigners entirely from its constitutional process might stamp itself as decidedly insular, even somewhat suspect."[9] Although the rule of law initiatives of international financial organizations have been controversial, with some praising and some criticizing their policies,[10] the point here is the potential impact these regimes may have on domestic constitutions and constitutional law.

Convergence or Fragmentation?

That these influences toward convergence exist should not obscure the fact that there may also be important sources of diversity, even fragmentation, concurrently at work. Identity-based social movements have grown in importance.[11] These may involve ethnonational, linguistic, or religious identities not recognized by present national borders, or other groups that have suffered social or legal discrimination, whose identity-based claims are in some respects facilitated by the same technological developments that facilitate forms of cultural and legal convergence. There are contests over what norms should have ascendence; international and national law may be subject to important claims and pressures "from below," as social movements in the "third world" resist economic globalization and its impositions on local values and communities of solidarity.[12] Multiple legal orders and regulatory pressures reflect and respond to the pushes and pulls manifested in the growth of global capitalism, global criminal networks, global NGOs, transnational social movements, and transnational religious movements—a set of "clash[ing] globalizations."[13] Among these clashes, though, are some forces also working to produce transnational legal norms—for example, to respond to harmful activities that transcend national boundaries (crime, environmental harms) or to recognize claims of local indigenous communities. Competition for capital, human resources, and technological and communications development may reinforce some diversities and at the same time contribute to the spread and "pull" of converging transnational norms.

Convergence in Law or As Interpretive Posture

Having said this, the meaning of "convergence" requires further specification. Convergence in constitutional rules may be simply an outcome, a fact that is produced, not from deliberate efforts to seek convergence or from deference to transnational norms, but from parallel responses to similar phenomena—including the demands of judicial review and the pressures and incentives of economic globalization. It may be partial, more notable in some areas and on some issues than others; it may result from economic pressures targeted at states, subnational entities, or business interests within a state to induce compliance with international norms.[14] Convergence, though, may also be a normative interpretive posture, working to conform national constitutional interpretation to international law or transnational legal consensus. It is with the latter that this chapter is primarily concerned.

Some proponents of convergence as a normative posture view domestic constitutional law as a site for the implementation of international law. National constitutions can manifest a cosmopolitan approach to rights by incorporating international law or specific international human rights treaties into their constitutions or treating them as having constitutional stature, sometimes for reasons based on the hierarchic superiority of international law. But convergence may also be associated with regional supranational instruments, as in Europe. Other forms of convergence involve a more decentralized approach, in which foreign comparative law may play a greater role. Support for this form of convergence might be based on an understanding of each national system as a participant in a decentralized but normatively progressive epistemological process of transnational norm convergence, which may be based on theoretical conceptions about constitutions as much as on ideas about international or supranational law.[15]

Postures of convergence might apply to methods of constitution-making and interpretation, as well as to the substantive rules or institutional designs of constitutional systems. David Beatty's and Robert Alexy's arguments might be taken to imply that a particular methodology—proportionality analysis—is inherent to the nature of constitutional rights or constitutional adjudication.[16] Democracy theorists propose that constitution-making is no longer legitimate without popular participation in the process through means ranging from wide consultation to acceptance at a referendum. Each of these positions is, in a sense, about a possible methodological convergence—for proportionality in the interpretation of rights, or for democratic participation in the formation of legitimate constitutions. One can, in theory, be a proponent of methodological convergence without necessarily being a proponent of substantive convergence (as Beatty at times claims to be). Yet the two are not quite so distinct as this. The reasons underlying methodological or process commitments are not without substantive, normative content themselves.[17] Outcomes inconsistent with that substantive basis for a method of constitutional interpretation or lawmaking may be viewed as arising from defects in the application of the method, thus drawing together methodological commitments and valid substantive outcomes.[18]

B. CONVERGENCE POSTURES AND THEIR NORMATIVE OR JURISPRUDENTIAL FOUNDATIONS

In a small but increasing number of countries, constitutional texts require constitutional interpretation to converge or accord with one or more international legal instruments. For example, article 93 of the 1991 Political Constitution of Colombia requires that domestic constitutional rights "be interpreted in accordance with" international human rights treaties ratified by Colombia. Section 75(22) of Argentina's Constitution now specifically states that close to a dozen named international and regional human rights instruments—including the Universal Declaration of Human Rights, the ICCPR, the ICESCR, and the CEDAW—are of "constitutional hierarchy." The 1993 Constitution of Peru states that "Norms relating to the rights and freedoms recognized by the Constitution are interpreted in accordance with the UDHR and with international treaties and agreements on those rights that have been ratified by Peru."[19]

Such provisions are not limited to the constitutions of South America. Section 10 of the Constitution of Spain declares, in terms quite similar to those used in Peru, that "[p]rovisions relating to the fundamental rights and liberties recognized by the Constitution shall be construed in conformity with the Universal Declaration of Human Rights and the international treaties and agreements thereon ratified by Spain." And Romania's Constitution of 1991 provides, in Article 20(1) concerning international human rights treaties, that "[c]onstitutional provisions concerning the citizens' rights and liberties shall be interpreted and enforced in conformity with the Universal Declaration of Human Rights, [and] with the covenants and other treaties Romania is a party to."[20]

A wider phenomenon is the incorporation of rights, drawn from international human rights instruments, into the language of discrete provisions of national constitutions. A study of Latin American constitutions found significant, though not consistent, inclusion of rights similar to those set forth in international instruments.[21] Another scholar wrote that "[e]ffective juridification of international law is advancing in a decentralized manner. Thus, the same penetration of domestic institutions by the rules of international law is present in many of the new constitutions emerging at the end of the Cold War," whose constitutional courts "easily speak a transnational language" and "analyze claims of rights by drawing freely on international, comparative, and domestic sources."[22] (South Africa's constitutional provisions, widely discussed in the literature, can better be understood as involving aspirations of engagement, not convergence, and will be discussed in the next chapter.)

Where a constitutional text requires that interpretation be "in accord" with international human rights law, or incorporates specific human rights instruments as being of "constitutional stature," it does not raise issues of interpretive legitimacy for a court to look at those instruments and how they are interpreted elsewhere. Even a formalist jurisprudence, or one grounded in deep commitments to positivism, would implement such constitutional directives. The purposes of these constitutional provisions, as expressed by their drafters,[23] have been to align their country's practices with those required by international human rights law and to mark a clear departure from prior regimes.[24] The Colombian Constitution of 1991 was intended as part of a serious effort at constitutional "transformation,"[25] with the aim of "sav[ing] Colombia."[26] Its constitutional court has made use of international as well as comparative law in interpreting the constitution in somewhat transformational ways,[27] although the seriousness of such transformational reasons for including human rights conformance provisions may differ in other countries.[28]

Transformational purposes may overlap with those motivating jurists in other countries who, lacking explicit mandates in the constitutional text, nonetheless argue for a presumption in favor of convergence with international law or international human rights law. Perhaps the best-known proponent of this view is Justice Michael Kirby, of the High Court of Australia. Justice Kirby has long argued for applying the principles of the Bangalore Declaration of 1988.[29] These principles, as they have developed and been elaborated, hold that domestic law, including constitutional provisions, should where possible be interpreted as consistent with international human rights law, including not only treaty law ratified by the countries but also principles of customary law.[30] Justice Kirby has sought to apply this presumption in his decisions on the High Court of Australia.[31] For example, in *Kartinyeri v. Commonwealth of Australia*, he relied on this presumption to interpret the federal constitutional power to legislate with respect to races as authorizing only benign, and not invidious, legislation.[32] In a case involving the government's right to take property without compensation in federal territories, he likewise relied on this presumption in construing the constitution to require that compensation be paid.[33] As of 2005 he was the only member of the Australian High Court to take the position of consistently inquiring whether the constitution could be read in a manner consistent with international human rights law, a position that has evoked active disagreement by other members of that Court (including Justice Callinan, quoted in Chapter 1).[34] However, an interpretive presumption that ambiguous constitutional provisions be interpreted in accord with binding international obligations of a country has been accepted by judges in other countries as well, as reflected in both majority and minority opinions in a 2004 Privy Council decision concerning the constitution of Trinidad and Tobago. Thus, Lord Bingham wrote:

> [I]f a provision of a state's domestic law is ambiguous and permits of two interpretations, one of which will accord with the state's international obligations and the other of which will involve a violation of those obligations,

> a court will so far as possible adopt that interpretation which will accord with the state's international obligations. . . . [This] proposition[] appl[ies] to constitutions as to other domestic law. . . .

And, Lord Bingham went on to emphasize, the presumption applied "even if the international obligations were undertaken after the date of the constitution."[35]

In the United States, perhaps the foremost proponent of a legal approach leading to some convergences is Yale Law School Dean Harold Koh. Unlike Justice Kirby, Dean Koh argues not so much for the prioritization of international law, but for a more decentralized form of law, transnational in character, that emerges from what he calls "transnational legal process."[36] If Kirby's focus is on an interpretive presumption in favor of consistency with international law, Koh's is on transnational legal *process*. Yet this process centers on the development of international norms, and Koh is plainly a proponent of international law not only being considered but also influencing constitutional interpretation. Koh's vision suggests that international law and domestic constitutional law will, and should, by dialogue and discussion converge on sufficiently similar results at least on human rights issues to result in a well-functioning international system.[37]

A number of reasons for convergence postures are offered by these and other scholars. Some are grounded in a moral/philosophical commitment to the existence of universalist human rights norms or in the legitimacy and compliance pulls of processes of identifying and developing such norms. Other reasons are more epistemic in character, having to do with the probable "rightness" of answers to legal questions reached by many different countries. A further set of arguments view international or transnational law as a form of constraint on interpretive discretion, adding legitimacy to the decisions of domestic judges. Arguments from judges' roles, of greater and lesser ambition, are advanced, focusing on the benefits of building an international legal system, or on the possibility that commitments to transnational legal norms may help judges constrain the possibility of dreadful departures within their own countries. Some arguments, finally, rest on expanded notions of positivism or textualism.

Universal Moral Rights

The UN Charter declares the existence of "fundamental human rights"; the UDHR, agreed to by the members of the United Nations in 1948, asserts in general terms what those rights are; and two major human rights covenants of 1966, along with many others, provide further specifications and offer means by which countries can consent to those specifications and agree to "soft" forms of enforcement against themselves. The UDHR has been referred to as a "Bill of Rights for the world," "the international Magna Carta," a "moral code that hallowed individual human worth and dignity," and a "universal moral code."[38] For one scholar, "a human right by definition is a universal moral right, something which all men everywhere, at all times ought to have, something of which no one may be deprived without a grave affront to justice, something which is owing to every human being simply because he is human."[39] Louis Henkin describes human rights as the only "political-moral idea that has received universal acceptance;"[40] for Harold Koh, "human rights norms are universal: they belong to everyone. . . ."[41]

The universalist assumptions of these rights, deriving from the nature of human beings and human societies,[42] are not grounded on notions of state consent or even on particular lawmaking processes. Indeed, Henkin argues that human rights norms are becoming like jus cogens norms, that is, norms of international law that are based not on the consent of the states but on their universally compelling nature.[43] According to Gerald Neuman, "The central purpose of international human rights law is to call into question positive legal practices that fail to respect universal values."[44] Jerome Shestack maintains that "the conflict between universalist and relativist theory has been rendered moot by the Declaration and its progeny. . . . [F]undamental human rights have become universal by virtue of their entry into international law as jus cogens, customary law, or convention."[45] While many refer to the widespread acceptance of these norms as evidence of their universal character,[46] their moral force derives not from state consent but from the nature of human beings.

Critics, however, argue that international law—to the extent it has any force—necessarily rests either on each state's consent and/or the consent of a sufficient number of states. Others attack the very concept of a universal understanding of human rights, because the rights individuals need or want will depend on the kinds of societies in which they live.[47] Still others attack the particular iterations of human rights found in the UDHR and related UN covenants as grounded in Western, rather than multicultural or cosmopolitan, conceptions.[48] Yet there are powerful arguments, as suggested above, for some form of universal conception of rights grounded in the moral quality of being human.[49]

How does this relate to domestic constitutional law? As Sujit Choudhry has suggested, one "interpretive mode, universalist interpretation, holds that constitutional guarantees are cut from a universal cloth, and, hence, that all constitutional courts are engaged in the identification, interpretation, and application of the same set of norms. Those norms are comprehended as transcendent legal principles that are logically prior to positive rules of law and legal doctrines."[50] Professor Neuman's suggestion of the "suprapositive" character of rights is an effort to capture the same idea, that constitutional rights may be seen as manifestations of more universal moral truths or human rights–based commitments, which all countries should strive to achieve or fulfill.[51] The increasing number of constitutions that assert as one of their purposes or principles to be in accord with international human rights law lends considerable positivist force to this claim.[52] Many post–World War II constitutions were framed in light of and adopt language from the UDHR and/or its related human rights covenants. And case law under some older constitutions—including that of the United States—suggests the aspiration to develop law in accordance with that of "civilized" nations (perhaps implying both the transnational character of some constitutional aspirations and the historic identification of international law with the interests and ideologies of the more powerful).[53] Positive constitutional texts may reinforce a sense that constitutions should be interpreted in the light of those rights that all human beings should be deemed to have, which are recognized in international human rights law. The purposes of constitutions, then, should be understood to give effect where possible to these fundamental and universal moral norms.

Epistemic Arguments

Jeremy Waldron, and Cass Sunstein and Eric Posner, have offered two versions of what I would call epistemic, rather than moral-universalist arguments, for why constitutional interpreters should give weight to transnational consensus on legal issues. Both accounts conceive of law as having "right answers" (or at least having the possibility of "right" or "better" answers), and of certain kinds of consensus as providing reliable (though not infallible) evidence of what the right answer is.

For Posner and Sunstein, an argument can be derived from Condorcet's Jury Theorem, which (to simplify) holds that, with respect to an issue on which any one decision-maker has a more than 50% chance of correct decision, the greater the numbers of independent decision-makers reaching the same result, the more likely the decision is to be correct.[54] As the authors recognize, the assumptions of the theory are significant; in areas of strong normative contest it may be impossible to say whether the first condition is met, and distinguishing independent decisions from those influenced by the decisions of others may also be quite difficult. For Waldron, transnational consensus (among "'civilized'" or "'freedom-loving'" countries) can function as a kind of "ius gentium," suggesting—by analogy, not to mathematical formula, but to the scientific process of sharing, accumulating and testing information—that if repeated iterations of decentralized decision-making by multiple legal decision-makers reach the same answer to a legal problem, that answer may well be the better one and is at least deserving of considered weight.[55] Such epistemic claims assume that guidance to answers on open questions relevant to constitutional judgment can be found in the accumulation of third party decision-making (like that of juries or scientific communities) by multiple national legal systems. Theories based on such claims may assume that the institutional character of the decision-maker is not relevant to the interpretation of whatever constitutional norm is at issue,[56] for consensus-based epistemic approaches must posit that the decision-makers are answering the same question.[57]

If international legal instruments were taken as evidence of epistemic agreement, they would have force in supporting a general posture of convergence. Many human rights instruments have gained ratification by the vast majority of nations in the world: for example, the ICCPR and ICESCR have each been ratified by well over 150 state parties, the CEDAW by over 180, and the Convention on the Rights of the Child by an even larger number.[58] Yet the reported gaps between ratification and improved compliance,[59] the possibility of ratification without incorporation into effective domestic law, and the possibility that some ratifications were based neither on independent judgments nor on the merits of each of the rights contained therein, weaken such epistemic claims.[60] If, on the other hand, epistemic claims for the normative value of a legal consensus were limited to areas in which deeper indicia of compliance (and/or of independent judgment) were required, the range of human rights issues on which a serious transnational consensus would emerge is much narrower. To identify such deeper indicia, resort might be had to the domestic law (including constitutional law) in rights-protecting, democratic rule-of-law countries (perhaps in part on the assumption that decision-making in free and democratic countries may reflect broader, deeper, or wider deliberation).[61]

Interpretive Discretion and Legitimacy

A different set of arguments in favor of presumptions of convergence are based on the role of the judge. For example, Justice Kirby has argued that considering the views of others will give constitutional court judgments greater legitimacy; sounding in discourse theory, Kirby suggests that the process of respectful consideration of others' views dealing with similar questions will increase the legitimacy of the decision. Further, Sir Sydney Kentridge suggests that, particularly when construing new bills of rights, looking at "[c]omparative jurisprudence enables the judge to test his or her value judgment against the judgments of other courts which have grappled with similar provisions," to assure that the judge is not simply having the constitution "mean whatever we want it to mean."[62] However, these arguments do not necessarily support a presumption of convergence, rather than of engagement with comparative or international sources.

A second argument may do so. By committing to interpretation consistent with international law, where possible, the judge has (arguably) constrained his or her discretion to a greater extent than if the standard were simply one of fair consideration. This constraint might take different forms. For example, according to the Romanian Constitution, international human rights act as a floor, but constitutional provisions more favorable to the rights holder will apply,[63] while the Argentine Supreme Court has, arguably, treated international human rights law as both ceiling and floor.[64] However, any claim for constraint of interpretive discretion from any such presumption depends on the degree of determinacy provided by the international body of law. While international human rights law may have fairly determinate application on some issues—for example, the prohibition on torture—given the breadth of human rights provisions and the absence of hierarchically final decision-makers to resolve the meaning of those provisions there is considerable room for national discretion in the interpretation of these rights and thus for indeterminacy.

Arguments from Judges' Roles

Anne-Marie Slaughter has argued that judges ought to participate in a shared process of articulating transnational norms to be enforced by judges around the world: "[I]mproving the capacity of government officials [including judges] to . . . govern" is essential for the creation of a stable world order, and international law can provide a "backstop" to support the judging capacities of judges.[65] These transnational judicial networks may be a mechanism that produces degrees of convergence on some issues—notably including the desirability of independence in judging—but the justifications offered in their support sound more in the normative posture of engagement, and will be more fully discussed in the next chapter. The idea of international law as a "backstop" resonates with the argument that interpretive presumptions in favor of international law can prevent serious abuses within domestic systems, discussed below.

Support for the International Legal System

A strong argument for convergence or harmonization of domestic legal systems with international law is the desire to promote the development of the international legal system, avoiding wars and promoting individual security, freedom, and economic well-being. The crux of Justice Kirby's argument is that "the failure of courts to give meaning to the law and the Constitution that accord, so far as possible, with international law, may itself contribute needlessly to State failures" to comply with their obligations under international law.[66] National courts ought to presume in favor of consistency with international law, lest they "contribute" to state breaches of international law. While he recognizes that "[o]ccasionally, disconformity will be unavoidable," he expresses hope that "this will be relatively rare and . . . courts will play a part in avoiding unnecessary instances." For judges to act toward this goal "is no more than a rational contemporary response to the accommodation of the nation, and its laws, to the environment of international law in which every nation now operates."[67]

As his elaboration of this idea makes plain, it is a concern with the vibrancy of international law as a system (and the inadequacy of existing international tribunals) that undergirds this argument. Thus Kirby writes, "international law would be grievously injured if national courts, out of a sense of their own superiority or proclaimed ignorance, were to reject the rules and influence of the international legal order."[68] The argument is premised on the idea that promoting an international legal system is a good to be desired: because nations are now "more inter-dependent,"[69] they have a greater stake in the development of a strong system of international law, to which the presumption Kirby argues for would contribute. The need for a more vigorous system of international law, or a "new world order," to harmonize or coordinate increasingly interdependent sets of states and regulators and to respond to increasingly transnational threats (environmental, crime, terrorism) is a theme sounded by many.[70]

This argument raises a number of questions. First, are the areas where coordination is needed so encompassing as to warrant a presumption of constitutional conformity with international law, given all of the functions of constitutional law? Second, Kirby's effort is to harness the legitimacy and power of domestic courts to implement international law. But depending importantly on what the domestic contexts of the courts are, might presuming in favor of a transnational legal norm undermine the very legitimacy that internationalists seek to draw upon?[71]

Harold Koh, who echoes many of Kirby's concerns in his arguments for U.S. courts considering international law in constitutional interpretation, envisions a somewhat more complex relationship between national and international law, a transnational process in which parallel domestic and international norms interact with each other in an interdependent and decentralized process of norm harmonization and convergence.[72] Like Kirby, Koh argues that "domestic courts must . . . advance the broader development of a well-functioning international judicial system," "look[ing] beyond narrow U.S. interests to the 'mutual interests of all nations in a smoothly functioning international legal regime,'" and that such courts, "whenever possible, should 'consider if there is a course that furthers, rather than impedes, the development of an ordered international system.'"[73] In Koh's terms, courts do so by "*coordinating* U.S. domestic constitutional rules with rules of foreign and international law."[74] Koh's transnational process accommodates the possibility that human rights will be protected sometimes at the level of international law and sometimes at the level of national law, while acknowledging the need for legal processes to help define and incorporate human rights into law.

As Karen Knop and others have suggested, the effect of encouraging domestic courts to consider international law in adjudication may well be a diversification, indeed fragmentation, of the meanings of international law in a range of areas, or a tendency to treat international law as a source that, like comparative law, is less a form of binding than of persuasive (or, in Mayo Moran's term, "influential") authority, thereby possibly diluting its force.[75] On its own terms, then, it is not clear that a presumption to interpret constitutional law in accord with international law will promote a stronger international legal system. As may be illustrated by the practice of the political branches in the United States of attaching reservations and understandings to international human rights treaties, national courts might interpret international law so as to conform to domestic law to a greater extent than the converse.[76] Finally, some might disagree with the premise that strengthening the present international legal system is beneficial, at least absent change in its structure, in light of concerns about the legitimacy of the substantive lawmaking capacities of the international system (including the democratic deficit in the processes and rules by which assent is manifested or formal action taken).[77]

Notwithstanding these questions, the idea that all states have a constitutional stake in a just and effective international legal system is powerful. States—and their associated constitutions—are in some respects defined by their coexistence in a world system of states whose authority is recognized by other states. All states have an interest in how their members are treated when in other states (or at least the great majority of states that allow their citizens to exit) and thus to support some minimal core of international human rights, as well as to respect international rules against aggressive use of force—for all states have, or should have, an interest in avoiding wars and genocides.

Checks against Horrific Conduct or Backsliding from Democracy

Behind arguments to support the international legal system through postures of convergence may lie another notion: that presuming in favor of interpretations that accord with international human rights law (even while never arriving at convergence) will develop habits of decision-making that will (to the extent law can do so) help prevent the most serious kinds of violations of human rights from occurring. According to Justice Kirby, "What carries us forward is the memory of the terrible wrongs to human rights and knowledge of the dangers for the world we live in, absent international law."[78] That is, international law's importance is in preventing the "terrible wrongs to human rights and . . . dangers for the world," such as genocide and war. International human rights law, then, may be seen instrumentally as a means to prevent great moral evils. Full incorporation of international human rights law in domestic constitutions, or interpretive presumptions of convergence, may be overbroad measures toward these goals, but such overbreadth is arguably necessary in order to assure the habitual pull of these transnational human rights norms.

Commitments to international human rights law in domestic constitutions might be thought particularly important to check abuses against minorities, whose capacities to rely on democratic mechanisms may be limited. In legal systems without a strong and well-established tradition of independent and effective judicial enforcement of antidiscrimination norms, the use of international law as an external check may have strong functional justification. Of course, the premise that some "outside reinforcements" are helpful might also be served, for example, by consenting to the jurisdiction of international tribunals, or even by according constitutional stature to "outside" members of constitutional courts or other decisional bodies (as in Bosnia-Herzegovina).[79] But requiring constitutional interpretation to accord with international human rights law may provide both local legitimacy and a basis for external monitoring and comparison to other tribunals' views of the same human rights norms, to prevent, or protest, gross deviations from those norms.[80]

A worry is whether the international legal system will stand as a bulwark against humanity's propensity for evil. Kirby has argued that it will, in part because the content of international human rights law is strongly influenced by Anglo-American norms of the rule of law and protection of civil liberties.[81] Yet, a skeptic might say, perhaps this is a mere reflection of the power of these countries at a time when their interests were served by those values. Moreover, international human rights law recognizes a number of grounds of necessity for departures from many of its norms. As Kim Scheppele has noted, international law as a whole may be moving in a direction toward greater criminal law enforcement responsibilities, and in so doing may experience internal tensions (like those of national states) over the demands of effective cooperation in combating or preventing terrorism and the protection of the full range of human rights.[82] Anne-Marie Slaughter and William Burke-White have written of the "significant danger inherent in these new functions of international law," which "lies in the potential of national governments to co-opt the force of international law to serve their own objectives"; by requiring states to act and strengthening their capacity to do so, they suggest, "international law may actually make states more effective at the very repression and abuse the interference challenge seeks to overcome. . . . [and] may give national governments new license to undertake otherwise illegal or unjust policies"; they consider the potential for conflict between "human rights and state security" within international law a "danger."[83] Their solution is to argue for checks and balances within international law and for the need for international regimes to consider multiple values, to strengthen rather than abandon international law. Finally, as noted earlier, international human rights law has competing values, whose application to particular cases is somewhat indeterminate. For example, international human rights law recognizes collective rights of "peoples" to self-determination—rights that have been invoked not only to overcome colonial domination and ground claims for greater autonomy for distinct cultural groups, but also to flame the passions of ethnic nationalism and xenophobia.[84]

Positive Textualist Arguments

As already indicated, a presumption for interpretive convergence might follow from a different set of premises based in positive understandings of law or a view of legal texts as having a kind of shared meaning and autonomy. These arguments exist on two levels, that of domestic constitutional law and that of international legal obligations.

Apart from explicit textual mandates to interpret in accord with some aspects of international law, implicit textual license or requirements for convergence might be found in domestic constitutional texts. Constitutional ideas have never been developed in isolation, and constitutions of one or more countries often influence the design and words used in others. As David Law has observed about the United States, "if any of the ideas or values enshrined in the Constitution were ever unique, this nation has endeavored only to spread them, not to monopolize them."[85] Many constitutions share parallel provisions, inspired in part by provisions of older constitutions and of human rights covenants.[86] If these are understood in a positive sense as intended to have similar meanings, then interpretive presumptions in favor of following a transnational consensus on their meaning might be advanced.

Such an account might require a view that those adopting such provisions committed to the specific evolutionary path followed by other comparable texts—that is, they are "autonomous" from being affected by other features of their constitution, but the autonomy is a "shared" one insofar as their interpretation should remain the same as those of other similarly worded provisions in other legal instruments. This reasoning also rests on a view that the rights provisions of a constitution can and should be interpreted relatively unaffected by other aspects, of government structure and allocation of powers, which differentiate constitutions from one another. That values or texts are shared, however, does not necessarily mean that others have interpreted them "correctly," either in some acontextualized sense or in the context of particular constitutional orders. And assuming the shared evolutionary autonomy of constitutional rights is not only heroic (at least in some systems), but also in some tension with a broader understanding of the functions of their domestic constitutions, as discussed below in Chapter 5.

An alternative basis in positive law for a normative obligation to interpret constitutions in accord with international law might be found in a nation's ratification of the UN Charter (Articles 55 and 56 of which commit members to work toward the protection of human rights), or in other international instruments, including human rights covenants. Hints of such a positive basis may be found in many decisions. In the United States, four justices relied in part on the UN Charter to hold unconstitutional discriminatory restrictions on property ownership by Japanese-Americans; one of the opinions observed,

> [W]e have recently pledged ourselves to cooperate with the United Nations to "promote . . . universal respect for, and observance of, human rights and fundamental freedoms for all without distinction as to race, sex, language, or religion." How can this nation be faithful to this international pledge if state laws which bar land ownership and occupancy by aliens on account of race are permitted to be enforced?[87]

Yuval Shany urges that international human rights treaties, once ratified, should be read to require some form of constitutionalization.[88] He argues that both "effective remedy" clauses, and requirements that states "ensure" or "secure" the rights guaranteed within them, require such constitutional incorporation, in part to have a basis for invalidating domestic statutes that are inconsistent with the international norms to which the country has agreed by ratifying the treaty.

Arguments for interpretive convergence grounded in international legal commitments, however, are controversial. Within such "dualist" systems as New Zealand, Australia, or Canada, treaties not implemented by the parliament conventionally have been without domestic legal force.[89] In nominally "monist" systems, as in the United States, whose Constitution's Supremacy Clause makes treaties the "law of the land," ratifying instruments sometimes declare or opponents may argue that specific treaties are not "self-executing" and should not be considered in judicial decision-making. And in either kind of system arguments may arise over whether treaties can "change" the meaning of the constitution, with resistance by some jurists to be expected.

* * *

Thus, we have seen that—as was the case with resistance to transnational influences on constitutional law—postures of convergence can rest on different normative grounds. These include universalist views of rights and the role of law in protecting rights (associated with universalist understandings of human nature, human societies, and justice), or more cautious epistemological positions that hold that the weight of practice is likely to represent a wisdom worth following. Domestic constitutional law may be viewed as a site for the implementation of international legal norms, or, alternatively, as a mechanism for the decentralized, interactive development of avowedly transnational legal norms. Convergence postures might also be based on positivist commitments, on a desire to strengthen the international legal system, or on the hope of forestalling the truly horrific.

C. DOCTRINAL IMPLICATIONS AND MANIFESTATIONS

After noting various forms in which a presumption for convergence may be articulated, this section considers possible doctrinal manifestations of convergence postures: first, efforts to apply norms extraterritorially; second, the use of a margin of appreciation doctrine; and third, reliance on proportionality analyses to resolve constitutional conflicts. It concludes by explaining why formal "monism" with respect to the relationship of international and domestic law may be, but is not necessarily, associated with postures of convergence.

Different Presumptions?

Doctrinal expressions of a convergence posture could take different forms. One is that international law in ratified treaties should be treated as *superior* to the constitution—that is, as the ground norm against which all other laws are evaluated. Yuval Shany refers to this approach as "supra-constitutionalism," under which international law overrides inconsistent constitutional law; he distinguishes it from "constitutionalization," under which international law has a status equal to that of the constitution (as in Argentina).[90] As noted above, Shany argues that international law itself requires such approaches, which call for giving legal force within domestic constitutional interpretation to at least some international norms. Another approach, already discussed, is for a presumption of constitutional harmony with international law. On this account, a constitution should be interpreted in a manner consistent with international law, if it is possible to do so within the interpretive framework of the particular constitution.

Thus, if international law condemns the execution of juveniles, that would be a strong independent reason to interpret the domestic constitution to do so.

A weaker presumption, one perhaps more compatible with a posture of engagement, is that a constitution be interpreted so as not to put the country in *breach* of its international obligations. As long as a constitution is open to the political branches' conforming national conduct to international norms—for example, by abolishing the juvenile death penalty—then a failure to construe the constitution as itself requiring this result would not necessarily put the country in breach of international law. This weaker presumption would not necessarily result in convergence between the meaning of the constitution and international law, but it would not be without force and could facilitate national practice coming into consistency with the requirements of binding international law. For example, it might favor interpreting a national constitution as affording the national government power to require compliance with judgments of the International Court of Justice taken pursuant to binding treaty obligations.[91] Or, perhaps even weaker, courts might presume that their constitutions be interpreted in accord with minimal standards of the behavior of "civilized" societies.[92] Without a commitment to all manifestations of current international human rights law, such a presumption would nonetheless provide a benchmark, however weak, of interpretive guidance (though one subject to objection by those who would regard this as a back door way of privileging only selective and contestable norms).

Extraterritorial Effects

Commitments to postures of convergence with the transnational may be reflected in a willingness to apply those norms with some extraterritorial force. Doing so can serve as both expression of and contributor to norm convergence—at least on some issues. Perhaps the clearest examples are found in foreign case law on extradition, including decisions of the European Court of Human Rights having extraterritorial effects on countries outside of Europe.[93]

In *Soering v. United Kingdom*,[94] the ECtHR held that the United Kingdom would violate its obligations under the ECHR by extraditing the defendant to face capital murder charges in Virginia, because doing so would expose the defendant to a serious risk of harm (suffering "death row phenomenon"),[95] in violation of the Article 3 bar on torture and inhuman or degrading treatment. The ECtHR reviewed in detail the nature of the criminal justice proceedings in Virginia and the conditions of confinement on death row, including the size of the cells and the number of hours of exercise, and the average length of time between conviction and exhaustion of appeals and habeas review. Although recognizing that "it is common ground that the United Kingdom has no power over the practices and arrangements of the Virginia authorities which are the subject of the applicant's complaints," the European Court continued, this fact could not "absolve the Contracting Parties from responsibility under Article 3 for all and any foreseeable consequences of extradition suffered outside their jurisdiction."[96]

Although the ECHR states that its application is limited to the jurisdiction of the member states,[97] the Court reasoned that the Convention's "special character" as a human rights treaty required a special approach to interpretation:

> In interpreting the Convention regard must be had to its special character as a treaty for the collective enforcement of human rights and fundamental freedoms.... Thus, the object and purpose of the Convention as an instrument for the protection of individual human beings require that its provisions be interpreted and applied so as to make its safeguards practical and effective....

Moreover, the Court indicated, the ECHR should be interpreted as part of a phalanx of international human rights agreements, some signed by different communities than were signatories to the European Convention:

> Article 3 makes no provision for exceptions and no derogation from it is permissible under Article 15 in time of war or other national emergency. This absolute prohibition of torture and of inhuman or degrading treatment or punishment under the terms of the Convention shows that Article 3 enshrines one of the fundamental values of the democratic societies making up the Council of Europe. It is also to be found in similar terms in other international instruments such as the 1966 International Covenant on Civil and Political Rights and the 1969 American Convention on Human Rights *and is generally recognised as an internationally accepted standard.*[98]

Accordingly, the Court found that the United Kingdom would be in violation of its Convention obligations were it to extradite the defendant to the United States without obtaining assurances that the defendant would not be sentenced to death. Extraditing defendants from the more than forty-five states that are parties to the ECHR to face the death penalty has become difficult if not impossible under *Soering* and its progeny.[99]

It is not only in Europe that extradition case law has sought to encourage convergence on issues of punishment. Twelve years after *Soering* was decided the Canadian Supreme Court found that, other than in "exceptional cases," it would violate the Canadian Charter to extradite someone to face capital punishment in the United States.[100] Although the causal nexus between extradition and imposition of the death penalty was not close enough to warrant finding a violation of Section 12 of the Canadian Charter of Rights and Freedoms (prohibiting "cruel and unusual punishments"), the Court instead found a violation of Charter Section 7, which provides, "Everyone has the right to life, liberty and security of the person and the right not to be deprived thereof except in accordance with the principles of fundamental justice." That Canada's own statutory abolition of the death penalty reflects "fundamental" Canadian principles of justice, the Court wrote, is "corroborate[d]" by the trend toward abolition in other democratic countries.[101] Imposing the risk of the death penalty on the eighteen-year-old defendants before it, the Court said, was inconsistent with Charter Section 7 for several reasons, including that "The Abolition of the Death Penalty Has Emerged as a Major Canadian Initiative at the International Level, and Reflects a Concern Increasingly Shared by Most of the World's Democracies."[102] As this text not so subtly proclaims, it is not merely that Canada itself does not have a death penalty, but that Canada is committed to a leadership role in promoting other countries' abolition of the death penalty.[103] It is not enough for Canada, or other countries, to "merely . . . take into account international law," but rather, all "'[n]ational legal systems should make sure they were in compliance with international laws and rights, in particular when it came to the right to life.'"[104]

In both of these cases, the respective courts denied that they were sitting in judgment upon or attributing liability to the United States. In both, however, the courts were willing in effect to afford some extraterritorial reach to their own constitutional commitments, creating incentives for the United States to offer assurances against imposition of the death penalty where extradition is sought from such countries. (The ECtHR has in other cases extended its case law concerning extradition of defendants to face conditions, not involving the death penalty, that in its view would amount to "inhuman or degrading treatment or punishment.")[105] The resort in the opinions to universal standards to support the respective courts' efforts to extend their internal rights commitments to other nations is an unusually clear example of a mechanism for influencing constitutional norms beyond national or regional borders. These decisions at once illustrate how domestic (or regional) court decisions may affect transnational behavior or norms and how transnational norms may affect domestic constitutional understandings. Doctrinal willingness to give extraterritorial effect to a human rights norm in this way not only influences and constrains domestic government conduct but also the conduct of other governments, not formally bound by the same domestic or regional instruments.

Margins of Appreciation

Given the absence of hierarchically superior binding articulators of international law in many areas, interpretive questions are likely to loom large in convergence postures. Along with universalist commitments to basic norms or values, doctrine developed within this posture would need mechanisms for managing or legitimating deviations in practice among different legal cultures. A key doctrinal component for judicial implementation may include the idea of a margin of appreciation, or margin of discretion, needed to make workable a commitment to universalism in the face of profound diversities.[106] The European "margin of appreciation" illustrates such a doctrine,[107] though the form that doctrine would take in a more decentralized context might well differ.

The "margin of appreciation" is a judge-made doctrine, not found in the text of the ECHR, and initially developed in cases involving member states' claims to derogate from the protections of the Convention because of an emergency.[108] It is now used in interpreting not only the derogation clause but also several of the "limitations" clauses found in Articles 8–11 of the ECHR (for example, with respect to rights of religious freedom, permitting only "such limitations as are prescribed by law and are necessary in a democratic society in the interests of public safety, for the protection of public order, health or morals, or the protection of the rights and freedoms of others").[109] The doctrine is variously described as providing national states "room for manoeuvre" in complying with the obligations of the European Convention,[110] as reflecting the superior competence of national authorities in evaluating the meaning of the rights and the necessity of limitations on rights,[111] or as a form of deferential review of what the treaty rights mean or how they apply, one that encompasses room for mistakes by national authorities that escape review.[112] It is also described as a "boundary between human rights and state sovereignty";[113] or as a form of "structural incorporation of local discretion into the legal doctrines of international human rights."[114] It has been applied and discussed in well over 700 cases,[115] some involving quite controversial or difficult social issues.[116]

The doctrine is subject to critique as having no clear analytical core, as a "tool" for resolving particular cases rather than a broader concept, leading to inconsistent or unprincipled usages.[117] In *Şahin v. Turkey*, the Grand Chamber of the European Court of Human Rights invoked the margin of appreciation in support of its decision to uphold Turkey's ban on the wearing of Muslim headscarves by university students.[118] As the Court explained it, among the roughly forty-five member states of the European Convention at the time, only three—Turkey, Azerbaijan, and Armenia—had prohibited headscarves for students at the university level. The Court noted the importance of secularism in Turkey's constitutional history and its relationship to women's equality, reported on the range of approaches within Europe to whether religious garb was permitted or prohibited in educational institutions, and referred as follows to the "margin of appreciation":

> Where questions concerning the relationship between State and religions are at stake, on which opinion in a democratic society may reasonably differ widely, the role of the national decision-making body must be given special importance. This will notably be the case when it comes to regulating the wearing of religious symbols in educational institutions, especially (as the comparative-law materials illustrate) in view of the diversity of the approaches taken by national authorities on the issue. It is not possible to discern throughout Europe a uniform conception of the significance of religion in society, and the meaning or impact of the public expression of a religious belief will differ according to time and context. Rules in this sphere will consequently vary from one country to another according to national traditions and the requirements imposed by the need to protect the rights and freedoms of others and to maintain public order. Accordingly, the choice of the extent and form such regulations should take must inevitably be left up to a point to the State concerned, as it will depend on the specific domestic context.[119]

In addition, the Court referred to the presence of "extremist political movements in Turkey that seek to impose on society as a whole their religious symbols and conception of a society founded on religious precepts" to justify its upholding Turkey's rigid insistence on the secularity of university space.[120] Under the reasoning in *Şahin,* then, it is possible that a similar ban in another country—for example, France—lacking well-organized "extremist" political parties of the type mentioned in *Şahin,* could be evaluated quite differently.[121]

The *Şahin* case ignited a wave of criticism that built on earlier critical evaluations. As many critics, including the one dissenting judge, noted, the Court did not seriously consider whether there were less restrictive alternatives to promote Turkey's goal with less harm to the religious liberty and educational interests of the petitioner. Its focus was primarily on the government interests, which the Court described as

> protection of the "rights and freedoms of others" and the "maintenance of public order" in a country in which the majority of the population, while professing a strong attachment to the rights of women and a secular way of life, adhere to the Islamic faith. Imposing limitations on freedom in this sphere may, therefore, be regarded as meeting a pressing social need by seeking to achieve those two legitimate aims, especially since, as the Turkish courts stated . . . , this religious symbol has taken on political significance in Turkey in recent years.[122]

The fact that the majority of the population adhered to the faith, some of whose members' religious liberty was being restricted, was considered primarily as bearing on the interest of the government in pressing the restriction, rather than on the interests being restricted. Indeed, the Court engaged in no serious efforts at balancing or proportionality analysis to consider the effects of the regulation on the petitioner,[123] nor did it fully explain why the diversity of approaches in Europe was relevant to whether Turkey's restrictive approach was justified even under the margin of appreciation.

Whether the margin of appreciation is understood as a device to recognize significant differences in the nature of government interests among the member nations, or as a mechanism for deferential review of national decisions in areas lacking in consensus, the prospects for different results on similar issues in different member states seems more than possible. Yet is some mediating principle not required in order to effectively apply a nominally universal norm across widely varying legal and cultural settings?[124] Consider the Colombian Constitutional Court's decision indicating that while the texts of international human rights covenants are part of the "Constitutional Bundle" and that constitutional rights must be interpreted in harmony with those covenants, interpretations of those covenants by, for example, UN committees or other international tribunals, though a "relevant guide," were *not* part of the "Constitutional Bundle."[125] On this basis, a national court could retain interpretive autonomy that would enable it to fit the international norm to the particular circumstances of its own country.

Despite its somewhat indeterminate and undertheorized basis, the margin of appreciation seems in no danger of disappearance from the ECtHR's doctrinal repertoire.[126] Its persistence and wide use in that Court's jurisprudence may be taken to reflect that it is a necessary concomitant of an effort to enforce a single standard of individual rights protection across so large a range of cultures and states with divergent histories as exists in Europe. The European Convention was in a sense the first effort to concretize in a legal format the guarantees of the UDHR; its terms bear strong similarities to those later embodied in the ICCPR. If a margin of appreciation is still used in Europe more than fifty years after the Convention came into effect, the necessity of some comparable doctrine in other contexts of seeking convergence around supranational human rights norms seems undeniable.

Proportionality, Balancing, and Means-End Analysis

Proportionality analysis is applied by many courts around the world to test the legality of government action. Under leading versions, the judge who has found that a government measure infringes on protected rights to some degree must ask whether the measure was prescribed by law, and for an important and pressing purpose in a democratic society. These are requirements of legislative judgment and legitimate end, familiar in many systems. Assuming there is a law, and that the law has a proper purpose, the inquiry goes on to ask whether the means chosen are rationally related to the goal, whether they impair the protected right as little as possible ("minimal impairment"), and whether the benefits toward the proper purpose are proportional in light of, or outweigh, the burdens on the protected right. Although there are some variations in the stringency with which this test is articulated and applied, for present purposes this summary is indicative of its general outlines.

The widespread use of proportionality analysis manifests a degree of convergence in the method of analysis in constitutional decisions; what is less clear is whether and to what degree it contributes to substantive convergences as well. Analytically, some claim, its use inheres in the idea of constitutional guarantees of rights. In some respects, proportionality may serve the role of the margin of appreciation doctrine, insofar as the weight of governmental interest may vary from one country to the next, justifying different results on what otherwise appears to be a similar issue. Yet, somewhat paradoxically, its minimal impairment tests might also serve as an engine of constitutional convergence, in contexts noted below.

Scope of Its Use Courts or tribunals in Canada, Colombia, Germany, the European Court of Human Rights, the European Court of Justice, India, Ireland, Israel, South Africa, and elsewhere invoke the concept of proportionality to review not only the propriety of sanctions, but also the legality of a wide range of government conduct.[127] Distinguishing features of proportionality analysis are its eschewal of doctrinal subcategories, its commitment to returning to foundational questions of constitutional purpose in structuring analyses of challenges to government action, and its requirement that the government come forward with justifications for statutes that infringe on protected rights.

Canada has played an influential role in the transnational development of proportionality analysis in constitutional law; its 1982 Charter of Rights introduced a "salvage" or limitations clause, leading to a two-stage analysis of Charter rights claims. First, the court asks whether there has been an infringement of a right specified in the Charter, such as rights of freedom of expression, or freedom of religion. If an infringement is found, and if the government action has been authorized by law, the Court then decides whether the challenged act can be "salvaged" or saved through analysis under Section 1 of the Charter. Section 1 provides that: "The Canadian Charter of Rights and Freedoms guarantees the rights and freedoms set out in it subject only to such reasonable limits prescribed by law as can be demonstrably justified in a free and democratic society." It is applied in Canada under the structured analysis set forth in *R. v. Oakes* and its progeny.[128]

Although the *Oakes* test is widely referred to outside of Canada, there are other versions of proportionality in use in constitutional courts around the world.[129] There are analytical differences in the formulations: judicial review that turns on an evaluation of the importance of the objective measured against its infringing effects on protected rights is likely to be more deferential than judicial review that is, in addition, based on an evaluation of whether the means chosen will produce proportionally greater results toward the government objective than harm to the protected right.[130] In Israel, the highest court at times has used an even more demanding standard, requiring that the marginal benefit of one choice over another to the government's interest must outweigh the marginal detriment to protected rights.[131] In U.S. constitutional law, the language of proportionality is used only in limited areas (criminal punishment, punitive damages, takings, and some federalism issues), though in other areas (such as strict scrutiny under a "compelling interest" standard) something akin to proportionality review may occur.[132]

Proportionality Inherent in Constitutional Review? Theoretical work suggests that use of proportionality analysis may inhere in constitutional rights adjudication, at least where the rights in question are understood to stand for a general principle rather than a discrete rule. Robert Alexy has argued that the idea of proportionality is an essential aspect of the conception of rights, at least as used in the German Basic Law and perhaps more broadly.[133] For Alexy, rights should be understood, for the most part, as *principles* that require *optimization.* This conception may be contrasted with several other ideas about rights: the idea of rights as "trumps," or as involving specific legal "rules," or as excluding certain justifications for government action.[134] Rights understood as optimization principles require a form of balancing or proportionality analysis to determine how, in different situations, the principle for which the right stands can be "optimized" while at the same time permitting the optimization of other rights. Constitutions of positive duties and positive rights are more likely to develop collisions of rights than negative rights constitutions.

David Beatty has argued that proportionality is the "ultimate rule of law," one that provides the appropriate analytic framework for the analysis of virtually all constitutional questions that can arise under virtually all constitutions, especially in the area of rights (both negative and positive).[135] For Beatty, the normative force of proportionality derives not from the nature of rights, but from proportionality's capacity to give equal respect to claimants on all sides of a question, with a court objectively deciding how to weigh these claims against one another. Proportionality review, Beatty asserts, turns "conflicts about people's most important interests and ideas into matters of fact, rather than matters of interpretation or matters of moral principle," as courts, aided by an objective evaluation of the parties' claimed subjective harm, apply a uniform standard of proportionality to discern where the balance lies in a just, neutral and relatively determinate form of analysis.[136]

Although these normative claims have not gone uncontested,[137] the broad attraction to proportionality review in constitutional courts around the world does call out for explanation. According to several accounts, it is the demand for justification of government action that is the bedrock of constitutional analysis. David Law attributes the phenomenon of "generic constitutional law" to features internal to constitutional adjudication:

> First, constitutional courts experience a common theoretical need to justify the sometimes countermajoritarian institution of judicial review. This concern, and the stock responses that courts have developed, amount to a body of *generic constitutional theory*. Second, courts employ common problem-solving skills in constitutional cases. The use of these skills constitutes what might be called *generic constitutional analysis*.[138]

As Professor Law writes, "there may only be so many ways to perform judicial review of legislation," and the "[g]eneral patterns" are similar. Rights established in constitutions, he says, "are inevitably subject to such restrictions as courts consider justifiable. In deciding whether a particular restriction is tolerable, courts employ the two means of problem solving that are perhaps most familiar to lawyers, balancing and means-end analysis,"[139] both of which are aspects of proportionality review. Similarly, in the context of understanding the relationship of different sources of law in the European Union, Gráinne de Búrca and Oliver Gerstenberg write that international human rights law should be understood as essentially involving duties of justification: "international law obligates states merely to justify those local practices that deviate from a shared, publicly evolving, cross-community set of standards," an "obligation [that] may be triggered in part by individual claims."[140] This duty of justification is central to all accounts of proportionality, or balancing and means-end analysis.

At a normative level, proportionality captures a kind of common sense view of justice—that greater harms should mean greater punishment, that greater burdens on individuals require greater justifications. Part of its attraction is the universality of such conceptions of justice, and their correspondence to common understandings of the function of constitutionalism. Explicit attention to proportionality arguably increases the transparency of judicial decision, framing a structure for exploring concerns likely to be relevant to judges and lawyers in a significant swathe of constitutional decision-making. One of the purposes of constitutionalism is to provide for government that is both effective in governing and respectful of individual rights; proportionality focuses on questions that seem to go directly to this purpose. Its attention to the individual parties' claims of injury or entitlement, to the legitimate governmental purposes at stake, and to the means available and chosen to satisfy those purposes, corresponds to widely held conceptions of fairness and of how tensions between the individual and her government should be resolved.[141] And its attention to particular facts might allow it to function as a flexible tool for protecting rights and maintaining constitutional law as an effective legal constraint on government over time.

Less compelling is the claim that proportionality is the only doctrinal tool needed. However important the inquiries of proportionality (into means-end analysis and balancing) may be, other doctrinal approaches remain important. These include the kinds of categorical analyses associated with U.S. First Amendment rights, or the rules of federalism by which some means (e.g., commandeering) but not others (e.g. conditional spending) are simply prohibited.[142] Constitutional interpretation, to be legitimate, may need to pay more attention to specific texts, and to what Carlos Santiago Nino has called the "historical constitution" of each country[143]—a framework of conventions that, while not necessarily fully based in democratically legitimate processes, are sufficiently accepted that they help make possible a constitutionalism oriented toward (if never perfectly achieving) democracy and human rights protection. Nonetheless, what Professor Law sees as the "sheer ubiquity" of balancing and means-end analysis suggests that these techniques are in some sense necessary to the project of constitutional interpretation—they are, he suggests, "naturally occurring" aspects of an "enterprise . . . defined not by common results, but by the problem-solving skills shared by lawyers everywhere."[144]

Will this methodological convergence—constrained as it is by divergent constitutional texts and institutions as well as by considerations of precedent in both common law and civil law systems[145]—lead to convergences of result?

Divergent Predictions Proportionality or balancing analyses have the potential to justify divergences *or* to lead to convergences of results across an array of constitutional issues. They also might come to serve the function presently served by the margin of appreciation doctrine in Europe.[146] Proportionality analysis could in theory give differing weight to interests asserted by different governments in different contexts (for example, secularism in Turkey versus secularism in France) in evaluating similar regulations. Indeed, such proportionality analysis might result in more clearly reasoned decisions, and thus more predictability and consistency, than the mere assertion of a margin of appreciation.

However, the methodology—or at least some features of it—may also have the opposing tendency to produce a convergence of results. The Canadian Court has made use of the experience of other free and democratic countries to test whether a restriction "minimally impairs" the protected right.[147] In *Charkaoui v. Canada*,[148] the Canadian Supreme Court concluded that a provision for the trial judge to view classified evidence in making a determination whether an alien was a dangerous terrorist (and thus "inadmissible" on security grounds) violated Canada's constitutional protections for procedural justice. The Court pointed not only to other aspects of Canadian law providing procedures for security-cleared counsel to view classified material, but also to similar procedures in use in the United Kingdom, to support its conclusion that the existing statute did not "minimally impair" and was a disproportional and hence unconstitutional intrusion on the defendant's procedural due process rights. The logic of minimal impairment may tend toward requiring a "least restrictive" approach that could be used to move toward convergence if each country's governmental interest is assumed to be roughly the same and if the measure of permissible infringement is set by the least restrictive means chosen by any similar, comparator country.

Thus, proportionality analysis has the potential either to contribute to a diversity of results, if similar asserted interests are given varying weights in different countries for contextual reasons, or to convergences, depending on the conditions and assumptions of the judges using the method and on the availability of information about less restrictive practices in other similarly situated countries.

Dualism/Monism and Convergence

In international law, "monism" refers to the idea that there is one universe of law, and that international law is a part (and a superior part) of domestic law. "Dualism" refers to the idea that international law is a separate legal system from domestic law, having no necessary hierarchic relationship to it, and that it remains "outside" the domestic system until some specific positive act of the discrete domestic system brings it within that system. While it has been argued that "monist" regimes (in which a constitution makes treaties part of internal law) would tend to greater convergence with international law, or to more openness to the influence of international law within the domestic system,[149] the matter is more complicated than such arguments suggest.

First, the division of the world into "dualist" and "monist" nations fails to capture the complexity of doctrines that condition whether international law in fact becomes binding and enforceable domestic law. As Tom Ginsburg notes, "a state can be monist with regard to treaty law but dualist with regard to customary international law"; conversely, some countries are "monist" with respect to "general principles of law" and dualist with respect to treaties.[150] And some, like the United States, are nominally "monist" but with regard to non-self-executing treaties are in effect "dualist."[151] Monism and dualism do not capture the complex array of hierarchical positions in which international law may stand—at the same status as statutes, superior to statutes, at the level of the constitution, and so on.

Second, to the extent that categories—ratified international treaties, unratified treaties, customary international law, and foreign legal practice—are being blurred in some countries' jurisprudences, the formal differences between monism and dualism may not correspond to the influence of the transnational on domestic adjudication. Whether this is called "creeping monism,"[152] or interpretive "constitutionalization,"[153] formal distinctions between monism and dualism can be undermined by the interpretive approaches of courts. Third, the incentives to abide by international law may be greater for smaller, weaker countries; and a country that is effectively "monist" at one point may become more dualist as it becomes more powerful (as may have occurred in the United States).[154]

Finally, some scholars argue that more rigorous requirements for bringing international obligations into the domestic legal system may sometimes predict a *greater* level of commitment with respect to those norms that are adopted. Professor Ginsburg found that the "democratizing constitutions" of countries in transition from autocracy to democracy "are more likely to give treaties superior status and to involve more actors in the treaty process than are constitutions written in either established democracies or autocracies."[155] If constitutional requirements for multiple steps to ratify (or implement) treaties are used to signal a greater commitment to treaties undertaken, then it could be a mistake to expect any connection between monism (or a general assumption of incorporation) and actual convergence.

D. INTERPRETIVE APPROACHES AND CONVERGENCE POSTURES

In Chapter 1 we saw how resistance to transnational influence in constitutional interpretation has many roots and can find expression in a number of different interpretive approaches. The same is true with respect to convergence.

Multiple Interpretive Roots

Some advocates of conforming constitutional law to international human rights law argue that the approach is consistent with a "living constitution," interpreted according to evolving social understandings. A common law, evolutive approach to constitutional interpretation may provide space for the consideration of international human rights laws, but would not necessarily treat them as hierarchically superior. Using international human rights law as a minimum standard may be more compatible with natural law theories of constitutional interpretation in which justice or morality, derived from human reason, play a central role. Although the dominant understanding of international law lies in the positive consent of states, human rights law—though grounded in that consent—has also been conceived within an older natural law tradition of international law. If reason is the basis for constitutional interpretation and for international human rights law, constitutional interpreters would in essence be drawing on outgrowths of the same source whether they looked at international human rights law or at constitutional law.

Across the jurisprudential spectrum, some scholars argue that originalism may support a presumption to interpret the U.S. constitution in conformity with international law.[156] Martin Flaherty, for example, argues that the "law of nations" had great influence on the Framers, and that the law of nations and constitutional law were complementary in their "purpose, method and result"; "principles of justice that informed the law of nations also informed domestic thought precisely because of the two projects' parallels."[157] Whatever the scope for this argument, the original understanding of at least some constitutional terms may well require interpretations that would be reciprocally recognized in the international community.[158]

Finally, textualism may support convergence with respect to many recent constitutions, at least on some issues. The parallel language in many modern constitutions and in international human rights instruments has been the subject of considerable commentary. A focus on constitutional texts, along with consideration of their "genealogical" influences, may support a presumption in favor of parallel interpretation.[159] As noted earlier, however, such presumptions would need to be premised on the idea that these texts share a kind of autonomy with their parallel cognates, relatively unaffected by other portions of the domestic constitution. Shared texts by themselves may provide only a basis for interested comparison; more is required to arrive at a presumption of convergence.

The Necessary Incompleteness of Convergence as Interpretive Approach

Convergence, then, is a posture that can be embraced within a number of different interpretive theories. As an interpretive theory by itself, however, convergence would be incomplete. There are relatively few areas of human rights law where a strong transnational consensus has developed; it is clearly lacking in such areas as regulation of religious garb in the public sphere, of abortions, of access to information and many others. The nature and scope of protection of private property (including compensation for takings) remains contested and largely unaddressed by the two major international human rights conventions.[160]

A major source of disagreement among nations in the twentieth century, both before and after World War II, was the normative status of private property and contract rights, when asserted to obstruct government welfare measures or as against other rights protected by constitutions. The European Convention on Human Rights, for example, initially *excluded* property protection from its reach, offering only an optional protocol protecting the "peaceful enjoyment of [one's] possessions," now in effect.[161] Although some scholars have argued for acceptance of a range of trade- and property-related rights as part of international law more generally,[162] the nature of the obligation to compensate for takings of property has for decades been a significant point of difference between more and less developed countries.[163] To be sure, rights of private property protection are increasingly found, both in domestic constitutions and in legal regimes protecting foreign investors.[164] Whether the prevalence of bilateral investment treaties has created customary international law protecting investor expectations is disputed.[165] Such protections, which may also be found in proposed multilateral treaties and in conditions imposed by world financial institutions,[166] may exert considerable pressure on what space is available for domestic constitutional differentiation and national policy-making.

At the level of constitutional law, however, there is reason to think that quite different concepts of property still exist even where a right to own property is recognized and even if study is limited to Western Europe and the United States.[167] As the Grand Chamber of the European Court of Human Rights wrote in 2007, "It is a characteristic of property that different countries regulate its use and transfer in a variety of ways. The relevant rules reflect social policies against the background of the local conception of the importance and role of property."[168] Asserting that states enjoy a "wide margin of appreciation" in deciding whether there is a "fair balance" between the general interest in the use of property and the adversely affected individual private property interests, the closely divided Grand Chamber rejected a challenge to loss of registered land through twelve years of adverse possession under British law. Although in some respects the world's constitutional systems have seemed further from convergence on economic principles than on the issues addressed in the two 1966 human rights conventions, it should be noted that economic liberalism (and the property and contract rights on which it is based) may attract greater adherents or exert greater practical force in some parts of the world than do the rights set forth in those covenants.[169]

Looking now at governance structure, while commitments to democratic decision-making through elections have clearly spread, they are manifest in a wide range of governance structures and voting schemes. Perhaps customary international law has come to recognize a right to democracy, as Thomas Franck has argued,[170] but governance structures at present are as much marked by diversity and particularity as by commonality, as are methods for constitution-making, despite some tendency toward the use of popular ratification as measure for testing or enhancing legitimacy.[171] There may well be a far more limited capacity for convergences in structural choices, as discussed in Chapter 8 below.

* * *

Convergence, if any, can only be partial, and its dynamic character will require a more complex interpretive approach than may at first glance appear. Even postures of convergence are likely to produce different interpretations of the same international human rights. As long as no hierarchically final and authoritative interpreter of international human rights law exists, more cannot be expected. In Europe, the margin of appreciation, or differential application of proportionality analysis, allow room for difference, and possibly more room for difference in the application of basic rights than one sees in federal nations with nationally enforced rights, such as the United States or Germany. Outside of Europe, convergence will be more difficult even to approach in the absence of a hierarchic decision-maker, in part because of the expressive and symbolic functions of constitutions and constitutional law and the divergent institutional contexts in which rights exist.

Moreover, the dynamic nature of both constitutional law and international law suggests that an end-state of convergence is unachievable and indeed, might be unhealthy for the development of both constitutional law and international law. New rights or new understandings of old rights will emerge, new claims will be made, and new social movements will arise, leading to new mobilizations for changes in understandings. Constitutions may be amended; so, too, international law and its interpretations may change. And they will of necessity do so unevenly, at first with outlier interpretations, which may or may not persuade or attract others. Indeed, some scholars argue that "if the categories of public international law, foreign law and domestic constitutional law were to collapse entirely to the point of indistinguishability, then the critical-transformative, participatory, and re-contextualizing dimension of international law would be threatened or altogether lost."[172] Yet the reasons for convergence are, to many, compelling; there is no denying that interest by governments in the constitutional law of other countries has dramatically increased, as evidenced by the Italian Senate's participation as an intervenor in the Canadian *Burns* decision, or the European Union's participation as an amicus in U.S. death penalty litigation.[173] Such efforts and influences can be expected to increase national courts' attention to sources of international or transnational law.

In evaluating the forces working toward convergence, one must also consider those factors that may be working toward a fragmentation of constitutional design and rights. One factor may be the democratization of politics, which may produce incentives for differentiation rather than for convergences. Few democratically elected leaders are likely to want to say that the design of their constitution "follows" any other one; rather there are incentives to claim that the product is uniquely designed for its own particular country. These may be related to the more general postmodern interest in self-identity and differentiation that has been discussed in another setting by Professor Franck.[174] Indeed, with respect to institutional design, rather than seeing convergence on one or more ideal types, what some scholars comment on is the increasing diversity of the government structures being organized, especially in postconflict societies.[175] Yet as I explore in the final chapter, it is in postconflict societies that international law and constitutional law may interact most closely, in ways that may influence the future course of both.

In those countries that adopt postures of convergence, these postures will in all likelihood function as rebuttable presumptions, in order to allow for national distinctivenesses in particular areas. But many countries will find it more compatible with their national constitutions to adopt postures of engagement, as discussed in the next chapter.

3. ENGAGEMENT WITH THE TRANSNATIONAL

A third set of postures are embraced by the term "engagement." If the posture of resistance is primarily concerned with national particularity, and the posture of convergence with creating or adhering to a harmonized transnational legal order, this third stance is primarily concerned with the self-reflective elements of constitutional adjudication. Engagement is founded on commitments to judicial deliberation and is open to the possibilities of either harmony or dissonance between national self-understanding and transnational norms. The focus here is on heightening judges' capacities for more informed and impartial deliberation about the content of their own constitutional norms; international and foreign law may both be considered, but as reflective tools rather than hierarchic demands. Engagement in a more relational mode also entails some recognition that domestic constitutional law may not be wholly domestic in its effects or that in sustaining constitutionalism states in the transnational community are interdependent.

Some scholars refer to these postures of engagement as "dialogical,"[1] which implies a conversation, a form of reciprocal intellectual give and take. While there is ongoing dialogue among some judges of national and international courts,[2] the posture of engagement may or may not imply felt obligations of reciprocity. A court may engage the work of other courts, or the experiences of other polities, or international human rights instruments, without any necessary expectation of response. For this reason I speak of "engagement" rather than "dialogue."

In contrast to the hierarchic obligation to apply "binding" law, "persuasive authority" is said to "attrac[t] adherence as opposed to obliging it."[3] But the reasons for reference to transnational sources extend well beyond those suggested by such a definition, which may obscure some distinctive aspects of the practice. There are important "negative" uses of foreign precedents (i.e., as "aversive" rather than "persuasive" authority),[4] as well as self-reflective references to foreign sources that are not "negative" precedents but are distinguishable from the domestic setting in a way that illuminates its assumptions. Such uses fit well within Professor McCrudden's broader definition of persuasive authority as any "material . . . regarded as relevant to the decision which has to be made by the judge, but . . . not binding on the judge under the hierarchical rules of the national system determining authoritative sources."[5]

If international law and transnational consensus (especially among rights-respecting constitutional democracies) play a dominant role in convergence postures, engagement postures are more open to considering the particular legal practices and reasoning of other countries. Courts that engage with foreign law in this way may be as (if not more) likely to distinguish foreign practice as to rely on it more affirmatively.[6] There are, to be sure, important differences between international and foreign law as sources; as discussed in Chapter 6, international law can bind the country externally and may need to be considered in interpreting particular constitutional terms; foreign constitutional court judgments, which necessarily raise questions of comparison, are also embedded in a system of ongoing government in ways that may affect their persuasive value. But both may be resources for engagement.

This chapter identifies two modes of engagement—deliberative and relational. As discussed in Part A below, in a primarily *deliberative* mode of engagement there is no general obligation to consider foreign or international law; the emphasis is on the transnational as a *permissive* source, rather than on presumptions of following international law or transnational consensus. In the hierarchy of sources considered, the transnational is likely to be lower on the scale of importance. Comparative questions, moreover, loom larger than in convergence models, given the focus on persuasion and reasoning (rather than on the presumptive normative force of international law or transnational consensus), and the need for more particularized, contextual judgments. Judges may, but usually need not, consider international or foreign law or legal experience, and may choose to agree or to disagree with its implications. In more *relational* modes of engagement, a felt relationship to international law or to other states, courts, or legal systems, motivates the deliberative consideration of transnational sources; there may even be a felt, or express, *obligation to consider* transnational sources. This felt obligation may also give rise to some duty to explain divergence from international law or strong transnational consensus, moving this form of engagement somewhat closer along the spectrum to a mild "convergence" approach. Both modes of engagement also carry expressive implications, as citation of a particular foreign source may be seen (whether so intended or not) as a form of affiliation.[7]

Part B explores the jurisprudential foundations of these postures of engagement. First, positive law, in the form of constitutional text or judge-made constitutional doctrine, may require or contemplate engagement. Second, pragmatic, consequentialist approaches to law may be informed by considering foreign experience. Third, understanding law as a form of "inquiry" (rather than only as a form of sovereign "command") supports a posture of engagement in the search for "better answers" to legal questions. Finally, because constitutions are situated among a plurality of legal orders, they may be seen as both a product of and influence upon an increasingly transnational normative community of constitutional actors. If constitutions both help constitute and are constituted by an international community, as well as a specifically national community, engagement may be a necessary requisite of constitutional interpretation.

Part C explores doctrinal sites or manifestations of these postures. Interpretive approaches that are multisourced, as exist in many constitutional courts, readily accommodate engagement with transnational sources. Questions about the role of courts in democracies may also provide occasion for engagement with other courts or constitutional systems. Some constitutional texts—for example, those concerned with prohibitions on cruel and unusual or inhuman and degrading punishment or treatment—seem to invite comparison. And the texts of some "limitations" clauses, which limit restrictions on protected liberties to those compatible with a "free and democratic society," may require it.

Finally, Part D examines positive influences toward engagement. A considerable number of cases decided by constitutional courts, and regional human rights tribunals, "engage" with the analogous law of other jurisdictions.[8] Many of the forces discussed in the prior chapter on convergence, may be at work, including globalization and the effects of prior colonial empires. Traditions of judicial reason-giving, together with the inevitability of comparative knowledge, also play a large role in explaining this model.[9] Judicial "networks," that may advance the personal and institutional interests of judges, promote engagement. But judges may also be normatively committed to the idea of independent judging as a distinctive activity, an idea reinforced by international law, which contributes to their willingness to engage.

A. ENGAGEMENT: DELIBERATIVE AND RELATIONAL MODES

Considering foreign and international law within a framework of learning by engagement—assuming neither convergence nor disagreement—can be defended as a legitimate interpretive tool offering modest benefits to the processes of constitutional adjudication. On this view, foreign or international sources are not treated as binding authority on constitutional interpretation, nor as presumptively to be followed. But neither do interpreters put on blinders that exclude consideration of foreign sources and experience. Transnational sources may be seen as interlocutors, offering a way of testing understanding of one's own traditions and possibilities by examining them in the reflection of others. A range of other uses of foreign law and experience, some including a mere passing mention, others empirical, still others a treatment of foreign decisions as a serious form of persuasive authority, exist within this posture.[10] As Australian scholar Cheryl Saunders has explained, "while the insights of comparative constitutional law may serve to highlight differences from the comparator jurisdiction, they may reveal similarities as well."[11]

Deliberative Engagement: Australia, the United States, Canada, and Japan

The Australian High Court has relied on the constitutional law of other countries (including the United States) in a number of cases, perhaps nowhere more interestingly than in its decisions implying individual rights from the Australian constitution's commitment to representative democracy. Thus, a right of freedom of political communication, not found as such in the Australian constitution but derived from its commitments to representative democratic government, was set forth in *Australian Capital Television Proprietary Ltd. v. Commonwealth.*[12] The Australian Court found that the implied right of political communication required invalidating a statute that prohibited political advertising on television or radio and mandated free air time for political candidates based on a formula that favored incumbent political parties. As Saunders wrote, "[f]oreign sources played a critical role" in the Court's opinions in establishing the necessary link between freedom of communication and democratic government: "deductions about the behavior of similar governing institutions, drawn from logic, history, or both, influenced by a shared belief in the value of freedom of speech," were used to support the argument that the principle of free political expression was implicit in the provisions for a free representative government, notwithstanding the absence in the Australian Constitution of an express individual right of expression.[13] Chief Justice Anthony Mason's opinion on this point relies on case law from Canada, England, the United States, and the European Court of Human Rights (ECtHR),[14] at the same time acknowledging a range of foreign legislative approaches to campaign advertising in electronic media (some permissive, some prohibitive, and some allocating free time) that did not "refute the proposition that [the contested statute] impairs freedom of discussion of public and political affairs."[15]

In other cases, notably including *Lange v. Australian Broadcasting,*[16] involving defamation and political figures, the Australian Court rejected the *New York Times v. Sullivan* approach to the nature of the defense in a defamation case involving political speech,[17] and placed more emphasis on how different the Australian constitutional context was from the American.[18] On issues concerning the scope of a defense to such defamation actions, foreign cases "were used largely . . . to assist in shaping Australian doctrine by reference to what it was not"; although "[f]oreign solutions were, for the most part, rejected, they nevertheless had an influence on the outcome."[19] More recently, in 2007, Chief Justice Murray Gleeson of the Australian High Court considered foreign law both to identify important similarities in values and differences between the Australian constitution and others on the issue of prisoner disfranchisement; his judgment in *Roach v. Electoral Commissioner* held unconstitutional a recent expansion of the statutory scope of disfranchisement (to apply to all prisoners serving sentences, even very short ones) as inconsistent with the constitutional requirements that members of the legislature be "'directly chosen by the people.'"[20] These cases reveal, as Saunders has said, that foreign sources may "appear at some, but not all steps, in the reasoning," "some are used in support of a particular proposition, while others are distinguished," a "mixed use of foreign sources" that is "typical of a dialogic approach."[21]

The foundational case on judicial review in the United States is itself illustrative of a deliberative mode of engagement. In *Marbury v. Madison,* the written character of the Constitution was used to differentiate the U.S. Constitution from Britain's and to justify the legitimacy of judicial review. Thus, the Court wrote that making a constitution is an act that

> organizes the government, and assigns, to different departments, their respective powers. It may either stop here; or establish certain limits not to be transcended by those departments. The government of the United States is of the latter description. . . . To what purpose are powers limited, and to what purpose is that limitation committed to writing, if these limits may, at any time, be passed by those intended to be restrained?

Its reference to a constitution that imposes limits and is written, so "that those limits may not be mistaken, or forgotten," implicitly invokes comparison with the unwritten British constitution of parliamentary supremacy, from which the U.S. Constitution was most emphatically to be distinguished. Yet, in the same opinion, the Court also drew affirmatively on British legal traditions of suing the King, to define the "essence of civil liberty" as "consist[ing] in the right of every individual to claim the protection of the laws, whenever he receives an injury. . . . In Great Britain the king himself is sued in the respectful form of a petition, and he never fails to comply with the judgment of his court."[22]

This third model of transnational comparison as engagement is also illustrated by *Roper v. Simmons*,[23] a 2005 decision invalidating the juvenile death penalty in the United States as a violation of the Eighth Amendment's prohibition on cruel and unusual punishments. Both the majority and Justice Sandra Day O'Connor, in her dissent, were in principle willing to look to outside law and practice to interrogate their judgment of whether that punishment for those offenders was constitutionally disproportionate in the United States, but only after considering more important factors, including state law and practice. For Justice Anthony Kennedy, international and foreign law, practice, and reasoning—though not "controlling"—helped to "confirm" the Court's judgment based on the weight of domestic state practices and its view of the moral capacities of adolescents.[24] Justice O'Connor resisted any categorical division of U.S. law from global currents: "this Nation's evolving understanding of human dignity certainly is neither wholly isolated from, nor inherently at odds with, the values prevailing in other countries."[25] Foreign law, however, did not affect her view that no domestic consensus against the juvenile death penalty yet existed, nor did it persuade her that the death penalty would be morally disproportionate for all seventeen-year-olds. Each of these justices preserved an Eighth Amendment methodology in which the law and practices of the U.S. states held first place in the analysis—not a stance conducive to a commitment to converge with international or transnational norms. Yet the willingness to look outside—for confirmation, for challenge, to check one's own judgment—illustrates the way in which foreign practice can function as an interlocutor of domestic law, particularly when it has arrived at the unusual degree of consensus in law and practice that existed with respect to the juvenile death penalty.

Turning to Canada, in a number of cases raising issues of "freedom of expression" under the Canadian Charter of Rights and Freedoms, the Canadian Supreme Court considered U.S. First Amendment cases, sometimes to distinguish and sometimes to agree with their conclusions. For example, the issue in *R. v. Keegstra* was the constitutionality of a law prohibiting the willful, public promulgation of hatred against racial and religious groups. The majority opinion discussed U.S. case law, touching on strands of law suggesting that it would prohibit such statutes as well as on strands that suggested otherwise; the Canadian court concluded that, to the extent that U.S. law would prohibit such a statute, it was not persuasive in Canada, given, inter alia, Canadian constitutional commitments to multiculturalism.[26] Canada's Supreme Court was sharply divided in *Keegstra*, and the lead dissent by Justice Beverley McLachlin relied on arguments from the U.S. case law and literature on the "marketplace of ideas" to emphasize the risks of such laws being used to censor legitimate public speech.[27] On other issues, for example, whether different standards apply to review the constitutionality of bans on leafleting and picketing, respectively, the Canadian Court found U.S. case law persuasive and adopted a similar approach.[28]

A final example of "engagement" with transnational comparison comes from a court known for its restraint and hesitation to invalidate statutes. According to two of its leading scholars, in the Supreme Court of Japan the "study and use of precedent, including foreign judicial decisions (especially of U.S. and German courts), has become a common feature of judicial life."[29] In 2008, the court referred to foreign and international law in its reasons for holding unconstitutional a provision imposing added requirements for attaining citizenship on the nonmarital children of Japanese fathers.[30] In an older case, the Japanese court rejected a challenge to a criminal statute imposing restraints on the campaign activities of public employees, prosecuted in the case for posting and distributing partisan political material during off-duty hours.[31] Notwithstanding the Japanese Constitution's guarantee of freedom of expression, which the court recognized as "the political foundation of a democratic state," the court upheld the statute as intended to assure the "neutral management of public administration."[32] The lower court in Japan had held that "when less restrictive means can be chosen to achieve the purposes of regulation, broader constraints are unconstitutional," and, relying on foreign precedent, found the criminal ban unconstitutional as applied to such minor acts. The Supreme Court disagreed, noting:

> [A]lthough there are points of agreement in the provisions of various countries' constitutions, the historical experiences and cultures of nations are diverse. Peoples differ in their rights consciousness and sensibility regarding freedom. Standards of judgment about the reasonableness of regulations regarding fundamental human rights are not formed in isolation from the social foundations of those countries. . . . Accordingly, although the legislative precedents of other countries are one important reference source, it is never

a correct attitude towards constitutional judgment to ignore that diversity of social conditions and to hold [foreign precedents] applicable as is to our country."[33]

Thus, the Supreme Court of Japan at once affirmed the legitimacy of looking at foreign authority and denied that foreign authority, as such, was necessarily applicable, given differences among countries.

The above-described usages of foreign and international law fit within a "deliberative," self-reflective model of engagement. On this view, judges may consider the laws and practices of foreign nations, as they may consider the writings of scholars, as aids to the deliberative process (though such foreign sources may have a different bearing or weight). The arguments for such deliberative use of comparative or international law rest in part on their value in helping judges to open a critical distance on a shared problem.[34] Transnational sources offer the reasoning of other thoughtful jurists confronting similar issues,[35] or may simply provide confirmation of conclusions supported by domestic sources;[36] they may address specific questions raised by constitutional text, or provide empirical information from comparative experience about the consequences of alternative interpretations. Transnational judicial discourse reflects an open deliberative process that draws on a range of sources for challenge and critique of analytical assumptions, for elaboration of common normative values in different institutional settings and for development of understandings of national distinctiveness. This kind of "constitutional cross-fertilization" is not necessarily reflected in citations.[37]

Expressive and Affiliative Functions of Engagement

In addition to enhancing deliberation, these references may serve other functions. Thus, some courts refer to or rely on other courts' decisions in order to enhance their own internal legitimacy, or to avoid adverse reputations in international or transnational communities, or even to reflect shifting political relationships between countries.[38] Consideration of foreign or international law may be part of an expressive project, in which references help establish that a country is breaking from a troubled past by showing concern for international human rights law (or contrariwise, that a country's view of itself is highly exceptionalist and excludes some international norms). Citations to foreign authorities may also reflect a national court's effort to distinguish itself from countries or legal norms with which it disagrees.[39] These expressive and signaling uses of foreign citations may be analogized to the choice of precedents on which to rely in common law systems, through which a court seeks both to promote its own legitimacy and to reflect alignments with favored or disfavored doctrines of the past. And whether or not an expressive use is intended, foreign references may well be received by the audience(s) for the opinions as expressing something about national identity through the perceived assertion of affiliations with other countries.[40]

Relational Engagement: South Africa and Elsewhere

Engagement may sometimes involve a set of relational obligations felt by constitutional court judges toward transnational sources of law, in ways that may differ from any felt duty, for example, to consider scholarly writing. This "relational" or "obligatory" consideration of transnational sources of law is illustrated by the unusual interpretive provisions of the South African constitution.

The South African constitution *requires* its courts to *consider* international law in deciding bill of rights issues and *authorizes* the courts to consider foreign law in so doing.[41] This requirement of *consideration* is quite distinct from constitutional provisions that require interpretive consistency with, or incorporate, international human rights treaties.[42] In South Africa, the constitution does *not* purport to require interpretive conformity with international law. The requirement is procedural, not substantive: the courts *must consider* international law, but the constitution does not require conformance. By contrast, another article of the South African constitution requires that *statutes* be interpreted, wherever possible, in accordance with international law.[43] But even this form of presumptive directive is lacking in the Constitution's treatment of the interpretive rule for its own interpretation. Rather, as explained by the President of the South African Constitutional Court in *State v. Makwanyane*, "[W]e are required to construe the South African Constitution, and not an international instrument or the constitution of some foreign country, and . . . this has to be done with due regard to our legal system, our history and circumstances, and the structure and language of our own Constitution. We can derive assistance from public international law and foreign case law, but *we are in no way bound to follow it.*"[44]

South Africa's constitution thus strikes a posture of *obligatory* engagement with international law and *permissive* engagement with foreign law.[45] Three examples will illustrate its workings. In *Government of South Africa v. Grootboom*,[46] the court was asked to interpret a constitutional provision securing the "right to have access to adequate housing," in light of the "right . . . to adequate housing" in the ICESCR. The court declined to follow what the UN Committee on Economic, Social and Cultural Rights described as a "minimum core obligation" to assure "minimum essential levels," explaining that the concept developed by the UN Committee was based on more than a decade of experience in evaluating reports submitted by parties to the Convention; the court said it lacked the experience needed to define what any "minimum core" would be in South Africa. Moreover, the differences in the texts of the rights were significant: the right of *access* language in the constitution, the court wrote, "recognises that housing entails more than bricks and mortar," and "suggests that it is not only the State who is responsible for the provision of houses, but that other agents within our society, including individuals themselves, must be enabled by legislative and other measures to provide housing." The court implied that determining a "minimum core" where the right is one of "access" to housing was more complex than the task the UN Committee faced, since it included questions about persons needing land, persons needing land and housing, and persons needing financial assistance. Under the Constitution, the key question was "whether the measures taken by the State to realise the right afforded by section 26 are reasonable."[47]

In *Makwanyane*,[48] the South African Constitutional Court concluded that imposition of the death penalty was unconstitutional under a clause in the interim constitution prohibiting "cruel, inhuman or degrading treatment or punishment."[49] The court found that the death penalty was not inconsistent with public international law, noting human rights treaties protecting the right to life that made specific exceptions for death penalties lawfully imposed. It considered foreign law on issues of both interpretive method and substance, suggesting that national courts had upheld the death penalty only in jurisdictions with an explicit preservation of the possibility of the death penalty in their constitutional texts.[50] In a detailed treatment of death penalty challenges in the United States, the South African court noted majority and dissenting views, considered the constitutional arguments made (including those addressing concerns about its arbitrary imposition), and even discussed decisions of state courts, including California's, on the death penalty and a subsequent state constitutional amendment to override the court decision.[51] It also discussed India, which retains the death penalty, and the Hungarian Constitutional Court's decision against the death penalty, as well as developing case law or views in Canada, the ECtHR, and the UNHRC, engaging with the reasoning of foreign tribunals and with particularities of texts as compared with the South African Constitution.[52] Ultimately the court concluded that the death penalty was prohibited, in part because of the abusive history of its use in South Africa.

Finally, in *Minister of Home Affairs v. Fourie*,[53] the South African constitutional Court concluded that under its constitution, limitations of marriage to exclude same sex couples were unconstitutional. It recognized that international law did *not* afford protection to same sex marriage, but concluded after reviewing international instruments and the views of the UNHRC that nothing in international law *forbade* recognition of such marriages. The South African constitution, by contrast, specifically listed sexual orientation as a presumptively prohibited basis for legal discrimination, and, as interpreted in the court's prior decisions, forbade the limitation in marriage law.[54] As these three examples illustrate, the "consideration" of international law required by the South African Constitution does not result in a formulaic following but in a serious and varied engagement.

Even in countries without an explicit constitutional mandate to consider international or foreign law, judges sometimes express a felt obligation to consider international law or foreign constitutional approaches.[55] The Chief Justice of Norway in 1998 wrote of "the duty of national courts—and especially in the highest court in a small country—to introduce new legal ideas from the outside world into national judicial decisions,"[56] even absent explicit invitation to do so in the constitution. Particularly outside the United States, there is beneath the surface of contemporary transnational constitutional discourse a sense of persuasive authority, embedded in a broader sense of a common venture.[57] Although New Zealand relies on an unentrenched Bill of Rights,[58] its case law—even before adoption of the Bill of Rights in 1990—has advanced the idea that courts have an obligation to consult international human rights law in resolving domestic legal questions. Yet at the same time that New Zealand judges assert, for example, that comments of the UNHRC "and similar statements emerging from other committees monitoring UN human rights instruments" can provide assistance, they also assert that they are not binding in New Zealand courts.[59] Similar decisions can be found in other countries that lack clear constitutional directives for compulsory engagement, as in India[60] or Botswana.[61]

Several distinctive features of relational modes of engagement emerge. First, for some judges there is the sense of joint purpose, of being embedded in a community of nations making decisions about similar issues under similar domestic constitutional instruments, and at times of an overarching legal order that recognizes international human rights norms that, whether domestically incorporated or not, provide reason to strive to meet international standards and to be mindful of other interpretations in doing so.[62] Second, relational engagement may involve the simultaneous acknowledgment of the nonbinding character of external sources of law and an obligatory sense that they must be considered. A third feature, found as well in "convergence" approaches based on transnational consensus, is that international human rights law and foreign constitutional decisions may both be referred to, reflecting a "blurring of international law into comparative law."[63] While the sense of relationship to international instruments can be understood as reflecting an effort to avoid putting one's country into breach of its existing, or possible future, external obligations, the gravitational pull of other countries' constitutional law and experience may require a theory of constitutional law that depends less exclusively on concepts of binding law and legal sanctions.

* * *

To summarize: The permissive, deliberative mode of engagement is not incompatible with relatively strong senses of the autonomy of national law, to the extent that transnational sources are simply used to better understand or develop national law. (Open references to foreign law may also be used, or taken, to imply expressive affiliations or disaffiliations.) A somewhat stronger, "relational" version of engagement embraces deliberative benefits but also includes a relational presumption in favor of considering widely shared norms. If requiring consideration of international law enhances the likelihood that national courts will be persuaded by it in constitutional interpretation, this mode falls close to the weaker versions of convergence discussed in the prior chapter. What relational engagement may instead embody, though, is an idea that providing justifications for following or departing from transnational norms is a means to enhance the normative legitimacy of legal decisions.

B. NORMATIVE OR JURISPRUDENTIAL FOUNDATIONS

Engagement can be understood to rest upon a range of jurisprudential foundations.

Positive Law

First, positive law in the form of constitutional text may require engagement. Even without such an explicit positive command, the drafting and ratification history of a constitutional instrument in the post–World War II era may suggest a connection to other constitutional or international instruments, with an assumption that there is some likelihood of benefit from considering the decisions of international or domestic tribunals implementing parallel norms. Indeed, this assumption seems at least as plausible as any assumption favoring convergence, discussed in Chapter 2. In drafting bills of rights premised on the UDHR, the ICCPR, or the ICESCR, nations were not necessarily committing themselves to convergence in meaning and application over time, but rather to a shared set of principles, values or aspirations, whose applications in different national contexts might vary but whose interpretation could benefit from considering those of others.

Pragmatism or Consequentialism

Second, a jurisprudence of pragmatism or consequentialism may support informed consideration of foreign experience or international law. Richard Posner is a leading advocate of pragmatism as an approach to judging, arguing that a pragmatic judge looks to make the best all-things-considered judgment, unconstrained by independent normative commitments to precedent or history.[64] On his approach, at least as articulated in the mid-1990s, foreign legal judgments matter in assessing pragmatic questions:

> If I were writing an opinion invalidating the life sentence in my hypothetical marijuana case I would look at the punishments for this conduct in other states and in the foreign countries, such as England and France, that we consider in some sense our peers. If a law could be said to be contrary to world public opinion I would consider this a reason, not compelling but not negligible either, for regarding a state law as unconstitutional even if the Constitution's text had to be stretched a bit to cover it. The study of other laws, or of world public opinion as crystallized in foreign law and practices, is a more profitable inquiry than trying to find some bit of eighteenth-century evidence . . . [about the framers.][65]

Although Posner later disavowed the relevance of foreign law in resolving an Eighth Amendment "cruel and unusual punishment" issue similar to the one discussed in his example,[66] the benefit of considering foreign laws as "facts" in the world relevant to assessing constitutional standards such as "cruel and unusual" or "reasonableness" has been asserted or assumed by many jurists.

More clearly consequentialist uses of foreign experience are represented, for example, by Canadian Justice Bertha Wilson's conclusion that litigation experience under U.S. First Amendment doctrine on union dues demonstrated that "nothing could be more incompatible with the promotion of collective bargaining."[67] Likewise, consider Justice Breyer's use of foreign federal systems in analyzing an issue of U.S. law in the *Printz* case: "[Notwithstanding differences, their] experience may nonetheless cast an empirical light on the consequences of different solutions to a common legal problem—in this case the problem of reconciling central authority with the need to preserve the liberty-enhancing autonomy of a smaller constituent governmental entity."[68] In the kind of case discussed by Posner, "world opinion" in the form of widely adhered-to bans on punishment may be relevant to assessing the meaning of the value-laden term, "cruel and unusual"; on the issues addressed by Wilson and Breyer, other countries' experiences bear on the functional, empirical consequences of different interpretations for constitutional values of freedom of expression or federalism.

Law as Inquiry

A third jurisprudential underpinning for a posture of engagement is a view of law as being a form of "inquiry," rather than or in addition to being simply a binding sovereign command. According to Patrick Glenn, "law as enquiry" is an understanding of law that embraces "use of non-binding and non-national sources of law," in an effort to reach better ways of interpreting and implementing fundamental law, or to enhance judicial self-awareness.[69] On this account, law itself is viewed not as the concrete and fixed product of a particular sovereign, but as a project of inquiry. Although Glenn regards the idea of law as inquiry as historically in opposition to the idea of law as the binding directives of a specific sovereign national state, he recognizes that "use of persuasive authority is not necessarily incompatible with the concept of binding law."[70] In its contemporary iteration, Glenn describes a view of law in which

> the use of extranational persuasive authority is . . . indicative of freedom in the choice of law on the part of legal officers. To the extent that the law used by these officers is not definitely made and imposed upon them but is rather chosen by them in an ongoing process, the underlying notion of law is that of enquiry. There is never a closing of sources, never a declaration of satisfaction with existing knowledge, never a pure process of deduction from a single given, never an entire commitment to an exclusive paradigm of law.[71]

This view of law, he says, is found in Canada, and is "widespread . . . in the contemporary world. [Notwithstanding] contemporary nationalism . . . the practice of much of the world is to remain continuingly receptive . . . to extranational legal experience."[72]

Objections to the idea of "law as enquiry" may focus on its harm to local legitimacy, its asserted incompatibility with the idea of constitutions as "settlements," and the possibility of incoherence or undue discretion in the proliferation of sources. Yet while "law as enquiry" and "law as [binding and specifically] national response" rest on distinctive jurisprudential foundations,[73] what we know about law and legal development suggests that the two are not polar opposites but in actuality may work together. As Sarah Harding suggests, "[a] dialogic/comparative approach does not undermine the common law norms of certainty, predictability, and uniformity[, but] proceeds on the assumption that . . . settled expectations are more likely to occur through the persuasion that comes with open dialogue and shared responsibility for constitutional interpretation."[74] Thus, she writes, "there is no necessary connection between comparative judicial reasoning and the dialogic model or between a rejection of comparative reasoning" and an "enforcement model . . . centered on local, independent, and final decision-making": "Comparative analysis neither undermines local authority nor disconnects legal analysis from its local origins when encompassed in a larger dialogic model."[75] Glenn, as well, concludes that "[c]ontemporary State law is . . . entirely compatible with the notions of persuasive authority and law as enquiry."[76]

Suggestions of this "inquiring" character of modern public law, under multiple "persuasive" influences, is widespread in contemporary scholarship. Thus, for example, Robert Ahdieh has focused on the "rhetorical nature of the relationship between international and national courts [that] affirms the prospective orientation of their interaction [to offer] counsel for future cases."[77] Judith Resnik has written of the "dialectical transnationalism" and "translocal internationalism" involved in iterative exchanges of ideas and influences on lawmaking and legal decisions at multiple levels.[78] And Paul Berman argues that in a "plural world," "claims to coercive power, abstract notions of legitimacy, and arguments about legal authority are only part of an ongoing conversation, not the final determining factors," and thus "law is an *ongoing process* of articulation, adaptation, re-articulation, absorption, resistance, deployment, and on and on."[79]

Although Glenn characterizes the United States as committed to the inquiry model before 1850, and to a more formalist, law-as-specifically-national-response model thereafter, these two approaches may coexist and be combined. A late nineteenth-century U.S. case clearly echoes Glenn's conception of "law as enquiry" in the constitutional context. In *Hurtado v. California*, the Court wrote:

> [I]t is better not to go too far back into antiquity for the best securities for our "ancient liberties." It is more consonant to the true philosophy of our historical legal institutions to say that the spirit of personal liberty and individual right . . . was preserved and developed by a progressive growth and wise adaptation to

> new circumstances and situations of the forms and processes found fit to give, from time to time, new expression and greater effect to modern ideas of self-government.
>
> ...
>
> ... Due process of law ... is not alien to that code which survived the Roman Empire as the foundation of modern civilization in Europe.... There is nothing in Magna Charta, rightly construed as a broad charter of public right and law, which ought to exclude the best ideas of all systems and of every age; and as it was the characteristic principle of the common law to draw its inspiration from every fountain of justice, we are not to assume that the sources of its supply have been exhausted. On the contrary, we should expect that the new and various experiences of our own situation and system will mould and shape it into new and not less useful forms.[80]

Autopoiesis An alternative to Glenn's articulation is offered by the literature on "autopoiesis" and law. The idea that a constitution is made for an indefinite and changing future, amenable to the ascertainment of "new," "wise," or "progressive" interpretations over time, accords with a concept of the law of the constitution as both fixed and open, a "national" response to cosmopolitan input. The national constitution might be seen, in Niklas Luhmann's terms, as an "autopoietic" system of law, "normatively closed but cognitively open."[81] While one must recognize the potential instability of such attempted divisions between norms and facts, the idea of normative closure and cognitive openness nonetheless captures a sense, however provisional, of the degree of constitutional autonomy and constraint experienced by judges engaged in constitutional interpretation over time.[82] Whether understood in these terms, or as a form of reflexive "living constitutionalism," the idea of law as inquiry can coexist with a view that an exercise of national sovereignty is involved in judicial interpretation of the national constitution. If the emphasis were on the idea of a "*common* law" that transcends national boundaries, this concept would lean toward convergence. But the idea of law as a form of inquiry that is open to ideas for improvement while at the same time constrained by national texts and histories seems a distinctive jurisprudential foundation for postures of engagement, one perhaps best captured by the Canadian metaphor of the constitution as a "living tree," capable of growth yet rooted in a particular national text. And it is consistent with the multi-valenced form of common law constitutional interpretation found not only in the United States but in a number of other constitutional systems, as discussed further below.

Process and Justification Another variation on the idea of law as inquiry, in terms of a jurisprudential foundation for engaging with the transnational, is related to the legitimating force of deliberative processes.[83] In the context of judicial decision-making and interpretation, major forms of process include public identification of the issue, public and adversarial contesting of the issue, and issuance of reasoned decisions. As noted earlier, knowledge of foreign and international law is increasingly unavoidable, especially in those countries in which judges are routinely supplied with electronic access to legal materials. To the extent that reason-giving is foundational to the legitimacy of interpretive constitutional law, and to the extent that judges have in mind comparisons with other countries or with a rule of international law in deciding the scope or meaning of a contested provision, a presumption in favor of judicial candor suggests that explaining the weight of these materials contributes to the legitimacy of the product.[84] Beyond these factors the relational model of engagement may itself be premised on an assumption that offering justifications to a transnational as well as domestic legal audience enhances the normative legitimacy of domestic law. This may be particularly salient where a country departs from a widespread practice.

Constitutional Law as Mediating the Domestic and the Global

A fourth jurisprudential basis for engagement might conceive of a constitution neither in strictly positivist terms, nor in the nationally specific forms of organicity associated with von Savigny's views, nor as a set of universalist moral principles, but rather as a form of law that constitutes a country both internally and as a member in a world of nations—that is, as a form of law that by its existence commits its polity to some form of engagement with others, in order to sustain the quality of being a nation in a world of nations. This idea assumes that international law speaks to the requisites for national statehood, as it does, and can accommodate international law speaking to the requirements of legitimate government, as it may be beginning to do. In this model, constitutions (and their associated judicial decisions and practices) serve as mediating institutions—mediating, that is, between the global and the national (as well as between the national and the local). On this view, although constitutions are "constituted" by their particular polities, the act of constituting a constitution takes place within a framework of international expectations, incentives, and relationships as well as domestic exigencies.

As a practical matter, constitution-making is framed not only by domestic "upstream" and "downstream" constraints,[85] but also by constraints of acceptability among and anticipated reactions by other nations.[86] Understanding constitutions as sitting between specifically national organic or positive law and universalist versions of law as reason allows one to see constitutions both as a form of law constituting the permeable boundaries of a nation, internally and within an international community of states, and as a product of and influence upon an increasingly transnational normative community of constitutional lawyers, jurists, and other constitutional and juridical actors. If constitutions are mediating institutions of law, designed to both provide for internal governance and create an effective interface with other national states—even if only by explaining differences in constitutional commitments—then it is perhaps easier to see why courts might feel some obligation to consider the constitutional law and systems of other nations as well as international law.

Positivism, pragmatism, law as inquiry and justified reasoning, and the interdependences of constitutions and the international system, then, all may serve as jurisprudential frameworks for understanding different forms of engagement.

C. DOCTRINAL OR INTERPRETIVE MANIFESTATIONS

Doctrinal manifestations of engagement are found in several areas. First, constitutional texts or doctrines that require judgments about whether limitations are compatible with a "free and democratic society" virtually require some comparison with other free and democratic countries, and other constitutional texts or doctrines invite comparison. Second, engagement is compatible with interpretive approaches that are multi-sourced or, in Mark Tushnet's words, "eclectic," and that allow for interpretive change in constitutional understandings.[87] Though perhaps not properly called doctrinal, discussions of a constitutional court's role, the degree of deference (if any) it owes other branches, and its authority to decide constitutional questions, are often the site for comparison. Finally, the multiple hierarchies of law found in Europe invite a complex form of engagement that verges on convergence, but holds open the possibility of multi-vocal constitutionalism in the jurisprudence concerning the compatibility of EU law with national constitutional law.

Texts That Call For or Invite Comparison—Limitations Clauses and Other Examples

As discussed in Chapter 2, the Canadian Charter of Rights and Freedoms includes a "salvage" or limitations clause, permitting a court to uphold statutes found to infringe on Charter rights, provided that the legislation meets the procedural ("by law") and substantive ("demonstrably justified in a free and democratic society") requirements of the provision. Canada is not alone in adopting such a clause, which derives from the earliest of the twentieth-century human rights instruments.[88]A somewhat more flexible and limited predecessor, which included the phrase, "reasonably justifiable in a democratic society," appeared in Nigeria's 1960 constitution,[89] which was inspired by language in the ECHR, which in turn was inspired by the UDHR. (Several other Commonwealth nations adopted post-independence provisions that use similar language.[90]) More recent constitutions have been influenced by earlier ones: South Africa's Constitution provides that "The rights in the Bill of Rights may be limited only in terms of law of general application to the extent that the limitation is reasonable and justifiable in an open and democratic society based on human dignity, equality and freedom. . . ."[91] (Not only the parallel terms but the drafting processes by which constitutional ideas and terms migrated might provide positive support for considering the interpretations of other polities.)

The Canadian clause was intended to ratchet up the standards of justification in order more effectively to assure the protection of the Charter's rights and freedoms.[92] Determining what limitations are justified in "a free and democratic society" requires some degree of comparison, for the words "free and democratic" imply a contrast with societies that are not, and a commonality with other "free and democratic" societies. As Lorraine Weinrib has written, in Canada "comparative analysis is regarded as internal to the activity of constitutional adjudication."[93] Similarly, the South African Court has on occasion treated its salvage clause as requiring something approaching a baseline of the practices of other "open and democratic" societies.[94] Although such clauses do not require resort to any particular foreign jurisdiction, they do require an understanding of the practices of other democracies and thus of some foreign law. Indeed, according to David Beatty, a leading Canadian scholar, "[t]he importance of the legal practice of other free and democratic societies in providing benchmarks for the possibilities of our own constitutional order has been one of the few subjects on which almost all legal academics are agreed."[95]

Although lacking the explicit constitutional mandate to consider international law found in South Africa, the Canadian court considers not only the practices of other democratic countries, but also the provisions of international human rights instruments. Professor Melissa Waters has noted that "the use of human rights treaties to interpret limitations provisions in domestic bills of rights" is increasingly common.[96] Section 7 of the Canadian Charter secures "[e]veryone . . . the right to life, liberty and security of the person and the right not to be deprived thereof except in accordance with the principles of fundamental justice." Waters points out that the Canadian Supreme Court "frequently utilizes the ICCPR and other treaties to interpret the 'reasonableness' and 'fundamental justice' limitations."[97]

While the Canadian court has its own divisions,[98] a significant number of constitutional opinions look to practices of other free and democratic societies. In an opinion concerning whether a prohibition on public solicitation to prostitution (not itself prohibited) met Section 1 standards, Justice Antonio Lamer noted the far more "draconian" measures in some American states to support his conclusion that the law was "reasonable and demonstrably justified in a free and democratic society."[99] Another opinion concerning mandatory union dues stated, "our courts have found the experience in other 'free and democratic' societies useful in determining whether means adopted in this country are the best alternative. . . ."[100] And in notable post-9/11 cases, the Canadian court has looked to foreign or international law to interpret its own constitution: in *Suresh v. Canada*,[101] for example, looking to international law to give effect to the "fundamental justice" limitation in Charter Section 7 to conclude that generally, deportation to face a risk of torture is barred, and in *Charkaoui v. Canada*,[102] looking to British law to conclude that an anti-terrorism statute did not meet the "minimal impairment" requirement of Canadian proportionality doctrine. Other countries with similar constitutional "limitations" clauses also consider foreign experience in evaluating what "free and democratic" or "open and democratic" societies do.[103] Even without a constitutional limitation clause that furnishes a textual basis, justices on the U.S. Supreme Court—including Justice Scalia—have on occasion referred comparatively, for example, to what "free but civilized societies" do.[104]

Other constitutional texts may also invite engagement with foreign law. Thus, Professor Calabresi has noted, "foreign court judgments might be relevant . . . when one is interpreting provisions of the U.S. Constitution that provide open-ended considerations of 'reasonableness'. . . [including] the Fourth Amendment, which bans 'unreasonable searches and seizures' and the Eighth Amendment which bans 'cruel and unusual punishments' and 'excessive' fines or bail."[105] As he elaborates, "[b]y calling for a modern day assessment of what searches are reasonable or what punishments are cruel and unusual, these clauses seem to invite us to look at contemporary practices both in the United States and in other Western legal systems that are closely related to our own."[106] References to foreign law, to support or to critique constitutional rules relating to criminal procedure, are found in the opinions of both liberal and conservative justices in the United States,[107] and of many judges in Commonwealth jurisdictions.[108]

Multi-Valenced Interpretation

A number of constitutional courts employ multi-valenced analytical techniques that typically involve resort not only to text and intent but to prior decisions (even in systems not formally built on judicial precedent), constitutional structure and purpose, the likely consequences of alternative interpretations, and international law or the experience of other democracies. Indeed, a recent comparative study of constitutional interpretation in six countries—Australia, Canada, Germany, India, South Africa, and the United States—found that "[i]nterpretation everywhere is guided by similar considerations, including the ordinary or technical-legal meanings of words, evidence of their originally intended meaning or purpose, 'structural' or 'underlying' principles, judicial precedents, scholarly writings, comparative and international law, and contemporary understandings of justice and social utility."[109] An eclectic, muli-valenced interpretive mode is readily compatible with the consideration of foreign or international law.

According to Donald Kommers, the German Constitutional Court generally draws on sources including unwritten principles of German constitutionalism, the written constitutional text, the history of the constitution, judicial precedents (though rejecting the principle of stare decisis as such), academic writings, and comparative and international materials.[110] Consider the first German Abortion Decision (1975),[111] which reached a result strikingly different from that in the United States, in an opinion that relied on a number of sources and forms of argument. The Court concluded that the government had an affirmative duty to protect fetal life and that a statute *permitting* abortion in the first twelve weeks was unconstitutional. Placing weight on the text of the Basic Law, which declares "human dignity" to be "inviolable" and provides that "every person shall have the right to life," the Court supplemented its understanding of the text by discussing the drafting history of the right to life clause from when the Basic Law was adopted in 1949. But the Court did not rely only on text and original understandings. Referring to its own past decisions ("constant judicial utterances") and its value-oriented approach to interpreting the Basic Law (involving an "objective ordering of values"), the Court also concluded that where the mother's own right to life and "sphere of intimacy" is at stake, requiring continuation of the pregnancy was not constitutionally "exactable" from the mother where it would pose a danger to her life or a grave danger to her health.[112] Accordingly, the legislature must provide exceptions from the ban on abortions at least in those situations and could provide exceptions for reasons of comparable gravity.

Explaining further why the statute was unconstitutional, the Court reasoned consequentially and based on comparative experience that permitting the abortion to be performed by the same physician who provided counseling (about social assistance to encourage continuation of the pregnancy) would be ineffective in preventing abortions. As experience in England showed, doctors could be found who would perform counseling with an eye, not to discouraging but to allowing abortion, for reasons of either financial self-interest or ideological commitments to women's emancipation or self-determination. At the same time, the Court considered but rejected arguments from the liberalization of abortion laws in other Western countries, because abortion regulations were sharply contested everywhere and because the Basic Law's principles could "be understood only in light of the historical experience and spiritual moral confrontation with the previous system of National Socialism,"[113] demonstrating how foreign law did not have binding or even presumptive authority on constitutional interpretation, but was among a set of sources to be considered.

In Canada, the Supreme Court considers a broad range of legal arguments and factors in making constitutional decisions and allows for the evolution of its constitutional law, viewing the Constitution as a "living tree." One example involved the court's shift between 1991 and 2001 on whether extraditing a person to face a possible death penalty would violate the Charter, in the later case finding that, generally, extradition to face the death penalty would be inconsistent with the "principles of fundamental justice" protected by Charter Section 7.[114] The court explained its change of position in light of intervening developments, including change in other state practices, and accelerating concern over wrongful convictions in both Canada and the United States. Although the "basic tenets of [Canada's] legal system . . . have not changed since 1991 . . . their application in particular cases (the 'balancing process') must take note of factual developments in Canada and in relevant foreign jurisdictions."[115] In other constitutional cases the Canadian court has analyzed the *consequences* of upholding certain common law police authorities (drawing in part on foreign experience), considered the *concept* of human dignity as applied to disenfranchisement (with different justices considering different foreign approaches), and narrowed its earlier approach to the extraterritorial reach of the Charter, found to pose "practical and theoretical" challenges, in light of international law and the need for international cooperation to combat transnational criminal activity.[116]

Australia is an interesting contrast because its judges, for the most part, have not explicitly embraced the "living tree" approach to constitutional interpretation found in Canada. Although some justices have argued that the Australian Constitution should be interpreted as a "living force," a number of the judges over time have been committed to what Professor Goldsworthy calls "moderate originalism," or "legalism," in which the words of the Constitution are understood to mean the same thing now as when they were enacted.[117] The Australian case law, however, while giving great weight to text as originally understood, also pays attention to "structural principles and implications," which may be unwritten, and "policy" concerns of "justice, utility and good government,"[118] which leave room for consideration of foreign (often U.S.) constitutional decisions. In addition to the implied freedom of political communication cases discussed above, consider, for example, *Street v. Queensland Bar Ass'n*,[119] where the Court reconsidered a question decided ten years earlier—whether the Constitution permitted a state to impose either a residency or a primary practice requirement for an attorney licensed in another state to become a member of the bar. The Court unanimously, but in separate opinions by the seven justices, disavowed earlier interpretations of Section 117 of the Australian Constitution, finding that it was more consistent with the purpose of making a unified country to interpret the ban on discrimination based on state residence more broadly. Justice Mary Gaudron wrote that the prior decisions interpreting Section 117 "do not reflect recent developments within the field of anti-discrimination law which have led to an understanding that discrimination may be constituted by acts or decisions having a discriminatory effect or disparate impact (indirect discrimination) as well as by acts or decisions based on discriminatory considerations (direct discrimination)," relying on both Australian and American case law.[120]

As will be discussed further in later chapters, the U.S. Court also relies on multiple modalities of interpretive argument.[121] Although it has not been as likely to use transnational legal sources as some other courts, the U.S. Court has, for example, invoked foreign experience, both positively and negatively, in resolving various constitutional challenges to confessions made during custodial interrogations;[122] its justices have drawn on transnational legal experience, foreign and international, to evaluate claims of presidential power.[123] The multi-sourced modes of U.S. constitutional analysis pose many openings for the consideration of foreign law—on the consequences of alternative interpretations, on the original understandings of the text,[124] and on the question of how a constitutional text should now be understood and applied.[125]

The Judicial Role, Constitutionalism, and Interpretive Approaches

There are a set of common themes, or antinomies, about judging and interpretation in a democracy, which have engaged judges across national lines for years.

Thus, in a leading Indian case on affirmative action, Justice V.R. Krishna Iyer referred to the U.S. Supreme Court's decision in *McCulloch v. Maryland*[126] on the standard for reviewing legislative action, and asserted the necessity for the constitution to be a living, "organic" document.[127] Looking in a different direction, in Canada's leading case on the permissibility of abortion regulation under the Charter, dissenting Justice William McIntyre argued that the majority was in error to strike down the law enacted by Parliament and focused in his dissent on the judicial role.[128] He noted that "'[c]ourts and legislators in other democratic societies have reached completely contradictory decisions when asked to weigh the competing values relevant to the abortion question,'" and argued that "the courts must confine themselves to such democratic values as are clearly found and expressed in the Charter and refrain from imposing or creating other values not so based"; accordingly, "the task of the court . . . is not to solve . . . the abortion issue, but simply to measure the content of [the challenged statute] against the Charter." To support his concept of the limited character of judicial review, he quoted at length from U.S. Supreme Court Justice Oliver Wendell Holmes's views, in *Lochner* and other cases, and argued that the principle was one that was "essential . . . in a constitutional democracy."[129]

Debates over the relationship between democracy and judicial review are played out in debates over interpretation—between formalist and evolutionary approaches, between "legalist" or "originalist" and more conceptual or teleological approaches. Constitutional texts rarely give positive indications of the range of interpretive norms that judges should employ. As judges determine what interpretive approaches are best suited to making constitutional judgments, it is thus not surprising to see them interested in, though not necessarily following, what other judges have done.

Legal Hierarchies and Multi-Vocal Constitutionalism in Europe

Although the effects of supranational regimes, especially those in Europe, have been discussed above in connection with convergence, I turn now to a more subtle possibility. The primacy of European Union law over conflicting national statutes is well settled by decisions of the ECJ.[130] By the logic of these ECJ decisions, the same principles would extend to national constitutions. Yet in a number of decisions dealing with the force of European law on conflicting national constitutional provisions, some national constitutional courts have refused to accept the principle that EU law is supreme over national constitutional law. Rather, national courts have taken stances at once sympathetic to the development of a uniform and coherent body of EU law and maintaining distance—or the possibility of distance—between EU law and national constitutional law.

Europe has two major supranational legal regimes enforced by regional judicial tribunals. One is the European Convention on Human Rights (ECHR), a regional human rights treaty inspired originally by the UDHR. The ECHR is enforced by the ECtHR, which sits in Strasbourg (and decided the *Soering* case, discussed in Chapter 2). The forty-seven parties to the ECHR (which include all members of the EU) are subject to the ECtHR's jurisdiction (which extends to individual petitions). The Court's decisions are binding, but depend on national law to be given effect. Member states have generally good records of compliance, though sometimes particularities of national law—for example, lack of authority to reopen proceedings—have proved to be obstacles to providing effective relief.[131] Other forms of resistance are not unheard of. For example, two recent cases involving complaints against Germany led to decisions that were quite controversial within Germany.[132] One, involving a child custody determination made by a German family court, resulted in a German Constitutional Court decision requiring consideration of a Strasbourg court decision but also asserting the supremacy of the German constitution over the Convention, suggesting that "the validity of international law within the internal legal order is susceptible to a constitutional reservation."[133] The Constitutional Court thus asserted that, in the event of an interpretation of the ECHR inconsistent with the fundamental rights norms of the Basic Law, the Basic Law—not the ECHR—would control.[134]

Unlike the ECHR, which designates a set of human rights and freedoms and machinery to protect them, the EU and the several treaties that constitute its legal basis not only protect rights relating to economic freedoms but also authorize a system of governance over delegated competencies. The EU has power to issue directives, which member states must implement through national measures, and regulations, which apply directly as law within member states and may apply to private conduct across a wide range of areas. Compliance with EU treaties and the secondary regulations issued thereunder is supervised by the European Commission, the administrative arm of the EU, and a court of last resort, the ECJ, hears cases brought by the Commission and also matters referred by national courts. Although the original treaty documents were silent on these points, the ECJ developed in its case law the principles of the direct effect and supremacy of EU law over the member states' laws. While the supremacy of EU law over member states' statutes is well accepted, as noted earlier the priority of EU law and national constitutions is unsettled and contested.

Yet to see this primarily as a terrain of resistance is incorrect. What is resisted is the claim of supremacy, not the benefits of or aspirations to harmonized interpretations. A term used in the literature to describe this relationship is "cooperative constitutionalism," understood to express a notion of a pluralistic set of legal orders, conceived not hierarchically but in overlapping relationships.[135] To illustrate, consider the German Constitutional Court's three major decisions on the relationship of the EU legal order and the German Basic Law. In the first of these, a case known as *Solange I* ("solange" means "so long as"), the Court held that because the EU legal order did not provide as much protection for fundamental rights as the German constitution did, EU law would be given effect within Germany only "so long as" it did not violate fundamental rights protected by the German Basic Law. As Mattias Kumm explains, in moving from *Solange I* to *Solange II*, decided twelve years later, the German Constitutional Court

> determined that the ECJ had significantly developed its review of EU legislation and held that the standard applied by the ECJ was essentially equivalent to the protection provided by the [Court's] interpretation of the German Constitution. For so long as that remained the case, the [Court] would not exercise its jurisdiction to review EU law on national constitutional grounds. Because the ECJ through its own jurisprudence, provided the structural guarantees that fundamental rights violations by EU institutions would generally be prevented, it conditionally accepted the authority of EU law.[136]

The shift from *Solange I* (1974) to *Solange II* (1986) was, then, a move from an assertion that the German Court would determine, case by case, whether an EU rule was incompatible with the German Basic Law's protection of fundamental rights, to a position that assumed that the ECJ was generally protecting fundamental rights and eschewed individual case review on that assumption.[137] Yet the German Court retained the possibility of determining that ECJ jurisprudence ceased generally to protect fundamental rights and of then retreating to its former position in *Solange I*.

Finally, in the *Maastricht Treaty Case* (1993), the German Court, while concluding that the Basic Law did not bar Germany from ratifying the Treaty, once again asserted its authority, "[b]ased on the premise that democratic legitimacy on the European level is derived from the empowerment of the Community by the national parliaments"; the German Court could "review 'legal instruments' of European institutions or agencies to determine whether such instruments remain within the limits of the sovereign rights conferred on them."[138] In upholding the Treaty, critics have noted, the German Court sought to influence the construction of a treaty meant to govern all member nations of the European Union through its implicit assertion that only on its interpretation could the treaty constitutionally be implemented in Germany: "By giving the Treaty an authentic interpretation to which the European institutions must abide in order to avoid the risk that the FCC [Constitutional Court] will declare EU acts void for Germany, the FCC sets itself up as a guardian of the constitutional framework of the EU."[139] In so doing, the German Constitutional Court was engaged with the jurisprudence of the ECJ in an effort to influence it to conform with the German Basic Law.[140] This activity might be viewed as illustrating the complexity of the mechanisms for convergence of laws in Europe, or instead as an unusually intensive form of engagement, generally committed to cooperative harmonized interpretations but resistant to the ECJ's claim of competence to determine the scope of convergence on its own authority.

Although the German Constitutional Court's decisions may be the best known, they are by no means unique; constitutional courts in France,[141] Italy,[142] Spain,[143] Denmark,[144] and Poland[145] likewise have contemplated the possibility of conflicts between national constitutions and legal efforts at European integration. Although there is debate whether the apparent possibility for finding a conflict is real, the possibilities of national influence on the interpretation of supranational law, and of supranational influence on national constitutional interpretation, appear inherent to this model. Although some have suggested that whatever the appearance of resistance to recognition of the supremacy of European law over domestic constitutions may be, it is unlikely to lead in fact to disparate results, in at least one instance thus far it apparently did: after the Polish Tribunal found legislation implementing the European arrest warrant's requirements unconstitutional, the Parliament amended the Polish Constitution to better accommodate the European arrest warrant but provided for "double criminality" as a condition for extradition.[146]

So while the ECJ and the ECtHR are forces pushing toward convergence, they also can generate resistance.[147] National constitutions are asserted as a basis for possible resistance to EU or European Convention law, but this possibility is articulated in a complex form of engagement, presuming in favor of a Europe-friendly interpretation but insisting that national constitutional values are at some level more important than full consistency with European law. Engagement in a complex plurality of constitutional orders characterizes this legal phenomenon,[148] in which the question of supremacy and priority as between European law and the national constitutions cannot be dealt with at one blow but requires a nuanced set of exchanges. In this setting, as one scholar suggests, "constitutional courts insist that it is the national constitutions, instead of the Court of Justice or the EC Treaties, that mediate the relationship between Community law and national law."[149]

A central feature of the judicially expressed concern about the purported supremacy of EU law has focused on its capacity to protect fundamental human rights, both under the European Convention and under national constitutions. The potential for conflict is illuminated by *Schmidberger v. Republic of Austria*,[150] a case decided by the ECJ. The case involved a planned demonstration by an environmental group along the Brenner Motorway, an important route through the Alps. Permission was granted by the local authorities, who agreed to close the motorway to traffic during the demonstration. Schmidberger, a company based in Germany that used the motorway to transport steel and timber between Germany and Italy, complained that the closure interfered with the free movement of goods in violation of rights guaranteed under EU treaties.[151] After the Austrian courts referred the issue to the ECJ, it rejected the challenge to Austria's decision to allow the demonstration and close the road. A balancing test, in which "the interests involved must be weighed having regard to all the circumstances of the case in order to determine whether a fair balance was struck between those interests," should leave national authorities a wide margin of discretion to decide whether banning such a demonstration would have constituted an "unacceptable interference" with the fundamental rights of the demonstrators.[152]

The *Schmidberger* decision and others (including the *Omega* case) suggest a role for national constitutional law in resolving tensions between the EU regime and domestic and supranational human rights regimes.[153] The larger point is that forms of engagement in the European context are complex, and—unlike elsewhere in the world—are framed within plausible claims of supremacy and direct effect at the EU supranational level. Notwithstanding legal structures that push strongly toward convergence, at least some national courts seek to engage, constructively, without acquiescing to the strongest claims of convergence.

D. POSITIVE INFLUENCES

As we have seen, there are multiple forces—intellectual, political, economic, cultural, and religious, as well as legal—that may push toward either resistance or convergence with transnational legal norms, and thus toward harmonization or fragmentation of various spheres of normative legal activity. These same forces may be at work in supporting postures of engagement. Here I comment specifically on globalization and the increased interaction among plural legal orders it creates, the continued effects of past colonial regimes and of the Commonwealth in promoting interchange about constitutional interpretation, instrumental and institutionalist reasons for engagement, the inevitability of increases in comparative knowledge among judges, and globalization of the norm of independent judging as factors that conduce toward the various forms of engagement.

Globalization, Transnational Disputes, and Plural Legal Orders

For the countries in Europe—especially for the twenty-seven members of the European Union, but also (though perhaps to a different degree) for the additional states that are parties to the ECHR but not are members of the EU—there are compelling reasons of law, politics, and economics to require strong forms of engagement, with mandatory consideration of European law. Whether this should be viewed within a convergence model or a strong engagement model is debatable. From the ECJ and ECtHR perspectives convergence is required; from some national courts' viewpoint, it is generally contemplated but not necessarily required. For the present, European jurists are dealing with some degree of legal pluralism.

Within and beyond Europe, moreover, globalization of economic activity, of social networks and movements, of criminal activity and environmental harm, pose challenges and promote change in the role of the territorial national states, on whose existence the idea of both constitutions and international law rest. For this reason, in part, interest in "constitutionalism" as a set of transnational norms disconnected from particular national constitutions has grown. Some scholars see a rise in the "*decentered* and *deterritorializing* apparatus of rule that progressively incorporates the entire global realm within its open, expanding frontiers."[154]

But while there may be some degree of "collapse" of the "territorial membrane" of the state,[155] globalization may be thought of as changing more in degree than kind the "interconnectedness" between national states and the international society of states that has long existed.[156]

National states and their courts, however, are being confronted with an increasing range of cases arising from transnational interactions. As global economic trade increases, more transactions can be expected to lead to more transnational adjudications, that is, cases in which the parties and law to be applied span more than one national jurisdiction. Some studies have found an association between cross-boundary trade and the states most likely to have references made to the ECJ.[157] (Whether to see these as mechanisms of engagement or convergence, in the case of the European Union, is complicated, as noted earlier.) Decisions about whether jurisdiction can be exercised in a manner consistent with the domestic constitution, as well as with international comity, may require domestic judges to become familiar with both some elements of international law and some foreign law.[158] Without suggesting what approach should be used to resolve, manage, or respond to these increasing confrontations among the world's jurisdictions, there seems little doubt that the process of transnational dispute adjudication will expose domestic judges more frequently to transnational sources of law, thereby increasing knowledge and making comparisons in constitutional cases more likely.

Past Colonialism and the Commonwealth Nations

In addition to the effects of globalization, the continuing influence of colonialism, and in particular, of the British empire on its former colonies' patterns of legal development, argument, and interpretation is a powerful force for constitutional engagement. This is so for several reasons (in addition to those already noted). A number of postcolonial constitutions in commonwealth nations were drafted with the assistance of British government offices, which encouraged inclusion of provisions for independent courts.[159] Commonwealth influence in the development of legal systems and judges was felt in other ways as well. Some national constitutions, for example, in Botswana, have specifically authorized the judges of other Commonwealth countries to be appointed to sit as a judge on the national high courts.[160]

Also of importance is that the Privy Council, when it engaged in judicial review of issues arising under the constitutions of members of the Commonwealth, would sometimes refer to cases involving other similar constitutional instruments. By drawing on arguments from multiple jurisdictions in construing the different members' constitutions, Privy Council decisions may have modeled and made ordinary such comparisons in the course of constitutional interpretation. This interpretive practice also created incentives for the courts of commonwealth nations and lawyers arguing cases before them to be more broadly aware of others' decisions.[161] Moreover, by articulating a view of national constitutions (even if formally enacted as British statutes) as "living trees" the meanings of which could evolve over time,[162] some Privy Council jurisprudence helped legitimize a range of interpretive sources similar to those used in multi-valenced constitutional interpretation, including foreign and international law. While living constitutionalism need not embrace the consideration of transnational sources, it is more open to them than, for example, highly intentionalist, originalist modes of interpretation.

In recent years, as the Privy Council's jurisdiction has been ending, the Secretariat of the Commonwealth continues to function in informal ways to maintain reasonably intensive levels of communication between judges of the courts of different independent commonwealth nations, through sponsored meetings and a formal organization of judges.[163] The Commonwealth Secretariat indicates that fifty-three countries in the world, with a combined population of nearly 2 billion persons, are members of the Commonwealth.[164]

Increases in Comparative Legal Knowledge

The Commonwealth Secretariat's work is a reflection of a broader phenomenon, to which the globalization of electronic information has also contributed, with more legal materials being produced and with greater access to those materials. In an environment where information flows quickly and remains available through the Internet, the incentives and opportunities for legal engagement increase, as the search costs for doing so decline. To put the matter strongly, knowledge of comparative and international law is increasingly inevitable; the option of not comparing because the "other" is unknown is increasingly declining, especially among those court systems with reasonable access to electronic and Internet resources. And even if only a small number of judges engage seriously with comparative materials,[165] their work is likely to become known and familiar within their own systems.

Institutional and Strategic Concerns, Mandatory Consideration as Soft Monitoring

As noted in prior chapters, states seeking to domesticate adherence to international human rights law for institutional or strategic purposes may incorporate that law into the constitution. A more flexible approach is to bind the state to *consider* international or foreign law in interpreting rights provisions. Such commitments may help a country align itself with the substantive positions of particular foreign allies, or qualify for financial assistance from international financial institutions, or even establish itself as a law-abiding "state" for international purposes.[166] In newly emerging democracies, such commitments may be a mechanism to solidify a break from the past, or to enhance the status or independence of the domestic court through its engagement with the decisions of other courts. Particularly where courts are relatively new and fragile, reliance on the views of other, better established courts (while maintaining a posture of independent judgment) may contribute to the reputation and independent adjudicatory capacity of the court within its own country.[167]

Mandatory consideration requirements may even be seen as a (very) soft form of having an independent monitor. For example, some scholars have criticized the South African Constitutional Court's *Grootboom* decision for refusing to adopt, as integral to interpreting the right of access to housing under Article 26 of the South African Constitution, the "minimum core" approach adopted by the UN monitoring committee for the ICESCR.[168] By *requiring* consideration of international law, South Africa in a certain sense invites and authorizes critique by international bodies when its interpretations depart from their own.

Independent Judging Gone Global: Judicial Networks and the Ideology of Judging

Finally, the idea of independent judging has gone global. The force of this idea, together with increases in institutional networks of judges and increased communications among courts, promotes, in various ways, a willingness to consider and refer to foreign and international legal materials, but in a spirit of engagement rather than convergence.

The Idea of Independent Judging in International and Constitutional Law The UDHR includes only one article that explicitly addresses a specific form of governance. Article 10 provides: "Everyone is entitled in full equality to a fair and public hearing by *an independent and impartial tribunal*, in the determination of his rights and obligations and of any criminal charge against him."[169] While the UDHR also states, in cautious language, that the legitimate authority of government must derive from the will of the people expressed in regular elections (without going quite so far as to say that a *democratic* form of government is required),[170] the requisite "independent and impartial tribunals" are central to the UDHR's commitment to the protection of human rights through the rule of law.[171]

The UDHR's commitment is echoed and given more concrete legal shape in the ICCPR, which, for example, states that "In the determination of any criminal charge against him, or of his rights and obligations in a suit at law, everyone shall be entitled to a fair and public hearing by a competent, independent and impartial tribunal established by law," and which encourages the creation of a specifically judicial remedy for violation of protected rights.[172] These provisions do not speak directly to whether judges should engage in constitutional review of laws, but they plainly imply the need for an independent judiciary that can adjudicate individual claims, especially in cases involving human liberty. The aspiration is also reflected, for example, in the creation of a UN Special Rapporteur on Judicial Independence (motivated by the gap between aspirations toward independence and performance on the ground),[173] and in the provisions of regional human rights instruments.[174]

The pervasiveness of this norm is reflected in transnational adjudication. Supranational tribunals evaluate the "independence and impartiality" of national judicial systems, sometimes requiring significant changes.[175] Indeed, the ECtHR's case law provided, if not the impetus, an external justification for major constitutional changes in the United Kingdom, including the impending replacement of the Law Lords by a Supreme Court. And national constitutional courts on occasion review international tribunals for their compliance with norms of independence and impartiality in judging, as occurred, for example, when the French Conseil Constitutionnel approved the provisions of the Statute for the International Criminal Court designed to protect the impartiality and independence of its judges.[176]

At the specifically constitutional level, increasing numbers of the world's constitutions provide in some way for the independence of the judiciary.[177] Of course the mere presence of provisions purporting to protect judicial independence does not in fact secure it. A particularly chastening example is that of Argentina, whose nineteenth-century constitution included provisions modeled on those of Article III of the U.S. Constitution.[178] During the twentieth century, however, practices of executive dominance of the Argentine Supreme Court developed, including the removals of judges through impeachment proceedings and court-packing expansions of membership.[179] Yet the spread of formal commitments to independent judging is relevant to show the force of the idea, an idea reinforced in some respects by economic aspects of globalization (as, perhaps, in China's willingness to try to develop more independent courts to participate in the World Trade Organization (WTO)).[180]

Judging as an Activity with Supranational Elements This globalization of an idea of judging that emphasizes judicial independence, not only from the parties but more generally from other forms of state authority, supports postures of engagement with the transnational in several ways.[181] First, it suggests that judging is itself an activity with "supranational" elements, that is, with elements common to the activity of judging that transcend national boundaries. Although this idea is an ancient one, it has also had its competitors, in which judging is seen as a more administrative duty legitimately supervised by responsible state authorities.[182] With the aspiration toward independent as well as impartial judging now in the human rights canon, and its infiltration into increasing numbers of national constitutions (as a goal if not yet a reality), judges may feel legitimate interests in understanding and promoting independent judging abroad.

Autonomy and judicial control of interpretive sources Second, the idea of judicial independence suggests that the task of judging must have a degree of autonomy, and that the judges must control the methods and sources of interpretation. Judges of constitutional courts not only meet with each other, and cite each other's opinions, but also defend the idea of at least some judicial autonomy over the sources of interpretation and develop interpretive theories that promote such autonomy. Even Justice Scalia, who has opposed referring to foreign law in constitutional interpretation, has stated his opposition to legislative efforts to constrain judges from so doing.[183] Transjudicial dialogue may reinforce norms of judging as at least a semiautonomous, discrete, and distinct activity.[184]

Human rights law's protection of judicial independence Third, the commitment of international human rights instruments to the idea of independent judging might help attract judicial attention to those instruments as generally useful sources of authority. As noted, while these instruments say very little about the organization of other parts of government, they do specify the need for independent and impartial courts. Judges may agree as a normative matter on the importance of judicial independence, and as an institutional matter they may be inclined to lend weight to those international human rights instruments that provide for independent judging by referring to them more generally as persuasive sources of authority.

Independence of judges from each other Finally, the idea of independent judging also suggests the idea of the independence of judges from one another.[185] One would predict that judges around the world would differ on legal issues no less than, and perhaps more than, judges within any one country. The idea of judicial independence from political branches may (though it need not necessarily) reinforce a norm of intrajudicial independence. Judges who believe that independent judging means that each judge should independently determine for himself or herself the best understanding of the law may not be disposed to follow their own colleagues, much less other judges in the world, if their own assessment of the law differs. Thus, judges may find the posture of engagement with the transnational more attractive—in being compatible with their own sense of independence—than the posture of convergence.

Judicial Networks The global ideal of independent judging is both reflected in and encouraged by the phenomenon of judicial networks that Anne-Marie Slaughter and others have observed.[186] Though the number of participants is small relative to the number of judges in the world, a body of judicial "networks" now exists. These networks include a set of constitutional court judges who communicate with each other and meet at conferences and fora around the world. While some scholars raise concerns about these networks and their contribution to what Professor Waters has termed "creeping monism,"[187] Dean Slaughter has argued that judges ought to participate in a shared process of articulating transnational norms to be enforced by judges around the world: "[I]mproving the capacity of government officials [including judges] to govern" is essential for the creation of a stable world order, and voluntary networks across national lines "perform a range of functions that enhance the effectiveness of domestic governance":

> They build trust and establish relationships among their participants that create incentives to establish a good reputation and avoid a bad one. They regularly exchange information about . . . different approaches to common legal issues. Finally, they offer technical assistance and professional socialization to members—whether regulators, judges, or legislators—from less developed nations. . . . In effect, government networks communicate to their

members everywhere the message that the Zimbabwean chief justice understood when he was under siege and commented, "I am not alone."[188]

The notion that judges of domestic courts should see themselves as actors in transnational networks of influence raises a number of questions. On the one hand, developing a professional identity as a judge serving as a check on government action that threatens human rights can have positive effects; being committed to the protection of the rule of law may be particularly important in times of emergencies when executives might be tempted to overextend their powers. However, it is not clear that judges developing strong identification with judges in other countries is necessary to fulfill this purpose, and it may carry costs of its own. Judges need to be attuned to the particular context of their national constitution and legal community to function well. They must do so at a minimum for pragmatic reasons, and, on some theories of constitutional interpretation, for normative reasons as well. Any understanding that judges may share some similar roles must be balanced with a recognition that they exercise them in very different contexts.

But Slaughter's reference to sharing "different approaches to common legal issues" contemplates a stance quite different from convergence. The "reputation"-enhancing incentives of networks are not necessarily reserved for those who produce results favored by a transnational consensus, but would support a self-conception of judges as independent of their governments—rights-protectors who are "not alone" in their efforts to resist pressures by their own governments. Something of this kind of socialization to a particular professional role is expressed by the International Commission of Jurists, founded in Berne, Switzerland in 1952, which, while "dedicated to the primacy, coherence and implementation of international law and principles that advance human rights," also has a "special emphasis on the independence of judges and lawyers."[189] A core concern, then, is for the independence of the courts themselves.

Courts Constructing Influence? Australian Justice Michael Kirby has written that "engaging in the analysis of analogous points, with the opinions of judges and other writers in many countries, helps ensure a national supreme court against intellectual isolation and, consequentially, a diminished influence of its own in the world of ideas."[190] Implicit in these remarks is that courts have an interest in exercising influence in a "world of ideas" that transcends national boundaries, or that courts play a role in the more general presentation of a country to the rest of the world. The effort at influence might be understood to take, as a measure of success, eliciting engagement by (or citation by) other courts as a sign of influence.

References to transnational sources may thus have strategic institutional purposes, as well as expressive purposes related to the judge's normative commitments. Engagement with other courts' decisions may be designed to manifest the relationship of courts to each other in the development of law, promoting an autonomous professionalism of independent courts (to which end the display of knowledge alone may have some perceived value) or the autonomous content of law under the interpretive control of judges. Recognizing other decision-makers may be thought to add to their legitimacy within their own legal orders.[191]

In addition to dignitary forms of citation designed to recognize or enhance the stature of particular courts or countries, transnational citations might also be used to express agreement with the content of decisions of other courts in ways that tend to enhance the precedential value of a decision. This function may be linked to the idea of the autonomous development of law; however, the ideological or substantive values of the decisions may be the most important factor behind such citations, rather than their autonomous development by courts as such. For example, when the Canadian Supreme Court addressed discrimination based on sexual orientation in employment in *Vriend v. Alberta*,[192] it quoted with approval from the U.S. Supreme Court decision in *Romer v. Evans*,[193] but did not refer to *Bowers v. Hardwick*.[194] By contrast, the South African Constitutional Court canvassed constitutional decisions both affirming and rejecting the validity of the death penalty in the *State v. Makwanyane* decision, exploring their reasoning before deciding that in South Africa the death penalty was barred by its Constitution.[195]

The increased practice of translating domestic constitutional court decisions (or summaries thereof) into English by the constitutional courts themselves is an indicator that the judges see some value to making their decisions more widely accessible to other jurists and lawyers. The German Constitutional Court, an important and influential one, now provides English summaries or translations of some of its most important decisions and its website has links to the websites of other constitutional courts around the world (and not just to European or English-speaking countries).[196] The Israeli High Court also has English translations of some of its cases on its website.[197] These English translations can be seen as an effort to influence and engage other communities of law,[198] expanding a global conversation about common legal issues that also occurs in seminars, conferences and informal exchanges among judges, academics and lawyers.[199]

Yet a desire for "influence," or even the development of a convergent sense of the importance of an independent judiciary, will not necessarily lead to or justify substantive convergence on legal rules. Rather, judges' interest in a wider audience is more likely to lead to the kind of transnational judicial discourse, or engagement with the work of judges in other countries and in supranational adjudicatory bodies, that we have in fact come to see.

4. CONSTITUTIONAL ADJUDICATION IN THE U.S. SUPREME COURT

Why Engage the Transnational?

Should the United States seek to bring its constitutional law into harmony with that of a transnational community of nations? Should it resist efforts to do so as a matter of first principle, rejecting even the consideration of foreign or international sources as bearing on constitutional meaning? The first approach, a convergence posture, risks ignoring the singular and long history of the U.S. Constitution; the second, a posture of general resistance, would deny to our judges the many benefits of considering foreign and international law arising from constitutions, treaties, and human rights instruments to which the United States has contributed. Engagement offers important insights for constitutional adjudication, both from a deliberative perspective concerned with improving the decision-making of the U.S. Supreme Court, and from a relational perspective in accommodating and mediating the developing relationships among and between constitutional and supranational legal systems.

As I show below, the U.S. Court and its justices have been involved in deliberative engagements with foreign and international law episodically over the course of our constitutional history, and in many of our most important constitutional decisions. It is thus emphatically not "foreign to our Constitution" to engage with the constitutional approaches of other nations.[1] And there is more reason in the twenty-first century to look to outside sources as an aid to interpretation than in the past, both because there are more transnational legal resources that bear on problems of constitutional interpretation in the United States and because the legitimacy of national states in the international community depends more than in the past on their adherence to transnational norms of democracy, the rule of law, and the protection of individual rights. I discuss deliberative engagement in Part A, and relational engagement in Part B below.

A. DELIBERATIVE ENGAGEMENT: AN INTERNAL PERSPECTIVE

The deliberative model of engagement is grounded in longstanding interpretive practices of the U.S. Court. It may be justified within a domestic perspective that is entirely self-referential—meaning that the rules for legitimate constitutional interpretation and constitutional change are determined within the legal system and by reference to its own practices. As noted above, on one account the basic norms of a constitution may be understood as "closed," that is, defined and subject to redefinition or change only within the self-referential system, while being more or less "cognitively open" to information generated by outside sources, even as it is self-referential in deciding what weight or significance should be given to such outside information.[2] On other accounts, the distinction between norms and information is necessarily unstable, or the interpretive practice has long been open to changed understandings of basic norms as well as to revised understandings of how existing norms apply.[3] For those who insist that the basic constitutional concepts and norms must be regarded as fixed (until changed by formal amendment), foreign and international law may nonetheless contribute to judges' decisions of how to apply and "implement" those concepts, by demonstrating alternative doctrinal approaches and contributing to functional understandings of the consequences of those alternatives.[4] Under any of these accounts, the focus is on engagement with the transnational as a means of improving the deliberative quality of domestic decision-making.

As the U.S. Court's jurisprudence suggests, deliberative uses of foreign and international law serve many legitimate roles in constitutional interpretation. Comparison is an inevitable part of the project of national self-expression that is so distinctive a feature of constitutions and constitutional law. To the extent that constitutions commit their polities to the protection of "inalienable" human rights, or to a common ideal of governance (for example, separation of powers, or judicial independence), constitutional interpreters are engaged in what is, in some sense, an overlapping project from which reciprocal learning is likely. Outsider perspectives, moreover, can help provide a check on error, as illustrated by the Court's allusions to avoiding totalitarian practice in its mid-twentieth-century decisions,[5] as well as by some justly famous dissents, noted below. Constitutional law is also in part about solving functional problems of governance; these functions are sometimes addressed by other countries similar enough to offer useful experience or information, and the U.S. Court has looked to that experience from time to time. Finally, because the role of an independent judge interpreting a written constitution in a democracy is a common one exercised under varying institutional and legal frameworks, considering such comparative sources of law may improve judging by providing a distinctive external perspective or lens through which familiar problems can be reexamined. In short, knowing more is generally better than knowing less. And judicial candor through written justification generally contributes more than silence to the legitimacy of the judicial process. These points are elaborated below.

Reflective Comparisons and Expressive Aspects of Interpretation in U.S. Constitutional History

The U.S. Constitution functions as something more than a binding legal instrument. As often observed, it has taken on over time something of the character of a civic religion—in the sense that commitment to the Constitution is a central, indeed constitutive, element of national identity. Pride in its existence and longevity, a tendency to conflate the Constitution with the normative good, and a recognition of the Constitution's text as what David Strauss calls a "common ground" are all characteristic of its role.[6] Although many constitutions express a national identity, the United States Constitution is viewed not only as expressing national identity but also as helping to construct it.[7] Constitutional interpretation then, in some ways, helps define who the "we" in the American "We the People" are, and who we are not. Its expressive role is an important one; what the Court says matters. While its decisions are surely not the only source of national identity, the Court's existence and work is an important strand in American self-understanding.

Transnational comparisons have long reinforced the expressive aspects of the Court's work. If national states are in some respects "imagined communities,"[8] they can exist as communities only where "others" exist or are envisioned. Understanding of a "self"—whether of an individual or collective entity—may require some sense of differentiation from the "other." The differentiation may consist only of geographical or territorial space, and the imagined community may share many values or characteristics of other communities—or it may be imagined as entirely exceptional and distinctive. In either case, or those falling in between, awareness of the "other" is implicated in the process of national self-definition.[9] That being so, comparison is an essential part of the project of national identity and self-expression, in constitutional as in other terms.

Self-expression in governance cannot be based on an uninformed imagination. If the United States is to be a "city on a hill," as some proponents of American exceptionalism argue it has been and should remain,[10] the surrounding terrain must be known: one cannot be a "city on a hill" if one is not surrounded by valleys or plains. One cannot be a "beacon of light" if one operates below the terrain of those who are supposed to see it. One cannot be a leader in the protection of freedom if one ignores baselines of freedom elsewhere or resorts to the procedures of dictatorships.[11] The assertion of American exceptionalism as a basis for resisting comparative inquiry is thus internally inconsistent.

American constitutional identity (including its exceptionalist strands) has been linked to elements of our experience viewed comparatively in constitutional adjudication. Examples in five areas are suggestive.

Freedom and Equality In *Plessy v. Ferguson*,[12] the Court rejected a challenge under the Fourteenth Amendment to a state law requiring racial segregation in public transportation, legitimating a regime of racial separation and subordination that lasted as a formal matter for nearly six decades (until *Brown v. Board of Education*[13]), a regime whose vestiges, some believe, continue to this day. As the sole dissenter in *Plessy*, Justice John Marshall Harlan wrote that state-mandated racial segregation "is a badge of servitude wholly inconsistent with the civil freedom and the equality before the law established by the Constitution," that "cannot be justified upon any legal grounds." This well-known statement would now be accepted by virtually all U.S. lawyers as embodying a core constitutional principle.

But Justice Harlan went on, in a comparative vein, stating, "We boast of the *freedom enjoyed by our people above all other peoples.* But it is difficult to reconcile that boast with a state of the law which, practically, puts the brand of servitude and degradation upon a large class of our fellow-citizens, our equals before the law."[14] Harlan's reference to the freedom of "our people above all other peoples" cuts to the heart of the comparative nature of exceptionalism: how, he asks, can the United States profess an ideology of freedom and liberty superior to all others while at the same time failing to extend that freedom and liberty to all of its own citizens?

In more modern times members of the Court have referred to transnational law to reflect on issues of personal freedom and race equality. References to the avoidance of totalitarianism in U.S. conceptions of personal freedom are found in cases like *Griswold v. Connecticut,* dealing with marital privacy and the right to use contraceptives.[15] In a 1990 dissent, Justice Kennedy quoted from a South African apartheid-era government document to support his argument for "strict scrutiny" of all racial classifications, even those purportedly justified by benign motivations, implying that we should take care not to end up like apartheid-era South Africa;[16] the Court has since adopted Kennedy's position on strict scrutiny.[17] More recently, in 2003 the Court in *Lawrence v. Texas* invoked European conceptions of personal freedom in striking down a Texas law prohibiting homosexual sodomy and Justice Ruth Bader Ginsburg relied on international human rights covenants in her concurrence in *Grutter v. Bollinger,* to support the compatibility of temporary race-conscious special measures in law school admissions with core commitments to equality.[18]

Due Process and Criminal Procedure Justice Harlan's comparative vantage in *Plessy* was in a lone dissent. In *Miranda v. Arizona,*[19] an iconic case from the 1960s, it was the Court itself that spoke in a comparative vein. The issue involved the constitutionality of custodial interrogation of a suspect without the presence of counsel. The Court held that, in order to protect the Fifth Amendment right against self-incrimination, statements made by a suspect in custodial interrogation—absent prior police advice of the constitutional rights to remain silent and have counsel—were not admissible. Invoking the traditions of American exceptionalism as a reason to embrace learning from the experiences of nations such as England, Scotland, India, and Ceylon (which at the time evidently provided greater protections for custodial interrogations), the Court wrote: "[I]t is consistent with our legal system that we give *at least as much protection to these rights* as is given in the jurisdictions described. We deal in our country with rights grounded in a specific requirement of the Fifth Amendment of the Constitution, whereas other jurisdictions arrived at their conclusions on the basis of principles of justice not so specifically defined."[20]

Executive Power The Court's opinion in *Miranda,* like Harlan's dissent in *Plessy,* can be read to express a vision of American exceptionalism—the idea of the United States as a "city on a hill," with its liberty-protecting Constitution[21]—as a positive reason to look at how U.S. practices compare to those of other countries. But the importance of comparison, the inevitability of comparison in the project of self-definition, and the utility of negative comparisons, are illustrated in many other cases. Justice Felix Frankfurter's concurring opinion in the *Youngstown Steel* case observed:

> It is absurd to see a dictator in a representative product of the sturdy democratic traditions of the Mississippi Valley. The accretion of dangerous power does not come in a day. It does come, however slowly, from the generative force of unchecked disregard of the restrictions that fence in even the most disinterested assertion of authority.[22]

Comparing Harry Truman and recent "dictators" (Hitler, Mussolini, Stalin) by denying that one is doing so (a form of rhetorical preterition) should not obscure the aversive use of comparison here:[23] "We" are a country of "sturdy democratic traditions" and not a country of "dictators"—but we risk becoming what we are not and do not want to be, if we abandon the fences that check power.

Citizenship and Immigration In closely divided cases, contested visions of national identity have been played out through invocation of foreign comparisons. In *Fong Yue Ting v. United States*,[24] the Court upheld a statute authorizing the deportation of Chinese laborers who did not possess a required residency certificate unless, on the testimony of at least one "white witness," they met the conditions to excuse them from the certificate requirement. In so ruling, the majority began by noting the universal practice of sovereigns to retain the right to expel aliens, "an inherent and inalienable right of every sovereign and independent nation" that the Court found unconstrained by the Constitution.[25] For four pages the majority opinion addressed international law, as enunciated by treatise writers, and the laws of both England and France concerning the power to expel aliens.[26]

While the majority in *Fong Yue Ting* invoked the practices of other sovereigns as a positive reason to read the U.S. Constitution to provide such powers, the dissenting justices invoked American exceptionalism. According to Justice David Brewer, "[t]he expulsion of a race may be within the inherent powers of a despotism. . . . [The] framers [of this Constitution] were familiar with history, and wisely . . . they gave to this government no general power to banish."[27] Justice Field also dissented, denying that the majority had correctly described the powers of other countries, and arguing that in any event, other countries' practices

> would have no bearing in these cases . . . Spain expelled the Moors; England, in the reign of Edward I, banished fifteen thousand Jews; and Louis XIV, in 1685, by revoking the Edict of Nantes . . . drove out the Huguenots . . . Within [the last] three years Russia has banished many thousands of Jews, and apparently intends the expulsion of the whole race. . . . All the instances mentioned have been condemned for their barbarity and cruelty, and no power to

> perpetrate such barbarity is to be implied from the nature of our government, and certainly is not found in any delegated powers under the Constitution. The government of the United States is one of limited and delegated powers. It *takes nothing* from the usages or the former action of European governments, nor does it take any power by any supposed inherent sovereignty.[28]

Thus, two contrasting narratives: "We the People" are not constituted under a basic law that permits barbarism, cruelty or despotism, in the dissenters' view; or, according to the majority, "We the People" have equivalent powers to other sovereign peoples around the world.

Cruel and Unusual Punishment In a number of cases involving Eighth Amendment issues, the Court has compared U.S. practices to those of other "civilized" nations. In at least one case, however, the foreign origin of a punishment, its "alien source," helped demonstrate that it was "barbarous" and "cruel and unusual" within our system.[29] In several other cases, an international consensus against a practice helped establish or confirm that a U.S. practice should be regarded as cruel and unusual. In *Trop v. Dulles*,[30] for example, four members of the majority concluded that imposing the loss of citizenship as punishment for a crime violated the Eighth Amendment, noting that "[t]he civilized nations of the world are in virtual unanimity that statelessness is not to be imposed as punishment for crime." Thus, not only do we "take nothing" from the practices of barbarous European dictators, but our practices ought to accord with those of the "civilized nations of the world" in order to assure the stature of the United States as among those "civilized nations."

* * *

In short, the Constitution and constitutional law express or help constitute a national identity, which is understood, in part, in comparison with that of other nations. As these and many other cases show, "we" are not a country hospitable to "despotism" or dictators; we are part of the group of "civilized nations" in the world. We have those powers "inherent in sovereignty," which can be determined by examining the powers and practices of other nations. And we are a freedom-loving country, that should do "at least as" well in protecting liberty as other countries. All of these assertions require some degree of reflective comparison.

Overlapping Normative Commitments and Constitutional Justice Seen from Outside

Closely related to the expressive and constitutive resort to comparative law to illuminate U.S. constitutional values and commitments is the possibility of shared knowledge and learning from other polities that have similar constitutional commitments. The degree of normative overlap between the U.S. Constitution and those of many other liberal democracies is considerable. One need not believe that there are, as an ontological matter, universal human rights across all human societies in order to see that many constitutions incorporate shared legal concepts, rights believed to be necessary for "liberty" or "justice" or "equal protection," which it is the task of written constitutions to help secure. Notwithstanding claims of American constitutional "exceptionalism,"[31] there are similarities between the rights-protecting provisions of the U.S. Constitution and those found in many other liberal democracies—in due process protections of liberty, in requirements for fair hearings before impartial decision-makers, in equal protection and in bans on cruel and unusual punishments.[32]

That such similarities exist should come as no surprise. Government actors, lawyers, and academics have urged adoption of provisions found in the U.S. Constitution in other countries. The United States played an important role in promoting the development of modern human rights commitments, embodied in the UDHR (and then in the two human rights covenants that went out for signature in 1966). These "archetypes" of rights protection in turn have influenced many post–World War II constitutions, many of which include parallel or cognate texts. These texts are, to be sure, rooted in different processes of legal consent and adoption among different constituencies; they may have significant differences in wording; and they may contemplate different institutional contexts of interpretation and enforcement. But they also may have what Gerald Neuman has called a "suprapositive" aspect—that is, a normative legal value "independent of [its] embodiment in positive law"[33]—contributing to the possibility that decisions applying one provision may offer normative insights into the application of their cognates in other jurisdictions. Thus, Gary Jacobsohn, a scholar acutely appreciative of the particularities of different constitutional systems, can nonetheless write of constitutional equality law that "it is possible to accommodate particularism (or at least leave its fundamental commitments unchallenged) while pursuing those universalistic aspirations that are compatible with both the nation's own promises and the increasingly predominant internationally held view on equal treatment under the law."[34]

In the first case holding that a criminal sentence authorized by law violated the Eighth Amendment, the Court noted the important "difference between unrestrained power and that which is exercised under the spirit of *constitutional limitations formed to establish justice*."[35] If one function of written constitutions is—as ours proclaims—to "establish Justice,"[36] taking into consideration outsider perspectives on contested practices might offer a kind of check against constitutional moral error. A number of Supreme Court opinions later determined, by political or legal processes, to have been serious constitutional errors were issued over dissents that sought to invoke "outsider" perspectives on shared values to forestall the error. The two dissenters in *Dred Scott* invoked then-contemporary European laws to challenge the majority's conclusion that Scott remained a slave;[37] as already noted, Justice Harlan appealed to a comparative sense of American commitment to freedom to condemn the Court's approval of state-imposed racial segregation in *Plessy*; and in *Lochner v. New York*, Justice

Harlan invoked the concerns of "civilized peoples" about working hours in support of the New York law struck down by the majority.[38] And even Justice Scalia, arguing that foreign legal materials are "hardly ever" relevant to constitutional interpretation, has acknowledged that they may be helpful in deciding whether "a particular holding will be disastrous."[39]

Foreign experience will not, of course, always point in more just directions, or in only one direction.[40] The question is, always, what is the best reading of our own constitution? Reflective comparisons may assist decision-makers in finding the answer. Implicit in this claim is an understanding of law, and specifically of constitutional law, as having a certain reflexive quality to it, permitting change in interpretations over time. True, constitutional law is often thought of as performing important settlement and coordination functions, both of which require stability and predictability. But at the same time the legitimacy of our constitutional law—its capacity to be regarded as legitimate in a social, legal, and moral sense—requires that even apparently settled understandings, such as the permissibility of classifying women as unfit for "male" occupations,[41] or of racial segregation, be open to "unsettlement,"[42] to "normative disturbances" toward better constitutional understandings.[43] To the extent that our Constitution shares values with others, outsider perspectives may prove helpful in efforts toward improved constitutional self-understanding.

Implementing the Constitution: Functionality and Doctrine

Functional comparisons can cast light on how to solve emerging constitutional problems and provide empirical information relevant to doctrinal questions that U.S. constitutional law asks, illuminating both more, and less, successful approaches. Legal concepts may need filling in,[44] and constitutional doctrine may make relevant the likely consequences of a challenged law or practice, or alternatives thereto, as well as the reasonableness of the government's basis for action, on all of which foreign law, practice, or experience may bear.

Fortuity may determine what polity first begins to address new problems, as technological, social, or political changes create apparently new constitutional issues.[45] For example, when U.S. state governments began to enact mandatory vaccination laws at the turn of the twentieth century and a constitutional challenge arose, the Court looked to practice in several European countries to satisfy itself that the restraints on liberty entailed by the law were reasonable in light of current understandings of scientific knowledge and the practices of other governments.[46] Foreign solutions may be deemed unsuccessful, illustrating the negative consequences of accepting a particular claim, as was the case in the Court's considerations of foreign law permitting assisted suicide in *Washington v. Glucksberg*,[47] or they may be inapposite due to constitutional differences.[48] Foreign practice is also relevant in assessing the constitutionality of legislation designed to coordinate with foreign regulation.[49] The following discussion notes several areas in which justices have invoked transnational sources for such purposes.

Change, New Problems, Health and Safety Regulation Empirical references to foreign experience are found in some of the leading constitutional cases dealing with challenges to government health and safety regulations. In *Lochner v. New York*,[50] *Muller v. Oregon*,[51] and *Jacobson v. Massachusetts*,[52] the constitutional litigation challenged innovative legislation regulating conditions that in some sense did not exist at the time of the Framing—in the first two cases, conditions of industrial work (development of which had accelerated in the latter part of the nineteenth century) and in the third, newly developed medical capacities to prevent the spread of harmful disease.[53] Thus new issues were presented to the Court arising out of newly perceived problems.[54]

In each of these cases, foreign experience (though not necessarily constitutional law) was invoked to support the constitutionality of the challenged state laws. Justice Harlan, for example, argued in his *Lochner* dissent that comparative experience suggested that the statute was not "extreme or exceptional" but "occup[ies] a middle ground," and plainly bore a substantial relationship to health and should be upheld.[55] In *Muller*, a majority of the Court found persuasive Brandeis's argument that foreign practice in adopting statutes limiting women's working hours supported the reasonableness, and hence the constitutionality, of the limitation on contractual freedom. Although foreign experience and legislation were not, "technically speaking, [legal] authorities . . . ," they were nonetheless relevant because "when a question of fact is debated and debatable, and the extent to which a special constitutional limitation goes is affected by the truth in respect to that fact, a widespread and long continued belief concerning it is worthy of consideration."[56] The existence of multiple other jurisdictions adopting similar legislation spoke to the constitutional standard for determining the validity of state regulation that limits individual freedom—in *Jacobson*, whether the law was "necessary" to control the spread of smallpox; in *Muller*, to show that the limitation of women's working hours was not an "unreasonable, unnecessary and arbitrary interference" with liberty of contract because it was (believed to be) well-founded in differences between the sexes. *Muller* is also a caution that a transnational "consensus" at one time may come to be seen as mistaken, reinforcing arguments for postures of engagement, not convergence.[57]

Criminal Procedure In 1957 Sanford Kadish observed that comparison with other Anglo-American countries was one of several techniques being used for determining the meaning of the Due Process Clause.[58] Resort to foreign experience worked both for and against expansion of protections, depending on the question. Justice Frankfurter's opinion for the Court in *Wolf v. Colorado*,[59] declining to extend the exclusionary rule to the states, relied on a survey of ten Commonwealth jurisdictions that found none of them excluded evidence obtained by unlawful searches. Yet Frankfurter also relied on foreign law to move ahead of his fellow justices in opposing the admission into evidence of a confession obtained through coercion as a violation of the Constitution.[60]

Although Frankfurter was off the Court by the time it was decided, *Miranda v. Arizona* reflected his willingness to consider foreign law, not only on shared constitutional values, as discussed above, but also with a more pragmatic focus on consequences. The Court reasoned that the existence of restrictions on custodial interrogations in the countries under study suggested that it would not harm law enforcement to require the police to give warnings.[61] The Court did not adopt any of the particular practices of the foreign countries it described in their detail, but rather modeled the constitutionally required warnings on those already in use in the United States by the Federal Bureau of Investigation.[62] Foreign practice was not considered a form of binding precedent, but a useful, "outside" example shedding light on how as a functional matter to implement the constitutional prohibition on coerced self-incrimination. Since *Miranda*, foreign law has been invoked by members of the Court on other criminal procedure issues involving the Fourth Amendment and the retroactivity of decisions concerning jury trial rights.[63]

Separation of Powers Justice Robert Jackson, whose concurrence is the most influential of the opinions in the *Youngstown Steel* case, made intensive use of foreign constitutional experience to explain some of the functional reasons for his decision. The interpretive question—the extent of the President's implied or emergency powers, in light of the Korean conflict, to seize the domestic steel industry to avert a labor stoppage—was one, Jackson concluded, on which clear historical evidence and judicial precedent were lacking.[64] In the face of this open question, he reasoned structurally, textually, and from comparative experience. Drawing on Clinton Rossiter's book, *Constitutional Dictatorship*, and other sources for descriptions of the constitutional means by which power was centralized in the executive in the United Kingdom, France, and Germany in the years leading up to and during World War II, Jackson concluded that contemporary experience suggested that "emergency powers are consistent with free government only when their control is lodged elsewhere than in the Executive who exercises them."[65] And resort to foreign experience on separation of powers issues has not been confined to Jackson's *Youngstown* opinion.[66]

Federalism In federalism cases, early references to the law of nations might be regarded as casting light on the original intentions of the framers,[67] but more contemporary uses are plainly functional and consequentialist in tenor. Thus, in *Wickard v. Filburn*, upholding a federal regulation that controlled the amount of wheat that could be grown for home consumption on family farms, the Court noted that "[t]he four large exporting countries of Argentina, Australia, Canada, and the United States have all undertaken various programs for the relief of growers . . . designed, in part at least, to protect the domestic price received by producers. Such plans have generally evolved towards control by the central government."[68] In a footnote, the Court commented, "[i]t is interesting to note that all of these have federated systems of government, not of course without important differences. In all of them, wheat regulation is by the national government."[69] Although the Court does not make explicit the connection, the evident purpose of the foreign comparison is to suggest that as a functional matter, for the United States to be able to feed its people and stay competitive in the world market, national regulation of wheat production is necessary and thus within the scope of the commerce power. A more recent effort to draw explicitly consequentialist comparisons was made by Justice Breyer, in his dissent in *Printz v. United States*.[70] Whether federal law could impose duties on state officers was a question that Breyer saw as open under specific constitutional text and past decisions of the Court. Considering the experience of other federal polities—including Switzerland, Germany, and the European Union, which not only permit but generally require that most central government laws be implemented only by officials of the constituent member entities—Breyer suggested that the consequences of requiring state officials to administer federal law were not inconsistent with a healthy federalism. Justice Scalia, by contrast, argued that comparative practice was of relevance in making, but not in interpreting, constitutions.[71]

Yet functional comparisons, while perhaps among the least controversial as a normative matter within the U.S. debate, are among the most difficult to make in constitutional law—whether in federalism or in other areas. As noted in Chapter 1, "omitted variables"—that is, distinguishing features of different constitutional systems that are omitted in analyses—act as confounding factors, and thus the ability to draw reliable causal inferences is weakened.[72] In *Printz*, the causal inference Breyer sought to draw might not be correct given other important differences, such as the direct popular election of senators in the United States, compared with the participation of members of the subnational governments in the upper house of the national legislature in Germany.[73] Some knowledge is no doubt better than none, but it must be used with caution in light of its complex and contestable empirical base.

The Law of Nations in the Constitution There are terms in the Constitution whose evident function demands some degree of contemporary reciprocity of understanding with other nations—terms like "Ambassadors," "Treaties," or the "Law of Nations." Here, the functional reason for comparison is at once also an originalist and purposive reason; these terms simply cannot be interpreted, or construed, without regard to understandings of the contemporary international community referenced by the very vocabularies used.

Given the object of establishing the United States as a sovereign in the community of nations, it seems implausible that framers or ratifiers would have intended to freeze the details of then-current understandings of "Offenses against the Law of Nations."[74] On the scope of the Treaty Power, most scholars would consider not only how treaties were understood at the Framing, but also how treaties are now generally understood in the contemporary international legal environment; the constitutional purposes of enabling and enforcing agreements with other countries through treaties would be ineffective if its meaning did not correspond to the ongoing nature of international relations.[75] And the Court has on occasion explicitly recognized the need to understand such terms in light of the evolution of international legal and economic relations.[76] This is not to say, of course, that the only interpretive source that should matter is contemporary international understandings; such a position risks ignoring U.S. history and the way in which these provisions fit within the broader constitutional structures. But even some of the most persistent critics of reliance upon transnational sources contemplate the use of international law to give meaning to such terms.[77]

Inevitability of Comparison, Multiple Perspectives, and Ethical Judging: Reflective Comparison and Impartiality

Finally, engaging with transnational sources of constitution-like law may strengthen both the quality of decisions and the power of reason-giving as a mechanism of accountability for politically independent judges. Comparison today is inevitable. It is almost impossible to be a well-informed judge or lawyer now without having impressions of law and governance in countries other than one's own. These impressions, which may influence views of U.S. constitutionalism, could be incorrect or subject to interpretive challenge.[78] A recent sequence of decisions provides an example. Chief Justice Warren Burger's 1986 concurring opinion in *Bowers v. Hardwick*[79] implied that homosexual sodomy was universally condemned in Western civilization. Seventeen years later, the Court in *Lawrence v. Texas* responded by noting that, several years *prior* to *Bowers*, the European Court of Human Rights had held that such a prohibition violated the ECHR.[80]

This sequence suggests that judges' reliance on what they think they know about other systems is inevitable, and illustrates that overt references to such reliance can be a form of accountability, permitting correction of errors.[81] It also suggests that if judges are influenced by but do not refer to transnational legal sources,[82] there could be significant costs to one of the principal mechanisms of judicial accountability—written reasons and public evaluation thereof. For the working mechanisms of ongoing accountability at the federal level lie not in the possibility of judges being removed from office, but rather in the constraints of reasoned response: how do the Court's decisions and reasons fare among the legal community, the general public, and knowledgeable commentators? Although there are settings in which courts do not give reasons for their decisions—for example, in granting or denying certiorari—on the whole judicial candor about reasoning is to be preferred to nondisclosure.[83] Comparison is a fact of legal life; when it influences a judge's deliberated decision it is (usually) better for him or her to say so.[84]

In a more positive vein, comparison can be a useful way to achieve some reflective distance, improving impartiality and objectivity about interpretive questions. As has been said about the benefits of consulting the "constitutional views of our predecessors," "the more varied the participants in the [constitutional] conversation the richer it will be and the more satisfactory will be its results."[85] Confronting the power of others' ideas about common legal problems or concerns can, in other words, contribute to a better intellectual product, and can also impose the discipline of explanation upon the decision-maker.[86] Even if the reasoning of a foreign court ultimately is rejected, explaining why it is inapplicable or wrong may improve the quality of the Court's reasoning, making its choices more clear to the audience of lawyers, lower courts, legislators, and citizens. It is sometimes said that dissent and separate opinions improve the quality of decision-making over the long run, as debate and discussion are provoked and informed by their existence.[87] So may transnational discourses of constitutional decision-making provide a broader arena for constitutional conversation. Reflective awareness of alternative constitutional approaches, then, may improve a judge's distance on the interpretive problem before the court.[88]

Engaging with the reasoned decision of other constitutional courts may be particularly helpful to professionally ethical judging in the United States. Although on this point norms vary widely in the world,[89] U.S. judges are ethically required to avoid discussion of pending cases with outsiders (except in the presence of the parties' counsel).[90] Such ethical rules reflect aspirations for decisions based on judges' impartial, reasoned views of the best understanding of the law. Achieving this understanding may require a judge to distance herself from her own first reactions, testing them for prejudice and subjecting them to reasoned interrogation.[91] Given aspirations for U.S. judges to maintain isolation from the immediate legal community in deciding cases (an isolation that is particularly weighty for judges on a court of last resort), considering "outsider" perspectives found in transnational sources of law can be particularly helpful.

Reflective comparisons can challenge assumptions that existing ways of proceeding are necessary or "natural," and thus can help "mitigate the effect of [a judge's own] idiosyncrasies."[92] Looking to foreign law thus expands opportunities for ethical engagement with the views of those having equivalent responsibility and aspiring to similar impartiality, providing a partial intellectual substitute for conversation, a testing from outside that may be particularly helpful on the most controversial and apparently value-laden choices. Comparative law in this sense can be the judge's "experienced friend," as Aharon Barak, then President of Israel's highest court, put it.[93] In these ways, reflective comparison offers the hope of more, rather than less, impartiality, as judges use foreign decisions as a way of distancing themselves from and checking their own first reactions.

Some might argue that reading the parties' briefs and the lower courts' opinions and discussing issues with one's law clerks are parts of the deliberative process that adequately provide for the kind of intellectual interchange that undergirds good judicial decision-making. But these activities are not equivalent to engaging as equals with others who bear a similar weight of decision. Moreover, opportunities for interchange within the U.S. Supreme Court are limited by, inter alia, the small number of justices. Although the state and lower federal courts write decisions with which the Supreme Court justices can engage, bound as they are by the Court's past decisions these lower courts are more constrained in exploring hard new constitutional questions than are the highest constitutional courts of foreign countries. As one foreign justice explained: "The essential question is . . . the degree to which a judge has freedom to choose. In this respect, the position of a judge within a hierarchy, where parties can obtain supervision through appeals, differs from that of a judge on a supreme court."[94]

This observation raises a further point: The judges of the highest constitutional courts for their respective countries face, in particularly acute form, the general tension between respect for democracy and the output of democratically elected legislatures and the need to treat constitutional rules as constraints on current legislation. As Professor Neuman has noted, "an argument that has already proven persuasive to an impartial body responsible for striking a balance between the claims of order and liberty" may be more persuasive to courts than "self-serving advocacy" or "normative speculation."[95] Or as Aharon Barak has suggested, the questions of judicial role in interpreting a constitution in a democracy are shared,[96] though the answers may be distinct. Understanding how different judges in other constitutional democracies have answered questions about the judge's role can lead a judge to a more conscious analysis of her own role and thus to a greater capacity for the kind of impartiality to which the best judges aspire.

Finally, deliberation and reason-giving are of most importance to the legitimacy of constitutional law on issues regarded as open. That some issues come to be regarded as open is beyond question; how they do so is the subject of an interesting literature that cannot be fully canvassed here.[97] These open questions call for processes of epistemic validation, that is, a decision process designed to reduce errors in making choices among interpretations that are plausibly supported by conventional strands of domestic authority.[98] In open cases these authorities apply or fit together with some degree of uncertainty. Traditions are multiple and may "becom[e] . . . a resource from which reasons for change may be derived . . . [t]he past is mobilized to invent a future."[99] Law must, in these settings, function as a form of "inquiry,"[100] open to learning from its own past and from the experiences of others.[101]

* * *

To summarize the reasons for deliberative engagement, apart from that it is already part of our interpretive practices: first, comparison facilitates a better understanding of one's own constitutional tradition, either with a view to preserving and advancing that tradition or with a view to re-understanding or reconstructing it. To the extent that one regards the expression of a nation's aspirations and commitments as a valid purpose of constitutional interpretation, awareness of other constitutional traditions may be helpful as both positive and negative forms of inspiration. As we have seen, historically, many U.S. references to other constitutional systems seem wrought up in a project of American constitutional exceptionalism that is expressive and self-constituting in nature; constitutional law may not only be expressive of traditional identities or aspirations, but also available for reconstructive projects. Comparative experience can provide both an illuminating mirror, "clarify[ing] our picture of ourselves," and a set of alternative visions for those who seek to change existing legal cultures.[102]

Second, understanding how roughly comparable bodies have interpreted roughly similar constitutional provisions can help illuminate constitutional commitments to shared constitutional values, like the idea of limited government or of freedom of speech.[103] Moreover, comparative reflection may be a safeguard against severe constitutional error, providing a lens or mirror through which our own understandings and practices may be viewed at a distance, without the command of (presumptive) conformance found in the convergence model. Third, the experience of other nations has utility for legal interpretation by demonstrating different approaches to similar "functional" questions; it can help provide "a basis for predicting the factual consequences" of different reasonably justifiable interpretations plausibly open to the decision-maker and suggest "whether those consequences are compatible with the commitments of a free society."[104]

Finally, considering comparative experience or international law can broaden and deepen the perspectives a judge of a court of last resort brings to the weighty responsibility she exercises in constitutional cases, thereby improving her capacity for impartial, objective decision-making. The very idea of an independent judge implies an aspiration toward impartiality, and wherever courts are vested with the power of constitutional review of legislation, tensions may arise between constitutionalism and democracy. Judicial consideration of foreign decisions by other constitutional courts or tribunals, or of constitutional practices of other Western democracies, or of widely subscribed to international norms, can provide diverse perspectives on the inevitable new questions, and revisitings of old questions, of which constitutional adjudication before the Supreme Court consists. The knowledge base for good constitutional decision-making is thus kept vibrant, as the judge—in deliberating beyond her first intuitions—must meet and consider the challenges posed by others' approaches. Given the inevitability of implicit comparison (and the potential for error therein), finally, open engagement can be a salutary check.

B. RELATIONAL ENGAGEMENT: CONSTITUTIONAL SYMBIOSIS IN A GLOBALIZING LEGAL WORLD

The deliberative model of engagement has an internal focus, using foreign or international law to develop the best understandings of a constitution as domestic law and from the perspective of domestic constitutional constituencies.

However, as discussed in Chapter 3, engagement may be motivated or justified not only by the possibilities for improved deliberation but also by a more relational understanding of constitutional law, an understanding that national constitutional systems exist in relationships with those of other countries and with international legal orders. The implications of this relationship may be expressed in a felt obligation to consider international or foreign law, even where it is understood not to be binding.

The U.S. Constitution has no provision comparable to South Africa's mandate to consider international law and authorization to consider foreign law; except where its provisions draw their definition in part from the practices of other nations, the U.S. Constitution cannot readily be construed as implicitly providing such a general directive. The Constitution is largely silent on the methods of its own interpretation, although its preamble invites a purposive reading of the text that follows to achieve the listed goals—"establish Justice," "provide for the common defense" and so forth.[105] To be sure, U.S. constitutional practice has long included references to foreign or international law, but it would be difficult to draw from that any general obligation to consider foreign or international law.

Yet felt obligations to do so might arise out of particular perceptions of national or institutional self-interest. A sense of relationship might reflect some limited recognition of the moral claims of those outside the polity whose interests are affected by domestic constitutional law. Countries and courts with power, it might be argued, ought at least to consider other countries' views in forming their own (on open questions), because their decisions impose externalities or their position generates expectations of due consideration from others. Alternatively, a more relational attitude may reflect a changing understanding of the jurisprudential underpinnings of modern state law or of the role of constitutional judges in democracies; given the impact of globalization on the sociology and epistemology of law, courts simply *are* acting within a set of transnational influences, and it is better to be conscious about it through consideration and reason-giving. In this setting, transnational engagement in constitutional interpretation may help legitimate liberal democratic national states and strengthen their ability to be effective influences.

Strategic or Institutional Goals, Weak State–Strong State Differences?

Some of the strategic goals relatively weak or newly democratizing states may have in binding themselves to consider international or foreign law will not have much traction in the United States, whose task is primarily to sustain rather than to create commitments to the constitutional rule of law. Indeed, there is an argument to be made that in sustaining domestic rule of law commitments, selective resort to the U.S.' own constitutional past may be a particularly powerful tool. Yet there may be other strategic goals served by a more relational posture.

One is to strengthen the rule of law elsewhere by implicit recognition of the role of independent judges, as Justice Breyer may have been doing by citing to an opinion of a Zimbabwean judge.[106] Judges in powerful democratic nations have legitimate interests in promoting the independence of the judiciary to support the rule of law elsewhere, if for no reason other than the impact of dominant scripts on the ability of each nation over time to sustain those commitments. Whether to do so in their judicial opinions, however, raises more complex questions of audience and affiliation.

A different set of instrumental reasons for engagement arises out of the changed character of international law. If once it applied primarily to inter-state relations, international law now also applies to the relationships between a state and its own citizens or residents, and the legitimacy of national states is increasingly measured by their compliance with transnational norms of democracy and human rights. International law, moreover, is now concerned not only with the obligations of states as such but also with the obligations of individual actors, including government officials, against whom claims or prosecutions may be brought in foreign or international fora (including criminal prosecutions for crimes against humanity or war crimes). Considering international law in construing our own Constitution and laws, especially insofar as they concern such grave conduct, allows U.S. courts to evidence concern for those rules and, in saying what they are, to influence understandings of international legal standards.[107]

Moral Obligations and Claims of Outsiders

From a moral point of view one might argue that all nations, and particularly powerful ones, have *obligations* to consider the views of outsider transnational communities on issues before domestic courts where the domestic decisions may affect those communities.[108] Do the decisions of the United States Supreme Court affect other nations? Yes, and in at least two distinctive ways; but as we shall also see, the implications for what the justices should feel obligated to consider are in most cases uncertain.

A Transnational Court? First, cases before the U.S. Supreme Court increasingly have come to concern what constitutional or other rights citizens of foreign countries have when they are in the United States or are being held by arms of the U.S. government in other parts of the world. Looking at the issues before the U.S. Supreme Court in recent years might even lead one to call it a "transnational court," at least from the perspective of those other countries whose nationals' rights and status are being determined by the U.S. Court.[109]

In addition to the ongoing docket of cases involving immigration and nationality law,[110] there have been two other significant sources of the increasingly transnational cast to the Court's constitutional docket in recent years. First, noncompliance by state and local law enforcement officers with obligations under the Vienna Convention on Consular Relations led to several cases involving foreign countries (Paraguay, Germany, and Mexico), including the recent *Medellín* case that was before the Supreme Court twice.[111] Second, the "war on terror," the U.S. practice of holding foreign nationals in Guantánamo, and asserted abuses of the security and rights of foreign nationals by or at the behest of the U.S. government, have generated a number of cases involving foreign nationals, with more pending in the lower courts.[112] It is no wonder that foreign governments and foreign legal scholars have increasingly participated, through amicus filings or otherwise, in cases on the Court's docket.[113]

These cases involve not only the asserted rights of foreign nationals, but also claims under international (as well as constitutional) law.[114] They can thus be regarded as multiply "transnational." Do the interests of foreign nations in the outcomes of litigation before the Court—whether based on their concern for their own nationals or for the development of international law—give rise to a duty on the Court's part to consider the legal views of outside members of the world community in these circumstances?[115] There are some reasons to say yes, where relatively direct interests are at stake, such as those of a foreign state with the treatment of its nationals, or concerning the United States' international obligations, for example, under a multilateral treaty in whose enforcement and effect many others have an interest. Yet any duty of fair consideration might be satisfied with fairly minimal attention and may not be reflected in any specific response.

An Influential Court? A second way in which the U.S. Court's work has transnational effects is that, given the longstanding role of the Court as a source of constitutional jurisprudence, its decisions may influence jurists in other parts of the world, thereby influencing other countries' domestic law,[116] and possibly even having an effect on customary international law.[117] Amicus filings, as Dean Alex Aleinikoff has written, reflect the views of foreign jurists "that the world beyond the United States has a direct and concrete interest in the resolution of the legal issues in [cases like] *Boumediene* because decisions of the U.S. Supreme Court are likely to influence the development of international law," by which other countries consider themselves bound.[118] The content of customary international law depends, in part, on state practice; so constitutional courts when deciding questions of interest to the transnational community are potential contributors to evolving norms. With international law now affecting how states treat persons within their jurisdiction, all states arguably have some stake in the decisions of other states about how to treat persons within their jurisdiction.[119] Given the reputation of the U.S. Court and the power of the United States, it is likely that the U.S. Court's decisions will continue to be of interest to courts in other countries.[120] Jurists in countries that wish to maintain a relatively high commitment to rights protection, then, may see themselves as having an interest in the legal position of the United States; countries that want more latitude in dealing with persons within their jurisdiction, likewise, may have an interest (perhaps not so readily expressed) in avoiding decisions that could help ratchet up transnational standards of treatment. These interests are quite diffuse; many nations, many international law experts, might share in them. Does this more diffuse set of interests give rise to any duty on the part of the Court to give consideration to their views?

Relational Constitutionalism and Minimal Cosmopolitanism? Adopting a stance of what one might call minimal procedural cosmopolitanism has some intuitive appeal. Although the Court's primary obligation of reason-giving is to account to the people of the United States for its decisions, there is arguably some basis in the legitimate expectations of outsiders for a need to explain decisions under the U.S. Constitution in ways that others, with different constitutional commitments, can understand. Extending the obligation of reason-giving to include what we might think of as an external audience—one that has no claim in the polity-bound representative democracy to be "counted" but which *is* nonetheless affected by the Court's judgments—would be consistent with the nature of the Court as a principled legal decision-maker whose authority is grounded, at least in part, in its public accounting for its decisions.[121] Indeed, the same expansion of the scope of international law (and acceleration of its pace of development) that undergirds some arguments against treating international law as an automatically binding part of federal law,[122] may make it *more* important for courts to consider and be aware of the divergent interpretations of seemingly cognate provisions, at least in arenas where national decisions may shape future understandings of customary law.

But the matter is more complicated. If there is any duty to give appropriate consideration to the legal concerns of external audiences, this may in fact occur without any reference in the Court's public opinions; and the process of providing some response may raise concerns for the Court's internal domestic audience. Moreover, the Court's response may not be regarded as a serious effort at engagement. For example, in *Sanchez-Llamas v. Oregon*,[123] the Court may have been attempting to provide reasons to a transnational audience why, given distinctions between the U.S. legal system and others, the remedy of excluding evidence in criminal cases was not appropriate to give effect to U.S. treaty obligations under the Vienna Convention on Consular Relations, and why, contrary to the conclusion of the ICJ in a different case, a defendant's procedural default of a claim that his consular rights had been violated should not be excused.[124] While the Court acknowledged the need to give "respectful consideration" to the International Court of Justice (ICJ) judgment, it engaged with the ICJ's reasoning about the treaty only to a limited extent.[125]

I have thus far discussed only a possible procedural obligation of consideration and response, not whether the Court has a moral obligation to take into account the effects of its decisions elsewhere as a substantive reason for decision. Whatever arguments there are in justice and moral theory for and against taking account of such "externalities," operationalizing any such obligation would be very difficult. It is difficult enough to be confident of the effects of a judgment within one domestic system;[126] it is far more difficult to be able to anticipate the effects of a judgment on a world of countries whose own laws and legal practices span a very wide range.[127] To the extent that legal judgments rest on particularities of one's own system, moreover, there is the risk of their being misunderstood, or applied inappositely, by other countries. If other countries follow "convergence" approaches in interpretation, predicting effects from decisions of influential courts might (in theory) be possible; but many (indeed, I will suggest in the final chapter, most) countries in practice and over the long term will adopt postures of engagement, rather than of convergence, with transnational legal understandings. Predicting the effects over time of a decision from a single, albeit influential, court, is even more difficult in a legal universe of engagement rather than convergence. One might be tempted to say that, assuming arguendo some moral obligation to consider the interest of other countries, it is too difficult to translate this obligation into legally useful information for a court making a constitutional decision; any focus on consequences must be limited to the court's own polity.

There may nonetheless be a small number of issues in which the likely effects of judicial decision are so clear as to warrant some substantive attention to the effects of one's judgment on other countries and peoples—for example, in cases involving the treatment of refugees, would-be asylum seekers, or other foreign nationals (or where there is an asserted violation of both constitutional and jus cogens norms). So I would hesitate to say that a concern for the effects of one's judgments on those outside the polity ought never to be considered; but in most cases the nature of those effects across the potential universe of affected countries is likely to be so diffuse and indeterminate as to be incapable of providing any guidance.

Judges and National Legitimacy in a Transnational Environment

Understanding the best decision for one's *own* polity may no longer permit a court to stand on national sovereignty, to treat the legal views of the international community (even their arguments about what a particular national constitution means) as requiring no response. The felt sense among others of the need for explanation is pervasive. I do not mean to suggest that the world has moved to viewing states as legitimized more by their adherence to human rights than by their connection to the democratic decisions of their own people, although emphasis on human rights compliance has grown in normative significance in the last half century. Nor do I suggest that the specifically consensual aspects of national sovereignty and national constitutions are without force; to the contrary, they are an essential grounding of a constitution in a specific people whose consent can actually be imagined or constructed. The United States is not in the position vis-à-vis supranational norms that European states are;[128] whatever the precise relationship of national constitutions to European law, it is plain that some considerable amount of effective national governance authority has been transferred to European-level organs, and this has not occurred (at least not nearly to the same degree) in the United States with respect to a transnational authority. At the same time, legal orders at the supranational level have expanded their claims against national governments, including the United States, in ways that virtually insist on a relationship and are likely to require more serious efforts to explain why the United States' legal position accords or differs from those expectations. Regardless, then, of obligations in cosmopolitan morality, obligations to do well by one's own country may favor at least the respectful consideration of the legal positions of others, to the extent that they are brought to the Court's attention.

The argument that the Court should feel some obligation to engage because foreign nationals, governments, and international organizations care about its decisions and are affected by them may not, of course, be persuasive to those still attached to a view of each national state as operating in a fully independent sphere. For those who believe that the relations between countries and the effects of one (powerful) country on others provide no theoretical warrant for even a minimally cosmopolitan attitude—or that as between countries, law is no more than a set of discourses through which power relations are played out[129]—there may yet be instrumental reasons to think the U.S. Court should in appropriate constitutional cases give respectful consideration to transnational legal sources. Failing to do so may impose subtle costs, whose adverse effects on the United States and its citizens may be difficult to trace, but nonetheless present. The dense network of legal, economic, and cultural connections that exist in a globalized environment make some degree of reciprocal influences of constitutional and transnational legal systems upon each other inevitable; over time the Court's failure to consider the approaches of international instruments, or of other constitutional systems, on analogous constitutional questions may appear less a matter of ignorance, and more a deliberate affront.

Judges as Diplomats? It has sometimes been argued that constitutional adjudication should be viewed as a positive *opportunity* to advance national interests in promoting specific forms of constitutional law (that may provide benefits to the Court in sustaining its own influence, or to the nation in terms of world peace, or national security, or congenial business markets, or to the nation's citizens by better protecting them from mistreatment when they travel),[130] or to develop a well-coordinated set of pluralized legal orders particularly in areas where conflicts of laws may arise.[131] Courts may be seen functioning as judicial diplomats, advancing their own countries' interests, whether through developing expectations of reciprocity ("we consider your approaches so you consider ours") or through the sheer power of their country of origin or the stature or reasoning of the court.[132] But I am somewhat skeptical of a court's competence to play a directed "diplomatic" role. Apart from serious questions of diplomatic competence, a national court is likely to be seen by other countries as naturally aligned with its government's views, at least in any case it decides in its favor; in periods and places of anti-American feeling, this may make it very difficult to calculate how what the Court says will be received elsewhere.[133]

Diffuse Instrumentalism, Diffuse Legitimacy But instrumental national concerns may be more diffusely affected by the attitude of the nation's highest court. When Justice Sandra Day O'Connor referred to "rely[ing] increasingly on international and foreign law" as a way to improve domestic decisions that would also "create that all-important good impression,"[134] she may have had something like this in mind. Rather than seeking to advance particular national goals—where a court's ability to foresee the likely immediate consequences is limited, requiring general knowledge and skill in predicting backlash that diplomats are more likely than jurists to have—Justice O'Connor may be read as more generally urging seriously respectful consideration of other approaches and reasoned explanation of important differences.[135] The harm from foreign perception of U.S. indifference to international standards of humane treatment is suggested by the report that, in order to extradite a terrorism suspect from the Netherlands, in 2007 the United States had to agree to return the defendant to the Netherlands to serve his sentence (if he were convicted).[136] A judicial reputation for respectful consideration of foreign views may promote reciprocity in the administration of international criminal justice, an area of increasing concern with the growth of international crime and terrorism and one in which aspects of the U.S. legal system have raised obstacles in recent years.[137] And there remains the possibility, not to be discounted, that the persuasive force of reasoning about constitutional rules—whether they concern the limits on government power to regulate speech or expenditures of monies in elections, or the scope of constitutional protection of private property—may over time change minds.

Jurisprudential Change and Constitutional Interdependence

More fundamentally, the asserted dichotomy between the internal and the external may be a misleading one.

Permeable Boundaries For one thing, the conventional domestic materials of legal interpretation may themselves require consideration of international law or the divergent legal perspectives of other nations in facing the interpretive choices before a U.S. court. These sources include both original understandings and a sense of constitutional purpose. As one conservative jurist wrote about the U.S. Constitution in a First Amendment case in the 1980s, "Implementation of the law of nations by the American government was seen as crucial to the conduct of our foreign relations, a subject of pervasive concern in the Constitution."[138]

That a constitution empowers its government to deal with foreign powers does not necessarily imply that constitutional provisions for internal governance should be interpreted in a particular way, but it may rule out some interpretations that would be inconsistent with a purpose to be able to make and enforce agreements with foreign powers. Likewise, that provisions bearing on international relations (such as "Treaties" or "war") may need to be interpreted in a way that relates to how other nations view the topic in order to be effective toward their anticipated end does not necessarily imply that other provisions—for example, specifying rights of persons within the territory—need to be as well. However, understanding a constitution's purposes to include establishing a country as a respected member of the community of nations might support some consideration of how "civilized" countries are constrained in treating those within its jurisdiction. Given the Court's recognition of the more "global nature of the economy and the extent to which actions in other parts of the world affect our own national security,"[139] the transnational context of interpretive choices—in light of the Constitution's purposes—could legitimately be considered by the Court as a matter of its ongoing interpretive practice.

Notwithstanding overheated rhetoric to the contrary, the Court's considering transnational legal norms cannot plausibly be seen as a "contamination" of a previously "pure" domestic discourse.[140] As Dean Mayo Moran of Toronto has observed, both constitutional and international law can exert a form of influence beyond the boundaries of their binding force.[141] Social interactions around legal issues and controversies diffuse, adapt, change, reinforce, and spread values and/or rules.[142] Domestic discourses have for years been influenced by "transatlantic" or global ideas.[143] Moreover, threats to that discourse swim around us, and may emanate from within as well as without, as when the U.S. Department of Defense linked those "who employ a strategy of the weak using international fora [and] judicial processes" with "terrorism" in challenging American strength.[144] Giving reasons why, for example, a constitutional value is shared but an operational rule is not, or why shared values lead to similar rules, or why values are not shared, are not contaminations of an autonomous local discourse. Rather, they are an effort to bring the skills of legal reasoning—logical clarity, thoughtful marshaling of information, analogical analysis—to resolution of the problem at hand. And failure to deal respectfully with transnational views about U.S. constitutional law may be understood as an act of public disregard for the views of others, with potentially adverse consequences that may be quite indirect but no less injurious.

Pluralism, Courts, and Constitutional Self-Defense Constitutional law has come to stand in more complex relationships with other legal systems. Constitutional pluralism is a situation in which multiple legal orders of a constitutional nature (that is, providing norms or rules governing the same conduct regulated by domestic constitutions) overlap,[145] and it provides one important perspective for relational engagement. From an internal viewpoint, the domestic constitution assumes a degree of autonomy from the transnational. But that sense of autonomy is also something of a fiction. If we were "'unavoidably side by side'" two centuries ago,[146] in the years since migrations of peoples have grown, transnational transactions (public and private, commercial and personal) have also grown, and retention of national affiliations to more than one polity has become more common.

For these reasons, the likelihood of interjurisdictional conflicts of judicial judgment, in matters affecting constitutional law, has increased. Different tribunals (domestic or supranational) in different countries will render judgments on the same or related issues; how are these managed, or reconciled, and conflicts resolved? Courts will develop rules for these problems, at least in the absence of legislation, but such "conflicts of law" rules are only one approach to interjurisdictional judicial conflicts. Softer approaches—grounded, for example, in interpretive fair consideration of foreign judgments, or more aggressive approaches similar but not equivalent to appellate review—are available as well,[147] and require at least an awareness of other legal systems and tribunals.

Knowledge once thus acquired does not simply disappear. More generally, ideas have never respected national boundaries, and modern communications technology facilitates the rapid spread of ideas and processes of permeation that can make origins difficult to track. Supreme Court justices, no less than lawyers and citizens, are influenced by the world of ideas in which they live, a world interpenetrated with traveling sources of ideas. Not only do ideas about law travel, but law and law-like norms are being produced by increasing numbers of national states, by subnational, supranational, regional, and international institutions, by nonstate affiliated entities and transnational movements, as well as by and within small cultural communities.

William Twining has written that "globalisation and interdependence challenge 'black box theories' that treat nation states or societies or legal systems as discrete, impervious entities. . . . In so far as our stock of theories of law assumes that municipal legal systems are self-contained or that public international law is concerned solely with external relations between states, such theories just do not fit the modern facts."[148] Twining notes the growing "disengagement of law and state," whether in the development of human rights, a transnational lex mercatoria, or the reemergence of Islamic law, all cited as examples of "the amorphous category 'non-state law.'"[149] Some go so far as to claim that we now already have forms of "global law without a state," particularly in the norms regulating commercial relationships,[150] and other scholars have argued that transnational businesses, criminal organizations, NGOs, and religious movements are important loci of power that operate beyond the regulatory capacities of single states or that may harness state power to facilitate their own objectives.[151]

Putting aside the wide range of arguably legal norms that emerge out of nonstate or even nongovernmental communities, the plethora of legal orders sponsored or constructed in various ways by national states is astounding. Local, state, and national government lawmaking is supplemented by the thousands of treaties and international agreements to which the United States is a signatory that may impose different or additional obligations on the government. The NAFTA regime is a prominent example, in which multi-member panels apply the law of the treaty between the United States, Mexico and Canada to govern challenges to government regulatory decisions that are claimed to bring into play the investor protection and antidiscrimination rules of NAFTA, in ways that may influence and be influenced by national law.[152] Treaties may also establish additional mechanisms for government regulation of private conduct, including the WTO regime, which can result in economic sanctions affecting private business.

The mere existence in the world of alternative and overlapping systems for declaring and protecting individual rights changes constitutional adjudication,[153] as normative claims based on alternative sources of law are developed and argued for. In increasing numbers of cases, the possibility exists of domestic decisions being seen as in conflict, or in harmony, with transnational regimes of rights protection, or even, potentially, of governance,[154] and this opens up new avenues of critique and evaluation and expands the scope of justification. The increasingly plural legal environment within which national constitutions operate necessarily affects how constitutions are understood and makes the task of maintaining the fiction of their autonomy cognitively more difficult. Each legal system may, from its own internal vantage point, assert hierarchic superiority where rules conflict, yet may not be in a position to insist;[155] a situation of "constitutional heterarchy" may thus exist.[156]

A leading theorist of globalization and law, Boaventura de Sousa Santos, can be understood to argue that the social fact of increased legal pluralism requires a revised focus in jurisprudence on the way in which "legal orders interact at all levels from the global to the very local. From a global perspective, the coexistence and interaction of legal orders at different levels is one reason why the phenomenon of legal pluralism must become central to general jurisprudence."[157] Santos has developed the term "interlegality" to refer to interactions between coexisting legal orders,[158] noting that the coexistence of these multiple legal orders does not imply either conflict or autonomy but embraces a wide range of relationships. The fact of increasing pluralism is captured by a number of other metaphors and vocabularies. Paul Berman has written on "hybridity,"[159] and Alex Aleinikoff has described how international transactions engage the laws of different domestic legal systems in a space that is "more web than pyramid," where legal "actors see themselves . . . as engaged in a common enterprise of working out norms"[160]—imagery that suggests actions by one country having effects on other parts of the web that will ripple through the web, perhaps in ways hard to predict. Others have referred to a kind of multilayered quilt, embracing the global, the national, and the local as separate but connected domains.

The organs of national states inevitably make decisions in the context of the sociolegal realities of their day. Those realities include streams of discourses across cultures about legal ideas, and indeed struggles between different constitutional regime ideas for the hearts and minds of various transnational communities. For the United States, this means that—whether with formal government consent or not—international human rights law, international commercial law, and international environmental law, as well as nonstate sources of law, are making claims to apply, control, or influence our law that call for responses.

Courts are in a sense forced into taking positions on these complex new relationships and demands. Domestic constitutional law may be seen, in some parts of the world, as competing with other legal systems and with other sources of power.[161] National territorial states are now only one of several locations for the exercise of political power, legal constraint, and communal self-expression.[162] A new paradigm of law is emerging, one in which communities of people exist in both hierarchical and nonhierarchical patterns whose connectedness, permeability, and differential allocation of functions to different levels of governance challenge the very idea of national sovereignty itself.[163] All branches of government are affected, but courts may play quite a special role, among constitutional actors, in giving shape to this new paradigm, because they are the institutions of constitutional governance with consistent obligations of justification, of public and principled reason-giving,[164] and because a wide range of parties may call on courts to react—in a reason-giving mode—to these new currents.

Rather than focusing unproductively on claims of sovereignty, in a period in which devolutions of power through privatization and through supranational governance are unmistakable, those seeking to sustain the efficacy of national states should be concerned with their states' *legitimacy*. And in the midst of pressures of globalization, national states may strengthen each others' positions as legitimate producers and enforcers of law by reciprocal recognition of constitutional coexistence and interdependence.[165]

Constitutional Coexistence and Interdependence What do I mean by the idea of constitutional interdependence? The dominant form of governance—whether representative democracy or autocracy—is likely to create an environment in which it is easier to maintain that form.[166] Aspects of globalization pose distinct threats to the rule of law, to the role of public law, and to the very idea of distinctive national constitutions and national constitutional law as significant forces in their societies.[167] If globalization implies an increased plurality of legal orders,[168] globalization in a competitive world market also entails transnational economic pressures, which may be seen as overtaking, or capturing and using, the apparatus of states to transform national law into an instrumentality of global trade and commerce. Globalization in a world of transnational communities organized around religious affiliations may both enrich law and decenter states as sources of law. Globalization in a world of transnational environmental problems engenders transnational legal responses, often requiring coordination and enforcement at the supranational level. Globalization of crime and global terrorism likewise threaten the security of national states and their centrality to the process of responding, as pressures exist to globalize solutions.[169] Even the globalization of discourses of human rights might be seen to threaten the maintenance of distinctive constitutional systems.[170] And yet without those national legal systems, effective and democratically legitimate responses to these various aspects of globalization will be difficult to achieve.

National states can no longer assume that they will be the exclusive sites for the organization of political power or the production of law; newer forms will coexist with national states. And though the United States will remain one of the more powerful states, it may not retain the position of hegemony it enjoyed in the latter decades of the twentieth century. As other states or supranational entities, such as the EU, or China, gain power, the competition for allegiances and ideological and economic power is intensified. Over the next quarter century, the arguments in favor of a more relational U.S. approach to engagement, grounded in the facts of jurisprudential change and constitutional interdependence, are likely to grow stronger.

In this setting, taking into account the views and reactions of others, explaining differences, and being open to persuasion on open points within one's own system, may promote, rather than detract from, a state's legitimacy and power in the world. Indeed, failing to do so may in the long run make it harder for the United States to retain force and shape as the distinctive national entity many believe it to be, one of power and influence in the world. Part of the national self-identity of the United States is that of a country respected in the world; the respect of others was a signal motif in the American Revolution, and has been a dominant motif through our history. Our capacity to influence others may depend, in part, on our taking seriously what others say and do, supporting a strategic conception of relational engagement. Further, the sociological facts on the ground make inevitable the fact of mutual influences, of constitutional coexistences and interdependence. We have no choice but to influence and be influenced by others, and doing so consciously enables us to have greater control over what we choose to be influenced by, the accuracy of our understandings, and how our actions are perceived.

* * *

As discussed in the next chapter, domestic constitutions can perform their functions only if they remain grounded in their particular polities, a proposition that may limit the degree to which judges should consciously seek to interact with the transnational and that makes relevant the nature and degree of positive authorization for more intense forms of transnational engagement. The absence of positive license only reinforces the objections to insisting too quickly on an overtly relational mode of engagement in the United States—however relational much of constitutional adjudication has in fact now become. As an older constitutional order, the United States has a richly developed jurisprudence in many areas; the benefits of engagement with transnational sources in any across-the-board way are likely to be relatively low; there are stronger reasons to consider foreign or international law in some areas—as where a broad and deep transnational consensus exists—than in others. Moreover, while moral concerns and the changing face of jurisprudence might support a more relational mode of engagement, other factors that are important in relatively new constitutional regimes are less so here (although recent departures by the United States from its rule of law traditions in the pursuit of terrorists might be thought to warrant some additional forms of self-reflection). It would be unrealistic to expect the U.S. Court always to feel obligated to explain our differences from others, given the already well-developed internal constitutional jurisprudence of the United States. For a country like the United States, which began in revolutionary separation from another, perhaps deliberative engagement is what can be expected—a "decent respect," as it were, for the opinions of others combined with an insistence on independence, rather than expressing stronger relational obligations to others in the interpretation of our Constitution.

But while the case for a relational model of engagement in the United States is not as compelling today as in some other countries, over the next quarter century the U.S. Court may well shift into a more relational way of engaging with nonbinding transnational sources of law. To the extent that the Court's relative insulation from transnational engagement reflects perceptions of its unique power and responsibilities, this may change; the future holds prospects for a more "multipolar" than "unipolar" world.[171] Moreover, the sheer increase in the volume and percentage of their time that U.S. lawyers and jurists spend on matters that are transnational in character (with disputes involving foreign parties in everything from family law to tort law to commercial transactions, or with issues governed by international or foreign law) will affect how lawyers and judges think about legal comparisons. "As the profession itself becomes transnational, its manner of thought . . . becomes (more) comparative, even for cases that are seen as domestic or internal."[172] Transnational "norm entrepreneurs," in NGOs and law practices, will also promote transnational awareness.[173] Deliberative engagement over time may also increase a sense of connection to shared legal problems.

Constitutional democracies committed to empowering a democratic government and to constraining its actions all have a stake in the idea of law as a constraint on political and economic power, especially as the demands for transnational intergovernmental cooperation increase.[174] Indeed, constitutional democracies may be in a symbiotic relationship with each other. Apart from the increasing proliferation and fragmentation of legal systems, law itself is, in a sense, under assault from many sources—globalization, markets, consumerism, transnational crime, terrorism—the material demands of which may threaten a domestic legal system's capacity to sustain a significant regulatory and expressive role for public law. If that is correct, then constitutional democracies around the world have a general, if indirect, stake in the continued salience and workability of public law around the world. Each country, in other words, has a stake in the success or failure of constitutionalism in others. This may be the strongest relational reason for engagement. Not only do we benefit from using foreign law as a critical lens on the necessities and values of our own system, but inviting multiple relationships of engagement, evaluation, critique, and appreciation may enable the constitutional democracies of the world each to improve their systems and thereby to sustain the capacity of public law generated within national states to continue to play an important role in actually regulating conduct and expressing particular national values.

5. ENGAGEMENT, U.S. INTERPRETIVE THEORY, AND MULTIFUNCTIONAL CONSTITUTIONS

If the case for engagement, in either a deliberative or a relational mode, is persuasive, why have references to foreign and international law in U.S. Supreme Court decisions generated so much recent controversy? What are the distinctively legal objections to this practice? How persuasive are these objections in the context of constitutional interpretation?

Objections to engagement come from at least two directions—those who think that transnational sources are rarely or never relevant or legitimate to consider, and those who believe that the national constitutions should generally be interpreted in accordance with international law or transnational consensus. Although the first objectors have been louder in the United States, the second pose important questions as well. After situating engagement in the dominant, practice-based approach to interpretation in the United States in Part A, I address objections from both resistance and convergence postures in Parts B and C, explaining how the multiple functions of and concepts within a domestic constitution lend support to postures of engagement.

A. ENGAGEMENT AND LEADING INTERPRETIVE APPROACHES

As shown above in Chapter 4, interpretive practices of the U.S. Court already have embraced transnational legal sources for a range of purposes, and considering transnational sources is beneficial in a variety of ways. But history, practice, and functional benefits are only a partial answer to those who challenge the theoretical legitimacy of considering transnational sources. As I will show, transnational engagement may contribute to each of the major approaches to legitimate interpretation in the United States, though more so to some than to others, and generally does so not as a novel factor but by speaking to criteria for judgment that are already a part of the framework for interpretive analysis.

There are, roughly speaking, three major schools of thought about how, as a normative matter, to interpret the U.S. Constitution. First, there are approaches that sound in a kind of historical positivism. These are text-focused within particular historical moments, or, in the case of Bruce Ackerman's work, atextually focused on specific historical "moments" in which constitutional change occurs by virtue of popular authorization; the interpreter is understood as an agent carrying out those historical commands. Second, there are approaches dominated by a kind of teleological or purposive assumption, connecting the Constitution's text with larger values, which in turn guide interpretive judgment. Here, the interpreter is serving as the agent of purpose or value understood (at a fairly general level) as embedded in the Constitution, rather than more historically specific commands. Finally, there are multi-valenced, practice-based theories of interpretation that draw on history and purpose, text and precedent, values and consequences, to guide interpretation. The legitimacy claims of these approaches are rooted, in part, in their existence in the ongoing and long-accepted practices of the legal institution.

Text- or "Moment"-Focused Positivism, Originalism, and Intentionalism

The first set of theories are those that focus on the text of the written Constitution as it was understood at the moment of adoption or amendment, or on atextual but specific-in-time "constitutional moments." "Meaning" for these purposes may be determined by the intentions of the drafters and/or by contemporaneous understanding; according to leading scholar Randy Barnett, the "public meanings" among those who would have ratified or otherwise democratically expressed their acceptance of text should control.[1] Under Akhil Amar's "intratextualism" approach, asserted internal coherences among the Constitution's textual provisions reflect their interrelated and historic meanings.[2] For Bruce Ackerman, constitutional moments of high mobilization around proposals and resistance to revised constitutional understandings can mark out decisive, popular constitutional regime changes in which the Constitution's meaning is in effect amended other than by formal textual amendment.[3] Although each of these theories is distinct, and may reach different conclusions on the same constitutional question, their inquiries resonate with the idea of the Constitution as a form of law fixed by the prior acts of a national constituency, adopted through specified methods (in theory democratic, or more so than judicial decisions), and connected with a particular national polity at a particular time.[4]

For those who are strong originalists, although comparative legal materials that bear on understanding original intent or meaning may properly be considered, contemporary foreign or international law will *not* be relevant when original sources are felt to provide a determinate answer to a constitutional question. Where originalist sources give out,[5] however, transnational experience might be helpful for some originalists. Many judges are originalists in the sense of identifying constitutional meaning understood at some level of generality, and applied to contemporary issues through methods informed by a number of other sources. Such "moderate" originalists may distinguish between "enactment intentions," having to do with the meaning and purpose of a text, and "application intentions" about how the provision would be applied, treating the former but not the latter as constraining,[6] and looking to a larger range of sources in determining how to apply the constitutional norm. As originalism comes closer to purposivism, the benefits of transnational engagement increase.

Even the more stringent originalist approaches, which would generally treat foreign or international law as irrelevant, might well recognize at least two important exceptions. First, if an original term was believed by the adopters to refer to a general concept that is universal or supranational in character, or was intended by the authorized constitution-makers to evolve over time or by reference to contemporary general (transnational) norms, a positivist or originalist should regard it as legitimate to look. Some provisions of the U.S. Constitution appear to be of this character, as already discussed.[7] Second, in a precedent-based system, original meanings may conflict with doctrine as developed over time;[8] the choice of which to follow may depend in part on understanding the functional consequences of either choice, which could be informed by comparative experience.

Purposivism

A second set of approaches involve more purposive interpretive frameworks, less concerned with implementing the specific intentions behind or the particularist historical meanings of the text, and more concerned with identifying and interpreting the Constitution in light of overarching purposes. Resort to general concepts rather than specific conceptions will require more reliance on other sources to fill in decision-making. Here, the interpreter identifies a set of values—of process and/or substance, institutional allocation or role—rooted in, or expressed in, the Constitution, or inferred from the Constitution's structure and functions and elaborated as the basis for interpretation. Key values for some may be democracy and self-governance, participation and/or representation, where the Court's role is primarily facilitative or protective of democratic or pluralist politics.[9] Others would place more weight on liberty and libertarian values, and/or on the protection of private property, as central constitutional purposes.[10] For still others, substantive versions of fairness and/or "constitutional justice," based on commitments to human dignity and equality,[11] or as defined by impartial jurists through appropriate process and principled judgment,[12] have a central place. Although this summary overgeneralizes, each of these approaches is defined by an understanding of some central sets of contemporary constitutional purposes in the world,[13] or rests on a commitment more generally to purposive readings of constitutional texts.[14]

Purposive theories of constitutional interpretation are open to considering international and foreign law, at least insofar as they may be concerned with advancing similar purposes. Thus, for example, Justice Breyer has referred to foreign practice in regulating campaign finance, which can be seen as bearing on his effort to explore what "active liberty" in U.S. constitutional practice requires or permits.[15] Foreign law may illuminate how constitutional values or purposes should be understood in particular applications, as in the Court's reference to European human rights law in *Lawrence v. Texas*.[16] Moreover, comparative experience with different constitutional approaches may yield legal information about the likely consequences of interpretive choices—information that may be relevant to assessing whether constitutional purposes would be defeated or advanced by one or another choice, as in Justice Breyer's reference to European federalisms in *Printz*.[17]

Multi-Valenced ("Common Law") Practice-Based Approaches

Still a third set of approaches looks to ground the legitimacy of constitutional adjudication within a discourse of ongoing interpretive practices. Most American judges draw on a multi-sourced approach to constitutional interpretation,[18] supported by common law legal traditions of independent judging. Within this interpretive matrix, the Constitution's text functions as "common ground," while the Court's own precedents are powerfully authoritative tools of interpretation.[19] Yet standing alone, these two sources—text and precedent—do not resolve all constitutional questions, nor do they provide an account of legitimate interpretive change, which depends importantly on larger understandings of constitutional purposes. For those who see the Constitution as an "institution," which as it endures over time is defined less by its specific words than by the set of governance practices that come to be seen as basic,[20] subsequent history—including engagements with and by the political branches[21]—sheds light on what Aharon Barak calls "objective" constitutional purpose and structure.[22] Legitimate modes of interpretive argument in the Court's ongoing practice also include original meanings, constitutional structure, values or "ethos" (informed by efforts over time to provoke, or resist, re-understandings of those values) and functional (or prudential) considerations of the consequences of alternative considerations.[23]

The relationships of these sources and modes of argument are not linear but interactive and interdependent.[24] This multi-valenced interpretive practice is to some extent self-legitimating; that is, in significant part it derives its legitimacy as interpretation from its continuity in practice over time. Its legitimacy is reinforced by its connection to the authoritative legal document, by its openness to multiple perspectives on that document's meaning, and by the continued process of justification that it engenders. Its functionality is suggested by the similar eclecticism in the jurisprudence of a number of constitutional courts around the world that engage in active judicial review and whose decisions are respected within their own systems.[25]

A central feature of these approaches in the United States is their reliance on both judicial precedents and processes of analogical, consequentialist, and values-based reasoning about their continued force. These approaches characteristically accept a range of eclectic sources; they reflect a historicism in the sense of valuing the past and ongoing practices; and they are open to changing interpretations. Some refer to this as "common law" constitutionalism, a term with the capacity to mislead insofar as it focuses on past precedent and stare decisis (rather than on the multiple sources—importantly including precedent—through which decisions are reached), and thus I use the term "multi-valenced" interpretation.

A number of legal scholars defend practice-based, multi-valenced forms of interpretation. Philip Bobbitt, for example, argues that constitutional law is legitimated by its basis in six "modalities" of argument, including arguments from text, history, structure, precedent (doctrine), prudence (or consequences), and "ethos" (based not on general morality but on values peculiar to the Constitution).[26] For Bobbitt, these constitutional modalities cannot be prioritized ex ante; they do not occupy hierarchical relationships, and different forms of these arguments may be more suitable for different problems or functions. For Richard Fallon, constitutional interpretation proceeds through several forms of argument, mostly similar to those discussed by Bobbitt.[27] Unlike Bobbitt, Fallon argues that there is a hierarchy among these sources, with text coming first, but he also recognizes the normative pull of other sources (especially policy or moral values) so that the text (hierarchically ranked first) may be understood in light of those sources. For David Strauss, constitutional adjudication is essentially a form of common law adjudication, characterized by "rational traditionalism," and informed by a sense of intergenerational humility; while paying some attention to text and original intentions, it is more typified by the "priority of doctrine [or precedent] over text," the "preferred position" of some parts of the Constitution, the "role of moral judgments," and what he sees as "nontextual" constitutional amendments.[28] In Professor Strauss' words, this approach permits "innovation" and the rejection of "morally unacceptable traditions," even as it presumes not to disturb existing understandings without good reason.[29]

Under each of these approaches, constitutional interpretation is open to arguments from a range of sources—not only text and precedent, but also history, structure, practice, consequences, and values linked to the Constitution. Some process-oriented theoretical approaches are also consistent with multi-valenced interpretation, focusing less on details of interpretive method and more on the relationships of the Court, the political branches, and the public in developing constitutional meaning.[30] Robert Post and Reva Siegel's concept of "democratic constitutionalism," a jurisprudential view of constitutional law as entailing a deep interdependence of law and politics, plainly contemplates interpretive engagement with contemporary understandings and conflicts; they argue that constitutional law loses its legitimacy if the Court seeks to cut itself off from changed understandings that emerge out of political contest.[31] And historicist approaches, such as that of H. Jefferson Powell, suggest that "constitutional law is an historically extended tradition of argument," drawing upon text, conventions of legal reasoning, and moral, political, and prudential factors.[32]

Notwithstanding their different emphases, all of these accounts view resort to arguments from multiple sources as within the compass of legitimate interpretive inquiry. Part of the appeal of such accounts is that they more closely match current practice than do others. These approaches also imply that the realm of legitimate decision is broader than any particular set of "right answers," and accept that constitutional law is legitimately open to change. The legitimacy of this multi-valenced approach rests not only in its correspondence with long-standing practice, and in the incrementalism and humility it encourages, but also in its benefits in bringing multiple perspectives to bear on constitutional interpretation, in providing bridges between our national past and present, and in allowing "losers" in one arena, or at one time, to legitimately advance arguments from within constitutional discourse for different results.

* * *

In multi-valenced approaches, transnational legal materials need not be regarded as a new and separate source, but rather as bearing on *existing* factors—helping to clarify our own understandings of constitutional purposes and values, and illuminating the consequences of alternative interpretations. Even Justice Scalia has invoked foreign law to suggest that the consequences of a constitutional interpretation would be consistent with "enhancing democratic elections."[33] Yet some scholars have argued that foreign and transnational sources are inapposite under most established approaches to constitutional interpretation. Professor Alford suggests that foreign law would be relevant primarily within pragmatist, or natural law approaches, but not with respect to what he identifies as either "conservative" or "activist" majoritarianisms, nor with respect to originalism.[34] But self-expressive uses of foreign experience cut across all domains of interpretation, and even originalism, as discussed above, may see resort to contemporary transnational sources in some cases on some issues. Approaches concerned with reinforcing democratic decision-making (a form of "majoritarianism"), for example, might find relevance in transnational sources—first, on the common problem of identifying obstructions to well-functioning democracy, and second, on the role of courts in remedying those obstructions.[35] Purposive approaches that focus on the Constitution's commitments to individual rights or limited government may find it helpful to compare and contrast similar ideas embodied in international instruments, or other nations' experiences (positive or negative) in implementing comparable values.

The nominally distinct interpretive schools of originalism, purposivism, and multi-valenced interpretation in fact overlap considerably with each other; differences amongst jurists are to a considerable extent over the weight or priority of the different sources of law that make up the practice of interpretive constitutionalism. Foreign and international law's salience will vary, for most judges, in tandem with their more general interpretive views. No U.S. Supreme Court justice has argued for a "convergence" posture, nor even that the Court should always feel *obligated to consider* international or foreign law on constitutional questions. What the United States has seen are occasional references, "comparative side-glances," to transnational sources, or discussions used to supplement other sources of interpretation, in ways compatible with most (though not all) interpretive approaches seen on the Court.[36] In this light, the very passionate resistance to references to foreign and transnational law articulated by some members of the U.S. legal community in recent years calls for explanation.

B. REJECTING RESISTANCE: LEGITIMATE INTERPRETATION IN THE UNITED STATES

The sources for the particularly aggressive resistance to foreign and international law in the United States over the last ten years are complex and overdetermined. Waves of xenophobia are not unusual in the history of the United States, notwithstanding and perhaps related to its large capacity to absorb immigration. Anxieties about the border and illegal immigration and changes in American cultural identity have been heightened in recent years; the 9/11 attacks exacerbated fear of the foreign. In the longer run, challenges to U.S. hegemony by the growth of other powers may be producing reactive U.S. assertions of preeminence reflected in claims that the United States could learn nothing from the rest of the world. It is anxiety-producing for those who imagine that the United States represents the best and highest forms of constitutionalism to be confronted with approaches elsewhere that are different and that claim to be better, in a number of areas of civil and criminal justice. In a perhaps contradictory vein, to the extent that the United States has assumed military responsibilities around the world, these responsibilities may reinforce a sense of exceptionalism, of it being unreasonable to expect the world's "police force" to put its personnel at risk before the International Criminal Court or be held to standards asserted by those in foreign nations who benefit from the U.S. military role.

In the politics of the first several post-9/11 years, many would locate the controversy over transnational references in constitutional interpretation in much larger "culture wars" over the role of courts, universalism and relativism, unilateralism, multilateralism and the meaning of patriotism.[37] The foreign became enmeshed in these ongoing "culture wars" over a range of issues: between "traditional" values and equality claims of women, gays, lesbians, and transgender persons; between pro–death penalty and anti–death penalty advocates; and over compliance with internationally defined legal rules, in areas ranging from criminal justice to the environment. What Professor Resnik has called "law as affiliation" helps to account for these multiple phenomena, emphasizing as it does the identity-constructing, identity-affirming characteristics of which law is treated as controlling, or of relevance, or inapposite.[38]

Yet these sources of resistance are also a reflection of the necessarily more globalized contexts in which legal and other decisions are made. They are evidence that contestation on a range of constitutional issues is now being conducted at the transnational level simultaneously with its emergence in many national polities. The replication in Australia of the debate between Justices Breyer and Scalia on this question only emphasizes the degree to which constitutional interpretation in one country is likely to influence interpretation—at the level of method or result—in others.[39]

As John Bell observes, "the distinctiveness of public law in individual countries . . . revolve[s] predominantly around institutions which arise not only from deliberate design . . . but also from history and underlying social problems. . . ."[40] Among the different sources of domestic public law, constitutions are often most sensitively identified with national identity. In the United States, the Constitution is very difficult to amend and the justices serve for long periods; the Court's constitutional decisions have a rare kind of finality and importance. It is thus not surprising to find strong contests about national "affiliation" being played out around the realm of constitutional interpretation and through more distinctively legal discourses of resistance to roles for foreign or international law in constitutional interpretation.

Fear of Being Bound

Concerns about the impact of international commitments or transnational consensus on democratic self-rule, sovereignty, the separation of powers, and federalism emerge in a number of settings: the effect of international treaties on the scope of constitutional powers;[41] the self-executing character vel non of treaties that the United States has ratified;[42] the legal significance of ratified but non-self-executing treaties;[43] and the content, status, and application of customary international law.[44] Scholars argue with some force that there is a tension between the U.S. constitutional system of checks and balances, designed to make government action more difficult and cumbersome, and allowing new binding norms to be developed through customary international law outside of those structures of checks and balances.[45] Moreover, critics add, reliance on foreign or international law in various forms of adjudication may be inconsistent with constitutional provisions allocating treaty-making authority to other branches in ways designed to respect the federal character of the U.S. Constitution.[46]

Much debate has concerned the *binding* force and scope of the international norm—that is, whether U.S. courts should consider themselves obligated to apply that norm directly, or to interpret domestic law to conform to that norm. In constitutional adjudication, it is the possibility that references to transnational sources herald a new theory requiring convergence with universal norms that especially concerns some critics.[47] In an engagement model, however, transnational norms function as forms of *persuasive* authority, generally nondispositive but available sources, which may (or on some issues should) be considered, but which need not be followed. This distinction is key to understanding why many of the objections to considering international or foreign law—to the extent that these objections differ from a more general set of interpretive disagreements in U.S. constitutional law—are ultimately without force.

Originalism and Formalism

As noted above, some versions of originalism, especially those focused on specific founding intentions, would eschew transnational legal sources—along with other contemporary sources. It is their premise that, both to constrain judicial discretion and for reasons of political legitimacy, only those sources that relate to understandings or intentions at the time the Constitution was ratified or amended are legitimate to consider. Where an original intent or meaning cannot be discerned, moreover, some originalists would simply defer to the decisions of the elected branches, based on default principles of democracy. Such originalists would find fewer occasions on which legitimately to engage with transnational legal sources in constitutional interpretation, for the same reason that they would eschew contemporary sources more generally. But few, if any, of the justices are (or can be) rigid originalists or intentionalists. Even Justice Scalia has termed himself something of a "faint-hearted" originalist, who recognizes the importance of stare decisis and settled expectations about constitutional law.[48]

Moreover, there are reasons to doubt originalism or intentionalism as a comprehensive constitutional theory. Over time the democratic valence of constitutional text as it was understood by those engaged in its framing and legally significant acts of ratification loses its legitimating force—though what the text has come to stand for may have acquired legitimacy through more organic processes. And if the original process of constitution-making was not a fully inclusive one—as the processes of the older U.S. Constitution were not—its claim to democratic legitimacy in binding the future, especially with very rigid amending procedures, is in more doubt. Apart from the difficulties of ascertaining the original intentions of collectivities of people who lived in very different historical circumstances, there are considerable challenges (and indeterminacies) in determining the level of generality at which to consider original understandings binding. As more time passes, memories are lost and circumstances change so that there is greater difficulty in applying approaches based on original understandings. Thus, the constraining effect diminishes as our ability to recapture past understandings fades and is challenged by new developments not encompassed within founding generations' specific views.

Formalists might favor limits on the sources to be considered in interpretation, on different grounds. A formalist approach might place substantial weight on settlement and favor relatively strong adherence to stare decisis, which would diminish the importance of sources other than the Court's own precedents; alternatively, formalists might support the articulation of rules over standards (development of which rules might be illuminated by resort to transnational sources). To the extent that formalists are particularly concerned with constraint, the ruling out of sources may appear to reduce the courts' discretion. But this objection, like that from originalism, does not relate to the specifically transnational character of the source; it might apply as well, for example, to resort to current opinion within the polity, or to the views of the political branches, or to reliance on social science research.[49] Formalism is thus in tension with changes in modern legal consciousness and the multiple functions of constitutions, discussed further below.

Democracy, Self-Rule, and Sovereignty

Those objecting to the use of transnational legal sources from the perspective of democratic self-rule treat judicial review as a deviant institution and may be skeptical of the very idea of a constraining constitution. Some would reconcile self-rule with constitutional constraint on a theory of popular sovereignty, with popular consent embedded in the constitutional instrument. The people may constrain their future decisions by constitutional consent, but anything to which "the people" had not consented could not be invoked to bind their future political decisions.[50] Democratic theory thus reinforces originalist or positivist approaches in ways that might exclude contemporary views or materials from influencing constitutional understanding, to avoid illegitimate judicial "amendment" of a constitution. This line of argument, however, is not specific to transnational sources, and excludes the possibility that interpretive evolution by the courts was itself consented to.[51]

Democratic self-rule, it is said, is particularly threatened if national sovereignty is also undermined, as when U.S. law is "controlled" by outsiders through judicial reliance on foreign or international law, or when "elitist" and "unelected" judges use foreign law to justify their efforts to "impose" the views of a transnational legal "elite."[52] Judges, however, do not conceive of themselves as imposing their own (or foreign) values, but as working to identify the values, concepts, and rules of the Constitution and how to implement them. Moreover, as Sarah Cleveland, Harold Koh, and others have shown, the idea that international law as such should be regarded as an entirely "outside" source ignores the degree to which the United States has been a major contributor to the development of international legal norms and the degree to which international law has been a part of American law.[53]

Yet, some critics argue, if U.S. constitutional law comes to depend on foreign or international law, this gives foreign governments the power to determine U.S. constitutional law. But foreign governments, or international tribunals, do not determine the relevance or weight of their own law in U.S. interpretation. Transnational legal sources can only influence the interpretation of U.S. judges if the U.S. judge—appointed in the manner specified in the U.S. Constitution or state constitution, as appropriate—decides it is relevant. It is hard to see a question of *sovereignty* being at issue in reliance on sources, viewed as nonbinding, in a decisional process the binding force of which depends entirely on the decisions of U.S. judges.[54] This objection from sovereignty, then, is more rhetoric than substance: the use of foreign and international law in constitutional interpretation does not permit outsiders to control anything, any more than citations to scholarly articles empower faculties to rule. Decisions about interpretation are made by U.S. judges, selected in accord with our own Constitution.

Putting aside the sovereignty objection, there are genuine tensions between popular self-rule and judicial review by unelected life-tenured judges, between democracy (understood as self-governance) and constitutionalism.

These tensions would surely be magnified if the primary basis for judicial rulings were a source of law beyond the control of members of the judges' own polity.[55] Arguments that ignore the objections from self-rule risk undermining important values of democratic decision-making. Democratic participation in decision-making in smaller communities is in some respects a good in itself, and one that can be threatened by external constraints. Moreover, the efficacy of human rights norms is importantly determined by the mobilization of domestic constituencies—within the domestic polity—to effect change on the ground and by the development of a legal culture that supports the practice of rights. And there is much that is attractive about the epistemological humility and value-pluralism behind approaches designed to enhance the quality of participatory decision-making within the domestic polity, envisioning a three-way interpretive dialogue between the people, the political branches, and the courts about constitutional meanings.

The tensions between democratic self-rule and judicial review under the Constitution, though real, are also complicated. The Constitution is the product of a prior and quite partial democratic consent, and specifies a procedure for its own amendment that puts the text well beyond ordinary democratic change. Although the 1789 Constitution was consented to, consent came from a very limited group that did not include women or slaves. Extension of the vote to minorities and women in the nineteenth and early twentieth centuries does not of itself provide democratic legitimacy to the very high threshold for amendment of the rest of the Constitution, in large part fixed by a polity that excluded them.[56] Thus, while the Constitution is law and entitled to respect as such, to treat its text, as originally understood, as the continued embodiment of "the people's" choices prioritizes decisions made by a less democratically legitimate group of people long gone over today's (more inclusive) majorities, a result difficult to justify through a theory of democracy and self-determination alone. The Constitution's continued normative force does not rest solely on those past acts of ratification or amendment, but on a continuing course of history and interpretive practices.

Democratic objections from a distinctly nonoriginalist perspective have also arisen. Neither foreign law nor international law, it may be argued, necessarily bear on what current majorities in the United States believe; to the extent that constitutional law is a "living tree," it must be one rooted in the United States.[57] Rosalind Dixon has sought to meet this objection by arguing that looking to foreign law in some circumstances may assist the Court in identifying stable trends of democratic opinion within the United States; she argues for "dynamic-reflective comparison" to illuminate "changes in U.S. constitutional standards, traditions or values in a given specific context over a particular period of time" by considering whether comparable nations subject to similar social movements are moving in a similar direction.[58] Professor Dixon justifies this "co-evolution" approach as helping identify "blockages" in domestic politics that might obstruct legislative manifestations of evolution in public views.[59] Transnational social movements have indeed shifted constitutional norms in many countries (for example, on slavery, women's rights, racial justice, and environmental protection), and it is not illogical to reason that responsive change in other liberal democracies might foreshadow or confirm the significance of similar changed understandings here. Yet few if any justices would find it appropriate to rely on foreign developments to reveal or confirm democratic preferences in the United States, in part because doing so has the potential to diminish the space for actual democratic decision-making within the polity.[60] For most judges the best evidence of what stable current majorities think (to the extent relevant to constitutional interpretation) is likely to be the nation's own laws and decisions, not those of other countries.[61]

Nonetheless, interpretive consideration of the views of foreign legislatures or courts, or of forms of international law to which the United States has agreed, may at times enhance democratic self-rule. Considering *ratified* treaties in interpreting the Constitution brings to bear the judgments of the President and Senate that undertook the obligations and presumably believed in doing so that they were consistent with the Constitution.[62] Moreover, where domestic laws are challenged as violating the Constitution, transnational law may provide support for upholding contemporary legislation, as in *Jacobson v. Massachussetts* and *Muller v. Oregon*.[63] True, sometimes looking to transnational law will reinforce serious questions about the constitutionality of contemporary decisions, as in Justice Jackson's consideration of foreign law in *Youngstown*.[64] Yet it surely cannot be the case that the Court may "look" at, consider, and refer to international or foreign law only when it supports the constitutionality of challenged legislation[65]—for until one looks one does not know, and having looked, to forbid a justice from being influenced by knowledge in one direction but not the other seems logically inconsistent and cognitively challenging.

In sum, referring to foreign and international law does not systematically make judicial review more, or less, consistent with democracy.[66] It simply provides another set of perspectives for U.S. judges to consider in reaching their best judgment of the U.S. Constitution. More generally, the point is this: the foreign or external source of legal authority does not warrant the categorical exclusions of consideration of materials that, were they *domestic* in origin, would be considered. Certainly the decisions of U.S. state courts and lower federal courts about the meaning of cognate provisions of state constitutions, or the decisions of legislative bodies and elected representatives, may be given more weight, since they are part of the broader sociolegal context (including the Supremacy Clause of the U.S. Constitution) in which domestic judges operate. But in the hardest of cases these domestic sources will often point in divergent directions. In such cases, foreign law should be seen, not so much as a "tie-breaker," but as a reflective mirror that helps the justices sort out better answers.

Interpretive License

Mark Tushnet has raised a different version of this problem, the question of constitutional "license"—whether courts need to be able to identify something in the Constitution or constitutional system that authorizes them to consider foreign or international law.[67] One response is to say that the core of judging is to exercise interpretive authority over adjudicatory issues before the court; courts no more need to point to a specific authority to consider foreign law than they need an authority to consider original intentions, or constitutional values, or the consequences of different interpretations.[68] Or, one might say, by creating a court and making it independent of the political branches, the constitution-makers must have contemplated the court's having a significant degree of independence in the core function of adjudication, which includes interpretation. At least in the absence of clear interpretive directives in the Constitution, the question of "license" is one of fit and suitability to the task at hand.

The Court's interpretive practices, as shown above, have included transnational materials, which is hardly surprising given the understandings of many in the founding generation that the Constitution was a rational design, informed by comparative experience and intended to enable the United States to function as a respected nation in the world. Larger opportunities for comparative learning have been created by experience under the many post–World War II constitutions drawing on international human rights instruments and on the U.S. Constitution or constitutions inspired by it; as Judge Guido Calabresi famously said, "[w]ise parents do not hesitate to learn from their children."[69] This Constitution, like many, leaves unaddressed, and thus to the courts, what sources generally to consider in constitutional interpretation. But if the Constitution's text does not support a general posture of convergence, it certainly does not support a general posture of resistance, a posture that would be inconsistent with the Court's earliest interpretive practices and thus implausible from a positivist perspective on interpretive license.

Separation of Powers, Federalism, and the Treaty Power

But there are other objections to consider: Are there features of the U.S. system of separation of powers, and federalism, that would be undermined by the Court's engagement with transnational law, or would make objections from democracy and sovereignty more intense? Does engagement risk giving international law an effect in constitutional law that it would not otherwise have domestically in a way inconsistent with the constitutionally specified processes of federal lawmaking? Is there merit to Chief Justice Rehnquist's dissenting view in *Atkins v. Virginia*,[70] that considering foreign law (or the views of NGOs, or public opinion polls) is "antithetical to considerations of federalism, which instruct that any 'permanent prohibition upon all units of democratic government must [be apparent] in the operative acts (laws and the application of laws) that the people have approved'"? While Rehnquist's rhetoric elides the language of the Eighth Amendment to the Constitution condemning "cruel and unusual" punishments, which is itself a "permanent prohibition" on inconsistent laws,[71] other kinds of challenges should be addressed.

The Constitution specifies a different procedure for making a treaty than for enacting a law, one that involves only the Senate—the house of Congress most associated with protection of the interests of the states as such—and the President. Does this specification in the Constitution of treaty-making by the President and Senate reflect a constitutional judgment against binding the United States to international norms through judicial judgment? The long interpretive tradition by which the Court has assumed the "law of nations" to be a part of American law,[72] should give one pause in so concluding. Moreover, Supreme Court decisions referring to foreign or international law in interpreting the U.S. Constitution do not "bind" the country to international norms, in ways that establish international obligations of the United States, breach of which can result in international sanctions. What is being given effect is the Court's best understanding of the Constitution, not international (or foreign) law. This objection from separation of powers and federalism, then, should not preclude deliberative engagement with international (or foreign) law as nonbinding sources.

Critics have further argued that the consideration of *unratified* treaty provisions undermines both federalism and separation of powers commitments in the treaty-making process. A particular target has been the Court's reference, in Part IV of *Roper v. Simmons,* to the Convention on the Rights of the Child, unratified by the United States, and to the ICCPR, which the United States ratified with a specific reservation to its provision barring the death penalty for offenses committed by those under eighteen.[73] Critics argue that the Court erred in giving any weight at all to the provisions of these instruments on the juvenile death penalty in its analysis.[74] The Court, however, did not invoke the ICCPR as evidence of domestic views or legal practice, or as having binding force as an international obligation on the United States. Rather, it discussed the ICCPR as evidence of the decisions taken by *other* countries that confirmed the Court's judgment, based on its analysis of domestic laws within the United States and its independent evaluation of the proportionality of imposing the death penalty on an adolescent. The Court thus treated the provisions in the ICCPR and Convention on the Rights of the Child as a form of comparative law, rather than as a form of binding international law. In so doing, it did not undermine the constitutional authority of the political branches to decide what binding international obligations to assume.[75]

The objections from democratic self-rule (intensified by federalism) and the separation of powers to judicial imposition of outside norms are not without force, even if they are complicated by the "democracy deficits" of U.S. constitutional history.[76] Other considerations also caution against efforts to bind the polity through judicial incorporation of international norms that have not been agreed to by more democratic internal processes; the legitimate interests of the states in a federal system raise serious questions about recognition of the preemptive force of law made other than through the constitutionally specified processes of legislation or treaty ratification.[77] However, in constitutional interpretation there is no question of binding the polity to follow foreign or international law; the question is only what persuasive value, if any, foreign or international law or practice may have in the task of interpreting the Constitution.

National Ethos and the Perils of Pragmatic Comparative Inquiry

Some critics are concerned that a deeply comparative commitment might lead the Court to seek an "international equipoise," in which U.S. constitutional law is brought more generally into alignment with the trends of other countries across a wide range of issues.[78] Professor Alford argues that if this were so, our distinctively national constitutional values would be adrift in ways that would be damaging. In an engagement posture, however, the goal is not "international equipoise" across constitutional issues. There is no reason why a willingness to give weight to a transnational consensus as clear, broad, and specific as it was on the juvenile death penalty to confirm a conclusion based on domestic sources, should have such implications for the range of other issues—abortion, religious freedom, defamation, and so forth—that Alford identifies as ones where the United States is out of step with other countries.[79] Not every issue will be amenable to comparative analysis, or to the same kind of comparative analysis, as discussed further below.[80]

Rule of Law, "Persuasive Authority," and Judicial Discretion

An important component of constitutionalism is the commitment to the rule of law. The stability and consistency generated by adherence to the rule of law, including the rules for change in the law, offer important benefits to all members of the polity; "hard" features of established law provide benefit to existing rights-holders in their ability to invoke law to protect those rights. The rule of law also facilitates democracy in that it specifies the procedures by which democratic decision-making proceeds.[81] These rule of law values should not preclude resort to international or foreign law (including decisions of non-U.S. tribunals) as an effort at genuine interpretation of existing U.S. legal texts, including the Constitution,[82] as occurred in some of our oldest cases in which the Court resorted to the "law of nations" as an interpretive aid to constitutional meaning.[83]

It is true that foreign law—unlike the law of lower courts and bodies within the United States—is constrained neither by an obligation to abide by this particular national constitution nor by a theory of precedent within our hierarchical legal system. Professor Charles Fried has argued that a judge, unlike a scholar, is constrained (by virtue of having the power of judgment) to engage only in interpretation of legal materials; as noted in Chapter 1, he has suggested that "expand[ing] the canon of authoritative" sources for constitutional interpretation to include comparative materials would threaten that constraint.[84] But considering transnational sources does not expand the canon, for as we have seen, historic usages go way back, although there is more transnational law available today, and interpretive canons can and do change. Rather than increasing judicial discretion by expanding the sources available to be considered, a practice of considering other courts' approaches to analogous issues may, by eliciting reasoning about distinctions or similarities between U.S. constitutional commitments and conditions and those of others, increase the deliberative quality and accountability of judging.

A perhaps related criticism, voiced by John McGinnis and others, stands against treating foreign or international law as any form of "persuasive authority."[85] Focusing on cases in which the Court referred to transnational legal sources in opinions striking down a law—as occurred in *Atkins, Lawrence,* and *Roper*—McGinnis argues that while foreign law may be used for its "informational value," it should not be used for its "disposition value;" that is, he objects to "reliance on propositions that have weight by virtue of their status as international and foreign law." The argument suggests that the idea of "persuasive authority" is an oxymoron, that the word "authority" implies a form of command or a force wholly unrelated to content.[86]

One difficulty with the purported binary distinction here is that part of the "information value" of a foreign judicial precedent is that a court said what it said to its own government. The information value of an international legal norm is not simply the norm and reasons for it but that it is enforced as law in other countries;[87] in other words, its "status" as law is relevant to the "information" the source provides. Yet the "law" status of a transnational source is quite different from the "law" status of a prior Supreme Court decision, or the "law" status of a clear domestic constitutional text. It does not speak, as law, to the domestic court; but the fact that it speaks as law in other locations communicates information about the context in which it occurs, that places it in an arguably different status than a scholarly article as a tool for comparative reflection.

A number of scholars argue that resort to foreign or international law, especially to illuminate substantive aspects of rights in morally contentious areas, illegitimately expands judicial discretion, raising the dangers of a return to Lochnerian natural law or the overempowerment of the judiciary.[88] When domestic interpretive sources align, foreign or international law will not move U.S. judges toward a different result; when internal sources are more ambiguous or contested, judges' disciplined reflection on foreign law does not so much expand discretion as provide a perspective on the best resolution within what is plausible in U.S. constitutionalism. The most "morally" controversial cases often are genuinely "hard"; indeed, deep controversy helps define the parameters of those cases understood to be hard. It is not surprising that good judges would read particularly widely on such issues.[89] In such cases, however, the tension between prudential silence (omitting reference to transnational sources even if they were helpful) and reasoned discussion may also be especially acute.[90]

As noted earlier, some scholars and jurists argue that permitting consideration of foreign sources would allow judges to give effect to their preferences under the name of law, expanding the range of views for which some precedent can be found and inviting "cherry-picking" of authorities around the world.[91] Multiplying the number and direction of authorities might, in theory, increase the range of permissible constitutional judgment, especially if the decisional process is imagined in mathematical terms. But constitutional law is underdetermined, not wholly indeterminate;[92] the range of plausible interpretive choices is not infinite, but bounded by the constraints of the national normative community of which judges are a part. Rather than treating each separate source as a mathematical "factor," multiplication of which yields many more possibilities for decision, constitutional interpretation in the common law tradition treats the modalities of argument as interactive; the strength of each depends in part on the nature of the issue, and in part on the relationships among the arguments.

Because transnational sources would be considered only on questions open within our system, and only insofar as they fit with interpretive questions relevant under the judges' more general methodology, they are unlikely dramatically to change the range of interpretive choices even if they influence which one is chosen. Use of foreign legal sources would be bounded by preliminary considerations of comparability; countries that are not highly comparable are unlikely to be persuasive sources of influence.[93] To the extent that foreign and international law are "in the mix" as persuasive authority it is, of course, possible that their consideration would affect choices among otherwise available interpretations, given the judicial drive toward coherence among sources. A judge's instincts, however, are conditioned by the legal system in which she functions; it seems unlikely that a judge would be predisposed to a result that had little support already in her own tradition (or that judges would act upon such a view on finding foreign support).

Moreover, foreign or international law would not necessarily function as an "additional" source comparable to text, precedent, original understandings, and so forth. In some cases, foreign experience would provide additional information about a source—for example, the consequences of alternative interpretations—that judges otherwise resort to. And in many cases—including those regarded as morally difficult—international and foreign law would function as a kind of "de-biasing device," producing decision-making more aware of the possibility and implications of interpretive choices, and thus more likely to respond by reasoning rather than by an instinctive assumption that one has the right answer.[94] Objections from rule of law and concerns for judicial discretion in these cases are answered by Professor Glenn's observation that having to confront foreign decisions offers far greater opportunity for critical reflection on one's own first instincts than otherwise;[95] to similar effect, Jennifer Nedelsky has argued that efforts to engage with perspectives from beyond helps judges "enlarge" their mental vision and check their own biases.[96] Transnational legal sources used in this way will function to constrain judges by adding a perspective through which the problem is considered.

Expertise and Bounded Rationality

Another set of objections derive from limitations of expertise and competence, and the opportunity costs of becoming sufficiently expert in comparative analysis. U.S. judges, it is argued, are not well trained to analyze foreign or even international law as it may bear on constitutional interpretation, and the time required for such training poses insurmountable difficulties. It is probably the case that most U.S. judges today were not educated about international and foreign law (although increasingly law schools offer students significant exposure to international and comparative law). Contextualized understandings of other countries' legal systems are important for fair use of foreign cases; there is a significant risk that doctrines, rules, or principles that make sense in one context will change meaning or lose value in another. Legal vocabulary may seem familiar but have different conceptual connotations; reading decisions in translation leaves one dependent on the language and legal skills of the translator. Although international law is relatively accessible, there are risks of sheer confusion about the scope and content of international law, as well as about how to understand constitutional decisions of other courts.

On the other hand, lawyers and judges are in a sense well trained to master new bodies of law. They are experienced in reasoning by analogy—and by disanalogy. Without denying the challenges or the risks, it is worth noting that two recent empirical studies of Canadian and South African usage of international or foreign law found little error or unfairness, and suggest that barriers of expertise can be overcome[97]—though again, legal education or law practice may differ in ways that make this more difficult in the United States.

Given the varying degrees to which international or foreign law is likely to be helpful in resolving domestic constitutional issues, judges may be understandably reluctant either to invest the time needed to feel comfortable relying on those sources or to risk error in relying on them without that investment of time. Judges' rational decisions are necessarily bounded ones, in a world exploding with legal information.[98] Professor David Strauss suggests that the benefits "from drawing on the accumulated wisdom of many societies would be outweighed by the unmanageability of the task."[99] This conclusion is overdrawn: not all appropriate uses of foreign law will involve a comprehensive survey, and there is a developing infrastructure of scholarship on foreign and especially on international law for attorneys to draw on and for judges to consider. Yet the undoubted difficulties in getting foreign law right warrant caution, as further discussed below in Chapter 6.

Comparability Challenges

A number of scholars have suggested that the basic criterion of comparability, important in functional uses of transnational experience, may be very difficult accurately to determine or even impossible to achieve. Political scientists may find it challenging enough to compare multiple constitutional systems, needing to determine what variables to include, and judges are not trained in the kinds of analyses necessary to make these kinds of comparisons. As noted in Chapter 4, the possibilities of comparison may be confounded by variables not studied. Some would go further, and argue that the United States is unique—no other country combines its size, its culture, its systems of federalism and presidentialism, its particular traditions of liberty, and the longevity of its constitution and of its highest court, and thus comparisons to foreign law can be ruled out.

Every country is in some sense unique; no two are identical in terms of population, structure, or history, though many share elements. The difficulties of drawing firm conclusions in making comparisons is an important reason why legal analysis should remain largely grounded in domestic traditions and histories and why postures of engagement, rather than convergence, make sense. But it is hard to believe that judges will make better decisions with less accurate knowledge of other systems. For that is the choice: most justices already believe that they know something about other legal systems, and, as shown by Chief Justice Burger's overdrawn claim in *Bowers v. Hardwick,* discussed earlier,[100] it is easy to be mistaken in what one thinks one knows without careful checking.

The challenges of comparability should not obscure the fact that reasoning analogically and by comparison is at the heart of what common law judges do.[101] Judges draw analogical comparisons quite regularly in their reasoning.[102] To know what to compare requires a sense of the purpose of the comparison. The purposes of many U.S. provisions are similar to those of other countries—to prevent barbarism by the government even as to those lawfully confined; to maintain a competitive democracy by, inter alia, preventing those who hold power from oppressing the speech of their political opponents—and the possibility of reasoning by analogy and comparison does not seem remote in such areas.

Constitutional Situation Sense, Contextualized Judgment, and Socialization

Apart from the familiar concerns of bounded rationality and limited information gathering and processing capacities, there is at least one further caveat to the proposition that knowing more is generally better than knowing less. To the extent that the task of being a constitutional court judge depends on a well-developed knowledge of and familiarity with one's own constitutional tradition, and on the acquisition of a sense of legal judgment about the role of the courts in the polity over the course of its history, one would expect the best Supreme Court judges to be in some sense practitioners who had at least at one time been deeply enmeshed in the practice of American constitutional law and/or constitutional politics. Karl Llewelyn famously wrote of the importance of "situation sense" in commercial law and statutory interpretation.[103] Although he did not extend this analysis in so many words to constitutional interpretation, he did argue that the Constitution was not a "document" but an "institution," that constitutional law was legitimate because of practices of interpretation as "part of our going Constitution," and that the working constitution consisted of the interlocking "ways" of government actors, interest groups, and the people.[104]

The constitutional "situation sense" that arises from long experience in working within a system, then, would be an important aspect of that which is called "good judgment" in law, comparable to the kind of expertise that arises from multiple cumulated experiences in other areas.[105] Situation sense is necessary in constitutional law to know what the parameters of plausible interpretation are and to exercise judgment on the best constitutional answer, an exercise that rests on familiarity with the details of the norms, institutions, and the histories of the particular system. The practice of being a good judge, of seeking to decide according to law—understood to exist apart from the judge's personal policy preferences—requires both knowledge and respect for the law and a kind of "practical wisdom."[106] The demands of practical wisdom, arising from knowledge and experience in the domestic system, pose challenges in at least two directions.

First, they help explain some of the risks of misunderstanding of comparative materials. If a highly developed situation sense is necessary to enable U.S. justices to make decisions reflecting sound constitutional judgment, how much of a situation sense is necessary properly to understand decisions from other countries? Bilingualism is difficult to achieve and takes years of practice; bi-legalism—developing a situation sense of multiple legal systems—likewise may be expected to take years to develop. While there are benefits to be had from comparison without being so fully enmeshed, the risks of errors of understanding are greater and steps must be taken to counteract these when foreign materials are considered by those without deep-country expertise. For this reason, it is difficult to expect judges to be ahead of the advocates or the scholarly literature in their willingness to consider and use foreign law (although international law may not pose these same risks to the same degree).

Second, the need to sustain one's own expert situation sense imposes limits on the time and personal intellectual resources that can be applied to the study of other systems. Might being *too* engaged with the transnational threaten a judge's maintaining a "feel" for the U.S. constitutional system? It is not clear how much of a problem this is, or how to distinguish the beneficial intellectual engagement with the foreign and international from the possibility of "losing touch" with the system one is rooted in. With an experienced lawyer or judge who has spent decades working in the U.S. system, spending some time with the intellectual challenge of confronting other systems can be a healthy check to unthinking complacency. In this there is a balance. But the tensions between maintaining the situation sense of the local, while challenging one's own sense of the natural through exposure to other systems, are to some extent inescapable, and impose constraints on how much comparative expertise can be expected to be developed. For this reason, as well, engagement—rather than a commitment to convergence—is the better posture for judges to take.

Some of the critiques of transnational judicial dialogue might be understood as concerns about the socialization effects on judges of spending time with judges from other countries. Does exposure to foreign ideas on balance have a negative effect, causing judges to lose track of the interpretive traditions and normative understandings of their own polity?[107] Do "transnational discourse" and meetings among constitutional court judges lead to a sense of overempowerment that might cause judges to misjudge their own system? The empirical judgment entailed in such claims is a complex one; but I am skeptical that judges who are educated and come of age in the United States, and have served as judges on American courts, would lose their moorings because of summers at Salzburg.[108] Indeed, comparative knowledge might conduce to more humility, awareness of the risks of judicial overextension, and appreciation of the fragility of the rule of law even in a longstanding constitutional democracy.

* * *

To summarize: arguments for resistance are found in democratic theory and concerns for sovereignty, in concerns for judicial competence and interpretive license, discretion and constraint, and in concerns about the epistemology of comparisons, and the relationships between a constitution, its judges, and its constitutional culture, and the practices of working constitutionalism. These concerns are serious ones, some of which tend strongly to support a fairly high degree of caution, but none preclude resort to transnational law as nonbinding authority.

Here I would add only two points. First, maintaining an attitude of resistance by an entire court is probably not possible, given the diversity of views on multimember courts, the inevitability of some comparative knowledge and influence, and the declining possibility of a legal consciousness that views law's autonomy as natural and unproblematic. The plausibility of claims that texts have entirely fixed meanings has come under assault not only in law but in literature and history; and there has been a related decline in lawyers' and judges' abilities to see formalism as a representation of legal reality, as a result of the critiques of Legal Realism and Critical Legal Studies. All of these phenomena contribute to a decline in confidence in the determinacy of any one source and increase the felt need to respond, in a justificatory mode, to competing sources and normative claims.

Second, the posture of unmitigated resistance to the transnational in constitutional interpretation does not fit well with the multiple purposes of constitutions, including the goal of maintaining an effective national sovereignty in an environment of increasing legal pluralism. One of the purposes of a constitution, very much including the U.S. Constitution, is to enable its country to be a respected member of the international community. For this purpose the

Constitution enables the federal government to make treaties and receive ambassadors, and enables its courts to entertain cases involving ambassadors or cases that arise under those treaties. The Constitution has at times been viewed as embodying the Declaration of Independence's most universalist claims, that all human beings "are created equal and endowed . . . with certain unalienable rights,"[109] a position that would suggest the possibility of normative overlap with many other constitutional systems and, indeed, of some form of joint or common venture in interpreting law to fulfill those universalist claims. To hold that judges should not even consider international or foreign laws that may illuminate how our own constitution should be understood—both in its specific relationships with other nations,[110] and in its commitments to (some) relatively universal normative understandings—is to close one's eyes to an important set of constitutional purposes that would be ill-served by such willful indifference or ignorance.

C. QUESTIONING CONVERGENCE: CONSTITUTIONS AS EMBODIMENTS OF NATIONAL DISTINCTIVENESS AND PLURAL FUNCTIONS

In contrast to "resisters," some jurists argue for postures of convergence, under which all countries should strive to converge with respect to major elements of constitutional and international law, especially those dealing with the protection of human rights, respect for the rule of law, and democracy. Postures of convergence would give substantial hierarchic effect to international law as such, or to emerging transnational consensus; such postures differ from those of even the more relational forms of engagement in the effort they contemplate to construe domestic constitutions in accord with international or transnational consensus.

As set forth in Chapter 2, Professor Shany has argued that ratified human rights treaties should be understood to require incorporation of their norms at the domestic constitutional level. Disputing the conventional understanding that such treaties allow states a wide range of ways to implement their obligations, he argues, the principle of "effective interpretation," as well as specific treaty clauses on effective remedies, require domestic enforcement at the constitutional level (especially where international enforcement mechanisms are relatively weak); he also notes the benefits of harmonizing interpretations of binding legal sources.[111] Justice Kirby of the Australian High Court has argued more broadly that domestic constitutions—like other domestic law—should be interpreted in accord with international law whenever possible.[112] This concept, shared by a number of judges in Commonwealth nations,[113] is reflected as well in the incorporation of human rights instruments into some national constitutional texts.[114]

Despite the appeal of these arguments, they are not entirely persuasive in the context of U.S. constitutional interpretation. Arguments for postures of convergence have special appeal for regimes that seek new departures from authoritarian pasts by binding their polities to protect human rights measured by international standards. But absent a clear commitment by constitution-makers to this approach, it is difficult to justify as an across-the-board position in constitutional interpretation. Constitutions serve multiple purposes. They function not only as entrenched operating rules for a legal system but also as forms of national self-expression, providing the framework for the working out within a particular "nomos" of its contests, commitments, and identity.[115] Constitutional interpretation, although it occurs in many societies and has common elements and concerns, is also and at the same time an intensely national act, and must be so understood to retain legitimacy within a particular polity. By invoking primarily universalist standards, convergence postures may undermine the transformative or constraining capacities of law based on distinctively national constitutional aspirations. And the transnational itself is a complex, at times double-edged, sword.

Compromise and Constraint in Constitutional Design

Constitutions embody both general principles and pragmatic compromises. Historically contingent compromises may be most likely to appear in federal constitutions,[116] but they are in theory fully anticipatable in any constitution-making process. As Jon Elster has argued, in moments of constitution-making there are usually upstream constraints, imposed by those who currently hold the power to convene a constitution-making process, and downstream constraints, imposed by those who must approve or accept the constitution.[117] These upstream and downstream constraints are likely to diverge as existing power holders seek to protect their power or existing arrangements against new demands, resulting in compromises. Compromises limit the application of more general constitutional principles, though in ways that can be highly contested. "Fit" with the particularities, textual and historical, of the polity, as well as requirements (sometimes competing) of principled justification, both operate as constraints on legitimate interpretation.[118]

Local Authorship and Universal Reason

Yet, it might be argued, if not on all issues, at least on issues of individual rights, the Constitution should be understood to be aiming at the same values protected by much of modern human rights law; it would thus be a fulfillment of that constitutional purpose to adopt a presumption of concordance. But multiple constitutional purposes create other tensions, for example, between local authorship and universal reason as constitutionally legitimating factors. By local authorship I mean the sense of constitutional belonging that can be created by processes of drafting or ratification, or by longstanding local traditions, or by working with particular constitutional institutions.[119] By universal reason I mean constitutional appeals to principle. Both may be required for a constitution to be experienced as a fundamental and self-constitutive law, in the way that the U.S. Constitution sometimes is seen to be. The perception of local authorship may be needed to anchor universal aspirations.[120] Engagement with comparative and international law permits the national court to mediate between the demands of the local and those of the universal. And it is a posture that embraces a diversity of constitutional views and practices, a diversity that may be valuable to the cause of constitutionalism itself.[121]

Textual, Institutional and Practice-Based Distinctions

A presumption of convergence with transnational consensus is in considerable tension with the precedent-based interpretive practices dominant on the U.S. Supreme Court. As noted in Chapter 4, Professor Neuman suggests that some rights, protected in national constitutions and international covenants, have "suprapositive" aspects particularly conducive to cross-national discussion; but, he also argues, these rights have aspects of legitimacy derived from the consent of particular peoples or political actors, and conditioned on specific institutional contexts for their interpretation and enforcement.[122] Language differences, or differences in understanding by ratifying generations, or in bodies of precedent that have been built up over time, thus legitimately may constrain interpretation of otherwise similar rights. Moreover, not all rights have "suprapositive" overlap; international law or foreign jurisprudence may on particular issues be inconsistent with established U.S. constitutional rights protections, in ways that should caution against *presuming* the desirability of convergence at the constitutional level, as opposed to taking the more open posture of engagement.

Institutional differences can affect the appropriate choice of doctrine to implement rights in particular societies,[123] and the institutional setting for rights enforcement in the United States is distinctive in several ways. To begin with, the United States is an older constitutional order, with many layers of complex doctrine around many constitutional issues. These layers of existing doctrine are themselves an "institutional" feature that constitutional interpreters in the United States must take account of, given rule of law commitments. Second, "case or controversy" limitations on justiciability distinguish the U.S. courts from some other systems that may permit "abstract" review, or that have more generous "standing" requirements, and may skew or shape the arena for judge-made doctrine.[124] Third, the United States' large size and federal character mean that there are laws and rules that can be promulgated and enforced by a wide array of decision-makers at federal, state, and local government levels; criminal prosecution at the state level is notably decentralized, and populist, with many states relying on elected attorneys general or district attorneys.[125] The decentralized nature of governance and of criminal prosecution can give rise to cases with many factual variations and create serious challenges of monitoring compliance with national norms (even with the extensive federal and state courts of the American judicial system), creating circumstances in which prophylactic rules to implement the Constitution may be seen as an appropriate constitutional strategy. Thus, application of "proportionality" standards on a case-by-case basis, as occurs in some other constitutional democracies, may have real drawbacks as a rights enforcement approach in the United States.

Furthermore, the net institutional benefit of a presumption of convergence may not be as great within the United States as elsewhere. International human rights law may be a helpful "backstop" where the rule of law is weak.[126] Tying constitutional interpretation to an international norm empowers domestic judges whose ability to command compliance with their decisions may be weak and provides an external measure of the correctness of decisions that may aid human rights–monitoring groups seeking to hold the court to its constitutional role. The rule of law, in the sense of compliance with judicial decisions, is not weak in the United States (although problems on occasion arise); the judges—at least those who sit on federal courts—feel fully empowered. Moreover, Professor Neuman concludes, "the less intense engagement of the United States in the international human rights regime currently results in fewer institutional benefits from coordination."[127] And, as suggested above, in some areas in which U.S. individual rights law departs from international human rights understandings, the U.S. approach is embodied in a sufficiently large body of precedent that the likelihood of change, even in the presence of a presumption of convergence, is low, and the risks to rule of law values in making a change nontrivial.[128]

Treaties, Presumptions, and Sub-Constitutional Implementation

Compliance with our international legal obligations furthers many important goals,[129] but the demands of international law may be satisfied domestically without necessarily resorting to constitutional interpretation. A ratified treaty embodying an international obligation is *a* reason to choose, as among alternative interpretations otherwise supported by the range of domestic sources, a constitutional interpretation that avoids breach of that obligation. For one thing, ratification represents the views of the President and Senate that the treaty is in the interests of the United States and might be taken to represent their views that it is lawful under the Constitution. But while these views of the political branches are a source of understanding constitutional meaning, they could be no more dispositive than are the presumed views of the whole Congress and the President with respect to *statutes*. Reasoning from representation-reinforcing theory, treaties might be entitled to *less* of a presumption of constitutionality than statutes, given the nonparticipation of the House of Representatives in approving treaties. On the other hand, reasoning from the national interest in having an effective voice in international affairs, treaties might have a *stronger* claim to such a presumption than statutes, because of the adverse consequences to the United States of having made a binding obligation that it cannot fulfill. Invalidating a statute does not cause the United States to breach an obligation to foreign nations; invalidating a treaty, or preventing it from being implemented, may do so, and that is (at least arguably) a more serious matter.

But saying a treaty (like a statute) is presumptively constitutional does not necessarily imply that the Constitution should itself be interpreted to embody the substantive rules of a treaty, even one providing for individual rights. First, treaties may be abrogated by legislation, or, possibly, by the President acting alone; constitutional law cannot be. Moreover, treaties and other international obligations generally can be fulfilled in a variety of ways;[130] interpreting the Constitution to require what a treaty does is not the same as interpreting the Constitution to permit the treaty to be implemented, either by judicial interpretation (in the case of self-executing treaties) or through legislation. There are stronger reasons for a presumption that the Constitution does not prevent compliance with treaty obligations than for a presumption that the Constitution itself should be interpreted to require what a treaty requires.[131] The range of ways treaty compliance can be achieved means there is some real distance between recognizing a treaty as binding law and interpreting the Constitution itself to require what the treaty does; and enforcement of international obligations through means other than constitutional interpretation has some distinctive benefits.[132]

International Law and Interpretive Space

The nature of customary international law, and a fortiori, of any emerging transnational consensus, also supports a posture of constitutional engagement rather than convergence in considering their implications for constitutional interpretation. Customary international law is constructed and evolves through the actions and beliefs of national states. Its content is influenced by pushes and pulls within the transnational community of nations; and a state that is a "persistent objector" is not bound by a rule of customary international law.[133] Constitutions are forms of "precommitment" and are intended to be more deeply entrenched than other forms of law. To link swathes of constitutional meaning to an evolving body of law constructed by multinational pushes and pulls—a process in which the United States may be pushing one way while others pull in a different direction—is arguably inconsistent with the character of a national constitution in its settlement and precommitment capacities. To the extent that customary international law is illuminating of what shared legal ideas require, courts may consider and rely on it—free, however, to conclude that a customary international law rule is not embodied in the national constitution. More generally, postures of engagement rather than convergence leave more space for national constitutions to provide a basis for resisting international legal rules or decisions that have less legitimate or persuasive normative pull.[134]

Elusiveness of Goal

Finally, as noted in Chapter 2, even those legal systems that aspire to convergence will find that goal elusive, and for reasons that are endemic to the decentralized, nonhierarchical set of institutions in the legal orders in play.[135] The divergent views of the Israeli High Court and the International Court of Justice (ICJ) on the legality, under international law, of a "security fence" or "wall" around Israel's borders may be an illustration.[136] As noted previously, the Colombian Constitutional Court, notwithstanding a mandate to interpret its rights provisions in harmony with certain human rights covenants, distinguished between the covenants and their interpretation: while international human rights treaties themselves were part of the "Constitutional Bundle" that controlled, this bundle did not include the jurisprudence of the UN's interpretive bodies—thus asserting a degree of national control over the interpretation of these international instruments.[137] As these examples suggest, international law in the hands of national courts may become something more like comparative law than a strongly uniform and binding body of international law.[138] In the absence of an authoritative final interpreter of these international instruments, strong degrees of convergence seem unlikely to emerge.

* * *

For these reasons, then, a posture of engagement seems on the whole best suited to the task of interpreting the U.S. Constitution in the early decades of this twenty-first century. Convergence as a general posture is inconsistent with the multiple purposes of the U.S. Constitution—which include not only fostering compliance with international law but also honoring the terms of specific commitments made for the domestic community. It also ignores the degree to which a government's capacity to serve as a strong enough location for the self-identity of a polity, and for effective governance and the protection of rights, depends on its generating quite local attachments, as well as its adherence to more universal values.

6. ENGAGING THE TRANSNATIONAL

A Contextual Framework

As we have seen, the use of international and foreign law in U.S. constitutional jurisprudence is not a novel form of judicial activism but an ongoing part of the interpretive traditions of the Court, evident in many of its most important decisions. From its earliest cases, U.S. Supreme Court justices, sometimes writing for the Court, sometimes alone, have invoked international or foreign law or experience as an aid to constitutional interpretation, a form of nonbinding but sometimes persuasive authority. While foreign or international law is neither available nor relevant in every constitutional case, the dramatic increase in these sources now requires a more thoughtful approach to their use lest courts and litigants be overwhelmed, or misled by inapposite comparisons.[1]

As earlier chapters have shown, there are recurring uses of foreign and international law in the Supreme Court's decisions: First, there are reflective, expressive uses, in which foreign or international law is invoked, by way of positive or negative comparison, to clarify or check understandings of basic constitutional commitments. Second, foreign or international law, or the experience of other countries, may be considered to assist in "implementing" constitutional values, whether by illustrating different doctrinal approaches to accommodating similar values, or by providing information on the likely or possible consequences of alternative interpretive choices.[2] Third, the Constitution's text (or doctrine) may require some resort to international law, as in addressing treaties, war powers, or the "law of nations," or may invite consideration of transnational sources in evaluating a quality, such as "cruelty" or "reasonableness," on which the practices of other nations shed helpful light.

Within these categories of use, there are three substantive considerations that should guide courts in deciding whether resort to transnational sources would be appropriate: the nature of the domestic issue, the nature of the transnational source in relation to its proposed use, and the comparability of the source with the issue in the United States. These are discussed in Part A below. Part B addresses the requirements of fair-mindedness and the need for procedures to promote fair and accurate use of foreign and international materials. Part C considers two other questions, relating to the use of transnational sources in lower courts and the occasions for "prudential" silence on transnational legal sources.

A. THREE CONTEXTUAL CONSIDERATIONS

Three basic considerations, simple to state but not always easy to apply, should guide judicial consideration of foreign or international law in constitutional interpretation. First, the nature of the domestic issue is important, for not all issues will be equally amenable to transnational engagement. Second, the nature of the transnational legal source, in relation to its proposed use in interpretation, matters. Whether the transnational source is a judicial decision or a foreign statute, for example, or is a foreign constitutional decision or a rule announced by an international tribunal may affect its persuasive value. Third, for some interpretive purposes comparability is quite important; deciding what is comparable is a complex inquiry, requiring knowledge not only of legal systems but also of the societies in which they are situated.

The Nature of the Issue and of Domestic Sources of Interpretation

The legitimacy of looking to international or foreign law or experience will vary with the domestic issue, depending on the specificity and history of our constitutional text, the degree to which the issue is genuinely unsettled, and the strength of other interpretive sources.[3] Just as some constitutional texts seem to demand a degree of reciprocity with international understandings, other constitutional issues are grounded in highly specific rule-like provisions, or in nationally distinctive constitutional commitments, on which foreign and international law are either silent or irrelevant. In contrast to the Eighth Amendment's ban on cruel and unusual punishment, or the Constitution's commitment to protecting "liberty" through "due process of law," other provisions—the age requirements for public office, the provisions for presidential pocket veto of legislation, the Fifth Amendment's grand jury requirement, the Second Amendment's right to bear arms,[4] and, possibly, the Establishment Clause of the First Amendment—might each be regarded as having that kind of specificity or distinctiveness (or both) that make transnational sources irrelevant, or less relevant, to plausible interpretive questions. I discuss five areas briefly, below, to illustrate this distinction.

Fifth Amendment Grand Jury Clause The Fifth Amendment requires that all federal criminal prosecutions for "capital, or otherwise infamous" crimes be initiated by a grand jury. Even if analysis of the criminal procedure in other countries might lead to a view that a grand jury is a superfluous or less than ideal check on prosecutorial discretion, these conclusions are largely irrelevant. The text of the Fifth Amendment is clear, and the required use of a grand jury in serious federal criminal prosecutions is a settled issue. On the other hand, issues of the scope of the grand jury requirement might be affected by one's evaluation of comparative law: whether the requirement should extend to state criminal prosecutions, an issue left less clearly settled by specific text, is one on which foreign experience might be, and indeed was, consulted.[5]

Establishment Clause To take another, more complex, example: Although most Western democratic countries have constitutional provisions that protect religious liberty, fewer have a constitutional text analogous to the Establishment Clause of the U.S. Constitution, a text that over the last several decades has been elaborated in a number of cases as requiring relatively strict forms of government neutrality toward religion and religious institutions.[6] Some Western democracies with relatively good protection of religious liberty have official established churches, including the United Kingdom, Norway, and Denmark.[7] On the other hand, France has no official church and the 1958 Constitution describes the French Republic as "secular."[8] Yet this has not prohibited direct state subsidies to private religious schools, upheld based on the principle of freedom of education.[9]

Moreover, of the constitutions that include provisions arguably analogous to the U.S. Establishment Clause, some include other constitutional texts that plainly contemplate a different meaning. Thus, for example, while the German Basic Law incorporates provisions of the Weimar Constitution that prohibit a "state church," other incorporated provisions envision a substantial relationship between churches and the state, including authorizations to churches to levy taxes (a power that many churches delegate to their state governments, which then pay the taxes over to the church).[10] Indeed, the German Basic Law's provisions also specifically state that "[r]eligious instruction shall form part of the regular curriculum in state schools, with the exception of non-denominational schools," and that "[p]arents and guardians shall have the right to decide whether children shall receive religious instruction."[11] Provisions for religious instruction during regular classes in public schools would be widely regarded as inconsistent with the U.S. Establishment Clause, whether understood through Thomas Jefferson's "wall of separation" metaphor or in more flexible terms.[12] Knowledge of foreign legal practice and of foreign experience under different approaches might be helpful in thinking through how to reconcile the Establishment Clause with the Free Exercise Clause, and there may be some convergences in constitutional doctrine that already exist, notwithstanding apparent textual differences. But because of significant variations in approaches elsewhere and the distinctive history and considerable precedent available for interpreting the American clauses, foreign sources, even those involving similar constitutional texts, can be of only limited assistance and must be used with considerable caution.[13]

Eighth Amendment By contrast, the Eighth Amendment to the U.S. Constitution, prohibiting "cruel and unusual" punishment, has from its earliest interpretations by the Supreme Court been viewed as inviting comparison with the practices of foreign countries. In 1879, the Court rejected a challenge to a sentence of death by shooting in the Utah Territory in part because "corresponding rules [that] prevail in other countries" supported the practice.[14] Since then in a number of cases foreign practices and international views were evaluated as a part of the Court's substantive "cruel and unusual" inquiry.[15] It was thus a notable turn when Justice Scalia, in 1989, wrote for the Court that "it is *American* conceptions of decency that are dispositive," not the "sentencing practices of other countries," which could be considered only after a determination of U.S. consensus was made.[16] This apparent resistance to considering foreign law lasted only until 2002, when the Court returned to a less resistant posture, in *Atkins v. Virginia*, and then in 2005, with more extensive consideration of foreign and international law in *Roper v. Simmons*.[17]

Security and Liberty The Executive Branch of the U.S. government, for a period of time after the terrorist attacks of September 11, 2001, took positions that sought to justify indefinite detention without trial, without access to attorneys and without judicial review—in short, without any of the accoutrements of legal proceedings or due process of law. The government also sought to justify the use of extremely harsh interrogation techniques, asserted that the President could not be constrained by law not to use torture, and more generally argued for what some characterized as "lawless enclaves," or legal "black holes."[18] There was little precedent for this phalanx of legal positions, in part because the basic premises of American constitutionalism should have made it unthinkable. The link between the idea of the Constitution as "law of the land" and the requirements of due process is longstanding, and the importance of judicial review is emphasized by the provisions of Article I, Section 9 securing the privilege of the writ of habeas corpus.[19]

Yet, at a time of justifiable fear, it can be difficult for the courts—whose judges sit in the same polity as executive branch decision-makers—to evaluate such executive claims with the same commitments to disinterested interpretation of the law that they ordinarily aspire to.[20] When a country has been attacked and its leadership argues for recognition of less bounded executive powers, domestic courts have struggled to retain the distance and balance needed to insist that law serve as a check on power. Interrogating one's instincts through alternative perspectives is particularly important to achieve impartiality in a time of fear.[21]

Other constitutional democracies have overlapping commitments to the protection of liberty, many in fact inspired by provisions in the U.S. Constitution; indeed, the protection of human liberty from arbitrary executive treatment is one of the commitments at the core of the Western liberal tradition. The practices of other liberal democracies that have had to respond to terrorist attacks can serve as interlocutors, an aid to more dispassionate decision-making in times of crisis,[22] and advocates have brought these to the attention of the Court. For example, an amicus brief in *Rumsfeld v. Padilla* focused on the approaches of other liberal democracies that faced movements using terrorist tactics (including Great Britain, Spain, and Israel), showing a range of special measures for suspected terrorists, all of which, however, provided for set (though in some cases renewable) time limits, access to counsel, and judicial review of the claimed bases for detentions.[23] Although *Padilla* was not resolved on the merits by the Court, the material brought forth in the briefing raised grave questions about the claim that, on a President's say-so, a citizen could be detained militarily, for years, and denied access to counsel or any minimal process to test the accuracy of the asserted basis of detention. Looking comparatively at other nations' practices today would not answer some questions of U.S. constitutional law—for example, whether an implication of the Treason Clause is that, absent a suspension of habeas corpus, a citizen may not be indefinitely detained without criminal trial.[24] But it could provide a helpful external perspective on the claims of executive authority that were made in some stages of *Padilla* and in other litigations arising out of the detention and treatment of prisoners in the "war on terror" held both in the United States and at Guantánamo.[25]

International Law as Embedded Element in Constitutional Terms As discussed in Chapter 4, some constitutional provisions invite or require resort to international law. Congress's power to "define and punish . . . Offenses against the Law of Nations," for example, must be understood as having some independent content derived from customary international law to serve its constitutional purpose, and likewise the term "treaty" and its scope. Beyond this, international law has been drawn on in a wide range of contexts over the course of U.S. constitutional history.[26] For example, the Court has treated contemporary international law as internal to its analysis of presidential powers in the past, and in 2006 it assumed that Congress could constitutionally limit the President to acting within the constraints of international law.[27]

* * *

Thus, the relevance and legitimacy of looking to international or foreign law will vary depending upon the domestic legal issue, the clarity of the constitutional text, and our interpretive traditions of analyzing that text. Whatever the foreign practice, the Fifth Amendment to the U.S. Constitution requires a grand jury for serious federal prosecutions. By contrast, terms referring to relations with other countries may require consideration of how those terms are understood by others, even if they are not entirely determined by reference to international law. One might think of this first question as a threshold inquiry of whether it is sensible to devote time and resources to considering international or foreign law in resolving an open question of domestic constitutional law.

Transnational Sources and "Open" Questions It might be asked whether transnational sources have any role in defining when a question is open. International or foreign law will no doubt influence this perception, but in indirect ways that cannot be doctrinally cabined or recognized. If the sense of what arguments are "off the wall" is "a matter of social practice and convention,"[28] the processes by which law, and specifically constitutional law, are seen as "open" or subject to change rest on a complex of influences, reactions, assimilations, rejections, modifications, or adaptations of ideas and advocacy. Given the force of stare decisis, it is unlikely that changing views elsewhere will affect the perception of an issue as open or closed until such time as ideas, concerns, or experiences are "brought home" and become part of U.S. legal culture.

Alan Watson argues that legal change is most commonly the result of what he calls "borrowing" of ideas from within or without an existing legal system, borrowing that may be driven not only by functional considerations but also by "chance."[29] But something less wholesale and clear than "borrowing" is likely to be at work in interpretive developments in constitutional law. In the "migration" of constitutional ideas, ideas may influence developments without yielding a clear rule or system that is "transplant[ed]," or "borrowed."[30] Influence may occur not only through a shifting sense of what is reasonable but also through aversive reactions, as Kim Scheppele has shown, and in other ways not captured by the metaphor of transplantation or borrowing.[31]

No jurist can escape exposure to international law and some foreign legal ideas, for "legal traditions . . . are in constant contact with one or more . . . other legal traditions."[32] Chance, however, plays an important role in precisely what kinds of sources, with what degree of accuracy of understanding, are in play. Exposure may be below the level of conscious thought about constitutional law, blending into a mélange of ideas, derived from multiple sources, that may influence how judges construct the clarity of issues and how they resolve what is "open" and closed. So while foreign and international law may play some role, along with many other sources, in influencing sociolegal or cultural understandings that in turn affect evaluation of what issues are "open," their force is likely to be indirect, uncertain, implicit, or unconscious.[33]

The Nature of the Transnational Source and its Proposed Use

Assuming that a U.S. constitutional issue is reasonably open to considering foreign or international law, whether to consider a transnational source will also depend on what that source is, and the purpose for which it is invoked. On occasion, a legal opinion by a single judge may provide such insight into the nature of a problem that by force of its reasoning, it persuades or illuminates an issue for another judge. Reliance on such a source, like reliance on a scholarly article, is based on the quality of its reasoning.[34] Like literary sources that have appeared in U.S. Supreme Court opinions, foreign sources may also be used for their eloquence or concision of expression on a subject that bears on the constitutional problem under consideration.[35] But this captures only a small portion of the uses of transnational legal sources.

A single foreign source may also provide an occasion for reflecting on the demands of one's own system, perhaps challenging assumptions that a particular way of proceeding is necessary in all democratic societies; even a sample of one might expand the range of doctrinal alternatives to be thought through and thereby improve deliberation. However, if functional claims are made as to the consequences of one interpretive approach over another, based on the experiences of other countries, some effort to consider a range of comparable polities, or otherwise carefully to select cases for comparison, would be needed in order to draw reliable causal inferences.[36] A strong transnational consensus in law and practice may by itself prompt deeper reflection on the nature of one's own constitutional commitments. But the persuasive value of a transnational source will often depend on a combination of its reasoning, the comparability of its context, and its institutional origin, including its particular form of authority, when considered in light of its proposed use.

The institutional context of a particular source, its provenance, then, may matter, though in complex ways: the processes leading to judicial decisions differ from those for legislative or treaty texts; the context of international or regional tribunals differ amongst themselves and from domestic courts; and a wide range of enforcement and interpretive authorities may exist, each with its own context. To illustrate the potential significance of such context, I discuss below two sets of institutional differences: those between legislation and constitutional decisions by courts, and those between foreign law and international law. In different settings the one, or the other, may have more persuasive force; and foreign constitutional law from comparable rule of law states may have a distinctive kind of seriousness in the deliberations of other judges facing similar problems.

Authority and Institutional Setting: Courts and Legislatures Different institutional processes for the production of law convey different information. The institutional authority of a legislature lies primarily in its expression of current popular views, filtered through the democratic representative process. Statutes thus convey a kind of democratic legitimacy on moral and social judgments in a particular moment; they may also reflect legislative judgments on social and economic tradeoffs, informed by the broad empirical inquiries legislatures are capable of.[37] Foreign statutes addressing a similar problem in a similar way may be a powerful indication that a practice cannot be regarded as irrational or unreasonable,[38] or may rebut claims that legal attitudes on a subject are universal.[39] That is, of course, a different matter from the ultimate constitutional question of whether a statute or challenged practice is or is not constitutional in the foreign state in question,[40] though the continued operation of a statute may be some evidence that it is constitutionally accepted.

Judicial decisions are, at least in theory, more likely to rest on some effort at legal consistency over time in the application of the entrenched commitments of a national constitution; their mode of reasoning is more likely than the language of statutes to correspond with the analytical questions faced by other judges, in ways that facilitate evaluation and comparison. Of course, legislative decisions may sometimes represent serious deliberation, just as judicial decisions may sometimes provide evidence of widespread views of a polity.[41] But judicial decisions offer a greater possibility than legislation of consistent reasoning, based on fair procedures, and (especially where they strike down acts of political branches with some popular support) a quality of judgment I call "seriousness." The idea of "seriousness" entails the fact that court judgments not only have authorized coercive effects on the parties before them, but also, at least in polities where statutes are more easily amended than constitutions, judicial judgments on constitutional issues may restrain future legislatures from acting. The quality of "seriousness" also derives from the willingness to review the acts of an ongoing government of which the judges are a part, and from the relatively clear responsibility of the typically small numbers of judges involved in each decision, as discussed further below.

Some scholars have argued for the parity (or even the superiority) of legislative decision-making on constitutional issues, with respect to the information before the decision-makers, their quality of deliberation and reasoning, and the democratic legitimacy of the value judgments expressed.[42] Legislators, however, do not necessarily see themselves as deciding constitutional issues but as developing and passing legislation. Moreover, legislative bodies—at least in the United States—lack many of the mechanisms for reasoned consistency, or efforts thereat, found in judicial decision-making processes. Even though some legislators engage in serious public reasoning, casting a yea or nay vote need not be accompanied by reasons and frequently is not. Judicial traditions of reason-giving imply a duty of deliberative, principled decision-making across cases. Legislators, moreover, are properly concerned with being re-elected, in contrast to judges on constitutional courts whose tenure and appointment provisions are typically set up to provide a capacity for independent judgment, conducive to a longer-run view. Thus, judicial decisions of foreign constitutional courts represent a distinctive form of authority, involving a longer-run view and principled constitutional reasoning that accounts for past decisions and that will apply to future cases. The institutions of judicial and legislative decision-making remain distinct in their procedures, in their responsibilities, and in their dominant styles of acting; thus statutes and constitutional court decisions may convey somewhat different kinds of information. Bearing such differences in mind, both may legitimately be considered.[43]

Authority and Source of Law: International and Foreign Law International law and foreign law each take different forms and each can function as a deliberative resource in domestic constitutional interpretation. The diverse forms of international law can be categorized across a number of dimensions, including the degree to which they rest on state consent and the procedures by which such consent is given at the domestic level, and the nature of the process at the international level by which the law is created.[44] Treaties are binding international legal obligations with respect to state parties that consent to them; customary international law binds all nations (except those that clearly dissent from a rule), and is formed by a more diffuse process (one to which widely subscribed to treaties may contribute). Sources of international law are especially protean, and may include nonbinding expressions (General Assembly Resolutions, statements or views of other UN bodies, for example) that contribute to the development of customary international law or to treaty interpretation.[45] The decisions of international tribunals may bind only the parties,[46] yet these decisions may be treated as evidence of a rule of customary international law or of the meaning of a treaty. And while most forms of international law rest on the consent or acquiescence of state parties, jus cogens norms apply regardless of state consent.[47]

That different forms of international law derive from differing processes may bear on the normative or informational weight they should have as persuasive authority in constitutional interpretation. For example, General Assembly resolutions reflect the views of many nations—but not necessarily the views of similarly situated nations, nor of popular majorities, given voting rules in the General Assembly and the absence of well-functioning democratic procedures in some member states.[48] Treaties that are widely ratified by national governments may in some respects be more persuasive as authority than the evolving views of expert bodies established under those treaties, bodies that have no general governmental responsibilities and whose authority is based more on delegation and expertise than democratically accountable judgments. Domestic law, of course, also takes different forms, though its formation is more readily subject to democratically influenced change than are most bodies of international law. There are written constitutional instruments in most states, which arise out of differing processes, subject to different amendment rules. Constitutional law itself is reflected in the decisions of courts, whose judges are typically appointed within the polity, and in the actions of elected political branches of governments.

Bearing in mind variations *within* the two categories of international and domestic law, it is nonetheless possible to identify some differences *between* them that may bear on their role in constitutional interpretation. The sections that follow discuss six possible distinctions. First, much international law is binding, or potentially binding, on all nations, and for the most part (at least in theory), through processes of state consent; comparative foreign law is not. Second, issues of selection and comparability loom larger in relying on foreign law than on international law. Third, international law has been regarded as "part of our law" in ways that distinguish it from foreign law. Fourth, however, international law remains of limited scope, compared to what most constitutions address. Fifth, in some areas international law is stated at a very high level of generality and lacks authoritative final decision-makers capable of generating clear and specific operative rules, in some contrast to domestic constitutional systems with effective judicial review. Finally, international and foreign law may have differing gravitational pulls or legal "seriousness" for constitutional court judges, in ways that bear on their persuasive value.

International law as binding or potentially binding International law may be binding on a state; foreign law virtually never is. Moreover, international norms not yet binding on a state may become binding by virtue of custom and official practice or acts. There is considerable benefit to rule of law principles (including clarity, predictability, and coherence of law and legal obligations) if domestic law is interpreted to facilitate compliance with the binding international legal obligations of its polity, under both treaty law and customary law.

Just as there may be reasons to avoid interpreting statutes to place a country in violation of its international obligations, so, it has been argued, there may be reasons to avoid constitutional interpretations that would do so.[49] There are powerful reasons to think that national constitutions are designed to facilitate rather than obstruct compliance with international law. Constitutional interpretations that would put a country in breach of its obligations are to be avoided, for many reasons, including interests in the rule of law (although deciding that a constitution does not itself forbid an act prohibited by an international treaty would not necessarily place the country in violation of its international obligation, if that obligation can be fulfilled otherwise).[50] Where international law has been made binding on the United States through constitutional processes,[51] presumptions of constitutionality that apply in the legislative setting arguably support a similar presumption that the international obligation can be constitutionally implemented.[52]

Not all forms of international law are binding. Some may be nonbinding because they have been rejected, or not accepted, by the political branches of the nation; there may also be domestic law obstacles to the judicial enforcement of binding treaty law.[53] But foreign law as such is never binding, nor does it, as such, become so; ignoring or acting contrary to foreign law will not put a state in violation of its own legal obligations. Ignoring or acting contrary to international law may well do so.

International law and questions of comparison International law, moreover (at least in the form of customary law or treaties open for signature to all nations) is less likely to raise questions of comparison. Customary international law is presumptively applicable to all nations, while foreign law always contains an implicitly comparative question. Except where a state has specifically indicated its disagreement with a norm, customary law is considered a binding obligation of all states.[54] Of course, many questions about customary law arise. Its normative content may be hotly disputed;[55] some scholars question the capacity even to identify customary international law in a world in which the practices of the better part of almost 200 countries must be studied to infer its content;[56] others raise questions about the extent to which customary international law has moved away from treating as "practice" what happens on the ground (rather than the statements of governments).[57] The particular applications of international law norms may vary as they are considered and applied in different national courts;[58] the remedy available for violation of the norm may depend more on domestic than on international law; and questions may arise about whether a particular country has objected to the norm so that it is not binding. But ordinarily no question of comparative judgment about the norm itself arises.[59]

Resort to specific foreign law, in contrast to customary international law or law based on treaties widely subscribed to, almost always involves questions of comparability, of how to choose what to look at. Each national state and its constitutional order is to some extent distinct. Even a right expressed in identical terms in two different nations may have different enforcement mechanisms or institutional implications;[60] structural provisions that are designedly interdependent pose particular difficulties for efforts to compare with respect to only a single element.[61] By the time *Roper v. Simmons*[62] was before the Court, a relatively clear, specific ban on the execution of juveniles asserted in the ICCPR in 1966 had become an almost universally adopted position, reflected in the law and practice of the overwhelming number of countries in the world. To have this kind of specific, broad, and deep consensus among the nations of the world on how to operationalize a particular rule against inhumane punishment is very rare.[63] Where foreign practices are in conflict—even among nations that are similar in their commitment to liberal democratic values—comparison must be particularly cautious and self-aware in identifying why a particular foreign country is, or is not, an appropriate comparator on a particular issue.

International law as "part of our law" International law has long been referred to by the Court as a "Part of Our Law."[64] The United States has helped to construct international law and international law has played a significant role in the application and interpretation of our own; indeed, as noted earlier, resort to international law is necessary to interpret some constitutional provisions.[65] Interpretation is not a one-way street; in order to interpret a constitution in light of international law courts must also interpret and construe international law, thereby potentially affecting its content. In these ways, international law is distinct from "foreign" law of other nations. Foreign law will rarely be so integral a part of the Constitution's correct interpretation, except perhaps where, as with older British law, it has what Sujit Choudhry calls a "genealogical" or historic relationship to a constitutional provision.[66]

The limited scope of international law On the other hand, international law simply does not address many important constitutional issues having to do with the structure of government, questions that are addressed by the domestic constitutions of many other countries. Thus we have Justice Robert Jackson's concurrence in *Youngstown* discussing the relationship between executive and legislative power in the context of three other countries;[67] or the debate between Justices Breyer and Scalia in *Printz* about the relevance of foreign federal systems to the question of the federal government's power to require subnational governments to enforce national laws.[68] All of these cases dealt with issues about which international law has had little to say.

International law is not entirely bereft of norms of governance. Major human rights instruments do require that there be independent courts to adjudicate certain kinds of claims;[69] they declare the right of "peoples to self-government," and recognize the rights to vote, to participate in the conduct of public affairs, and to have equal access to the public service; they may even provide a basis for ultra vires review of government action, by providing for government action "by law."[70] But international human rights treaties are otherwise silent on forms of government organization or relationships between executive and legislative power.[71] True, international institutions like the World Bank and IMF promote "rule of law" and good governance initiatives designed to promote development; their empirical benchmarks may over time contribute to the development of further legal norms,[72] but domestic constitutions provide a clearer set of legal frameworks for resolution of structural constitutional questions that sometimes come before the courts. Although international law may be moving toward the development of customary criteria for government structures,[73] international law is still of limited scope in addressing structural issues of major importance to domestic constitutions.

General, aspirational, or conflicted norms; clarity and enforceability Some international norms are more aspirational than enforceable in character; they may be general (or vague) rather than precise; and they may be intended to be enforced through diplomatically negotiated solutions or implemented progressively over time. Some international legal sources consist of "soft" law, that may, in the words of a critic, reflect only "fragments of international practice and international opinion," but not binding obligations.[74] But even binding human rights treaties have sometimes been described as particularly vague relative to other international norms,[75] although their terms are not necessarily dissimilar to those found in many constitutional bills of rights.

Depending on the breadth of their genuine consensual basis in the international community, and the degree to which their substantive content coincides with domestic constitutional values, general or aspirational norms and interpretations thereof by expert international bodies may be helpful in testing or illuminating understandings of basic constitutional commitments. Yet different sources of international law—different treaties or covenants—may conflict with each other, without reliable rules of legal hierarchy or a centralized authoritative decision-maker to resolve them.[76] While domestic constitutional rights may be framed at comparable levels of generality or vagueness, and can come into tension with each other, they are also given more specific content through internal institutional processes, in ways that differ from the processes of international fora. Many treaty enforcement mechanisms are not designed to function with the force and immediacy of binding court judgments; in the human rights area their efficacy is contested and viewed as doubtful by some.[77] The enforcement mechanisms for domestic constitutional law are designed (at least in the United States and a number of other systems) to function, through judicial decisions, with more force and immediacy than the enforcement processes of the monitoring committees of international human rights law.[78] Both the interpretive and enforcement mechanisms of international law may differ enough from those for domestic norms to create some hesitation as to their weight on the part of national courts, which must render enforceable judgments.

Gravitational pull and seriousness among rule of law constitutional democracies The gravitational pull of international law resides in important part in its claim of legal bindingness; this pull may be increased through the kinds of "transnational legal processes" described by Harold Koh.[79] But there is a distinctive gravitational pull of the legal practices of countries, or groups of countries, with commitments to human rights, democracy, and the rule of law roughly comparable to ours. These legal practices, whose force within their own polities is reinforced by daily iterations of interaction and dialogue, interpretation, internalization, and obedience, would include not only constitutional jurisprudence but also statutes and executive practices, at least to the extent that they are treated as valid within their systems. Some courts might understandably attach more positive persuasive value in constitutional interpretation to the legal practices of comparable rule of law democracies than to international law sources, whether as to the empirical consequences of doctrinal rules, the legitimate justifications for government action, or the implications of basic constitutional commitments.

The gravitational pull of the laws of other constitutional democracies is in part based on reason and persuasion, in part on the transparency and accessibility of legal procedures in other rule of law states. The gravitational pull may also be based on what Goodman and Jinks have described as "mimicry," or forms of institutional isomorphism that may not be functional or entirely based on reason but rest instead on a transnational sociolegal sense of legitimacy, of what legitimate states do.[80] The pull may be particularly strong among countries already seen as relatively like-minded in their commitments to liberal democracy.[81] Although it might be thought that threshold requirements of correspondence mean that transnational sources in fact can have no influence other than to confirm what already exists in domestic law, this thought rests on too reified a notion of what is "in" a constitution, ignoring how reflection back and forth among sources can affect a judge's understandings. While threshold questions of comparability are important, it is a mistake to assume that the factors being compared have preformed essences that are entirely exogenous to the comparison.[82]

Among the practices of other liberal democracies, constitutional law in a rule of law system—one in which the law actually functions to constrain the government—might have greater persuasive value to judges of other domestic constitutional courts than some international legal sources (such as the international human rights covenants, as interpreted by their monitoring committees), for at least three additional reasons.

First, as noted earlier, international law is sometimes regarded as more like "law-on-the-books" than "law-in-action." Even written treaties, created to impose binding obligations on the signatories, may vary in their apparent weight, depending on the enforcement mechanism contemplated by the treaty. This gap between what is said and what is done is viewed as quite large in some areas of international human rights law, which is among the forms of international law most often invoked in constitutional litigation.[83] True, the correspondence between the stated legal norm and the practice will vary in both international law and domestic law, from country to country and even from issue to issue. Domestic systems face gaps as well; scholars have asked whether significant parts of the U.S. Constitution were, for a time, a "sham."[84] Simply because a constitutional court announces a decision does not mean it will be complied with.[85] "Seriousness"—to the extent that it refers to the relationships between "words" of law and "action" on the ground—may be a feature of constitutional law in some systems and not others; it may also be a feature of some forms of international law, where there is a high degree of correspondence between the stated norm and practice on the ground. While the opposition between international law and domestic law with respect to correspondence with practice is not a sharp one, it nonetheless may be telling on some issues.

Second, the practices of written judicial opinions, and the relatively small numbers of members of constitutional or supreme courts, as compared, for example, to the many legislators and executives often involved in creating treaty law, may create a greater sense of personal responsibility and accountability for the decisions that are produced.[86] This sense of responsibility is enhanced by the requirements of principled, consistent public reason-giving in producing opinions that mark what judges, as distinct from legislators, routinely seek to provide. Judges on international courts, or possibly members of expert monitoring committees, may feel a similar sense of responsibility, but in a very different context.

Third, to the extent that part of the special responsibility of judging comes from the power of giving a coercive or effective judgment *within* a governmental system, domestic courts may find more reason to pay attention to what their judicial counterparts in other countries have to say (both about international law and about constitutional law) than to the views of international monitoring committees, or even some international tribunals.[87] Domestic courts make decisions for an ongoing system of governance of which they are a part; their decisions, enforcing limits while sustaining an effective national government, may be regarded by courts of other countries as in that sense particularly weighty. But the International Court of Justice (ICJ) does not function as part of an ongoing government; and the UNHRC, which has monitoring and interpretive responsibilities for the ICCPR, is not a court, but a committee, and it is a committee of the United Nations, which does not have general governmental responsibilities comparable to national states.[88] While expert reports, views, or guidelines that do not emanate from courts may be useful to consider in expressive value-clarification or value-checking ways,[89] they may not carry the same gravitas as a coercive decision of a domestic court, enforcing law against its own government, and their authority grounded in democratic consent appears far more attenuated.[90]

Both the source of the rule and the involvement of a national rather than international tribunal are relevant to "seriousness." Foreign *constitutional* law involves the possibility of judicial constraint of the action of an ongoing government. Such rulings may have more persuasive weight to other domestic courts than international legal norms standing outside the system of domestic enforcement.[91] In contrast to concerns that ratifications of human rights treaties may be a form of "cheap talk,"[92] there is a level of seriousness if one is dealing with a national rule of law system in which decisions of a constitutional court are treated as having binding force.[93] The seriousness of decisions is reinforced by the fact that the judges enforcing the rule live in the country in which the rule is applied and, as part of the system of governance, are subject to institutional reactions of other parts of the government and the public reactions of a particular polity.[94]

This is not to deny that constraints exist on the formation and interpretation of international treaties, if they are to obtain agreement of a significant number of states and establish and implement norms (even if aspirational) in ways that can be complied with. But it might be thought that a *role difference* exists between international law—at least in the area of human rights—and domestic constitutional law. Concerns for workability in context and for enforcement of and respect for particular constitutional compromises may hold a higher place in constitutional law, and concerns for correct formulation of the aspirational norm, and, over a longer time frame, for its realization, may hold more importance for international law.[95]

Seriousness and cosmoskepticism: Breard, Sanchez-Llamas, and Medellín Distinctions between norms applied by international tribunals and those applied by domestic courts may be reflected in recent Supreme Court decisions, interpreting the Constitution and treaties of the United States in ways distinctly inhospitable to the domestic enforcement of international law as declared by supranational adjudicators. In *Breard v. Greene*,[96] the Court denied relief requested by both the prisoner and his state of Paraguay. The request for relief was based in part on the ICJ's order requesting the United States to take measures to assure that a death sentence was not carried out pending ICJ resolution of Paraguay's challenge to the failure of a U.S. state to comply with the Vienna Convention on Consular Relations ("Consular Convention").[97] The U.S. Court found that procedural default and possibly Eleventh Amendment immunity doctrines precluded its issuance of any such order. In *Sanchez-Llamas v. Oregon*,[98] the Court held that U.S. courts had no obligation to exclude evidence from criminal trials where the evidence resulted from a failure to advise defendants of their rights under the Consular Convention. In so doing, the Court referred to foreign practice to support its claim that most other signatory nations did not treat failures to provide consular warnings as a basis for excluding the defendant's incriminating statements from his criminal trial.[99] The Court also held that, notwithstanding the contrary views of the ICJ in the *Avena* case,[100] the "full effect" clause of the Consular Convention did not overcome procedural default rules, and the courts were not required to consider Consular Convention claims that had been forfeited under state procedural law.[101]

More recently, in *Medellín v. Texas*,[102] the Court construed treaties, including Article 94 of the UN Charter, *not* to create a "self-executing" obligation to comply with the ICJ's decisions, noting that at the time of U.S. ratification of the UN Charter (creating the ICJ) the Executive Branch's understanding was that ICJ adjudication would result only in a "'moral obligation,'" not the "automatic enforceability of ICJ decisions in domestic courts."[103] The Court further held that the President lacked power to require state courts to reopen their consideration of defendants' claims in order to comply with the ICJ's judgment.[104] The case involved a defendant whose particular situation had been before the ICJ in the *Avena* case brought by Mexico, but the Court gave relatively little weight to the ICJ decision itself.[105] The five-justice majority opinion, written by the Chief Justice, relied in part on "postratification" understandings concerning the status of ICJ judgments in domestic courts among nations signatory to the Consular Convention and its Optional Protocol.[106]

The attention given to other countries' practices—and the relative *lack* of attention given to the ICJ's reasoning, or to the original purposes of the Supremacy Clause of the U.S. Constitution in describing treaties as part of the "Law of the Land"—is notable. Indeed, one scholar has already suggested that the Court's reasoning may place most treaties beyond judicial enforcement, notwithstanding the Supremacy Clause.[107] To the extent the Court moved away from generally treating treaties as domestically enforceable law, its decision moved the United States closer to the "dualist" regimes characteristic of, for example, Commonwealth nations. Why did the Court give so much weight to the practices of other nations, and so little to the original Constitution's apparent purpose (to assure other nations that the United States would comply with its treaty obligations by making them justiciable in its courts)?

Although there are no doubt many reasons, one possibility is that the increasingly inclusive character of international sources of law may evoke more resistance than in the past. When the UDHR was adopted by the General Assembly of the United Nations in 1948, there were fifty-six countries voting—forty-eight in favor with eight abstentions. In 1958 the Court referred, in *Trop v. Dulles*,[108] to an international survey of some eighty-four countries of the world, a group still more dominated by the United States and its European allies than any comparable survey today would be, with more than 160 countries signatory to the ICCPR and 170 or so countries signatory to the Consular Convention. It may be one thing to align with the practices of the "English-speaking world," or the "Anglo-American" tradition that the Court on occasion referred to in resolving criminal procedure cases in the 1940s and 1950s, and a different matter to align with today's "international community," including all the many countries of the post-colonial, arguably more democratic world.

Further, behind the apparent skepticism about international law as articulated by international tribunals may lie a fear that international fora are hostile to, or unreliably impartial in adjudicating claims against, the United States, perhaps especially in cases involving the death penalty.[109] Decisions of other national courts, enforcing comparable treaty obligations against their own governments, might be viewed as better sources of impartial authority because they would not be motivated by a hostility toward the world's "super-power."[110] And part of the resistance to the *Avena* judgment might derive from a perception that violations of the Consular Convention are widespread in the world and traditionally remedied through apology, and that the ICJ's willingness to go as far as it did in requiring internal judicial redress was related more to U.S. retention of the death penalty than to any particular recalcitrance in U.S. efforts to comply with the Consular Convention requirements. On this account, the ICJ judgment may have been viewed by the majority as so unreasonable an application of the treaty that it commanded little respect.[111]

Explanation is not the same as justification. For the United States not to have complied with the *Avena* judgment does harm to the international legal system—reinforcing the views of those who believe international law is no more than "organized hypocrisy" on behalf of the most powerful,[112] and is a disturbing result for a nation that has historically promoted international law and the jurisdiction of the ICJ.[113] That the international community now reflects a broader set of views might be seen, on the whole (and notwithstanding democracy problems noted earlier), as contributing to the significance or persuasive value of those international norms with broad support. At the same time, the greater variety of views represented in the international community has arguably increased the distance between new international consensuses and the norms embodied in the U.S. Constitution.

* * *

For these reasons (some normatively attractive, some not), foreign constitutional court decisions (especially from other rule of law democracies) may hold at least as much potential as decisions of international tribunals, or international legal texts standing alone, for use as persuasive sources in interpreting the Constitution, notwithstanding the formally obligatory character of much international law. International and foreign law, we have seen, may exert different kinds of pulls or influences on different kinds of constitutional issues. Some factors may favor giving weight to international law; others may favor giving more weight to foreign constitutional law or legal experience. Both, however, offer a potentially valuable "outsider" or alternative perspective on domestic legal issues, with deliberative benefits—by way of contrast or positive comparison—to U.S. constitutional decision-making.

It is worth noting, moreover, that foreign and international law are not necessarily entirely autonomous and distinct. Customary international law (or the "law of nations") reflects the general, consistent practice that nations engage in because of a felt legal obligation, thereby making national legal practice—including that of the United States—of some relevance to the determination of customary international legal norms; "general principles of law," another source of international rules, include "principles that exist in the national laws of states worldwide."[114] A strong transnational consensus on a shared value, even if not part of customary international law, may also have a persuasive value that goes beyond that which considering other countries' practices singly would have, in part because it may foreshadow an emerging customary norm, and also because knowledge that many other reasonable actors have reached a different conclusion on the same normative question, contested within one's own country, may prompt deeper reflection on the reasons why. International and domestic sources may overlap in other ways, for example, when countries implement international human rights covenants through their constitutions.[115] The vocabulary of distinct forms of law, foreign or international, should not obscure their often interrelated and overlapping content.

Comparability: Normative and Functional Concerns

Comparability matters more for some purposes than for others and matters particularly in considering *foreign* law and experience.[116] Use of a foreign decision because of the persuasive internal logic of its reasoning may not require any showing of comparability, though a good jurist will consider whether the provenance of even a well-reasoned opinion may elicit negative reactions from her domestic audience. Expressive, value-clarifying, or value-checking uses of foreign law may be designed to show, in an expository or "interlocutory" way, how the United States is similar to or different from another country, or how the United States understands its own values; such usages do not necessarily require similarity, but they do entail the identification of shared or distinct constitutional systems and values.

Considerable controversy has been engendered by this value-clarification, value-checking mode of comparison. The Court's approach has sometimes been misunderstood as one of adherence to a normative consensus of other nations, or of treating foreign decisions as "precedents" comparable to U.S. decisions. Rather, what is going on in cases such as *Lawrence v. Texas* is the use of other nations' experiences to interrogate U.S. interpreters about the best understanding of their own Constitution.[117] This "normative" use of foreign law is not as precedent (which in a common law system is generally to be followed absent a good reason not to), but rather as a reflective mirror, helping judges clarify the nature of U.S. constitutional values, by reflecting on what the law is in other countries. For this reason, considering the experiences even of countries that might be regarded as negative models may also help in constitutional value-checking and clarification.

Comparability in the sense of *similarity* is most important when transnational law and experience are being considered as suggesting the answer to a functional question relevant under existing U.S. doctrine (such as whether a statute is the "least restrictive means" in cases involving "strict scrutiny") or because they may illustrate the likely consequences of alternative interpretive approaches and thereby help the Court determine what doctrine will best implement an agreed-on U.S. constitutional value. In these cases, to determine what is comparable requires knowledge beyond the immediate question—and even beyond the field of law, if an effort fully to understand the likely effects is entailed; that is, both law and related experience will be important to the inferences that can be drawn.[118] Although such functional uses of foreign experience are in some ways less controversial, they pose empirical challenges and require caution in drawing inferences.[119]

To complicate matters, sometimes functional and "normative" (that is, value-checking or value-clarification) uses of transnational law are blended. For example, in *Lawrence v. Texas*, one of the references to the case law of the ECtHR asserted that "The right the petitioners seek in this case has been accepted as an integral part of human freedom in many other countries. There has been no showing that in this country the governmental interest in circumscribing personal choice is somehow more legitimate or urgent."[120] The language of "legitimacy" here is the language of values, suggesting that the Court has concluded that the "human freedom" to which the United States and Europe are each committed must be understood to include the liberty of adults to choose to engage in private homosexual conduct; the language of "urgency" might be taken to indicate that a functional case for prohibiting private consensual adult noncommercial sodomy could not be established. Although this reference has been criticized by some scholars for ignoring differences in the relevant "constitutional" texts,[121] neither *Lawrence* (and the line of substantive Due Process cases in the United States) nor the ECtHR's decision in *Dudgeon* were primarily about close textual analysis, nor could they have been. Rather they were about whether a general principle embodied in the dispositive text—"respect for . . . private . . . life" under Article 8 of the ECHR, and "liberty" in the United States Due Process Clause (a term long understood to embrace some protection of "private" life)—required re-evaluation of a proscribed activity.[122]

Some scholars have taken a position of "hyperparticularity"—that each country is so unique, or the United States is so unique, that no other country is sufficiently comparable; they focus on differences in the wording of similar texts, on different national experiences, and on the "exceptionalism" of the United States' founding, aspirations, or religiosity. Some see only the exceptional and miss the many commonalities; some acknowledge both, but argue that a scientifically verifiable process for understanding how law works in each society is beyond accomplishment. This view would deny the possibility of learning from history, as much as of learning by comparison, and while historical or comparative knowledge is always and only partial, it can supplement other less informed and even more partial views.[123] While there are obstacles to accurate comparison,[124] hyperparticularity is too pessimistic a view of the possibilities of learning—and one inconsistent with the rationalist, ameliorative perspective of the U.S. Constitution.

Other scholars would address the challenges of comparison by the use of threshold standards. Professor David Fontana has suggested that a "judge should use . . . comparative legal materials only if the contextual differences are relatively minimal."[125] "Minimal difference" may be too narrow a standard, however. There are important differences between any two nations and this approach would exclude those comparisons that may be aversive precedents or that may help clarify differences. Constitutional approaches from quite different societies, moreover, might well be illuminating in reflecting on one's own constitutional commitments.

Yet functional comparisons designed to cast light on how to solve common problems or on the consequences of alternative interpretations of the Constitution are most likely to be of value if they come from similarly situated societies. An initial point of comparison is whether countries are committed to democratic forms of government, with respect for liberal rights, under a rule of law system. This requires some degree of political and sociological, as well as legal, knowledge. Even those who might argue for looking primarily at legal texts[126] could not realistically deny the need for some extralegal analysis of the sociological conditions of legality and respect for rights that must play a role in the selection of comparators for functional purposes. Doing so may require resort to independent ratings, like those of Freedom House's Annual Survey of Political Rights and Civil Liberties.[127] Under these kinds of criteria, the United Kingdom would be among a group of countries that could be a useful comparator as to the substance of some constitutional rules: although it does not have a written constitution that is judicially enforceable as against parliamentary legislation, the British do have a rule of law constitutional system, with a well-functioning democracy that has lasted over a long period of time, and a shared legal system out of which many U.S. constitutional values grew.

Indeed, the United Kingdom might be more comparable to the United States—notwithstanding the absence of a single written constitution or of U.S.-style judicial review of legislation—than, say, Argentina (even though Argentina's nineteenth century constitution was modeled on that of the United States and Argentina is a large federal nation), or certainly than Russia, an even larger federal nation but one with a poor record for democracy, and political and civil rights.[128] Yet, if parliamentary supremacy survives as part of the British constitution, comparisons will need to confront institutional questions. If the question is, what kind of legislation is justified and necessary in a liberal, rule of law society confronting problems of terrorism, a British statute in effect for some time might be a helpful resource in identifying the consequences of the presence or absence of particular procedures for both security interests and individual due process rights.[129] If the question, however, is, what force has a decision of the highest court in Britain declaring a statute incompatible with the Human Rights Act, the persuasive force of the court's reasoning is but one factor; the U.S. Court would also need to be mindful that judicial review in Britain is, at least formally, a "weak form" of review that allows legislative departures from the court's ruling.[130]

Thus, a second criterion to consider is whether the country has a tradition of entrenched written constitutions, enforced by courts. Such countries are more likely to have confronted not only the substance but also the institutional role questions the U.S. Court faces in resolving constitutional issues. Many constitutional rights provisions are designed to protect similar understandings of rights and values—understandings only partially revealed by their text, because their social meaning and institutional context will also be necessary for accurate comparison. Where it is a court that is authorized to provide the constitutional answer, analysis will be grounded in a more comparable institutional arrangement, though attention to the possibility of legislative override or change through amendment also might be relevant to evaluating institutional comparability.[131]

Third, in determining what is comparable, one should look not only at legal and political systems but also at societal characteristics.[132] Without taking sides in the general debates over whether law necessarily mirrors society,[133] one must surely consider the broader context in which law develops and operates in evaluating the comparability of foreign law for constitutional purposes. Aspects of understanding this broader context include the history and culture of legal traditions and language (as when Justice Frankfurter referred to the Anglo-American tradition, or the "English-speaking world"), the size and heterogeneity/homogeneity of the country (including linguistic, ethnic, and/or religious affiliations),[134] and the material and economic commitments of the state (for example, whether it is a "social state"). Comparisons of social norms of moderation and tolerance, which Karol Soltan argues are essential features of "constitutional patriotism,"[135] might be important in looking at issues, for example, of speech regulation, or religious tolerance or accommodation; and, as Professor Dixon's work suggests, a history of active social movements around constitutional issues may also be a relevant measure of comparability.[136] But these comparisons must also be linked with the particular constitutional commitments of the polity, for sometimes constitutions are designed to constrain historically dangerous societal tendencies.[137]

On a range of issues involving individual rights as well as structure,[138] countries that are large, federal, and heterogeneous may offer more persuasive analogies than countries that are small and homogeneous, and that do not confront to the same extent the diversity of views and backgrounds that the United States embraces. These three factors may be related. Larger countries are likely to be more heterogeneous; federalism is more prevalent among larger polities,[139] and may be a form particularly likely to be used when strong differences divide national populations. Internal heterogeneity, federalism, and the greater difficulties of securing compliance with legal rules across larger areas, are characteristics that may influence the shape of doctrine. More generally, cultural, social, and economic factors affect how constitutional law can be implemented. "Prophylactic" or bright-line rules of procedure, for example, may be less necessary to protect underlying constitutional values in societies that either rely heavily on informal resolution of criminal matters or have a homogenous and well-trained national police and prosecution force capable of adhering to legal norms without resort to such prophylaxis. Likewise, the effectiveness of informal norms in producing remedies for government wrongdoing—for example, by resignation in the face of scandal—may bear on other questions of constitutional remedies. Moreover, economic resources may bear on what levels and forms of procedures for legal justice are possible, or indeed on what kinds of questions are treated as legal issues or not.

Fourth, foreign or international law can be considered for functional purposes only if it has addressed the topic at hand. So, for example, countries that have had long histories of dealing with purposeful violence targeted at civilian populations will be more likely to have thought about and addressed the question of whether routine criminal procedure law or more specialized procedures are needed to respond. To the extent that democratic, rights-protecting nations have considered and reached solutions, other countries experiencing similar problems could benefit from considering the solutions accepted, and rejected, in such other nations.[140]

A separate question, perhaps implicit in some strands of American exceptionalism, is whether the *power* of a country in the community of nations is relevant in analyzing comparability. To be sure, all other things being equal, a powerful nation with a normatively attractive body of law is likely to have more influence on other nations' laws—by virtue of familiarity, accessibility, and interest in studying it—than a smaller nation with an equally normatively attractive body of law. This does not imply that the laws of a powerful nation cannot benefit from comparisons with less powerful nations.[141] Considerations of power might, however, play a cautionary role for those pursuing rationales relating to "judicial diplomacy." Great powers are likely to have a capacity to influence, by what they do and are seen do to and by what they demand of themselves and others; "if global culture matters, the 'double standards' employed by some powerful states can have negative effects."[142] But obvious efforts to influence or instruct other countries may backfire.[143]

One further caveat: Functional comparison is appealing and seductive. But it assumes that comparable functions can be identified across countries and can be so identified from primarily legal materials. As Günter Frankenberg argues, if we look at foreign law only from the perspective of what we already know about our own country, we will miss much. To assume one can tell what "functions" exist and whether they are similar may be to assume the answer; to ask the question only from the U.S. perspective may obscure the very different contexts in which other countries operate. For these reasons, Frankenberg argues that in making legal comparisons, scholars should engage in what he calls "distancing" as well as "differencing," efforts to shift the perspective from which comparisons are made.[144] Although Frankenberg warns against taking "shortcuts" in constitutional comparison,[145] adjudicators must ultimately make decisions in real world time. It is for scholars to create the infrastructure of learning on which judges can draw—always with caution, because, as the work of comparativists implies, there will always be more that we do not and cannot know.

* * *

The work of identifying principles of guidance on the relevance or weight of foreign and international law in constitutional interpretation has only begun, but progress has been made. As I and others argue, the nature of the domestic constitutional question is critical, with some more open than others to being informed by transnational sources.[146] Second, the nature of the transnational source matters across several dimensions. As Professor Cleveland suggests with respect to international law, the *universality of a norm in law and practice* goes to its persuasive force;[147] transnational consensus on an issue that is broad, deep, and specific may call for consideration, in ways that the regimes of particular countries do not. Next, as Professor Kumm's work also suggests, the *process* by which an international norm is formed, as well as its *substantive character*, bears on the degree of consideration it should attract.[148] The institutional *provenance* of norms, rules, and decisions also matters, with legal practices and especially constitutional decisions of other courts in rule of law democracies having, for example, a distinctive form of seriousness. Whether and how the U.S. *political branches* have accepted (or rejected) an international legal norm may affect the nature of its persuasive value:[149] their acts may express the judgment of other constitutional actors on the constitutionality of implementing an obligation and might also speak directly to the perceived relationship between treaty norms and substantive constitutional norms.[150] Finally, the *degree of comparability* with respect to democracy, rights-protection and the rule of law, among other factors, matters for the self-reflective uses, positive and negative, of foreign law and experience, especially for normative value-checking and clarification or to shed light on empirical questions asked by U.S. doctrine.

While these considerations are not simple "rules of thumb," together they offer a start at identifying how courts should decide to consider transnational sources in constitutional adjudication. Consistent with a posture of engagement, they offer a "graduated" approach:[151] one that does not treat foreign or international law as an undifferentiated mass to be either rejected or embraced, that is open to both positive and "aversive" uses of foreign law or experience,[152] and that is sensitive to the varying normative contexts of both the domestic issue and the foreign or international source.

B. FAIR USAGE, FAIR PROCESS, AND RECENT CONTROVERSIES

It is more challenging to understand a foreign legal system than one's own. The growth of international law and proliferation of interpretive bodies and fora pose their own challenges. These challenges may call for additional attention to procedures to promote fair and accurate consideration.

Fair and Accurate Usage: Death Penalty and Gay Rights Cases

As Michael Ramsey has written, a basic imperative of legal analysis is to be accurate in describing the relevant facts and law, including the law of other countries if one is going to rely on it.[153] Chief Justice Burger's concurrence in *Bowers v. Hardwick* arguably fell below that standard, revealing (in its implication that homosexuality was universally condemned in Western civilization) an apparent lack of knowledge of the ECtHR's prior *Dudgeon* decision.[154] And according to Professor Ramsey, an amicus curiae brief in *Atkins v. Virginia*[155] may have gone beyond its sources in asserting that China did not execute persons who are mentally retarded,[156] while another amicus brief, he argues, relied on an inadequate study of world practices in asserting the rarity of death sentences for the mentally retarded.[157]

Accuracy and fairness are essential, but not all omissions are equally concerning as a matter of accuracy. Soon after it was decided, the Court's *Roper* decision was criticized for indicating that the United States stood virtually alone in permitting imposition of the death penalty for crimes committed by juveniles under the age of eighteen, because, it was explained, Japan, a constitutional democracy that has the death penalty, "allows the execution of 18- and 19-year-olds, but explicitly categorizes them as 'juvenile offenders,' since, in Japan, the age of majority for most purposes . . . is 20."[158] Although the Court did not discuss Japan, the asserted facts about Japan are not inconsistent with the view that no other democratic country in the world permitted the execution of those seventeen years of age or younger at the time of the crime. Overt consideration of Japan is thus unlikely to have changed the evaluation of the overwhelming consensus that existed on this point in international law, especially given the specific age cutoff reflected in Article 6(5) of the ICCPR, prohibiting—in those states that allowed the death penalty—execution of those younger than eighteen at the time of the offense, and its correspondence with the ages used in U.S. state laws for various purposes identified by the Court.[159] Accuracy is important, but judicial opinions are not legal treatises.

Apart from issues of accuracy, legitimate legal argument requires fair treatment of sources, including respect for the context of decision, appropriate recognition of divisions of opinion, and a reasoned basis for selecting comparators.[160] But what is fair treatment will depend on what use is being made of a transnational source. There is a difference between using foreign law to establish, or to rebut, a universal proposition, for example.[161] To the extent that a rights-protecting provision in our Constitution originated in English law, as did the Cruel and Unusual Punishment Clause, the development of this concept in Britain would be relevant to show at least one plausible interpretation of the concept; evaluating whether a punishment today is "cruel and unusual" also may benefit from a relatively comprehensive survey of those countries that prohibit cruel or inhuman punishments, or a subset of those nations that, like ours, are constitutional democracies with effectively limited government.

A serious transnational consensus on an issue, like that established in *Roper*, may quite reasonably prompt self-reflection,[162] without being understood to call for convergence. Some scholars have argued that the Court should "avoid false shortcuts to world 'consensus,'" and not rely on the views of UN agencies, or even the decisions of the European Court of Human Rights, as representing the views of the nations within its jurisdiction.[163] It is important to be careful in asserting claims of consensus, and to recognize the difference between nonbinding "soft law" expressions by UN-related bodies and binding international legal obligations. Yet reports of UN agencies are not irrelevant to identifying developing international views, and surely the decisions of the ECtHR represent a useful source of legal understandings, as U.S. Supreme Court decisions, which have been widely influential in other countries, were so regarded even when they were not unanimous or met resistance in the U.S. states.[164]

Moreover, many helpful forms of engagement with transnational materials do not depend on "consensus" or require comprehensive surveys, but can be fulfilled through careful reflection on legal materials from systems on which there is a substantial scholarly literature in English, to provide an appropriate framework for understanding foreign law in its context. Reflective comparisons for value-checking or clarification may be prompted not only by a widespread transnational consensus, but by the approach of a single comparable nation. And it can be illuminating to consider contrary foreign views. Thus, for example, Professor Dixon suggests that in *Lawrence*, the Court's analysis might have been strengthened had it considered not only the European countries bound by *Dugdeon*, but also the practices of a constitutional democracy that did not prohibit the criminalization of sodomy, as in India, or of a "neighboring constitutional opposite such as Pakistan."[165] By including such countries in a reflective comparison, she suggests, observers might see a connection between that prohibition and more general persecution under law of gays and lesbians: "the clear distance between the Indian or Pakistani experience and U.S. norms in this context . . . might have clarified at least the lower bounds of U.S. commitments to same-sex privacy or equality. . . ."[166] (Perhaps the Court's earlier references distinguishing the Constitution's commitments from the practices of totalitarianisms might be understood as playing a related role).[167] This point may be generalized: even if a country is not an established Western democracy, looking at its rules, or at its reasons for a particular rule or practice, can be illuminating.[168]

Comparisons for purposes of value clarification, moreover, will also benefit from drawing on multiple examples from a range of practices represented in otherwise comparable countries. If some of the most comparable countries have constitutionally prohibited a practice that others have upheld, honest acknowledgment of the divergence and the reasons therefor would bear on their weight in evaluating what U.S. values require. This is important to "fair treatment" in order to avoid the potential distortion that may arise from looking only at what first comes to mind, which may mislead a court as to the need for or consistency with democratic practices of a particular approach. For there are few issues in the world on which there is likely to be the kind of overwhelming consensus on a specific position as existed with respect to the juvenile death penalty at issue in *Roper*.

Considering comparator countries on both sides of a contested issue also helps respond to concerns about judicial "cherry-picking" of foreign authorities. Although he did not appear to give weight to either, Chief Justice Rehnquist in his dissent on an abortion regulation question referred to both the German and Canadian abortion decisions, which look in very different directions.[169] Considering foreign law in one case or on one issue does not mean one must consider it in others, given the ways in which domestic issues differ from each other; but unfair "cherry-picking" may arise when the Court considers international or foreign law in an inconsistent or partial way on one issue.[170] Professor Cleveland, for example, argues that if the Court looks to international law to shed light on the necessary powers of a national government (as it has done in the past), the Court should also consider the limitations on such implied powers also implicit in international law.[171] As courts become more self-aware about the criteria being used implicitly to decide what foreign or international law sources to consider, they should be encouraged to apply those criteria with more consistency.[172]

Finally, fair usage will often require understanding of the broader constitutional, institutional, and historical contexts of the decision being considered.[173] As previously noted, the problem of understanding foreign law in its context may be particularly difficult in dealing with a constitution, "which to a greater extent than other laws, is likely to be embedded in the life of its national community and may have evolved over an extended period of time."[174] In order to gain an appreciation of foreign constitutional court decisions, awareness of the critical literature within that country on the decision may be helpful, particularly in courts in which separate opinions are not permitted or customarily written.[175]

Hate Speech and the Importance of National Context

An example will illustrate some of these points. A Canadian decision upholding a law criminally punishing "hate speech" arose in a context with many similarities to the United States: both are federal nations, both influenced by British legal traditions, with some similar, though not identical, constitutional rights-protecting provisions.[176] The Canadian decision has been relied on by scholars arguing in favor of the constitutionality of hate speech regulation in the United States.[177] But, as Mark Tushnet points out, "in Canada's federal system, criminal enforcement is centralized in each province's Attorney General," leading to a lower potential for abuse and chilling of speech through the multiple prosecutions that may occur in a more decentralized system of criminal law enforcement like that of the United States.[178] One might generalize to suggest that prophylactic rules of constitutional doctrine may be more necessary in a large, heterogeneous, federal system with large numbers of state and local governments that carry out overlapping general government functions, than in smaller and differently organized polities, where the capacity to apply a doctrine requiring more individualized assessment of particular circumstances and to do so in a uniform and fair way may be greater.[179] Whether a country relies on elected prosecutors and judges (as in many states in the United States) might also affect the context in which constitutional doctrine is formed.[180]

Reliance on foreign practice to determine the consequences of hate speech prohibitions (or their absence) is difficult, as evidenced by disagreements between the majority and the dissenting members of the court in the Canadian case, over whether the hate speech ban in Canada will diminish racist views and practices and how much such a ban risked chilling legitimate political speech or literary works.[181] Apart from institutional differences, Canadian constitutional commitments to "multiculturalism" embody a national ethos distinct from the U.S. tradition of "robust, uninhibited" speech.[182] National legal cultures thus "express" themselves in the contours of what "expression" they protect and what they do not, in ways that may confound conceptual or functional comparisons.

Fair-Mindedness and the Multi-Directionality of Transnational Law: The Exclusionary Rule

Transnational legal sources are themselves diverse, even among liberal constitutional democracies. They will not necessarily align with each other, nor will they always point in more "liberal" or more "conservative" directions, as measured by domestic lines of division.[183] In an engagement posture, both "liberal" and "conservative" sources may be considered. Indeed, fair-minded consideration of transnational sources may challenge one's own assumptions about the best interpretations of U.S. law, in different directions.

However, the suggestion that if one considers foreign law at all one must take the "bitter with the sweet"—in the sense of following supposed transnational consensus on a range of issues—is incorrect.[184] A worldwide consensus is, first of all, quite rare. Most examples proffered in recent dissents or scholarship of areas where the United States is assertedly out of step, such as abortion, or religious establishment, do not come close to establishing the kind of specific, concrete, broad and deep transnational consensus that existed at the time of *Roper* against the death penalty for juvenile crime.[185] More important, the presence of a transnational trend, or even a strong consensus, is at best only a part of an argument to reconsider, and not necessarily to reject, one's own distinctive view. International law, or foreign law from even comparable countries (as on defenses to defamation, or prohibitions of certain forms of "hate speech"), may point in directions that differ significantly from U.S. understandings of the rights protected by the Constitution, or that would modify or contract remedies designed to implement those rights.

Insistence that it is the U.S. Constitution being interpreted entails careful attention to its own history and context. Even in *Roper* the Court first concluded, based on domestic sources, that the juvenile death penalty could no longer be upheld as consistent with the Eighth Amendment, and only then discussed transnational legal sources as confirming that judgment.[186] Although the Court should be open to reconsidering prior views in the face of serious and reasoned domestic constitutional contest, which may be informed by a strong transnational consensus on an issue, there may be good reason to reject the persuasive force of any such consensus here. Both points are illustrated below.

Chief Justice Burger and Justice Rehnquist argued repeatedly in the 1970s that the fact that no other country had adopted a purportedly mandatory exclusionary rule for illegally seized evidence supported reconsideration of the exclusionary rule in the United States; they emphasized the uniqueness of the rule and argued that experience elsewhere suggested that a mandatory exclusion rule was unnecessary.[187] More recently, Justice Scalia and others have suggested that the United States remains unique in the mandatory character of its exclusionary rule for illegally seized evidence (notwithstanding the development of significant exceptions in the last twenty-five years).[188]

In evaluating an argument for change based in part on comparative experience, such as that advanced by Burger and Rehnquist, one would want to know what other mechanisms exist to control police illegality in the countries being compared, and what other remedies (including civil lawsuits) are available and effective here to protect the substantive Fourth Amendment "right of the people to be secure in their persons, houses, papers, and effects, against unreasonable searches and seizures."[189] One would want to consider how practicable other mechanisms would be here, a large federal country with multiple concurrently acting police forces and with some history of police abuse, especially against minority populations. One would also want to consider how deeply embedded the exclusionary rule is in judicial and police practice, whether interests in the stability and predictability of law would caution against overruling,[190] and whether the size, heterogeneity, and multiple levels of police investigatory authority might require a more stringent set of remedies to constrain government behavior.

Yet it cannot be the case that one may only consider transnational law when it goes in one direction—whether it be to uphold rather than to strike down a statute, or to expand or contract understandings of rights and their implementation. There may be sound reasons in general for the Court to be more hesitant to retrench constitutional doctrines protecting rights, especially if those doctrines were developed over many years in response to experiences in the United States.[191] Reflective consideration does not mean following a transnational consensus that would impair rights protected under the U.S. Constitution. But there is no reason to exclude consideration of transnational sources of law and comparative experience where a new constitutional issue arises or where an existing rule of constitutional law becomes unsettled within U.S. constitutional discourse.

* * *

As we have seen, appropriate use of foreign and international law in constitutional interpretation cannot be reduced to a single rule of thumb, nor captured in simple formulae. Indeed, some degree of judicial "bricolage"—a drawing on transnational sources that depends on the contingencies of what is "at hand" in the parties' briefs or the judge's accumulated legal knowledge or the lower court opinions (reflecting some other judge's accumulated knowledge)—is to be expected.[192] Fair usage will depend on the issue and the purpose. It would, of course, be a mistake to rely on one's knowledge of constitutional law or practice in, say, Germany, or South Africa, or Australia, and to generalize from that—whether as to a consensus on an issue, or as to the likely consequences of an interpretive choice. Deep contextual knowledge is important to an accurate understanding of what other courts have held; analysis of multiple comparators is likely to improve the accuracy of predictive, functional comparisons. But, knowledge of even a single other system may enhance a judge's critical objectivity, providing a reflective mirror for better understanding U.S. law, as long as there is some disciplined attention to differences, as well as similarities, in the context of the issues being discussed.[193] And attention to process, discussed next, may be able to improve both the accuracy and fairness of judicial consideration of transnational legal sources.

Procedures for Gathering and Considering Transnational Legal Sources

Reliance on international law as a persuasive source in constitutional interpretation may be thought to raise no special issues of competence, since the Supreme Court justices have long had occasion to address international law. Yet the sources of international law have grown increasingly complex; and whatever the justices' familiarity with international law, foreign law raises further challenges.

Some proponents of comparative constitutional law have suggested that it should be introduced into trial level decision-making over contested constitutional issues and adjudicated according to rules of procedure relating to proof of foreign law.[194] Another approach would rely on court or library personnel to improve justices' knowledge of foreign laws; some constitutional courts now routinely hire foreign lawyers to work as law clerks.[195] Still another approach is taken by the 2001 Practice Direction issued by the Lord Chief Justice of England and Wales, designed to cut down the numbers of cases and authorities cited.[196] Most of its provisions concern citation of domestic authority. But a clause directed at authority from "other jurisdictions" says that "[c]ases decided in other jurisdictions can . . . be a valuable source of law in this jurisdiction," but "such authority should not be cited without proper consideration of whether it does indeed *add* to the existing body of law."[197] This Practice Direction thus views foreign law primarily as "additive" authority on open propositions, and suggests a presumption against using foreign authority simply to "confirm" what domestic authority also suggests, though it does not entirely rule it out.[198]

Such developments raise the question whether, to assure fair and accurate use of transnational sources, the U.S. Supreme Court should consider any adjustment of its own practices and procedures. In some recent cases, accidents of the briefing schedule and rules concerning amicus briefs might have inhibited the ability of the Court to receive a full airing of the relevant foreign or international law. In *Roper v. Simmons*, for example, the state supreme court had upheld the defendant's challenge to his death sentence.[199] Thus, in the Supreme Court, the warden was the petitioner and the death-sentenced prisoner was the respondent. Amicus briefs filed in support of the respondent invoked foreign and international law, some quite extensively.[200] However, under the Supreme Court's rules, amicus briefs cannot be filed at the time of the reply, and the petitioner's reply brief is much more limited in length.[201] Thus, once the respondent's side amici briefs had been filed, the petitioner's side had no further opportunity under the Court's rules for its own amici to respond.[202] It is not unreasonable for the Court to rely on responsible amicus briefs as a guide to its own research and analysis, but at least under the current rules, the parties and amici may not always provide a full adversarial discussion.[203]

The extent of the adversarial briefing in those cases where foreign or international law are raised as persuasive authorities, however, is not fully accounted for by briefing schedules under the Supreme Court rules. The amicus brief of Human Rights Watch in *Lawrence v. Texas*, though filed on the petitioner's side, went unanswered in any of the sixteen amicus briefs filed in support of respondent in that case.[204] No brief in *Lawrence* brought to the Court's attention the situation of India with respect to the punishment of sodomy, which Professor Dixon argued ought to have been considered (though it seems unlikely that the Court was misled on whether there were countries that retained punishment for sodomy).[205] Although the *Atkins* Court has been criticized for relying on weakly supported amicus briefs to conclude that the "world community" condemned executing the mentally retarded,[206] no opposing party or amici disputed their claims.

In such situations, it could increase the fairness, transparency, and, possibly, the accuracy of the Court's consideration if an opposing party or amicus, or a court-appointed unaligned expert, were able to respond to efforts to invoke foreign or international law as persuasive authority. Although U.S. legal ethics rules impose duties on counsel to disclose to courts adverse authority, this obligation is one limited to disclosure of "legal authority in the *controlling* jurisdiction not disclosed by opposing counsel and known to the lawyer to be *dispositive* of a question at issue. . . ."[207] Foreign and international law would rarely, if ever, be "controlling" or "dispositive" on constitutional questions.[208] To be sure, accurate and fair use are likely to be promoted by the opportunities for critique, private and public, afforded by the decisional processes of a multi-member court. But at least for cases in which the Court is considering relying on transnational authority (especially foreign law) in a significant way, it should consider whether existing procedures for briefing are adequate, or whether additional briefing from court-appointed experts, or permitting the filing of amicus briefs in reply, or otherwise, would be advisable.[209] Assuring that the Court has within its institutional apparatus personnel with sufficient education and expertise to assist in research on issues of foreign or international law would be another step toward assuring fair use, and a possible substitute for full adversarial briefing.[210]

Further, to the extent that the Court is able to articulate explanations for its choice of comparator countries, it may help focus lawyers' arguments on those likely to be of most assistance to the Court. Criteria to be considered were suggested above; but to some extent likely comparator countries will emerge from the Court's past constitutional cases, which have referred to British and other English-speaking common law jurisdictions, including Canada and Australia, but also on occasion to other countries such as France. Selection of comparators based on jurisdictions with which a country "typically regards itself as having most in common, generally, and in relation to questions of democracy and liberty," and with which lawyers and judges are "most familiar," is a not unreasonable judicial practice.[211] Other European sources—including the respected German Constitutional Court, interpreting a Basic Law adopted initially under constraints imposed by the allies under U.S. leadership—might be further referred to in the future,[212] as well as the two supranational European courts, whose opinions are accessible in English.[213] Some constitutional courts from democracies outside of Europe are becoming influential, at least in part by virtue of the quality of their reasoning and accessibility of their case law, and decisions from such courts on particular matters may also be useful to consider.[214]

Providing mechanisms for effective adversarial briefing and/or increasing the expertise of the Court's staff on issues of foreign or international law seem preferable to the approach of the Practice Direction on the Citation of Authorities.[215] A requirement that the parties separately address (and potentially argue about) the bases for citation is likely, at least in the United States, to promote "side issue" litigation about whether to cite, rather than what, if any, bearing the citations have. Moreover, the Practice Direction's focus on "additive" authority, to establish propositions of law, might exclude both functional and the very important expressive uses of foreign law discussed earlier. As for requiring foreign law to be raised and briefed in lower courts,[216] while appellate courts benefit from lower court consideration of such sources, the resources that would be needed to sustain such an evidentiary approach at the trial level, across the board, may be out of proportion to the net likely benefit, especially considering that foreign and international law are rarely likely to be of central importance to the federal constitutional questions before those courts.

C. INSTITUTIONAL CONSTRAINTS AND PRUDENTIAL SILENCES: LIMITS ON ENGAGEMENT?

The above discussion does not exhaust the considerations that might reasonably constrain or affect judges' decisions to consult or discuss transnational legal sources. What court the judge sits in may affect the general utility of engagement with foreign and international law. And prudential factors may in some cases support "silence" over candor in the discussion of transnational sources.

Lower Courts as well as Supreme Court?

Some lower federal and state courts already make use of foreign and international law, in constitutional interpretation and in other kinds of cases. Indeed, state level officers may be more receptive to international or foreign law, on some issues, than the federal courts.[217] Many legal disputes now arise in transnational settings, and there are increasing numbers of lawyers and NGOs engaged in transnational legal norm entrepreneurship who bring these materials to the lower courts. One of the benefits of the decentralized and overlapping jurisdictions of the United States is that state courts provide what Professor Resnik has called "multiple ports of entry" for the diffusion and testing of legal ideas.[218] There is surely some potential benefit (including for the Supreme Court) in having the thoughtful reflections of lower court judges on the bearing of international or foreign law on a difficult constitutional issue. State courts, moreover, may be more accustomed than federal courts to comparative analysis, through looking at other state court decisions on common law issues (as well as occasionally on issues of state constitutional interpretation). And some state constitutions bear strong affinities to foreign constitutions on issues of positive rights not textually present in the federal constitution, and on those issues state courts might have particular reason to consider foreign or international law.[219]

But considering foreign and international law as a judge in a lower court differs from doing so as a member of the Supreme Court. Considering foreign and international law has opportunity costs: it takes time to learn what that law is, and with respect to foreign law it takes time to determine whether a country or countries are appropriate comparators, and for what purposes. Most lower courts differ from the Supreme Court in several relevant respects: their dockets are much broader; they have many more cases and many more issues to decide; they do not have as much control over their dockets; and in recent decades they have been persistently concerned with delays in the disposition of pending litigation. The percentage of their cases in which foreign or international law would be appropriate to consider is lower than in the Supreme Court; in a much higher percentage of lower court cases the controlling legal rule will be governed by stare decisis. Routine consideration of international and foreign law across constitutional cases would add to the costs of litigation, and might increase the impact of imbalances in advocacy resources associated with wealth.[220] Risks of error would be greater, given time constraints and the more limited opportunities for multi-member collegial checking, especially at the trial court level.

Having control over its own merits docket, the Supreme Court is able to set its own substantive agenda to a much greater extent than the lower federal courts; indeed, it has so reduced its "argued cases" docket in recent years that concerns have shifted from whether the Court is overworked to whether the Court is underworked.[221] In many cases in which there is a controlling Supreme Court decision, the task of the lower courts is to follow and apply it; in the Supreme Court, open questions, or an issue whether a prior decision can be overruled, arise more often than in the lower courts. Given the higher percentage of relatively open constitutional cases in the Supreme Court as compared to lower federal or state courts, the Court has more time it can put to developing familiarity with international and foreign legal materials. To a greater extent than lower court judges, then, Supreme Court justices can develop familiarity both with the methods and challenges of comparison and with a small number of jurisdictions whose decisions are likely to be regarded as of greater comparative value. So the opportunity costs of foregone analysis and research on other topics are lower; the likelihood of being able over time to acquire a reasonable degree of competence in relevant transnational law is higher; and the percentage of cases that might benefit from such consideration is also greater. Given the finality and power of Supreme Court decisions in constitutional cases and the difficulty of amendment to correct these decisions, reading more broadly on a wide range of perspectives is a more justified use of judicial time at this level. Absent a particularly interested or knowledgeable judge in the lower courts, the likely returns are lower compared to the potential opportunity costs.

This is not to say that it is improper for lower courts to consider foreign sources and international law in resolving constitutional issues. Some state court judges have done so, not only in determining issues under the federal constitution but also in determining issues under the state constitutions.[222] But the mix of benefits and costs of encouraging judges to engage in this inquiry is decidely different in the lower courts than in the U.S. Supreme Court.

Prudential Noncitation, "Silent Dialogues,"[223] and Internal and External Legitimacy

Deliberative engagement does not itself require public citation. There are constitutional systems, for example, France, in which the established practice is not to refer explicitly to foreign law but for it to be presented in the materials before the court in ways knowledgeable observers understand to influence decision.[224] And in other systems, such as Taiwan's, an influential jurist's view holds that foreign law should be cited only in footnotes or quotations but not in the Court's reasoning as such; a recent study found only four cases in which foreign law was explicitly referred to in majority opinions, though with more such references in concurrences or dissents.[225]

But in the U.S. system, norms of judicial candor ordinarily favor overt acknowledgment of legal influences on the judge's decision-making.[226] Whether the Court's reasoning contributes to its legitimacy is a subject of considerable debate; social scientists find much less public knowledge of the courts' reasoning than of the results of its decisions.[227] Yet within the community of lawyers and jurists, reasoning matters, and while it matters in diffuse ways, a failure of reasoning will over time detract from the view of law as a principled activity, an important element of its legitimacy.

Some of the relational purposes of engagement may require citation, as in invoking the approaches of allied countries to reinforce a reciprocal receptivity to different views of shared norms, or to explain a divergence from international law or transnational consensus. But while judicial review may serve, in this transnational era, to enhance a nation's legitimacy in the world community,[228] the principal audience for a constitutional court's decisions is domestic; without domestic acceptance and legitimacy in a democratic polity, external legitimacy will not matter. And, as noted earlier, there may be occasions when prudence will support silence, rather than disclosure, of a judge's awareness of and reactions to foreign or international law.

In *Boumediene v. Bush*,[229] upholding the right of Guantánamo detainees to seek habeas corpus relief in federal courts, the Court did not explicitly refer either to international law or to the contemporary approaches of other liberal democracies to the rights of detained asserted terrorists.[230] The reasoning was grounded principally in a discussion of the Suspension Clause, of its English history, and of analysis of the Court's own precedents, notwithstanding amici briefing on contemporary transnational legal sources.[231] Perhaps prudence favored a focus on historical and domestic sources, since the Court for the first time invalidated national legislation under the Suspension Clause and at the same time sought to remind the Congress of its traditional role of protecting liberty through the writ.[232] Yet perhaps there are echoes of the reflective mirror provided by commitments of other free nations in the Court's definition of "freedom's first principles" to include "freedom from arbitrary and unlawful restraint."[233] Insofar as it upholds judicial review, moreover, the decision is compatible with the thrust of the arguments before the Court grounded in international law and transnational practice, thus arguably requiring no special explanation from an external perspective.

In another 2008 decision, *Kennedy v. Louisiana*,[234] the Court upheld an Eighth Amendment challenge to use of the death penalty to punish those convicted of raping a child, but without any specific discussion of the practices of foreign nations. Although the Court's description of Eighth Amendment method included a passing reference to the role of international materials,[235] Justice Kennedy, writing for the Court, did not refer to information in an amicus brief about foreign and international law. Perhaps, in light of the controversy over the discussion of foreign law in *Roper*, this should be viewed as a wise prudential decision, or, alternatively, as a reasonable omission, given the absence of as strong a transnational consensus against the proportionality of this punishment for this crime as in *Roper*.[236] On the other hand, could it be regarded as an unwise departure from a fairly consistent past practice of referencing the laws of other countries in considering substantive challenges to the death penalty? Especially in light of *Roper*'s assertion that the practice of Britain was of special relevance, and the focus of the amicus briefing on Britain's experience in abolishing the death penalty for all forms of rape more than 120 years before it abolished the death penalty entirely, it is tempting to see this omission as a mistake, insofar as the Court departed without explanation from the methodology previously adopted.

The larger point remains, however, that many of the benefits of engaging with comparative materials may be present even if the Court does not refer explicitly to doing so. But there is nothing illegitimate in such open references—and norms of judicial candor, and the accountability that public reason-giving promotes, should generally favor overt discussion where there is consideration. Efforts to move toward a more disciplined approach to foreign and international law in constitutional adjudication would favor consistency in approach, at least absent substantial prudential reasons to do otherwise.

7. ENGAGEMENT, EQUALITY, AND OLDER CONSTITUTIONS

Equality before the law is closely associated with the rule of law. Most modern liberal constitutions include provisions guaranteeing equality of persons before the law or prohibiting certain discriminations. And yet most countries struggle with how to overcome historic injustices directed at groups based on their gender, race, ethnicity, language, or religion. The U.S. Constitution prohibits states from denying to any person the "equal protection" of the law and, as interpreted, prohibits many forms of discrimination, including invidious classifications based on race or gender. Its case law on equality, however, has been more insular than its Eighth Amendment case law, even though U.S. equality decisions like *Brown v. Board of Education* have been influential resources for other countries' constitutional decisions.[1] Internal aspects of U.S. equality law doctrine—including highly elaborated distinctions in the level of scrutiny (for example, race classifications receiving "strict" scrutiny, gender classifications receiving "intermediate scrutiny")[2]—and internal struggles within U.S. constitutional discourse between formal and substantive understandings of constitutional justice, may have contributed to the relative insularity of U.S. discourse.

The age of this Constitution and of its equality case law may also have contributed to this relative insularity. Newer constitutional systems generally stand to benefit more from engagement than older ones; well-established constitutional orders will already have deep lines of precedent and practice unlikely to be influenced by what others do. However, on issues relating to equality there may be a real benefit to U.S. constitutional law, in both value-clarification and doctrinal implementation, from engagement with the jurisprudence of other constitutional democracies.

The U.S. Court's understandings of equality under the Fourteenth Amendment have had to evolve over time, since enactment of the Fourteenth and other Civil War Amendments between 1865 and 1870. In the twentieth century, many national constitutions were adopted for transformational purposes, some to overcome past racial or ethnic subordination, and included explicit provisions (often inspired by international human rights instruments or other constitutions) addressing issues of equality. From their inception these newer constitutional systems have combined commitments to liberty with commitments to equality and have had to integrate those commitments together in their constitutional jurisprudence. Their courts have elaborated on equality norms in relationship with other rights less encumbered by the need to overcome late-eighteenth-century, or mid-nineteenth century, assumptions. Their jurisprudence might thus be of particular assistance to developing understandings of how to integrate the relatively newer commitments to equality into the law and practice of the older U.S. Constitution, and especially its longstanding commitments to liberty.[3]

There is particular reason to look outside, as well as within, in resolving constitutional claims that relate to racial and gender equality. The legal movements for abolition of slavery, for women's suffrage, and for gender equality in the United States developed in conjunction with similar movements in other countries, and were the subject of a rich transnational discourse. Today, most nations profess adherence to norms of racial and gender equality, although there is significant divergence both in practice and in the legal justifications offered for deviations from stated norms. Racial and ethnic inequality was at the core of Nazi ideology and is at the core of what modern human rights regimes reject; and given the widespread subordination of women and their exclusion from domestic or international power until the mid-twentieth century, many polities have had to grapple in roughly the same time period with how to realize newfound constitutional commitments to gender equality.

The presence of deep controversy over internal norms, as is often encountered in equality issues, might be itself a particular reason to look outside—not for the purpose of adopting external norms, but rather to critically interrogate our own "instincts" or predispositions of which it is so important to become aware before coming to judgment in deeply controversial cases. Reflective comparison with external sources and practices has a particular capacity to challenge deeply entrenched assumptions about what is "necessary" or "natural," and thus deliberative engagement holds real potential for benefit.[4] As Gary Jacobsohn argues, all constitutions are to some extent aspirational and necessarily imperfect in achieving their aspirations; comparative self-reflection, attending to the differing contexts in which different constitutions operate, "illuminates the jurisprudential challenge inherent in the gap between actual and ideal conditions."[5] Comparisons with other equality-committed jurisdictions can be helpful in identifying such "gaps," as well as in casting light on whether differences that appear "natural" are instead socially constructed forms of subordination. Engagement with the work of other national courts under constitutions committed to liberty and equality might thus be helpful reflective mirrors, notwithstanding particularities of the U.S. constitutional context.

Part A explores the Court's treatment of the impact of the newer equality commitments on the older Constitution and draws on foreign constitutional law in discussing how better to integrate equality commitments into the more general interpretive framework in cases such as *Morrison v. United States*.[6] Part B discusses the Court's 2001 decision in *Nguyen v. INS*,[7] upholding gender discrimination in citizenship, in light of related case law in other countries. Parts C and D then consider how "engagement" with transnational law might come into play in analyzing two other issues in contemporary U.S. constitutional law, abortion regulation and affirmative action. Comparison among constitutional democracies reveals a wide range of approaches on abortion; it suggests that the *absence* in the United States of a strong constitutional concept of positive duties of government reinforces the importance of a large sphere for autonomous decision-making. Finally, comparison raises questions in several directions about the constitutional law of affirmative action, confirming Jacobsohn's caution that law's aspirations for equality can only be imperfectly met.

A. EQUALITY AND INTERPRETATION OVER TIME: FEDERAL POWER TO REDRESS GENDER INEQUALITY

With its basic power-distributing structures established in 1789 and with an unusually difficult amending process, the U.S. Constitution relies significantly on interpretation to secure the flexibility needed for the basic work of a liberal, democratic national constitution—that is, to provide a framework for governance that is both effective and protective of human rights, and to express fundamental national commitments and self-understandings. The Constitution's initial concern with protecting human liberty from improper restraint or coercion (as well as protecting existing property rights) was supplemented through the amendment process by constitutional commitments to equality of citizenship, the centrality of voting, and the rights of all persons to the "equal protection of the laws."

Constitutional amendments provide legitimate occasions for interpretative change. But how one comes to understand and construct what an amendment means is a complex process: the text itself, evidence of original understandings, precedents, and historical practices all play a role, as does the fact that the authoritative text is amended at different times and by different generations, each bringing its own set of understandings of what the text means and what the amendment is to accomplish. It is the task of constitutional interpretation to integrate those many understandings into a workable whole.

One approach has been to read amendments in relatively narrow terms, as involving only the most specific concern that gave rise to the change. Examples abound, as in the *Slaughter-house Cases*,[8] which read the Fourteenth Amendment as focused on the status of the recently freed slaves and thus unavailable as a basis for challenges to the fairness of state economic regulation. Another approach has been to treat amendments more purposively, and to allow them to infuse understandings of the entire Constitution. It is this second approach that is more appropriate for a constitution that is so difficult to amend, at least when amendments assert general principles concerning the "equal protection of the law" or extend the fundamental right to vote.[9]

Reading the U.S. Constitution Holistically

Treating the more recent amendments as interpretive lenses for the older parts of the Constitution, rejecting a "clause bound" approach,[10] is justified by a metaconstitutional value of democracy. Among reasonable interpretations, those most consistent with how the weight of the Constitution has changed as popular commitments have shifted and been expressed in more recent amendments should be favored. This does not, of course, resolve what those newer amendments mean, a subject on which there remains considerable conflict even today—does the Fourteenth Amendment stand for a proposition of government "color blindness" or for a normative ideal of a more substantive equality? However its central meaning is understood, this holistic approach means that some newer constitutional texts must be understood as "changing" the whole Constitution—as infusing the interpretive project more generally—rather than merely adding to or subtracting some discrete portion of what came before it. The Court has in some respects reasoned holistically about the Constitution and equality, but in discrete arenas, rather than more comprehensively, as shown below.

In the original Constitution of 1789, equality of persons was at best a subordinate theme and plainly was not understood in terms of racial or gender equality.[11] Deepening commitments to a basic norm of equality of citizenship and to the foundational character of popular election only come later—in Amendments Thirteen, Fourteen, Fifteen, Seventeen, Nineteen, Twenty-Three, Twenty-Four, and Twenty-Six.[12] A substantial jurisprudence of equal protection grew up, protecting not only voting rights but rights to be treated with fairness and equality, regardless of race or gender, in a range of public settings. Most of the cases in which these developments occurred have entailed claims of individual right grounded in the Fourteenth Amendment and asserted against *state* laws or actions. It is in the application of these Fourteenth Amendment equality principles to the *federal* government or to *federal* powers under Article I (part of the original Constitution), that one can sometimes see a holistic effect of the Civil War amendments.

Justice Holmes famously wrote, in a case dealing with the treaty power, of the need to interpret older portions of the Constitution in light of "what this country has become."[13] Plainly the Court did so in deciding, in *Bolling v. Sharpe*,[14] that what the Fourteenth Amendment's Equal Protection Clause required of the states under *Brown v. Board of Education*,[15] the Fifth Amendment's Due Process Clause—originally ratified in 1791—required of the *federal* government, which controlled the schools of Washington DC. *Bolling* was emphatically not an "originalist" decision; it did not apply the specific original understandings of framers or ratifiers of the Fifth Amendment, nor of the Fourteenth Amendment; rather, it rested on an attribution of a more general purpose to the Fourteenth Amendment, one whose power swept back through earlier parts of the Constitution to inform understandings of the original Due Process Clause.[16] Racial equality had moved from a subordinate to a dominant constitutional value, and perhaps in part because of the adverse perception of American racial injustice among the community of nations the United States sought to influence in the early days of the Cold War.[17]

A similar movement occurred in respect of equal citizenship and voting. After *Baker v. Carr*[18] upheld the justiciability of challenges to state legislative districting under the equality requirements of the Fourteenth Amendment, the Court extended very similar requirements of equality in apportionment to congressional districts and state legislative districts. *Wesberry v. Sanders*,[19] which held that Article I, Section 2 required congressional districts to adhere to the one-person one-vote rule, followed the Court's earlier decision that the Fourteenth Amendment's guarantee of "equal protection of the laws" required such a rule for statewide office.[20] Once again, part of the original Constitution was read in light of more recent commitments to full equality. Indeed, the Court specifically rejected analogies to the Electoral College (and its incorporation of the per-unit representation rule for states in the Senate) as based on a "conception of political equality [that] belongs to a bygone day" in light of the enactment of the Fifteenth, Seventeenth, and Nineteenth Amendments.[21]

More than a century after the Fourteenth Amendment proclaimed an obligation on the states to provide equal protection of the laws to all "persons," the Court for the first time struck down a gender classification in *state* law in its 1971 decision in *Reed v. Reed*.[22] The Court then moved quickly from the *Reed* decision under the Fourteenth Amendment to hold unconstitutional a gender discrimination in *federal* military benefits law in *Frontiero v. Richardson*.[23] The Due Process Clause of the Fifth Amendment now was found to impose on the federal government an obligation of equal treatment of women and men comparable to that which the Fourteenth Amendment imposed on the states.[24] In all three sets of cases, a principle of equality law was applied to the states or state offices under the Fourteenth Amendment; the same principle was then extended to federal office or used to constrain the federal government through interpretations of older, pre-existing parts of the Constitution.

The Morrison Case: Federal Power and Gender Equality

In *Morrison v. United States*,[25] however, the older and newer parts of the constitution were treated as entirely disconnected. The issue was the constitutionality of a provision in the federal Violence Against Women Act of 1994 (VAWA) that provided a civil rights cause of action against perpetrators of gender-motivated violence. The act had been passed after a four-year process of legislative consideration, including extensive hearings on the adverse effects on women's well-being and equality of so-called "domestic" violence—violence that often went unredressed by state criminal justice systems. The Court evaluated the challenge to VAWA's civil rights cause of action under the standards of *Lopez v. United States*,[26] which distinguished between "economic" and other activity for purposes of determining whether conduct sufficiently affected interstate commerce to come within Congress's powers under Article I, Section 8 to regulate such commerce. Because the regulated act in VAWA was understood as an act of private violence, not limited to or necessarily entailing a commercial setting or economic motive, the statutory provision could not be sustained under the Commerce Clause.[27] Nor could it be upheld as a valid exercise of Congress's powers under the Fourteenth Amendment, because the remedy was directed against the private perpetrators of violence, not against the assertedly deficient state processes or the officials responsible therefor.[28]

The Commerce Clause of the Original Constitution The Court was concerned, especially in its Commerce Clause analysis, with the need to identify limits on Congress's legislative power to regulate private acts, in a world in which with some degree of plausibility any act in any location can be said to "affect" the interstate markets. There must, the Court, said, be some line between "what is truly national and what is truly local."[29] Yet it failed to explore a possible limiting rationale that would have treated the Commerce Clause power and the Fourteenth Amendment powers of the Congress as acting together, rather than as separate and disconnected, and in so doing, provided a basis to uphold the legislation without creating the possibility of limitless congressional power. The argument, implicitly advanced by an amicus brief,[30] was that the equality norms most highly protected in the Fourteenth Amendment case law—under which race classifications are subject to the strictest scrutiny, and gender classifications to a high level of scrutiny—should be understood to inform the power to regulate commerce, so as to permit Congress to rely on a longer chain of inferences when it exercises its Commerce Clause powers to redress racial or gender inequalities that serve as barriers to full and equal participation in the national economy.

Would it have been appropriate for the Court to have considered international or foreign materials in evaluating this argument? There was no very specific or unique constitutional text the interpretation of which would control the outcome; this was not a case under, for example, the Second Amendment, which is quite unusual. Rather, *Morrison* involved application of two general constitutional principles shared by many federal systems—that the federal government's enumerated powers, while broad, are not unlimited, and that women, like men, are owed the "equal protection of the laws." That the issue of congressional power is embedded in a particular federal system does raise cautions about the complexity of comparisons across national lines, as discussed in Chapter 8 below. Nonetheless, the nature of the domestic issues did not rule out the possible relevance of transnational sources.

There remains the question whether there was any transnational legal source on point and what, if any, authority it offers. Putting aside such questions as whether U.S. ratification of the ICCPR provided a treaty-based source of power to enact the legislation (discussed below in Chapter 8), international law (including customary international law) would generally *not* speak to the question of the competence of the national government to enact legislation, because international law for the most part does not concern itself with the internal allocations of legislative powers. Thus, while many sources of international law would encourage and support legislation to prevent violence against women, linking the problem of violence with more general questions of women's equality, they would not directly speak to the question of which level of government was empowered to enact regulatory legislation.[31]

Turning to foreign constitutional law, the question of national power depends on an interpretation of the power-conferring clauses of the Constitution and, under the Fourteenth Amendment, of the scope of protection afforded by the rights it provides. The U.S. Constitution was a federal constitution before it was an equality-rights-protecting constitution. Are there analogous legal situations in roughly comparable jurisdictions? Very few. There are only about two dozen formally federal national constitutional systems in the world; of these, most of their constitutions were newly written after World War II and typically include both specifications of rights (including equality rights) and power-allocating provisions.[32] Of the older federal constitutions still in effect, Australia's constitution, though modeled in part on the American, does not include many rights-protecting provisions (and includes no general equality-protecting clause) and others sufficiently differ in context and history from that of the United States as to substantially confound comparative analysis of this question.[33]

Canada's constitutional structure and history offer more parallels for these purposes: Canada's federal constitution, like that of the United States, was adopted long before rights provisions guaranteeing equality were added by way of amendment. The "federal" Canadian Constitution Act dates to 1867; Canada's Charter of Rights and Freedoms, including a guarantee of equality, was not enacted until 1982.[34] As in the United States, the Canadian constitutional instruments have long been interpreted and enforced by courts respected for their independence. On the other hand, national government powers in Canada have been construed somewhat more narrowly than comparable clauses in the U.S. Constitution, in part because of the Privy Council's interest in early case law in protecting an area for the French-speaking province of Quebec to operate with some degree of autonomy. Moreover, the Canadian national government has some enumerated powers—including the power over criminal law—that are not enumerated to the national government in the U.S. Constitution. Notwithstanding the need for caution in making comparisons, a 1998 decision of the Alberta Court of Appeals might have been illuminating on the possibility that later equality-rights provisions might influence understanding of earlier power-granting clauses.

In *Reference re Firearms Act*,[35] the issue before the Canadian courts was whether the licensing and registration provisions of a comprehensive national firearms law were within the federal jurisdiction over "criminal law" under Section 91(27) of the Constitution Act, 1867, or instead intruded upon the provinces' legislative jurisdiction over "property and civil rights" pursuant to Section 92(13) of the Constitution Act, 1867. (Automobile registration, for example, was conducted by the provinces and understood to be within their jurisdiction over "property and civil rights.")[36] In an opinion upholding the national law, the chief judge of the

Alberta Court of Appeals sought holistically to combine the 1982 Charter's commitment to gender equality with interpretations of the earlier divisions of powers. Indeed, Chief Justice Catherine Fraser described at some length the "importance of interpreting the Constitution Act, 1867 . . . in a way which is consistent with constitutionally guaranteed equality rights [under the 1982 Charter]."[37] Under the "pith and substance" doctrine,[38] Fraser concluded that neither the purpose nor the primary effects of the law intruded on provincial powers, but rather were directed to public safety goals within the scope of the federal criminal law power. She relied in part on the "gender dimension" of gun violence to support her interpretation of the scope of the federal criminal law power,[39] noting evidence from both Canadian and U.S. studies showing that firearms "have been used—and continue to be—to threaten, intimidate, and hurt women."[40] Arguing that the Charter had already been found to have a "pollinating" effect on common law and statutory interpretation, Chief Justice Fraser saw "no reason to exclude the Charter, a part of the Canadian Constitution—the supreme law of the land—from an interpretation of the division of powers provision in the Constitution Act, 1867."[41] The court of appeals decision, issued over a dissent by two judges, was affirmed by the Canadian Supreme Court (albeit without reference to this argument).[42] But it shows the possibility, in Canada, of resort to later-enacted rights-related amendments to inform contested understandings of the federal distribution of powers under earlier parts of the constitution.[43]

Would this source have been helpful in considering the interpretive question in *Morrison* had it been brought to the U.S. Court's attention? Perhaps the Court would have thought not, since it was the reasoning only of a lower court judge in another country (although supreme courts in other countries, including Canada, refer on occasion to foreign lower court decisions, including those of lower federal and state courts in the United States).[44] Moreover, it was an interpretation of a national government power (over criminal law) that does not have a cognate in the U.S. Constitution. And the fact that Canada has no provision equivalent to the U.S. Second Amendment might also bear indirectly on the U.S. Court's willingness to consider the reasoning in a Canadian case dealing with national gun registration.[45] On the other hand, the Canadian jurisprudence's longstanding willingness to construe national powers (for example, the "trade and commerce" power) narrowly to protect provincial authority might have given added force to the willingness to consider Charter commitments to equality in a more generous construction of another federal power.

Perhaps the Canadian case might have caused some justices to rethink whether the Commerce Clause power could have supported this legislation on grounds that could be cabined to equality-promoting legislation—*not* because a Canadian judge did so, but because what Chief Justice Fraser wrote in 1998 resonated with what the U.S. Court had itself done in earlier cases. In *Heart of Atlanta Motel v. United States*[46] and *Katzenbach v. McClung*,[47] the Court rested its finding of congressional power on the effect that discrimination by restaurants and hotels had on the capacity of African-Americans to travel and participate on equal terms in the national economy. Although the acts involved commercial enterprises, given the Court's emphasis on the effects of the discrimination on African-Americans' ability to participate in the economy, the reasoning of these cases could have been extended to support the constitutionality of VAWA's civil rights provision. Interpreting the Commerce Clause of Article I in light of the equality commitments of the Fourteenth Amendment has older roots. In 1918, the Court wrote that the Fourteenth Amendment "completely . . . broadened the national scope of the Government under the Constitution by causing citizenship of the United States to be paramount and dominant instead of being subordinate and derivative, and therefore, *operating as it does upon all the powers conferred by the Constitution,* leaves no possible support" for a challenge to federal power to use a draft to raise armies.[48] Surely one could have found the Fourteenth Amendment to provide added support for using the Commerce Clause power to remove barriers to women's participation in the national economy resulting from gender-motivated violence. Although only a lower court decision, the Canadian case might have called more attention to the possibilities *within* U.S. constitutional doctrine for upholding the statute on a rationale that did not extend unlimited powers to Congress under the Commerce Clause.

Yet the Court's opinion in *Morrison* does not appear to struggle with the issue; it is self-assuredly confident that notwithstanding the legislative record, Congress lacked power to enact the civil rights remedy of the VAWA.[49] With a Court so self-assured, it is doubtful that experience elsewhere would have been of interest even if it had been brought to the Court's attention, which it was not. With a more open-minded Court, though, foreign law might have caused more reflection on the relationships between the Commerce Clause power and our later constitutional commitments to equality.

The Fourteenth Amendment Under current doctrine, Congress's power to enforce the Fourteenth Amendment must be directed at preventing or remedying conduct the Court would agree violates the Constitution; that is, Congress has only a remedial power under Section 5 of the Fourteenth Amendment, not a power to help define what "equal protection of the laws" in Section 1 means.[50] And the Fourteenth Amendment as interpreted applies only to "state action,"[51] the principal basis on which the *Morrison* Court found that the civil rights remedy provided by VAWA was beyond the scope of Congress's powers under that Amendment (because the remedy ran against private persons who committed gender-motivated assaults). The Court did not accept the argument that the remedy was needed to compensate for state governments' failures aggressively to prosecute and punish gender-motivated assaults. Although the "state action" issue has been the subject of considerable jurisprudence by other constitutional courts,[52] these were not brought to the Court's attention;[53] given existing U.S. constitutional doctrine, as well as the confident tenor of the majority opinion in *Morrison,* it is doubtful that additional comparative sources would have been thought helpful in this case. While the state action doctrine has support in precedent dating to the nineteenth century, other interpretations of the Equal Protection Clause, for example, as prohibiting only intentional discrimination (and not action that merely has a disparate effect) based on race or gender, are of more recent vintage.[54] The doctrinal experience over time of foreign jurisdictions that take different approaches might be illuminating on the degree to which a sharp line should be maintained between intent and effect in giving meaning to the Equal Protection Clause.[55]

Doctrinal Specificities and the Hibbs Case

Different constitutions may yield complex and highly particular doctrine not easily amenable to transnational comparisons. The question in *Nevada Department of Human Resources v. Hibbs*[56] was whether the Family and Medical Leave Act (FMLA) could be regarded as Fourteenth Amendment legislation in order to authorize suit for violation against the state. Under the Court's case law, this question turned on tests of the "proportionality" and "congruence" of the statutory means to a constitutional purpose, an analysis to be based in significant measure on the nature of the record before the Congress.[57] There was no discussion in the Court's opinions of the wide range of European and other approaches to achieving more gender equality in the distribution of employment and family responsibilities and benefits.[58] Foreign experience was mentioned only briefly in amici briefs, and only in those opposed to the constitutionality of the law.[59] The complexity of U.S. jurisprudence on the constitutional questions presented, and its internal focus on what Congress considered,[60] may help account for the silence of the advocates and the Court on transnational sources on the role of different forms of family leave in promoting gender equality.[61]

B. CITIZENSHIP AND GENDER: NGUYEN

In *Nguyen v. INS*,[62] the U.S. Court essentially ignored efforts by amicus groups to bring transnational human rights sources to bear in resolving domestic constitutional questions, as it had in *Morrison* (decided one year earlier). *Nguyen* provides a notable example of a decision whose reasoning and result might well have been improved, within the Court's own doctrinal framework for decision, by engagement with comparative constitutional decisions.

Nguyen upheld gender discrimination in the capacities of U.S. citizen mothers and fathers to pass on U.S. citizenship for children born out-of-wedlock abroad.[63] Under the relevant federal statute, children born abroad to an unmarried U.S. citizen father had to meet requirements for citizenship that went beyond those imposed on children born abroad to unmarried U.S. citizen mothers, including, for those claiming citizenship through unmarried fathers, a requirement that formal proof of parentage was established before age eighteen.

The Court, in a five to four decision, upheld the statute.[64] It concluded that the gender distinction was justified because it was designed to assure a biological connection between the child and a U.S. parent and to assure that there was an opportunity for parent-child relationships to develop in the case of fathers.[65]

As the facts in Nguyen's case suggested, the statutory means were not a close fit to these goals: the child had in fact been raised in the United States by his U.S. citizen father since the age of six, and thus had a biological connection and a parent-child relationship with the U.S. citizen male parent. (The father had successfully established formal proof of biological parenthood, but after the child was eighteen, and in this respect outside of the statutory requirements.) The dissent argued that there were sex-neutral methods of achieving those goals, and urged that assuming the mother's presence at birth to be sufficient to establish opportunity for a relationship was a gender-based and overbroad stereotype. Moreover, even if the physical differences between the sexes in childbirth justified differential proof requirements as to biological parenthood, it is hard to see a justification for the age-eighteen cutoff that applied to fathers' proofs in cases—like that before the Court—where the father and child had been in a sustained familiar relationship well before that age. The result in *Nguyen* was in considerable tension with what many believed to be the requirements of "intermediate scrutiny" of gender classifications, as the dissent vehemently argued.[66] Indeed, the result was somewhat surprising in light of prior case law.[67]

The statutory classification was arguably inconsistent with the ICCPR, to which the United States is a party. Any such inconsistency would not by itself necessarily invalidate the statute, given that the ICCPR was ratified subject to a non-self-execution clause, which may have been intended to deny the treaty the status of judicially enforceable law (absent implementing legislation) and to preclude application of the last-in-time rule (insofar as it would permit judicial invalidation of an earlier-enacted statute as inconsistent with the later treaty).[68] But might the ICCPR, and how it was interpreted elsewhere, bear on understanding the constitutional question, as one amici curiae brief argued?[69]

Several factors would go to its weight. In addition to the non-self-execution declaration, the ICCPR was ratified with certain "understandings," including that the ICCPR's ban on discrimination would not prohibit certain classifications that would be upheld under U.S. equal protection law.[70] Although the effect of such an "understanding" on the binding, legal force of an international instrument is contested, to the extent ratification matters because of recognition by the political branches of the binding force of an international norm, the interpretation given by those branches to the norm might also matter, in this case possibly detracting from its weight on constitutional meaning.[71] Second, the application of the international norm to the challenged citizenship rule was not clear from the face of the treaty, although the UNHRC, interpreting the ICCPR, had found some gender distinctions in national laws relating to citizenship and residence to be prohibited.[72] Third, state practice with respect to citizenship laws, even among signatories to the ICCPR, was by no means uniform in rejecting gender distinctions; the most widely criticized of the gender distinctions in nationality and citizenship laws have been those disqualifying *women* from passing on citizenship to their children.[73] The degree to which other countries had in fact brought their citizenship laws into compliance with gender equality norms—or not—at the time of the decision might have led jurists to discount the value of the ICCPR and other international instruments as relevant, persuasive authority; the underdeveloped application of the international norms to heightened requirements for males passing on citizenship remains a limitation. And Congress itself could modify the statute to come into compliance with emerging international law, so upholding the statute would not necessarily put the United States in breach of an international obligation.

Nonetheless, the issue was one on which a treaty binding on the United States arguably spoke, and emerging lines of decision were in the direction of viewing distinctions based on sex with greater skepticism. At the time of the *Nguyen* decision, several national or regional tribunals had questioned or invalidated gendered rules relating to citizenship or residency.[74] None of these involved the precise issue in *Nguyen*, however, and arguable support for the majority's reasoning might have been found in a 1984 decision on paternity contests by the European Court of Human Rights.[75] In other jurisdictions, including Bangladesh[76] and Pakistan,[77] gender discriminations in citizenship law had been upheld as against equality challenges. Consideration of foreign constitutional approaches, then, would have yielded no consensus, but would have informed the U.S. Supreme Court that in at least some democratic countries with arguably analogous legal regimes and roles of courts (including Canada, which, like the United States, is a country that is a net recipient of immigrants),[78] gender discriminations in citizenship laws had been held invalid under constitutional equality provisions.

An amici brief in *Nguyen* placed special emphasis on decisions by Canadian and Botswanan courts, each of which invalidated under their domestic constitutions laws that prevented *female* citizens from passing on citizenship to their children on the same terms as male citizens, and each of which emphasized how incompatible such distinctions were with women's full equality. The brief argued that such cases were evidence of an emerging norm of customary international law,[79] an understandable effort to establish binding "customary international law" but one that might have cost an opportunity to invite the judges simply to reflect on the reasoning and arguments of these cases from two constitutional democracies in very different parts of the world.[80] In the *Unity Dow* case in Botswana, the court interpreted the constitution (itself somewhat ambiguous on gender as a prohibited classification)[81] in light of the gender equality commitments of international human rights law, including the UDHR, to invalidate a statute providing that mothers (but not fathers) who marry noncitizens cannot pass Botswanan citizenship to their children; the court emphasized that custom and tradition are not static and must "yield to the Constitution."[82]

Arising in the context of citizenship for born-abroad children, as in *Nguyen*, the Canadian decision emphasized the lack of equality between men and women that was conveyed through a gender discrimination in the ability to pass on citizenship to a child born abroad. Invalidating a statute that provided for easier acquisition of Canadian citizenship for children born abroad to Canadian fathers than for those born abroad to Canadian mothers, the Court in *Benner v. Canada* wrote, "this legislation continues to suggest that, at least in some cases, men and women are not equally capable of passing on whatever it takes to be a good Canadian citizen."[83] The U.S. Court, by contrast, ignored the expressive meaning of gender distinctions as to the capacity to pass on citizenship. Yet because the Canadian statute disadvantaged women, not men, the potential numbers of children claiming citizenship on the basis of their relationship to the disadvantaged gender might have been presumed to be lower. This was a point that may well have concerned the U.S. Court,[84] and might have led its justices to find the conclusions in Canada and Botswana inapposite.

Yet the reasoning in these two decisions about the message of gender inequality conveyed by such statutes would still have been helpful to consider. *Nguyen*'s subject matter was of international concern, with results that could affect other nations. Gender equality cases may be particularly likely to raise challenges to deeply ingrained attitudes and beliefs derived from custom, tradition, family experience, and/or religion, and thus their consideration might particularly benefit from "outsider" perspectives. The Court's willingness in *Nguyen* to accept the mother's supposed opportunity based on physical childbirth to develop a relationship with the child as a basis for excluding fathers who in fact had developed such relationships from passing on citizenship for failure to meet the formality of establishing paternity by age eighteen may reflect at least a tolerance for such ingrained and stereotypical attitudes. Where such deeply held attitudes are in conflict with emancipatory equality commitments, a judge's greater knowledge of how other courts around the world have responded may help clarify reasoning about both human rights and judicial roles.

Cases vindicating gender equality as against traditional norms may have persuasive value through the force of their reasoning combined with respect for the particular tribunal's willingness to issue and reach a judgment of condemnation. Identifying the range of constitutional views held by otherwise useful comparator countries may improve reflective comparisons by enabling a domestic court more fully to appreciate its own context.[85] But awareness of foreign decisions from countries less comparable in their effective constitutional commitments might also encourage more impartial stances, by making explicit the biased premises behind their gender-based citizenship distinctions.

In the *Sharifan* case from Pakistan, a country quite different from the United States across many vectors of comparison,[86] a judge on the Lahore High Court rejected a challenge to the constitutionality of allowing foreign wives of Pakistani husbands to claim Pakistani citizenship while access to Pakistani citizenship based on marriage was denied to the husbands of Pakistani wives.[87] A significant aspect of the court's reasoning was that a woman's domicile must follow that of her husband under "private international law," recognized in (older) commonwealth case law.[88] Invoking decisions requiring a woman's domicile to follow that of her husband, parts of the opinion suggest the naturalness of gender discriminations relating to marriage and the association of marriage with a view of women as male property.[89] To support gender discrimination in access to citizenship based on marriage, this foreign court chose sources that embraced a rule that women's domicile must follow that of their husbands, offering reasoning based on highly gendered traditions. For those with "eyes to see," such a decision might prompt reconsideration of how other gender distinctions should be regarded in societies, like that of the United States, that would reject rigid gender-based rules of marital domicile.

Given the physical differences in the two sexes' role at birth, some form of statutory distinction in methods of proof of biological relationship where citizenship turns on fatherhood or motherhood might be sustainable under a proper application of intermediate scrutiny in *Nguyen*. Had the Court considered the reasoning of other countries' recent decisions involving gender classifications in citizenship, perhaps it would have been inclined to apply the more searching inquiry to this particular statute that intermediate scrutiny of gender classifications has generally required.[90] And had it done so, it might have thought differently, at least about whether the requirement that proof of paternity have been formally established *before* age eighteen was in fact sufficiently "substantially related" to the goal of trying to assure the potential for or an actual relationship between the citizen-parent and the child.[91]

C. ABORTION, REPRODUCTIVE FREEDOM, AND EQUALITY

In the above examples, we have seen how reflective engagement with the laws of only a small number of countries may illuminate understandings of equality and of national power to advance equality. That there are a range of approaches to constitutional issues of equality, reaching divergent results, does not detract from the use of those sources as reflective mirrors, casting different lights on the domestic constitutional issue to enable the domestic interpreter to see more clearly the specificities of her own constitutional context as well as what values are shared across national boundaries. Fears by "resisters" that looking at the transnational will serve only as a "one-way ratchet" to a liberal progressive agenda, driving U.S. law inexorably in a single (and contested) direction, are plainly misplaced. The materials are often divergent, and their implications subject to argument and disagreement. Perhaps nowhere is this more true than with respect to regulation of abortion, an issue raising important questions of liberty and equality, life and health.

In his dissent in the juvenile death penalty case, Justice Scalia criticized the Court for its inconsistency in considering foreign law, as part of his larger argument against resort to foreign law or any assumption that U.S. constitutional law should conform to transnational consensus. He noted that "the Court's abortion jurisprudence . . . makes us one of only six countries that allow abortion on demand until the point of viability."[92] To the extent the Court in *Roper* considered a transnational consensus on the juvenile death penalty issue, it was acting in an unprincipled way, he implied, because "[t]hough the Government and amici in cases following *Roe v. Wade*, 410 U.S. 113 (1973), urged the Court to follow the international community's lead, these arguments fell on deaf ears."[93]

Apart from the specific interpretive traditions of the Eighth Amendment, a serious worldwide consensus on other shared issues of constitutional concern may well call for consideration, though it should not, of course, necessarily be followed. But it is a mistake to imply that there is a consensus, comparable to that in *Roper*, on the regulation of abortion. There is no clear, specific international legal norm but rather a real diversity of regulatory and constitutional approaches to this difficult subject, and spectrums of regulation that must be understood across multiple axes: Are abortions generally prohibited or permitted? Is there a right to choose to have an abortion? Are there "indications" or reasons required for legal abortions and, if so, what are they, and who decides on their presence? Is there a time period during pregnancy after which abortions are legally more restricted? Are there counseling, or informed consent, or third-party notification or consent requirements? Is there a right to be free from coerced abortion?[94] Is access to contraception, abortion services and other medical care provided by law?

The relationship between formal law and its effects in this area is particularly problematic. Although obtaining accurate information on abortion rates is difficult, especially where abortions are illegal or highly restricted, many experts believe that abortion rates are not particularly sensitive to legal regimes regulating abortion.[95] Canada, for example, has had no criminal prohibition of abortion since 1988, yet it appears in some years to have had a lower abortion rate than the United States;[96] and in both countries roughly 90% of abortions reportedly occur in the first trimester.[97] A recent study cosponsored by the World Health Organization and the Guttmacher Institute found evidence suggesting that the legal regime did not influence the rate of abortions, but that highly restrictive regimes were associated with adverse effects on women's health and mortality.[98] Laws that substantially limit or prohibit abortions, then, may not produce their intended results, a lack of correspondence that may be important for evaluating the constitutional rights at stake. Characterizing a country as an "outlier" on the "laws on the books" criterion may thus provide less information about the material effects of the law than at first appears.[99]

With these cautions, the discussion below will demonstrate the wide range of positions taken on abortion regulation among the countries and constitutional courts of the world; a significant diversity exists even if one limits comparison to Western liberal democracies. Within this diversity, in most such countries there is some recognition of the need to protect a pregnant woman's life or health in the regulatory regime (though there are some departures). Comparative reflection leads to three other potentially useful insights. First, there may be a range of regulatory approaches that are, on balance, as compatible with women's equality as the current *Roe-Casey* regime, although it is important to recognize that abortion rights relate not only to women's equality but also to liberty-autonomy values. Second, changing the basic structure of U.S. abortion law in protecting women's right to choose, in favor of some European approaches, could substantially impair women's equality here, given the absence of constitutional duties on government to redress gender inequalities associated with pregnancy. Finally, the absence of positive state duties, and its relationship to the structure of U.S. constitutional analysis, contributes to the "rights" discourse around abortion, including pressure for recognition of fetuses as "persons" with rights under the Fourteenth Amendment.

The Absence of Worldwide Consensus

There is no transnational consensus on abortion remotely comparable to that on the juvenile death penalty. Indeed, in his dissent in *Casey*, Chief Justice Rehnquist specifically noted the range of views represented by Germany and Canada, the German Court invalidating a new abortion law because it was too liberal in permitting abortions, and the Canadian court invalidating a statute permitting abortions for health reasons where the procedural requirements were too restrictive in preventing such therapeutic abortions.[100] The call to check constitutional intuitions that might arise from true consensus—among similar and quite different countries, or even among established liberal democracies—is thus simply not present with respect to abortion.

According to the Center for Reproductive Rights (whose 2004 study was referenced by Justice Scalia in his *Roper* dissent), there were five major approaches to the regulation of abortion in early 2008: in the most restrictive category, sixty-eight countries, with 26% of the world's population, generally prohibit abortions altogether or allow them only to save the pregnant woman's life; fifty-six countries, with just over 39% of the world's population, are in the "least restrictive" category, and permit abortions "without restriction as to reason," generally within a specific time period.[101] Canada—one of the six countries referred to in the sources cited in Justice Scalia's dissent—has imposed no criminal prohibitions on abortion since its earlier statute was invalidated in 1988. The abortion regime in Great Britain permits abortion up to 24 weeks for a wide range of reasons, including socioeconomic concerns, and has been characterized as essentially providing for elective abortions.[102] And within the single country of Australia (another English-speaking developed state in the common law legal tradition, with a record of democracy and respect for civil and political liberties), the legal abortion regimes of the different states have varied widely, from restrictive limitations on the grounds for abortion to virtually complete decriminalization.[103]

Even within regions there are divergent patterns of regulation. In North America, U.S. constitutional law protects a pregnant woman's right to choose an abortion up to the time of fetal viability, but states may regulate to advance interests in protecting fetal life or the pregnant woman's health provided they do not impose an "undue burden" on her choice; after viability the states may prohibit abortions except where necessary to protect the pregnant woman's life or health.[104] Canada, as noted, has had no national regulation of abortion through criminal law since 1988 and its constitutional law would impose some limits on government regulation.[105] In Mexico, according to the Center for Reproductive Rights, most states prohibit abortion except in cases of rape or fetal impairment or to save the woman's life.[106] In these three federal systems, regulation not only varies substantively but takes place (or not) in quite different ways as between national and subnational levels.[107]

Within Europe, abortion is also subject to widely different regulatory regimes. The German Constitutional Court has had considerable influence. In its 1975 decision, the (then West) German court insisted that a fetus is protected by the constitutional right to life beginning fourteen days after conception, that the state is obligated to protect that life, and that this implies that abortions cannot be treated as legal in the absence of a determination that a specific circumstance or "indication" justifying abortion, such as a serious threat to the pregnant woman's health or life, exists.[108] In the 1990s, at least two constitutional courts in Eastern Europe addressed abortion, in each case invalidating legislation as too permissive in allowing abortions. The Constitutional Court of Hungary struck down administrative regulations of abortion, in an opinion suggesting that a more restrictive regime would be constitutionally required, while indicating that neither a complete ban on abortions nor unrestricted availability of abortions would be constitutional;[109] the court subsequently held unconstitutional a provision permitting abortion in the first twelve weeks if the pregnant woman decided she was in an emergency situation, requiring more procedural limitations.[110] In Poland, the Constitutional Tribunal invalidated one ground for abortion provided by the legislature (where the woman was in "difficult financial and personal circumstances"), limiting the lawful grounds for abortions to cases involving rape, fetal genetic defects, or threats to the pregnant woman's health or life.[111]

In France, however, under a 1975 law, abortion was permitted during the first ten weeks (amended in 2001 to twelve weeks), provided the woman believes herself to be "in distress" and undergoes counselling and a waiting period.[112] The French Conseil Constitutionnel rejected a constitutional challenge to the statute as too permissive, concluding that it did not disregard, inter alia, the principle of protection of children's health.[113] The Italian Constitutional Court, in 1975, held unconstitutional the *absence* of a broad enough exception for therapeutic abortions to protect women's health, writing that "there is no equivalence between the right not only to life but also to health of one who—like the pregnant woman—is already a person, and the safeguard of an embryo which has yet to become a person."[114] And the Austrian Constitutional Court rejected a challenge (similar to that which was successful in Germany) to a liberalized abortion statute permitting abortions by medical doctors within the first three months, not accepting arguments that the provision violated the right to life protected by Article 2 of the European Convention on Human Rights or equality rights.[115] As recently as 2007, the European Court of Human Rights noted "that legislative provisions as to when life commenced fell within the State's margin of appreciation," and that court's recent case law has similarly "noted that the issue of such protection was not resolved within the majority of the Contracting States themselves and that there was no European consensus on the scientific and legal definition of the beginning of life."[116] Variations in regulatory approaches are also found among the countries of South America and of Africa.[117]

Not surprisingly given these variations, there are no widely subscribed-to general human rights covenants that either establish express rights to abortion or expressly require states to prohibit abortions sought by pregnant women, although one regional instrument defines the right to life as beginning, "in general, from the moment of conception."[118] A fortiori there is no international law instrument itself specifying a period beyond which abortion should be prohibited, or before which it must be permitted. In this respect the abortion issue stands on a quite different footing in the international community from that of the juvenile death penalty, which had been subject to an age limit chosen by the drafting parties of the ICCPR in 1966 and agreed to over the next four decades by most states around the world. Although a number of international and regional human rights bodies have expressed concerns over the effects of restrictive abortion laws on women's lives, health, dignity, and equality,[119] there is at present no international consensus on the conditions and term within which abortions should be legally permitted comparable to that embodied in the ICCPR ban on the death penalty for those under age eighteen.[120]

The reasoning in constitutional court decisions relating to abortion, even among liberal democracies formally committed in some form to gender equality, likewise varies considerably; indeed, the decisions of the German, Irish, and Canadian courts proceed from fundamentally divergent premises.[121] Canada's Supreme Court addressed the pregnant woman's Charter right to "security of the person," finding it unnecessary to evaluate any claim of fetal rights. Instead, the principal opinion in *R. v. Morgentaler* considered whether the statute, having determined that women whose life or health were threatened by continuation of pregnancy should be able to have an abortion, in fact made it too difficult in fact for them to do so; it concludes that "to the extent that [the statute] is designed to protect the life and health of women, the procedures it establishes may actually defeat that objective," making it impossible to obtain such abortion or imposing "great trauma, expense and inconvenience" on the woman.[122]

The German Constitutional Court, by contrast, concluded that, especially in light of the disregard for human life under the Nazis, the provision of the Basic Law that "'everyone'" has the right to life obligated the state "to furnish protection for" the fetus,[123] and was violated by a statute's implication that first trimester abortions were lawful: "The legal condemnation of the interruption of pregnancy required by the constitution must clearly appear in the legal order existing under the constitution."[124] Although women's constitutional rights to "free development of . . . personality" were recognized, the right to life had priority.[125] However, the legislature could permit abortions to go unpunished where continuing the pregnancy would burden the woman more than a usual pregnancy, such that requiring her to continue the pregnancy against her wishes could not reasonably be justified. The court indicated that exceptions must be made where continuing the pregnancy would represent a threat to life or serious impairment of health, and were also permissible for reasons of "similar gravity" concerning "eugenic" issues (presumably relating to fetal malformation or illness), pregnancies resulting from criminal acts, or cases where the "general social situation" of the pregnant woman and her family would make the sacrifice too grave.[126] The Irish constitution is more explicit than Germany's in providing for the "right to life of the unborn."[127] In the X case, however, the Irish Supreme Court reasoned that, where "there is a real and substantial risk to the *life*, as distinct from the health, of the mother," from possible suicide if the pregnancy continues, abortion was permissible.[128] Thus, even among free, liberal constitutional democracies, there is nothing approaching the consensus that existed on the juvenile death penalty on this issue.

Health, Autonomy, Multiple Perspectives and Gonzales v. Carhart

As noted earlier, there are increasing expressions of concern by human rights bodies and in some constitutional court judgments about the adverse effects of highly restrictive abortion regimes on women's health.[129] When Nicaragua in 2006 enacted legislation to eliminate all exceptions from its prohibition of abortion, its decision to do so was condemned by many involved in the enforcement of regional and international human rights treaties, and has reportedly been challenged on constitutional grounds in Nicaragua.[130] The Colombian Constitutional Court in 2006 found a similar statute to be unconstitutional, drawing on international and foreign law to conclude that the absolute ban violated women's constitutional rights to life, to health, to reproductive autonomy, to equality, and to human dignity.[131] In the 2007 *Tysiąc* case, the European Court of Human Rights—in reasoning similar to the Canadian *Morgentaler* decision—held that Poland had violated the requirement of respect for private life found in Article 8 of the European Convention. Polish law permitted abortions where the pregnant woman's life or health was endangered; its violation consisted in not having in place "effective mechanisms capable of determining whether the conditions for obtaining a lawful abortion" had been met.[132] While the ECtHR did not address whether the ECHR itself provides for a right of abortion, the court's analysis demonstrated substantial concern over the health effects for pregnant women of restrictive approaches to abortion.[133] Indeed, there may be some trend in the reasoned decisions towards recognizing that some accommodation must be made for pregnant women's decision-making, at least where pregnancies result from criminal conduct or the pregnant woman's life or health is at stake,[134] though struggles over norms in national and international fora persist.[135]

It is not surprising to find the United States among those countries that allow more room for decision by the pregnant woman and that do not require justification through a state-specified list of reasons, given the longstanding commitments to liberty characteristic of U.S. constitutional jurisprudence. Moreover, as Professor Laurence Tribe suggests, the special concern in the United States for bias against minority populations in the exercise of administrative discretion provides further support for the existing U.S. approach, one not based on government evaluation of the reasons for previability abortions.[136] For all the controversy *Roe v. Wade* has engendered, the conclusion that the challenged state statute, which made no exception for the pregnant woman's *health,* was inconsistent with her constitutionally protected liberty (and, as more recent cases indicate, equality) has enjoyed wide support. Yet a goal of some in the U.S. pro-life, anti-abortion movement is to limit legal grounds for abortion to the protection of the pregnant woman's *life.*[137]

To prohibit pregnant women from terminating a pregnancy that threatens their own health would pose a substantial threat to their well-being and to their equality, liberty, and human dignity.[138] The 2007 decision in *Gonzales v. Carhart*[139] raises questions about the stability of the Court's prior doctrine on the need for "health" exceptions in abortion regulation.[140] The Court there upheld a criminal prohibition on a particular abortion procedure that made no exception for cases in which the procedure was necessary to protect the health of the pregnant woman, in a retreat from its conclusion seven years earlier, in *Stenberg v. Carhart,*[141] that a ban that lacked such an exception was unconstitutional. Notwithstanding reason to doubt the reliability of legislative "findings" that the procedure was never medically necessary,[142] the Court upheld the federal "Partial-Birth Abortion Ban" act against a facial challenge, indicating, however, that it would be open on future "as applied" challenges to consider whether in particular cases the ban functioned as an "undue burden" on the right to terminate a pregnancy.[143] Although U.S. constitutional doctrine remains that governments may not impose "undue burdens" on the right to choose to end a pregnancy up until viability, the Court's shift from *Stenberg* to *Gonzales* on the health exception, and its reasoning, raise questions about the future stability of the basic framework of abortion doctrine.[144]

Reflective comparisons with the constitutional approaches of other jurisdictions—including those liberal democracies that recognize, as the United States does not, a fetal right to life or a state duty to protect fetal life—may yield useful insights on the difficult questions that arise around abortion regulation. Countries whose social characteristics and legal systems are most similar to those of the United States generally recognize at least some exceptions for threats to health as a basis for legal abortion.[145] In Europe, Ireland is the only sizable member that nominally prohibits all abortions except those justified by threats to the woman's *life*.[146] Ireland's strong religious traditions—reflected in the distinctive preamble to its constitution[147]—may help explain why it has the unusually limited regulatory regime it does;[148] the abortion regime in Ireland, moreover, is sustained by the availability of abortions in Great Britain and the now constitutionally protected ability of Irish women to travel to obtain abortions there.[149] Although there are important variations in approaches to health, a number of constitutional systems that recognize affirmative government obligations to protect the potential life of the fetus nonetheless require some legal access to abortion to protect women's health.[150] With its constitutional commitments to liberty and women's equality, the United States should surely hesitate before retreating from its own doctrine allowing abortions to protect women's health.[151]

Social Rights, Social Reasons, Equality, and Abortion

Twenty years ago Professor Mary Ann Glendon argued that approaches to the regulation of abortion in Europe ought to provide a model for the United States. In Europe, she wrote, there are statutes that "name[] the underlying problem as one involving human life, not as a conflict involving a woman's individual liberty or privacy and a non-person," and that try to make the pregnant woman "aware of alternatives without either frightening or unduly burdening her." She argued that the abortion issue is one on which "political compromise is not only possible but typical," and that "European countries have been able to live relatively peacefully with [such abortion] laws without experiencing the violence born of complete frustration . . ." found in the United States.[152] Moreover, she reasoned, "[i]f we are to move from abortion on demand to reimposition of restrictions on abortions in certain situations, we should review the entire complex of laws that bear on maternity and child-raising. . . . [T]hose who would restrict or deny abortion should be prepared to give the pregnant woman every possible form of assistance . . . not only during pregnancy but also after childbirth."[153]

In social welfare states that provide support, as a matter of right, for the health care needs of pregnant women and their children—including adequate education about sex and pregnancy prevention, as well as ready access to health care when needed—and that make a serious effort to allow women truly equal opportunity for market work by also providing generous support for the process of raising children and by working to encourage men to share in child-raising responsibilities, the effects of more restrictive time periods, or of limited reasons for abortion, might be less harmful to women's equality.[154] Better availability of health services, for example, might mitigate the effects of a shorter time period in the first part of pregnancy for choosing abortions (with appropriate exceptions when health issues develop or are discovered later in pregnancy). Some Nordic countries, which have reasonably strong commitments to gender equality and to social welfare supports, and which have female labor market participation rates among the highest in the developed world,[155] apply a term approach for elective abortions that is shorter than that employed in the United States.[156]

Even in Germany, with its willingness to condemn abortion statutes as unconstitutional because too permissive, the constitution commits the government to maintaining a "social . . . state" and to taking positive steps to overcome the disadvantage imposed on women by the facts of pregnancy and child-rearing. In the second German abortion decision in 1993, the Constitutional Court in important part (though not entirely) upheld the thrust of a scheme to decriminalize first trimester abortions if they follow counseling with a view to persuading the woman to continue her pregnancy. Although the state could not as a matter of course pay for such abortions, the German court held, it could do so if the woman's financial condition would make it difficult for her to pay—and recent reports are that about 80% of abortions in Germany are paid for by the state.[157]

The German Constitutional Court was explicit in suggesting that the state should "protect women against educational and occupational disadvantages resulting from pregnancy and child rearing, especially considering the obligation under Article 3(2) of the Constitution to further the equal participation of men and women in working life."[158] It thus emphasized that the affirmative duty of the state was not only to encourage women to continue their pregnancies, but also to act positively to prevent pregnancy from adversely affecting the capacities of women in the workplace, as by providing social support for child-rearing.[159] To fulfill its obligation to prevent pregnancy from imposing unreasonably on women, the Court suggested, the state should take measures such as financial subsidies, preventing disadvantage in employment and education, amending the social security law "to take account of periods spent in uncompensated childrearing," legislating to prevent landlords from terminating leases due to a new child, and/or modifying credit laws to relax repayment schedules after birth of a child.[160] It is not at all clear how much of this is happening on the ground, and the availability of abortion may be quite limited in some parts of country; but the articulated constitutional vision demands that, if the state encourages or requires women to carry pregnancies to term, it must act affirmatively to try to overcome the disadvantages thereby imposed.

The U.S. Constitution is not typically read as imposing affirmative obligations on governments to "provide substantive services for those within its border[s]";[161] indeed, the Court has said, "nothing in the language of the Due Process Clause itself requires the State to protect the life, liberty, and property of its citizens against invasion by private actors."[162] As an older constitution, it embodies greater commitments to "first generation" rights designed to constrain governments from acting in ways inconsistent with private ordering than it does to later-developed rights concepts that require more affirmative government action.[163] In the last three decades the U.S. Court has shown little inclination to develop positive and judicially enforceable obligations on the government to act in the social and economic sphere based on the protections of liberty and equality that the Constitution does embody,[164] nor has the political process advanced in developing fundamental political commitments to social welfare supports—if anything, it has moved in the opposite direction. Whether other approaches would be sustainable as interpretations of this Constitution is a serious question; but for the foreseeable future these are not likely to gain traction in the Court.

Professor Glendon recognizes that in some European case law, "there is the notion that what the pregnant woman can be required to sacrifice for the common value is related to what the social welfare state is ready and able to do to help with the burdens of childbirth and parenthood."[165] But the United States is, constitutionally, not at this time a social state; and pragmatically it is much less of a social state than many of the European comparators. The United States is behind most European countries in providing for paid parental leave, for example, and is behind a number of other countries in providing state support for quality child care; medical care is regarded as a state obligation in much of Europe, but not to the same extent in the United States. These facts are related to the absence of a constitutional commitment to being a "social" state, a commitment without which the burdens of enforced pregnancy pose a greater threat to women's equality than they would in the presence of a more robust system of social supports.

Whatever the appeal of the approaches in some European social states, the difference in constitutional regimes makes it more important in the U.S. context that women who find themselves with unwanted pregnancies have wide room for autonomous decision-making about whether they can go forward or need to terminate the pregnancy. In the United States, more restrictive abortion laws—significantly shortening the time period for elective abortions, for example, or limiting the reasons for which abortions may be sought—cannot be justified by reference to the experience of other countries with more secure social support. Having a child imposes not only substantial physical intrusions on the body of the pregnant woman but also (for most) a lifetime of responsibility for another person. These responsibilities make it more difficult for women, if they become the primary parent, to compete successfully in the labor market under current conditions. To prevent a pregnant woman from having an abortion, then, imposes considerable costs on her, not only for the duration of the pregnancy but also (in many cases) for years thereafter.

To impose those costs through more restrictive state laws without compensating mechanisms to protect her health and mitigate some of the burdens of childbearing and childrearing would raise serious concerns with respect to requirements for "equal protection" and nondiscriminatory treatment of women and men. It is one thing to impose some limits on lawful abortions in settings where the medical costs of pregnancy and other health care are provided for, where there are subsidies and support for childcare and child-raising, and where the state is obligated to take affirmative steps to counteract, at least in part, pregnancy-related disadvantages to women's equality in the economic sphere. It is a different matter for the law to say, in effect, that the state will require women to continue pregnancies without state support for any of the associated disadvantages and costs.

Liberty and Equality at Stake

But this should not be taken to suggest that, with adequate social support, no "right" to terminate a pregnancy need be recognized. To the contrary, the unique burdens of being pregnant, the impositions on a woman's bodily integrity and physical liberty, call for recognition of a pregnant woman's decisional authority to end her pregnancy, especially in its early stages. The context of social support may matter somewhat more to equality-based than to liberty-based rationales for the right to choose. But even with a more "social" state women retain important interests in their own bodily integrity, and in the liberty to structure their own lives, that are protected by a realm of autonomous decisional authority, which at the same time enables women's participation, socially, economically, and politically, on more equal terms.

The Absence of a "Positive" State and the "Optionality" of Government Interests

The absence of developed ideas of government duties under the Constitution influences or structures the conceptual discourses of both "pro-life" and "pro-choice" proponents, as well as the Court's decisions. This structure not only places considerable pressure on rights-based arguments for autonomous decision-making by the pregnant woman (advanced by the pro-choice community), but may also tend to reinforce an individual rights framework of argument by those who believe government has an obligation to protect fetal life. Under *Roe* and *Casey*, states *may*—but need not—prohibit nontherapeutic abortions after viability.[166] If it is entirely up to governments to choose whether or not to protect interests in the potential life of fetuses—that is, if states do not, as a constitutional matter, owe an enforceable duty of protection[167]—then those who regard fetal life as so closely related to human life that it must receive protection will be drawn to arguments from individual rights and to characterizations of the fetus as a constitutional "person" with "rights" against state action (such as laws allowing abortion) that can be asserted in opposition to the pregnant woman's rights, as is reflected in some of the pro-life anti-abortion rights literature in the United States.[168]

As Professor Glendon argued, the *expressive* features of abortion law matter.[169] For those in the polity who believe that fetal life requires some degree of protection, the current structure of U.S. constitutional law—under which states may, but need not, legislate to advance interests in the potential life of the fetus—must be deeply troubling (as are paternalistic arguments for restricting women's decisions for those committed to women's rights to control their own bodies). In some jurisdictions with reasoned constitutional decisions on abortion, courts have held that a fetus, though not a person with an individual right to life, is a form of life within the constitutional *value* of life that the state was required to protect.[170] Recognition of a distinction between individual *rights* and constitutional *values* in life on which the government must act gives greater weight to the moral views of those who view fetal life as deserving of protection while still allowing a capacity in law to recognize the rights of women who seek abortions.[171] Such an approach, however, is not likely to develop in the United States given other commitments of U.S. constitutionalism, discussed further below.

* * *

Laws and social conditions that restrict women's ability to choose abortions have an enormous effect on their equality. Pregnancy imposes health risks, physical changes, and in some cases physical constraints on the woman for many months; childbirth compounds the health risks.[172] Having a child is not a discrete and isolated event; it leads to others that become constitutive of and demanding on one's life and time. Although parenting should be a two-person obligation, it is all too easy for fathers to be uninvolved, a situation that has proved obdurate even in the face of marginally successful legal efforts at change (as in Norway).[173] The obligations of parenting, while bringing to many rewards of transcendent meaning and value, are associated with women having lower earning capacity and less advancement than comparably educated and situated men. To blink these facts away is not acceptable in a constitutional system committed to gender equality.

The social interests in recognizing the connection between fetal life and born human life have undeniable force. But they can be advanced in a variety of ways, including perhaps most importantly through public health and education measures,[174] and do not by themselves answer whether women's choices to remain pregnant—a matter of enormous personal import—should be limited by law. Restrictive limitations of abortion timing may undermine a regulatory regime's goals, by leading some women to travel to obtain abortion outside the jurisdiction or to seek illegal (and hence less safe) abortions. Reasons-based regimes, even those that include the criteria found in the more liberal regimes,[175] are in tension with autonomy; they may obstruct performance of abortions (even those substantively meeting the reasons requirement of a legislative scheme), especially if implemented through onerous third-party evaluations. Although some other liberal democratic societies assert interests in restricting abortions to reasons of a certain gravity, or limit the period for choosing abortion more than in the United States, many of them mitigate the effects of these restrictions through various social supports. Comparative reflection thus suggests the need for a more autonomy-based model here to sustain acceptable levels of gender equality (or to avoid unacceptable forms of inequality), especially given the U.S. constitutional approach to social support for children and their parents.

D. OPTIONAL BUT "COMPELLING" STATE INTERESTS IN U.S. CONSTITUTIONAL LAW: AFFIRMATIVE ACTION IN THE UNITED STATES AND INDIA

In the previous section, a paradox in U.S. constitutional law was identified: some "state interests" (such as the interest in fetal life) are treated as important or compelling enough to justify intrusions on individual rights otherwise protected by the Constitution, but those same interests are treated as optional for governments to decide whether to pursue. Reflecting comparatively on constitutional approaches to affirmative action to improve the situation of groups historically discriminated against brings this paradox into view. Consider *Grutter v. Bollinger*,[176] in which the U.S. Court upheld a public university law school's authority to consider race in admissions, in light of a compelling state interest of promoting diversity in its classrooms. Justice Clarence Thomas argued in dissent that the state had no compelling interest in having a public law school at all, or in having an academically elite law school which required special consideration of race to maintain the desired diversity, as evidenced by the facts that many states had no law schools or no elite law schools.[177] Plainly the Court's majority envisions compelling interests in a different way, as more optional—as interests that may, but need not, be invoked by governments, but which, if they are invoked, are of the highest order in justifying otherwise prohibited classifications.

This oddly optional character of "compelling" government interests results from at least two important features of U.S. constitutional law: first, its commitment to the idea that there are no, or few, judicially enforceable "positive" government obligations, and second, its commitment to federalism and democracy, to affording some latitude for decision-making in state and local governments. If compelling interests were regarded as mandatory, courts would be called on to enforce and monitor their implementation.[178] The structure of equal protection analysis is not derived simply from the need to elaborate interpretive standards for its judicial enforcement, but from the need to do so in a setting divorced from a complementary interpretive tradition of government obligations and committed to (relatively) decentralized decision-making (at least in some policy areas).

Another factor—the age of the U.S. Constitution—is also worth noting in understanding this body of law. Many modern constitutional texts reflect choices to be more explicit than the U.S Constitution in describing the bases on which discrimination is prohibited and in authorizing affirmative measures.

International human rights agreements, likewise, specifically authorize the use of temporary measures that employ otherwise prohibited categories (e.g., of race or gender) in order to advance the position of subordinated groups.[179] Authority in positive law sometimes matters to the meaning and remedial mechanisms of rights: in Canada the constitution's text authorizes affirmative action programs, and in India, the text *requires* some such programs, for example, through reservation of seats in legislatures.[180]

Of course, the relative opacity of the text of the U.S. Constitution is only one factor in understanding the hesitation of U.S. constitutional law to uphold affirmative action based on race. Original understandings of the Fourteenth Amendment are ambiguous.[181] Equal protection law in the United States has become over the last thirty years increasingly symmetrical, treating the prohibited act as that of classifying according to a criterion (such as race or gender) regardless of whether the classification is claimed to burden men or women, whites or blacks, in tension with more substantive understandings of constitutional equality.[182] Social beliefs play a significant role; to the extent that social recognition of the presence (and harms) of discrimination is lacking, efforts to change the status quo may appear unjust.[183]

Constitutional Solidarity, Societal Discrimination, and Individualized Consideration

More generally, the constitutional basis for the kind of solidarity that might support affirmative measures is much weaker in the United States than, for example, in India, a large, diverse, democratic country with more than a half century of experience with constitutionally required or authorized forms of affirmative action.[184] The Indian Constitution was conceived as a transformational instrument, designed to overcome a feudal system of hierarchical inequality embodied in the caste system that had been nurtured by an intermeshing of religion, culture, and sociolegal practice.[185] The constitution names "untouchability" under the caste system as the object of its prohibitions, and specifies that "its practice in any form is forbidden"; it also includes a number of provisions directed at "private" practices of subordination, including denials of access based on caste to shops, restaurants, drinking wells, or places of public entertainment.[186] In the United States, by contrast, notwithstanding the Thirteenth Amendment's abolition of slavery and the Court's interpretation that Congress's power to enforce that amendment extends to "'all badges and incidents'" of slavery,[187] continuing "societal discrimination" based on race—which can be traced back to the race-based system of slavery—has been rejected in several opinions as a basis for upholding affirmative action (or, by implication, for establishing a constitutional violation from the government's failure to act affirmatively).[188]

On the one hand, comparative perspectives might be relied on to challenge the idea that equality under law can be vindicated without greater affirmative attention to "societal discrimination," or that the effort to ban government discrimination as a mechanism to overcome a historic legacy of discrimination based on race, or caste, must be joined with an effort to uproot the social practices with which past discrimination was entwined. But given the absence of a clear positive basis in the U.S. Constitution's text for affirmative action, a comparative perspective might suggest more caution, especially in the absence of strong social consensus. The existing requirements in the case law for affirmative measures to meet rigorous requirements for use, including requirements of individualized consideration of each application, might be understood as reflecting such caution.

Even overtly transformative constitutions, such as India's, have struggled with how to define equality in a situation of ongoing inequalities associated with one's birth position. Some members of the Indian Supreme Court have read the authorization for affirmative uses of caste or class as exceptions to a general equality principle of merit-based government employment and educational access.[189] Others have read the general equality provisions as themselves being compatible with (or even requiring) affirmative action to provide an equalizing lift to those who are members of historically disadvantaged social classes.[190] Concerns for whether the use of criteria of discrimination to afford benefits helps overcome, or further instantiates, material disadvantages, stereotypes, and polarities among groups exist in both the U.S. and Indian discourses. The evidence in India suggests that affirmative measures may help bridge gaps in material access to social goods and positions, but leaves in question the role of such measures in overcoming, reinforcing, or increasing, stereotypes and class polarities or even violence.[191] Requirements of individualized consideration, as the U.S. case law demands, might be thought to mitigate the potential harm that flat-out quotas or reservation of seats may do in reinforcing divisions.[192]

Temporary Measures?

A more specific kind of remedial issue is also illustrated by India, one raised by the U.S. Supreme Court's 2003 decision indicating that race-conscious measures must have durational limits.[193] When first enacted in 1950, the Indian Constitution provided for reservations of seats in legislative bodies for members of disadvantaged castes, subject to a ten-year limitation. These reservations have been regularly extended by constitutional amendment every ten years, and remain in force.[194] One might read this course of events in different ways. The repeated extensions might be seen as appropriate responses to intransigent inequalities related to a caste system in place for millenia. Or one might view the extensions as related to the entrenchment of interests based on group membership among the legislators whose responsibility it is, under the Indian constitution's amendment provisions, to adopt constitutional amendments—suggesting that reliance on time limits to assure the temporary character of such measures may not be effective. Although bargaining and agreement with other groups was in all likelihood necessary to secure these extensions, these groups may have self-interested as well as public-interested motivations for agreement. It will thus be very difficult to tease apart these narratives. The court-supervised durational limits of U.S. law present a very different institutional setting, in which court-ordered terminations of such programs appears a real possibility.

Super-Classifications and Specially Subordinated Groups

Comparative experience looks in other directions as well. U.S. equal protection jurisprudence does not distinguish between African-Americans—the racial group that suffered the most severe, persistent, and long-standing forms of legalized subordination through the institution of slavery—and other racial groups; indeed, U.S. constitutional law imposes a requirement of even-handedness in the level of judicial scrutiny any use of race is given, regardless of its purpose.[195] The Indian Constitution distinguishes among different categories of disadvantaged social groups.[196] In one Indian Supreme Court opinion, Justice Krishna Iyer suggested that the Indian Constitution should be interpreted to accommodate greater degrees of affirmative action for those who are members of the most consistently subordinated groups—the Scheduled Tribes and Scheduled Castes ("dalits," or "harijans," formerly called "untouchables")—whose experience lay at the heart of the past the Indian Constitution sought to reject. However, he would not treat in the same way the members of the "other backward classes," also referred to in the Constitution as eligible for special treatment, because the "Constitution itself makes a super-classification between harijans and others, grounded on the fundamental disparity in our society and the imperative social urgency of raising the former's sunken status."[197]

Does this kind of reasoning open the possibility that the very specific experience of African-Americans, who became the unique objects of a brutal system of slavery and legalized subordination in ways that differ in extent and duration from the treatment of other racial or ethnic groups, might have warranted a different course in the development of U.S. equal protection law?[198] Could the Thirteenth Amendment's abolition of slavery and the Fifteenth Amendment's references to race, color, or previous condition of servitude have served as textual markers of a special recognition of the super-subordinated status of those whose race and color identified them as slaves or descendants thereof?

Too much time and too many precedents may by now establish the generality of application of the U.S. approach to the equal protection clause for this to be, on the whole, an acceptable interpretive move. Apart from questions of doctrinal stability, social changes, including immigration and intermarriage in the generations since slavery, would greatly complicate any effort now to introduce such an approach. Although the basic structure of U.S. equal protection analysis is so well-established that its outlines are unlikely to change, seeing the question through the eyes of another country's constitutional system may provide a new lens on evaluating those optional but compelling interests that may be asserted within U.S. equal protection law, including interests in overcoming the effects of the entwined governmental and societal discrimination that so pervasively subordinated African-Americans for so long.[199]

* * *

Given the great stain on the American Constitution wrought by slavery and the *Plessy* era, there are compelling reasons to be open to rethinking how our constitutional doctrine on racial equality might be improved. More generally, on issues of equality likely to arise in the future—women's service in military combat positions, gays and lesbians serving openly in the military, same-sex marriage, reparations for slavery, regulation and contest over new assisted reproduction technologies—women and men, as lawyers and in governments, legislatures and courts, will be called on to decide what equality means and requires, what human liberty means and requires, what are legitimate (or compelling) government reasons for drawing distinctions or for regulating private choices, and what are appropriate means of doing so. These are efforts that can benefit from all the thinking and rethinking—in local, national, and transnational locations, informed by the experience of others—that can be mustered. Looking to well-reasoned judgments of other comparable jurisdictions, as well as to the uses made of these exclusionary categories by other regimes, can provide forms of checking on our own moral and constitutional blindness—the blindness that beset the six justices who formed the majority in *Goesaert v. Cleary* in 1948 to uphold exclusion of women from "male" professions like bar-keeping,[200] or the eight justices who voted with the majority in *Plessy* to uphold state-mandated segregation of the races.

8. CONSTITUTIONAL PARTICULARITIES, FEDERALISM, AND THE TRANSNATIONAL

If engagement with the equality law of other constitutional democracies affords multiple perspectives on shared constitutional problems and aspirations, engaging with the constitutional law of other governments' structures offers somewhat less accessible but nonetheless interesting perspectives on ideas of well-organized constitutional government. A post–World War II model of constitutional federalism has emerged, of a form promoted by the United States and the victorious Allies in post-war Germany. This model has at least two salient characteristics: As federal states, these countries have two or more levels of constitutionally secured government, one national, the other subnational, each of which has jurisdiction based on territory and exercises some general powers of government with respect to the people in each territory. Second, these federal states have a relatively robust set of rights guaranteed by a constitution to the people of the entire country, which rights are given national interpretation and enforcement through some form of constitutional court.[1]

But as striking as is this post–World War II model of federalism, so too are the many variations among federal systems. Federalism, while standing for a common idea of shared governmental power over the same territory, can take many different forms. Because of these variations, the benefits to courts of looking to comparative constitutional law on specific issues of federalism are likely to be more limited than in some other areas of comparative constitutional law, as this chapter explores in Part A. Different federal systems, moreover, will have courts that are more, or less, open to the transnational in constitutional interpretation, for reasons that relate in part to the nature of the most pressing issues in particular federal constitutional system, as explored in Part B. A comparison of case law in the United States and Canada in Part C illustrates these points, and explains how the federal character of the U.S. system reinforces arguments in favor of engagement, rather than convergence, as the posture that in the United States best "fits" with the Constitution and its rich, complex, and in some respects troubling history.

A. FEDERALISM AND THE LIMITS OF INTERPRETIVE ENGAGEMENT

Some of the U.S. Court's early engagements with foreign and international law occurred in the context of federalism issues. In the eighteenth and nineteenth centuries, justices invoked foreign or international law in federalism cases involving the judicial power, Indian tribes, the Commerce Clause, and state powers of taxation.[2] In the twentieth century, Justice Frankfurter argued in at least two cases that the constitutional law of intergovernmental tax immunity in the United States ought to follow the approaches taken in Australia or Canada.[3] Writing for the Court in *Wickard v. Filburn*,[4] Justice Jackson alluded to the powers of the federal governments in other countries that were also major wheat exporters in implicit support of his conclusion that the national government had power to regulate wheat production, even on family farms. And more recently, Justice Breyer relied on the experience of other federal systems to argue in dissent that federal "commandeering" of state or local government officials is constitutional.[5]

Yet as we shall see, drawing inferences from other courts' conclusions about federalism issues within their own system poses a particular set of challenges. It is not that comparison can never offer illumination, but the task of "getting it right" in understanding another system's decisions is more difficult and the likely benefit of comparison on particular issues of doctrine may be smaller. Three key features distinguish engagement with issues of federalism from engagement with many issues of individual rights.

Historically Contingent Compromises

First, constitutional federalisms are historically contingent, emerging out of necessarily political compromise among existing power holders, corresponding to a particular array of issues at a particular moment in time. These arrays of power and their translation into federalist bargains are likely to differ, at least in some important details, among different federalisms (even as it is clear that some functions, such as defense, are typically allocated to central governments in federal systems). Because most federal systems are created through intensely political processes designed to accommodate the competing demands for power, recognition, autonomy, and authority of groups of existing power holders, federalisms are peculiarly the product of political compromise in particular historically situated moments, designed as practical rather than principled accommodations of competing interests.

Constitutional courts have acknowledged these compromises with remarkable candor. Thus, in South Africa, the Constitutional Court explained that one of the constitutional principles to which the new constitution had to adhere, guaranteeing no diminution in "[t]he powers and functions of the provinces," was designed "to encourage political formations which had refused to participate in the transition process to change their minds and to support the transition to a new political order."[6] Some thirty years earlier, the U.S. Supreme Court in *Reynolds v. Sims* had explained that the U.S. Senate was "conceived out of compromise and concession." Thus, the Court held, the Constitution's allocation of two Senators per state regardless of population did not stand for a more generalizable principle allowing the states to rely on similar apportionment methods in designing the upper chambers of state legislatures.[7] The fact that the constitutional rule for the Senate reflected a compromise meant that it did not stand for a broader constitutional principle.

The Canadian Supreme Court as well has recognized how compromises that inhere in the initial federal bargain may be at odds with more general constitutional principles. In 1996, that court rejected an argument that the equality clause of the 1982 Charter of Rights and Freedoms required government funding of denominational schools for Jewish or non-Catholic Christian children on the same terms as for Catholic denominational schools.[8] Section 93 of Canada's 1867 Constitution Act guaranteed the existing rights of certain "dissentient" or minority denominational schools (such as Catholic schools in predominantly Protestant Ontario, or Protestant schools in Quebec). After the Charter became effective in 1982, Ontario's funding for Catholic schools was challenged as a violation of the Charter's religious freedom rights and equal protection guarantees; the gist of the plaintiffs' claim was that the failure to fund Jewish schools or certain non-Catholic Christian schools in Ontario violated these Charter rights. Rejecting plaintiffs' efforts to challenge the special status of Catholic schools, the Court essentially treated the provisions of Section 93 as an important foundational compromise, a "'solemn pact,'" or "'cardinal term' of Union [without which] there would have been no Confederation."[9] As these examples suggest, each federal bargain is in some respects unique to the parties' situations, in ways that constitutional prescriptions based on the universal, or natural, or necessary rights of women and men as persons are not.

Interdependent Federal Balances

Not only are federal systems agreed to as a compromise, but the compromise typically constitutes an interrelated *package* of arrangements. A common theme in constitutional court decisions on federalism is that of the "balance" between central and subnational governments. This balance consists of multiple interdependent features, which may include, among others, the allocation of legislative powers, the allocation of executive powers, the structure of court systems and allocation of jurisdiction, the makeup of the "federal" house of the national legislature, the particular responsibilities, powers, or duties of that house, the specific prohibitions on subnational or national authority designed to protect distinctive interests, and the role of the subnational units in amendment of the constitution. No one element of the package of arrangements can be compared to an ostensibly similar element in a different federal system without more broadly considering the comparability of the "packages" and of the role of the particular element within that package.

Thus, for example, in Canada the national government has an enumerated power over "trade and commerce," which in isolation might be read as similar to the power given to the U.S. Congress to "regulate Commerce . . . among the several States." Indeed, the Canadian constitutional text lacks any explicit limitation to "interstate" or "interprovincial" trade or commerce, and thus standing alone might be read as even broader than the federal power over commerce in the United States. Yet the Canadian clause has been read more restrictively than the U.S. commerce clause, in light of the specific enumeration to the provinces of powers, for example, over "property and civil rights" and the Privy Council's broader concern to leave room for the exercise of provincial powers, especially in French-speaking Quebec.[10] The U.S. Constitution does not contain any equivalent enumeration of the powers of the states, nor was the U.S. Court faced with the dominant challenge in Canada of holding together in a single federation two different language communities, linked by history, law, and religion to different foreign states. Interpretation of specific power-granting clauses, then, is necessarily framed by the larger constitutional contexts in which they rest.

Another example emerges in a comparison between German and U.S. federalism, advanced by Justice Breyer in his dissent in *Printz v. United States*.[11] The issue before the U.S. Court was whether Congress could require state and local governments to implement the administration of a federal law (there, by requiring local law enforcement personnel to perform background checks required to purchase handguns under a federal statute). The majority held not, that such "commandeering" was inconsistent with the constitutional plan for the federal government to legislate and act directly on its citizens, rather than through the states. In dissent, Justice Breyer argued that the experience of other federalisms, including Germany's, suggested that such a national power was not incompatible with a healthy federalism.

Justice Breyer's point is surely true as far as it goes, but it did not fully address important differences in the two federalisms. In Germany, members of the länder governments (which were organized prior to any national government after Germany's defeat in World War II) sit in the upper chamber of the national legislature, which has a right to veto those laws—and only those laws—that impose administrative responsibilities on the länder. Administration of federal law is seen as a protection of the interests of the länder, both in preserving its members' legislative veto and enabling them to control how the law is administered. The dynamics of issues such as "commandeering" are thus quite different in Germany than in the United States, where the Senate does not nearly so directly represent the interests of the subnational governments, especially since the senators are directly elected for that office by the people of the state.[12] Federal commandeering of states that are not directly represented, in their governmental capacity, in the national legislature might be thought to pose a somewhat different set of questions for constitutional federalism; commandeering where subnational units have the exclusive power to administer the law, again, affects the federal balance of power differently from situations in which power to administer is held concurrently or is exclusively allocated to the national government.[13]

No Transnational Archetype

Third, federal systems cannot draw in their design or interpretation on well-established and detailed "archetypes," or templates in the way that modern constitution-makers have used the Universal Declaration of Human Rights, or the two major international human rights covenants, as templates for the design of their own bills of right. The individual rights provisions in most constitutions drafted and adopted after World War II have "a common core of human rights provisions that are strikingly similar," often derived from international or regional human rights conventions.[14] International law has far less, for the moment, to say about government organization—-and especially about federal organization—than it does about human rights.[15] The inescapable ubiquity of human beings as the central concern of any system of governance may contribute to the far greater specificity of international law concerning the content of human rights than the forms of governance.

The two dozen federal systems in the world afford almost as many models of government design, notwithstanding some similarities, for example, in generally having a bicameral legislature in which one house represents the interests of the constituent parts. But the differences loom large. There are significant variations in the allocation of powers, and in the degree to which such allocations function as fixed poles or as default rules.[16] Some federal systems reflect a momentum of integration of formerly separate or dispersed territorial governments, while others are more devolutionary in character.[17] Many federal systems are consciously designed to accommodate territorially based ethnic or linguistic minorities, or other similarly distinctive communities with special histories and cultures; others, though, cannot be understood on this basis.[18] Some federal constitutions allocate powers to only one level of government, with a residuary clause for the remainder; some allocate to two or more levels of government, with or without residuary clauses. Most federal systems rely on a court to adjudicate federalism controversies, but some, like Switzerland, preclude judicial review of the constitutionality of national laws, permitting such review only of subnational laws. And while most federal constitutions do not provide for the withdrawal of member states, some have done so at least in formal terms.[19]

For all of these reasons, it is more plausible to envision reciprocal influences on the development of individual rights provisions than of federalism features.[20] Rights provisions in national constitutions and international human rights instruments display considerable overlaps, which may be attributed not simply to the international archetypes that exist but to the fact of their having human beings as their subjects, as compared with the very divergent ways in which societies organize their own political functioning. Prohibitions or rights relating to fundamental aspects of human freedom (and experience therewith) might be thought particularly suitable to transnational comparisons (positive or negative) because of their subject matter, to the extent that they deal with attributes believed to be in some sense innate to the human condition and across societies.

To be sure, the rights provisions of different national constitutions, even if worded identically, operate within distinctive contexts of specific national cultures and constitutions,[21] and within what may be distinctive institutional mechanisms for the implementation and enforcement of these rights. And while on many issues of individual rights there are international archetypes reflecting widely shared aspirations, as we saw in Chapter 7 this is not always the case, as there is significant disagreement on values concerning the status of the fetus that affects legal approaches to abortion.[22] But with respect to federalism, and despite a possibly emerging shared transnational value of subsidiarity,[23] international law is silent on federal design and structure; the foreign constitutional law of federalism is varied because the underlying federal bargains are varied. And the legal issues that come before courts in federalism cases concern an always socially constructed context, and not a shared human experience (of life and death, pregnancy and birth) to which democratic constitutional commitments of equality, liberty, and fair treatment speak. For a wide range of rights there is still a greater possibility for a common core of meaning than there is for the meaning of particular allocations of powers in particular federal systems.

Comparative experience of courts in resolving specific federalism issues may thus have less to offer other courts engaged in constitutional interpretation than do comparative rights decisions. This does not necessarily mean, however, that the courts of federal systems have nothing of value to learn from comparative constitutional federalism: knowledge of comparative federalism may contribute to a better-informed attitude toward judicial enforcement of federalism provisions than would otherwise exist, as discussed below in Part D. Nor does the fact of federalism imply that a system will be less (or more) open to engagement or convergence with the transnational on other issues. Indeed, international legal norms have particular salience in some federal systems. Not surprisingly, federally organized nations may have quite different postures toward the transnational, explainable by aspects of history, culture, and more general legal orientation as well as by particularities of their federal organization, as discussed in the next section.

B. FEDERAL SYSTEMS' VARYING POSTURES TOWARD THE TRANSNATIONAL

Theoretical Tendencies?

Is there any systematic tendency that could be predicted about the relationships between a federal national system and the attitude of that constitutional system to engagement with or influence by transnational law? There are competing theoretical possibilities. First, it might be thought that federalism's commitment to pluralized legal orders within one polity would condition a more generalized comfort with multiple legal orders and hence facilitate interest, receptivity, and willingness to engage. In the United States, important participants in the constitution-drafting process engaged in comparative exercises in the founding period, finding the experience of other confederal and would-be democratic polities to be helpful guides—both those occurring in the then-state governments and those that had occurred in other polities through history. The constitutional framework that was established permits each of the states to maintain its own legal system, based either on common law or on civil law traditions, and allows that state law to operate as long as it does not conflict with federal law. Many transactions or activities are subject to concurrent regulation by state and federal law. Whether because of founding comparisons or ongoing experience with multiple legal orders, one can imagine that an orientation to plural legal orders would comfortably expand to looking outside at a variety of nonbinding sources of law.

Second, there is a competing and logically incompatible possibility that the complexity of the pluralized legal orders of a federal system will drive constitutional thinking and judicial decision-making inward. In large federal polities there may be a wealth of internal materials and legal norms, perhaps the product of complex negotiations, which will need to be considered in the deliberations of the country's courts in order for decisions to have legitimacy. Accounting for the complexity of internal law may take all the time reasonably allocatable to particular decisions. Moreover, as noted above, federal systems are highly interdependent and unique products of particular politically contingent arrangements. The contingency of federal systems may be associated with an insistence on the specificity of their own compromises. To the extent that the legitimacy of a federal system is seen to depend on a careful calibration of internal authorities, it is possible that overt references to transnational legal sources, or to particular foreign sources, would be destabilizing.[24]

Third, federalism may by itself make international law more salient insofar as international law addresses rights of self-determination. A nation that is already federal may be more at risk of secessionary movements, or of independent complaints by its subparts to international sources of legal authority. Both of these moves would tend to make members of subnational elites, as well as national elites—which are likely to include members of the judiciary—more aware of international law, if only as a tool by which to respond to these possibly unwanted moves by subnational parts.[25] To the extent federalism is used as a form for protection of minority rights, it may be particularly likely to be associated with subnational unit elites who speak the language of the human rights international law jurisprudence that forms a basis for such appeals to external recognition and remedy. As we shall see this possibility may play a role in Canadian attitudes.

Finally, perhaps it is the case that federalism simply tends to make debates about the relevance and character of foreign and international law more explicit. Federalism in its various forms produces multiple and overlapping points of decision-making. These multiple decision points may include the courts, as in the United States, with the concurrent and overlapping jurisdictions of the state and federal courts. With multiple locations for the exercise of governmental, and specifically judicial, authority, there are arguably more complex possibilities for reception, resistance, and dialogue about transnational/international law.[26] There are glimmerings of this effect in both the United States and Canada, as discussed below. Thus, perhaps all that can be said is that different federalisms tend to yield particularized and complex political and historic practices that influence and are influenced by diverse categories of thought that show up in judicial discourses. Such judicial discourses, then, function as both reflective pools and synthesizers of domestic narratives of federalism.

Federalism Tropes and the Transnational in the United States and Canada

A comparison focused primarily on the United States and Canada will try to illuminate how differing federalisms may affect courts' interpretive postures toward transnational sources of law. For if federal constitutional systems can fruitfully be compared in ways that would illuminate constitutional interpretation, these two democratic countries would be a promising place to start, in light of the factors discussed in Chapter 6 above.

Each country has a written constitution, with a long history of judicial interpretation and enforcement of constitutional provisions against other branches of government. Each country has had a federal form of government for over a century, and the U.S. Constitution and U.S. experience played some role in the drafting of the federalism provisions of the Canadian counterpart. As noted in Chapter 7, each had a federal, structural constitution that in some respect predated constitutional extension of nationally guaranteed individual rights to all governments within the polity. Each has a "generalist" Supreme Court, with jurisdiction over a wide range of issues decided by lower courts, that acts as the final adjudicator of issues of national—including constitutional—law.[27] Each court is regarded as relatively independent, in adjudication, from the appointing authorities of the judges or other obviously improper influence. Each court writes substantial, reasoned opinions, in the common law tradition, explaining its judgments, which are sometimes unanimous and sometimes rendered as multiple separate opinions or judgments of its members, concurring or dissenting.

Although some of these conditions hold in other federal countries, such as Australia, the absence of a robust constitutional bill of rights in Australia distinguishes it from both Canada and the United States. The U.S. Constitution strongly influenced mid-nineteenth century Argentine constitution-making, but Argentine constitutional history over the same time period has had neither the continuity of rule of law nor the stable electoral politics as a basis for change in government power that the United States and Canada have had, nor has its court enjoyed the practical independence from political control of those in Canada and the United States.[28] In contrast to the model of engagement being explored here, the Argentine Supreme Court for a time treated U.S. Supreme Court precedents as controlling, based on the genealogical connections between the two systems,[29] arguably a form of what Michael Dorf calls "dynamic incorporation of foreign law"[30] that was quite unusual even in its time; early case law in the Canadian and Australian systems rejected any view that U.S. authority would be controlling in the interpretation of their national constitutions.[31]

Although there are important constitutional similarities between the United States and Canada, their interpretive practices, otherwise similar, diverge markedly in their propensity to refer to foreign and international law. The Supreme Court of Canada is more inclined to refer, without apology, to foreign and international legal material, and to discuss these materials at some length, than is its counterpart in the United States.[32] This tendency is notable not only in constitutional decisions, but in other areas of law.[33] It is not that the Canadian court always, and the U.S. Court never, refers to foreign or international law in constitutional cases. To the contrary, throughout the history of the U.S. Court there are episodic discussions, some quite thoughtful, about foreign or international law as it bears on constitutional issues, as discussed in earlier chapters, and there are many Canadian Supreme Court cases on constitutional law that discuss only Canadian sources. Nonetheless, the Canadian court has more discussions that engage at some length with the reasoning of foreign decisions than are found in the U.S. Reports; it has indicated that "Canada's international obligations can assist courts charged with interpreting the *Charter's* guarantees";[34] and the general phenomenon of considering foreign or international law is far less controversial in Canada than in the United States (perhaps in part because of a different relationship to the international and in part because of the Canadian court's sophistication in distinguishing, as well as relying on, foreign precedents considered). Many of these discussions are in cases involving questions of individual rights, rather than questions of allocation of powers among the two levels of government in Canada.[35]

Moreover, in Canada, as we shall see, an increasingly important trope of constitutional discourse is that of participation and negotiation as foundations for the legitimacy of law. In the United States, by contrast, there is more of an emphasis on laws as rules, rights as trumps, and winners-take-all in adjudication and in elections, a system in which formal boundaries may be of greater importance.[36] These differences in style relate to standard tropes in the conversations about each nation's own federalism, as the next sections will hopefully further show.

Constitutional Commonalities

The larger constitutional positions and histories of Canada and the United States provide the context for what kind of relationships the courts would have, in each of these democratic and federal nations, to transnational legal development. Some substantial shared common characteristics are, as already noted, that both Canada and the United Sates have a federal form of government, entrenched in a written constitution, the boundary lines of which have been interpreted, evolved, and enforced in part through a course of judicial decisions.[37] These three characteristics—a federal union, under a written constitution, enforced by courts—are supplemented by others.

Both nations share a background as British colonies,[38] and more specifically a legal background in the British common law. Both nations, moreover, have a substantial degree of constitutional regime continuity—the Constitution of 1789 is still regarded as binding, except as modified, in the United States, and the same is true for the Constitution Act, 1867 in Canada. In a somewhat more complicated way, both nations had a substantial history of judicial review of structural limitations on the two levels of government *before* their courts began to enforce a national bill of rights against the subnational levels of government.[39] In addition, both have had traditions of judicially independent national judges, including the members of their respective Supreme Courts. Because of the regime continuities in both countries as longstanding constitutional federations, it is doubtful that resort to international or transnational law has been perceived as necessary to repudiate past political or legal regimes, as may have been the case in countries such as Spain, Argentina, and South Africa, or in Central and Eastern Europe.

In both countries, treaties may be entered into or ratified by the national government without automatically becoming judicially enforceable as domestic law, although for somewhat different constitutional reasons. At a textual level, the U.S. Constitution looks to be more "monist" than "dualist" in declaring in Article VI that treaties made under the authority of the United States are "the law of the land." Yet the doctrine of "non-self-executing treaties" has long meant that some treaties of the United States are not judicially enforceable without implementing legislation, and as a result of the 2008 *Medellín v. Texas* decision, it is possible that many (if not most) treaties will now be treated as non-self-executing.[40] Moreover, although it has been strongly argued that treaties were intended to be enforceable as such as a form of law,[41] the practice of the U.S. government in recent years has been to adopt human rights treaties with reservations or declarations that seek to limit their domestic force.[42] Indeed, in several cases spanning administrations of different parties, the Executive Branch took the position that state procedural rules could apply to block consideration of treaty violation claims, a position the Court has accepted.[43] Thus, notwithstanding the Supremacy Clause, a treaty may not be directly judicially enforceable as law. (If a treaty is effectuated by federal implementing legislation, however, the rule of *Missouri v. Holland*[44] permits such legislation even in areas otherwise reserved to the states.) In Canada, as a formal matter, the government exercises the prerogative power to enter into treaties without the approval of the parliament.[45] Yet the national government in Canada lacks power (without provincial agreement) to implement treaties in areas otherwise reserved to the provinces, as a result of the Privy Council's much-criticized decision in the *Labour Conventions* case.[46] Thus, despite some differences in the constitutional treaty-making power and in its internal effects, in both Canada and the United States it is possible for some treaties ratified by the national government to remain internally unenforceable by national courts.

Distinctive Constitutional Histories and Federal Bargains

Yet there are other marked differences in constitutional origins, structure, and history, which one might expect to generate very different interactions with transnational law. To begin with, the United States began in the eighteenth century, in a moment of strong rupture from Britain, and ensuing constitutional lawmaking proceeded with an intensely self-aware sense of autonomy. The initial development of the federal structure in Canada did not arise from arguably independent states but rather from British colonies; the 1867 Constitutional Act was originally enacted as a British statute, called the British North America Act, 1867.[47] Relatedly, the sense of each subnational unit as equally vested with its own sovereign powers is not nearly so pronounced in the Canadian as in the U.S. tradition. The revolutionary backdrop of U.S. constitutional developments and the relatively developed political and constitutional theory that emerged in the United States in the years of and following the Revolution stand in contrast to the far more incrementalist development from colony to independent nation seen in Canada. Canada did not have to reject its ties with the British Empire to pursue its own constitutional development. Nor did it develop so elaborated a political theory as that found in the Federalist Papers in defense of the constitutional structure of the 1867 Act.[48]

Five structural differences between U.S. and Canadian constitutionalism bear on the nature and enforcement mechanisms of the federalism balance. First, Canada relies on a parliamentary, rather than presidential, system of governance, a form sometimes associated with weaker rather than stronger federalisms.[49] Relatedly, a second difference (perhaps more salient) is that the Canadian legislature's upper house is quite unlike the U.S. Senate. In Canada, members of the Senate are not selected by or elected in the provinces, as U.S. senators are in the states, but rather are federally appointed; numerical equality is achieved on a regional rather than a provincial basis. Reflecting the pre-existing powers of the states that banded together to form the new nation, the U.S. Constitution allocates "equal suffrage" in the Senate to each state (that is, two Senators per state), no matter how small or large the population, and Article V of the Constitution more deeply entrenches the rule of equal suffrage of the states than other parts of the Constitution.[50] Third, in Canada equality of representation in the Senate is maintained between Ontario and Quebec,[51] adding to the *asymmetry* in the treatment of the other provinces, implying that these two provinces are the central core of the nation and also suggesting a perhaps more flexible attitude toward political representation than is manifest in the more rigid formula of the U.S. Constitution. These features might suggest that the states would play a stronger role in constraining federal-level political choices in the United States than would the provinces in Canada, and/or that Canadian federalism would show more flexibility in dealing with the situations of the different provinces.[52]

Fourth, in contrast to the United States' legal autonomy from Great Britain, Canada's constitutional development emphasized continuity of connection with and continued attention to developments in Britain. Until 1982, as a formal matter, Canada could not amend its constitutional documents without the consent and affirmative action of the British parliament; in the United States the power of amendment was part of the original constitution, exercised in the first Congress to add the Bill of Rights and soon thereafter in the 1790s to overrule a Supreme Court decision.[53] Until 1949, the Canadian Supreme Court's decisions were subject to review by the Privy Council in London; the U.S. Supreme Court has functioned as the final court of review since its inception. These two aspects of Canada's constitutional history thus required attention to the decisions of another country's court, and negotiation with another country's legislative body to effectuate amendments and changes to Canada's own constitutional order. Moreover, the presence of Privy Council review may have softened objections to the jurisdiction of the Supreme Court of Canada over provincial matters.[54] And the early decisions of the Privy Council, in defense of provincial powers, meant that a somewhat "external" judicial body was early on seen as supportive of the interests of the provinces, rather than as oppositional.[55] Even today, Canada's membership in the Commonwealth may reinforce a willingness to be open to considering transnational legal materials.

A final point of contrast worth noting is in the organization of the judiciaries, which differs in at least two possibly relevant respects.[56] First, although there are provincial courts in Canada—that is, courts created and staffed by the provinces—the jurisdiction of these purely provincial courts is quite limited.[57] The more significant courts are the Section 96 and Section 101 courts.[58] Section 96 courts (which include the highest courts of the province) are created by the provinces, but their judges are appointed by the federal government.[59] In addition to the federal appointments to the higher provincial courts, and unlike in the United States, judges at all levels are appointed, not elected, though with some variation in whether provincial attorneys–general who make judicial appointments use nominating or screening commissions.[60] Both the influence of the federal government appointments at the provincial level and the absence of elections for judges at the subnational unit level may contribute to a more homogeneous attitude among Canadian judges, oriented toward the professional norms of other judges.[61]

Founding Divisions and Historic Momentum

The historic momentum of the federal compromises in the United States and Canada is another factor, one that is central to understanding the different postures of their modern era courts. In the United States, "states' rights" are inextricably associated with the institutions of slavery, segregation, and Jim Crow. This association is in important respects rooted in the founding compromises reflected in the notorious three-fifths rule and the Fugitive Slave Clause of the original U.S. Constitution. In Canada, provincial rights are associated with rights of self-governance and cultural preservation of a linguistic and religious minority, concerns likewise reflected in founding sections of the 1867 Act.[62] The goals associated with the states' rights idea in the United States were antithetical to international human rights, as evidenced by the political forces behind the near passage of the proposed Bricker Amendment to the U.S. Constitution by the U.S. Senate in the early 1950s.[63] The Bricker Amendment would have limited the effect of treaties on U.S. domestic law and was motivated in part by concern that UN-related legal commitments should not be given domestic effect to uproot racial segregation in the South or used to justify a federal anti-lynching law. The proposed amendment failed in the Senate in 1954, but only after the Eisenhower Administration offered assurances it would seek no ratification of human rights treaties.[64]

The U.S. states have long since abandoned their official support for segregation and Jim Crow, and one might have thought that signaling that abandonment might include a reversal in position with respect to international human rights law. Yet the historical antipathy in the United States between "states' rights" and international human rights has lingered on, albeit in a more diffuse context. By contrast, the linguistic and religious minority rights associated with provincial autonomy demands in Canada are for the most part consonant with the new emphasis in post–World War II international law on self-determination of peoples and minority rights protection.[65] Indeed, in litigating a recent advisory reference concerning the legality of unilateral secession in the event of a positive referendum, advocates of Quebec's secession relied extensively on international law to claim a right unilaterally to secede.[66] One would not be surprised, then, to see in Canada some who favor provincial autonomy claims also being sympathetic to the message of international human rights norms.

Age of Rights-Incorporating Texts

Another important difference between the Canadian and U.S. federal constitutional systems is when their formal constitutional texts providing for individual rights were adopted. There is a great difference between the late-twentieth-century political movement for adoption of the Canadian Charter of Rights and Freedoms, and the late-eighteenth-century moment of constitution-making in the United States, the period when the Bill of Rights enters the U.S. Constitution. There is also a considerable difference between the mid-nineteenth century, when the post–Civil War amendments to the U.S. Constitution were adopted, and 1982, when the Canadian Charter was adopted. Timing may have reinforced Canadian openness to other influences, particularly since the Charter was drafted, negotiated, and ultimately adopted shortly after Canada's 1976 ratifications of the ICCPR and the ICESCR. Apart from the substance of the texts adopted, judges in the United States in the 1980s already had a wealth of domestic constitutional precedents bearing on many issues, whereas Canada's relatively recent adoption of the Charter—at a time when there was a burst of both international human rights law and comparative constitutional law coming available—meant that the incentives for Canadian judges to consider foreign and international law were stronger.[67]

The affinity of those supporting provincial rights for the French-speaking minority in Canada, in sympathy with major normative commitments of international human rights law, moved in odd eddies and currents around the Charter of Rights movement in Canada. Quebec opposed patriation and the Charter, not because of hostility to the idea of constitutional rights designed to implement international human rights, but rather, in important part, because of the Charter's failure to recognize a special role for Quebec. Indeed, Quebec adopted its own provincial constitution, securing many of the rights provided for in the Canadian Charter and some of those set forth in the major human rights covenants (ICCPR and ICESCR).[68]

Geopolitics

Geopolitical factors also account for some differences in orientation between U.S. and Canadian judges. The United States has been a (if not the) major world power during the living memory of its judges. A nation of close to 300 million people, its size, its armed forces, and its economy are many times larger than those of Canada. As a smaller power, Canada may have greater incentives to be aware of and concerned with what judges in other countries say and think than do those who identify with the power of the United States. The idea that judges would at some subconscious level identify with the power position of their countries requires a number of contestable assumptions, but as a working hypothesis it seems important to consider. Daryl Levinson's work reminds us to be wary of strong claims that assume identity of interest between government, institutions, and their personnel,[69] but there are a number of possible mechanisms by which judges might identify with the power or prestige of their countries, especially insofar as it affects the prestige of their own offices. A smaller country will not usually gain prestige by its military force, but might by its reputation for international engagement and cooperation, and judges from Canada may experience satisfaction from being regarded as committed to a cooperative transnational project of judging and human rights.

Legal Culture: Rights and Negotiation, Written and Unwritten Constitutional Constraints

Finally, consider legal culture. The United States, it might be thought, has a somewhat greater commitment to the proposition that law's authority is based on its promulgation from some democratically legitimated source, and an associated commitment to forms of positivism that seek to attribute law to particular decisions by a particular sovereign. The *Erie* doctrine in the United States denies the possibility of a "general common law" and requires federal courts—notwithstanding the constitutional grant of jurisdiction to them based on diverse state citizenship—to follow the legal rule that a state court would determine based on state law; in Canada, as Professor Martha Field emphasizes, the highest national court has the "final word" on the development and meaning of the common law, as well as on interpreting provincial statutes.[70] And the strands of U.S. jurisprudence committed to textualism and originalism in constitutional interpretation stand in some contrast to Canada's greater ease with a more evolutive conception of law over time, of its constitution as a "living tree,"[71] and to constitutionalism as involving principles that exist outside of written legal commitments.[72]

In Canada, moreover, there is more familiarity and comfort with the idea of unwritten constitutional conventions than in the United States. Although a constitutional convention is commonly understood as a constitutional practice not subject to judicial enforcement, and thus perhaps not bearing on judicial interpretation,[73] tolerance of unwritten conventions and norms might bespeak a form of flexibility in which the writtenness of a constitution's text is not seen as the exclusive basis for determining what the country's constitution is. That is, the written text does not exclude the possibility of unwritten constitutional principles. At this level of generality, flexibility in understanding what the constitution is might translate into flexibility as to what sources can be consulted to determine what the constitution means.

Perhaps relatedly, there may be more of a tendency in Canada than in the United States to address political controversy over constitutional relationships through negotiations. It was Canadian negotiations at a series of conferences that resulted in a proposal to Britain enacted into law as the Constitution Act, 1867.[74] Canadian federalism has been referred to as a system of "executive federalism"[75] because of its reliance on conferences and discussions among the federal and provincial governments; indeed these processes are sometimes criticized for their lack of transparency.[76] Some commitment to negotiation as a basis for constitutional legitimacy is also reflected in Constitution Act, 1982, Section 35.1, which provides that

> The government of Canada and the provincial governments are committed to the principle that, before any amendment is made to [provisions of the Constitution Act, 1867 and the Constitution Act, 1982 Act concerning jurisdiction over and rights of aboriginal peoples] (a) a constitutional conference that includes in its agenda an item relating to the proposed amendment, composed of the Prime Minister of Canada and the first ministers of the provinces, will be convened by the Prime Minister of Canada; and (b) the Prime Minister of Canada will invite representatives of the aboriginal peoples of Canada to participate in the discussions on that item.[77]

This constitutional commitment to inclusive discussion of the relationship between aboriginal peoples and the rest of Canada may be seen as something of a forebear to the judicially articulated obligation of negotiation in the *Secession Reference* decision.[78] The Court's derivation of an obligation to negotiate was perhaps less creative than might appear on first reading, in part because the idea that negotiation is a foundation for constitutional legitimacy was not only already a part of the constitutional traditions of Canada but was also already expressed in the written constitutional text dealing with aboriginal peoples.[79]

The significance of negotiations in the practice of Canadian constitutionalism may also have been reinforced by the Privy Council decision in the *Labour Conventions* case, holding that the national government in Canada lacked power to implement Canadian treaties unless the subject area came within a specific enumerated head of power.[80] In practice this holding "does not mean that Canada is always precluded from signing, ratifying, or performing treaties upon subjects within the legislative competence of the provinces," in part because "[t]he federal government can consult with the provinces before assuming treaty obligations which would require provincial implementation. . . ."[81] By contrast, the accepted rule in the United States is that the national government has legislative power to implement treaties.[82] The weaker implementation powers of the national government in Canada may have further reinforced commitments to intergovernmental negotiation, made easier with a group of only ten provinces (and three territories) than it would be with the fifty U.S. states. Moreover, to the extent that the *Labour Conventions* rule gave the provinces more of a role in implementing international obligations, it may also have positively affected provincial willingness to engage with international norms.[83]

Legal Culture and Legal Education

In seeking to understand U.S. and Canadian federalisms, and how they affect their respective courts' willingness to consider foreign or international law as relevant in resolving constitutional cases, Canadian commitments to bilingualism and multiculturalism as they affect legal education and political culture should not be neglected. Whether cause, effect, or both, legal education in Canada is more comparatively and internationally oriented. Many law students are "bijural," learning both civil law and common law traditions.[84]

* * *

So, in accounting for the varying postures of the U.S. and Canadian courts to international and foreign sources in adjudication, among the most important explanatory factors are these. First, as part of the British empire (and now as a member of the Commonwealth), Canada was part of a legal tradition in which multiple nations were concerned with a common source of law, and was accustomed to having to interpret the decisions of the Privy Council even though it sat in Britain. Moreover, Canada's incremental progress toward independent nationhood lacked the rejection of British authority that characterized, however ambivalently, the early revolutionary period in the United States. Second, the attraction of international human rights law for Quebec nationalism significantly affects the valence of federalism in Canada and makes it as an institutional structure less hostile to "outside" influence than the United States. Moreover, reliance on the Civil Code in Quebec and language commonalities would work to encourage

French Canadians to be interested in developments in France and other French-speaking countries. The explicitly "multicultural" commitments of the Charter reflect (as well as challenge) the two language communities from which Canadian federalism was constructed;[85] civil law and common law are taught in Canadian law schools and become familiar to lawyers and judges there, who are thereby accustomed to understanding multiple legal systems. Third, as noted, the impact of the Charter movement (and its support by women's groups) followed in time and was plainly hospitable to Canada's international human rights commitments.[86] Fourth, Canadian culture is described by some as a less deeply positivist legal culture,[87] as discussed above. Fifth, Privy Council interpretations of the Canadian constitution to allow the federal government to enter into treaties that it could not itself implement may have created more of an emphasis on negotiation and the need to consult the provinces in entering international obligations, thereby perhaps involving and exposing provincial elites to aspects of international law.[88] Finally, the executive government of Canada seems to have taken more embracing stances than its U.S. counterpart toward international law and its binding character as law for the last three decades.[89]

By contrast, the United States as an independent nation was born of abrupt rejection of British rule, rather than worked out in an incremental way, over time, with British consent and cooperation. Although in its early years the United States had strong incentives to be attentive to international custom and the views of other countries in litigation, and this attitude is manifest in a number of Marshall Court decisions,[90] over time far more ambivalent strains were introduced that have been the subject of considerable commentary. The Court's episodic posture of ambivalent resistance during parts of its history, may, however, understate the influence of judges' and lawyers' knowledge of the practices of other countries even when they were not formally cited. Between 2003 and 2005, when the U.S. Supreme Court appeared to be somewhat less resistant and more receptive to considering the views of others in resolving constitutional cases, Congress took up the banner of resistance, with several bills or resolutions introduced to restrict federal courts' citation to or reliance on foreign or international law in constitutional interpretation.[91] The ambivalent attitude of the U.S. Congress toward the binding force of international law may be better captured by the fact that the Bricker Amendment was proposed than that it was rejected.[92]

C. FEDERAL SYSTEMS, CONSTITUTIONAL ADJUDICATION, AND TRANSNATIONAL SOURCES OF LAW

A review of Canadian and U.S. cases in several areas of constitutional law will deepen the comparison and show how the age and particularities of the U.S. federal system contribute to the conclusion that cautious engagement, rather than convergence or resistance, is the appropriate posture for the United States.

While there is comparative learning to be had, particularly at the level of general interpretive approach, considering foreign constitutional decisions on discrete federalism issues is more challenging and in some respects less likely to be useful than on other issue areas. These points are illustrated by considering several sets of decisions.

Secession

Both Supreme Courts faced questions about the legal authority of members of the federal union to secede. The decisions arose more than 120 years apart, a fact with implications for the legal context in which each case was decided.

In the 1869 decision in *Texas v. White*,[93] the United States Supreme Court rejected the argument that Texas, by virtue of its secession and taking up arms against the United States, was no longer to be regarded as a state of the union able to prosecute lawsuits in the national courts. Texas remained a state of the union because the Constitution contemplates an "indestructible Union, composed of indestructible States."[94] In so reasoning, the Court briefly discussed the idea of a "state," implicitly drawing on transnational understandings.[95] The Court emphasized that the states retain rights of self-governance, but their relations with the Union were "indissoluble" except by revolution (which appears to be outside the realm of legality in this opinion), or "through consent of the States"[96]—an ambiguous reference, possibly referring to the amendment process of Article V.

More than a century later, in 1998 the Canadian Supreme Court decided the Quebec *Secession Reference* case,[97] rejecting claims that either international law or Canadian constitutional law recognizes a unilateral right to secede if the people of a province vote by referendum to do so. Reasoning that a vote only in Quebec would not reflect the relationships and interests of the rest of Canada of which Quebec was a part, the opinion emphasizes the organic development of the relations of the parts to the whole. Both opinions concluded that the expressed desire (or declaration) of a member state to withdraw is insufficient, given the interests of the whole. The Canadian decision placed considerably less weight than did the U.S. Court on any notion of provincial consent in joining the Union—understandably, since Quebec had not agreed to the Charter or the constitutional acts of patriation in 1982.

But the Canadian opinion went on to hold that, should there be a clear vote, on a clear question, in favor of secession, a duty would arise for the rest of Canada to negotiate in good faith with Quebec over issues of secession, under principles of democracy, federalism, protection of minorities and the rule of law. In the almost 130 years since *Texas v. White*, there had developed a substantial body of constitutional law on democracy and individual rights, and of international law concerning the right of self-determination of peoples, going beyond older writings on international law concerning limited defensive rights of secession.[98] Although the Canadian Supreme Court rejected Quebec's international law argument (that the right of self-determination entitled it to secede) because Quebec was not being denied rights of participation in the union nor was it an oppressed or colonial people,[99] the more general point is that this question arose at a time when a larger body of legal material discussing democracy, federalism, and minority rights in constitutional law, and self-determination and secession under international law, was available than at the time of *Texas v. White*. And while the decision was based on unwritten principles of Canadian law, the Court's construction of those principles—particularly its emphasis on the legitimacy of a democratic expression of a desire to secede, and on the protection of minority rights—have strong resonances with international human rights law. To the extent that legal styles of reasoning are path-dependent, the "firstness" of the United States in constitutional adjudication on this issue may well have limited the range of transnational sources available for consideration, in comparison to those available at the time of the Canadian *Secession Reference* case.

The Canadian case also illustrates another way in which federal systems may make international law relevant to internal constitutional decisions. Some scholars have argued against recognition of a right of secession based on referenda conducted within the lines of existing subnational units in a federation, because, they suggest, such a rule would create *disincentives* to use of the federal form, to the detriment of affording desirable degrees of self-governance to territorially identified groups.[100] Yet today, other incentives for devolution through various forms of federalism (and, perhaps as well, the incentives and the possibilities of smaller territories eventually seeking status as national states) have arguably increased.[101] Evolution of international law (and awareness of it) concerning secessionary rights might not only affect bargaining over federal balances in future constitutional negotiations, whether of national states or supranational unions, but also contribute to a kind of blend of international and transnational constitutional law concerning the processes by which membership and boundary issues are resolved, as discussed below in Chapter 9.

Commerce, Criminal Law, and National Power

In both the United States and Canada the supreme courts are asked to address whether legislative acts of the national government exceed that government's enumerated powers. Here, difference in the federal allocation of powers at first appear to play an important role in the two courts' decisions. On closer examination, however, it appears that other differences in the respective courts' orientations to constitutional change and the role of transnational sources in constitutional interpretation may also be at work.

In the 1990s, the U.S. Court for the first time since the New Deal struck down as beyond national power a federal criminal statute regulating private behavior. In *United States v. Lopez*,[102] the Court held that the national government's power to regulate interstate commerce and other activities that "substantially affect" interstate commerce did not extend to support a federal statute prohibiting the possession of a firearm within 1,000 feet of a school. The statute required no proof that some element of the crime itself was interstate in character and contained no findings showing a connection between the prohibition and commerce. Criminal law, the Court wrote, was generally for the states to regulate, as was education. And the rationales proffered by the federal government in support of the statute—that violence near schools interfered with the United States' ability to produce a competitive and educated citizenry and that the excess insurance costs and other costs of gun violence near schools were large enough to affect the national economy—were rejected as insufficient because they could be applied to virtually any subject Congress wished to regulate and were thus inconsistent with the idea that "enumeration presupposes something not enumerated."[103]

The effort to distinguish that which was "truly national" from that which was "truly local" drove both this opinion and the decision in *Morrison v. United States,*[104] in which the Court held that Congress lacked power, under either the Commerce Clause or the Fourteenth Amendment, to provide a civil rights remedy for victims of gender-motivated assaults. The majority opinions in these cases relied on founding intentions from the late-eighteenth century, and on cases decided during the post-Reconstruction period of U.S. constitutional history when the Fourteenth and other post–Civil War amendments were given relatively narrow readings. International norms or the practices of other nations received virtually no attention in the majority opinions and little in the lengthy dissents that were written.

In Canada, unlike in the United States, specific powers are enumerated to both levels of government, the provinces and the federal government; also in contrast to the United States, in Canada power over "criminal law" has been allocated to the national government. Although the national government has power over "trade and commerce," this clause has been given a narrower reading in Canada than its cognate in the United States, one designed to preclude federal regulation of intraprovincial trade or of "minute rules for regulating particular trades" and to preserve a meaningful area for provincial power under the provinces' enumerated power over "property and civil rights in the province."[105] Thus, the Canadian court's conclusions that matters lie outside the "trade and commerce" power would be of limited relevance in the United States, where there is no specific enumeration of powers to the states over "property and civil rights" and where, since the mid-twentieth century, a relatively stable core of doctrine has permitted federal regulation of almost any kind of commercial activity or transaction on the theory that they affect the entire national economy.

In the criminal law area, Canadian provinces have power over administration of justice in the province, including, according to Professor Peter Hogg, police and prosecution of offenses under the federal criminal code (over which the national government also has concurrent but unexercised authority).[106] The difficulty that the Canadian court has faced is whether the criminal law power means that the national parliament can legislate on any subject if its regulation is enforced through criminal sanction. The answer at a formal level seems to be no, but drawing the dividing line has been difficult.[107]

These tensions over federalist divisions of power are reflected in a Canadian case, already discussed in Chapter 7, involving a challenge to a national gun registration law as beyond the scope of national power. In addition to giving weight to the 1982 Charter value of gender equality in construing the earlier federalist allocations of power,[108] the chief justice in the majority on the Alberta court of appeals resorted to nonbinding international legal sources in ways atypical of U.S. decisions, commenting that "Parliament's increased efforts to strengthen and tighten gun control laws also happen to be consistent with Canada's international human rights commitments."[109] In discussing the "pith and substance" of the legislation, the opinion went on to describe recent recommendations by an expert committee to an international commission on crime prevention of which Canada was a member,[110] and to note the implications of the UN Declaration on the Elimination of Violence Against Women, a General Assembly Resolution from 1994.[111] Even though Canada had not incorporated this Declaration into its domestic law, the opinion invoked an interpretive presumption that "where legislation is open to two interpretations, one of which is more consistent with international human rights norms, then that interpretation is to be preferred," thereby suggesting that the scope of Parliament's power under the 1867 Constitution Act should be interpreted in light of international human rights law.[112] The long-standing idea in Canadian jurisprudence that the 1867 Constitution Act should be treated as a "living tree"—a phrase that originated in a gender equality case involving whether women were eligible to be appointed as senators in Canada[113]—may make it easier for judges to be open not only to considering subsequent internal constitutional developments but also international developments in construing the older 1867 Constitution Act's federalist divisions.[114]

On the other hand, in *Morrison* the U.S. Court did not even discuss whether the statute could be upheld as implementation of a ratified treaty. Yet one amicus brief in *Morrison* was devoted in significant part to arguing that the Violence Against Women Act (VAWA) could be regarded as implementing legislation under the ICCPR (which the United States had ratified in 1992) and thus, under *Missouri v. Holland*,[115] upheld as within Congress' powers, regardless of the scope of the Commerce Clause or Fourteenth Amendment. Several articles of the ICCPR prohibit sex discrimination, protect the equal rights of men and women, or address the need to provide "equal and effective protection against discrimination."[116] The amicus brief argued that the VAWA's remedy for gender-motivated assaults could be regarded as an implementation of the ICCPR's asserted requirement for affirmative government protection of individuals from private action (gender-based violence) infringing on their rights, especially in light of interpretations of the ICCPR by the UN Human Rights Committee and the UN General Assembly's Declaration on the Elimination of Violence Against Women.[117] Two opposing amici vigorously argued, however, that the issue was not before the Court, not having been raised in the "Questions Presented," and further, that the ICCPR was not relied on by Congress in its articulation of the constitutional grounds for action.[118] Although the Court has at times said a statute should be sustained on any "reasonably conceivable state of facts," in recent years where Congress specified the bases for its legislative acts, the Court has refused to consider grounds not asserted.[119] It is thus perhaps not surprising that the Court did not address this issue.

Yet the arguments for viewing the statute as a constitutionally valid means of implementing the ICCPR were not trivial.[120] The Senate Committee report accompanying Senate ratification had indicated that, in those areas where the ICCPR set a higher standard than domestic constitutional law, the "normal legislative process" would be the mechanism to effect change,[121] and VAWA was the product of a normal federal legislative process. On the other hand, the ICCPR is not focused on gender equality (as, for example, CEDAW is); and the VAWA statute does not refer to the ICCPR. Moreover, U.S. ratification of the ICCPR was accompanied by several reservations, understandings and declarations, including an understanding that the Covenant would "be implemented by the Federal Government to the extent that it exercises legislative and judicial jurisdiction over the matters covered therein, and otherwise by the state and local governments," as well as a proviso that the ICCPR would not require or authorize any legislation *prohibited* by the Constitution.[122] These provisions might be interpreted to mean the Senate sought to deny Congress any additional power to enact implementing legislation, as was recognized in *Missouri v. Holland*, although the effects of such understandings and provisos (or their application to this issue) are contestable.[123] So while there are understandable reasons in U.S. Supreme Court practice and recent constitutional decisions to explain the Court's failure even to discuss the treaty issue, the contrast between its stance and that of the Canadian courts is marked.

Rights and Federalism

In both countries it is somewhat more common to find references to foreign or international law in cases involving claims of individual rights, rather than disputes over federal allocations of powers. Yet federal divisions of power may influence how open or resistant a court is to foreign or international law respecting human rights issues.

Death Penalty and the Allocation of Criminal Jurisdiction Consider the death penalty. Under the federal allocations of powers as they are understood in the United States, jurisdiction over criminal law, and decisions whether to provide for, to seek, or to carry out a death penalty are largely within the jurisdiction of the states. In 2004, there were over 3,300 prisoners on death row in state criminal justice systems, and fewer than two dozen federal prisoners who had been sentenced to death.[124] In Canada, "criminal law" is an enumerated power of the national government. Canada abolished the death penalty by national legislation in 1976 (except for certain military offenses, for which the death penalty was abolished in 1998) and efforts to reinstate it thus far have failed.[125]

While the Canadian Supreme Court in recent years has identified Canada with evolving transnational standards opposing the death penalty, the U.S. Supreme Court has been much more ambivalent—both about the death penalty and about reliance on international standards.[126] Efforts to bring transnational standards to the attention of the Court have elicited extremely strong objections from several justices, including Justice Scalia, who famously wrote for the Court that "it is *American* conceptions of decency" that control in interpreting the Eighth Amendment's ban on cruel and unusual punishments.[127] Chief Justice Rehnquist wrote in dissent to condemn reliance on other countries' practices in death penalty cases,[128] as did Justice Thomas.[129] Although *Roper*, holding unconstitutional the imposition of the death penalty on offenders who were juveniles at the time of the offense, included an entire section discussing foreign and international law, it did so at the end of the opinion and in a clearly secondary status to its consideration of factors of domestic law; in its 2008 decision holding the death penalty unconstitutional as punishment for rape of a child, the Court did not address transnational legal sources, notwithstanding amicus briefing.[130] Although the Canadian court has been criticized by Canadian scholars for insufficient attention to international law in its decisions on extradition, its opinions have given considerably more attention to international and foreign law in evaluating constitutional issues relating to extradition to face the death penalty.[131]

A prominent aspect of the U.S. Court's jurisprudence on the death penalty has been the degree to which the decision is viewed as committed to the different states and the implicit valuing of federalism in allowing different states, through democratic institutions of governance, to make different choices on this matter. The fact that thirty-five or more states in the United States have allowed the death penalty has been repeatedly invoked by its defenders on the Court. These state laws—over a matter on which the states have legislative competence under U.S. federalism understandings—lend a democratic legitimacy to the death penalty laws that heightens the "countermajoritarian" character of a decision to invalidate its use. A telling statement was Justice O'Connor's opening assertion in an opinion for the Court, in a case dealing with whether a federal court would hear on the merits a challenge to a state court conviction and death sentence, that "This is a case about federalism."[132]

In Canada, the provinces do not have constitutional power to enact criminal laws with the death penalty.[133] The Canadian federalist allocations thus constrain the legislative expression of the range of views on the death penalty that emerge in duly enacted state statutes in the United States.[134] Because the allocation of jurisdiction places criminal law at the national level in Canada, the Canadian court's constitutional analysis of the death penalty (to the extent legitimately influenced by domestic legislative decisions), is thus not informed (as it is in the United States) by multiple subnational legislative approaches, but only by the national government's decision by legislation to abolish capital punishment. The federalist allocation of power to enact criminal laws with death penalties in the United States thus shapes the context for the U.S. Court's decisions in ways that the Canadian court does not face.

Group Rights, Group Remedies, and Federal Compromises The U.S. Constitution has been interpreted to require government neutrality in its treatment of racial and religious groups. The government must be neutral as among religions;[135] laws using racial classifications are subject to the same strict standard of review whether they are claimed to benefit, or disadvantage, members of racial minority groups;[136] even gender classifications are subject to the same level of scrutiny whether they are claimed to disadvantage women or men.[137] Remedial measures employing suspect classifications are themselves suspect and subject to review under the most careful scrutiny.[138] And in recent years the U.S. Court has relied on commitments to federalism to narrow the scope of Congress' s power to enact remedial legislation to secure the "equal protection" of the laws.[139]

Canada's federal history, including the 1867 Constitution Act's provisions of special rights to "dissentient" minority religions in particular provinces, may shed light on its rather different approach, in ways that make it in some respects resistant to and in other ways receptive to international human rights norms. As noted above, under Section 93 of the 1867 Act, the rights of religious minorities protected through state funding of education that existed at that time were to be preserved. A constitutional challenge to Ontario's failure to fund Jewish (and non-Catholic Christian) schools was brought under the equality provisions of the Charter, but rejected, in part because another section of the Charter specifically preserved Section 93 rights.[140] However, a subsequent challenge brought before the UN Human Rights Committee was successful before that committee, which concluded that the reasons given by Canada—including that funding for minority Catholic schools in Ontario was secured by a founding compromise necessary to create the Confederation and guaranteed in the constitution—did not justify the discrimination in treatment; the difference in treatment violated the ICCPR article 26 prohibition on discrimination.[141] The individual complaint procedure before the UN Human Rights Committee was available because Canada, unlike the United States, had ratified the Optional Protocol to the ICCPR (and the Committee's views evidently led to some increase in tax credits for minority religious education.)[142]

Although the Article 93 provisions for continued public funding of "dissentient" religions as they existed in 1867 are thus in some respects resistant to modern human rights law and to the force of the 1982 Charter's equality provision, their existence within the Canadian constitutional tradition may be related to Canada's greater constitutional acceptance of other international human rights approaches, including specifically affirmative action involving group-specific remedial measures. In the 1982 Charter, Canada (in important measure as a result of pressure from women's groups) adopted an equality and antidiscrimination provision explicitly referring to discrimination based on a number of axes (including "sex") and also adopted a provision indicating that the antidiscrimination provision did not bar ameliorative affirmative action programs. In case law developed since, the Canadian Supreme Court has relied on the authorization of Section 15(2) for affirmative action programs to help interpret what counts as a discrimination barred by Section 15(1). [143] In *Lovelace v. Ontario*,[144] the Canadian Supreme Court rejected a challenge by nonregistered First Nations people to a revenue sharing arrangement between Ontario and registered bands of First Nations peoples in connection with gambling operations. The court there treated Section 15(2) as helping to illustrate what is meant in Section 15(1) by discrimination;[145] if a classification has ameliorative purposes it is less likely to be found to impugn the dignity or status of those challenging classification.[146]

Affirmative action and other forms of temporary measures are specifically authorized by several UN human rights conventions concerned with discrimination. In *Lovelace*, the Canadian Supreme Court opinion casually cited a report by the UN Committee on Economic, Social and Cultural Rights along with other materials in connection with its discussion of the disadvantages aboriginal peoples have suffered.[147] In the United States, the constitutionality of affirmative action for racial minorities has been hotly contested and tightly constrained. The Court has held that affirmative action measures are subject to the same strict level of scrutiny as an invidious discrimination; between 2003 and 2007 it struck down Seattle's race conscious school assignment plan as well as the University of Michigan's undergraduate admissions program's use of race.[148] Although Justice Ruth Ginsburg in a concurring opinion in *Grutter v. Bollinger* that was joined by Justice Breyer referred to international human rights conventions' approval of temporary affirmative action measures in support of the Court's decision permitting the University of Michigan law school to take race into account in admissions, this reference did not elicit engagement by other justices but did provoke some hostile public responses opposing use of foreign and international law.[149]

The Canadian Charter, enacted in 1982, affirmatively recognizes the validity and distinctiveness of ameliorative programs in a way consistent with post–World War II human rights instruments. But in addition to the modernity of its rights-recognizing constitution, the older history of Canadian federalism may be thought to conduce to a different set of views on issue of preferences or accommodations for disadvantaged groups. The boundaries of Quebec are designed to provide some degree of autonomy and protection for the French-speaking minority in Canada. Given the Canadian history of accommodating both French and English communities, including, for example, the rule that at least three judges of the Canadian Supreme Court be from Quebec, and the special constitutional treatment of "dissentient" religious schools,[150] the foundations of Canadian federalism are in some ways compatible with an understanding of individual rights that allows for affirmative action or distinctive treatment of minority groups.

There has long been a certain asymmetry in Canadian federalism in the formal representation of the provinces and in their governance structures.[151] In the United States, by contrast, the constitutional tradition is more strongly one of formally symmetrical federalism.[152] The formal equality of the states in the U.S. federal system might be thought to be ideologically connected to the appeal of "color blindness" as an acontextualized principle of formal equality.

D. TOWARD MODERATING CERTAINTIES ABOUT FEDERALISM

Knowledge of comparative constitutional federalisms may enhance capacities for constitutional self-awareness and judicial impartiality in resolving cases raising federalism issues. This is so even though foreign and international law is likely to be of more limited use in resolving discrete constitutional issues—for example those relating to the meaning of one or another allocation of power to one or another level of government—given the package-like quality of federalist bargains. One might contrast Justice Breyer's argument from the experience of other federalisms on the issue of "commandeering" (one that may carry less force when evaluated in the context of the entire federal package of arrangements in the different systems) with the suggestion made in Chapter 7, that awareness of the Canadian *Firearms Reference* decision might have highlighted the possibilities immanent in U.S. constitutional law—notably in the cases upholding the public accommodations provisions of the 1964 Civil Rights Act[153]—for a more holistic reading of the U.S. Constitution's Commerce Clause. To the extent that federalism cases require reasoning from what Charles Black called the "structures and relationships" of the Constitution,[154] understanding more about the nature and experience of other successful liberal democratic constitutional federalisms may be helpful, in a more diffuse way, in informing the "stance" of reviewing courts toward federalism-based claims about national power in the United States.

Comparative study might have a moderating effect on U.S. federalism discussions. Predictions of dire consequences if the Court upholds national legislation, challenged on federalism grounds, from time to time have reached a fevered pitch in the United States.[155] A calmer, more moderate stance might ensue if judges were more aware of how broad the powers are that states in the United States continue to exercise, especially in the realm of taxation and finance, when compared to those of subnational units in other Western federal democracies.[156] On the other hand, some argue that federalism in the United States is a nonfunctional vestige of the past that should influence neither statutory interpretation nor constitutional decision-making.[157] Such arguments, however, overlook the possible benefits of judicial doctrine that at least holds open the prospect of enforcing federalism-based limits against efforts dangerously to centralize power at the national level (perhaps not to be expected but theoretically possible). A knowledge that as the Nazis rose to power in Germany, abolition of the self-governing capacities of the Länder was a prelude to the consolidation of totalitarian rule (and the extermination of large parts of the population), and that the German constitution now guarantees as unamendable that Germany will remain a federal state, might well be relevant, for example, should a claim arise that an emergency requires the national government to replace or take over state governments.[158] Having a sense of perspective born of greater knowledge of the ways in which federal governments are constituted, preserved, and succeed or fail elsewhere may be important to informing the fundamental attitude that judges bring to federalism problems.

Comparative constitutional study may bear on a judge's stance in reviewing federalism challenges to legislation in another way as well. Understanding foreign constitutional systems would entail knowledge of the procedures used to amend foreign constitutions, thus emphasizing how much more difficult it is to change the U.S. Constitution through formal amendment than to change the constitutions of many other countries, including other strongly federal nations. While judicial review is quite commonly described in the United States as "countermajoritarian," the U.S. amendment process is in a sense also deeply "countermajoritarian" in the degree to which it allows small minorities to prevent formal constitutional amendment.[159] Given this difficulty in the formal amendment process, some degree of evolutionary potential allowing for "play in the joints" probably has been necessary to allow this Constitution to continue to provide a framework for governance. Awareness of the greater power of its own decisions to forestall majoritarian decision-making (relative to other constitutional courts in countries with easier-to-amend constitutions) could bear on the Court's willingness to give some deference to national legislative decisions in its own constitutional analyses.

Finally, as we have seen, divergent founding circumstances of federal systems[160] can be reflected in how their legal systems relate to transnational legal sources, even many decades (or centuries) after that founding. For the United States, the founding circumstance of slavery—and the post–Civil War agitation to protect the states' "rights" to maintain an immoral system of human degradation—continue to shadow efforts to promote the full embrace of modern human rights norms. Because these circumstances are so woven into the history of the United States, the resistance to transnationalism extends well beyond the pernicious systems that gave special power to that resistance. "States' rights" has, evidently, ceased to be regarded as a disreputable code for racism; it has been advanced as a basis for progressive state initiatives on gay rights, affirmative action, and environmentalism.[161] A deep commitment to localism and decentralized democratic decision-making is also characteristic of U.S. constitutional politics, and in recent years federalism has been deployed on the right and on the left as a basis for state experimentation and distinctiveness.

These orientations make it more difficult here to argue in favor of convergence with transnational human rights norms, because the discursive framework of federalism in the United States is one of a decentralized freedom of state and local governments to make different choices. Awareness of the roots of some hostility to international human rights law can serve as a helpful brake on the more extreme and unhelpful forms of unilateralist resistance to considering such transnational sources of law. But engagement (not convergence) with the transnational is what can most realistically fit into this constitutional tradition of federalism—a tradition that, however malevolent some of its strongest sources of inspiration may be, nonetheless appears to be deeply ingrained in the constitutional and political discourse, and which offers positive features of decentralization of, and thus checks on, power, and openness to decentralized, experimentalist approaches to law and legal regulation.

* * *

Neither in this chapter nor in Chapter 7 have I discussed comparative engagements that are simple, or whose implications for U.S. law are entirely clear. Engagement, done well, is complex, and perhaps more so than I have been able to capture. Even when there is a broad, deep and concrete transnational consensus, as on the juvenile death penalty, or when the constitutional practices of comparable liberal democracies caution against acceptance of broad claims of executive power, there is far more to good constitutional interpretation than simply going along; interpretation must remain rooted in national text, precedents, purposes, ethos, and history. Where foreign comparisons are more complex and ambiguous, like those discussed in this chapter, skeptics might argue that transnational comparisons are just not useful to judges. But knowing more about how constitutional law works elsewhere may contribute to a degree of humility about what we think we know and of open-mindedness to argumentation about the best way to interpret our own Constitution. These are qualities of mind to cultivate for all judges, and perhaps especially for life-tenured judges on a court of last resort.

9. CONSTITUTIONS AS MEDIATING INSTITUTIONS, TRANSNATIONAL CONSTITUTIONAL VALUES, AND ENGAGEMENT IN TWENTY-FIRST CENTURY CONSTITUTIONAL INTERPRETATION

Looking to foreign and international law, we have seen, has been a legitimate feature of the U.S. interpretive canon. And there is more reason in the twenty-first century to look to outside sources in interpreting the U.S. Constitution, both because there are more transnational legal resources that bear on common constitutional problems and because the legitimacy of national states depends more than in the past on their respect for transnational values of democracy, human rights, and the constitutional rule of law. Constitutional law does not always coincide with international law, or with transnational consensus on particular points, but respectful consideration of those transnational sources can help dispel the appearance of disregard for what are properly viewed as shared legal concerns.

Constitutions more generally function as sites of engagement between domestic and transnational norms and between domestic and transnational audiences, and they do so increasingly through the process of judicial interpretation. The pluralism of legal orders with respect to constitution-like norms calls out for the legitimizing force of justificatory reasoning; constitutional law will be called on to accommodate or to justify differences between national and transnational legal requirements. Increasing awareness of shared constitutional values among liberal constitutional democracies, as well as increasing numbers of jurisdictional conflicts of a constitutional character, will demand national responses,[1] reinforcing a deepening awareness of how domestic constitutional decisions are perceived by audiences abroad as well as at home.

Charles Black famously argued that judicial review performs not only a checking function, but also a legitimation function in validating contested laws.[2] People will disagree in good faith, he argued, and need a process in which they may participate that will give them an impartial answer whether the government actions with which they disagree are legitimate. His argument thus rested on the need to maintain the trust and confidence of the people in a functioning, democratic, national polity. The legitimating function of judicial review vis-à-vis other countries or the international community rests on quite different premises. Yet judicial review by independent courts itself may be legitimating, under international legal norms, and the effort to persuade, by good faith, public reasoning may contribute to the state's stature and negotiating power in the international community.[3] To the extent judicial review helps promote compliance with international norms that are also embodied in domestic law, it will have regime-legitimizing effects. But even where domestic constitutional law diverges from transnational norms, explaining—taking seriously transnational norms—may contribute toward a more diffuse form of legitimacy.

Judicial review by a domestic court will not, of course, have the same kind of legitimating force in the international sphere as in the domestic. To the extent that Black's argument was based not only on the Court's relative impartiality, but also on the opportunity of those within a polity to participate in a fair process, including influencing who sits on the courts, the argument does not apply to those outside the polity. Even where foreign citizens or states participate in litigation, as parties or through amicus briefs, they are not *of* the polity and do not have the opportunity through elections to participate in the making of laws or the selection of public officers who select justices. But while divergences from international norms may not be accepted by outsiders regardless of the justifications offered, the legitimacy of the process and the seriousness of consideration may go some of the way toward strengthening the legitimacy of the state. Moreover, the issues that come before the Supreme Court are often ones on which the American public is divided. To the extent that some of the American people are aware that practices of other democracies support their views of what the U.S. Constitution means (and they are likely to become more aware over time), there will be a legitimacy benefit within the polity from explanations for divergences.

Engagement with the transnational is at heart a project of constitutional self-definition, which also has the possibility of influencing, and being influenced by, developing transnational norms. Indeed, this closing chapter argues that domestic constitutions should be understood as inevitably in a relationship with international law and the constitutional approaches of other members of the international community, and not merely in the sense that constitutions provide rules (be they monist or dualist) for the incorporation of international law as domestic law, or in their approach to interjuridisctional conflict, or even in how expressly open they are to influence by transnational sources. International law and national constitutions are in a sense co-constituted; each depends in important ways on the other. At the same time, there are important variations in the nature of these relationships, with implications for the role of transnational legal sources in constitutional interpretation, which caution against arguments for any single cross-national model.

As discussed in Part A, domestic constitutions have long been designed to establish their countries as *states* in an international community. Conversely, the requirements for state recognition in international law depend on features typically addressed by national constitutions. Undergirding these phenomena is an interdependence between national constitutions and international law. Insofar as international law embodies transnational expectations of legitimate state behavior, those expectations have become thicker and more concerned with internal matters, not only in human rights, but in government organization. Such interdependent relationships between international law (and its state actors) and domestic constitutions provide support for conceiving of the role of international law in domestic constitutional interpretation within the terms of engagement models.

Moreover, the interdependencies of constitutional and international legal systems, in some ways logically entailed in the relationships of modern constitutions and international law, have deepened; they are perhaps most visible in moments in which existing state boundaries are in question, or in which subnational political entities begin to assume a more active role in transborder relations. As discussed in Part B, in situations involving the definition of states and membership in them, the dividing lines between domestic constitutional law and international law appear more permeable than ordinarily. Constitutions and constitutional law may be called on to facilitate the adjustment of legal relations, and even boundaries, among countries—functions sometimes considered the province of international law—thereby illustrating a blending of the roles of constitutional and international law. Distinctions between postures of engagement and convergence become less relevant in these settings as linkages and requirements are worked out between domestic constitutional law and international law or transnational legal norms. The relationships between domestic and transnational public law in settings of potential new state formation, and in the more complex federalisms that are populating our sociolegal context, are suggestive of an emerging form of transnational constitutionalism, which, I argue, is best understood as a set of shared values rather than shared legal rules.

In Part C, I revisit the sociolegal context for engagement. Not only is transnational engagement an increasingly inevitable feature of modern constitutional life, but it also offers the possibility for strengthening both the legitimacy and the effectiveness of domestic constitutional law in a world rife with other claims of norm-producing and regulatory authority and real threats to the security of national states. Efforts to account for the cross-national spread of legal norms and institutions, whether through processes of iterative persuasion or less instrumental forms of institutional isomorphism or acculturation, suggest the important stake that constitutional democracies have in the success of other constitutional democracies. For all of these reasons, the ambivalent resistance at times displayed by the U.S. Court to considering transnational sources of law in constitutional interpretation should be rejected in favor of a cautious embrace of the benefits of engagement.

A. THE INTERDEPENDENCE OF CONSTITUTIONAL AND INTERNATIONAL LAW

The U.S. Constitution of 1789, like other national constitutions that came later, had many purposes—among them, establishing a relationship to the transnational, to other countries, and to the international law governing states. The Constitution was intended to solve particular problems in foreign relations, including the important goal of securing state compliance with the Treaty of 1783, breaches of which provided occasion (or excuse) for British refusal to withdraw troops from U.S. territory.[4] More generally, the Constitution was intended to reinforce the standing of the United States as a state among others. To be a state among others in the world requires the agreement of other states, both for "constitutive" and practical purposes.[5] Indeed, it has been suggested that in contrast to "'the French Revolution, the American Revolution was not a nationalistic affront to international stability,'" because the Declaration itself implied that the independence being declared therein, the statehood within a community of national states, "could only come into force if it was accepted by other members of the international community. . . ."[6] But there are reasons to think that national constitutions are more generally designed to facilitate rather than obstruct compliance with the expectations of the international community.

Although, a written constitution has not historically been necessary to gain recognition as a state, a functioning (if nonentrenched) "constitution," or accepted ground-rules for governance, probably has been.[7] Today, moreover, almost all countries have written constitutions (many of which are, as a formal matter, entrenched and increasingly are subject to interpretation and enforcement in adjudication). Among the purposes manifest in the text of most written constitutions is to enable the country to deal externally with other countries, to enjoy respect from other countries as having a legitimate government. Constitutions provide for the making and enforcement of treaties and for the prohibition of acts in violation of international law. To the extent that constitutions are "constitutive" of their states and identified with them, constitutions and the international community have been in a sustained legalized relationship for centuries, one that is growing closer-knit through sociological and political processes as well as purely legal ones.

Recognition of States

From Westphalia to the present, international law has been contingent on the existence of states, even as it defines criteria for recognition as a state. Even today, states remain the dominant (if no longer exclusive) actors and subjects in international law. International law does not require that states have particular constitutions, written or otherwise, but it does require as indicia of recognition a number of characteristics that are intimately associated with the functions of constitutions. These indicia for recognition are often embodied in national constitutions that explicitly proclaim the "sovereignty" of their countries.[8]

Thus, one of the requirements of international law is that a state must have "competence, within its own constitutional system, to conduct international relations with other states. . . ."[9] Constitutional frameworks typically define the offices and procedures by which the "local" national community "treats" with other countries or international organizations—allocating powers, defining competencies, establishing procedures for the exercise of those competencies, and providing mechanisms by which international obligations are observed by and within the national community.[10]

In addition to having the "competence . . . to conduct international relations with other states," there are three other accepted minimal conditions for being recognized as a state in international law: a specific territory, a "permanent population," and a government that is effectively in control.[11] Modern constitutions are almost always written with a view to establishing status as a state in the international community under these traditional requirements. The condition that there be a functioning government in control of a territory and population is closely connected to fundamental constitutional purposes. While effective control is not necessarily secured by a written constitution, the purpose of a domestic constitution is to design and enable not only legitimate, but also effective government, through provisions specifying lawmaking power, powers of execution and administration of the laws, and providing for control over the use of coercive force. Constitutions seek establishment of a sufficiently empowered government to effectively maintain order and control over the national territory by, inter alia, specifying a hierarchy of legal norms and allocating authority over police and military forces for both internal and external matters.[12] The requirements in international law for a definite territory and permanent population are also typically assumed or addressed in national constitutions when they speak on behalf of a "people" or "peoples" in a specific territory.[13]

International Law and Domestic Constitutional Compliance

International law may also look to compliance with domestic constitutions on some issues of international law,[14] including recognition of successor governments. Regime change in accord with formal constitutional requirements may be a factor in international recognition of a successor state or government. Regime change through constitutional means typically raises no question of successor status or recognition of governments. However, the *unconstitutionality*, within domestic law, of a change in government may raise a question of recognition for countries that do engage in "recognition" of governments.[15] Though incipient norms favoring change by constitutional electoral means are not applied consistently,[16] on at least one occasion in recent years the unconstitutionality of a change in governments (a military coup against the elected president of Haiti) contributed to the international community's refusal to give recognition to the new government.[17]

Regional pockets of international lawmaking capacity also appear to be moving to include additional requirements for the recognition of new or successor states (or governments). In 1991, the European Community (EC) issued "Guidelines on the Recognition of New States in Eastern Europe and in the Soviet Union," which conditioned recognition, inter alia, on the new states having "constituted themselves on a democratic basis . . . [and] accepted the appropriate international obligations, . . . especially with regard to the rule of law, democracy and human rights," including the rights of ethnic and other minority groups.[18] According to Professor Sean Murphy, "[t]he European Community and United States recognized the statehood of the republics of the former Soviet Union based on these principles."[19] The EC developed similar guidelines for the recognition of new states emerging from the former Yugoslavia (under which recognition of Croatia was reportedly in question because of an absence of constitutional guarantees for minority group rights).[20] The Organization of American States (OAS) also appears to be developing norms generally aimed at promoting democracy, to deter and penalize "an unconstitutional interruption of the democratic order or an unconstitutional alteration of the constitutional regime that seriously impairs the democratic order in a member state."[21] These actions may be seen as an extension of the concern over the content of domestic constitutions evidenced in the UN's policy of nonrecognition of Southern Rhodesia, because it was established by a "racist settler minority," and of the OAS and the UN in response to the overthrow of elected President Aristide in Haiti.[22] These developments suggest that the ideas of self-determination of peoples, and of a right to democracy in international law, as elaborated by Thomas Franck's influential article,[23] might lay a foundation for future nonrecognition of new states, or sanctioning of existing ones, that deny the vote or other forms of participation to minority groups.

Moreover, as the Canadian *Secession Reference* case suggests, compliance with domestic constitutional obligations in dealing with potential secessionary situations may bear on the international community's willingness vel non to recognize a new state if an attempt at secession is made.[24] Distinguishing the principle of "effectivity" in recognition of new states in international law from any "right" to secede, the Canadian court observed that "foreign states may . . . take into account . . . an examination of the *legality of the secession according to the law of the state* from which the territorial unit purports to have seceded."[25] Thus, both longstanding requirements for being recognized as a state in international law—with the ensuing rights and obligations—and newer expectations that may be emerging for recognition or good standing in the international community, are based on factors of state character (and possibly compliance with substantive norms) typically embodied in national constitutions.[26]

Thus, for international law and the international community, domestic constitutions are an increasingly legitimate object of outside scrutiny. To be sure, this scrutiny is likely to be most aggressive with respect to weaker members of the international community, which may be a feature of international law more generally (and some would say, of law more generally).[27] But even if true, that does not detract from the significance of the point here—that is, the expansion of the arena of legitimate international concern with respect to the content and interpretation of domestic constitutions.

Overlapping Subjects

The fact of overlap between the goals and subjects of constitutions and of international law cannot be ignored, not only on human right issues, but on requirements for independent courts (and possibly on other separation of powers requirements), as well as on issues of trade and commerce. For example, both international human rights law and the constitutional law of most Western constitutional democracies value freedom of expression, religious freedom, liberty, fair trial process, and equality of treatment without regard to religion, race, or gender. Understanding those values and determining the best ways to apply them is at once a shared—and a specifically national—project.

With respect to the possibly emerging requirements for international recognition of states based on respect for democratic self-governance, the rule of law, protection of human rights, and commitment to the principle of non-aggression, it should be noted, constitutions typically specify the forms of self-governance to be followed in the constitution of their government, which might now be subject to evaluation under international requirements for democracy, the "self-determination of peoples" and the protection of minorities. Following the American model, many written constitutions now address the protection of specific individual rights. These typically overlap with (though they may not exactly correspond to) the "human rights" provided for in international law, which were developed from and have since served as an archetype for, constitutional bills of right.[28] Because of the possibilities of evaluation by other countries and international organs, national states may benefit from being able to point to protections in their constitution and laws for such rights.

International law now condemns the aggressive use of force by one state against the territorial integrity of another, and constitutions may also explicitly limit their own use of force with substantive criteria that embody the nonaggression principle (with perhaps the most prominent example being the renunciation of war and rights of belligerency in the constitution of Japan).[29] Even if they do not limit their country's use of force, constitutions in liberal democracies typically allocate responsibilities for its use in ways that may promote accountability under international nonaggression norms.[30]

International Incentives for Domestic Constitutional Change

International legal developments may provide incentives unrelated to recognition for other forms of domestic constitutional design or interpretation. Although the European legal order is admittedly quite distinct and more highly integrated than any other supranational regime, it is nonetheless noteworthy that many countries in Europe decided to modify their own constitutions in order to be able, legally, to ratify the Maastricht treaty.[31] France has recently amended its constitution to be able to ratify protocols to international human rights covenants prohibiting the death penalty.[32] (The EU also uses its economic leverage to encourage change in developing countries in governance and human rights.[33])

Other new international organs, such as the International Criminal Court (ICC), might be viewed as providing incentives for having adequate domestic mechanisms for prosecuting crimes that are also within the ICC's jurisdiction, through the "complementarity" provisions limiting prosecution before the ICC to those situations in which a state is "unwilling or unable genuinely to" investigate and prosecute a case.[34] And the World Trade Organization's existence establishes strong economic incentives for membership and appears substantively to affect state behavior, even if WTO sanctions are rarely (thus far) awarded.[35]

Interlock and Overlap

National constitutions, international law, and the attitudes and behavior of foreign states and foreign influences, then, have long been in interaction. National constitutions are framed in part with the international community in mind; international law's requirements depend, in part, on features typically defined in national constitutions. National constitutions have been "engaged" with the transnational from their inception. Increasingly (and particularly in Europe), more robust forms of interaction have emerged, going beyond the traditional requirements of state recognition toward a more demanding set of expectations.[36] International law and legal regimes and domestic constitutions and constitutional interpretation thus have both points of *interlock* (for example, with respect to criteria for recognition) and areas of *overlap* (to the extent that they address similar subjects).

In addition, constitutional law and customary international norms tend to develop in an interactive relationship. Customary international law is explicitly built on the practices felt to be obligatory by national states, but there may be a fine line between what is felt to be obligatory by virtue of domestic constitutions and what is felt to be obligatory by international law. As noted earlier, some constitutions have built explicit linkages to international law, incorporating particular international instruments as of constitutional stature, or incorporating some general principles of international law as a superstatutory norm.[37] If the same judges are interpreting and applying international as well as constitutional law on the same subject, some convergences of interpretation may be expected over time, but with influences likely running in multiple directions at once, from national courts to international adjudicators and back.[38] And many scholars believe that the formal hierarchy between international and constitutional is becoming less important in light of the increasing practice of interpretation in light of international law.[39] More points of interlock and overlap may be expected.

B. BOUNDARIES AND TRANSITIONS AT THE INTERSECTION OF INTERNATIONAL AND CONSTITUTIONAL LAW: TRANSNATIONAL CONSTITUTIONAL VALUES?

Although this chapter claims that constitutional law and international law are interdependent, in so doing it has assumed that they are separate bodies of law developed in different settings, grounded in distinctive decisional processes, and applicable to noncongruent populations. In some settings, however, international and constitutional law intersect more intensively, revealing deeper interconnections and suggesting the development of a transnational form of constitutionalism at their intersections. Where state boundaries are contested, as in Quebec and Northern Ireland, or transitions to new regimes take place, as in South Africa, the permeability, overlaps, and mutually reinforcing pulls of constitutional and international law may be particularly intense. The legal reconstruction of states may involve both transnational legal norms and domestic constitutional interpretation or the construction of new norms blending the international and national.

An incipient form of transnational constitutionalism is most clearly glimpsed in these seemingly anomalous moments, reflecting an emerging "shared law," or, perhaps better, a set of "shared values" of constitutionalism, which may contribute to both constitution-making and constitutional interpretation and to international legal developments.[40] Understanding transnational constitutionalism as a set of legal values, rather than clear legal rules,[41] I will suggest below, is a more accurate reflection of this development and is more compatible with approaches of engagement.

Boundaries, Membership, and Secession

Secessionary movements to create new states have often been resolved through civil wars as a matter primarily of power and international recognition.[42] With modern efforts to ban the aggressive use of force, civil wars have not come to an end, but international supervision of efforts to bring hostilities to a close has played an increasing role and with it a resort to law, including proposed constitutions.[43]

Under international law, a right to secede is not implied simply from the right of self-determination; rather, secession is generally regarded as justified only in colonial situations, in other settings of foreign oppression, or where there is a claim by a distinct people that their rights of self-determination have been seriously violated by the existing state, as by denial of meaningful access to government to pursue their own development, and there are no other effective remedies available.[44] Constitutions generally do not provide specifically for rights to secede, although it is not entirely unheard of. For example, the constitution of St. Kitts and Nevis specifies that on a two-thirds vote in Nevis to secede, it may do so and the 2003 Constitutional Charter of the State Union of Serbia and Montenegro included a clause permitting either party to withdraw after three years upon meeting certain procedural requirements, a measure used by Montenegro in 2006.[45] The constitution of the former USSR (Union of Soviet Socialist Republics) contained procedures for secession (not in fact used in the breakup of the Soviet Union), as did the constitution of Yugoslavia (which did not prevent violence in connection with some of the secessions from Yugoslavia).[46] And the constitution of Ethiopia includes provisions nominally permitting secession.[47] Some theorists favor secessionary rights, either on principles of democratic self-determination, or as a remedial measure where just cause exists.[48] Other scholars are more skeptical of the benefits of recognizing secessionary rights at all, analogizing nonconsensual secession to unhappy divorces with "joint custody" of populations and assets in ways that make irredentism, ethnic cleansing, and forced migrations more likely; Cass Sunstein, for example, has argued that a constitutional right of secession is inconsistent with the basic function of a constitution as a form of precommitment that enables and protects the democratic process.[49]

When a portion of a state breaks away, it necessarily implicates the domestic constitution (written or unwritten) of the prior state, the new state's own future constitution, and international law and relations. Consent of both populations, under authorized domestic procedures, if accompanied by protections for human rights in both parts, will have validating effects under both domestic constitutional law and international law. In the *Secession Reference Case* discussed in Chapter 8, the Canadian court rejected claims that, were there a referendum in favor of secession in Quebec, the province would have a right under international law to secede, finding no persistent rights violations in how Quebec was treated and noting that Quebec and its people participated in democratic decision-making in Canada. However, the court also held that if there were a "clear majority" vote on a "clear question," the unwritten but basic principles of Canadian constitutionalism would require the rest of Canada to negotiate with Quebec with respect to its position. In these negotiations, the court contemplated, due account would need to be taken for the protection of minority rights and respect for the rule of law (presumably, by adopting the terms of withdrawal according to the constitutional procedures for amendment), as well as for democracy and federalism. In its emphasis on the legitimating force of consent, the Canadian court echoed what some see as an emerging requirement in international law concerning the need for democratic consent to constitutions;[50] in its emphasis on the need to assure the protection of human rights, the Canadian court located its own unwritten constitutional principles in a stream of discourse compatible with post–World War II international law norms.

The Belfast (or "Good Friday") Agreement adopted for Northern Ireland ten years ago, though widely regarded as "constitutional" in character,[51] also has strong elements of an international agreement.[52] After decades of violence between the Catholic, Republican population, who favored union with Ireland, and the Protestant, Unionist population, who favored remaining part of Great Britain, the Agreement committed all parties—the United Kingdom, the Republic of Ireland, and the leading political factions in Northern Ireland—to the principle of consent of the people of Northern Ireland as the basis for any change in its legal status.[53] The agreement recognizes that although substantial numbers of people in Northern Ireland favor union with Ireland, at present the majority favors remaining part of the UK. It commits all sides in the future to "recognise the legitimacy of whatever choice is freely exercised by a majority of the people of Northern Ireland with regard to its status, whether they prefer to continue to support the Union with Great Britain or a sovereign united Ireland."[54] The agreement of both existing national states—Ireland and the UK—and of the leadership of the major factions within Northern Ireland to this process might be seen as a way of at once internationalizing and constitutionalizing the process of state boundary definition.

Rather than being determined by physical force, political compromise, or an international tribunal's or arbitrator's determination of historic claims or of which government has most shown a "'continuous and peaceful display of the functions of State'" within the territory,[55] the matter will be decided by constitutional processes of referendum, by which the voice of the people can speak. This approach at once enhances the legitimacy of whatever state boundaries result in the future and has the potential for destabilizing state boundaries in other parts of the world.[56] Is this a "constitutionalized international" law, or an "internationalized constitutional law"? The very line between the domestic and the transnational is at issue.[57]

Agreements such as the Good Friday Agreement, or the procedures and criteria for negotiating over secession defined by the Canadian court, are at once profoundly constitutional—providing, as they do, for the allocation of a most fundamental aspect of governance authority, namely, territorial jurisdiction—and profoundly uncharacteristic of one of the hallmarks of constitutions, insofar as they do not, indeed cannot, assert a distinct and definite national identity. In some respects, such agreements or approaches are the antithesis of a traditional national constitution, sounding more in the regularization of international procedures for the resolution of transnational disputes. A commitment to the protection of minority rights, and reliance on voting procedures in state-definition and membership contests, then, may sound in both constitutional law and international law in state boundary contests.

Transitional and Transnational Constitutional Processes

Although occupying or colonial powers have in the past imposed constitutions or constitutional conditions, constitution-making in recent decades has become both more "transitional" and more "transnational."[58] Not only in countries riven by civil war, but in a range of countries undergoing significant regime change, new forms of constitution-making are taking place—more deliberately transitional, incrementalist, and staged in character;[59] and more transnational, involving consultations with (if not management by) international actors (governmental and nongovernmental organizations), concerning constitutional design (including voting systems), constitutional rights, and constitutional enforcement mechanisms. The more transitional nature of these new constitution-making episodes reflects an understanding of a certain open quality of constitution-making, of being able to rely on provisional or interim agreements as more information is gathered about how those arrangements work, and as some degree of trust and mutual tolerance hopefully develop among those who are working the interim constitutional arrangements together. The more transnational approach in these new constitution-making episodes is but another reflection of the extent to which the vitality of public law, of constitutional law, and of some forms of international law are wrought up with the success of particular national states in making, living under, and effectively governing under their own domestic constitutions.

The South African process and the constitution that emerged from it exemplify the degree to which constitution-making—and the constituting or reconstituting of national states—has become a more transnational process. Although the leadership of the South African movement was indigenous, the influence of international law and of other liberal, democratic constitutional systems was obvious in the research and consultations performed. International pressures, through boycotts and sanctions, were over the long run important pressures on the white government to yield power, as were the contacts established between foreign jurists (including American lawyers like Sam Dash of Watergate fame) and members of the South African liberation movement. The African National Congress (ANC) drew legitimacy from the self-determination principles of international law and at the same time came to embrace commitments to the protection of minority rights embodied by international law and the ideas of constitutionalism in Western states.[60]

The South African example emphasizes important elements of the possibly emerging transnational constitutional order. Prominent among them is a simultaneous commitment to the legitimating force of judicial review by an independent court and the legitimating force of democratic decision-making—including constitution-drafting—by representative and referenda forms of democracy. The relationships of constitutions to democracy are complex. Constitutions facilitate democracy by establishing fixed ground rules for basic structures and elections and by protecting the preconditions for democratic decision-making, such as free speech; constitutions are designed to respect the outcomes of democratic decision-making when they do not threaten constitutional values; and constitutions are intended to constrain democratic outputs when they do cross constitutional lines. Illustrating the tensions between the *democracy-facilitating*, *democracy-respecting*, and *democracy-constraining* aspects of constitutionalism is the innovative role of the South African Constitutional Court in approving the final constitution.

The interim constitutional agreement in South Africa was negotiated by unelected representatives of the black majority with members of the existing government (who had come into office through undemocratic elections that excluded voting by the black majority). Under the Interim Constitution, the Constitutional Court was established and required to review the constitutionality of the Final Constitution, to see if it complied with the thirty-four basic principles agreed to in the multiparty (but not democratically elected) negotiating group.

South Africa's successful completion of the constitution-making process, drawing on both democratic processes and the independent constraint of judicial review, is thus a new blend of constitutionalism, which rests not only on the formality of prior legitimate consent, but on transnational substantive norms—democracy, the protection of minority rights, and respect for human equality and dignity—that draw their legitimacy from both substantive political morality and the clear approval of a majority of South Africans. South Africa both drew on and contributed to these transnational norms, not merely of human rights protection, but of the broader organization of a structure of governance designed to secure their protection. After South Africa's constitution-making of the 1990s, it is easier to say that particular governments or particular practices violate emerging transnational norms of constitutionalism.[61]

International interventions in recent years have encouraged the adoption of constitutions, including rights protections.[62] Without a core commitment to the protection of human rights, and enforceable mechanisms to secure those rights, the principle of democratic self-determination alone may have the potential to lead to ethnic conflagrations and oppressions, rather than to more peaceable and deliberative democracies.[63] International participants, an independent constitutional court, and international controls have been resorted to as mechanisms to promote rights protection in recent civil conflicts.[64] In a sense, then, the success of both domestic and international law in these settings is dependent on independent guarantors—mechanisms, internal or external, to secure the enforcement of these rights—a classic function of (at least Western) constitutions, enforced through judicial review, and now interlocking with the interests of the international community and echoed in the international law of human rights.

Federalism and the National/International Border

Federalism may be a significant site of the blending of international and constitutional law for at least three reasons. First, federal systems by definition include internal boundaries that might some day become (or, once were) international boundaries. These internal boundaries may not remain stable throughout time and their renegotiation may invoke parallel courses of international and domestic constitutional law. Second, federal systems illustrate that government authority can be shared, that "sovereignty" in this sense need not be exclusive—an insight that lies at the foundation of much of the concurrent regulation that now exists between supranational and domestic legal systems and that is at the foundation of the Northern Ireland agreements. And third, federal systems raise the possibility of nonstate actors, that is, subnational governments and their officials, participating in dialogue about the content of international law in ways that challenge conventional understandings of the exclusive role of states, secure on an internally sealed constitutional footing, as the creators of international law.

Thus, the Good Friday Agreement is of interest not only in its commitments to the principle of democratic consent to resolve a state boundary issue and to the protection of human rights whoever exercises sovereignty over the territory, but also in its creative cross-boundary forms of governance. Under Strand Two of the Agreement, a "North-South Ministerial Council" was established, made up of ministers from the Republic of Ireland, a national state, and from the new, democratic government of Northern Ireland, established under Strand One; Northern Ireland remained, as a legal matter, part of the United Kingdom, but was to be represented on this council by its own first minister and deputy first minister (positions designed to be shared by Unionist and Nationalist/Republican parties). This Council was not only consultative, but was intended to formulate common policy, by agreement of all concerned, for the entire island of Ireland.[65] Under Strand Three of the Agreement, an East-West group, the British-Irish Council, was also to be established, including representatives of the Westminster government, of all devolved parts of the United Kingdom, of Northern Ireland, and of the Republic of Ireland, to work by consensus on matters of common interest, including education, culture, agriculture, and EU matters.[66]

As devolutionary pressures increase in the foreseeable future, innovative forms of shared governance are more likely to emerge. As they do, the capacity of nonstate, subnational, or regional political entities to contribute to the formation not only of domestic constitutional law, but also of international law, may increase as well. As parts of federal states become or seek to become actors in transnational discourse and agreements, their positions may at once contribute to the development of domestic (subnational and national) and international law, suggesting that these two fields are related in the sources from which they draw and by which they are influenced.

Do these developments have any connection to the United States? After all, the United States in recent years has been identified with considerable "resistance" to the idea of considering foreign or international law in constitutional interpretation; it has resisted, in the name of the Constitution, efforts to require subnational implementation of decisions by international tribunals under ratified treaty instruments, as in the recent *Medellín* litigation.[67] Yet, even in the United States there is a reservoir of constitutional interpretation that could facilitate transfer from national to international status for territories, reflecting the porosity of legal boundaries to transnational influence; revisionist readings of the *Insular Cases*, for example, place weight on their authorization of "territorial deannexation" to achieve independence for the territories.[68]

Although secession of states (or territories) does not seem a likely event in the relatively close-knit legal order of the United States,[69] the possibility of state and local actors participating in the formulation and reformulation of international law is perhaps more foreseeable. Increasingly, states (and even local governments) in the United States pursue interests in foreign policy and relations with foreign states, even if their legal initiatives are sometimes found to be "preempted" by national power or statutes.[70] In a form of what Judith Resnik calls "translocal internationalism," state or local governments have endorsed human rights treaties, notably including the CEDAW, which the national government has not ratified, and taken steps to implement the Kyoto Protocol on control of greenhouse gases, also unratified by the United States;[71] and state courts independently consider human rights instruments, or the decisions of foreign constitutional courts or of international human rights tribunals, in resolving issues of state law.[72] These developments in the United States, and comparable or more intense forms of subnational interactions elsewhere,[73] suggest that although national states may remain in formal control of binding international law, the process of transnational value development is a broader one, with many more governmental (and nongovernmental) participants.

Contemporary constitutionalism in federal states, moreover, at once rests on the possibilities for consensual, democratic lawmaking and rights protection within traditional state boundaries and undermines strong claims of territorially based exclusive sovereignty. In federal systems, ultimate "sovereignty" is shared based on a consensually specified divisions of jurisdiction; the United States, with the first modern constitution of a national state, in Justice Kennedy's words, "split the atom of sovereignty"[74] in establishing a uniquely federal form of organization. These divisions of jurisdiction may be dynamic (as reflected in the federalism-related amendments to the German Basic Law in 2006)[75] and are not so far a step from sharing of governmental power across the boundaries of traditional national states. Once the "atom of sovereignty" has been split, cross-border governance, "shared sovereignty," and other forms of concurrent or overlapping jurisdiction, allocated differently for different functions, all become conceptually possible.[76]

Modern constitutions contemplate the use of legal processes to determine boundary issues, both within the national state (for example, under Article III of the U.S. Constitution the Supreme Court has jurisdiction over interstate boundary disputes) and, perhaps now, with respect to the existence of national state boundaries.[77] New transnational arrangements are emerging (albeit, thus far in only a small number of areas) in which the very boundaries of the "state" are regulated and subject to change in the name of some legal constitution-like instrument, through referenda-like processes, as in Northern Ireland. This phenomenon raises the question whether the idea of democratic participation in constitution-making, which some see as an emerging international norm, may lead to more porosity or contingency of the boundaries of the national state: Of course, Northern Ireland is, to a considerable extent, *sui generis*, its arrangements marked by innovation and creativity. But its approach is widely known and studied throughout the world; with increased interest in devolution, increasing regional autonomy or independence movements (as in Catalonia, or the Basque country), and the development of "shared sovereignty" arrangements (especially for weaker states),[78] its arrangements may well have influence elsewhere.

If domestic constitutions are read to include provisions governing the redefinition of the state itself, the boundaries between national and international law become more of a continuum than a sharp line. Transnational norms may be reconstituting our understanding of what legitimates governmental states; if constitutions were once dependent on pre-existent territorial entities, in the future the territorial boundaries of states themselves may become more fluid and depend on the outcome of quasi-constitutional norms and processes. Given that some subnational entities (California, for example, with its 37 million people) are larger than many national states, and that some subnational entities, notably in Belgium, have powers to conduct what looks like foreign relations (for example, exercising jurisdiction over export policies and work permits for foreign workers, with power to make treaties with foreign governments on matters within their jurisdiction),[79] the authority of subnational sources of law in contributing to understandings of international legal norms may be expected to grow. Moreover, the possibilities of subnational entities becoming separate states is becoming more legalized, and in ways that invite a blend of constitutional values and international law. It would thus not be surprising for international law to begin to look to subnational sources of law to help identify state practice, or for international and national law, working together, more generally to authorize subnational entities to make international agreements.[80]

Risks of Transnational Constitutionalism: Law or Values?

Although on issues relating to boundaries and membership it may be possible to see something like a transnational constitutional law of democratic self-determination at work, an intersectional blend of international and constitutional law, transnational norms more generally should be conceptualized as a set of overlapping or "shared values," rather than "shared law."[81] For while the presence of shared values among the constitutional democracies of the world is undeniable, moving too quickly to the conclusion that there are transnational legal rules risks undue diminution of the national spaces for deliberative democratic decision-making. A possible example of these risks is provided by Professor Tom Ginsburg's account of conflict between the Constitutional Court in Mongolia and the elected branches of its government.

Mongolia has judicial review under a written constitution and has been categorized as a "free" country by Freedom House for the past sixteen years.[82] Although the first government under the 1992 Mongolian constitution was formed from members of parliament,[83] after the 1996 elections the Constitutional Court declared it unconstitutional for members of the elected legislature to serve in the cabinet. In other words, the court found, parliamentary forms of governance with shared executive and legislative powers were unconstitutional. Arguments before the court invoked comparative practice, both of the United States and of parliamentary systems in Germany, Japan, and Britain, with counsel arguing that the presidential system in the United States should not be regarded as a model for interpreting the Mongolian constitution (which provided for both an elected president and a prime minister).[84] Professor Ginsburg has criticized the court's decision as inconsistent with rule of law considerations: it altered the rules of the political game just after an election in which the parties had detrimentally relied on prior practice; it was inconsistent with past practice; and it was inconsistent with the drafting history and text of the constitution, which rejected a complete ban on concurrent holding of posts for members of the parliament for a provision that said members could not hold other posts "'other than those assigned by law.'"[85]

After efforts to challenge the court's decision through a new statute specifically authorizing the holding of cabinet posts by members of parliament was rejected as unconstitutional by the court,[86] Mongolia in late 1999 passed its first amendment of the 1992 Constitution with "the support of all major political parties."[87] In March 2000, however, a panel of the court ruled that the constitutional amendment was itself incompatible with the constitution's separation of powers principle; the new parliament's leadership announced that it would nonetheless form the government out of members of parliament and expressed the view that it would not formally respond to the court decision, because doing so would imply "acceptance of the illegal action of the Constitutional Court in ruling a constitutional amendment unconstitutional."[88] Although it is unclear what effect transnational sources may have had, the nature of the argument described raises at least the possibility that the court disregarded the implications of its own constitutional text based on an understanding, influenced by transnational sources, of the necessary character of either "separation of powers" or of a system with a directly elected president.

Unlike the clear international norm in favor of independent courts discussed above in Chapter 3, and the international norm of some form of democracy as the basis for legitimate government, neither of the two principal human rights covenants speaks with specificity to the separation of legislative and executive power in constituting the government. There is no well-established transnational consensus among constitutional democracies prohibiting parliamentary forms of governance, or banning legislators from serving in other government positions,[89] and there is significant debate in the comparative government literature over the advantages of the different systems in promoting an effective rule-of-law democracy.[90]

To be sure, there is an increasing transnational discourse, among national governments and international organizations, concerned with governance structures and checks and balances.[91] On occasion, foreign states (including the United States) or international bodies have drawn on this discourse to take positions asserting national governments' violations of their own domestic constitutional orders. Such actions of foreign states or international bodies bespeak a confidence that there is something outside the constitution that permits a distinction between "sham" and "real" compliance with overarching norms of separation of powers and legitimate constitutional amendment, norms that are embodied in, but perhaps not fully defined by, discrete national texts. The willingness to look beyond the form of law (especially in condemning constitutional amendments as unconstitutional),[92] implies a capacity to judge the internal constitution and compliance therewith of other states. But this posture raises serious questions of constitutional theory, concerning both the source of normative law being applied and the basis for external actors to pronounce on it.[93]

Efforts to develop thick concepts of transnational constitutionalism pose some risks to democracy and to a perhaps desirable diversity in governmental structures, given how much is contested in our knowledge of how different systems of organization work. Engagement with the practices of other democracies seems a sounder basis for proceeding than efforts to prematurely articulate concrete standards around which constitutional democracies are expected to converge. Although courts are particularly charged with assuring constitutional justice, they must do so in a way that also advances democracy within their own polity. Democracy at any level bears risks of biases or prejudices operating, or simple failures to attend to the effects of general rules on vulnerable minority populations. Looking at constitutional problems from a transnational perspective can remind interpreters of how more universalist commitments are applied elsewhere, helping a court to distinguish between the legitimate products of representative government and those infested with bias. But as courts seek to implement the constraining features of constitutionalism, they must also remain grounded in the democracy-facilitating and democracy-respecting functions of domestic constitutions.

In this way, postures of engagement may be linked to a recognition that constitutionalism involves at once universalist principles and commitments to a particular community—loyalty to which comes not only from shared principles, but from working "with others in a common effort" to improve particular institutions in particular communities.[94] Postures of engagement, to the extent that they contemplate that the transnational may function as an intellectual check on constitutional moral blindness, are consistent with those attitudes of moderation and humility, of not being too sure one is right, that are regarded as fundamental to the tolerance a constitutional state in a heterogenous community must rest on,[95] and which may be necessary as well for effective international monitoring of the presumably greater diversity of approaches among different countries to issues of constitutional structure.

For all these reasons, therefore, the content of the emerging transnational constitutionalism ought to be conceived more in terms of shared *values* and shared problems than shared law.[96] A value or principle of avoiding undue concentrations of power, at the core of the idea of separation of powers and checks and balances, is one thing; a specific rule favoring parliamentary over presidential systems or vice versa is another. A shared value of having an independent judiciary is one thing; specific rules are another matter. Temporary judgeships may be prohibited by norms of independent and impartial judging in some jurisdictions and specifically permitted in others.[97] Decisions in Europe that judges may not simultaneously hold certain executive positions,[98] or the Canadian constitutional decision, based on unwritten norms, that prohibits legislative setting of judicial salaries without an independent commission,[99] may have less weight in less wealthy countries (where the resources to produce multiple levels and forms of governance may not be as great) or in countries that provide other forms of protection to the independence of judges (through, for example, specific recusal rules or constitutional guarantees that salaries cannot be diminished). Such rules are best regarded as specific instantiations of a more general transnational constitutional value of judicial independence. Engaging with the *values* of transnational constitutionalism, rather than seeking to discern and follow specific *rules*, is more likely to promote a good balance between national specificity and more universalist aspirations and to sustain the democratic legitimacy of domestic constitutional interpretation.

C. THE FUTURE: THE GRAVITATIONAL FORCE OF THE TRANSNATIONAL AND THE RANGE OF CONSTITUTIONAL RESPONSES

International law and the constitutional systems of the world are interdependent; each has a stake in the success of others. These interdependencies, manifested in the actions of the international community of possible nonrecognition or intervention, imply a mediating role for national constitutions between the global and the national. The interdependencies are explained, in part, by important work in international theory, both through the "transnational legal processes" of persuasion and acculturation that Harold Koh, Ryan Goodman, Derek Jinks, and others describe,[100] and by the relatively new state-building functions international law has begun to take on. Moreover, the legal pluralism created by the increasing overlap between the subjects of domestic constitutional law and the subjects of international law will tend to increase the occasions for influence back and forth as well. Yet these interactions may lead in multiple directions. The diverse situations of the nations of the world caution against efforts to impose a single rigid theory, descriptive or normative, on their constitutional postures toward the transnational. Engagement is a capacious approach, which embraces a range of variations in the postures actually taken.

Interdependence and Interpretation: Mediating the National and the Global

It might be objected that the relationships and influences between international law and national states do not have any necessary bearing on how domestic *constitutional* provisions should be interpreted by their own national courts. Even if some forms of domestic law, including treaty interpretation, provide avenues for a mediating function, constitutions are distinctive and may not necessarily be suited to play the same role. A constitution, it might be argued, could enable a state to continue to meet international criteria for recognition and comply with major elements of international law, while still being interpreted in a formalist or originalist way that excludes consideration of contemporary foreign or international law or practice. But this is not necessarily so.

First, modern constitutions designed to comply with international human rights law may well be understood to contemplate evolutionary understanding of their major elements, within certain large limits. And there is some reason to believe this would be true as well for at least some aspects of the (older) U.S. Constitution with respect, for example, to Congress's power to define offenses in violation of the law of nations, or the prohibition on cruel and unusual punishment. One might cabin the consideration of international or foreign law to discrete texts or issues and, as suggested earlier, foreign and international law are more relevant to some constitutions than others. But to assume that the external and internal functions of a constitution can be segregated into discrete compartments is less true than once it was, as the subjects of concern to international law have expanded. Although there are risks to the democratic legitimacy of constitutional law from being too closely tied to evolving transnational or foreign norms,[101] there are also risks to constitutional functions in ignoring that evolution.

Second, if a constitution is drafted or amended in the modern era, it is likely that its drafters were influenced by their consideration of foreign and international law, in ways that make it appropriate to consider the evolution of those sources of law as issues arise under the new constitution. Particularly for constitutions that emerge out of transnational constitution-making efforts, with deliberate modeling on aspects of foreign constitutions or international human rights law, the early years of interpretation after adoption of a new constitution may see resort to transnational sources that help explicate the new commitments. Even when constitutional change is less wholesale, transnational influences in constitution formation may be significant. In the United States, at least two major transnational movements contributed to constitutional change by formal amendment: the abolitionist antislavery movement was transnational in character, as was the women's suffrage movement, which grew out of and followed abolitionism.[102] Professor Resnik has thus challenged the conception of constitutional law as itself an entirely "domestic" category, arguing instead that the Constitution and evolving understandings of its meaning developed not in isolation from, but in conversation with transnational influences.[103]

Third, over time, shifts in understanding of basic concepts embodied in constitutional texts and international law are likely to occur, regardless of founding circumstances. Constitutions must both constrain and respond to developments. Different constitutions are designed to do so in different ways, with a different balance of amendment and interpretation as means of evolution.[104] If constitutional values are linked to maintaining status as a law-abiding member of the international community in a system that relies heavily on interpretation over time, its interpreters will necessarily be concerned with views of other countries.

International law, in turn, will be influenced by the reasoned interpretations and practices of national states, including the decisions of their courts.

Domestic constitutions, insofar as they shape official conduct and advance national self-definition, can function as "mediating institutions" between the global and the local (national) communities.[105] Constitutions are designed both to establish their nations as members of the international community and provide the basis and space for democratic politics internally; they are committed to some universal values and to some very particular national values. Their authorized interpreters thread the way among these functions. On this account, strong versions of resistance to *considering* international and transnational sources of law must be seen as incompatible with important purposes of the domestic constitution, both functional and expressive. Most nations' courts will, at times, disagree with others' interpretations of international obligations (raising the "competence-competence" issue with respect to the content of international obligations) or feel themselves obligated in any event to follow particularities of their own constitutional order for reasons already discussed. And whether to adopt a moderate posture of convergence through some presumption of constitutional consistency with international law or transnational consensus, or a posture of relational engagement with obligations to consider and respond to international law or transnational consensus, or a posture of deliberative engagement to consider such materials when they are brought before the court and appear useful in resolving some open issue of domestic law, raises questions on which reasonable minds may disagree. But that is a different matter from whether to rule out consideration of international or transnational norms—a possibility that is increasingly illusory, at least for jurists in the free world.

It would be a mistake to see national constitutions as merely transmission vehicles for some broader international legal system or values. It is the function of national constitutions to be interpreted for their particular polity, enforcing principles associated with that polity, however informed by transnational standards they may be. The mediating function of constitutions is to maintain connections both to the grounds for local legitimacy and principle and for transnational legitimacy. Although such mediation may produce coordination and coherence, it may not do so across the board. Constitutions that aim to promote democratic and effective government allow latitude for elected leaders to make decisions, and there may well be space between constitutional requirements and how to meet the country's international obligations that must be filled in by a democratically accountable leadership. That space can be provided by postures of engagement.

Constitutional Interdependence, Transnational Legal Process, Acculturation, and Changing Threats

Understanding some of the reasons for increasing degrees of constitutional interdependences reinforces the case for postures of engagement. Harold Koh has detailed a "complex process of institutional interaction whereby global norms are not just debated and interpreted, but ultimately internalized by domestic legal systems," through processes of dialogue, reasoning, persuasion, decision-making, and internalization of the norms that are thereby constructed.[106] While Koh's work focuses on the development of international or transnational legal norms, Professors Goodman and Jinks focus on the degree to which constitutive features of national states are influenced by a global culture that develops and spreads expectations of how a state functions; a culture in which "orthodoxy" is "the causal mechanism that drives the emergence and diffusion of global scripts (rather than habitualization and persuasion)."[107] Goodman and Jinks argue that "several constitutive features of the modern state (including the very notion of being an autonomous actor) are socially constructed at a global level," a "perspective [that] directly challenges the normative appeal and conceptual coherence of state resistance to other potentially conflicting global norms."[108]

Their work powerfully shows how the sense of legitimate government action is influenced by dominant norms. Whether cultural orthodoxy or iterative processes of persuasion are understood as the more central mechanisms, the relevance for this project is how entwined global influences necessarily are in the formed expectations and understandings of the subjects of public law in each national state (at least those that are committed to open discourse, as in liberal democracies).

Constitutional interdependence is grounded not only in the sociology of national and international norm development and adaptation in the realm of governance, but also in the national security interests of existing states. As Professors Anne-Marie Slaughter and William Burke-White suggest, "[t]he external security of many nations depends on the ability of national governments to maintain internal security sufficient to establish and enforce national law."[109] For Slaughter and Burke-White, this entails the need for international law to help build effective national governments, to "backstop" them, and, at times, to coerce their action, especially in adopting appropriate legal standards.[110]

If the main threats to world peace today derive from failing states (and the human rights violations, humanitarian disasters, massive and concentrated migrations, and attacks on neighboring states they spawn),[111] or if, as Philip Bobbit argues, a principal threat to democratic states is from nongovernmental terrorist organizations,[112] the implications are not only for international law, but for comparative constitutional law. International law is not a sufficient "backstop"; it does not purport to function within a framework of general governance. Threats to security from failed states and threats to democratic decision-making from the influence of nonstate actors provide reason for a considerable degree of engagement with the constitutional law of other states in an effort to reinforce, educate, learn from, and be part of a community of influence toward sustaining constitutional states that can maintain peace and advance justice within the world community.

As Goodman and Jinks write, "if global culture matters, the 'double standards' employed by some powerful states can have negative effects."[113] If major states ignore or treat contemptuously apparently relevant international standards or transnational consensus, their conduct may suggest to other states that a "go it alone" approach is what states do.[114] Such attitudes may be counterproductive, eliciting reactive refusals by other states to consider genuine security issues or reactive impositions of extra procedural hurdles designed to protect against future violations of transnational standards of treatment (as in the report of Dutch insistence, before extraditing a terrorist suspect to the United States, on an agreement requiring his return to the Netherlands to serve any sentence that might be imposed).[115] Security interests are at stake not only in obvious moments of state breakdown or affiliative identity conflict, discussed below, but more generally in sustaining or building constitutional democracies.[116]

Constitutional Diversity and the Mediating Role

Constitutional systems do not function as self-contained institutions, but work in a sociolegal environment affected by both national histories and cultures and by international legal orders and the constitutional approaches of other nations. A constitution provides a legal framework within which the competing demands of domestic and international law are reconciled, managed, or decided on; a constitution also provides a location for contest, within the polity, over what the country stands for and against, what its national identity is. That national legal identity is necessarily defined, in part, in contrast and comparison to the international community of which the state is a part. If, as Alex Aleinikoff suggests, the central question today is not *whether*, but "*how* do we mediate between and among normative systems,"[117] the answer, this book suggests, will to some extent vary among constitutional systems.

The range of variations in the relationships between national constitutions and international law, for example, are not captured by older dichotomies between monism and dualism. As discussed in Chapter 2, understanding these relationships requires an approach at once more granular and more general, which focuses on the degree of engagement or convergence with transnational sources of law by the system as a whole. For example, convergences might be sought by dualist systems through enactment of statutes requiring or encouraging compliance with international law, as much as or more than in systems that are "monist" with regard to ratified treaties, but ratify very few, or treat those they ratify as "non-self-executing." Judges may treat customary international law as relevant only to filling in "gaps" in domestic law, or to statutory interpretation but not constitutional interpretation, or to all of these. Such variations, as well as the age and depth of a particular constitutional regime, may influence which posture of engagement (or convergence) with international law in constitutional interpretation is the best fit with the particular national constitution. Systems may be more or less receptive (or resistant) to emerging international economic norms, than to international human rights norms.

As for foreign law, a similar range of postures is conceivable. A clear transnational consensus over a public law norm among constitutional democracies may particularly warrant consideration. Even absent such consensus, engagement is likely to increase in response to the sense of common venture in giving meaning to similar values, even if those values may be implemented in different ways. Different courts may develop patterns of looking at some foreign courts' decisions more than others, depending on other patterns of connection and influence, legal and otherwise; foreign judges who have studied in Germany, or Canada, or the United States, for example, may be more likely to refer to the jurisprudence of those courts than others.[118] In European countries, both high courts and lower-level courts have a rich set of incentives and institutional interrelationships that engage them with the decisions of the two European courts, which also have influence beyond Europe.[119]

Increased Interactions, Litigation, and Technology

Apart from the choices courts may make about their postures, the sheer likelihood of some degree of engagement with foreign law is increasing as a result of the growth of public law litigation involving multinational parties or situations. Situations of conflicts of public law are likely to occur with more frequency in today's world of travel, the boundaryless features of the Internet and contemporary communications technologies, multinational businesses, and the rise of dual citizenships. Conflicts that arise from the forms of legal pluralism created by interactions across boundaries in a transnational legal environment will yield contests over issues of jurisdiction, choice of law, and enforcement of judgments, which will call for the development of doctrinal approaches for coordination or priorities.[120] Constitutional law has already been deployed as a (contested) basis for jurisdictional coordination in the well-known Yahoo litigation;[121] constitutional law may in the future form a basis for invoking public policy exceptions to conflicts of law approaches grounded in private transactions, though other rules for public law conflicts may over time develop.[122] It will be impossible for courts (or legislatures) to resolve these kinds of issues without considering how other countries' courts (or legislatures) are likely to treat the same issue when it arises in the converse setting, and how they are likely to react to the U.S. rule.

Moreover, domestic and foreign constitutional law is likely to be invoked in litigation arising out of supranational dispute resolution[123] and the findings of supranational adjudicators under bilateral or multilateral investment treaties may influence U.S. judges and lawyers' views of their own practices.[124] Other constitutional issues cutting across boundaries, for example, involving the rights or status of foreign nationals, will also challenge courts to understand foreign public law: the interest of other nations in the treatment of foreign nationals under domestic constitutions of other states is obvious (as are the possibilities of tit-for-tat interpretive moves). But constitutional law might also be called on, together with international law, to limit the territorial reach of national law.[125] More generally, lawyers in large international law firms, local officials in transnational organizations, members of national government agencies, and activists in transnational social movements are all likely to be exposed to a wide range of transnational legal materials that may influence their views of domestic constitutional law.[126] And it is not only judges and lawyers but, at least in some cases, citizens sitting on juries who will increasingly be exposed to divergent constitutional approaches, as illustrated by a federal district court's decision to allow a jury to consider a communication from the South African Constitutional Court concerning its views respecting the removal of a person from South Africa for trial in the United States.[127]

It is not only through law and legal norms that transnational influence on constitutions is felt. Changes in technology and communication, nonstate global forces (including transnational businesses, cultural and artistic phenomena, terrorist movements, religious movements, ethnic nationalisms, transnational NGOs), growth in human migrations, diasporas, and increases in persons of multiple nationalities are all nonlegal forms of transnational influence on national and transnational organs and institutions, including national constitutions. Some of these forces exert influence toward more coordinated or harmonized legal regimes, while others may seek or create reactions toward more marked diversities. With increased communication, greater exposure to legal ideas and norms from around the world is inevitable (and so, too, are implicit comparisons). These phenomena do not necessarily imply across-the-board convergences, though given the relationships between global culture and national law there are likely to be some. Rather, they imply the possibility of change in national cultures, possibly including constitutional cultures, in a diversity of ways.

Future Choices and the Enduring Significance of National Constitutions

Given the kinds of interactions and processes described above, are we likely to see more areas in which constitutional law converges—not because courts or constitution-makers consciously decide to do so, but because of the impact of a globalizing legal culture in which courts participate? Are we likely to see more open engagement with foreign and international law as sources? Are domestic constitutions likely to diminish in significance? The answers are maybe, yes, and (probably) no.

More convergence around particular issues is certainly possible as cultural, political, social, as well as legal phenomena contribute to the spread of common problems and development of common ideas of how to handle them. Convergence may emerge not only with respect to substantive issues, but also with respect to interpretive methodology. Some courts may take postures of convergence with binding international law and of engagement with foreign law.

"Generic" constitutional law,[128] in both substance and methodology, or a "ius gentium" of public law,[129] may emerge in some areas, though the force of such moments of convergence within any particular constitutional system will depend on factors internal to that system as well.

Yet, globalization can be expected to produce not only convergences but fragmentations, particularly likely to emerge around identity-based movements that may be nationalistic in character. The rise of interest in sharia law at the constitutional level is only one example of a potential line of marked divergence among constitutional systems, but there are a number of others, especially in light of the ongoing tensions between neoliberal economic ideas (under considerable assault at the time of this writing in the fall of 2008) and more social and community-based concepts of rights in the global South. Moreover, one cannot ignore the threats that exist to liberal democratic constitutional orders from outside of law and secular conceptions of law—from terrorism, from fundamentalisms of various sorts, and from the economic powers of multinational business activities. These threats to the centrality and power of law reinforce the stake that liberal constitutional democracies have in one another's success; they also will affect different countries in different ways. Hence, a decided "maybe" to the question of likely convergences.

More important than specific convergences or divergences will be the continued processes of inquiry and learning from other systems, deliberation, and reasoned, public justification in response. Constitutions will continue to be important foundations of state-centered public law; indeed, they may contribute to the development of more constitutionalized forms of international law, and they are likely to assume greater importance as expressions of national identity, even as they are being continuously informed by developments in international law and in other countries' constitutional systems. One can thus expect to see more engagement and of greater variety. Learning cannot be cabined; high court judges on listservs with one another, the circulation and widespread availability of opinions in English translations (English becoming something of a lingua franca of law)—all this will only accelerate the learning process. Absent an unforeseeable "dark age" in which the digital/electrical connections between producers of law are suddenly and substantially disrupted, law will continue to develop at multiple levels, through multiple, interdependent loops of knowledge and influence, positive and negative. Whether formally committed to reflexivity in constitutional learning and interpretation, through modes of democratic experimentalism, or otherwise,[130] constitutional systems and their courts, including the Supreme Court of the United States, will inevitably be influenced—the questions are only ones of degree, both of influence and of directed self-awareness in the process.

National constitutions are likely to endure as important legal instruments. They are perhaps likely to assume greater importance as expressions of national identity, as they are under more pressure to allow or produce some degree of convergence with economic coordination systems and with human rights norms. Despite moments and episodes of the "postnational" in the highly integrated setting of Europe,[131] for the most part "this global era [is one] of the universal extension of state formation to all the peoples of the world. The universal extension of state formation reflects the establishment of a post-colonial standard of political legitimacy," in a global society.[132] That is, constitutional states—states based on law, constrained, engaged with, and influenced by a transnational community of law in other states and at the supranational level—are likely in the future to coexist with the development of supranational or international legal orders. These supranational orders, however, are not likely to displace constitutional states as principal organs of general governance and of political identity.[133]

As noted, the transnational is by no means a unitary phenomena; globalization in Europe is different and may have quite different relationships with domestic constitutions than globalization in South America, for example, or the United States. Convergence of human rights and constitutional rights is a different matter than convergence with respect to business and commercial regulation. Postures of either engagement or convergence can allow national constitutions to play the mediating role discussed earlier. As we have seen, even constitutions committed to convergence or harmony with the transnational, at least thus far, have been interpreted to reserve to national authorities the meaning of the transnational norm, creating the possibilities for divergences. The mediating role is not only of significance to the internal law of the country, but may be of significance to the development of transnational legal standards; these standards, in turn, will need to continue to allow for and be influenced by the diversity of national orders under which the lives of human societies can be beneficially organized.

Does this imply that "engagement" may be the most attainable posture for the domestic constitutions of other nations, insofar as elements of diversity (as well as of relationship to the world order of nations) inhere in the very idea of a national constitution? The role of national constitutions in the twenty-first century differs in important respects from nineteenth- and early twentieth-century constitutions, in that national constitutions are no longer the exclusive (or necessarily principal) source of defining potentially binding legal norms of public law. And yet, they retain special functions performed by no other body of law in expressing distinctive national experience and particularities, while structuring, empowering, and constraining a general government. So, for example, Professor Slaughter suggests that justices of the U.S. Supreme Court might acknowledge that some U.S. First Amendment jurisprudence is quite different from that of most other Western democracies, as "an artifact of the particular history of this country," while at the same time explaining the comparative merits of the U.S. approach.[134] To the extent that the particularities of free speech doctrine might "legitimately differ"[135] in different countries, the point is that constitutional law can "mediate," in the sense of expressing respectful recognition of those differences without necessarily abandoning them.

Yet, articulating a single overarching model of the relationship between transnational law and domestic constitutional interpretation is probably not reasonable, since states are situated in quite different relationships to international law and transnational norms. If the model of resistance is based on the assumed superiority of national law, or the exclusive legitimacy of domestic sources in constitutional interpretation, and the model of convergence is based on the assumed superiority of transnational norms or the strongly persuasive value of transnational consensus, the model of engagement is one based on discursive and epistemic rather than hierarchic assumptions about constitutional interpretation and the role of the transnational. "Engagement" is an attractive model for a very wide range of states, itself embracing a range of locations between strong resistance to transnational norms and softer versions of convergence.

The permissive model of "deliberative" engagement is plainly useful for many constitutional orders and may be a particularly good fit with older constitutional regimes whose basic constitutional frameworks predate modern international law, and which may have accumulated substantial bodies of internal precedent and practice that constitutes their particular forms of constitutionalism. Considering transnational legal sources may at once identify important differences and important similarities between the domestic constitution and others; foreign or international law may have no effect on a domestic court's constitutional decision or simply prove unpersuasive; it may lead the court to conclude that its own situation is quite distinctive, thereby helping to illuminate in a deeper way the constitutional values and institutional particularities of the judge's own constitution; or it may prove helpful and persuasive in identifying, among a range of interpretations plausible within domestic resources, what the domestic judge concludes is the best interpretation of her own constitution.

Deliberative approaches to engagement consider foreign and international law primarily as an intellectual resource for improved decision-making about the national constitution, on the assumption that the national constitution is the fundamental legal norm of its particular country. The discourse is focused on heightening judges' capacity for better informed and even for more objective (in the sense of being able to bring to bear multiple perspectives) deliberation about the content of their own constitutional norms. International and foreign law are reflective tools, rather than hierarchic demands; depending on the nature of the issue, international law with its binding obligations, or foreign constitutional law from closely comparable polities, reflecting the lived judgments of judges who work within ongoing governments of countries in which they live, may at times have greater persuasive value, as to the role of the judge or as to better interpretive understandings of particular rights or powers in the national constitution.

Deliberative engagement with the transnational is distinct from, but may also over time contribute to a more *relational* approach as courts come to feel some obligation to consider—though not necessarily to follow—transnational legal sources that bear on the issue before them. An *obligation to consider* might arise not only from the possible deliberative benefits, but also from a felt sense of connection—whether to a transnational community of constitutional (or human rights–deciding) judges, whose professional role in some sense obligates them to consider and contribute to a corpus of law, or to the idea of law as a search for better ways to resolve common problems or implement common values, or to the people of the world, in recognition that the laws of any one country (and here, particularly of the more powerful countries) may have effects beyond its own borders.[136]

The relational pull—the sense of an obligation to consider—may be stronger with respect to international law than the domestic constitutional laws of other countries, depending on factors discussed earlier, including the formal legal status of the international norm within the domestic system, the nature of the processes by which it was adopted, its conformance, vel non, with fundamental rights protected in the domestic system, and its interpretive relationship to national constitutional texts.[137] The relational pull of other countries' decisions would depend, inter alia, on their commitment to a shared legal norm. The relational pull of a deep and broad transnational consensus on a point involving shared values might call for a public explanation or justification of why a particular country reaches or adheres to a different conclusion, although unlike in a convergence model, it may not provide an independent reason to adopt that view. An obligation to consider international or foreign law is more likely to produce greater knowledge by domestic decision-makers about such law, though whether that means it will produce more convergences depends on a number of other factors, including the degree of convergence already contemplated by the framers or the text of the constitution, and the willingness of judges to distinguish (as the South African court did in the *Grootboom* case discussed in Chapter 3) between the particularities of international and domestic law.

The first approach to engagement, grounded in its capacity for enhancing the quality of judicial deliberation about the meaning and application of the domestic constitution, may be more palatable especially to very powerful countries with long established and distinctive traditions. Assuming that judges can "engage in engagement" without losing a sense of the distinctiveness of their own system's norms, it raises fewer concerns about democratic legitimacy and self-government.[138] At the same time, it can inform domestic interpreters of those areas in which the choice of domestic interpretations may have implications for the international status or standing of the country—a legal fact that may, from prudentialist or consequentialist perspectives, be of some relevance. The second approach to engagement may require some external motivation (for example, a state's perceived need to align with others in its interpretive approaches, or some special license, as in constitutional directives as to interpretation, in order to enjoy domestic legitimacy). It is more likely to both result from, and to assure on an ongoing basis, at least some areas of intense overlap between local and transnational normative understandings.[139] A deliberation-enhancing model of engagement may coexist with a relational model, and the one may tend to lead to the other; yet there are distinctions in attitude and likely frequency of resort to transnational law between them that may result in a more incrementalist and cautious approach in the former model.

In either case the central idea is to engage, to consider, and not, necessarily, to follow or harmonize with. For as we have seen, there is a potential "dark side" of any legal regime. International law is made through processes that depend, at least in some cases, on decision-making by polities that may not be internally democratic, whose contributions to transnational norms are not weighted in accordance with their population or degree of internal democracy, and which represent a very wide and divergent range of legal cultures. As Slaughter and Burke-White suggest, the "new purposes of international law" to help "backstop, strengthen and compel" state governance—are a "double-edged sword."[140] A leading example of the potential "dark" underside of this sword are the provisions of UN Security Council Resolution 1373 which, inter alia, requires states to freeze the assets of terrorist groups designated as such by a Counter Terrorism Committee established by the Resolution,[141] but "with no international legal control over this determination whatsoever"[142] and arguably without appropriate procedural protections. The recent decision of the European Court of Justice in the *Kadi* case may be seen as an example of a supranational court's resistance, on behalf of its own and its member states' constitutional commitments to human rights, to the purportedly superior claims of international law.[143] The ECJ holding that Council orders implementing the UN Security Council resolutions on sanctions for terrorist financiers were in violation of fundamental European norms of procedural due process is suggestive of the benefits of interpretive space that engagement postures provide.

International law, like domestic state law, may be subject to forms of capture by multinational economic interests, as many would argue the Trade-Related Aspects of Intellectual Property (TRIPS) agreement on intellectual property represents.[144] Even international human rights and humanitarian law and movements may have their "dark side" of, inter alia, disfranchisement of community decision-making in the name of contested specifications of human rights,[145] or false claims of representation, or even legitimizing violence.[146] The transnational is no guarantor of wise judgment. Moreover, misapplying the values of transnational constitutionalism in a particular context is another risk. Thus, notwithstanding the uncertainty engendered by a posture of engagement, rather than by a presumption of convergence, the possibility of serious inquiry for what the transnational norm does or does not reflect about the domestic constitutional norm allows more space for domestic constitutions to police, as well as be influenced by, the international.[147]

For now, in much of the world (including the United States), domestic settings, framed by national constitutions, remain a better vehicle for the development and sustenance of meaningful democratic politics and representative decision-making than international or supranational settings. Although we are likely to see continued increases in legal systems' knowledge of and capacity to interact with foreign and international law in the development of domestic constitutional law, national constitutions will continue to provide the working framework for democratic governance and change within particular national polities. But they will also play an important role in mediating the national state's relationship to legal norms and values in the larger world community, norms and values that no one country can hope to control.

For all these reasons, candid embrace of engagement and commitment to engage in a disciplined and open-minded way should be the hallmarks of enlightened and enduring U.S. constitutionalism in the 21st century. For if the U.S. Constitution is still "intended to endure for ages to come,"[148] it must be able to navigate through the twenty-first century's expanded universe of law.

NOTES

INTRODUCTION: CONSTITUTIONAL COSMOLOGY

1. *See Constitution Restoration Act of 2004: Hearing on H.R. 3799 Before the Subcomm. on Courts, the Internet and Intellectual Property of the H. Comm. on the Judiciary*, 108th Cong. (2004); *see also Appropriate Role of Foreign Judgments in the Interpretation of American Law: Hearing on H. Res. 568 Before the Subcomm. on the Constitution of the H. Comm. on the Judiciary*, 108th Cong. (2004).

2. Practice Direction on the Citation of Authorities, (2001) 1 W.L.R. 1001 (Eng.) (issued by the Lord Chief Justice of England and Wales, Apr. 9, 2001), *available at* http://www.hmcourts-service.gov.uk/cms/814.htm.

3. S. AFR. CONST. 1996 § 39.

4. CONST. ARG. § 75(22).

5. *See* David Schneiderman, *Constitutional Approaches to Privatization: An Inquiry into the Magnitude of Neo-Liberal Constitutionalism, in* REGULATION 501, 524–26 (Colin Scott ed., 2003).

6. *See* Loi constitutionnelle de modernisation des institutions de la Ve République (1), arts. 29, 30, Law No. 2008-724 of July 23, 2008, Journal Officiel de la République Française [J.O.] [Official Gazette of France], July 24, 2008, p. 11890; 1958 CONST. art. 61-1 (Fr.), *English transl. available at* http://www.assemblee-nationale.fr/english/8ab.asp#TITLE%20VII; *see also* "France Backs Constitution Reform," BBC News, July 21, 2008, *available at* http://news.bbc.co.uk/2/hi/europe/7517505.stm; The French Political System—Constitutional Reform—2008, http://about-france.com/constitutional-changes-2008.htm. At this writing I am unaware whether a statute has gone into effect implementing this constitutional change.

7. The term "transnational" encompasses not only international law as it is traditionally understood (to embrace widely adhered to treaties, conventions, and customary international law), but also regional agreements and bilateral agreements, as well as the domestic law of foreign nations when considered, relied on, or distinguished in another tribunal's or lawmaking body's decisions. Transnational law may also include the domestic law of particular countries that seek to regulate transnational phenomena, such as migration, "trafficking," or citizenship.

8. *See, e.g.*, Rainer Nickel, *The German Federal Constitutional Court: Present State, Future Challenges, in* BUILDING THE UK'S NEW SUPREME COURT: NATIONAL AND COMPARATIVE PERSPECTIVES 175, 196 n.64 (Andrew Le Sueur ed., 2004); Neil Walker, *The Idea of Constitutional Pluralism*, 65 MOD. L. REV. 317, 337 (2002); *see also* Roderick A. MacDonald, *Metaphors of Multiplicity: Civil Society, Regimes and Legal Pluralism*, 15 ARIZ. J. INT'L & COMP. L. 69, 76 (1998).

9. *See* LAW AND GLOBALIZATION FROM BELOW: TOWARDS A COSMOPOLITAN LEGALITY (Boaventura de Sousa Santos & César A. Rodríguez-Garavito eds., 2005); BALAKRISHNAN RAJAGOPAL, INTERNATIONAL LAW FROM BELOW: DEVELOPMENT, SOCIAL MOVEMENTS AND THIRD WORLD RESISTANCE (2003).

10. *See generally* PHILIP BOBBITT, SHIELD OF ACHILLES (2002); THOMAS L. FRIEDMAN, THE WORLD IS FLAT (2005).

11. For a brief summary of writing on the "right of abode" cases arising in Hong Kong, and the "review" of judicial decisions exercised by the Standing Committee of the National People's Congress, see VICKI C. JACKSON & MARK TUSHNET, COMPARATIVE CONSTITUTIONAL LAW 269–70 & n.e (2d ed. 2006). On a decision concerning the right of education, which some hailed as China's *Marbury*, see Chris X. Lin, *A Quiet Revolution: An Overview of China's Judicial Reform*, 4 ASIAN-PACIFIC L. & POL'Y J. 180, 197 (2003); *see also* Benjamin L. Liebman, *China's Courts: Restricted Reform*, 21 COLUM. J. ASIAN L. 1, 14 (2007) (suggesting that Chinese "courts are playing more important roles than in the past . . . [and] courts confronted by [political instructions or] pressures are increasingly likely to try to use legal arguments to resist"); Ignazo Castellucci, *Rule of Law with Chinese Characteristics*, 13 ANN. SURV. INT'L & COMP. L. 35, 51–52 (2007) (describing tensions between the Supreme Court's interpretive rulings and NPC decisions). *See generally* Randall Peerenboom, *Law and Development of Constitutional Democracy in China: Problem or Paradigm?*, 19 COLUM. J. ASIAN L. 185, 218–219, 224–25 (2005) (discussing the increased role of the constitution, courts' resistance to supervision by the procuratorate, and public pressures for imposition of the death penalty); RANDALL PEERENBOOM, CHINA'S LONG MARCH TOWARD RULE OF LAW 121 n.119 (2002).

12. TOM GINSBURG, JUDICIAL REVIEW IN NEW DEMOCRACIES: CONSTITUTIONAL COURTS IN ASIAN CASES 26 (2003), *quoting* John W. Meyer et al., *World Society and the Nation State*, 103 AM. J. SOC. 144, 145, 149 (1997) (also discussing the influence of "worldwide models" and "standard scripts" in nation-state development and characteristics).

13. *See* H.W.O. Okoth-Ogendo, *Constitutions Without Constitutionalism: Reflections on an African Paradox, in* CONSTITUTIONALISM AND DEMOCRACY 65, 71 (Douglas Greenberg et al. eds., 1993).

14. RAN HIRSCHL, TOWARDS JURISTOCRACY: THE ORIGINS AND CONSEQUENCES OF THE NEW CONSTITUTIONALISM 44 (2004).

15. *See* Mathew C. Stephenson, *"When the Devil Turns . . . ," Political Foundations of Independent Judicial Review*, 32 J. LEGAL STUD. 59 (2003) (describing support for independent judicial review as resting on political competition); *see also* GINSBURG, *supra* note 12, at 18 (describing judicial review as "political insurance"); Mark Ramseyer, *The Puzzling (In)dependence of Courts: A Comparative Approach*, 23 J. LEGAL STUD. 721 (1994).

16. *See, e.g.*, Martin Shapiro, *The Success of Judicial Review and Democracy, in* ON LAW, POLITICS AND JUDICIALIZATION (Martin Shapiro & Alec Stone Sweet eds., 2002).

17. Commitment to international human rights agreements might serve similar purposes, or, as may be the case with domestic constitutions, might serve more self-interested elite purposes of creating the appearance but not the reality of future compliance.

18. *See* Cass Sunstein, *Constitutionalism and Secession*, 58 U. CHI. L. REV. 633, 637 (1991); *see also* JON ELSTER, ULYSSES AND THE SIRENS: STUDIES IN RATIONALITY AND IRRATIONALITY (1984). For Elster's afterthoughts on constitutions as precommitments, see JON ELSTER, ULYSSES UNBOUND (2000).

19. Sunstein, *supra* note 18, at 639. Sunstein suggests that constitutions may function to take a range of contentious issues off the table, such as with respect to property rights, religion, or abortion. *Id.* at 639–40. Experience suggests, however, that constitutions lack the capacity to take issues that remain truly contentious off the table for long. The provision in the U.S. Constitution prohibiting Congress from regulating the slave trade for twenty years until 1808 was arguably more effective toward the goal of building a union in the early decades than was its studied silence (or *Dred Scott*'s interpretation) on the legality of slavery thereafter.

20. C. F. STRONG, A HISTORY OF MODERN POLITICAL CONSTITUTIONS 155–56 (1963) (describing attitudes of the French toward their constitutions prior to the Third Republic), *quoted in* Albert P. Blaustein, *The Influence of the United States Constitution Abroad, in* EUROPEAN AND AMERICAN CONSTITUTIONALISM IN THE EIGHTEENTH CENTURY 120, 124 (Michal Rozbicki ed., 1990).

21. THE FEDERALIST NO. 43, at 293 (James Madison) (Jacob E. Cooke ed., 1961); *see also* Jon Elster, *Forces and Mechanisms in the Constitution-Making Process,* 45 DUKE L.J. 364, 388–90 (1995) (discussing the importance of secrecy and compromise); Vicki C. Jackson, *Principle and Compromise in Constitutional Adjudication: The Eleventh Amendment and State Sovereign Immunity,* 75 NOTRE DAME L. REV. 953 (2000).

22. *See* CHARLES L. BLACK, JR., THE PEOPLE AND THE COURT: JUDICIAL REVIEW IN A DEMOCRACY 34–86 (1960).

23. *See, e.g.,* Kim Lane Scheppele, *Aspirational and Aversive Constitutionalism: The Case for Studying Cross-Constitutional Influence Through Negative Models,* 1 INT'L J. CONST. L. 296 (2003); *see also* Judith Resnik, *Law as Affiliation: "Foreign" Law, Democratic Federalism, and the Sovereigntism of the Nation-State,* 6 INT'L J. CONST. L. 33 (2008).

24. *See* Okoth-Ogendo, *supra* note 13, at 67–68.

25. *See, e.g.,* S. AFR. CONST. 1996 pmbl. & § 39.

26. For example, decisions of the French Conseil Constitutionnel from 1999 onward were available on the Internet at least as of mid-2006. *See* Harvard Law Library (last visited Sept. 23, 2006), http://www.law.harvard.edu/library/services/research/guides/international/france/const.php. The website of the French Conseil Constitutionnel makes available not only the opinions, but the underlying materials, and includes a number of cases with English translations. *See* http://www.conseil-constitutionnel.fr/conseil-constitutionnel (click on icon for English)

27. In June 1994, Vernon Bogdanor and Bernard Rudden could write that Professor S.E. Finer's 1979 book, *Five Constitutions,* "was never reprinted and so the texts of major constitutions became once more hard to find." S. E. FINER, VERNON BOGDANO, & BERNARD RUDDEN, COMPARING CONSTITUTIONS vii (1995). Today, those who have access to a subscription to Constitutions of the Countries of the World can view the constitutions of close to 190 countries online, with information about amendment history. *See* http://www.oceanalaw.com/default.asp (visited Sept. 1, 2008). Those without a subscription can view, free over the Internet, the constitutions of some 89 countries translated into English thanks to the International Constitutional Law Project, *see* http://www.servat.unibe.ch/law/icl/index.html (last visited Sept. 1, 2008); foreign constitutions in various languages are also available at the University of Richmond Constitution Finder, http://confinder.richmond.edu/ (last visited March 4, 2009). And the website Constitutionmaking.org, a joint project of the U.S. Institute for Peace and the Comparative Constitutions Project, has a number of constitutions (current and historical) available in English translations.

28. The Venice Commission (the European Commission for Democracy through Law) is the advisory body on constitutional law to the Council of Europe; it was authorized in 2002 to accept non-European members and now has over 50 member countries. Its Secretariat has produced a regular *Bulletin on Constitutional Case-Law,* that along with its CODICES data base, reports on the constitutional case law of its members and some non-European courts as well as the ECJ and ECtHR. *See* http://www.venice.coe.int/site/main/Presentation_E.asp.

29. Progressive Policy Institute, Trade Fact of the Week (Sept. 3, 2003), http://www.ppionline.org/ppi_ci.cfm?knlgAreaID=108&subsecID=900003&contentID=252023 (from 57 countries in 1900 to 192 in 2000); *see also* SEAN D. MURPHY, PRINCIPLES OF

INTERNATIONAL LAW 3, 24 (2006) (45 states in existence in 1945, 191 in existence in 2005); Countrywatch, http://www.countrywatch.com/facts/facts_default.aspx?type=text&topic=SECNT (last visited Mar.4, 2009) (193 independent states in the world).

30. *See* DONALD S. LUTZ, PRINCIPLES OF CONSTITUTIONAL DESIGN 4 (2006) (fig. 1.1).

31. *See* JOHANNES MORSINK, THE UNIVERSAL DECLARATION OF HUMAN RIGHTS: ORIGINS, DRAFTING, AND INTENT 12 (1999).

32. *See* International Covenant on Civil and Political Rights (ICCPR) (visited Sept. 1, 2008), *available at* http://www.ohchr.org/english/countries/ratification/4.htm; International Covenant on Economic, Social and Cultural Rights (ICESCR), *available at* http://www.ohchr.org/english/countries/ratification/3.htm (visited Sept. 1, 2008).

33. The U.S. Constitution that came into force in 1789 is the first modern, written constitution of a national state; Poland and France both saw written constitutional instruments in 1791. On the influences on and among the eighteenth-century American, French, and Polish constitutions, see the essays in CONSTITUTION AND REFORM IN EIGHTEENTH CENTURY POLAND: THE CONSTITUTION OF 3 MAY 1791 (Samuel Fiszman ed., 1997); *cf.* MARK BRZEZINSKI, THE STRUGGLE FOR CONSTITUTIONALISM IN POLAND 39–45 (1998) (describing the influence of the English unwritten constitution and the 1789 draft of the French constitution on the 1791 Polish constitution).

34. Akhil Amar, *Some New World Lessons for the Old World,* 58 U. CHI. L. REV. 483, 483 (1991).

35. LEON FRASER, ENGLISH OPINION OF THE AMERICAN CONSTITUTION (1783–1798), at 55 (1915) (indicating that the Constitution was sent to the British Ministry "by the ship Peggy, Captain Wallace," on September 18, 1787, and that by October 30, 1787, copies of the Constitution had appeared in British newspapers).

36. *See, e.g.*, THE FEDERALIST NOS. 15, 16 (Alexander Hamilton), 18 (Alexander Hamilton & James Madison) (Jacob E. Cooke ed., 1961); DUMAS MALONE, JEFFERSON AND THE RIGHTS OF MAN 161 (1951); JACK RAKOVE, ORIGINAL MEANINGS 26–27 (1996); *see also* Amar, *supra* note 34, at 487–88 (discussing concerns for union to avoid internal and external wars).

37. Letter of the President of the Federal Convention, Dated September 17, 1787, to the President of Congress, Transmitting the Constitution, *available at* http://avalon.law.yale.edu/18th_century/translet.asp (signed by George Washington, President, By Unanimous Order of the Convention). For discussion, see Daniel Farber, *The Constitution's Forgotten Cover Letter: An Essay on the New Federalism and the Original Understanding,* 94 MICH. L. REV. 615 (1995).

38. *See* THE FEDERALIST NOS. 7 (Alexander Hamilton), 42, 43 (James Madison), 75 (Alexander Hamilton) (Jacob E. Cooke ed., 1961).

39. *See* Martin v. Hunter's Lessee, 14 U.S. 304, 334 (1816) (describing the jurisdiction that included "Cases affecting Ambassadors" as "of vital importance . . . to the national sovereignty").

40. *See* Glass v. The Sloop Betsey, 3 U.S. (3 Dall.) 6, 16 (1794) (stating "that no foreign power can of right institute, or erect, any court of judicature of any kind, within the jurisdiction of the United States, but such only as may be warranted by, and be in pursuance of treaties," and thus "the admiralty jurisdiction, which has been exercised in the United States by the Consuls of France, not being so warranted, is not of right").

41. 3 U.S. (3 Dall.) 199, 235–37, 244–45 (1796) (Chase, J.); *see* Carlos Manuel Vázquez, *The Four Doctrines of Self-Executing Treaties,* 89 AM. J. INT'L L. 695, 699 (1995).

42. *See, e.g.*, Worcester v. Georgia, 31 U.S. (6 Pet.) 515, 560–61 (1832) (referring to the law of nations in defining the status of Indian tribes within the United States); Holmes v. Jennison, 39 U.S. (14 Pet.) 540, 569–72 (1840) (Taney, C.J., opinion for four justices) (concluding that state governors lacked power to extradite the defendant to a foreign

nation in light of the national government's treaty power, which Taney interpreted in light of the practice of nations); Prigg v. Pennsylvania, 41 U.S. (16 Pet.) 539, 611 (1842) (noting that the fugitive slave clause in the Constitution marked a departure from the law of nations, which would have allowed one state to refuse to recognize slave property based on municipal laws in another state).

43. Okoth-Ogendo, *supra* note 13, at 67 (emphasis in original).

44. *See, e.g.*, Roper v. Simmons, 543 U.S. 551, 622–28 (2005) (Scalia, J., dissenting); Richard A. Posner, *Foreword: A Political Court*, 119 HARV. L. REV. 31 (2005).

45. *See supra* note 11; *cf.* Ran Hirschl, *The Question of Case Selection in Comparative Constitutional Law*, 53 AM. J. COMP. L. 125 (2005) (discussing five principles of case selection for small-n comparative constitutional studies).

46. Rough proxies for the rule of law can be found by working with several sources, including the rankings for respect of political and civil liberties provided by Freedom House, and categorizations by political scientists, for example, of countries that are "constitutional republics (democracies)," LUTZ, *supra* note 30, at 129–30 (discussing separation of powers and popular control as measures). Most of the countries in these categories rely on courts to provide some enforcement of constitutional or quasi-constitutional instruments; in some, courts lack power to invalidate national laws, though they are empowered otherwise to enforce constitutional or quasi-constitutional norms.

47. The ECJ and the ECtHR are regional supranational courts, dealing with questions that arise in their member states, under international covenants and agreements among those states and law developed under those agreements. Neither court is wholly analogous to a domestic constitutional court. Yet each issues binding decisions, interpretations, or judgments; their opinions are influential in national court systems, especially in Europe but beyond as well. Like constitutional courts, they decide questions affecting government powers and individual rights that "cannot be resolved merely by finding out what a contemporary majority" in a national state has decided, VICKI C. JACKSON & MARK TUSHNET, COMPARATIVE CONSTITUTIONAL LAW 194–95 (2d ed. 2006), and many of the issues they address parallel those that arise in domestic constitutional courts.

48. For a helpful introduction to U.S. debates on some of these issues, see CURTIS A. BRADLEY & JACK L. GOLDSMITH, FOREIGN RELATIONS LAW: CASES AND MATERIALS 427–43 (2002).

49. For helpful scholarly accounts of some of the terrain of resistance, from interpretive theory, democratic commitments, the challenges of accurate comparison, or skepticism about the predilections of judges, see Roger Alford, *In Search of a Theory for Constitutional Comparativism*, 52 UCLA L. REV. 639 (2005); Jed Rubenfeld, *Commentary, Unilateralism and Constitutionalism*, 79 N.Y.U. L. REV. 1971, 1999 (2004); Michael D. Ramsey, *International Materials and Domestic Rights: Reflections on Atkins and Lawrence*, 98 AM. J. INT'L L. 69, 77–79 (2004); Kenneth Anderson, *Squaring the Circle? Reconciling Sovereignty and Global Governance Through Global Government Networks*, 118 HARV. L. REV. 1255, 1307 (2005) (reviewing ANNE-MARIE SLAUGHTER, A NEW WORLD ORDER (2004)); Ernest A. Young, *Comment: Foreign Law and the Denominator Problem*, 119 HARV. L. REV. 148 (2005); Kenneth Kersch, *The New Legal Transnationalism, the Globalized Judiciary, and the Rule of Law*, 4 WASH. U. GLOBAL STUD. L. REV. 345.

50. *See generally* INTERPRETING CONSTITUTIONS: A COMPARATIVE STUDY (Jeffrey Goldsworthy ed., 2006).

51. On universalist or natural law approaches, see, e.g., David Held, *What Hope for the Future? Learning the Lessons of the Past*, 9 IND. J. GLOBAL LEGAL STUD. 381 (2002); Donald Kommers, *The Value of Comparative Constitutional Law*, 9 J. MARSHALL J. PRAC. & PROC. 685 (1976). On common law approaches, see Jeremy Waldron, *The Modern Ius Gentium*, 119

HARV. L. REV. 129 (2005); *see also* Paolo G. Carozza, *"My Friend is a Stranger": The Death Penalty and the Global Ius Commune of Human Rights,* 81 TEX. L. REV. 1031 (2003); Peter J. Spiro, *Treaties, International Law and Constitutional Rights,* 55 STAN L. REV. 1999, 2022–25 (2003); *cf.* David S. Law, *Generic Constitutional Law,* 89 MINN. L. REV. 652 (2005) (arguing that the nature of constitutional justification contributes to generic forms of argument); Jeremy Waldron, The Storrs Lectures, "'Laws Partly Common to All Mankind': Foreign Law in American Courts," Yale Law School (2007), *available at* http://www.law.yale.edu/admissions/podcasts.asp (visited Sept. 4, 2008) (developing a "bottom-up" argument for treating some rights as widely agreed-on in the world).

52. *See* David Held, *Cosmopolitanism: Globalization Tamed?,* 29 REV. INT'L STUD. 465 (2003); *cf.* Harold Hongju Koh, *International Laws as Part of Our Law,* 98 AM. J. INT'L L. 43, 56 (2002) (discussing interlinking processes of compliance); Harold Hongju Koh, *On American Exceptionalism,* 55 STAN. L. REV. 1479 (2003) (discussing adverse effects of U.S. "double standards"). On externalities, see Mattias Kumm, *Democratic Constitutionalism Encounters International Law, in* THE MIGRATION OF CONSTITUTIONAL IDEAS 256, 266–67, 271 (Sujit Choudhry ed., 2006) (arguing that subsidiarity may favor domestic incorporation of international law where it addresses transnational externalities).

53. *See* Yuval Shany, *How Supreme Is the Supreme Law of the Land?,* 31 BROOK. J. INT'L L. 341 (2006) (arguing for incorporating international human rights standards from ratified treaties in constitutional interpretation); *cf.* Harold Hongju Koh, *Transnational Legal Process,* 75 NEB. L. REV. 181, 206–07 (1996) (arguing that transnational legal processes promote both generation of and compliance with international norms).

54. *See, e.g.,* Nadine Strossen, *Recent U.S. and International Judicial Protection of Individual Rights: A Comparative Legal Process Analysis and Proposed Synthesis,* 41 HASTINGS L.J. 805, 825–27 (1990) (arguing that the United States' leadership role makes it appropriate that international human rights norms "be observed in domestic litigation at least to the limited extent of being considered in interpreting and applying ambiguous provisions of domestic positive law"); *see also* Brief of Amici Curiae Mary Robinson et al., Lawrence v. Texas, 539 U.S. 558 (2003) (No. 02-102), 2003 WL 164151, at 30 (suggesting that "parochial analyses" will "undermine U.S. influence"); Claire L'Heureux-Dubé, *The Importance of Dialogue: Globalization and the International Impact of the Rehnquist Court,* 34 TULSA L.J. 15 (1998) (exploring reasons for the relative decline in influence of the U.S. Supreme Court internationally, including as one its "failure . . . to take part in the international dialogue among the courts of the world, particularly on human rights issues"). *Cf.* Sarah H. Cleveland, *Our International Constitution,* 31 YALE J. INT'L L. 1, 102 (2006) (noting that the U.S. "is a major and active participant in the creation, development, and interpretation of international law").

55. For scholarly accounts of dialogue or engagement with the transnational in constitutional interpretation, see, for example, Sujit Choudhry, *Globalization in Search of Justification: Toward a Theory of Comparative Constitutional Interpretation,* 74 IND. L. J. 819 (1999); Cleveland, *supra* note 54; David Fontana, *Refined Comparativism in Constitutional Law,* 49 UCLA L. Rev. 539 (2001); Gary Jeffrey Jacobsohn, *The Permeability of Constitutional Borders,* 82 TEX. L. REV. 1763 (2004); Kumm, *supra* note 52; Frank I. Michelman, *Reflection,* 82 TEXAS L. REV. 1737 (2004); Cheryl Saunders, *The Use and Misuse of Comparative Constitutional Law,* 13 IND. J. GLOBAL LEGAL STUD. 37, 67 (2006); Mark Tushnet, *The Possibilities of Comparative Constitutional Law,* 108 YALE L.J. 1225 (1999); Melissa Waters, *Getting Beyond the Crossfire Phenomenon: A Militant Moderate's Take on the Role of Foreign Authority in Constitutional Interpretation,* 77 FORDHAM L. REV. 635 (2008).

56. *See, e.g.,* Vicki C. Jackson, *Packages of Judicial Independence: The Selection and Tenure of Article III Judges,* 95 GEO. L.J. 965, 1002 (2007) (suggesting that even though life tenure

for judges is, based on comparative constitutional experience, demonstrably not necessary for achieving effective levels of judicial independence, changing that ongoing system for federal judges in the United States now could have unforeseen and possibly adverse effects).

CHAPTER 1. RESISTING THE TRANSNATIONAL

1. John O'Sullivan, Op-Ed., *High Court Opposites Dazzling Off the Bench*, CHI. SUN-TIMES, Oct. 25, 2005, at 43; *see* Roger Alford, The Breyer-Scalia Road Show, Opinio Juris (Oct. 26, 2005), *available at*, http://lawofnations.blogspot.com/2005/10/breyer-scalia-road-show.html (last visited Jan 21, 2009).

2. *See* Mark C. Rahdert, *Comparative Constitutional Advocacy*, 56 AM. U. L. REV. 553, 558–59 (2007) (summarizing testimony).

3. *See* Jack Tsen-Ta Lee, *Interpreting Bills of Rights: The Value of a Comparative Approach*, 5 INT'L J. CONST. L. 122 (2007) (describing the "four walls" doctrine of constitutional interpretation for Malaysia and Singapore); *see also infra* note 88.

4. Carlos F. Rosenkrantz, *Against Borrowings and Other Nonauthoritative Uses of Foreign Law*, 1 INT'L J. CONST. L. 269 (2003).

5. Mary Ann Glendon, Op-Ed., *Judicial Tourism*, WALL ST. J., Sept. 16, 2005, at A14.

6. Mark Tushnet, *The Possibilities of Comparative Constitutional Law*, 108 YALE L.J. 1225 (1999).

7. The preamble to the Chinese constitution was amended in 1993, 1999, and 2004, suggesting its expressive importance in delineating ongoing Chinese history, ideology, and accomplishments. See XIAN FA (Constitution) pmbl. (1982) (P.R.C.), *translated in* 4 CONSTITUTIONS OF THE COUNTRIES OF THE WORLD: CHINA 1–3 (Rüdiger Wolfrum & Rainer Grote eds., 2005). For the language from the Iraqi constitution, see PERM. CONST. OF THE REPUBLIC OF IRAQ pmbl (2005), *translated in* 9 CONSTITUTIONS OF THE COUNTRIES OF THE WORLD: IRAQ 1–2 (Rüdiger Wolfrum & Rainer Grote eds., 2007).

8. Atkins v. Virginia, 536 U.S. 304, 348 (Scalia, J., dissenting) (quoting Thompson v. Oklahoma, 487 U.S. 815, 868–69 n.4 (1988) (Scalia, J., dissenting)).

9. Robert Post, *The Challenge of Globalization of American Public Law Scholarship*, THEORETICAL INQUIRIES IN LAW (online version), Vol. 2, No. 1, Article 11 (2001).

10. On the framers and natural law, see, e.g., Suzanna Sherry, *The Founders' Unwritten Constitution*, 54 U. CHI. L. REV. 1127 (1987); Thomas C. Grey, *Origins of the Unwritten Constitution: Fundamental Law in American Revolutionary Thought*, 30 STAN. L. REV. 843 (1978).

11. Western Australia v. Ward, (2002) 213 C.L.R. 1, 390–91 (Callinan, J.) (emphasis in original). For discussion, see Devika Hovell & George Williams, *A Tale of Two Systems: The Use of International Law in Constitutional Interpretation in Australia and South Africa*, 29 MELB. U. L. REV. 95 (2005); Hilary Charlesworth et al., *Deep Anxieties: Australia and the International Legal Order*, 25 SYDNEY L. REV. 423, 461–63 (2003).

12. RANDY E. BARNETT, RESTORING THE LOST CONSTITUTION: THE PRESUMPTION OF LIBERTY 89–117 (2004) (arguing that "original meaning" originalism is the best way to "'lock in' a constitution that is initially legitimate because of what it says").

13. *Id.* at 120–21; *id.* at 93 (discussing Ronald Dworkin, *Comment*, *in* ANTONIN SCALIA, A MATTER OF INTERPRETATION: FEDERAL COURTS AND THE LAW 116 (1997)).

14. Jeffrey Goldsworthy, *Originalism in Constitutional Interpretation*, 25 FED. L. REV. 1, 20 (1997); *see also* Jack Balkin, *Abortion and Original Meaning*, 24 CONST. COMMENT. 291, 292–93, 295–97 (2007) (distinguishing "expected application" from "original meaning").

15. On the nature of interpretive discretion as a legally bounded activity, see AHARON BARAK, JUDICIAL DISCRETION 18–20 (1989). *Cf.* KEITH WHITTINGTON, CONSTITUTIONAL INTERPRETATION: TEXTUAL MEANINGS, ORIGINAL INTENT AND JUDICIAL REVIEW 5–7 (1999) (characterizing, somewhat differently from Barnett, interpretation as "legal" and constuction as "political").

16. BARNETT, *supra* note 12, at 103–09.

17. On other forms of exegesis, see, e.g., ELLIOT DORFF & ARTHUR ROSETT, A LIVING TREE: THE ROOTS AND GROWTH OF JEWISH LAW (1988) (describing a change from prophecy to exegesis as the basis for Jewish law).

18. *See* Richard Posner, *Foreword: A Political Court*, 119 HARV. L. REV. 31, 86–87 (2005) ("To cite foreign decisions as precedents is indeed to flirt with the idea of universal natural law, or, what amounts to almost the same thing, to suppose fantastically that the world's judges constitute a single, elite community of wisdom and conscience.").

19. On the assertedly dominant role of "will" or popular consent, in American constitutionalism, see, e.g., Paul W. Kahn, *Comparative Constitutionalism in a New Key*, 101 MICH. L. REV. 2677, 2700 (2003); Paul W. Kahn, *Political Time: Sovereignty and the Transtemporal Community*, 28 CARDOZO L. REV. 259, 268–70 (2006); Jed Rubenfeld. *Unilateralism and Constitutionalism*, 79 N.Y.U. L. REV. 1971, 1999–2000 (2004). For an argument that interpreting an older constitution to be consistent with current international law would impermissibly change the constitution without resort to constitutional amendment procedures, see Al-Kateb v. Godwin (2004) 219 C.L.R. 562, 592 (Austl.) (McHugh, J.).

20. *See, e.g.*, Joan L. Larsen, *Importing Constitutional Norms from a "Wider Civilization": Lawrence and the Rehnquist Court's Use of Foreign and International Law in Domestic Constitutional Interpretation*, 65 OHIO ST. L.J. 1283 (2004); Kenneth Anderson, *Foreign Law and the U.S. Constitution*, POL'Y REV. 33, at 41 (June–July 2005). In past generations, intense social "value" issues in the United States would have included regulation of labor contracts, or permitting or prohibiting racial discrimination; in contemporary times, examples would include discrimination against homosexuals, the availability of abortion, or the death penalty.

21. Roger Alford, *In Search of a Theory for Constitutional Comparativism*, 52 UCLA L. REV. 639, 674 (2005); *see also* Ernest A. Young, *Comment: Foreign Law and the Denominator Problem*, 119 HARV. L. REV. 148 (2005).

22. 540 U.S. 93 (2003) (upholding campaign finance regulation), discussed in Alford, *supra* note 21, at 680.

23. Although the Court in *McConnell v. FEC* did not refer to foreign law, justices have referred to foreign constitutional approaches in other campaign finance cases. *See* Nixon v. Shrink Missouri Government PAC, 528 U.S. 377, 403 (2000) (Breyer, J., concurring) (noting Canadian and European constitutional approaches to evaluating campaign finance regulations). The Court did refer to foreign experience in addressing malapportionment in the 1960s, noting the British problem with rotten boroughs. *See* Reynolds v. Sims, 377 U.S. 533, 568 n.44 (1964) (characterizing the British experience of eliminating "rotten boroughs" as "interesting and enlightening"). And while it is true that foreign and international law have played only a subsidiary role in Eighth Amendment cases, the tradition of the Court's looking to those sources on substantive "cruel and unusual" punishment issues goes back to 1879. *See* Vicki C. Jackson, *Constitutional Comparisons: Convergence, Resistance, Engagement*, 119 HARV. L. REV. 109 (2005).

24. *See, e.g.*, Aharon Barak, *Foreword: A Judge on Judging*, 116 HARV. L. REV. 16 (2002); JUDGES IN CONTEMPORARY DEMOCRACY: AN INTERNATIONAL CONVERSATION (Robert Badinter & Stephen Breyer eds., 2004).

25. JOHN HART ELY, DEMOCRACY AND DISTRUST: A THEORY OF JUDICIAL REVIEW (1980).

26. *See* Alford, *supra* note 21, at 645, 675. For a different view on this point, see Rosalind Dixon, *A Democratic Theory of Constitutional Comparison*, 56 AM. J. COMP. L. 947, 976 (2008) (suggesting that foreign constitutional practices can help determine the "evolving content of U.S. standards").

27. *See* Rosenkrantz, *supra* note 4, at 269.

28. *See, e.g.*, Nelson Lund & John O. McGinnis, *The Boundaries of Liberty: Lawrence v. Texas and Judicial Hubris*, 102 MICH. L. REV. 1555, 1581 (2005) (asking, critically, "Can the Court really be implying . . . that the decisions of foreign courts have more authority than decisions of American legislatures or even prior decisions of the U.S. Supreme Court itself?").

29. Rosenkrantz, *supra* note 4, at 286.

30. *See, e.g.*, 1 BRUCE ACKERMAN, WE THE PEOPLE: FOUNDATIONS 23 (1991) (explaining theory of dualism, distinguishing between the people acting in their constitutional capacity in constitutional moments and the outcomes of ordinary politics); *see also* Paul Kahn, *Community in Contemporary Constitutional Theory*, 99 YALE L.J. 1, 22–23 (1989) (commenting on "community discourse" as an attempted resolution of will and reason, and stating: "The Court, then, represents the community's better self: It represents its public identity to its private constituents."); *cf.* Frank Michelman, *Foreword: Traces of Self-Government*, 100 HARV. L. REV. 4, 17 (1986) (suggesting that "if the Justices have any way to further the cause of our self-government, it lies through the exercise of their own").

31. *See* Jonathan Miller, *The Authority of a Foreign Talisman: A Study of U.S. Constitutional Practice as Authority in Nineteenth Century Argentina and the Argentine Elite's Leap of Faith*, 46 AM. U. L. REV. 1483, 1516–21, 1523–26 (1997); Rosenkrantz, *supra* note 4, at 272–73.

32. Rosenkrantz, *supra* note 4, at 277; *see* Miller, *supra* note 31, at 1547–61.

33. *See* H.W.O. Okoth-Ogendo, *Constitutions Without Constitutionalism: Reflections on an African Political Paradox*, *in* CONSTITUTIONALISM AND DEMOCRACY: TRANSITIONS IN THE CONTEMPORARY WORLD 65, 70–72 (Douglas Greenberg et al. eds., 1993). Law as autochthonous identity is related to expressivism, but emphasizes more the organic cultural and historical connections between a people and a constitution, rather than, for example, constitutional expression of transformative or universalist goals.

34. *See also* Rosenkrantz, *supra* note 4, at 293–94 (arguing that a constitutional culture can develop only when constitutional law is "perceived and experienced as a unique and final umpire in all the conflicts that may emerge among citizens of a democratic state").

35. Lund & McGinnis, *supra* note 28, at 1606–07.

36. Rosenkrantz, *supra* note 4, at 290, 295.

37. Charles Fried, *Scholars and Judge:, Reason and Power*, 23 HARV. J.L. & PUB. POL'Y 807, 817–19 (2000).

38. Posner, *Foreword*, *supra* note 18, at 86.

39. *See, e.g.*, Christopher McCrudden, *A Common Law of Human Rights? Transnational Judicial Conversations on Constitutional Rights*, 20 OXFORD J. LEGAL STUD. 499, 507 (2000); Yash Ghai, *Sentinels of Liberty or Sheep in Woolf's Clothing? Judicial Politics and the Hong Kong Bill of Rights*, 60 MOD. L. REV. 459, 479 (1997); Pradyumna K. Tripathi, *Foreign Precedents and Constitutional Law*, 57 COLUM. L. REV. 319, 343–44, 346 (1957); *cf.* Adam Smith, *Making Itself at Home: Understanding Foreign Law in Domestic Jurisprudence: The Indian Case*, 24 BERKELEY J. INT'L L. 218, 265–66 (noting Indian Court's "cherry picking" associated with aspirational uses of foreign law)

40. *Cf.* New York Times v. Sullivan, 376 U.S. 254, 280–82 (1964) (adopting as constitutional law the tort rule on defamation of public officials in Kansas, rather than that followed in some other states, including Alabama, where the case before the Court had arisen).

41. *See* Christopher McCrudden, *Human Rights and Judicial Use of Comparative Law, in* JUDICIAL COMPARATIVISM IN HUMAN RIGHTS CASES, at 16–17 (Esin Örücü ed., 2003) (describing advocate's reliance in ECJ litigation on U.S. gender equality cases but omission of relevant case, *Johnson v. Transportation Agency*); *cf.* Li-ann Thio, *Beyond the "Four Walls" in an Age of Transnational Judicial Conversations: Civil Liberties, Rights Theories, and Constitutional Adjudication in Malaysia and Singapore,* 19 COLUM. J. ASIAN L. 428, 487–89 (2006) (describing "misrepresentation" in courts' use of foreign law). On early post-Charter enthusiasm for, but mistakes in, the use of *international law* by Canadian courts, see Anne F. Bayefsky, *International Human Rights Law in Canadian Courts, in* INTERNATIONAL HUMAN RIGHTS LAW: THEORY AND PRACTICE 115, 137–40 (Irwin Cotler & F. Pearl Eliadis eds., 1992) (urging improved judicial and legal education).

42. *See, e.g.,* Young, *supra* note 21, at 165–67; David A. Strauss, *Common Law, Common Ground, and Jefferson's Principle,* 112 YALE L.J. 1717, 1738 (2003).

43. Tushnet, *supra* note 6, at 1266–67.

44. Rosenkrantz, *supra* note 4, at 283.

45. *See* Frederick Schauer, *The Politics and Incentives of Legal Transplantation, in* GOVERNANCE IN A GLOBALIZING WORLD (Nye & Donahue eds., 2000). Constitutional resistance occurs not only in courts. *See, e.g.,* Shiv Visvanathan & Chandrika Parmar, *Life, Life World and Life Chances, in* LAW AND GLOBALIZATION FROM BELOW (Boaventura de Sousa Santos & César A. Rodríguez-Garavito eds., 2005) (describing survival of British colonial idea of government ownership of forests in Indian constitution and continuing resistance of forest dwellers); *cf.* Balakrishnan Rajagopal, *Limits of Law in Counterhegemonic Globalization, in* LAW AND GLOBALIZATION FROM BELOW, *supra,* at 185–87, 209–10 (describing resistance by those whose homes in India were threatened by dam construction, and government's reliance on "human right" to development to support the dam).

46. Steven G. Calabresi, *"A Shining City on a Hill": American Exceptionalism and the Supreme Court's Practice of Relying on Foreign Law,* 86 B.U. L. REV. 1335 (2006).

47. *See* Chapter 4, below, suggesting that to be a "City on a Hill" requires ongoing comparison.

48. *See Appropriate Role of Foreign Judgments in the Interpretation of American Law, Hearing on H.Res. 568 Before the Subcomm. on the Constitution of the H. Comm. on the Judiciary,* 108th Cong. 26 (Mar. 25, 2004) (statement of Jeremy Rabkin, Professor of Government, Cornell University), *available at* http://commdocs.house.gov/committees/judiciary/hju92673.000/hju92673_0.HTM.

49. Okoth-Ogendo, *supra* note 33, at 67–68; *cf.* SHELDON WOLIN, POLITICS AND VISION 558–63 (expanded ed. 2004) (emphasizing role of constitution in constituting "the state as the most formidable power in society," a feature now challenged by postmodern growth in the power of transnational corporations, international agencies, nongovernmental organizations, a "superpower," and terrorism).

50. *See, e.g.,* S. AFR. CONST. 1996, ch. 2, §. 39; CONST. ARG. § 75 (22) (as amended 1994); *see also* Carsten Smith, *The Supreme Court in Present Day Society, in* THE SUPREME COURT OF NORWAY, 96, 133–35 (Stephan Tschudi-Madsen ed. 1998).

51. *See, e.g.,* Makau Mutua, *Savages, Victims, and Saviors: The Metaphor of Human Rights,* 42 HARV. INT'L L. J. 201 (2001); Makau wa Mutua, *The Ideology of Human Rights,* 36 VA. J. INT'L L. 589 (1996) (describing how the UDHR was drafted and adopted without the involvement of many then-colonies and by the affirmative vote of only 48 states); *see also* Raimundo Panikkar, *Is the Notion of Human Rights a Western Concept?,* 120 DIOGENES 75 (1982) (problematizing and complexifying the ideas behind "human rights" as they may be understood in different cultures); RAIMUNDO PANIKKAR & ARVIND SHARMA, HUMAN

RIGHTS AS A WESTERN CONCEPT 36–53 (2007). The ICESCR has long been criticized for not having an an individual complaint enforcement mechanism by those who see economic, social, and cultural rights as no less central than the civil and political rights protected by the ICCPR. For critical discussion of efforts to adopt such a mechanism, see Michael J. Dennis & David P. Stewart, *Justiciability of Economic, Social, and Cultural Rights: Should There Be an International Complaints Mechanism to Adjudicate the Rights to Food, Water, Housing, and Health?*, 98 AM. J. INT'L L. 462 (2004). As this book was going to press, the UN General Assembly adopted an Optional Protocol for the ICESCR, to open for signature some time in 2009. G.A. Res. 63/117, U.N. Doc. A/RES/63/117 (Dec. 10, 2008).

52. *See* Anderson, *supra* note 20, at 45; Roger Alford, *Misusing International Sources to Interpret the Constitution*, 98 AM. J. INT'L L. 57, 57–58 (2004); Roger Alford, *Roper v. Simmons and Our Constitution in International Equipoise*, 53 UCLA L. REV. 1 (2005).

53. John O. McGinnis, *Foreign to Our Constitution*, 100 NW. U. L. REV. 303, 309 (2006). On diversity, see also John Harrison, *Human Rights and American Exceptionalism: Uniformity, Diversity, and the Process of Making Human Rights Norms*, 3 U. ST. THOMAS L.J. 334 (2005).

54. Maintenance of diversity is often discussed in connection with the values of federalism. *See, e.g.*, Lynn Baker & Ernest Young, *Federalism and the Double Standard of Judicial Review*, 51 DUKE L.J. 75, 124 (2001); *see also* DAVID L. SHAPIRO, FEDERALISM: A DIALOGUE 75–107 (1995).

55. McGinnis, *supra* note 53, at 309.

56. *See* Scott Cummings, *The Internationalization of Public Interest Law*, 57 DUKE L.J. 891, 988 (2008). On activities of women's NGO groups before the UN CEDAW Committee, see Elizabeth Evatt, *Finding a Voice for Women's Rights: The Early Days of CEDAW*, 34 GEO. WASH. INT'L L. REV. 515, 534–35(2002). On participation before European courts of a conservative Christian U.S. NGO, see Rachel Morris, *Crusaders in Wingtips*, LEGAL AFF. (Mar./Apr. 2006).

57. It should also be noted that foreign or international law may influence not only judicial decisions but legislative and executive ones, which in turn may influence constitutional interpretation.

58. *See, e.g.*, Ken Kersch, *The New Legal Transnationalism, the Globalized Judiciary, and the Rule of Law*, 4 WASH. U. GLOBAL STUD. L. REV. 345 (2005).

59. *See, e.g.*, Lawrence v. Texas, 539 U.S. 558, 586, 594 (2003) (Scalia, J., dissenting) (arguing that "*Bowers* [*v. Hardwick*, 478 U.S. 186 (1986)] was right" when decided and should not be overruled).

60. ANNE-MARIE SLAUGHTER, A NEW WORLD ORDER 103 (2004); *see* Jeffrey Toobin, *Swing Shift: How Anthony Kennedy's Passion for Foreign Law Could Change the Supreme Court*, NEW YORKER, Sept. 12, 2005.

61. *Cf.* Schauer, *supra* note 45, at 260–61 (noting that judge's citations can have "symbolic effect" in expressing agreement with another country's court).

62. *Cf.* David Fontana, *The Next Generation of Transnational/Domestic Constitutional Law Scholarship: A Reply to Professor Tushnet*, 38 LOY. L.A. L. REV. 445, 457 (2004) (arguing that there are no "disagreements anymore about the relevance of transnational law," and that debate focuses on what uses are legitimate). Although Professor Fontana identifies passages in the writings of prominent opponents of the Court's references to foreign law that contemplate some legitimate uses, the arguments for "resistance" that are discussed above continue to have salience in contemporary discussions.

63. *See* H. Patrick Glenn, *Persuasive Authority*, 32 MCGILL L.J. 261 (1987).

64. Some constitutions are quite explicit in authorizing or even requiring that international or comparative law be considered in interpreting domestic constitutions. *See* Chapters 2 and 3 below (discussing, inter alia, the Colombian and South African constitutions).

65. Carlos Santiago Nino, *Transition to Democracy, Corporatism and Presidentialism with Special Reference to Latin America*, *in* CONSTITUTIONALISM & DEMOCRACY: TRANSITIONS IN THE CONTEMPORARY WORLD 46, 55 (D. Greenberg et al. eds., 1993).

66. *Id.* at 55 (describing von Savigny's views).

67. Harold Berman, *Toward an Integrative Jurisprudence: Politics, Morality and History*, 76 CAL. L. REV. 779, 789 (1988); *see also* Richard A. Posner, *Past-Dependency, Pragmatism, and Critique of History in Adjudication and Legal Scholarship*, 67 U. CHI. L. REV. 573 (2000) (observing that law is more oriented to the past than other disciplines, and that legal convergence among countries in the world is much slower than economic and technological convergence).

68. It was for these reasons that von Savigny wrote in opposition to efforts to codify German law in the nineteenth century. *See* Berman, *supra* note 67, at 789.

69. *See* Harold Berman, *The Historical Foundations of Law*, 54 EMORY L.J. 13, 18–19 (2005).

70. A possible example is found in the Basic Law of Germany, whose interpretation has been informed by a determination to keep Germany on a path unalterably opposed to Naziism. *See West German Abortion Decision: A Contrast to Roe v. Wade*, 9 J. MARSHALL J. PRAC. & PROC. 605, 662 (Robert E. Jonas & John D. Gorby trans., 1976) (German Constitutional Court's assertion that the Basic Law's principles with respect to abortion could "be understood only in light of the historical experience and spiritual moral confrontation with the previous system of National Socialism").

71. OLIVER WENDELL HOLMES, JR., THE COMMON LAW 1 (1881).

72. As an illustration, consider Paul Kahn's work, which combines an emphasis on "will" and "culture" in U.S. constitutional law. *See* Kahn, *Comparative Constitutionalism*, *supra* note 19, at 2677–78, 2699.

73. Rubenfeld, *supra* note 19, at 1971, 1995, 2005.

74. Anderson, *supra* note 20, at 48 (emphasis in original). The complexity of any modern society's "culture"—its necessarily plural, contested, and dynamic character—gives one some pause over such claims, as over those claims made by Professor Rosenkrantz. Is it the willingness of Justices Breyer, Ginsburg, O'Connor, and Kennedy to consider foreign and international law that best corresponds with American constitutional culture, or Justices Scalia's and Thomas's general unwillingness to do so? And one might question the characterization of "international constitutionalism" and European traditions in light of the attention given, for example, by Jürgen Habermas to the legitimating force of deliberative democratic decision-making. *See* JÜRGEN HABERMAS, BETWEEN FACTS AND NORMS: CONTRIBUTIONS TO A DISCOURSE THEORY OF LAW AND DEMOCRACY 170–71, 188–90, 287–302 (William Rehg trans., 1996).

75. *But cf.* Richard Frimpong Oppong, *Re-Imagining International Law: An Examination of Recent Trends in the Reception of International Law into National Legal Systems in Africa*, 30 FORDHAM INT'L L.J. 296, 321–22 (2007) (describing a 1993 change in the Zimbabwe constitution, "aimed at preventing courts from invoking international law"). The provision states: "'Except as otherwise provided by this Constitution or by or under an Act of Parliament, any convention, treaty or agreement acceded to, concluded or executed by or under the authority of the President with one or more foreign states or governments or international organizations . . . shall not form part of the law of Zimbabwe unless it has been incorporated into the law by or under an Act of Parliament.'" *Id.* (quoting CONST. OF

THE REPUBLIC OF ZIMBABWE art. 111B (1993)); *cf.* Lorraine Weinrib, *Of Diligence and Dice, Reconstituting Canada's Constitution*, 42 U. TORONTO L.J. 207, 220 (1992) (stating that there was an unsuccessful effort during drafting to cut off reliance on U.S. jurisprudence in interpreting the 1982 Canadian Charter); Thio, *supra* note 41, at 454–55 (stating that "constitutional and statutory amendments" were used in Singapore to overturn a judicial decision that, relying in part on foreign law, had subjected a ministerial preventive detention order to judicial review on an "objective" test).

76. *See* Kim Lane Scheppele, *Aspirational and Aversive Constitutionalism: The Case for Studying Cross-Constitutional Influence Through Negative Models*, 1 INT'L J. CONST. L. 296 (2003); Sujit Choudhry, *The Lochner Era and Comparative Constitutionalism*, 2 INT'L J. CONST. L. 1 (2004).

77. In common law countries, or others with a practice of separate opinions, divergent views are more readily identified with respect to the use of foreign law. A multi-member court that issues opinions only in the name of the court or without dissent could obscure differences in viewpoints on whether to consider foreign or international law.

78. 521 U.S. 898 (1997). For critical analysis, see Vicki C. Jackson, *Federalism and the Uses and Limits of Law: Printz and Principle?*, 111 HARV. L. REV. 2180 (1998). For "resistance" to foreign or international law in more socially controversial recent decisions, see Roper v. Simmons, 543 U.S. 551, 622–28 (2005) (Scalia, J., dissenting); Lawrence v. Texas, 539 U.S. 558, 598 (2003) (Scalia, J., dissenting) ("Constitutional entitlements do not spring into existence . . ., as the Court seems to believe, because foreign nations decriminalize conduct."); Atkins v. Virginia, 536 U.S. 304, 347–48 (Scalia, J., dissenting) (describing as "irrelevant . . . the practices of the 'world community,' whose notions of justice are (thankfully) not always those of our people"); *id.* at 322–24 (Rehnquist, C.J., dissenting); Knight v. Florida, 528 U.S. 990, 990–92 (1999) (Thomas, J., concurring in denial of certiorari) (criticizing Justice Breyer's references to foreign law as demonstrating the absence of U.S. legal support for his "neoteric" Eighth Amendment claim).

79. *But see* McIntyre v. Ohio Elections Comm'n, 514 U.S. 334, 381–82 (1995) (Scalia, J., dissenting) (relying on experience in other Western democracies in requiring disclosure of participants in electioneering to argue for upholding an Ohio law banning anonymous campaign literature in referenda); Glendon, *supra* note 5. For examples of resistance to international and foreign law expressed within a *statute*, see Military Commissions Act of 2006 [MCA], §3(a)(1), 10 U.S.C. §948b(g) (providing that no unlawful enemy combatant may invoke the Geneva Conventions as a source of right in a military commission proceeding); MCA § 5, 28 U.S.C. § 2241 note (providing that Geneva Conventions may not be invoked as a source of rights in habeas corpus or certain other civil proceedings); MCA § 6(a)(2), 18 U.S.C. § 2441 note ("No foreign or international source of law shall supply a basis for a rule of decision in the courts of the United States in interpreting the prohibitions enumerated in [the War Crimes Act, 18 U.S.C. § 2441(d)]").

80. 529 U.S. 598 (2000). For additional discussion, see Chapters 7 and 8, below.

81. *See* Brief Amici Curiae on Behalf of International Law Scholars and Human Rights Experts in Support of Petitioners, United States v. Morrison, 529 U.S. 598 (Nos. 99-5, 99-29) (arguing that ICCPR provides basis for a statute implementing obligations); Brief of Amicus Curiae Eagle Forum Education & Legal Defense Fund in Support of Respondents, United States v. Morrison, 529 U.S. 598 (Nos. 99-5, 99-29) (arguing that ICCPR provides no such basis given Senate reservations); Brief of the National Association of Criminal Defense Lawyers as Amicus Curiae in Support of Respondents, United States v. Morrison, 529 U.S. 598 (Nos. 99-5, 99-29) (to similar effect and arguing that question was not in any event before the Court). See discussion in Chapter 8, below.

82. *See* Al-Kateb v. Godwin (2004) 219 C.L.R. 562, 594–95 (Austl.) (McHugh, J.). For examples of Justice McHugh's engagement with foreign constitutional law, see *Re* Colonel Aird; *Ex parte* Alpert (2004), 220 C.L.R. 308, 321–22, 324 (Austl.); Chapter 3, notes 14, 19 below.

83. On Turkey, see Esin Örücü, *The Turkish Experience with Judicial Comparativism in Human Rights Cases, in* Judicial Comparativism in Human Rights Cases 134–37, 140–41 (Esin Örücü ed., 2003) (noting that the Constitutional Court "seldom" considers ECtHR case law and that when it does there is seldom a "full discussion"). There is also critical discussion concerning the Constitutional Court's apparent refusal to implement the Strasbourg Court's decisions. *Id.* at 137. On France, see Luc Heuschling, *Comparative Law and the European Convention on Human Rights in French Human Rights Cases, in* Judicial Comparativism in Human Rights Cases 23, 26, 27 (Esin Örücü ed., 2003) (stating that although the ECHR has become important in France there is still resistance especially to the case law of the ECtHR and noting the French view of the perfection and superiority of French law, and the view of law as embodied in statutes, as important explanatory factors). For further discussion of the citation practices of the French Conseil Constitutionnel, see Chapter 6, below.

84. *See* Chapter 3 below. These moments of resistance may not, however, represent a more general posture of resistance to the transnational.

85. *See* Lee, *supra* note 3, at 122–23; *see also* Andrew Harding, *Comparative Case Law in Human Rights Cases in the Commonwealth: The Emerging Common Law of Human Rights, in* Judicial Comparativism in Human Rights Cases (Esin Örücü ed., 2003) (discussing Malaysia).

86. Gov' of Kelantan v. Gov't of Malaya, [1963] 1 M.L. J. 355, 358 (Malaysia), quoted in Lee, *supra* note 3, at 124.

87. *See* Lee, *supra* note 3, at 125–27 (describing one Privy Council decision and several decisions of Singapore courts).

88. *See id.* at 130–31; *see generally* Thio, supra note 41, at 435, 477–508 (exploring how the "four walls" doctrine nonetheless permits some engagement with foreign law and distinguishing between using foreign law "selectively, even inaccurately, to serve instrumental purposes or buttress pre-determined statist conclusions," and its use as "a positive aid in developing normative reasoning, as a source of creative insight to enhance judicial reasoning by exposure to a broader range of ideas and experiences").

89. *See* Thio, *supra* note 41, at 468, 476, 486, 499–501.

90. *See generally* Vicki C. Jackson, *Ambivalent Resistance and Comparative Constitutionalism: Opening Up the Conversation on "Proportionality," Rights and Federalism,* 1 U. Pa. J. Const. L. 583 (1999). For other earlier work in which I explore and respond to resistances, from which parts of this chapter and later discussions are drawn in part, see Vicki C. Jackson, *Multi-Valenced Constitutional Interpretation and Constitutional Comparisons: An Essay in Honor of Mark Tushnet,* 26 Quinnipiac L. Rev. 599, 665–68 (2008); *Transnational Challenges to Constitutional Law: Convergence, Resistance, Engagement,* 35 Fed'l L. Rev. 161 (2007) (Austral.); *Constitutional Comparisons: Convergence, Resistance, Engagement,* 119 Harv. L. Rev. 109 (2005); *Transnational Discourse, Relational Authority, and the U.S. Court: Gender Equality,* 37 Loyola of Los Angeles L. Rev. 271, 325-49 (2003); *Narratives of Federalism: Of Continuities and Comparative Constitutional Experience,* 51 Duke L. J. 223, 263–71 (2001).

91. Fong Yue Ting v. United States, 149 U.S. 698, 757 (1893) (Field, J., dissenting) (emphasis added); *see id.* at 737 (Brewer, J., dissenting) ("[W]hatever rights a resident alien might have in any other nation, here he is within the express protection of the Constitution . . . ").

92. Jacobson v. Massachusetts, 197 U.S. 11, 31–33 & n.1 (1905); Muller v. Oregon, 208 U.S. 412, 419–20 n.1 (1908).

93. *See* Wickard v. Filburn, 317 U.S. 111, 125–26 & n.11 (1942) (referring to foreign law in case involving scope of national power to regulate commerce); Youngstown Sheet & Tube Co. v. Sawyer, 343 U.S. 579, 650–52 (1952) (Jackson, J., concurring) (referring to foreign law in case involving scope of the President's power to take property without legislative authorization).

94. *See* David Schneiderman, Constitutionalizing Economic Globalization: Investment Rules and Democracy's Promise (2008).

95. *See* David Schneiderman, *Investment Rules and the New Constitutionalism*, 25 Law & Soc. Inquiry 757, 765 (2000) ("The Calvo doctrine . . . emerged as a response by developing countries in Latin America to the power of international capital. The doctrine . . . stated that aliens were not entitled to a higher degree of protection in their claims against the host state than local investors, and that foreign, like local, investors were required to submit their claims to local courts rather than seek diplomatic protection from their home state."). For further discussion, see John Henry Merryman & David S. Clark, Comparative Law: Western European and Latin American Legal Systems 1173 (1978).

96. Schneiderman, *supra* note 94, at 117.

97. *See id.* at 159–63; *see also* David Schneiderman, *Constitutional Approaches to Privatization: An Inquiry into the Magnitude of Neo-Liberal Constitutionalism, in* Regulation 501, 524–26 (Colin Scott ed., 2003) (describing 1996 Colombian Constitutional Court decision holding unconstitutional two bilateral investment treaties, resulting in a constitutional amendment three years later in partial response).

98. *See* Stephen Gill, Power and Resistance in the New World Order 131–35, 166–67 (2003); *cf. id.* at 166, 131–32 (noting that the "new constitutionalism," which "confers privileged rights of citizenship and representation to corporate capital, whilst constraining the democratization process . . . ," may not necessarily imply "a general weakening of state capacity," but rather particular constraints from the neoliberal "new constitutionalist" economic policies).

99. *See* La Bugal-B'laan Tribal Ass'n v. Ramos, G.R. No. 127882 (S. C. December 1, 2004) (Phil.), *available at* http://sc.judiciary.gov.ph/jurisprudence/2004/dec2004/127882.htm (last visited Feb. 6, 2009), *reversing* 421 S.C.R.A. 148 (S.C., Jan. 27, 2004), *available at* http://sc.judiciary.gov.ph/jurisprudence/2004/jan2004/127882.htm (last visited Feb. 6, 2009). The major issue was whether a proposed service contract with a foreign-owned company to manage mining extraction operations violated a provision in the Philippines Constitution (art. XII) providing that use and development of "natural resources shall be under the full control and supervision of the State," which could "enter into co-production . . . agreements with Filipino citizens" or business entities if at least 60% of their "capital is owned by such citizens. . . ." The initial ruling found that the service contract needed to but did not meet the 60% rule; the later ruling disagreed, concluding that the constitutional provision was not intended to prevent the state from contracting with foreign companies, under another constitutional provision, for "technical or financial assistance" in managing extraction activities that the state lacked the resources to perform. The reasoning of the principal opinions was "originalist," focusing in detail on proceedings in the constitutional commission that prepared the 1987 constitution, and purposive. The challengers were a tribal group whose interest in the environmental conditions of the lands was threatened by the proposed extraction activities. (The provisions for control over natural resources may be understood as in part a reaction to the many decades of U.S. occupation, when natural resources could be exploited by U.S. citizens as well as Philippine citizens (*see* La Bugal-B'laan Tribal Ass'n (Jan. 27, 2004)).

100. *See* Vicki C. Jackson, *Comparative Constitutional Federalism and Transnational Judicial Discourse,* 2 INT'L J. CONST. L. 91, 102–08 (2004).

101. *Cf.* Katherine A Sawyer, *Rejection of Weimarian Politics or Betrayal of Democracy: Spain's Proscription of Batasuna Under the European Convention of Human Rights,* 52 AM. U. L. REV. 1531, 1559 (2003) (describing Turkish Constitutional Court's issuance of an order dissolving a political party for failure to abide by "principles of secularism" that were "enshrined in the Constitution as a pillar of the Turkish State"). For an argument that notwithstanding other countries' constitutional practices permitting the abolition of political parties in the name of "militant democracy," Spain's particular authoritarian culture and history of repression of speech should cause hesitation before adopting constitutional doctrine upholding such limitations (as had occurred in response to the terrorist activities of the ETA on behalf of Basque separatism and the Batasuna party), see Víctor Ferreres Comella, *The New Regulation of Political Parties in Spain, and the Decision to Outlaw Batasuna, in* MILITANT DEMOCRACY 133 (András Sajó ed., 2004).

102. Some courts have looked comparatively to reinforce conclusions that antiterrorism measures failed adequately to protect due process and equality rights. *See, e.g.,* A. v. Sec'y of State for the Home Dep't [2004] UKHL 56, [2005] A.C. 68 (appeal taken from Eng.) (U.K.) (finding that statute authorizing indefinite detention of foreign, but not domestic, terrorism suspects violates the Human Rights Act, with references to decisions in Canada and United States in, for example, Lord Bingham's judgment (paras. 30, 39)); *cf.* Yigal Mersel, *Judicial Review of Counter Terrorism Measures: The Israeli Model of the Judiciary During the Terror Era,* 38 N.Y.U. J. INT'L L. & POL. 67 (2005–06); Kim Lane Scheppele, *The Emergency Constitution in the Post–September 11 World Order: We Are All Post 9-11 Now,* 75 FORDHAM L. REV. 607 (2006) (suggesting cautious examination of foreign experience to aid in designing responses to terrorism without sacrificing liberty or unduly accreting executive power). Yet the need for caution in engaging with foreign and international law in constitutional interpretation, leaving open the possibility for resistance, is suggested by the possibilities that international or foreign law might move in harsh directions in response to perceived threats to national and international security. *See* Kim Lane Scheppele, *Other Peoples' PATRIOT Acts: Europe' s Responses to September 11,* 50 LOY. L. REV. 89, 90 (2004) (describing U.S. posture after September 11 as "inward-looking, unilateral, and self-absorbed," describing European responses as "supportive of and complementary to" that of the United States, and identifying human rights concerns over UN Security Council Resolution 1373). For further discussion, see Chapters 6 and 9, below.

103. Joseph Weiler, *Federalism Without Constitutionalism: Europe's Sonderweg, in* THE FEDERAL VISION: LEGITIMACY AND LEVELS OF GOVERNANCE IN THE UNITED STATES AND THE EUROPEAN UNION 54, 63 (Kalypso Nicolaides & Robert Howse eds., 2001); *see also* Kim Lane Scheppele, *A Realpolitik Defense of Social Rights,* 82 TEX. L. REV. 1921, 1941–49 (2004) (describing how the Hungarian Constitutional Court enabled Hungary to resist demands from the International Monetary Fund by finding rapid changes in the country's welfare laws to be unconstitutional). *But cf.* KAREN J. ALTER, ESTABLISHING THE SUPREMACY OF EUROPEAN LAW: THE MAKING OF AN INTERNATIONAL RULE OF LAW IN EUROPE 49 (2001) (arguing that some lower national courts use referrals to the ECJ to increase their own power vis-à-vis their own national high courts).

CHAPTER 2. CONVERGENCE WITH THE TRANSNATIONAL

1. Roper v. Simmons, 543 U.S. 551, 624 (2005) (Scalia, J., dissenting).

2. *See, e.g.,* BASIC LAW [GRUNDGESETZ] arts. 23, 24 (F.R.G) (authorizing participation in the EU and authorizing the transfer of sovereign power to international organizations).

On constitutional provisions that incorporate international law as having a higher legal status than statutes, see Vicki C. Jackson, *Transnational Challenges to Constitutional Law: Convergence, Resistance, Engagement*, 35 Fed'l L. Rev. 161, 164–65 (2007) (Austral.) (noting German Basic Law art. 25 and article 7 of the Costa Rica constitution). For earlier discussions of convergence from which some of this chapter is drawn, see Jackson, *Transnational Challenges, supra;* Vicki C. Jackson, *Constitutional Comparisons: Convergence, Resistance, Engagement*, 119 Harv. L. Rev. 109 (2005).

3. For a description of South American constitutions with rights provisions modeled on the ICCPR, see Janet Koven Levit, *The Constitutionalization of Human Rights in Argentina: Problem or Promise?*, 37 COLUM. J. TRANSNAT'L L. 281, 293–301 (1999). The model for enactment may then invite recourse to comparative and international sources in subsequent interpretation, *see, e.g.*, N. Reg'l Health Auth. v. Human Rights Comm'n, [1998] 2 N.Z.L.R. 218, 232–44 (H.C. Auckland) (1997) (discussing UN Human Rights Committee General Comment and U.S., Canadian and Australian equality law in interpreting the statutory N.Z. Bill of Rights Act 1990 and Human Rights Act 1993), which may in turn influence other tribunals in interpreting similar texts. On the influence of the UDHR on the ECHR (which has also influenced domestic constitutional law in Europe), see Minister of Home Affairs v. Fisher, [1980] A. C. 319, 328–29 (P.C. 1979) (appeal taken from Bermuda) (Lord Wilberforce).

4. Following the fall of the Soviet Union, not only were constitutional protections of human rights given a further boost, but in many countries economic property rights began emerging, subject to transnational pressures for convergences. *Cf.* Joel Trachtman, *The International Economic Law Revolution*, 17 U. PA. J. INT'L ECON. L. 33 (1996). For arguments in favor of recognizing economic rights, including rights of trade, as fundamental forms of human rights, see, for example, Ernst-Ulrich Petersmann, *Theories of Justice, Human Rights and the Constitution of International Markets*, 37 LOY. L.A. L. REV. 407 (2003); Steve Charnovitz, *The Globalization of Economic Human Rights*, 25 BROOK. J. INT'L L. 113, 116–17, 122 (1999).

5. On the role of the British Commonwealth Association and Interights (a human rights group) in sponsoring judges' meetings promoting a "rapprochement" of domestic and international law, see Melissa A. Waters, *Creeping Monism: The Judicial Trend Toward Interpretive Incorporation of Human Rights Treaties*, 107 COLUM. L. REV. 628, 643–50 (2007). On other regional human rights regimes, see James L. Cavallaro & Stephanie Erin Brewer, *Reevaluating Regional Human Rights Litigation in the Twenty-First Century: The Case of the Inter-American Court*, 102 AM. J. INT'L L. 768, 768–69 (2008) (noting that African Court on Human and People's Rights is just starting to hear cases and that with respect to regional courts such as the Inter-American Court of Human Rights, there can be a "vast gap between what regional courts order and what actually happens in a country"); *cf.* Jenny S. Martinez, *Towards an International Judicial System*, 56 STAN. L. REV. 429, 494, 498 (2003) (discussing domestic incorporation of decisions of the Inter-American Court).

6. *See* On Capital Punishment, Decision 23/1990: 31 October 1990 (CC) (Hung.), *translated in* CONSTITUTIONAL JUDICIARY IN A NEW DEMOCRACY: THE HUNGARIAN CONSTITUTIONAL COURT 118–38 (László Sólyom & Georg Brunner, eds., 2000); VICKI C. JACKSON & MARK TUSHNET, COMPARATIVE CONSTITUTIONAL LAW 648–49 (2d ed. 2006) (noting beliefs that the decision, made during Constitutional Court's first year, was motivated in part by Hungary's effort to be accepted into the Council of Europe).

7. The legal relationships between these two supranational courts and their member states differ in significant ways. For example, an important source of ECJ jurisdiction is

the preliminary reference, including from lower levels of national courts; exhaustion of domestic remedies is generally required before invoking the ECtHR's jurisdiction. *See* Laurence R. Helfer & Anne-Marie Slaughter, *Toward a Theory of Effective Supranational Adjudication*, 107 YALE L. J. 273, 291 (1997) (discussing preliminary references to the ECJ under Article 177); ECHR art. 35.1. The precise legal effect of the two supranational courts' judgments on domestic law may differ, especially in light of the ECJ's doctrines of supremacy and direct effect (see Chapter 3, note 130 below). *Compare, e.g.*, ANTHONY ARNULL ET AL, WYATT AND DASHWOOD'S EUROPEAN UNION LAW 526–27 (2006) (describing binding effect on national courts of ECJ interpretations on preliminary references) *with* Alec Stone Sweet & Helen Keller, *The Reception of the ECHR in National Legal Orders*, in A EUROPE OF RIGHTS: THE IMPACT OF THE ECHR ON NATIONAL LEGAL SYSTEMS 3, 7–8 (Helen Keller & Alec Stone Sweet eds. 2008) (noting questions about whether ECtHR judgments bind national courts and a range of processes by which those judgments impact national legal systems). Both courts employ doctrines (the ECJ's margin of discretion, the ECtHR's margin of appreciation) that may accommodate national differences. Although these courts and their legal regimes push toward convergences within Europe, at the national constitutional level the effects may be more complex. *See* Chapter 3 below.

8. *See* Oona Hathaway, *Between Power and Principle: An Integrated Theory of International Law*, 72 U. CHI. L. REV. 469, 505 n.85 (2005) ("the World Bank is now taking countries' records of 'governance' into account in its lending decisions. The Bank measures governance by estimating six factors: 'voice and accountability,' 'political stability and absence of violence,' 'government effectiveness,' 'regulatory quality,' 'rule of law,' and 'control of corruption.' The Bank uses eighteen separate sources for these indicators, including several measures of countries' human rights practices."); *see also id.* at 505 ("[N]ew guidelines for the European Union's Generalized System of Preferences, which grants trade preferences to 178 developing nations, require participants to ratify twenty-seven core governance, human rights, and environmental treaties by the end of 2008 in order to remain in the program").

9. Donald L. Horowitz, *Constitutional Design: Proposals Versus Process, in* THE ARCHITECTURE OF DEMOCRACY 15, 15 (Andrew Reynolds, ed., 2002).

10. *See* Thomas H. Hill, *Introduction to Law and Economic Development in Latin America: A Comparative Approach to Legal Reform*, 83 CHI.-KENT L. REV. 3, 22 (2008); *see also* Alvaro Santos, *The World Bank's Uses of the "Rule of Law" Promise in Economic Development, in* THE NEW LAW AND ECONOMIC DEVELOPMENT: A CRITICAL APPRAISAL 253 (Trubek & Santos eds., 2006). For an introduction to the "new comparative economics" that examines relationships between legal tradition (civil or common law) and economic development, see Emma Phillips, *The War on Civil Law? The Common Law as a Proxy for the Global Ambition of Law and Economics*, 24 WIS. INT'L L. J. 915 (2007); see also Richard A. Posner, *Law and Economics in Common-Law, Civil-Law, and Developing Nations*, 17 RATIO JURIS 66 (2004). For an overview of the literature on the "rule of law" and economic development, and of the obstacles to rule of law initiatives, see Ronald J. Daniels & Michael Trebilcock, *The Political Economy of Rule of Law Reform in Developing Countries*, 26 MICH. J. INT'L L. 99 (2004).

11. *See* Thomas M. Franck, *Clan and Superclan: Loyalty, Identity and Community in Law and Practice*, 90 AM. J. INT'L L. 359 (1996); Neil Walker, *The Idea of Constitutional Pluralism*, 65 MODERN L. REV. 317, 328–31 (2002).

12. For helpful treatments, see, for example, BALAKRISHNAN RAJAGOPAL, INTERNATIONAL LAW FROM BELOW: DEVELOPMENT, SOCIAL MOVEMENTS AND THIRD WORLD RESISTANCE (2003); LAW AND GLOBALIZATION FROM BELOW: TOWARDS A COSMOPOLITAN LEGALITY (Boaventura de

Sousa Santos & César A Rodriguez-Garavito eds., 2005) (a collection of essays focusing on the possibilities of "subaltern cosmopolitan legality").

13. I borrow the term from Stephen Gill, *Constitutionalizing Inequality and the Clash of Globalizations*, 4 INT'L STUD. REV. 47 (2002); STEPHEN GILL, POWER AND RESISTANCE IN THE NEW WORLD ORDER xvi–xvii, xix (2d ed. 2008) (discussing the "clash of globalizations," consisting of a dominant set of powers and a "transformative, global resistance").

14. Peter J. Spiro, *Globalization and the (Foreign Affairs) Constitution*, 63 OHIO ST. L. J. 649, 715–29 (2002) (exploring the combined effects of economic globalization and the disaggregation of state functions, which facilitate targeted pressures).

15. For a possible example, see Robert B. Ahdieh, *Between Dialogue and Decree: International Review of National Courts*, 79 N.Y.U. L. REV. 2029, 2123–39 (2004) (discussing the emergence of international norms of due process through dialectical exchanges among national and supranational tribunals).

16. *See* DAVID M. BEATTY, THE ULTIMATE RULE OF LAW (2004); ROBERT ALEXY, A THEORY OF CONSTITUTIONAL RIGHTS (Julian Rivers trans., 2002).

17. *See, e.g.*, Walter F. Murphy, *Consent and Constitutional Change*, *in* HUMAN RIGHTS AND CONSTITUTIONAL LAW (James O'Reilly ed., 1992) (arguing that the principle of equal human worth that underlies commitments to democracy may justify resistance to a democratic decision, e.g., amending a constitution, that is incompatible with equal human worth).

18. *See, e.g.*, Laurence H. Tribe, *The Puzzling Persistence of Process-Based Constitutional Theories*, 89 YALE L.J. 1063, 1064 (1980).

19. PERU CONST. (1993) (Final and Transitory Provisions, No. 4), *found at* http://www.parliament.go.th/parcy/sapa_db/cons_doc/constitutions/data/Peru/peru.pdf.; CONST. ARG. § 4(22), *available at* http://www.argentina.gov.ar/argentina/portal/documentos/constitucion_ingles.pdf; CONST. COLOM. (1991), *available at* http://confinder.richmond.edu.

20. *See also* ROMANIA CONST. (1991) (as amended to 2003), art. 20(2), *available at* http://www.cdep.ro/pls/dic/site.page?id=339&idl=2 (stating that in the event of "inconsistencies . . . between the covenants and treaties on the fundamental human rights Romania is a party to, and the national laws, the international regulations shall take precedence, unless the Constitution or national laws comprise more favorable provisions").

21. Levit, *supra* note 3, at 293–301.

22. Paul W. Kahn, *American Hegemony and International Law: Speaking Law to Power: Popular Sovereignty, Human Rights, and the New International Order*, 1 CHI. J. INT'L L. 1, 14–15 (2000).

23. *See* Levit, *supra* note 3, at 301.

24. *See* Jonathan M. Miller, *A Typology of Legal Transplants: Using Sociology, Legal History and Argentine Examples to Explain the Transplant Process*, 51 AM. J. COMP. L. 839, 854, 862–63 (2003) (arguing that incorporation in Argentina was a "legitimacy-generating" form of transplant, intended by its proponents to "link Argentina to the rights-respecting countries of the world, giving it the moral legitimacy of those states"); Levit, *supra* note 3, at 317 (suggesting that incorporation was designed as "a symbolic break from the past . . . [to] enhanc[e] Argentina's reputation and standing vis-à-vis Mercosur and other economic integration efforts").

25. *See* Ruti Teitel, *Transitional Jurisprudence: The Role of Law in Political Transformation*, 106 YALE L. J. 2009, 2062 (1997); *cf.* William C. Banks & Edgar Alvarez, *The New Colombian Constitution: Democratic Victory or Public Surrender?*, 23 U. MIAMI INTER-AM. L. REV. 39 (1991) (describing "extralegal" processes by which the new constitution was adopted and arguing that its success and legitimacy remained questions for the future).

26. *See* Martha I. Morgan with Mónica Maria Alzate Buitrago, *Constitution-Making in a Time of Cholera: Women and the 1991 Colombian Constitution*, 4 YALE J.L. & FEMINISM 353, 365 (1992) (quoting university students' slogan, "We Can Still Save Colombia").

27. *See, e.g.*, Translation of Excerpts of Decision C-355/2006, Colombian Constitutional Court Abortion Decision of May 10, 2006, published by Women's Link Worldwide (with Foreword by Rebecca J. Cook), *available at* www.womenslinkworldwide.org (click on "publications," click on C-355/2006, Excerpts of the Constitutional Court's Ruling That Liberalized Abortion in Colombia) [hereinafter *Case C-355, Colombian Constitutional Court Abortion Decision*]; *see also* Martha I. Morgan, *Taking Machismo to Court: The Gender Jurisprudence of the Colombian Constitutional Court*, 30 U. MIAMI INTER-AM. L. REV. 253, 272–73, 278, 289, 316 (1999) (noting the significance of international human rights law in constitutional litigation in Colombia).

28. The work of Professors Miller and Levit suggests that the constitutionalization of human rights in Argentina was only thinly supported by participatory processes of norm internalization and may thus risk failure. *See* Miller, *supra* note 24, at 862–65 (noting the "weakness of the debate," with only one legal provision (on the right of reply) receiving discussion on the floor of the convention); Levit, *supra* note 3, at 316–18 (noting that the question of human rights treaties was delegated to a subcommittee of the constitutional assembly that dealt more generally with the status of international law and before which debate was not about specific provisions, except for women's rights issues, but about whether to import wholesale international human rights treaties); *id.* at 319–21 & nn.181, 182 (observing that the work of deciding which human rights treaties to incorporate occurred in closed-door meetings, cutting off space for human rights organizations to participate); *infra* note 64.

29. *See, e.g.*, Michael Kirby, *International Law—The Impact on National Constitutions*, 21 AM. U. INT'L L. REV. 327, 334–36 (2006) (discussing the Bangalore Principles); *cf.* Tavita v. Minister of Immigration, [1994] 2 N.Z.L.R. 257, 266 (C.A.) (noting the Balliol Statement's reference to the "duty of the judiciary to interpret and apply national constitutions . . . in the light of the universality of human rights").

30. *See* 1 DEVELOPING HUMAN RIGHTS JURISPRUDENCE: THE DOMESTIC APPLICATION OF INTERNATIONAL HUMAN RIGHTS NORMS ix–x (Commonwealth Secretariat ed., 1988) (reproducing the Bangalore Principles, developed at Judicial Colloquium in Bangalore). The 1988 Bangalore Principles are also reproduced in M. D. Kirby, *The Role of the Judge in Advancing Human Rights by Reference to International Human Rights Norms*, 62 AUSTL. L. J. 514, 531–32 (1988). Later iterations of these principles place more weight on a "'*duty* . . . to interpret and apply national constitutions . . . in harmony with [both] international human rights codes and customary international law. . . .'" Waters, *supra* note 5, at 646 (quoting the 1998 Bangalore Principles) (emphasis added); *see also* Kirby, *supra* note 29, at 362 ("To the greatest extent possible, in constitutional as in other branches of the law, domestic courts should seek a reconciliation of the international and municipal legal regimes.").

31. *See* Al-Kateb v. Godwin (2004) 219 C.L.R. 562, 624 n.223 (Kirby, J., dissenting) (citing the Bangalore Principles). For Justice McHugh's rejoinder to Justice Kirby, see *infra* note 34.

32. (1998) 195 C.L.R. 337, 417–19 (Kirby, J., dissenting).

33. *See* Newcrest Mining (WA) Ltd. v. Commonwealth of Australia (1997) 190 C.L.R. 513, 657–661 (Kirby, J.)(Austl.). Justice Kirby has addressed international human rights law even where he concludes that it cannot be followed because it is inconsistent with clear and valid domestic law. *See* Minister for Immigration & Multicultural & Indigenous Affairs v. B (2004) 219 C.L.R. 365, 425 (Kirby, J.) (upholding detention of alien children);

see also Re Woolley, Ex parte Applicants M276/2003 (2004) 225 C.L.R. 1, 70, 71 (Kirby, J.) (same). For a recent case suggesting Justice Kirby's possible movement from a convergence posture to one of engagement, see Vasiljkovic v. Commonwealth (2006) 227 C.L.R. 614, 662 (Kirby, J., dissenting) ("In deriving implications from the language and structure of the Constitution, Australian judges . . . are entitled to inform themselves of the developing content of the international law of human rights. Such law does not bind them to particular outcomes. But it is often informative and helpful. . . ."). In this case, Kirby would have granted relief, which the Court denied, to a person challenging extradition to Croatia to face war crimes trials. *See id.* at 665, 673.

34. In addition to Justice Callinan's views, see, for example, Justice McHugh's statements in *Al-Kateb v. Godwin* (2004) 219 C.L.R. 562, 589–64 ("[C]ontrary to the view of Kirby, J, courts cannot read the Constitution by reference to the provisions of international law that have become accepted since the Constitution was enacted in 1900.").

35. Matthew v. The State, [2004] UKPC 33, ¶ 55, [2005] 1 A.C. 433 (appeal taken from Trin. & Tobago) (U.K.) (Judgment of Lord Bingham, Lord Nicholls, Lord Steyn and Lord Walker, dissenting); *see also id.* at ¶ 12 (Judgment of Lord Hoffmann, for the majority) (noting and relying on the "principle that domestic law should so far as possible be interpreted consistently with international obligations and the weight of opinion expressed in domestic cases decided in other jurisdictions" in construing sections 4 and 5 of the Trinidad and Tobago constitution); R. v. Hape, [2007] 2 S.C.R. 292, 324 (LeBel, J.) (Can.) ("In interpreting the scope of application of the *Charter*, the courts should seek to ensure compliance with Canada's binding obligations under international law where the express words are capable of supporting such a construction.") In *Matthew* a majority of the Privy Council reversed an earlier Privy Council decision, to hold that although a mandatory death penalty was inconsistent with the constitution's substantive rights, it was saved from invalidity by another constitutional provision (section 6) protecting pre-existing laws from invalidation. *Id.* at ¶¶ 12–14. The Judgment of Lord Bingham et al. disagreed with this conclusion. *Id.* at ¶¶ 41. Under Lord Hoffmann's judgment, however, the death sentence of the particular defendant, Matthew, was changed to one of life imprisonment, because he had expected an individualized review of that sentence which was no longer possible. *Id.* at ¶¶31–32.

36. *See* Harold Hongju Koh, *Transnational Legal Process*, 75 NEB. L. REV. 181 (1996).

37. *See, e.g.*, Harold Hongju Koh, *Can the President be Torturer in Chief?*, 81 IND. L.J. 1145, 1155–56 (2006) (arguing for an understanding of constitutional law as embracing checks and balances and "human rights universalism"). In recent writings Dean Koh has argued that in choosing among competing interpretations, judges should construe the Constitution "in a manner most consistent with a clear view of the global community of reason and rights." Harold Hongju Koh, *A Community of Reason and Rights*, 77 FORDHAM L. REV. 583, 602 (2008).

38. Jerome J. Shestack, *Book Review and Note (reviewing* JOHANNES MORSINK, THE UNIVERSAL DECLARATION OF HUMAN RIGHTS: ORIGINS, DRAFTING, AND INTENT (1999)), 94 AM. J. INT'L L. 600, 600–01 (2000).

39. Philip Alston, *Conjuring Up New Human Rights: A Proposal for Quality Control*, 78 AM. J. INT'L L. 607, 615 (1984), quoting MAURICE CRANSTON, WHAT ARE HUMAN RIGHTS? 36 (1973).

40. LOUIS HENKIN, THE AGE OF RIGHTS ix (1990).

41. Koh, *Torturer in Chief, supra* note 37, at 1155.

42. For an effort to ground human rights not in an unchanging natural law but in the lived contexts of human beings in today's world, see Allen Buchanan, *Human Rights and*

the Legitimacy of the International Order, 14 LEGAL THEORY 39 (2008). Many leading public philosophers engage themselves with the question of human rights. *See, e.g.*, Jürgen Habermas, *Kant's Idea of Perpetual Peace, with the Benefit of Two Hundred Years' Hindsight*, in PERPETUAL PEACE: ESSAYS ON KANT'S COSMOPOLITAN IDEAL 113, 146 (James Bohman & Matthias Lutz-Bachmann eds., 1997) (arguing for a cosmopolitan law of human rights secured through "the idea of the constitutional state"); *cf.* MARTHA NUSSBAUM, WOMEN AND HUMAN DEVELOPMENT: THE CAPABILITIES APPROACH 78–80 (2000) (developing Amartya Sen's idea and arguing that there are ten capabilities all human should be able to realize); Amartya Sen, *Capability and Well-Being, in* THE QUALITY OF LIFE 30 (Martha Nussbaum & Amartya Sen eds., 1993). Even if one accepts that legal systems should be organized toward realization of these capabilities, this goal is not necessarily linked to legal *rights*, if there are other ways to assure their realization.

43. *See* Louis Henkin, *Human Rights and State "Sovereignty,"* 25 GA. J. INT'L & COMP. L. 31, 37–39, 44 (1995).

44. Gerald Neuman, *The Uses of International Law in Constitutional Interpretation*, 98 AM. J. INT'L L. 82, 85 (2004).

45. Shestack, *supra* note 38, at 602.

46. *Cf.* Henkin, *Human Rights and State "Sovereignty," supra* note 43, at 40 (arguing that national constitutions contributed to the development of the rights set forth in the UDHR). Although the rights themselves may be grounded in universal understandings of the moral condition of human society, the process by which they are asserted is not irrelevant to their legitimacy. *See, e.g.*, Alston, *supra* note 39, at 618–21 (suggesting that given the difficulty of formulating substantive principles by which human rights can be identified, insistence on reliable procedures for the declaration of such rights is important to avoid dilution of the concept).

47. For description of some of this opposition, see EVA BREMS, HUMAN RIGHTS: UNIVERSALITY AND DIVERSITY, at 27–31 (2001) and Chapter 1, above.

48. *See* sources cited above in Chapter 1, note 51; BREMS, *supra* note 47, at 22–24; *see also* Yash Ghai, *Universalism and Relativism: Human Rights as a Framework for Negotiating Interethnic Claims*, 21 CARDOZO L. REV. 1095, 1095–98, 11135–40 (2000).

49. For an elaboration of "cosmopolitanism" as the moral basis for politics and the construction of political institutions in a globalized environment, see David Held, *Cosmopolitanism: Globalisation Tamed?*, 29 REV. INT'L STUDIES 465 (2003); *see also* DAVID HELD, GLOBAL COVENANT: THE SOCIAL DEMOCRATIC ALTERNATIVE TO THE WASHINGTON CONSENSUS 170 (2004) (identifying cosmopolitan principles for a new internationalism); Thomas Pogge, *Cosmopolitanism and Sovereignty*, 103 ETHICS 48 (1992).

50. Sujit Choudhry, *Globalization in Search of Justification: Toward a Theory of Comparative Constitutional Interpretation*, 74 IND. L.J. 819, 825 (1999).

51. *See* Gerald Neuman, *Human Rights and Constitutional Rights: Harmony and Dissonance*, 55 STAN. L. REV. 1863, 1868 (2003). Professor Waldron, while rejecting arguments from universal moral or "natural" law, has advanced an argument for consistency in the development of overlapping human and constitutional rights based on principles of fairness in how people in the world community are treated. *See* Jeremy Waldron, The Storrs Lectures, "'Partly Laws Common to All Mankind': Foreign Law in American Courts," Yale Law School (Sept. 10–12, 2007), *available at* http://www.law.yale.edu/news/5408.htm (available in writing in part at http://iilj.org/courses/2008iiljcolloqium.asp).

52. In addition to those constitutions discussed earlier, see, for example, BENIN CONST. pmbl., *available at* http://www.chr.up.ac.za/hr_docs/constitutions/docs/BeninC(englishsummary)(rev).doc (last visited Feb. 20, 2009) (asserting "attachment to the principles of democracy and

human rights" and referring to the UN Charter, the UDHR, and the African Charter on Human and Peoples' Rights); CAMEROON CONST. pmbl. (1996), *available at* http://confinder.richmond.edu/admin/docs/Cameroon.pdf (last visited Feb. 11, 2009) (stating "our attachment to the fundamental freedoms enshrined in the Universal Declaration of Human Rights, the Charter of the United Nations, and The African Charter on Human and Peoples' Rights"); MALI CONST. pmbl., art. 116 (1992), *available at* http://confinder.richmond.edu/admin/docs/Mali.pdf (last visited Feb. 11, 2009) (affirming commitment to the UDHR and the African Charter on Human and Peoples' Rights and giving ratified treaties "superior authority over laws of the State"). *See generally* Nsongurua J. Udombana, *Interpreting Rights Globally: Courts and Constitutional Rights in Emerging Democracies*, 5 AFR. HUM. RTS. J. 47, 59 (2005) (summarizing African constitutions with directives for constitutional interpretation in light of international law).

53. International law, that is, may not be seen as independent from particular national agendas. *See* Martti Koskenniemi, *International Law in Europe: Between Tradition and Renewal*, 16 EUR. J. INT'L L. 113, 117 (2005); BOAVENTURA DE SOUSA SANTOS, TOWARD A NEW LEGAL COMMON SENSE: LAW, GLOBALIZATION AND EMANCIPATION 317–20 (2d ed. 2002); *cf.* STEPHEN KRASNER, SOVEREIGNTY: ORGANIZED HYPOCRISY (1999); JACK GOLDSMITH & ERIC POSNER, THE LIMITS OF INTERNATIONAL LAW 3–14 (2005) (arguing for a state-centered rational choice model of international law).

54. *See* Eric A. Posner & Cass R. Sunstein, *The Law of Other States*, 59 STAN. L. REV. 131, 141, 144 (2006) (also indicating that decision-makers must act on 'private' information).

55. *See* Jeremy Waldron, *Foreign Law and the Modern Ius Gentium*, 119 HARV. L. REV. 129, 143–46 (2005).

56. For a discussion of this point in the U.S. context, see Nicholas Quinn Rosenkranz, *Condorcet and the Constitution: A Response to* The Law of Other States, 59 STAN. L. REV. 1281, 1303 (2007).

57. Institutional arrangements affect both *who* decides and *what* the question is. Statutes prohibiting the death penalty, for an institutionalist, may not "mean" the same thing, or be answering the same question, as constitutional interpretations that do so. *See* Chapter 6, below.

58. *See* Office of the UN High Commissioner for Human Rights, Ratifications and Reservations, http://www2.ohchr.org/english/bodies/ratification/4.htm (last visited Sept. 2, 2008) (showing 162 parties to the ICCPR, 159 parties to the ICESCR, 185 parties to CEDAW and 193 parties to the Convention on the Rights of the Child).

59. *See* Oona A. Hathaway, *The Cost of Commitment*, 55 STAN. L. REV. 1821 (2003); Oona A. Hathaway, *Do Human Rights Treaties Make a Difference?*, 111 YALE L.J. 1935 (2002); see Chapter 6, below for further discussion.

60. *See also* Posner & Sunstein, *supra* note 54, at 165–66.

61. *See also* Rosalind Dixon, *A Democratic Theory of Constitutional Comparison*, 56 AM. J. COMP. L. 947, 984–85 (2008).

62. Sir Sydney Kentridge, *Comparative Law in Constitutional Adjudication: The New South African Experience, in* JUDICIAL RECOURSE TO FOREIGN LAW: A NEW SOURCE OF INSPIRATION? 329, 330 (Sir Basil Markinesis & Jörg Fedtke eds., 2006); *see* Kirby, *supra* note 29, at 359–60.

63. *See supra* note 20; *cf. Re* Colonel Aird; *Ex parte* Alpert (2004) 220 C.L.R. 308, 337, 344–50 (Austl.) (Kirby, J. dissenting) (concluding that there was no international law or human rights rule to constrain the jurisdiction of military tribunals over off-duty acts by members of the armed services, but nonetheless interpreting the Australian constitution to so provide, thereby treating international human rights as a floor that the domestic constitution could exceed).

64. *See* Miller, *supra* note 24, at 865–66 (describing Argentina Supreme Court's holding (in *Bramajo*, 319 Fallos 1840, 1844–48 (1996)), refusing to enforce a three-year statutory limit on pretrial detention because the American Convention on Human Rights required only "reasonable" limits and in some cases more than three years could be reasonable). On the possibility that human rights regimes will be invoked to legitimate oppressive state practices, see *infra* text at note 83 and Chapter 9, note 146.

65. Anne-Marie Slaughter & William Burke-White, *The Future of International Law is Domestic (or, The European Way of Law)*, 47 HARV. INT'L L.J. 327, 334, 339–43 (2006). Under the EU model, the coauthors say, international law influences domestic politics and governance in three ways—by "strengthening domestic institutions, backstopping national governance, and compelling domestic action." *Id.* at 329.

66. Kirby, *supra* note 29, at 360.

67. *Id.* at 360–61.

68. *Id.* at 362.

69. *Id.* ("[In] the era of globalization, . . . we are at once freer but more inter-dependent").

70. *See, e.g.*, ANNE-MARIE SLAUGHTER, A NEW WORLD ORDER 34–35, 232–35, 257–60 (2004); Christopher C. Joyner, *Countering Nuclear Terrorism: A Conventional Response*, 18 EUR. J. INT'L L. 225, 229, 236–37, 250 (2007); Michael Bahar, *Attaining Optimal Deterrence at Sea: A Legal and Strategic Theory for Naval Anti-Piracy Operations*, 40 VAND. J. TRANSNAT'L L. 1, 7, 77–81 (2007); Aurelie Lopez, *The Protection of Environmentally Displaced Persons in International Law*, 37 ENVTL. L. 365, 407–09 (2007); Kimmo Nuotio, *Terrorism as a Catalyst for the Emergence, Harmonization and Reform of Criminal Law*, 4 J. INT'L CRIM. JUST. 998, 1006–07 (2006).

71. *See, e.g.*, Judith Resnik, *Foreign as Domestic Affairs: Rethinking Horizontal Federalism and Foreign Affairs Preemption in Light of Translocal Internationalism*, 57 EMORY L.J. 31, 88 (2007).

72. Harold Hongju Koh, *International Law as Part of Our Law*, 98 AM. J. INT'L L. 43, 53 (2004)("[O]ne prominent feature of a globalizing world is the emergence of a transnational law, particularly in the area of human rights, that merges the national and the international."). This "blurring" of national and international may pose its own risks. *See* Kent Roach, *Constitutional, Remedial, and International Dialogues About Rights: The Canadian Experience*, 40 TEX. INT'L L.J. 537, 564–75 (2005) (criticizing the Canadian court's refusal to articulate an absolute norm based on jus cogens against deporting a person to face torture in *Suresh v. Canada (Minister of Citizenship and Immigration)*, [2002] 1 S.C.R. 3 and attributing the court's action to the blurring of comparative and international law).

73. Koh, *supra* note 72, at 53–54 (quoting Justice Blackmun). Dean Koh is supportive of the universalist tradition of international law in domestic law, a tradition consisting of "a commitment to fundamental justice, international legal process, transnationalism, and human rights." Harold Koh, *Mark Janis and the American Tradition of International Law*, 21 CONN. J. INT'L L. 191, 192 (2006); *see also* Koh, *A Community of Reason*, *supra* note 37, at 602. Under his theory, the moral force of universal norms is not self-actualizing; international law has a positive side that must be activated, through transnational processes, in order to bring norms of justice into legally enforceable rules. *See* Koh, *Transnational Legal Process*, *supra* note 36, at 204–05 (describing the "normativity" of that process).

74. Koh, *supra* note 72, at 53 (emphasis added).

75. *See* Karen Knop, *Here and There: International Law in Domestic Courts*, 32 N.Y.U. J. INT'L L. & POL. 501 (2000); Mayo Moran, *Inimical to Constitutional Values: Complex Migrations of Constitutional Rights*, *in* THE MIGRATION OF CONSTITUTIONAL IDEAS 233, 234–35 (Sujit Choudhry ed., 2006). *Cf.* Roach, *supra* note 72, at 553–75 (describing a process of

"dialogue" between the UN Human Rights Committee and the Canadian courts; praising the Canadian courts' openness to international norms, but criticizing their refusal to recognize an absolute jus cogens norm against deporting a person to face torture). Roach's critique would favor more stringent adherence to international law; the implication of the work of Knop and Moran is that constitutional interpretation in light of international law is likely to be more of a two-way, than a hierarchical, process.

76. *See* David Sloss, *The Domestication of International Human Rights: Non-Self-Executing Declarations and Human Rights Treaties*, 24 YALE J. INT'L L. 129, 194 (1999).

77. *See, e.g.*, Ian Johnstone, *Legislation and Adjudication in the UN Security Council: Bringing Down the Deliberative Deficit*, 102 AM. J. INT'L L. 275, 276, 278 (2008); Stephen Sieberson, *The Proposed European Constitution—Will It Eliminate the EU's Democratic Deficit?*, 10 COLUM. J. EUR. L. 173, 206–07 (2004); Peter Lindseth, *Democratic Legitimacy and the Administrative Character of Supranationalism: The Example of the European Community*, 99 COLUM. L. REV. 628, 633–34 (1999).

78. Kirby, *supra* note 29, at 363.

79. The Constitution of Bosnia and Herzegovina, adopted as part of the Dayton Accords, *see* General Framework Agreement for Peace in Bosnia & Herzegovina art. V & annex 4, Dec. 14, 1995, 35 I.L.M. 89, required three of nine members of the Constitutional Court to be appointed by the President of the European Court of Human Rights. CONST. BOSNIA-HERZEGOVINA art. VI. *See also* CONST. OF THE REPUBLIC OF KOSOVO art. 152 (2008), *draft available at* http://www.kushtetutakosoves.info/?cid=2,1 (requiring, on a transitional basis, the appointment by the International Civilian Representative of three international judges, not from bordering countries, to the Kosovo Constitutional Court).

80. *See* Tom Ginsburg, *Locking in Democracy: Constitutions, Commitment and International Law*, 38 N.Y.U. J. INT'L L. & POL. 707, 757 (2006) (discussing constitutional incorporation of treaties as a precommitment device, and noting appeal of international law "where one distrusts outsiders less than one distrusts one's own compatriots"); *cf.* Andrew Moravcsik, *The Origins of Human Rights Regimes: Democratic Delegation in Postwar Europe*, 54 INT'L ORG. 217 (2000) (arguing that "[e]stablishing an international human rights regime . . . is a tactic used by governments to 'lock in' and consolidate democratic institutions, thereby enhancing their credibility and stability vis-à-vis nondemocratic political threats").

81. Kirby, *supra* note 29, at 354, 356.

82. *See* Kim Lane Scheppele, *The Migration of Anti-Constitutional Ideas: The Post-9/11 Globalization of Public Law and the International State of Emergency*, *in* THE MIGRATION OF CONSTITUTIONAL IDEAS (Sujit Choudhry ed. 2006); *see also* Slaughter & Burke-White, *supra* note 65, at 347–48 (agreeing that states have invoked "exceptions to international and domestic legal protections . . . under the cover of fighting terrorism," and noting "Tanzania, Indonesia, Russia, Pakistan, and Uzbekistan, each of which has undertaken 'draconian anti-terrorism laws' that compromise human rights and strengthen the hand of government vis-à-vis opposition groups"); Upendra Baxi, *Voices of Suffering and the Future of Human Rights*, 8 TRANSNAT'L L. & CONTEMP. PROBS. 125, 132 (1998) (noting concern that some human rights regimes may legitimize abuse "in the name of making human rights secure").

83. Slaughter & Burke-White, *supra* note 65, at 347; *see also* Roach, *supra* note 72, at 553–75.

84. *See, e.g.*, Russell A. Miller, *Self-determination in International Law and the Demise of Democracy?*, 41 COLUM. J. TRANSNAT'L L. 601, 608–17 (2003); Gerry J. Simpson, *The Diffusion of Sovereignty: Self-determination in the Post-Colonial Age*, 32 STAN. J. INT'L L. 255, 256–58 (1996).

85. David S. Law, *Generic Constitutional Law*, 89 MINN. L. REV. 652, 658 (2005).

86. In Henkin's terms, these constitutions are "genetically" related, in that they are drawing on similar models. The "genetic" relationships Henkin describes are a broader group than what Choudhry calls "genealogical" relationships, in which one constitution in a relatively tight sense grew out of another. *See* Choudhry, *supra* note 50, at 821, 825; Louis Henkin, *A New Birth of Constitutionalism: Genetic Influences and Genetic Defects*, 14 CARDOZO L. REV. 533, 534 (1993).

87. Oyama v. California, 332 U.S. 633, 649–50 (1948) (Black, J., joined by Douglas, J., concurring). *See also id.* at 673 (Rutledge, J., joined by Murphy, J., concurring) ("The Alien Land Law['s] . . . inconsistency with the Charter, which has been duly ratified and adopted by the United States, is but one more reason why the statute must be condemned").

88. Yuval Shany, *How Supreme Is the Supreme Law of the Land? Comparative Analysis of the Influence of International Human Right Treaties Upon the Interpretation of Constitutional Texts by Domestic Courts*, 31 BROOK. J. INT'L L. 341 (2006).

89. *Compare* Suresh v. Canada (Minister of Citizenship and Immigration), [2002] 1 S.C.R. 3, 38 (Can.) (recognizing that although treaty norms are not internally binding absent incorporation by statute, the constitution's meaning "may be informed" by such law and holding that absent extraordinary circumstances, deporting an alleged terrorist supporter to face possible torture would violate the "fundamental justice" standard of Charter Section 7) and Tavita v. Minister of Immigration, [1994] 2 N.Z.L.R. 257, 265–66 (C.A.) (describing the government's suggestion that New Zealand's obligations under the ICCPR and another human rights convention were irrelevant to interpretation of domestic immigration laws as "unattractive" in implying that the international obligations, assumed but not yet implemented by statute, were "window-dressing") *with* Kavanagh v. Governor of Mountjoy Prison, [2002] 3 I.R. 97, 127 (Ir.) (Fennelly, J.) (rejecting claim that court's decision on a constitutional question, involving right to a jury trial, should be influenced by Ireland's accession to the ICCPR or by the "views" of the UNHRC expressed on the appellant's claim and disagreeing with *Tavita*'s approach because under the Irish constitution "'[n]o international agreement shall be part of the domestic law of the state save as may be determined by' the legislature"). For different perspectives, see Reem Bahdi, *Globalization of Judgment: Transjudicialism and the Five Faces of International Law in Domestic Courts*, 34 GEO. WASH. INT'L L. REV. 555, 560 (2002) (characterizing reasoning in cases like *Tavita* as invoking a rule-of-law idea that even where a treaty obligation is not yet domestically enforceable, "the state must be held accountable for its promises made in international instruments"); Waters, *supra* note 5, at 695–704 (arguing for a more cautious approach, giving weight to current indicators of political support for unimplemented treaties in evaluating their force on domestic legal questions). On monism and dualism, see infra, text at note 149.

90. For Shany, the EU provides an example of "supra-constitutionalism," insofar as European Community Law trumps domestic constitutional law. Shany, *supra* note 88, at 356 & n.58. This hierarchy, however, though asserted by the ECJ, remains contested. *See, e.g.*, Mattias Kumm, *Beyond Golf Clubs and the Judicialization of Politics: Why Europe Has a Constitution Properly So Called*, 54 AM. J. COMP. L. 505, 523 (2006) (Suppl.) ("For the most part national courts have not accepted that EU Law is the supreme law of the land"); for further discussion, see Chapter 3, below. Shany's third category, "quasi-constitutionalization," applies when international law trumps all other domestic law with the exception of the constitution (as in how Germany treats certain customary international norms or Costa Rica treats treaties). *See* Shany, *supra* note 88, at 357 & n.60.

91. *But cf.* Breard v. Greene, 523 U.S. 371 (1998) (per curiam); Medellín v. Texas, 128 S. Ct. 1346 (2008). Neither case involved national *legislation* requiring state compliance

with the treaty obligations at issue, though each case was in some tension with the implications of the inclusion of treaties in the Supremacy Clause of the U.S. Constitution.

92. *See, e.g.*, Trop v. Dulles, 356 U.S., 86, 99–100 (1958) (plurality opinion) (Eighth Amendment requires that "power be exercised within the limits of civilized standards").

93. The ECtHR is not a domestic constitutional court, but a regional human rights court, whose judgments have proved more effective thus far than those of other international or regional human rights tribunals. *See* Sweet & Keller, *supra* note 7, at 3. The relationship of its judgments to the internal constitutional orders of the European member states is complex. *See id.* at 8–26; *see also* Chapter 3, below. For present purposes, however, it is a court, construing constitution-like rights, in ways that are understood to bind the parties before it to comply. *See* ECHR art. 46 (parties "undertake to abide" by final judgments and the Committee of Ministers "supervises" the "execution" of judgments). In its extradition case law, the ECtHR indirectly evaluates the lawfulness—under the European Convention (ECHR)—of practices in jurisdictions outside its reach, notably including the United States.

94. 161 Eur. Ct. H.R. (ser. A) (1989).

95. "Death row phenomenon" consists of the combination of dread and uncertainty about one's fate, and daily suffering under rigorous conditions of confinement, that results from long delays in carrying out death penalties caused by intervening legal processes. Eighth Amendment challenges on this basis have been raised but not yet heard on the merits in the U.S. Supreme Court, though some justices have indicated that the question posed is a serious one. *See* Smith v. Arizona, 128 S. Ct. 2997 (2007) (mem.) (Breyer, J., dissenting from denial of certiorari); Foster v. Florida, 537 U.S. 990, 991–93 (2002) (mem.) (Breyer, J., dissenting from denial of certiorari); Knight v. Florida, 528 U.S. 990, 993–94 (1999) (mem.) (Breyer, J., dissenting from denial of certiorari); Elledge v. Florida, 525 U.S. 944, 944–46 (1998) (mem.) (Breyer, J., dissenting from denial of certiorari); *see also* Lackey v. Texas, 514 U.S. 1045 (1995) (mem.) (Stevens, J., memorandum respecting denial of certiorari).

96. *Soering*, 161 Eur. Ct. H.R. (ser. A) at 34.

97. *See* ECHR, art. 1—Obligation to Respect Human Rights ("The High Contracting Parties shall secure to everyone *within their jurisdiction* the rights and freedoms defined in Section I of this Convention") (emphasis added).

98. *Soering*, 161 Eur. Ct. H.R. (ser. A) at 34 (emphasis added); *see also id.* at 35 (discussing the Torture Convention).

99. *See also* Bader v. Sweden, App. No. 13284/04, Eur. Ct. H.R. (Nov. 8, 2005), *available at* http://www.echr.coe.int/echr (concluding that relief from deportation was required where Bader faced death sentence imposed in absentia in Syria that would violate arts. 2 and 3 of Convention).

100. United States v. Burns, [2001] 1 S.C.R. 283 (Can.). *See also* Mohamed v. President of the Republic of South Africa, 2001 (3) SA 893 (CC) (S. Afr.), *available at* http://www.saflii.org/za/cases/ZACC/2001/18.html (discussing both *Soering* and *Burns* and concluding that the South Africa Constitution did not permit either extradition or deportation to face the death penalty).

101. *Burns*, [2001] 1 S.C.R. at 335; *see also id.* at 331 ("Canada currently is the only country in the world . . . that has abolished the death penalty at home but continues to extradite without assurances to face the death penalty abroad").

102. *Id.* at 330.

103. *See also id.* at 330–35 (emphasizing "important initiatives within the international community denouncing the death penalty, with the government of Canada often in the

forefront. These include: Extrajudicial, summary or arbitrary executions: Report by the Special Rapporteur, U.N. Doc. E/CN.4/1997/60, at para. 79; Extrajudicial, summary or arbitrary executions: Note by the Secretary-General, U.N. Doc. A/51/457, at para. 145; United Nations Commission on Human Rights Resolutions 1997/12 (Canada voted in favour), 1998/8 (Canada sponsored the resolution and voted in favour) . . . ").

104. *Id.* at 333 (quoting Canada's representative to the UNHRC in 1997) (internal citation omitted). *See also* Venezia v. Ministero Di Grazia e Giustizia, Corte cost., 27 Jun. 1996, n. 223, Gazz. Uff. 3 July 1996, *reprinted in* 79 RIVISTA DI DIRITTO INTERNAZIONALE 815 (1996), *summarized in* 91 AM. J. INT'L L. 727 (1997) (case note by Andrea Bianchi) (Italian Constitutional Court holds that extradition of a fugitive indicted for a crime for which capital punishment is provided by the law of the requesting state would violate the Italian Constitution, regardless of the sufficiency of the assurances provided by the requesting state that the death penalty would not be imposed).

105. *See, e.g.,* Salah Sheekh v. The Netherlands, App. No. 1948/04, Eur. Ct. H.R ¶¶ 148–49 (Jan. 11, 2007) (finding that expelling the petitioner to Somalia would violate Article 3 of the Convention, given conditions he would likely face there because he and his family had been targeted for abuse as minorities); Garabayev v. Russia, App. No. 38411/02, Eur. Ct. H.R. (2007) (finding violation of Article 3 from Russia's extradition of defendant to Turkmenistan where he faced severe conditions of confinement for three months); Shamayev v. Georgia & Russia, 2005-III Eur.Ct. H.R. 153 (finding violation in extradition of Chechen defendants from Georgia to Russia, notwithstanding assurances that no death penalty would be sought, given likelihood of poor conditions and abusive treatment), noted in Maria Gavounel, *International Decision: Shamayev v. Georgia & Russia, App. No. 36378/02 at* http://www.echr.coe.int. *(European Court of Human Rights, April 12, 2005)—ECHR Decision on extradition of Chechen rebels to Russia,* 100 AM. J. INT'L L. 674 (2006).

106. I am grateful to Mark Tushnet for a conversation some years ago on this point. The text discusses the "margin of appreciation" doctrine in the European Court of Human Rights. An arguably analogous doctrine concerning the "margin of discretion" is found in the jurisprudence of the European Court of Justice. *See, e.g.,* Case C-36/02, Omega Spielhallen- und Automatenaufstellungs-GmbH v. Oberbürgermeisterin der Bundesstadt Bonn, 2004 E.C.R. I-9609, described in Chapter 3, note 153, below. In light of these doctrines, one can debate whether to characterize the European regimes as regimes of "convergence" or of intensive "engagement."

107. For background on the margin of appreciation doctrine, see FRANCIS G. JACOBS, THE EUROPEAN CONVENTION ON HUMAN RIGHTS 201–02 (1975); HOWARD CHARLES YOUROW, THE MARGIN OF APPRECIATION DOCTRINE IN THE DYNAMICS OF EUROPEAN HUMAN RIGHTS JURISPRUDENCE 13–24 (1996).

108. *See, e.g.,* Lawless (Commission), 1 Eur Ct H.R. (Ser. B), at 82 (1960–61); Ireland v. United Kingdom, 25 Eur. Ct. H.R.(ser. A) at 78–79 (1978); *see generally,* YOUROW, *supra* note 107, at 15-17; J. G. MERRILLS, THE DEVELOPMENT OF INTERNATIONAL LAW BY THE EUROPEAN COURT OF HUMAN RIGHTS 137–38 (1988); Michael R. Hutchinson, *The Margin of Appreciation Doctrine in the European Court of Human Rights,* 48 INT'L & COMP. L. Q. 638, 639–40 (1999); Oren Gross, *"Once More Unto the Breach": The Systemic Failure of Applying the European Convention on Human Rights to Entrenched Emergencies,* 23 YALE J. INT'L L. 437, 456–57 (1998).

109. ECHR art. 9(2).

110. STEVEN GREER, THE MARGIN OF APPRECIATION: INTERPRETATION AND DISCRETION UNDER THE EUROPEAN CONVENTION ON HUMAN RIGHTS 5 (2000).

111. A classic statement is in *Handyside v. United Kingdom*, 24 Eur. Ct. H.R. (ser. A) at 22 (1976): "By reason of their direct and continuous contact with the vital forces of their countries, State authorities are in principle in a better position than the international judge to give an opinion on the exact content of these requirements as well as on the 'necessity' of a 'restriction' or 'penalty' intended to meet them."

112. *See* Neuman, *The Uses of International Law*, *supra* note 44, at 87 n.29 (suggesting that "decisions of th[e] court upholding a national practice against a human rights challenge [using the margin of appreciation] do not necessarily express an ultimate conclusion about the compatibility of the practice with the right"); *see also* Paolo G. Carozza, *Subsidiarity as a Structural Principle of International Human Rights Law*, 97 AM. J. INT'L L. 38, 61 (2003) (referring to the margin of appreciation as a "judicially created doctrine of self-restraint, which refers to the breadth of deference or error the Court will allow national bodies before it will declare a violation of one of the substantive guarantees under the Convention").

113. *See* Carozza, *supra* note 112, at 70.

114. *Id.* at 62; *see also* MERRILLS, *supra* note 108, at 157 ("[T]he margin of appreciation is a way of recognizing that the international protection of human rights and sovereign freedom of action are not contradictory but complementary"; the doctrine helps determine the boundary between them).

115. *See* GREER, *supra* note 110, at 5 (referring to more than 700 judgments as of the year 2000).

116. *See, e.g.*, Evans v. United Kingdom, App. No. 6339/05, Eur. Ct. H.R. (Mar. 7, 2006), *available at* http://www.echr.coe/int/echr (upholding, as within the margin of appreciation, a British statute specifying that if either party to the in vitro fertilization of eggs withdrew consent for their use, the eggs were to be destroyed, over the objection of a woman who had donated eggs before removal of cancerous ovaries); Pretty v. United Kingdom, 2002-III Eur. Ct. H.R. 155 (2002) (rejecting challenge to UK prosecutors' refusal to assure a very sick woman that if her husband helped her to die he would not be prosecuted and noting the wide margin of appreciation in this area of diversity in views). *But cf.* Smith & Grady v. United Kingdom, 1999-VI Eur. Ct. H.R. 45 (rejecting margin of appreciation defense and holding that it violated the Convention to investigate and discharge for homosexuality two members of the British armed services).

117. *See, e.g.*, James Sweeney, *Margins of Appreciation: Cultural Relativity and the European Court of Human Rights in the Post–Cold War Era*, 54 INT'L & COMP. L. Q. 459, 462–63 (2005); Paul Mahoney, *Judicial Activism and Judicial Self-Restraint in the European Court of Human Rights: Two Sides of the Same Coin*, 11 HUM. RTS. L.J. 57, 83 (1990). For a fairly positive assessment of the margin of appreciation doctrine's development as of the mid-1990s, *see* YOUROW, *supra* note 107, at 186–89, 197 (exploring and explaining the different application of the ECtHR's margin of appreciation doctrine across different fields of law, with the greatest discretion allowed in Article 15 derogation cases, and considerable discretion allowed in cases under Articles 8–11 and Protocol 1, Article I, as compared with a more rigorous drive toward uniformity in Articles 5 and 6 due process case law); *see also* Yuval Shany, *Toward a General Margin of Appreciation Doctrine in International Law?*, 16 EUR. J. INT'L L. 907, 922–26 (2005) (identifying various criticisms of use of margin of appreciation but also arguing that international law will need to develop something comparable).

118. Şahin v. Turkey, 2005-XI Eur. Ct. H.R. 173 (Grand Chamber) [hereinafter *Şahin II*]

119. *Id.* at 204 (citations omitted).

120. *Id.* at 206 (quoting from prior decision, Şahin v. Turkey, App. No. 44774/98, Eur. Ct. H.R., at para. 109 (June 29, 2004) [hereinafter *Şahin I*]; *see also Sahin II*, at 206–07

(stating that "'each Contracting State may, in accordance with the Convention provisions, take a stance against such [extremist] political movements, based on its historical experience'" [quoting *Şahin I*, at para. 109] and that "where the values of pluralism, respect for the rights of others and, in particular, equality before the law of men and women are being taught . . . , it is understandable that the relevant authorities should wish to preserve the secular nature of the institution concerned and so consider it contrary to such values to allow religious attire . . . to be worn").

121. *See* Jennifer M. Westerfield, *Behind the Veil: An American Legal Perspective on the European Headscarf Debate*, 54 AM. J. COMP. L. 637, 651 & n.62, 654, 678 (2006) (arguing that the *Şahin* judgments were partly motivated by "fear of militant Islam," and that if the ECtHR "address[es] a future French case concerning the headscarf," it "should not consider itself bound by" those judgments, nor should it extend the same "wide margin of appreciation"). *But cf.* Decision N° 2004-505 DC, Nov. 19, 2004, The Treaty establishing a Constitution for Europe, para. 18 (Conseil Constitutionnel) (Fr.) (referring to reasoning in *Şahin I* in explaining why provisions concerning religious rights in proposed Constitution for Europe would not interfere with France's constitutional commitment to secularism).

122. *Şahin II*, *supra* note 118, at 206 (quoting *Şahin I* at ¶108).

123. *See id.* at 207–08 (referring to procedures by which regulation was adopted in finding proportionality with respect to claim under Article 9); *see also id.* at 216 (with regard to claim under Article 2, asserting without analysis that the regulation did not hinder performance of habitual religious duties and referring to the procedures to adopt and enforce the regulation, of which petitioner was on notice when she applied).

124. *Cf.* Ghai, *supra* note 48, at 1099 (arguing that an understanding of human rights that is balanced between universalism and relativism, and recognizes some (but not all) rights as having universal aspects, can provide a framework for "mediating competing ethnic and cultural claims" in a multiethnic society).

125. *See Case C-355, Colombian Constitutional Court Abortion Decision*, *supra* note 27, at 45.

126. From time to time judges on the ECtHR have suggested that the doctrine would or should disappear from use. *See, e.g.*, Z. v. Finland, 1997-I Eur. Ct. H.R. 323, 357–58 (De Meyer, J., partly dissenting).

127. *See generally* BEATTY, *supra* note 16. For a helpful analytical treatment (published after this chapter had been written), see Alec Stone Sweet & Jud Mathews, *Proportionality Balancing and Global Constitutionalism*, 47 COLUM. J. TRANSNAT'L L. 72 (2008). For earlier work from which some of this section is drawn, see Vicki C. Jackson, *Being Proportional About Proportionality*, 21 CONST. COMMENT. 803 (2004) (reviewing DAVID M. BEATTY, THE ULTIMATE RULE OF LAW (2004)).

128. *See* R. v. Oakes, [1986] 1 S.C.R. 103. Under the *Oakes* approach, statutes found to intrude on Charter rights may nonetheless be upheld under Section 1 if (1) their purpose is consistent with a "free and democratic society" and of "sufficient importance to warrant overriding a constitutionally protected right or freedom," and (2) the statutory limits "are reasonable and demonstrably justified in a free and democratic society," *id.* at 129, 141, a standard designed to "ensure [] that the legislative means are proportional to the legislative ends." R. v. Morgentaler, [1988] 1 S.C.R. 30, 73–74 (Dickson, C.J.) (explaining the *Oakes* test). The proportionality requirement, in turn, has "three important components": First, "the measures adopted . . . must be rationally connected to the objective. . . . Second, the means, even if rationally connected to the objective in this first sense, should impair 'as little as possible' the right or freedom in question. . . . Third, there must be a proportionality between the *effects* of the measures which are responsible for limiting the Charter right or freedom, and the objective which has been identified as of 'sufficient importance.'"

Oakes, at 139. This third criterion is sometimes referred to as proportionality in the "strict" sense, and has been further elaborated in *Dagenais v. Canadian Broadcasting Corp.*, [1994] 3 S.C.R. 835 (Can.). The lead opinion concluded that when "the measure at issue, while rationally connected to an important objective, will result in only the partial achievement of this object . . . the third step of the second branch of the *Oakes* test requires both that the underlying *objective* of a measure and the *salutary effects* that actually result from its implementation be proportional to the deleterious effects the measure has on fundamental rights and freedoms." *Id.* at 887.

129. *See, e.g.*, Elisabeth Zoller, *Congruence and Proportionality for Congressional Enforcement Powers: Cosmetic Change or Velvet Revolution?*, 78 IND. L.J. 567, 582 (2003) (describing the German proportionality test in terms of costs and benefits, e.g., "the act must be proportionate strictly speaking (verhaltnismassig), which means that its costs must remain less than the benefits secured by its ends").

130. This distinction is emphasized in *Dagenais*. *See supra* note 128.

131. *See* HCJ 2056/04 Beit Sourik Village Council v. Gov't of Israel (The Security Fence Case) (High Court of Justice, June 30, 2004), *available at* http://elyon1.court.gov.il/files_eng/04/560/020/A28/04020560.a28.pdf (last visited Jan. 22, 2009).

132. *See also* District of Columbia v. Heller, 128 S. Ct. 2783, 2852 (2008) (Breyer, J., dissenting) (arguing that where constitutional interests are implicated in complex ways, the Court asks "whether the statute burdens a protected interest in a way or to an extent that is out of proportion to the statute's salutary effects . . . " and noting that such a "proportionality" approach is found in "various constitutional contexts"). For an argument to expand use of proportionality in U.S. law, see E. THOMAS SULLIVAN & RICHARD S. FRASE, PROPORTIONALITY PRINCIPLES IN AMERICAN LAW: CONTROLLING EXCESSIVE GOVERNMENT ACTIONS (2008).

133. *See* ALEXY, *supra* note 16, at 66–67.

134. *See* Matthew Adler, *The Moral Structure of American Constitutional Law*, 97 MICH. L. REV. 1 (1998) (arguing that "rights" are "rights against [certain] rules"); RONALD DWORKIN, TAKING RIGHTS SERIOUSLY xi (1977) (on rights as trumps).

135. *See* BEATTY, *supra* note 16, at 170–76. The rights or interests protected are almost atextual on Beatty's account, which favors "proportionality" analysis over "interpretivism."

136. *Id.* at 171.

137. For critique of claims for the impartiality and determinacy of this method, see, for example, Jackson, *Being Proportional About Proportionality*, *supra* note 127 (also questioning commensurability of the interests); some of the following discussion is drawn from this source.

138. Law, *supra* note 85, at 661; *see also id.* at 693–94 ("Around the world, constitutional courts apply different levels of scrutiny keyed to the importance of the interests at stake, but not all use the word 'proportionality' to describe this form of analysis.")

139. *Id.* at 696. Balancing, in Law's view, focuses on both the goals the government seeks to achieve and the other interests affected, while means-end analysis focuses on the efficacy of the means to assure the goal; in the former, courts "balance" not by "metrics," but by "analogy," and "the more important the [individual] interest, the less that unnecessary impairment of it will be tolerated." *Id.*

140. Gráinne de Búrca & Oliver Gerstenberg, *The Denationalization of Constitutional Law*, 47 HARV. INT'L L.J. 243, 244 (2006). Their analysis might be read to suggest that a process of convergence would be driven by the requirements of justification. *See id.* at 252 (suggesting that in Europe, "the relationship between human rights and constitutional rights can be understood as one of mutual backup and multi-layered justification," a form

of analysis that makes room for "de-nationalized persuasive authority," and thus contributes to what they call the "denationalization of constitutional law" through a comparative perspective on government justification).

141. Moreover, it is argued by some, structured proportionality review meets some of the criticisms of judicial balancing, *see infra* note 142, through its efforts to elicit attention to specific, nonformulaic justifications from the government.

142. For a general argument that proportionality analysis is inconsistent with U.S. understandings of rights as "trumps," see Neomi Rao, *On the Use and Abuse of Dignity in Constitutional Law*, 14 COLUM. J. EUR. L. 201, 246–54 (2008). For an influential critique of balancing approaches in constitutional law, see T. Alexander Aleinikoff, *Constitutional Interpretation in an Age of Balancing*, 96 YALE L.J. 943 (1987).

143. CARLOS SANTIAGO NINO, THE CONSTITUTION OF DELIBERATIVE DEMOCRACY 15 (1996).

144. *See* Law, *supra* note 85, at 697–98.

145. *See, e.g.*, Donald P. Kommers, *Germany: Balancing Rights and Duties*, IN INTERPRETING CONSTITUTIONS; A COMPARATIVE STUDY 161, 192–93 (Jeffrey Goldsworthy ed., 2006) (explaining that the role of judicial decisions in constitutional law is different than in the codified legal system, because the rulings have "the force of general law").

146. For an argument that the proportionality doctrine should be used to define the boundaries of the margin of appreciation, see YUTAKA ARAI-TAKAHASHI, THE MARGIN OF APPRECIATION DOCTRINE AND THE PRINCIPLE OF PROPORTIONALITY IN THE JURISPRUDENCE OF THE ECHR 14–18, 192–95 (2002).

147. The "minimal impairment" test under *Oakes* is similar but not necessarily identical to the American "least restrictive means" test; the rigor of the fit required under *Oakes* may vary depending on both the severity of the infringement and the importance of the government objective. *Cf.* R. v. Oakes, [1986] 1 S.C.R. 103, 139 ("A wide range of rights and freedoms are guaranteed by the Charter, and an almost infinite number of factual situations may arise in respect of these. Some limits on rights and freedoms protected by the Charter will be more serious than others in terms of the nature of the right or freedom violated, the extent of the violation, and the degree to which the measures which impose the limit trench upon the integral principles of a free and democratic society."). For a later case softening the demands of "minimal impairment," see R. v. Keegstra, [1990] 3 S.C.R. 697, 784–85 (Can.) (suggesting that the "minimal impairment" test does not necessarily require a nonpenal approach to hate speech).

148. Charkaoui v. Canada (Citizenship and Immigration), [2007] 1 S.C.R. 350.

149. *See, e.g.*, Louis Henkin, *Implementation and Compliance: Is Dualism Metastasizing?*, 91 AM. SOC'Y INT'L L. PROC. 515 (1997) (arguing that monism better promotes compliance with international law); *see also* ROGER FISHER, IMPROVING COMPLIANCE WITH INTERNATIONAL LAW 147 (1981) (arguing that "[c]onverting an international legal obligation into a domestic one drastically increases the forces toward . . . compliance"); *cf.* LOUIS HENKIN, HOW NATIONS BEHAVE 60–68 (2d ed. 1979) (emphasizing the importance of domestic legal institutions in securing compliance with international law). *But cf.* YUJI IWASAWA, INTERNATIONAL LAW, HUMAN RIGHTS, AND JAPANESE LAW: THE IMPACT OF INTERNATIONAL LAW ON JAPANESE LAW 288–311 (1998) (noting that Japanese courts are reluctant to find violations of international human rights treaties, even though Japanese law makes treaties directly enforceable and accords them a higher status than statutes). For a helpful introduction to the ideas of "monism" and "dualism," see Louis Henkin, *The Constitution and United States Sovereignty: A Century of Chinese Exclusion and Its Progeny*, 100 HARV. L. REV. 853, 864–66 (1987).

150. Ginsburg, *supra* note 80, at 714.

151. *See, e.g.*, Medellín v. Texas, 128 S. Ct. 1346 (2008). For description of a range of relationships between domestic constitutions and international law, see, for example, Thomas M. Franck & Arun K. Thiruvengadam, *International Law and Constitution-Making*, 2 Chinese J. Int'l L. 467 (2003).

152. Waters, supra note 5. *Cf.* Helen Keller & Alec Stone Sweet, *Introduction*, in A Europe of Rights: The Impact of the ECHR on National Legal Systems 20 (Helen Keller & Alec Stone Sweet eds. 2008) (noting that some dualist states have "nonetheless conferred on [European] Convention rights constitutional or quasi-constitutional status").

153. *See* Shany, *supra* note 88, at 356–57, 360–71 (distinguishing between explicit incorporation of international law through techniques of "supra-constitutionalism," "constitutionalization," and "quasi-constitutionalization," and more "interpretive" forms of incorporating international law in constitutional analysis).

154. *See* Ginsburg, *supra* note 80, at 757–58; *cf.* David Sloss, *When Do Treaties Create Individually Enforceable Rights? The Supreme Court Ducks the Issue in* Hamdan *and* Sanchez-Llamas, 45 Colum. J. Transnat'l L. 20 (2007) (showing that in the first fifty years of U.S. constitutional history the Supreme Court regularly afforded judicial remedies for breach of individual rights under treaties, embracing what the author calls a "transnationalist" view).

155. *See* Ginsburg, *supra* note 80, at 717–19, 744–45, 753–55.

156. Martin Flaherty, *Judicial Globalization in the Service of Self-Government*, 20 Ethics & Int'l Affairs 477, 479–80, 493–99 (2006); *see also* David Golove, *Treaty-making and the Nation: The Historical Foundations of the Nationalist Conception of the Treaty Power*, 98 Mich. L. Rev. 1075 (2000); *Panel, The Framers' Understandings of Originalism and International Law*, 11 Chap. L. Rev. 307, 313–18 (2008) (remarks of Professor Golove).

157. Flaherty, *supra* note 156, at 497. As he also argues, the enactment of the 1789 Constitution was in important measure prompted by a desire to be able to prevent violations of international law by the states. *Id.* at 497–98.

158. *See* Chapter 5, text at notes 6, 7, below (noting the question whether originalism, which often envisages intentions fixed at the moment of enactment, tethered to a specific understanding at a former time, can embrace an intent to have meaning evolve with the evolution of norms or moral values (or to require interpretation to conform to evolving customary international law), or whether such approaches should be understood as more "purposivist").

159. *See supra* note 86 (on Professor Choudhry's "genealogical" category).

160. The Universal Declaration of Human Rights asserts a right to own property, and not to be "arbitrarily deprived" of property. UDHR art. 17; *see also* UDHR art. 27 (2) (recognizing rights in scientific, artistic or literary works); *cf.* Baxi, *supra* note 82, at 147 (treating these provisions as examples of the "contradictory elements" of classic understandings of human rights and as laying a foundation for trade-related rights embodied in the WTO and in bi- and multi-lateral investment agreements). However, no right of compensation for deprivations of property is found in express form in either the ICCPR or the ICESCR, although the ICESCR does recognize in article 15(1)(c) a right to protection of moral and material interests in authored work. For discussion of the contested status of rights of property in international law, see Daniel Halberstam & Eric Stein, *The United Nations, the European Union and the King of Sweden: Economic Sanctions and Individual Rights in a Plural World Order* (Working Paper, Dec. 2008), forthcoming, 46 Common Market L. Rev. (2009), *available at* http://papers.ssrn.com/sol3/papers.cfm?abstract_id=1312082, at 41–43 (criticizing the suggestion that right to property is jus cogens norm and describing scholarly disagreements over whether property rights have now acquired the status of customary international law, outside of particular regions); Prudence E. Taylor, *From Environmental to Ecological Human Rights: A New Dynamic in International Law?*, 10 Geo.

INT'L ENVTL. L. REV. 309, 324–25 (1998) (describing the historically contested and compromised nature of the UDHR art. 17 property right, and the silent or more qualified approaches of subsequent human rights instruments).

161. The first protocol to the European Convention (Protocol to the Convention for the Protection of Human Rights and Fundamental Freedoms, opened for signature Mar. 20, 1952, art. 1, 213 U.N.T.S. 262) states that:

> Every natural or legal person is entitled to the peaceful enjoyment of his possessions. No one shall be deprived of his possessions except in the public interest and subject to the conditions provided for by law and by the general principles of international law.
>
> The preceding provisions shall not, however, in any way impair the right of a State to enforce such laws as it deems necessary to control the use of property in accordance with the general interest or to secure the payment of taxes or other contributions or penalties.

Interpretation of this provision has often involved the "margin of appreciation." *See, e.g.*, GREER, *supra* note 110, at 5, 12–13 (also noting that of all the ECHR rights, this right "is limited by the most wide-ranging restrictions").

162. *See, e.g.*, Petersmann, *supra* note 4; Ernst-Ulrich Petersmann, *Time for a United Nations 'Global Compact' for Integrating Human Rights into the Law of Worldwide Organizations: Lessons from European Integration*, 13 EUR. J. INT'L L. 621 (2002); Ernst-Ulrich Petersmann, *Human Rights and the Law of the World Trade Organization*, 37 J. WORLD TRADE 241 (2003); *cf. e.g.*, Peter Charles Choharis, *U.S. Courts and the International Law of Expropriation: Toward a New Model for Breach of Contract*, 80 S. CAL. L. REV. 1 (2006).

163. *See* Chapter 1 above (noting how Mexico and other countries in Latin America included "Calvo clauses" in their constitutions).

164. *See* XIAN FA art. 13 (1982) (P.R.C.) (amended Mar. 14, 2004) ("Citizens' lawful private property is inviolable"; "The state, in accordance with law, protects the rights of citizens to private property and to its inheritance"; "[C]ompensation" is required for private property that is "expropriated or requisitioned"), *available at* http://english.peopledaily.com.cn/constitution/constitution.html; DAVID SCHNEIDERMAN, CONSTITUTIONALIZING ECONOMIC GLOBALIZATION: INVESTMENT RULES AND DEMOCRACY'S PROMISE (2008) (describing the investor protections found in NAFTA and many bilateral investment treaties as quasi-constitutional in nature, consisting of long-term treaties requiring years of notice to withdraw, establishing nondiscrimination rules and according foreign investors rights against the regulatory diminution of investment-backed expectations through extensions of U.S.-style norm against takings of property without just compensation).

165. *Compare, e.g.*, Steffen Hindelang, *Bilateral Investment Treaties, Custom and a Healthy Investment Climate: The Question of Whether BITs Influence Customary International Law Revisited*, 5 J. WORLD INVESTMENT & TRADE 789, 804, 809 (2004) (making the case for "a minimum standard of protection in customary international law derived from BITs" insofar as they reflect a "common set of principles") *with* Andrew T. Guzman, *Why LDCs Sign Treaties That Hurt Them: Explaining the Popularity of Bilateral Investment Treaties*, 38 VA. J. INT'L L. 639, 643–44 (1998) ("[B]ecause BITs are signed by developing countries in pursuit of their economic self-interest rather than out of a sense of legal obligation, these treaties do no[t] support a rule of customary international law that incorporates the Hull Rule."). To the extent that the UDHR has become customary international law, it recognizes the right to own property. *See supra* note 160.

166. *See* Slaughter & Burke-White, supra note 65, at 338 n.46 (discussing efficacy of IMF/World Bank "conditionality"); *cf.* Poul Engberg-Pedersen & Brian Levy, *Building*

State Capacity in Africa: Learning from Performance and Results, *in* BUILDING STATE CAPACITY IN AFRICA 87 (Brian Levy & Sahr Kpundeh eds., 2004) (describing the World Bank's projects on "Public Sector Reform and Capacity Building" to improve governance in Africa).

167. *See, e.g.*, GREGORY S. ALEXANDER, THE GLOBAL DEBATE OVER CONSTITUTIONAL PROPERTY 97–98, 146–47 (2006).

168. J.A. Pye (Oxford) Ltd v. United Kingdom, App. No. 44302/02, Eur. Ct. H.R. ¶¶ 74, 75 (Aug. 30, 2007) (Grand Chamber), *available at* http://www.echr.coe.int/echr.

169. *Cf., e.g.*, Baxi, *supra* note 82, at 163–64 (worrying "that the paradigm of the Universal Declaration of Human Rights is being steadily supplanted by a trade-related, market-friendly, human rights paradigm"). Query whether the effect of divisions in legal views about property rights is different in kind from the effect of differences around the recognized human rights issue of gender equality, where gaps between formal legal commitments in international instruments and conventional domestic legal practices may remain quite large. If legal practice as well as formal law is considered, the areas of transnational consensus may narrow considerably.

170. Thomas M. Franck, *The Emerging Right to Democratic Governance*, 86 AM. J. INT'L L. 46 (1992).

171. *See* Vivien Hart, *Democratic Constitution Making* (U.S. Inst. Of Peace, Special Rep. 107, July 2003), *available at* http://www.usip.org/pubs/specialreports/sr107.html; Stephen J. Schnably, *Emerging International Law Constraints on Constitutional Structure and Revision: A Preliminary Appraisal*, 62 U. MIAMI L. REV. 417 (2008).

172. *See* De Búrca & Gerstenberg, *supra* note 140, at 261–62.

173. *See* United States v. Burns, [2001] 1 S.C.R. 283 (Can.); Atkins v. Virginia, 536 U.S. 304, 316 n.21 (2002).

174. *See* Franck, *Clan and Superclan*, *supra* note 11.

175. *See e.g.*, Horowitz, *supra* note 9, at 31–35 (observing the multiplication of forms of governance through conflicting transnational influences and models, resulting in "hybrid institutions").

CHAPTER 3. ENGAGEMENT WITH THE TRANSNATIONAL

1. *See* Sujit Choudhry, *Globalization in Search of Justification: Toward a Theory of Comparative Constitutional Interpretation*, 74 IND. L.J. 819, 835–38, 855–65 (1999); Cheryl Saunders, *The Use and Misuse of Comparative Constitutional Law*, 13 IND. J. GLOBAL LEGAL. STUD. 37 (2006); *see also* Sarah K. Harding, *Comparative Reasoning and Judicial Review*, 28 YALE J. INT'L L. 409, 424–27, 437–39 (2003).

2. *See, e.g.*, JUDGES IN CONTEMPORARY DEMOCRACY: AN INTERNATIONAL CONVERSATION (Robert Badinter & Stephen Breyer eds., 2004).

3. H. Patrick Glenn, *Persuasive Authority*, 32 MCGILL L.J. 261, 263 (1987); *see also* Anne-Marie Slaughter, *A Global Community of Courts*, 44 HARV. INT'L L.J. 191 (2003) (describing the growth of persuasive authority).

4. *See* Kim Lane Scheppele, *Aspirational and Aversive Constitutionalism: The Case for Studying Cross-Constitutional Influence Through Negative Models*, 1 INT'L J. CONST. L. 296 (2003); *see also* Sujit Choudhry, *The Lochner Era and Comparative Constitutionalism*, 2 INT'L J. CONST. L. 1 (2004).

5. Christopher McCrudden, *A Common Law of Human Rights?: Transnational Judicial Conversations on Constitutional Rights*, 20 OXFORD J. LEGAL STUD. 499, 502–03 (2000).

6. *See* C.L. Ostberg et al., *Attitudes, Precedents and Cultural Change: Explaining the Citation of Foreign Precedents by the Supreme Court of Canada*, 34 CANADIAN J. POL. SCI. 377,

392–94 (2001) (finding, between 1984 and 1995, some 702 references to U.S. law in Canadian Charter cases, but only four cases in which U.S. doctrine was followed, while in thirty other cases it was distinguished); Bijon Roy, *An Empirical Survey of Foreign Jurisprudence and International Instruments in Charter Litigation*, 62 U.T. FAC. L. REV. 99, 127–37 (2004) (concluding that in the thirty-four Charter cases between 1998 and 2003 in which foreign or international law was considered, in only one instance was foreign jurisprudence plainly "followed," with other references either involving "support" or a "survey" or being "distinguished"); *see also id.* at 104 (concluding that "external sources are very rarely, if ever, dispositive of Charter issues").

7. Judith Resnik, *Law as Affiliation: "Foreign" Law, Democratic Federalism, and the Sovereigntism of the Nation-State*, 6 INT'L J. CONST. L. 33 (2008). I thank Rosalind Dixon for sharing drafts of *A Democratic Theory of Constitutional Comparison*, 56 AM. J. COMP. L. 947 (2008), and The Constitution and Global Values: Different Models of Engagement (Aug. 2006 mss.) (discussing "cosmopolitan" and "deliberative" engagement) and for helpful exchanges from which my own thinking about "engagement" benefited.

8. *See, e.g.*, Sir Basil Markesinis & Jörg Fedtke, *The Judge as Comparatist*, 80 TUL. L. REV. 11, 57–58 (2005) (stating that from 1994 to 1998, there were more than 1,200 references to British, Canadian, European, Indian, or U.S. law in the Constitutional Court and Supreme Court of South Africa); *id.* at 36–38 (summarizing studies and concluding that the German Constitutional Court, though cautious in its usage, has been more willing to refer to comparative law than other German courts); Roy, *supra* note 6, at 123–24 (finding that between 1998–2003, there were references to foreign and international authority in thirty-four of the 402 Canadian Charter cases; of the eighty-seven references, sixty were to foreign law and twenty-seven to international sources); Ostberg et al., *supra* note 6, at 392–94 (finding that between 1984 and 1995, in close to half of all Canadian Charter cases studied there were references to U.S. law); William Binchy, *The Supreme Court of Ireland*, in JUDICIAL ACTIVISM IN COMMON LAW SUPREME COURTS 169, 178–79 (Bruce Dickson ed. 2007) (describing Irish constitutional cases referring to U.S., German, and Canadian jurisprudence); Adam M. Smith, *Making Itself at Home: Understanding Foreign Law in Domestic Jurisprudence: The Indian Case*, 24 BERKELEY J. INT'L L. 218, 252–55, 257–62 (2006) (discussing use of foreign and international law by Indian Supreme Court in constitutional cases and variances over time); *cf.* Gerald L. Neuman, *Import, Export, and Regional Consent in the Inter-American Court of Human Rights*, 19 EUR. J. INT'L L. 101, 108–16 (2008) (suggesting that the Inter-American Court of Human Rights might draw too heavily on the jurisprudence of the ECtHR without sufficient attention to its own regional context and state-party consent).

9. On the increasingly transnational character of both law practice and judging, see H. Patrick Glenn, *Comparative Law and Legal Practice: On Removing the Borders*, 75 TUL. L. REV. 977 (2001).

10. *See* Saunders, *supra* note 1, at 50 (describing a spectrum of uses of foreign law).

11. *Id.* at 52.

12. (1992) 177 C.L.R. 106; *see also* Nationwide News Pty. Ltd v. Wills (1992) 177 C.L.R. 1, 50 (Brennan J.), 72–73 (Deane and Toohey JJ).

13. Saunders, *supra* note 1, at 54.

14. *See Australian Capital Television*, 177 C.L.R. at 140 (Mason, C.J.); *cf. id.* at 240–41 (McHugh, J.) (arguing that the U.S. Constitution is a "more valid analogy" for Australia on freedom of political communication than approaches in Europe or other democratic countries relied on by the Commonwealth).

15. *Australian Capital Television*, 177 C.L.R. at 131 (Mason, C.J.) (referring to the Australian legislature's consideration of laws in such countries as the United Kingdom,

the United States, Canada, France, New Zealand, Norway, Germany, Sweden, Denmark, Austria, Israel, the Netherlands, and Japan).

16. (1997) 189 C.L.R. 520; *see also* Theophanous v. Herald & Weekly Times Lt, (1994) 182 C.L.R. 104, 135–36 (Mason, C.J.) (stating that *Sullivan* test "gives inadequate protection to reputation").

17. New York Times Co. v. Sullivan, 376 U.S. 254 (1964).

18. *See Lange*, 189 C.L.R. at 560, 563 (distinguishing Australia Constitution's relationship to the "one common law in Australia" from the United States, with its more fragmented state-by-state common law and its explicit First Amendment).

19. Saunders, *supra* note 1, at 56–58; *see also* APLA Ltd v. Legal Services Comm'r (NSW) (2005) 224 C.L.R. 322, 362 (McHugh, J.) (describing how "[r]eliance on the implied freedom [of political communication], identified in *Lange*, requires the opposite approach to that involved when" a defendant in the United States relies on the First Amendment freedom).

20. *See* Roach v. Electoral Comm'r, (2007) 233 C.L.R. 162, 177–80, 182 (Austl.) (Gleeson, C.J.) (analyzing decisions in *Sauvé v. Canada (Chief Electoral Officer)*, [2002] 3 S.C.R. 519 and *Hirst v. United Kingdom*, 2005-IX Eur. Ct. H.R. 187, which had found invalid certain disfranchisement laws in Canada and the United Kingdom, respectively, and concluding that a 2006 disfranchisement act that abandoned efforts to distinguish those prisoners guilty of more serious crimes "broke the rational connection necessary to reconcile the disenfranchisement with the constitutional imperative of choice by the people"); COMMONWEALTH OF AUSTRALIA CONSTITUTION ACT, 1900, §§ 7, 24. Chief Justice Gleeson warned of the "danger that uncritical translation of the concept of proportionality from the legal context of cases such as *Sauvé* or *Hirst* to the Australian context could lead to the application in this country of a constitutionally inappropriate standard of judicial review of legislative action," but at the same time acknowledged finding "aspects of the reasoning . . . instructive" in suggesting that disfranchisement be limited to serious criminal offenses, *Roach*, (2007) 233 C.L.R. at 177–80. *But see id.* at 220–21 (Hayne, J., dissenting) (finding there to be no similarity between the constitutional provisions being interpreted in "overseas" cases and the issue under the Australian constitution).

21. Saunders, *supra* note 1, at 56–57; *see also id.* ("The resulting doctrine and the justification for it are distinctively Australian. They are located in a wider international constitutional tradition, however, through which understanding of them is enhanced."). Australian scholars, including Saunders, have not been not wholly uncritical. *See id.* at 67–75 (raising concerns, not over legitimacy of considering foreign law, but over possible "unjustifable selectivity" in choosing sources and challenges of understanding foreign contexts); *see also* Adrienne Stone, *Freedom of Political Communication, the Constitution and the Common Law*, 26 FED'L L. REV. 219 (1998) (Austl); Eric Barendt, *Free Speech in Australia: A Comparative Perspective*, 16 SYDNEY L. REV. 149 (1994).

22. Marbury v. Madison, 5 U.S. (1 Cranch) 137, 163, 176 (1803). A critic might suggest that *Marbury*'s reference to British law was entirely "genealogical"—or "originalist"—in character, explaining what the original intent or understanding of the framers and ratifiers was. But *Marbury*'s invocation of British law reads at least as much like an illuminating contemporary comparison.

23. 543 U.S. 551 (2005).

24. *Id.* at 578.

25. *Id.* at 605 (O'Connor, J., dissenting).

26. *See* R. v. Keegstra, [1990] 3 S.C.R. 697, 743–44 (Can.)

27. *Id.* at 803 (McLachlin, J., dissenting).

28. *See* United Food & Commercial Workers Local 1518 v. KMart Can. Ltd., [1999] 2 S.C.R. 1083, 1118-21 (Can.) (agreeing with a distinction drawn in U.S. First Amendment law between leafleting and picketing). Canadian justices have likewise considered U.S. Fourth Amendment case law, sometimes to agree, sometimes not, in resolving issues under Charter Section 8. *See, e.g.*, R v. Kang-Brown, [2008] 1 S.C.R. 456, 501–02 (Binnie, J.); *id.* at 522, 545 (Deschamps, J., dissenting) (discussing foreign case law in connection with challenge to "dog sniff" search).

29. LAWRENCE W. BEER & HIROSHI ITOH, THE CONSTITUTIONAL CASE LAW OF JAPAN, 1970 THROUGH 1990, at 19 (1996).

30. *Case to seek revocation of the disposition of issuance of a written deportation order*, 2006 (Gyo-Tsu) No. 135, Minshū vol. 62, no. 6 (Sup. Ct. Jap., June 4, 2008), *English transl. available at* http://www.courts.go.jp/english/judgments/index.html (enter date, code and case number) (referring, in the "Reasons," ¶4(2)(c), to the practice of other states, the ICCPR and the Convention on the Rights of the Child); *see id.* (Izumi, J., concurring, ¶4) (referring to the ICCPR and the Convention on the Rights of the Child); *see also* Japan Federation of Bar Associations, Statement on Supreme Court Ruling Nationality Law Unconstitutional (June 4, 2008), http://www.nichibenren.or.jp/en/activities/statements/080604.html

31. *See* BEER & ITOH, *supra* note 29, at 522–43 (translating and explaining Japan v. Osawa [the "Sarufutsu Public Employees Case"], 28 Keishū 393 (Sup. Ct. Japan, Nov. 6, 1974)).

32. *Id.* at 525–26.

33. *Id.* at 530–31 (bracketed material in last line of quote is in the original translation).

34. *See, e.g.*, Banco Nacional de Cuba v. Sabbatino, 376 U.S. 398, 440 & n.1 (1964) (White, J., dissenting) (arguing that courts of other Western nations have not found it necessary to rely on the "act of state" doctrine to avoid deciding on the validity under international law of foreign sovereigns' actions).

35. *See, e.g.*, State of Kerala v. Thomas, A.I.R. 1976 S.C. 490, paras. 95–96 (India) (Mathew, J.) (noting views of U.S. justices, such as Justice Harlan's discussion of the concept of equality under the Equal Protection Clause); Translation of Excerpts of Decision C-355/2006, Colombian Constitutional Court Abortion Decision of May 10, 2006, published by Women's Link Worldwide (with Foreword by Rebecca J. Cook), *available at* http://www.womenslinkworldwide.org (click on "publications," click on C-355/2006, Excerpts of the Constitutional Court's Ruling That Liberalized Abortion in Colombia), *full opinion available in Spanish at* http://www.corteconstitucional.gov.co/relatoria/2006/C-355-06.htm (considering, among other foreign laws, the German, Spanish, and U.S. abortion case law); *see also* Anne-Marie Slaughter, *A Typology of Transjudicial Communication*, 29 U. RICH. L. REV. 99, 104–06 (1994); Laurence R. Helfer & Anne-Marie Slaughter, *Toward a Theory of Effective Supranational Adjudication*, 107 YALE L.J. 273, 367–73 (1997) (emphasizing benefits of a "global community of law" and transjudicial dialogue); G. L. Davies & M.P. Cowen, *The Persuasive Force of Decisions of United States Courts in Australia*, 15 AUSTL. B. REV., 1996 A.B.R. LEXIS 27.

36. *See* Roper v. Simmons, 543 U.S. 551, 575 (2005); Atkins v. Virginia, 536 U.S. 304, 316 n.21 (2002)

37. Slaughter, *Global Community, supra* note 3, at 193–204; *see also* Michael Kirby, *Think Globally*, 4 GREEN BAG 2D 287 (Spring 2001). Sometimes transnational considerations exist beneath the surface of an opinion. *Compare* Ruth Bader Ginsburg & Deborah Jones Merritt, *Affirmative Action: An International Human Rights Dialogue*, 21 CARDOZO L. REV. 253, 261–81 (1999) (describing status of affirmative action in the United States, India, and the European Union) *with* Grutter v. Bollinger, 539 U.S. 306, 344 (2003) (Ginsburg, J., concurring) (discussing international covenants contemplating temporary affirmative

measures); Gratz v. Bollinger, 539 U.S. 244, 298 (2003) (Ginsburg, J., dissenting). Neither of Justice Ginsburg's written opinions referred to foreign national practices, such as those in India described in her paper, although she asked Solicitor General Olson at oral argument in *Gratz* about constitutional experience with "positive discrimination" in other countries, including Canada, the European Union, and South Africa. *See* Transcript of Oral Argument at 24–25, Gratz v. Bollinger, 539 U.S. 244 (2003) (No. 02-516), *available at* http://www.supremecourtus.gov/oral_arguments/argument_transcripts/02-516.pdf.

38. *See* Frederick Schauer, *The Politics and Incentives of Legal Transplantation, in* GOVERNANCE IN A GLOBALIZING WORLD 253 (Joseph S. Nye Jr. & John D. Donahue eds. 2000) (exploring strategic and political uses of cross-national references); *see also* Robert B. Ahdieh, *Dialectical Regulation,* 38 CONN. L. REV. 863, 914 (2006); Reem Bahdi, *Globalization of Judgment: Transjudicialism and the Five Faces of International Law in Domestic Courts,* 34 GEO. WASH. INT'L L. REV. 555, 590–95 (2002).

39. *See* Schauer, *supra* note 38, at 260; Choudhry, *Globalization in Search of Justification, supra* note 1, at 888; Heinz Klug, *Model and Anti-Model: The United States Constitution and the "Rise of World Constitutionalism,"* 2000 WIS. L. REV. 597, 601–02 (2000).

40. *See* Resnik, *Law as Affiliation, supra* note 7, at 37 (describing state laws in the early United States prohibiting reference to English law in aftermath of the Revolution); Glenn, *Persuasive Authority, supra* note 3, at 280 n.51 (noting nineteenth century Swiss law forbidding reference to foreign law); Lindsay Farmer, *"The Genius of our Law . . . ": Criminal Law and the Scottish Legal Tradition,* 55 MOD. L. REV. 25, 25 (1992) (noting the importance for Scotland of assertion of its law's independence and distinctiveness from English law as reflected in the 1707 Treaty of Union); *cf.* ELIZABETH BORGWARDT, A NEW DEAL FOR THE WORLD 51 (2007) (suggesting that U.S. conceptions of human rights abandoned economic rights because of their association with Marxism during the Cold War).

41. S. AFR. CONST. 1996 § 39 (1) ("When interpreting the Bill of Rights, a court, tribunal or forum (a.) must promote the values that underlie an open and democratic society based on human dignity, equality and freedom; (b.) must consider international law; and (c.) may consider foreign law."). For earlier work on "relational" engagement, from which some of this discussion is drawn, see Vicki C. Jackson, *Transnational Discourse, Relational Authority and the U.S. Court; Gender Equality,* 37 LOYOLA L. A. L. REV. 271, 282–306 (2003).

42. See Chapter 2, above, discussing Argentina and Colombia.

43. S. AFR. CONST. 1996 § 233 ("When interpreting any legislation, every court must prefer any reasonable interpretation of the legislation that is consistent with international law over any alternative interpretation that is inconsistent with international law.").

44. State v. Makwanyane, 1995 (3) SA 391, 415 (CC) (S. Afr.) (emphasis added) (referring to Section 35 of the Interim Constitution); *see* S. AFR. (Interim) CONST. 1993 § 35(1) (in interpreting rights provisions, courts "shall, where applicable, have regard to public international law" and "may have regard to comparable foreign case law").

45. For a mandatory consideration requirement applicable to *both* international and foreign law, see CONST. OF THE REPUBLIC OF MALAWI 1994 § 11(2) (c) (requires the courts "where applicable, [to] have regard to current norms of public international law and comparable foreign case law"); *see also* CONST. LAW OF ANGOLA 1992, art. 21(2) (constitutional norms related to fundamental rights are to be interpreted in light of the UDHR and international treaties to which Angola adheres, even if not invoked by the parties); CONSTITUÇÃO DE LA REPÚBLICA DE CABO VERDE [Constitution of Cape Verde], art. 16(3), as amended by Lei Constitucional No. 1/V/99, Nov. 23, 1999 (requiring that constitutional norms concerning fundamental rights be interpreted and gaps filled in light of the UDHR).

46. Government of the Republic of South Africa v. Grootboom, 2001 (1) SA 46 (CC) (S. Afr. 2000).

47. *Id.* at 59–67 (covering all quotations in *Grootboom* in this paragraph).

48. 1995 (3) SA at 451–53.

49. S. AFR.(Interim) CONST. 1993 §11 (2).

50. *See Makwanyane*, 1995(3) SA at 415–17, 422–23 (noting the U.S. Constitution's Due Process Clause, which prohibits deprivations of "life" without due process of law, arguably contemplating that there could be deprivations of life with due process of law). *Makwanyane* was decided under the Interim Constitution. *See supra* note 44.

51. *Makwanyane*, 1995 (3) SA at 432–33 & n.113 (A. Chaskalson, P.).

52. *See, e.g., id.* at 430 (noting that Hungary's constitution prohibited only the arbitrary imposition of punishment and that South Africa's constitution provides stronger protection to the right to life); *id.* at 428 (concerning India: "The wording of the relevant provisions of our Constitution are different. The question we have to consider is not whether the imposition of the death sentence for murder is 'totally devoid of reason and purpose.' . . . It is whether . . . the death penalty is cruel, inhuman or degrading, and if it is, whether it can be justified in terms of section 33."). The court also referred to the American Convention on Human Rights and to jurisprudence from several other countries including Canada, the United States, and Germany.

53. Minister of Home Affairs & Others v. Fourie & Others, 2006 (1) SA 524 (CC) (S. Afr. 2005).

54. *See id.* at 569, 563–65.

55. Indeed, in *Makwanyane*, President Chaskalson expressed this idea: "The international and foreign authorities are of value because they analyse arguments for and against the death sentence and show how courts of other jurisdictions have dealt with this vexed issue. *For that reason alone they require our attention.*" 1995 (3) SA at 413 (emphasis added).

56. Carsten Smith, *The Supreme Court in Present-Day Society, in* THE SUPREME COURT OF NORWAY 95, 135 (Stephan Tschudi-Madsen ed., 1998).

57. Albie Sachs, *Social and Economic Rights: Can They Be Made Justiciable?*, 53 SMU L. REV. 1381, 1388 (2000); *see also* Slaughter, *Typology of Transjudicial Communication*, *supra* note 35, at 122; Slaughter, *Global Community*, *supra* note 3, at 193 (referring to a sense of "common judicial enterprise"); *cf.* A. v. Governor of Arbour Hill Prison, [2006] I.E.S.C. 45 (Sup. Ct. Ireland, 2006) (discussing the constitutional law on retroactivity of several non-European jurisdictions and concluding that the prisoner's claim—that one convicted under a statute subsequently declared invalid is necessarily entitled to relief from conviction—was "out of kilter with other constitutional systems and . . . our own").

58. The New Zealand Bill of Rights is regarded by the government as part of New Zealand's constitution. *See* The Constitution of New Zealand, *available at* http://www.gov-gen.govt.nz/role/constofnz.htm (last visited Feb. 13, 2009) (describing New Zealand as having a constitution, not set out in one single document, but consisting of court decisions, conventions of practice, the Treaty of Waitangi, and legal documents including the Constitution Act 1986, the State Sector Act 1988, the Electoral Act 1993, the Judicature Act 1908, the Ombudsmen Act 1975, the Official Information Act 1982, the Public Finance Act 1989, and the New Zealand Bill of Rights Act 1990, among others). *But cf.* Stephen Gardbaum, *The New Commonwealth Model of Constitutionalism*, 49 AM. J. COMP. L. 707, 728 (2001) (describing the New Zealand Bill of Rights as an "ordinary statute," with the unusual feature of requiring that all other statutes be interpreted in accord with it).

59. *See, e.g.*, N. Reg'l Health Auth. v. Human Rights Comm'n, [1998] 2 N.Z.L.R. 218, 233–35 (H. C. Auckland) (1997) (Cartwright, J.) (stating further that "none of the principles or statements are binding" but "[a]ny analysis of policy which may directly or indirectly discriminate must be done in the light of the international principles and experience . . . and, where appropriate, assistance may be drawn from overseas cases"); *see also, e.g.*, Quilter v. Attorney-General, [1998] 1 N.Z.L.R. 523, 530–31 (C.A.) (1997) (Thomas, J.); Van Gorkom v Attorney-General, [1977] 1 N.Z.L.R. 535, 542–43 (Sup. Ct. Wellington) ("[N]ew [legal powers]. . . . should not without compelling reason be taken to allow the introduction of a policy conflicting with the spirit of international standards proclaimed by the United Nations documents."); *cf.* Attorney-Gen'l v. Refugee Council of New Zealand, Inc., [2003] 2 N.Z.L.R. 577, 610 (C.A.) (McGrath, J.) (discussing the difference between a duty to "giv[e] effect" to an international obligation and a duty to "have regard" for it). On the status of the Bill of Rights Act in New Zealand, see *supra* note 58.

60. *See e.g.*, Vishaka v. State of Rajasthan, A.I.R. 1997 S.C. 3011 (Sup. Ct. India) (concluding that the state's failure to prevent rape and sexual harassment violated equality provisions of the Indian Constitution as well as the CEDAW, and asserting that "[a]ny international convention not inconsistent with the fundamental rights [of the Indian Constitution] and in harmony with its spirit must be read into these provisions to enlarge the meaning and content thereof, to promote the object of the constitutional guarantee"); *cf.* Grutter v. Bollinger, 539 U.S. 306, 344 (2003) (Ginsburg, J., concurring) (invoking CEDAW and the Convention on the Elimination of Racial Discrimination in support of "affirmative action" measures for a temporally limited period of time—even though the United States has not ratified CEDAW, and ratified the Race Convention with a reservation that it was not self-executing).

61. *See* Unity Dow v. Attorney-General, *reprinted in* 13 HUM. RTS Q. 614 (Bots. High Ct. 1991), *affirmed in relevant part*, Dow v. Attorney-General, 103 I.L.R. 128 (Bots. Ct. App. 1992) (striking down a statutory discrimination against female citizens' capacities to pass on citizenship to their children). Both courts relied on transnational legal sources, with references (by one or both courts) to the African Charter on Human and Peoples Rights banning sex discrimination (signed by Botswana but not yet implemented through domestic legislation), the UDHR, Privy Council decisions reviewing cases from Bermuda and Australia, case law from other countries, the UN Declaration on the Elimination of Discrimination Against Women (1967), and the "comity of civilised nations." *See also, e.g.*, Rattigan v. Chief Immigration Officer, 103 I.L.R. 224, 228–29, 231–34 (Zimb. Sup. Ct. 1994) (Gubbay, C.J.) (referring to *Unity Dow* and to decisions under the ICCPR and the ECHR in interpreting the Zimbabwe constitution). For further discussion of *Unity Dow*, see Chapter 7 below.

62. Professor Slaughter has emphasized the increasing role of courts as institutions engaging in dialogue and relationships with each other both in adjudicatory decisions and in nonadjudicatory collegial settings. *See* Slaughter, *Typology of Transjudicial Communication*, *supra* note 35, at 119–22; Slaughter, *Global Community*, *supra* note 3, at 193–95; *see also* McCrudden, *supra* note 5, at 506.

63. Karen Knop, *Here and There: International Law in Domestic Courts*, 32 N.Y.U. J. INT'L L. & POL. 501, 525 (2000); *see also* Knight v. Florida, 528 U.S. 990, 995–97 (1999) (Breyer, J., dissenting from denial of certiorari) (discussing decisions of the ECtHR, the Privy Council on the Jamaican death penalty, the Indian, Zimbabwean, and Canadian Supreme Courts, the views of the UN Human Rights Committee, and U.S. reservations to the International Covenant on Civil and Political Rights); *Quilter*, [1998] 1 N.Z.L.R. at 530–31 (referring to foreign constitutional law and international sources in evaluating a quasi-constitutional

challenge to the exclusion of same-sex marriages from statutory definition); *cf.* David Kennedy, *One, Two, Three, Many Legal Orders: Legal Pluralism and the Cosmopolitan Dream,* 31 NYU REV. L. & SOC. CHANGE 641, 646–54 (2007) (suggesting that international law does not always mean the same thing in different places and urging study of "comparative international law"). *See* Chapter 2, notes 73, 81 above.

64. *See, e.g.,* Richard A. Posner, *Pragmatic Adjudication,* 18 CARDOZO L. REV. 1 (1996); *see also* Richard A. Posner, *Past-Dependency, Pragmatism, and Critique of History in Adjudication and Legal Scholarship,* 67 U. CHI. L. REV. 573 (2000).

65. Posner, *Pragmatic Adjudication, supra* note 64, at 13–14.

66. *See* Richard A. Posner, *Foreword—A Political Court,* 119 HARV. L. REV. 31 (2005) (arguing that the use of foreign law in *Roper v. Simmons* was improper).

67. Lavigne v. Ontario Public Service Employees Union, [1991] 2 S.C.R. 211, 300 (Can.) (Wilson, J.) (explaining why she would not apply the rule of *Abood v. Detroit Bd. of Education,* 431 U.S. 209 (1977)).

68. Printz v. United States, 521 U.S. 898, 977 (1997) (Breyer J., dissenting).

69. Glenn, *supra* note 3, at 287–88, 283, 263.

70. *Id.* at 263; *see id.* at 279, 266–67.

71. *Id.* at 288.

72. *Id.* Indeed, Glenn argues that law as inquiry is "thus the dominant concept, both in space and time, in the continuation of Western law"; until the shift in the seventeenth through nineteenth centuries toward a view linking particular national states with the production of law as a system of control, all Western nations viewed law as inquiry. *Id.* at 288–89.

73. *See id.* at 278–79, 287.

74. Harding, *supra* note 1, at 457. Harding draws a parallel distinction between an "enforcement model" of judicial review, used by the U.S. Supreme Court, and law as "dialogue," which she associates with the Canadian Supreme Court.

75. *Id.* at 421, 464.

76. Glenn, *supra* note 3, at 289. For Glenn, the compatibility lies "in the sense that State law is taken as displacing but never entirely eliminating extranational sources . . . Law . . . precedes the State and continues to surround it." *Id.*

77. Robert B. Ahdieh, *Between Dialogue and Decree: International Review of National Courts,* 79 N.Y.U. L. REV. 2029, 2078, n. 214. (2004); *see also* Robert B. Ahdieh, *From Federalism to Intersystemic Governance: The Changing Nature of Modern Jurisdiction,* 57 EMORY L.J. 1, 23–24 (2007) (noting that "intersystemic governance" depends importantly on methods of persuasion, rather than coercion).

78. Judith Resnik, *Foreign as Domestic Affairs: Rethinking Horizontal Federalism and Foreign Affairs Preemption in Light of Translocal Internationalism,* 57 EMORY L.J. 31, 34, 54 (2007).

79. Paul Schiff Berman, *A Pluralist Approach to International Law,* 32 YALE J. INT'L L. 301, 329 (2007) (emphasis added) (discussing international law in a more pluralist setting).

80. Hurtado v. California, 110 U.S. 516, 530–31 (1884); *see also* Glenn, *supra* note 3, at 277, 283.

81. Niklas Luhmann, *The Unity of the Legal System, in* AUTOPOIETIC LAW: A NEW APPROACH TO LAW AND SOCIETY 12, 14, 20 (Gunther Teubner ed., 1988). Luhmann applies a concept from systems analyses to create a jurisprudential description of the nature of law and the legal system as a self-referential, self-producing system. The "closed" nature of the system, he says, consists "in that only the legal system can bestow legally normative quality on its

elements and thereby constitute them as elements," and that this "[n]ormativity has no purpose beyond this . . . [that is, the] continuous making possible" of itself. *Id.* at 20. In its operation, however, the system is "dependent on facts," and can "change its programs when the pressure of facts dictates this," and is in this sense "cognitively open." *Id.*

82. The idea of a system that is "normatively closed but cognitively open" is fragile in two directions, because each category destabilizes the other—the closure of norms will be threatened as "knowledge" enters, and existing norms and categories through which we receive information will limit the possibilities for how cognitively "open" any system can really be. Moreover, the idea that one can distinguish norms from their application may be illusory or subject to manipulation by the capacity to recharacterize a norm as an application and an application as a norm.

83. On legal procedures' relationships to the legitimacy of law, see, e.g., LON L. FULLER, THE MORALITY OF LAW (1969) (arguing that procedural norms of legality help protect against ad hoc decision-making and other failures to create real law); THOMAS M. FRANCK, THE POWER OF LEGITIMACY AMONG NATIONS (1990); Harold Hongju Koh, *Transnational Legal Process*, 75 NEB. L. REV. 181 (1996). *Cf.* Tom R. Tyler, *Trust and Law Abidingness: A Proactive Model of Social Regulation*, 81 B.U. L. REV. 361, 367–368, 377–78, 382 (2001) (showing that people's willingness to trust authorities varies with their perceptions of the fairness of the procedures those authorities use). For a far-reaching discussion of the relationships between deliberation and legitimate legal decisions in democracies, see JÜRGEN HABERMAS, BETWEEN FACTS AND NORMS: CONTRIBUTIONS TO A DISCOURSE THEORY OF LAW AND DEMOCRACY (William Rehg trans., 1996).

84. *See generally* David Shapiro, *In Defense of Judicial Candor*, 100 HARV. L. REV. 731 (1987). *But cf.* Scott Altman, *Beyond Candor*, 89 MICH. L. REV. 296, 302–03 (1990) (arguing for candor and self-awareness but against certain kinds of judicial introspection). For further discussion of prudential silence about transnational knowledge, see Chapter 6 below.

85. *See* Jon Elster, *Essay: Forces and Mechanisms in the Constitution-Making Process*, 45 DUKE L. J. 364, 373 (1992).

86. *See id.* at 390–92 (noting that threats of foreign intervention may be a factor in the bargaining over constitutions); *see also* Thomas M. Franck, *The Emerging Right to Democratic Governance*, 86 AM. J. INT'L. L. 46 (1992) (arguing that the Declaration of Independence's reference to world opinion was a radical recognition that the legitimacy of the new state depended on international acceptance, not just transfer of power from Britain). For a thoughtful account of the dominance of "geostrategic" concerns in the drafting of the U.S. Constitution, see Akhil Reed Amar, *Some New World Lessons for the Old World*, 58 U. CHI L. REV. 483 (1991). For additional discussion see Chapter 9, below.

87. *See* Mark Tushnet, *The United States: Eclecticism in the Service of Pragmatism, in* INTERPRETING CONSTITUTIONS: A COMPARATIVE STUDY (Jeffrey Goldsworthy ed., 2006). For discussion of constitutional interpretation based in common law or "multi-valenced" interpretive methods, see Chapter 5, below.

88. Article 29 of the UDHR includes a limitations clause, inspired in part by a proposal from an American Law Institute (ALI) Committee. *See* UDHR art. 29(2) ("In the exercise of his rights and freedoms, everyone shall be subject only to such limitations as are determined by law solely for the purpose of securing due recognition and respect for the rights and freedoms of others and of meeting the just requirements of morality, public order and the general welfare in a democratic society."); Louis Sohn, *The New International Law: Protection of the Rights of Individuals Rather Than States*, 32 AM. U. L. REV. 1, 44 (1982) (stating that the reference to "democratic society" in Article 29(2) of the UDHR was

inserted by the drafters, "on the basis of a similar clause in the statement of essential human rights, prepared in 1946 by a committee of the American Law Institute and presented to the United Nations by Panama"). For the ALI Committee proposal, see *Statement of Essential Human Rights*, 243 ANNALS AM. ACAD. POL. & SOC. SCI.18, 26 (1946). Article 29, in turn, inspired limitations clauses in other important human rights instruments including the European Convention on Human Rights and the ICCPR.

89. *See, e.g.*, CONSTITUTION art. 22(2) (1960) (Nigeria) (protecting privacy, family life, the home and correspondence, but preserving laws that "are reasonably justifiable in a democratic society" in the interests of safety, defense, order, morality, community economic well-being, or to protect the rights of others), *available at* http://www.nigeriacongress.org/resources/constitution/nig_const_60.pdf; *see also* Kenneth Roberts-Wray, *Human Rights in the Commonwealth*, 17 INT'L & COMP. L.Q. 908, 910, 916 (1968). The term "reasonably justifiable in a democratic society" appears in several other rights-protecting provisions found in articles 23-27 of the 1960 Nigerian constitution. *Cf.* John Momis et al., Papua New Guinea Constitutional Planning Committee Report 1974, Chapter 5, Part 1 (A), paras. 26-29 (*available at* http://www.paclii.org/pg/CPCReport/main.htm) (discussing proposed constitutional language permitting limits on rights only where "reasonably justifiable in a democratic society"). I am grateful to Loretta Wiatr, Georgetown University Law Center 2009, for her excellent research on this topic (Memo, June 26, 2007).

90. *See, e.g.*, CONST. COMMONWEALTH BAHAMAS art. 21(c); CONST. BOTSWANA art. 9(d); GRENADA CONST. ORDER art. 6(6) (Dec. 19, 1973); CONST. MALTA § 38(2); CONST KENYA art. 75(6); CONST. REPUBLIC MAURITIUS art. 8; CONST. REPUBLIC TRINIDAD & TOBAGO art. 13(1) ("reasonably justifiable in a society that has a proper respect for the rights and freedoms of the individual"); *cf.* BARBADOS INDEPENDENCE ORDER [Constitution] art. 12.2 (Nov. 22, 1966) (using phrase "reasonably justifiable); CONST. INDIA art. 19(2) (referring to "reasonable restrictions" on a right); CONST. JAMAICA art. 14(2) (using phrase "reasonably justifiable"); CONST. PAKISTAN art. 15 (using phrase "reasonable restriction"); CONST. INDEPENDENT STATE OF SAMOA art. 5(2) (using phrase "reasonably justifiable").

91. S. AFR. CONST. 1996 art. 36(1) (also stating that whether a limit is justified will depend on "all relevant factors, including . . . less restrictive means to achieve the purpose").

92. *See* Lorraine Eisenstat Weinrib, *Canada's Constitutional Revolution: From Legislative to Constitutional State*, 33 ISR. L. REV. 13, 29–31 (1999); *see also* CANADA'S CONSTITUTION ACT 1982 & AMENDMENTS: A DOCUMENTARY HISTORY (Anne Bayefsky ed., 1989), vol. I at 211, 214, 355, vol. II at 669, 678, 704, 745–46, 766, 788, 821, 907, 926 (showing the progression of language proposed for Canadian limitations clauses, from the 1971 language authorizing such "limitations as are prescribed by law and as are *reasonably justifiable* in a democratic society . . . ," to the enacted version, which permits only those "reasonable limits . . . as can be *demonstrably justified* in a free and democratic society") (emphasis added).

93. Lorraine E. Weinrib, *Constitutional Conceptions and Constitutional Comparativism*, *in* DEFINING THE FIELD OF COMPARATIVE CONSTITUTIONAL LAW 4 (Vicki Jackson & Mark Tushnet, eds., 2002).

94. *See, e.g.*, DeReuck v. Director of Public Prosecutions, 2004 (1) SA 406, 430, 432–36, 438–39 (CC) (S. Afr. 2003) (rejecting challenge to a child pornography statute, finding the restriction on freedom of expression to be justifiable under article 36); Coetzee v. Gov't of Republic of South Africa, 1995 (4) SA 631, 659 (CC) (S. Afr.); Ferreira v. Levin, 1996 (1) SA 984, 1025 (CC) (S. Afr. 1995).

95. David Beatty, *Constitutionalizing A Labour Code: Creative Uses of Comparative Law*, 8 COMP. LAB. L. & POL'Y J. 211, 227 n.42 (1987) (citing works by a number of scholars).

96. Melissa A. Waters, *Creeping Monism: The Judicial Trend Toward Interpretive Incorporation of Human Rights Treaties,* 107 COLUM. L. REV. 628, 675 (2007).

97. *Id.*

98. *See* Weinrib, *supra* note 93, at 22–26 (noting that the Canadian justices have to some extent replicated U.S. divisions between more purposive human rights-protecting conceptions of a constitution and more "nationalist" approaches to constitutional interpretation that seek to protect "traditional social mores"). Weinrib argues that comparativism in constitutional law is linked to a "shared commitment to human dignity," *id.* at 22, 24, though her work also shows how comparisons may be invoked by those committed to more particularist conceptions. *Id.* at 25–26 (describing as the "favored sources for comparison" by more traditionalist Canadian judges "American constitutional theory . . . consistent with Justice Scalia's" views).

99. Reference re ss. 193 and 195.1(c) of the Criminal Code (Man.) ("Prostitution Reference"), [1990] 1 S.C.R. 1123, 1200 (Can.) (Lamer, J.).

100. Lavigne v. Ontario Public Service Employees Union, [1991] 2 S.C.R. 211, 298 (Can.) (Wilson, J.) (citing Re Federal Republic of Germany and Rauca (1983), 41 O.R. (2d) 225 (C.A.)); *see also id.* at 322, 324, 330–33 (LaForest, J.) (discussing U.S. cases); *supra* note 67.

101. Suresh v. Canada (Minister of Citizenship and Immigration), [2002] 1 S.C.R. 3, 37–45.

102. Charkaoui v. Canada (Citizenship and Immigration), [2007] 1 S.C.R. 350.

103. *See, e.g.,* Union of Refugee Women & Others v. Director: Private Security Indus. Regulatory Auth. & Others, 2007 (4) SA 395 (CC) at 409–15 (S. Afr., 2006) (referring, inter alia, to a Canadian constitutional decision, *Andrews v. Law Society of British Columbia,* [1989] 1 S.C.R. 143, in addressing the constitutionality of a statute generally limiting certain security positions to citizens or permanent residents); Hopkinson v. Police, [2004] 3 N.Z.L.R. 704 (H.C. Wellington) (N.Z.) (discussing U.S. and Hong Kong case law on whether flag burning is protected by the right of freedom of association); *cf.* Pretty v. United Kingdom, 2002-III Eur. Ct. H.R.155, paras. 19–23 (2002) (discussing Canadian case law under Charter §§ 1, 7, in the context of rejecting a claim that the European Convention affords a right to assisted suicide).

104. RAV v. St. Paul, 505 U.S. 377, 382–83 (1992) ("From 1791 to the present, however, our society, *like other free but civilized societies,* has permitted restrictions upon the content of speech in a few limited areas. . . .") (emphasis added); *see also* McIntyre v. Ohio Elections Comm'n, 514 U.S. 334, 381–82 (1995) (Scalia, J., dissenting).

105. Steven G. Calabresi, *Lawrence, the Fourteenth Amendment, and the Supreme Court's Reliance on Foreign Constitutional Law: An Originalist Reappraisal,* 65 OHIO ST L.J. 1097, 1104 (2004).

106. *Id.*

107. *See, e.g.,* Miranda v. Arizona, 384 U.S. 436, 486–91 (1966); *id.* at 522–23 (Harlan, J., dissenting); *see also* Chapter 6 below (noting use of foreign practice to argue against the U.S. exclusionary rule).

108. For foreign courts' discussions of U.S. constitutional cases on criminal procedure, see, for example, R. v. A., [1994] 1 N.Z.L.R. 429, 433–35 (C.A.) (1993); R. v. Edwards, [1996] 1 S.C.R. 128, 156 (Can.) (La Forest, J., concurring) (discussing U.S. cases and emphasizing Katz v. United States, 389 U.S. 347 (1967)); R. v. Smith (N.M.), 94 N.S.R. 2d 361, 367–72 (Nova Scotia); Grollo v. Palmer (1995) 184 C.L.R. 348, 367–69 (Austl.) (Brennan, C.J.) (discussing *Katz v. United States* in upholding legislation authorizing federal judges to issue telecommunication interception warrants and rejecting arguments that such a function is incompatible with the exercise of judicial power).

109. Jeffrey Goldsworthy, *Introduction* to INTERPRETING CONSTITUTIONS, *supra* note 87, at 5. Earlier works from which this section is drawn include Vicki C. Jackson, *Constitutions as "Living Trees?" Comparative Constitutional Law and Interpretive Metaphors,* 75 FORDHAM L. REV. 921, 927-39 (2006); *Multi-Valenced Constitutional Interpretation and Constitutional Comparisons: An Essay in Honor of Mark Tushnet,* 26 QUINNIPIAC L. REV. 599, 620–31 (2008).

110. Donald P. Kommers, *Germany: Balancing Rights and Duties, in* INTERPRETING CONSTITUTIONS, *supra* note 87, at 189–96. The intentions of the drafters are in his view clearly secondary.

111. *See* Robert E. Jonas & John D. Gorby, *West German Abortion Decision: A Contrast to* Roe v. Wade, 9 JOHN MARSHALL J. PRAC. & PROC. 605 (1976) (translating the abortion decision of the Federal Constitutional Court [Bundesverfassungsgerichts], Judgment of Feb. 25, 1975, 39 BVerfGE 1 (F.R.G.)).

112. *Id.* at 624, 642, 648.

113. *Id.* at 659–62.

114. *See* Kindler v. Canada, [1991] 2 S.C.R. 779 (Can.); United States v. Burns, [2001] 1 S.C.R. 283 (Can.). *Burns* illustrates how Canadian interpretive methodology facilitates engagement; as discussed in Chapter 2, the case is also an example of attitudes of "convergence" on the death penalty issue.

115. *Burns,* [2001] 1 S.C.R. at 361; *see also* Canada (Attorney General) v. Hislop, [2007] 1 S.C.R. 429 (invoking "living tree" doctrine and considering U.S. case law on retroactivity and remedies for constitutional rights violations). The Canadian courts' "living tree" metaphor is an accepted part of the legal discourse in Charter cases and in structural constitutional cases under the 1867 Constitution Act. *See, e.g.,* Reference re Employment Insurance Act (Can.), ss. 22 and 23, [2005] 2 S.C.R. 669, 677, 702 (referring to the "living tree" and concluding that changes in women's participation in the labor market since 1940 justified a broader understanding of the scope of the federal government's constitutional power over "unemployment insurance"); Gosselin v. Quebec (Attorney General), [2002] 4 S.C.R. 429, 491–92 (McLachlin, C.J.) (noting that Charter § 7 may some day be interpreted, under the living tree approach, to embrace positive obligations on the part of the government even though it is not so interpreted in this judgment).

116. *See, e.g.,* R. v. Kang-Brown, [2008] 1 S.C.R. 456, 476 (LeBel, J.) (noting a dissenting opinion of U.S. Justice Souter in explaining adverse consequences of upholding a dog sniff search in circumstances presented); *id.* at 507–08 (Binnie, J.) (citing U.S. case law in explaining need for objective criteria for warrantless searches); *id.* at 522 (Deschamps, J.) (discussing Australian and U.S. experience); Sauvé v Canada (Chief Electoral Officer), [2002] 3 S.C.R. 519, 545–46 (McLachlin, C.J.) (referencing South African case on individual dignity and voting); *id.* at 588–94 (Gonthier, J., dissenting) (noting a wide range of foreign law to suggest that Canada's disfranchisement law is "quite moderate" and consistent with dignity); R. v. Hape, [2007] 2 S.C.R. 292, 339–46 (LeBel, J.) (noting "practical and theoretical" difficulties with older approach to Charter's extraterritorial application); *id.* at 347-48 (suggesting that Charter's extraterritorial application to Canadian officials' activities would make transnational cooperation in criminal investigations more difficult).

117. Jeffrey Goldsworthy, *Originalism in Constitutional Interpretation,* 25 FED. L. REV. 1 (1997). For a useful study contrasting Australian "legalism" with U.S. "originalism," see Jamal Greene, *On the Origins of Originalism* (unpublished manuscript Jan. 23, 2009) (on file with author). On the constitution as a "living force," see McGinty v. State of Western Australia (1996) 186 C.L.R.140, 200–01 (Austl.) (Toohey J., dissenting); Theophanous v. Herald & Weekly Times, Ltd., (1994) 182 C.L.R. 104, 173–74 (Austl.) (Deane., J.).

118. Jeffrey Goldsworthy, *Australia: Devotion to Legalism, in* INTERPRETING CONSTITUTIONS, *supra* note 87, at 121–36.

119. (1989) 168 C.L.R. 461 (Austl.).

120. *Id.* at 566 (Gaudron, J.).

121. *See* PHILIP BOBBITT, CONSTITUTIONAL FATE (1982) (describing six modalities of constitutional argument); Richard H. Fallon, Jr., *A Constructivist Coherence Theory of Constitutional Interpretation,* 100 HARV. L. REV. 1189, 1189–90 (1987).

122. *See, e.g.,* Ashcraft v. Tennessee, 322 U.S. 143, 155 (1944) ("[C]ertain foreign . . . governments . . . convict individuals with testimony obtained by police organizations possessed of an unrestrained power to seize persons suspected of crimes against the state, hold them in secret custody, and wring from them confessions by physical or mental torture. So long as the Constitution remains the basic law of our republic, America will not have that kind of government."); Miranda v Arizona, 384 U.S. 436, 486–90 (1966) (referring positively to foreign experience with procedural safeguards for custodial interrogations).

123. *See, e.g.,* Youngstown Sheet & Tube Co. v. Sawyer, 343 U.S. 579, 650–52 (1952) (Jackson, J., concurring) (discussing foreign constitutional approaches to emergency powers); *see also* Chapter 6, note 27, below.

124. *See, e.g.,* Loving v. United States, 517 U.S. 748, 759–69 (1996 (upholding the delegation of authority to the President to specify aggravating and mitigating circumstances to be considered in imposing the death penalty for military offenses prosecuted in courts martials). Most U.S. justices agree that foreign or international law, to the extent considered or known at the time of the Framing, may legitimately be considered in understanding original meanings of constitutional text.

125. *See, e.g.,* Roper v. Simmons, 543 U.S. 551, 575–78 (2005); Trop v. Dulles, 356 U.S. 586, 102–03 (1957) (plurality opinion); Muller v. Oregon, 208 U.S. 412, 419 n.1 (1908).

126. 17 U.S. 316 (1819).

127. State of Kerala v. Thomas, A.I.R. 1976 S.C. 490, paras. 131, 132, 156 (India) (Krishna Iyer, J.).

128. R. v. Morgentaler, [1988] 1 S.C.R. 30, 132–64 (Can.) (McIntyre, J., dissenting).

129. *Id.* at 137 (McIntyre, J., dissenting) (quoting Dickson, C.J., at 46); *id.* at 137–39 (McIntyre, J., dissenting) (noting Holmes's dissent in *Lochner v. New York,* 198 U.S. 45 (1905)).

130. *See* Case 6/64, Costa v. Ente Nazionale Per L'Energia Elettrica (ENEL), 1964 E.C.R. 585 (supremacy); Case 26/62, Van Gend & Loos v. Nederlandse Administratie der Belastingen, 1963 E.C.R. 1 (direct effect); *see also* J.H.H. Weiler, *The Transformation of Europe,* 100 YALE L. J. 2403, 2413–19 (1990).

131. *See, e.g.,* Michele Nino, *Court of Cassation, Section 1 Criminal (Corte de Caassazione, Sezione 1, Penale): Effect of Decisions of the European Court of Human Rights on Domestic Criminal Courts,* 71 J. CRIM. L. 406, 407 (2007) (explaining the difficulty in Italy of reconsidering criminal cases in response to ECtHR rulings).

132. *See* Von Hannover v. Germany, 2004-VI Eur Ct H.R. 41 (finding that the German legal system had failed to provide respect for the plaintiff's private life, as required by Article 8 of the ECHR, in refusing to enjoin publication of certain photos of the plaintiff); Görgülü v. Germany, App. No. 74969/01, Eur. Ct. H.R. (2004) (finding a violation of a nonmarital father's right to family life by German courts' refusal to consider his interests in denying his effort to block adoption and obtain visitation). *See also* Sahin v Germany, 2003-VIII Eur. Ct. H.R. 63 ((holding that German courts violated the equality guarantee of Article 14 of the Convention by allowing different treatment of fathers of nonmarital children than of divorced fathers of marital children); Sommerfeld v Germany, 2003-VIII Eur Ct. H.R. 137 (involving similar issues).

133. Matthias Hartwig, *Much Ado About Human Rights: The Federal Constitutional Court Confronts the European Court of Human Rights—Part I/II*, 6 GERMAN L.J. 869, 874–75 (2005); *see id.* ("The Federal Constitutional Court underscored that the ECHR . . . leaves it up to its member States how to guarantee respect for the obligations established by the treaty. . . . [The] Federal Constitutional Court rejected all proposals seeking to minimize the effects of the Convention, for example by declaring that it binds only the State internationally and not its organs internally. . . . However, the Federal Constitutional Court found that the convention does not enjoy the rank of constitutional law within the German system. . . .").

134. At the same time, the German Constitutional Court indicated that domestic courts must "duly consider" the ECtHR's decision, striking a posture of (at least) strong engagement. Felix Müller & Tobias Richter, *Report on the Bundesverfassungsherichts's (Federal Constitutional Court) Jurisprudence in 2005/2006—Part I/II*, 9 GERMAN L. J. 161, 167 (2008). For an English translation of the Constitutional Court's decision, see Order of the Second Senate of 14 October 2004, 2 BvR 1481/04, http://www.bverfg.de/entscheidungen/rs20041014_2bvr148104en.html. *Cf.* Müller & Richter, *supra*, at 170 (reporting on the lower court's continued resistance to sufficiently taking the ECtHR decision into account, resulting in further review in the Constitutional Court).

135. *See, e.g.*, Anneli Albi, *Supremacy of EC Law in the New Member States: Bringing Parliaments into the Equation of 'Co-operative Constitutionalism,'* 3 EUR. CONST. L. REV. 25 (2007); András Sajó, *Learning Co-operative Constitutionalism the Hard Way: the Hungarian Constitutional Court Shying Away from EU Supremacy*, 2 ZEITSCHRIFT FÜR STAATS-UND EUROPAWISSENSCHAFTEN 351 (2004); Oreste Pollicino, *Italy: Constitutional Court at the Crossroad Between Constitutional Parochialism and Co-operative Constitutionalism: Case note on judgments nos. 348 and 349 of 2007*, 4 EUR. CONST. L. REV. 363 (2008)]; Samantha Besson, *From European Integration to European Integrity: Should European Law Speak with Just One Voice?*, 10 EUR. L.J. 257 (2004); *see also* Samantha Besson, Sovereignty in Conflict, 8 European Integration Online Papers (EioP) (2004), *available at* SSRN: http://ssrn.com/abstract=594942 (discussing the idea of "cooperative sovereignty" in a "post-national constellation"). *Cf.* Marc Amstutz, *In-Between Worlds:* Marleasing *and the Emergence of Interlegality in Legal Reasoning*, 11 EUR. L.J. 766 (2005) (discussing EC decision, Case C-106/89, Marleasing [1990] ECRI-4135, requiring interpretation of national law in accordance with EU directives "as far as possible")

136. Mattias Kumm, *Beyond Golf Clubs and the Judicialization of Politics: Why Europe Has a Constitution Properly So Called*, 54 AM. J. COMP. L. 505, 525–26 (2006) (Suppl.) (discussing both cases and explaining that "[s]tructural deficits in the protection of fundamental rights on the European level were the reason for the FCC to originally insist that it should not accept the authority of EU Law, insofar as constitutional rights claims were in play. When those specific concerns were effectively addressed by the ECJ, the authority of EU Law extended also over national constitutional rights guarantees . . ..").

137. *See* Daniel Halberstam, *The Bride of Messina: Constitutionalism and Democracy in Europe*, 30 EUR. L. REV. 775, 783 (2005); *see also* Stephen Breyer, *Changing Relationships among European Constitutional Courts*, 21 CARDOZO L. REV. 1045, 1054–55 (2000); Kommers, *supra* note 110, at 204–05.

138. Manfred H. Wiegandt, *Germany's International Integration: The Rulings of the German Federal Constitutional Court on the Maastricht Treaty and the Out-of-Area Deployment of German Troops*, 10 AM. U. J. INT'L L. & POL'Y 889, 899 (1995).

139. *Id.* at 902. For another assessment, see Joseph Weiler, *Does Europe Need a Constitution? Demos, Telos and the German Maastricht Decision*, 1 EUR. L.J. 219 (1995).

140. *See also* Bundesverfassungsgericht [BVerfG] [Federal Constitutional Court] July 18, 2005, 2 BvR 2236/04, "European Arrest Warrant Case," *English translation available at* http://www.bundesverfassungsgericht.de/entscheidungen/rs20050718_2bvr223604en.html (finding that German statute implementing the European Arrest Warrant was in violation of German Basic Law); *cf.* ANTHONY ARNULL ET AL., WYATT & DASHWOOD'S EUROPEAN UNION LAW 502 (5th ed. 2006) (suggesting that the large numbers of preliminary references from Germany to the ECJ has "increased the impact of German law and legal thinking" on ECJ jurisprudence). On the ECJ's rapprochement with human rights norms, see Case 11/70, Internationale Handelsgesellschaft mbH v. Einfuhr-und Vorratsstelle für Getreide und Futtermittel, 1970 E.C.R. 1125; *see also* Case 4/73, Nold v. Comm'n of the European Communities, 1974 E.C.R. 491, 507 (indicating that the ECJ should draw on international human rights treaties in which its member states have participated or signed for developing guidelines within community law); Case 44/79, Hauer v. Land Rheinland-Pfalz, 1979 E.C.R. 3727, 3745 (considering a protocol to the European Convention on Human Rights and "ideas common to the constitutions of the member states" with respect to property rights). *Cf.* Clemens Rieder, *Protecting Human Rights within the European Union: Who Is Better Qualified to Do the Job—the European Court of Justice or the European Court of Human Rights?*, 20 TUL. EUR. & CIV. L.F. 73 (2005) (arguing for a more comprehensive human rights regime for the EU countries consolidated by ECJ jurisprudence); Bruno de Witte, *The Past and Future Role of the European Court of Justice in the Protection of Human Rights, in* THE EU AND HUMAN RIGHTS 859, 860–67 (Philip Alston ed., 1999) (discussing the ECJ's role in protecting fundamental human rights as "general principles of Community law," including unwritten principles drawn from common constitutional traditions of the member states as well as international human rights law).

141. CC Decision No. 2004-505DC, Nov. 19, 2004, Rec. 173, Traité établissant une Constitution pour l'Europe, www.conseil-constitutionnel.fr; *see* Guy Carcassonne, *France Conseil Constitutionnel on the European Constitutional Treaty*, 1 EUR. CONST. L. REV. 293 (2005); Loïc Azoulai & Felix Ronkes Agerbeek, *Conseil Constitutionnel (French Constitutional Court), Decision No. 2004-505 DC of 119 November 2004, on the Treaty establishing a Constitution for Europe*, 42 COMMON MKT L. REV. 871, 877 (2005) (describing the Conseil's recent decisions as establishing that "in the French legal order Community norms will have unconditional and immediate precedence, unless they come into conflict with certain fundamental principles protected by the French Constitution").

142. *See* Albi, *supra* note 135, at 26 (noting *Granital*, Decision No. 170, 1984; *Frontini*, Decision No. 183, 1973); *see also* Bruno de Witte, *Direct Effect, Supremacy and the Nature of the Legal Order, in* THE EVOLUTION OF EU LAW 177, 202–03 (Paul Craig & Gráinne de Búrca eds., 1999).

143. Constitutional Court of Spain, Declaration on the Consistency of the European Constitutional Treaty with the Spanish Constitution, DTC 1/2004, Dec. 13, 2004, *described and discussed in* Camilo B. Schutte, *Spain Tribunal Constitucional on the European Constitution*, 1 EUR. CONST. L. REV. 281 (2005) *and available in English at* http://www.tribunalconstitucional.es/jurisprudencia/Stc_ing/STC2007-dtc12004.html; Fernando Castillo de la Torre, *Tribunal Constitucional (Spanish Constitutional Court), Opinion 1/2004, of 13 December 2004, on the Treaty establishing a Constitution for Europe*, 42 COMMON MKT. L. REV. 1169 (2005); Ricardo Alonso García, *The Spanish Constitution and the European Constitution: The Script for a Virtual Collision and Other Observations on the Principle of Primacy*, 6 GERMAN L. J. 1001 (2005).

144. Carlsen v. Rasmussen, [1999] 3 C.M.L.R. 854, 861 (Sup. Ct.) (Den.) (noting powers of Danish courts should "extraordinary situation" arise of ECJ upholding an act extending

beyond limits of Denmark's constitutionally permissible "surrender of sovereignty" in act acceding to EU treaty); *see also* de Witte, *supra* note 142, at 198–200.

145. *See* Albi, *supra* note 135, at 37 (2007) (describing, inter alia, the Polish Constitutional Tribunal's decisions on the European Arrest Warrant legislation and the Cession Treaty case, in which the Court both asserted the supremacy of the Polish constitution and sought "to interpret the national provisions in an EU-friendly way"); Adam Łazowski, *Accession Treaty, Polish Constitutional Tribunal: Conformity of the Accession Treaty with the Polish Constitution, Decision of May 11 2005*, 3 EUR. CONST. L. REV. 148, 155–57 (2007) (noting Polish Court's reliance on decisions by German and Danish constitutional courts and describing its holding not only that Polish constitution has supremacy over EU but also its assertion of its power to evaluate secondary Community legislation for conformity with the Polish constitution).

146. Łazowski, *supra* note 145, at 160 (stating that the double criminality requirement was "contrary to EU law"); Angelika Nußberger, *Poland: The Constitutional Tribunal on the Implementation of the European Arrest Warrant*, 6 INT'L J. CONST. L. 162, 170 (2008). The ECJ in 2007 upheld the elimination of double criminality in the Council's Framework Decision on the European Arrest Warrant. *See* Florian Geyer, *European Arrest Warrant: Court of Justice of the European Communities, Judgment of 3 May 2007, Case C-303/05,* Advocaten voor de Wereld VZW v. Leden van de Ministerraad, 4 EUR. CONST. L. REV. 149 (2008).

147. *See* J.H.H. Weiler, *Federalism Without Constitutionalism: Europe's Sonderweg*, in THE FEDERAL VISION: LEGITIMACY AND LEVELS OF GOVERNANCE IN THE UNITED STATES AND THE EUROPEAN UNION 54, 63 (Kalypso Nicolides & Robert Howse eds., 2001).

148. *See* Kumm, *supra* note 136, at 529–30.

149. Albi, *supra* note 135, at 32; *see* de Witte, *supra* note 142, at 201 ("The thesis that Community law has absolute primacy, even over national constitutional provisions, is generally not accepted by national supreme courts.").

150. Case C-112/00, Schmidberger v. Austria, 2003 E.C.R. I-5659. With thanks to Nancy Dinsmore, a Georgetown University Law Center student, for excellent research assistance in preparing a memorandum on which I have drawn in this section.

151. On appeal, the Austrian court decided that the resolution of the case required an interpretation of Community law and referred the case to the ECJ for a preliminary ruling. Austria argued that the restriction of free movement of goods arising from a demonstration should be permitted where the obstruction is not permanent, particularly because the assessment of the interests should "lean in favour of the freedoms of expression and assembly," which are inviolable democratic rights. *Schmidberger*, 2003 E.C.R. I-5659, at I-5702 para. 17.

152. *Id.* at 5720 paras. 80–81.

153. *See* Case C-36/02, Omega Spielhallen-und Automatenaufstellungs-GmbH v. Oberbürgermeisterin der Bundesstadt Bonn, 2004 E.C.R. I-9609, paras. 31–33 (holding that European Community law on the free movement of goods and services does not invalidate a German restriction on a laser game involving "simulated killing of human beings" shot at with laser guns, in light of Germany's constitutional commitment to human dignity and the need to allow member states a "margin of discretion"); *see also* Craig T. Smith & Thomas Fetzer, *The Uncertain Limits of the European Court of Justice's Authority: Economic Freedom versus Human Dignity*, 10 COLUM. J. EUR. L. 445 (2004). *But cf.* Case C–341/05, Laval v. Svenska, 2007 E.C.R. I–11767 (upholding priority of EU free movement of service rules over national labor law, as applied to workers posted to Sweden, notwithstanding Sweden's constitutional protection of the right to take collective action,

which the ECJ interpreted not to preclude application of EU law); Ronnie Eklund, *Free Business Movement and the Right to Strike in the European Community: Two Views: A Swedish Perspective on* Laval, 29 COMP. LAB. L. & POL'Y J. 551 (2008).

154. MICHAEL HARDT & ANTONIO NEGRI, EMPIRE xii (2000) (emphasis in original).

155. Philip Bobbit, *Marketing the Future of the State, in* THE NEW STATESMAN (Jan. 17, 2003).

156. *Cf.* David Held, *Democracy, the Nation-State and the Global System, in* READINGS IN CONTEMPORARY POLITICAL SOCIOLOGY 311, 312, 314–15 (Kate Nash ed., 2000). Held is careful to distinguish between the argument that there are "elements of continuity in the formation and structure of modern states," and the "claim that there is nothing new"; and he identifies as new in the "modern global system . . . the chronic intensification of patterns of interconnectedness, mediated by such phenomena as the modern communications industry and new information technology." *Id.*

157. *See* Alec Stone Sweet & Thomas L. Brunell, *The European Court and the National Courts: A Statistical Analysis of Preliminary References, 1961–95*, 5 J. EUR. PUB. POL'Y 66 (1998), *available at* http://www.jeanmonnetprogram.org/papers/97/97-14-.html; KAREN J. ALTER, ESTABLISHING THE SUPREMACY OF EUROPEAN LAW: THE MAKING OF AN INTERNATIONAL RULE OF LAW IN EUROPE 35–36 (2001) (commenting on such studies). On the direction of the causality, if any, see also Jean-Yves Pitarakis & George Tridimas, *Joint Dynamics of Legal and Economic Integration in the European Union*, 16 EUR. J.L. & ECON. 357 (2003).

158. *See* Chapter 9, below.

159. William Dale, *The Making and Remaking of Commonwealth Constitutions*, 42 INT'L & COMP. L.Q 67, 68 (1993); *see id.* at 67–68, 75–76, 78 (stating that "Whitehall lawyers must have drafted at least 33" independence constitutions, which generally gave citizens the right to vote).

160. CONST. BOTSWANA § 100 (3)(a) (Court of Appeal); *see id.* § 96 (3)(a) (High Court); *see also* Sir Anthony Mason, *Reflections of an Itinerant Judge in the Asia-Pacific Region*, 28 INT'L J. LEGL. INFO. 311, 315–22 (2000) (describing his service after retiring from the Australian High Court, on the highest courts of Fiji, Solomon Islands and Hong Kong); Gregory Dale, *Appealing to Whom? Australia's 'Appellate Jurisdiction' Over Nauru*, 56 INT'L & COMP. L. Q. 641, 642 (2007) (describing three models by which foreign judges hear appeals: when "expatriate" judges are appointed to sit on national courts, as in Botswana; when appeals go to a supranational court, such as the Privy Council or the Caribbean Court of Justice; and when another country's court is authorized to act as the court of appeals, as in Nauru).

161. For a recent example, see Panday v. Gordon, [2005] UKPC 36, [2006] AC 427 (2005) (appeal taken from Trin. & Tobago) (U.K) (Judgment by Lord Nicholls of Birkenhead) (construing the Constitution of Trinidad and Tobago, against the "background" of defamation law in Australia, Canada, and New Zealand, not to override the common law of defamation).

162. *See* Edwards v. Attorney-General for Canada ("The Persons Case"), [1930] A.C. 124 (P.C. 1929) (appeal taken from Can.).

163. Whether similar effects are exerted among former French colonies, or colonies of other former powers (such as Spain, or Portugal), is beyond the scope of what is addressed here; the existence of a French language-based association of constitutional courts (created in 1997 and claiming more than 40 members), that sponsors conferences and exchanges of information, suggests that the question would be worthy of study. *See* Association des Cours Constitutionelles ayant en Partage l'Usage du Français (ACCPUF), at http://www.accpuf.org/ (click on "l'Association").

164. *See* Commonwealth Secretariat, Legal and Constitutional Affairs Division, http://www.thecommonwealth.org/Internal/1514709/lcad (last visited Apr. 17, 2008).

165. *Cf.* SIR BASIL MARKESINIS & JÖRG FEDTKE, JUDICIAL RECOURSE TO FOREIGN LAW 173–216 (2006) (discussing the impact of a judge's overall "mentality" on his or her inclination to consider foreign law and providing examples of both receptivity and hostility). On the availability of "sabbaticals" that enable some constitutional court judges to spend time abroad and learn in person about other constitutional systems, see Chapter 5, note 108, below.

166. *Cf., e.g.,* TOM GINSBURG, JUDICIAL REVIEW IN NEW DEMOCRACIES: CONSTITUTIONAL COURTS IN ASIAN CASES at 154–55 (2003) (suggesting that Taiwan Court's embrace of the "rhetorical standard of international practice" could be seen as part of a strategy to highlight differences between Taiwan and the PRC). Taiwan may have a special strategic interest in doing so, given its interests in gaining recognition from other states.

167. There may also be reasons for engagement more personal to the judges; concerns for reputation may make judges care about how they are regarded—not only at home but also abroad. *See generally* LAWRENCE BAUM, JUDGES AND THEIR AUDIENCES 103–04, 109–10 (2006). Although this possibility has elicited criticism, to the extent that concern for reputation abroad produces more careful reasoning and thinking it has advantages. As discussed in Chapter 5 below, it is unlikely that U.S. judges will be influenced so as to lose their grounding in the very strong U.S. constitutional culture.

168. *See, e.g.,* John Dugard, *Twenty Years of Human Rights Scholarship and Ten Years of Democracy*, 20 S. AFR. J.ON HUM. RTS. 345, 348 (2004); Geraldine Van Bueren, *Alleviating Poverty Through the Constitutional Court*, 15 S. AFR. J. ON HUM. RTS. 52, 57 (1999) (declaring that "it is the minimum core approach which provides economic and social rights with a determinacy and certainty"); *see also* Karin Lehmann, *In Defense of the Constitutional Court: Litigating Socio-Economic Rights and the Myth of the Minimum Core*, 22 AM. U. INT'L L. REV. 163 (2006).

169. UDHR art. 10 (emphasis added); *see also* UDHR art. 8 ("Everyone has the right to an effective remedy by the competent national tribunals for acts violating the fundamental rights granted him by the constitution or by law.")

170. *See* UDHR art. 21 ("(1) Everyone has the right to take part in the government of his country, directly or through freely chosen representatives. . . . (3) The will of the people shall be the basis of the authority of government; this will shall be expressed in periodic and genuine elections which shall be by universal and equal suffrage and shall be held by secret vote or by equivalent free voting procedures.").

171. UDHR pmbl. ("Whereas it is essential, if man is not to be compelled to have recourse, as a last resort, to rebellion against tyranny and oppression, that human rights should be protected by the rule of law . . . ").

172. *See* ICCPR arts. 14(1), 2.3(b).

173. *See* Param Cumaraswamy, Independence and Impartiality of the Judiciary, Jurors and Assessors and the Independence of Lawyers, Report of the Special Rapporteur, 1994/41, UN Doc. E/CN.4/1995/39 (Feb. 6, 1995) (describing the creation of the position in 1994 through the UN Commission on Human Rights); *see also* Param Cumaraswamy, Civil and Political Rights, Including Questions of: Independence of the Judiciary, Administration of Justice, Impunity, Addendum, Report of the Special Rapporteur on the Independence of Judges and Lawyers, UN ESCOR, 56th sess., at paras. 34–37, UN Doc. E/CN.4/2000/61/Add.1 (2000) (documenting attacks on the judiciary in Guatemala). On rhetorical support throughout the world for judicial independence, see also Seventh UN Congress on the Prevention of Crime and the Treatment of Offenders, Milan,

Aug. 26–Sept. 6, 1985, *Basic Principles on the Independence of the Judiciary,* UN Doc. A/CONF.121/22/Rev.1, at 58-62 (1986) (endorsed by General Assembly resolutions 40/32 of Nov. 29, 1985 and 40/146 of Dec. 13, 1985) (favoring judicial independence, addressing judicial tenure and the right of judges to form associations with other judges).

174. *See* American Convention on Human Rights (ACHR), art. 8(1) (guaranteeing rights to be heard before a "competent, independent and impartial tribunal, previously established by law"); ECHR art. 6(1) (stating that in the determination of civil rights or criminal charges, "everyone is entitled to a fair and public hearing within a reasonable time by an independent and impartial tribunal established by law"). *Cf.* African Charter on Human and People's Rights, art. 7(1) (providing for a right to have one's case heard and tried "by an impartial court or tribunal").

175. *See, e.g.,* McGonnell v. United Kingdom, 2000-II Eur. Ct H.R. 107 (2000) (finding that the Royal Court of Guernsey failed to meet impartial adjudication requirements because the Bailiff served in judicial, executive, and legislative capacities); *see also* Borgers v. Belgium, 214 Eur. Ct. H.R. (ser. A) 21 (1993); Vermeulen v. Belgium, 1 Eur. Ct. H.R. Rep. 224 (1996); Procola v. Luxembourg, 326 Eur. Ct. H.R. (ser. A) (1995); *cf.* The Loewen Group., Inc. v. United States, ICSID Case No. ARB(AF) 98/3, Award (June 26, 2003), para. 142 (finding that American state trial and verdict "were improper and cannot be squared with minimum standards of fair international law and fair and equitable treatment"), *available at* http://naftaclaims.com/Disputes/USA/Loewen/LoewenFinalAward.pdf.

176. *See* Beate Rudolf, *International Decision: Statute of the International Criminal Court, Decision No. 98-408 DC, 1999 J.O. 1317,* available at http://www.conseil-constitutionnel.fr/decision/1998/98408/98408dc.htm. *French Conseil Constitutionnel, Jan, 22, 1999,* 94 AM. J. INT'L L. 391, 393 (2000).

177. *See* M. Cherif Bassiouni, *Human Rights in the Context of Criminal Justice: Identifying International Procedural Protections and Equivalent Protections in National Constitutions,* 3 DUKE J. COMP. & INT'L L. 235, 271 (1993) ("At least thirty-two national constitutions provide explicitly that a criminal trial be before an independent and impartial tribunal. In another fifty-four constitutions, general provisions are made for an independent judiciary or court system without referring directly to the criminal trial.").

178. Jonathan M. Miller, *The Authority of a Foreign Talisman: A Study of U.S. Constitutional Practice as Authority in Nineteenth Century Argentina and the Argentine Elite's Leap of Faith,* 46 AM. U.L. REV. 1483, 1554–55 & n.519 (1997) (reproducing text of 1860 Argentine Constitution arts. 100, 101).

179. *See* REBECCA BILL CHAVEZ, THE RULE OF LAW IN NASCENT DEMOCRACIES: JUDICIAL POLITICS IN ARGENTINA 38–41 (2004); GRETCHEN HELMKE, COURTS UNDER CONSTRAINTS: JUDGES, GENERALS AND PRESIDENTS IN ARGENTINA 63–92, 146–52 (2005).

180. Accession to the WTO required China to develop an impartial and independent judiciary to review administrative disputes concerning WTO obligations. *See generally* Veron Mei-Ying Hung, *China's WTO Commitment on Independent Judicial Review: Impact on Legal and Political Reform,* 52 AM. J. COMP. L. 77, 78–79, 80–82 (2004) (concluding that notwithstanding its efforts to comply, China has thus far failed to solve the fundamental problems underlying lack of judicial independence, including Communist Party control of law and courts); *see also* Karen Halverson, *China's WTO Accession: Economic, Legal, and Political Implications,* 27 B.C. INT'L & COMP. L. REV. 319, 354 (2004). For discussion of the state of judicial independence and reform efforts toward its improvement, see RANDALL PEERENBOOM, CHINA MODERNIZES: THREAT TO THE WEST OR MODEL FOR THE REST? 32, 105–06, 212–16, 220–24 (2007).

181. *Cf.* Antoun v. The Queen (2006) 224 A.L.R. 51, 61 (Austl.) (opinion of Kirby, J.) (arguing that ratification of ICCPR "reinforced [a common law practice favoring impartial

judging] by a rule of international law which expresses the entitlement to an impartial tribunal as a fundamental right of the individual concerned. It is not simply an aspiration or guideline of good judicial practice. It is a basic *right*. . . .") (emphasis in original).

182. *See* Judith Resnik & Dennis E. Curtis, Representing Justice: Mapping the Rise and Fall of Judging from Renaissance Iconography to Twenty-First Century Courthouses (chapter on "Obedience: The Judge as the Loyal Servant of the State," discussing "judicial subservience and dependence") (forthcoming, Yale University Press, 2010).

183. *See* Charles Lane, *Scalia Tells Congress to Mind Its Own Business*, Wash. Post, May 19, 2006, at A19 (quoting Justice Scalia's comment on proposed legislation to restrict references to foreign law: "'It's none of your business,' he said, referring to Congress. 'No one is more opposed to the use of foreign law than I am, but I'm darned if I think it's up to Congress to direct the court how to make its decisions.'").

184. *See* Anne-Marie Slaughter, A New World Order 68, 69, 101 (2004); *see also* Slaughter, *supra* note 3, at 192–93 (arguing that transjudicial dialogue leads judges to "conceive of themselves as capable of independent action in both international and domestic realms").

185. It is possible to have a judiciary that appears to be relatively independent of external political controls but in which individual judicial decisions are tightly constrained, not only through the ordinary process of appeal but also through control within the judiciary of the job conditions and prospects for advancement of lower court judges. *See, e.g.*, J. Mark Ramseyer & Eric B. Rasmusen, *The Chief Justice and the Institutional Judiciary: The Case for Managed Judges: Learning from Japan After the Political Upheaval of 1993*, 154 U. Pa. L. Rev. 1879 (2006). Although institutional and individual independence play distinct roles, some of the normative arguments in support of each overlap. Some courts do not issue separate or dissenting opinions, a practice whose relationship to independence of judgment is complex. *Cf., e.g.*, Cyril Ritter, *A New Look at the Role and Impact of Advocates-General—Collectively and Individually*, 12 Colum. J. Eur. L. 751, 763 n.63 (2006) (stating that the ban on separate opinions by ECJ judges preserves their independence from their own national governments).

186. *See* Slaughter, *supra* note 184, at 65–103; Helfer & Slaughter, *supra* note 35, at 372–73. In addition to conferences and networks, legal mechanisms of inter-court referral promote the development of ideas about judging. *See, e.g.*, *id.* at 309–10; *see also* Alter, *supra* note 157, at 38 (arguing that the European legal order was created by judges talking to one another in a process of "doctrinal negotiation").

187. *See* Waters, *supra* note 96, at 646–47.

188. Anne-Marie Slaughter & William Burke-White, *The Future of International Law is Domestic (Or, The European Way of Law)*, 47 Harv. Int'l L.J. 327, 334–35 (2006). The co-authors argue that, under an approach begun in Europe but spreading beyond, international law influences "domestic outcomes" in three ways—by "strengthening domestic institutions, backstopping national governance, and compelling domestic action. . . ." *Id.* at 328–29.

189. *See* International Commission of Jurists, Website, http://www.icj.org (click on "What does ICJ do?," "About Us," and "Questions and Answers") (last visited Mar. 4, 2009).

190. Michael Kirby, *International Law—The Impact on National Constitutions*, 21 Am. U. Int'l L. Rev. 327, 360 (2006).

191. Justice Breyer's citation to a Zimbabwean decision may have had this purpose in mind. See Chapter 4, note 106 below.

192. Vriend v. Alberta, [1998] 1 S.C.R. 493.

193. Romer v. Evans, 517 U.S. 620 (1996).

194. Bowers v. Hardwick, 478 U.S. 186 (1986). Since *Bowers* was decided ten years before *Romer*, perhaps the Canadian Court was simply correctly reading the trend suggested by *Romer*; in 2003, the U.S. Court in *Lawrence v. Texas* overruled *Bowers*. On simply ignoring contrary authority, see *infra* note 195.

195. Ignoring contrary authority is subject to legitimate critique, see Chapter 6 below, although there may be some legitimate uses of even single opinions (for example, to show that a judge is not alone in holding a view, or for the elegance of expression of an idea).

196. *See* Website of the German Constitutional Court, "Update" page, http://www.bundesverfassungsgericht.de/en/index.html (listing "Recent Decisions and Press Releases in English"); *id.* at "Links" page, under "Constitutional Courts in other countries," and including Algeria, Benin, Bolivia, Ecuador, El Salvador, Taiwan, Thailand, and Venezuela, as well as other European countries and several English-speaking countries) (last visited Sept. 13, 2007).

197. *See* http://elyon1.court.gov.il/eng/home/index.html. (English-language Website, Supreme Court of Israel).

198. One could imagine more specific reasons, involving institutional or national self-defense, for such publications. Perhaps the German court publishes its decisions in English in order to increase its influence on the two European courts with which it is in something of a struggle over the question of "competence-competence," as discussed earlier in this chapter. Perhaps the Israeli court is engaged in an act of national self-defense by disseminating opinions its justices believe will show that Israel is a law-abiding, rights-respecting polity, to shore up support against the weight of many countries' views of the illegality of Israel's treatment of the Palestinians. *Cf.* Ronen Shamir, *"Landmark Cases" and the Reproduction of Legitimacy: The Case of Israel's High Court of Justice*, 24 L. & Soc'y Rev. 781 (1990) (arguing that high-profile cases tended to legitimate activities of the state without seriously constraining state action).

199. *See, e.g.* Judges in Contemporary Democracy, *supra* note 2; Kirby, *Think Globally*, *supra* note 37, at 291–92 (referring to Yale Law School's annual gathering of constitutional court judges and noting how the Internet makes "interconnection" easier).

CHAPTER 4. CONSTITUTIONAL ADJUDICATION IN THE U.S. SUPREME COURT: WHY ENGAGE THE TRANSNATIONAL?

1. *See* Chapter 1, note 53, above. For useful discussions of the Court's use of foreign or international law over time, see Sarah H. Cleveland, *Our International Constitution*, 31 Yale J. Int'l L. 1 (2006); Steven G. Calabresi & Stephanie Dotson Zimdahl, *The Supreme Court and Foreign Sources of Law: Two Hundred Years of Practice and the Juvenile Death Penalty Decision*, 47 Wm. & Mary L. Rev. 747 (2005); David Fontana, *Refined Comparativism in Constitutional Law*, 49 UCLA L. Rev. 539 (2001). For earlier work from which some of this chapter is drawn, see Vicki C. Jackson, *Constitutions as "Living Trees?' Comparative Constitutional Law and Interpretive Metaphors*, 75 Fordham L. Rev. 921 (2006); *Constitutional Law and Transnational Comparisons: The Youngstown Decision and American Exceptionalism*, 30 Harv. J. L. & Pub. Pol'y 191 (2006) [hereinafter *Youngstown Decision*]; *Constitutional Comparisons: Convergence, Resistance, Engagement*, 119 Harv. L. Rev. 109 (2005) [hereinafter *Constitutional Comparisons*]; *Narratives of Federalism: Of Continuities and Comparative Constitutional Experience*, 51 Duke L. J. 223, 247–63 (2001); *Ambivalent Resistance and Comparative Constitutionalism: Opening Up the Conversation on "Proportionality," Rights and Federalism*, 1 U. Pa. J. Const. L. 583 (1999).

2. *See, e.g.*, GERALD TEUBNER, LAW AS AN AUTOPOIETIC SYSTEM (1993); Niklas Luhmann, *Closure and Openness: On Reality in the World of Law*, in AUTOPOIETIC LAW: A NEW APPROACH TO LAW AND SOCIETY (G. Teubner, ed. 1988); *cf.* H.L.A. HART, THE CONCEPT OF LAW 91–96 (1961) (describing law's secondary rules of recognition, change, and adjudication, that prescribe how valid primary rules governing behavior in the world are made, identified, and applied within the system).

3. *See, e.g.*, Richard Lempert, *The Autonomy of Law: Two Visions Compared, in* AUTOPOIETIC LAW: A NEW APPROACH TO LAW AND SOCIETY, *supra* note 2, at 152, 178–80 (suggesting that "Anglo-American" views of the partial autonomy of law embrace "the idea that law is open to normative influences from extralegal sources of power and authority"). It is possible that judges' conception of their system as "normatively closed but cognitively open," however inaccurate, would have a healthy effect in supporting a constrained concept of the judicial role. *Cf.* Scott Altman, *Beyond Candor*, 89 MICH. L. REV. 296 (1990) (arguing for judicial behavior that is candid but not introspective).

4. On the idea of "implementation" as a major task of constitutional adjudication, see generally Richard H. Fallon, Jr., *Foreword: Implementing the Constitution*, 111 HARV. L. REV. 54 (1996). *Cf.* Benjamin C. Zipursky, *Pragmatic Conceptualism*, 6 LEGAL THEORY 457 (2000) (exploring the possibility of pragmatism in service of conceptual understandings of law).

5. *See, e.g.*, Kotteakos v. United States, 328 U.S. 750, 773 (1946); Ashcraft v. Tennessee, 322 U.S. 143, 155 (1944); *see also* Griswold v. Connecticut, 381 U.S. 479, 497 (1965) (Goldberg, J., concurring); Fikes v. Alabama, 352 U.S. 191, 199 (1957) (Frankfurter, J., concurring); Brown v. Allen, 344 U.S. 443, 512 (1953) (Frankfurter, J.); Wieman v. Updegraff, 344 U.S. 183, 194 (1952) (Black, J., concurring).

6. *See* David A. Strauss, *Common Law, Common Ground, and Jefferson's Principle*, 112 YALE L.J. 1717, 1738 (2003).

7. For an important discussion of the expressive function of constitutional law, see PHILLIP BOBBITT, CONSTITUTIONAL FATE 181–242 (1982).

8. BENEDICT ANDERSON, IMAGINED COMMUNITIES (2006 ed.); *see also* BOBBITT, *supra* note 7, at 222 ("[O]ur ethos may be contrasted with those of other . . . societies . . . ."); *cf.* J. H. H. Weiler, *Does Europe Need a Constitution? Demos, Telos and the German Maastricht Decision*, 1 EUR. L.J. 219, 246–47, 248 (1995) (discussing "belongingness" and "originality" as values of national identity).

9. *See* ANDERSON, *supra* note 8, at 205 (noting the modern need for "narratives of 'identity'" for persons and nations); *cf. id.* at 16 (noting the decline of the "unselfconscious coherence" of religious communities after the late Middle Ages).

10. *See* Stephen G. Calabresi, *"A Shining City on a Hill": American Exceptionalism and the Supreme Court's Practice of Relying on Foreign Law*, 86 B.U. L. REV. 1335 (2006). For earlier work from which this paragraph is drawn, see Jackson, *supra* note 1, *Youngstown Decision*, at 216–17.

11. *Cf., e.g.*, Sanford H. Kadish, *Methodology and Criteria in Due Process Adjudication—A Survey and Criticism*, 66 YALE L.J. 319, 333–34 (1957) (noting the use of "evidence of the inconsistency of a given procedure with due process in the historical association of similar procedures with tyrannical governments" to give objective content to evolving understandings of Due Process Clause; citing as an example Justice Black's dissent in *Shaughnessy v. United States ex rel. Mezei*, 345 U.S. 206, 217–18 (1953) (Black, J., dissenting) (discussing Russian laws of 1934 and German law under Hitler)).

12. 163 U.S. 537 (1896).

13. 347 U.S. 483 (1954).

14. *Plessy*, 163 U.S. at 562 (emphasis added).

15. Griswold v. Connecticut, 381 U.S. 479, 497 (1965) (Goldberg, J., concurring); *see also* MARY L. DUDZIAK, COLD WAR CIVIL RIGHTS 90–114 (2000) (discussing effect of the Cold War on discourses around *Brown v. Board of Education*, 347 U.S. 483 (1954)); RICHARD A. PRIMUS, THE AMERICAN LANGUAGE OF RIGHTS 177–233 (1999) (discussing role of anti-Naziism and anti-totalitarianism in shaping changed rights discourses after World War II).

16. Metro Broadcasting, Inc. v. Federal Communications Commission, 497 U.S. 547, 635 (1990) (Kennedy, J., dissenting) (suggesting that governments may claim benign purposes even when a racial classification is in fact being used invidiously). One response to Justice Kennedy's cautionary example is the presence of independent courts capable of looking, substantively, at evidence of the actual purpose and effects of such laws.

17. Adarand Constructors, Inc. v. Pena, 515 U.S. 200 (1995) (overruling *Metro Broadcasting, Inc. v. FCC*).

18. Lawrence v. Texas, 539 U.S. 558, 576–77 (2003); Grutter v. Bollinger, 539 U.S. 306, 344–45 (2003) (Ginsburg, J., concurring).

19. 384 U.S. 436 (1966).

20. *Id.* at 489–90 (emphasis added).

21. *See* Calabresi, *"A Shining City on a Hill," supra* note 10.

22. Youngstown Sheet & Tube Co. v. Sawyer, 343 U.S. 579, 593–94 (1952) (Frankfurter, J., concurring).

23. *See* Kim Lane Scheppele, *Aspirational and Aversive Constitutionalism: The Case for Studying Cross-Constitutional Influence Through Negative Models*, 1 INT'L J. CONST. L. 296 (2003).

24. 149 U.S. 698 (1893).

25. *Id.* at 711.

26. *See id.* at 707–11.

27. 149 U.S. at 737 (Brewer, J., dissenting).

28. *Id.* at 757 (emphasis added) (Field, J., dissenting); *cf.* Shaughnessy v. United States *ex rel.* Mezei, 345 U.S. 206, 217–18 (1953) (Black, J., dissenting) (invoking a contrast with the dictatorial laws of Russia and Nazi Germany to argue against unreviewable executive discretion to imprison an alien).

29. Weems v. United States, 217 U.S. 349, 368–69, 377 (1910).

30. Trop v. Dulles, 356 U.S. 86, 102–03 (1958) (plurality opinion).

31. *Compare* Calabresi, *"A Shining City on a Hill," supra* note 10, at 1379–82, 1410–14 (arguing the case for American exceptionalism and invoking popular culture as reason to avoid foreign citation) and Roger P. Alford, *Free Speech and the Case for Constitutional Exceptionalism*, 106 MICH. L. REV. 1071, 1082–86 (2008) (book review) (suggesting that all constitutional systems are exceptional in ways that limit comparison) *with* Stephen Gardbaum, *The Myth and the Reality of American Constitutional Exceptionalism*, 107 MICH. L. REV. 391, 393–97 (2008) (arguing that although the U.S. Constitution is exceptional in its age, brevity, and the content of some of its rights, its structure of rights is "well within the contemporary constitutional mainstream") and Rosalind Dixon, *A Democratic Theory of Constitutional Comparison*, 56 AM. J. COMP. L. 947 (2008) (arguing for "dynamic-reflective" comparisons based on the likelihood of "co-evolution" of constitutional values in otherwise similar democracies).

32. *Compare, e.g.*, U.S. CONST. amends. VI ("In all criminal prosecutions, the accused shall enjoy the right to a speedy and public trial, by an impartial jury . . . ."), VIII (prohibiting "cruel and unusual punishments") *with e.g.*, CANADIAN CHARTER OF RIGHTS AND FREEDOMS, 1982, §§ 11 ("Any person charged with an offence has the right . . . to be tried within a

reasonable time . . . [and] to be presumed innocent until proven guilty according to law in a fair and public hearing by an independent and impartial tribunal"), 12 ("Everyone has the right not to be subjected to any cruel and unusual treatment or punishment").

33. *See* Gerald L. Neuman, *Human Rights and Constitutional Rights: Harmony and Dissonance,* 55 Stan. L. Rev. 1863, 1868 (2003).

34. Gary Jeffrey Jacobsohn, *The Permeability of Constitutional Borders,* 82 Tex. L. Rev. 1763, 1786–87 (2004).

35. Weems v. United States, 217 U.S. 349, 381 (1910) (emphasis added).

36. U.S. Const. pmbl. Justices with very different substantive views have invoked this aspiration toward justice in interpreting the Constitution. *See, e.g.,* John Paul Stevens, *Is Justice Irrelevant?,* 87 Nw. U. L. Rev. 1121, 1121–22 (1993); Stenberg v. Carhart, 530 U.S. 914, 953 (2000) (Scalia, J., dissenting).

37. *See, e.g.,* Dred Scott v. Sandford, 60 U.S. (19 How.) 393, 534 (1857) (McLean, J., dissenting) ("[N]o nation in Europe . . . considers itself bound to return to his master a fugitive slave . . . "); *see also* Sarah H. Cleveland, *Foreign Authority, American Exceptionalism, and the Dred Scott Case,* 82 Chi-Kent L. Rev. 393, 397 (2007) (showing that foreign authority was a "valued sounding board" for the Court on the slavery issue in antebellum period). Commentary on *Dred Scott* disagrees on whether the decision should be regarded as mistaken because it was immoral, or because it relied too much on "intentionalist" reasoning, or because it did a poor job of identifying original intentions; there is even disagreement whether it was a correct reading of the Constitution as it then stood (I believe it plainly was not). *See generally* Mark Graber, *Desperately Ducking Slavery: Dred Scott and Contemporary Constitutional Theory,* 14 Const. Comment. 271 (1997).

38. *See* Lochner v. New York, 198 U.S. 45, 71 (1905) (Harlan, J., dissenting) (comparing average work hours in the United States and abroad and referring to work hours as "a subject of serious consideration among civilized peoples" and among those with "special knowledge of the laws of health"). In the New York Court of Appeals, more explicit reference was made to British law. *See* People v. Lochner, 69 N.E. 373, 382, 384 (N.Y. 1904) (Vann, J., concurring) (noting that the New York statute regulating bakers' hours was modeled on but went beyond an 1863 British act, and discussing British and U.S. health data to support the conclusion that regulation was justified as a health measure), *rev'd,* Lochner v. New York, 198 U.S. 45 (1905).

39. Justice Antonin Scalia, *Keynote Address: Foreign Legal Authority in the Federal Courts,* (address to the Annual Meeting of the American Society of International Law, Washington D.C., 2004), 98 Am. Soc. Int'l L. Proc. 305, 307 (2004); *see also* David Fontana, *The Next Generation of Transnational/Domestic Constitutional Law Scholarship: A Reply to Professor Tushnet,* 38 Loy. L.A. L. Rev. 445, 463 (2004).

40. *See, e.g.,* Fong Yue Ting v. United States, 149 U.S. 698 (1893), discussed above in text. For a critical analysis of the case, see Cleveland, *supra* note 1, at 39–41.

41. *See, e.g.,* Goesaert v. Cleary, 335 U.S. 464 (1948); Bradwell v. Illinois, 83 U.S. 130 (1873).

42. *See* L. Michael Seidman, Our Unsettled Constitution: A New Defense of Constitutionalism and Judicial Review (2001).

43. Jan-Werner Müller, *A General Theory of Constitutional Patriotism,* 6 Int'l J. Const. L. 72, 76, 85 (2008) (arguing that constitutional patriotism should see "constitutional culture as always open and incomplete").

44. *Cf.* Ran Hirschl, *The Question of Case Selection in Comparative Constitutional Law,* 53 Am. J. Comp. L. 125, 129–31 (2005) (describing "concept thickening through multiple description" in comparative constitutional analyses).

45. It can be difficult to distinguish between "new developments" problems and unresolved "open issues"—what makes an issue "open," even if it has been decided before, has to do with "newer" understandings or developments.

46. Jacobson v. Massachusetts, 197 U.S. 11, 28 (1905) (treating foreign laws requiring mandatory vaccination as evidencing "the knowledge . . . common to all civilized peoples touching" the problem (smallpox) at issue).

47. 521 U.S. 702, 734 (1997) (noting Dutch government report concerning possible abuses of vulnerable persons in administering legalized euthanasia in that country); *cf. id.* at 718 n.16 (noting varying positions taken by different countries concerning euthanasia).

48. *Cf., e.g.,* Raines v. Byrd, 521 U.S. 811, 828 (1997) (rejecting congressional standing to challenge line item veto, while noting that "there would be nothing irrational" in allowing such standing as is the case in some European constitutional courts, but stating that this approach is not one "that has obtained under our Constitution to date").

49. *See, e.g.,* Eldred v. Ashcroft, 537 U.S. 186, 205–06 & n.13 (2003) (upholding the legitimacy of Congress's rationale for extending copyright terms to ensure that American authors would get the same term of protection as European authors, and quoting a law review article cautioning against an "isolationist" reading of the Copyright Clause).

50. 198 U.S. 45 (1905).

51. 208 U.S. 412 (1908).

52. 197 U.S. 11 (1905).

53. *Lochner* involved an 1897 New York law, invalidated in 1905; in *Muller,* a 1903 Oregon statute was upheld in 1908; in *Jacobson,* a new ordinance, enacted under authority of a 1902 state statute, was at issue and was upheld in 1905.

54. As readers will note, whether something appears as a problem to be regulated or is seen as a "natural" and unchanging condition of life is itself malleable.

55. 198 U.S. at 70–73 (Harlan, J., dissenting). The majority held otherwise, in an opinion that is regarded by many as one of the Court's great errors, applying a paradigm of "free labor" related to arguments to end slavery, but without an understanding of human liberty and contracting in the industrial age. *See* William E. Forbath, *The Ambiguities of Free Labor: Labor and the Law in the Gilded Age,* 1985 WIS. L. REV. 767, 773–82. For other accounts of *Lochner,* see HOWARD GILLMAN, THE CONSTITUTION BESIEGED 10, 126–28 (1993) (viewing the Court's decision as reflecting opposition to class-based legislation); David E. Bernstein, *Lochner Era Revisionism, Revised: Lochner and the Origins of Fundamental Rights Constitutionalism,* 92 GEO. L.J. 1, 58–60 (2003) (arguing that *Lochner* reflected an appreciation of the importance of fundamental rights).

56. *Muller,* 208 U.S. at 420–21. In *Jacobson,* as noted, the Court rejected a challenge to a state mandatory vaccination law, in which counsel had argued about the practice in foreign countries. *See, e.g.,* 197 U.S. at 15–16. Plainly the import of foreign practice mattered to the Court. *See, e.g., id.* at 28, 31 n.1 (referring to "the knowledge which . . . is common to all civilized peoples touching smallpox," discussing foreign laws, and reviewing medical literature).

57. Constitutional interpretations that rest on "empirical" assumptions, as in *Muller,* must be open to revision as those assumptions are challenged and normatively re-understood. The normative reversal of the assumed validity of gender differentiation in *Muller* would take many decades.

58. Kadish, *supra* note 11, at 328; *see also id.* at 348–49.

59. Wolf v. Colorado, 338 U.S. 25, 30 (1949), *overruled by* Mapp v. Ohio, 367 U.S. 643 (1961); *see also* Culombe v. Connecticut, 367 U.S. 568, 588–92 (1961) (Frankfurter, J., announcing the judgment of the Court) (discussing mixed foreign approaches to rules on exclusion of confessions made during custodial interrogation).

60. Stein v. New York, 346 U.S. 156, 200 (1953) (Frankfurter, J., dissenting) ("I cannot believe that these confessions, in view of the circumstances under which they were elicited, would be admitted in a criminal trial in England, or in the courts of Canada, Australia or India"); *see also Culombe v. Connecticut,* 367 U.S. at 581–87 & n.24 (Frankfurter, J., announcing the judgment of the Court) (relying on historic and contemporary legal materials from Commonwealth jurisdictions that condemn secret interrogations and use of the "third degree" and provide protections against their occurrence, and noting that "continental countries" that had used torture to produce confessions have abandoned it).

61. Miranda v. Arizona, 384 U.S. 436, 489 (1966) ("Conditions of law enforcement in our country are sufficiently similar to permit reference to this experience as assurance that lawlessness will not result from warning an individual of his rights or allowing him to exercise them.").

62. *Id.* at 483.

63. *See, e.g.,* California v. Minjares, 443 U.S. 916, 919 (1979) (Rehnquist, J., dissenting from denial of stay) (referring to "comparative law" in questioning the Fourth Amendment exclusionary rule); Schriro v. Summerlin, 542 U.S. 348, 356 (2004) ("[T]he mixed reception that the right to jury trial has been given in other countries, . . . though irrelevant to the meaning and continued existence of that right under our Constitution, surely makes it implausible that judicial factfinding so '*seriously* diminishe[s]' accuracy as to produce an "'impermissibly large risk'" of injustice.") (citation omitted). Whether retroactivity doctrine is itself a form of constitutional law is a complex question. *See generally* Richard H. Fallon, Jr. & Daniel J. Meltzer, *New Law, Non-retroactivity and Constitutional Remedies,* 104 HARV. L. REV. 1733 (1991).

64. *See* Youngstown Sheet & Tube Co. v. Sawyer, 343 U.S. 579, 634 (1952) (Jackson, J., concurring) ("Just what our forefathers . . . would have envisioned had they foreseen modern conditions, must be divined from materials almost as enigmatic as the dreams Joseph was called upon to interpret for Pharaoh.").

65. *Id.* at 652.

66. *See, e.g.,* Banco Nacional de Cuba v. Sabbatino, 376 U.S. 398, 440 (1964) (White, J. dissenting). The Court held that in litigation involving title to property nationalized by the Cuban government, the U.S. courts were barred, by the act of state doctrine, from examining the validity of such expropriations under international law. Dissenting, Justice White invoked the law in several other democratic countries—including England, Netherlands, Germany, Japan, Italy, and France—to support his argument that: "No other civilized country has found such a rigid rule necessary for the survival of the executive branch of its government; the executive of no other government seems to require such insulation from international law adjudications in its courts; and no other judiciary is apparently so incompetent to ascertain and apply international law." *Id.*

67. *See, e.g.,* Holmes v. Jennison, 39 U.S. (14 Pet.) 540, 561, 569–72 (1840) (4-4 split) (Taney, C.J., opinion for four justices) (concluding, in light of the practice of nations, that the federal treaty power precludes a state governor from deciding to extradite a fugitive to Canada); Worcestor v. Georgia, 31 U.S. (6 Pet.) 515, 560–61 (1832) (relying on the law of nations to help determine Indian tribes' status); Gibbons v. Ogden, 22 U.S. (9 Wheat.) 1, 227 (1824) (Johnson, J., concurring) (referring to the law of nations in discussing the exclusivity of federal power over interstate commerce).

68. Wickard v. Filburn, 317 U.S. 111, 125–26 & n.27 (1942).

69. *Id.* at 126 n.27.

70. Printz v. United States, 521 U.S. 898 (1997).

71. *Id.* at 921 n.11 (Scalia, J., for the Court); *see id.* at 976–77 (Breyer, J., dissenting).

72. Mark Tushnet, *The Possibilities of Comparative Constitutional Law*, 108 YALE L.J. 1225, 1238–39, 1266–69 (1999); *see also* Kadish, *supra* note 11, at 355–56.

73. *See* Daniel Halberstam, *Comparative Federalism and the Issue of Commandeering*, *in* THE FEDERAL VISION: LEGITIMACY AND LEVELS OF GOVERNANCE IN THE UNITED STATES AND THE EUROPEAN UNION (Kalypso Nicolaides & Robert Howse eds., 2001). For further discussion, see Chapter 8, below.

74. U.S. CONST. art. I, § 8; *see also* Cleveland, *supra* note 1, at 36. One might regard this form of reasoning as an act of "translation," *see* Lawrence Lessig, *Fidelity in Translation*, 71 TEX. L. REV. 1165 (1993), or simply as a sensible understanding of the purpose of a constitution, one that must have been intended from the nature of the constitutional endeavor. *See generally* CHARLES L. BLACK, JR., STRUCTURE AND RELATIONSHIP IN CONSTITUTIONAL LAW (1969).

75. *Cf., e.g.*, David M. Golove, *Treaty-Making and the Nation: The Historical Foundations of the Nationalist Conception of the Treaty Power*, 98 MICH. L. REV. 1075, 1089–90 (2000) (discussing the treaty power as extending to "any subject appropriate for negotiation and agreement among states").

76. *See* United States v. Arjona, 120 U.S. 479, 485–86 (1887) (noting that the world economy had changed to rely more on the liquidity of public debt instruments, and concluding that the scope of Congress's power to define offenses against the law of nations should likewise extend to the forgery of such instruments, as it did in Vattel's time to forgery of public coin or bank remittances). For further discussion, see Chapter 6, below text at notes 25–27.

77. *See, e.g.*, John O. McGinnis, *"Outsourcing Authority?" Citation to Foreign Court Precedent in Domestic Jurisprudence: Contemporary Foreign and International Law in Constitutional Construction*, 69 ALB. L. REV. 801, 803–04 & n.2 (2006); Michael D. Ramsey, *Agora: The United States Constitution and International Law: International Materials and Domestic Rights: Reflections on Atkins and Lawrence*, 98 AM. J. INT'L L. 69, 71 (2004); *see also* Ronald Turner, *The Juvenile Death Penalty and the Court's Consensus-Plus Eighth Amendment*, 17 GEO. MASON U. CIV. RTS. L.J. 157, 195 n.240 (2006); Jackson, *Constitutional Comparisons*, *supra* note 1, at 118-19.

78. On the role of "informational, cognitive, and attitudinal blinders" in judging, see Chris Guthrie, *Misjudging*, 7 NEV. L.J. 420 (2007). Guthrie's critique assumes that each of these "blinders" increases the risk of misjudging, a claim that depends on the knowability of right answers. The existence of single right answers in constitutional law is often contestable, which makes it more difficult to identify what we might mean by "misjudging" in this arena.

79. 478 U.S. 186, 196 (1986) (Burger, C.J., concurring) (asserting that homosexual conduct has "been subject to state intervention throughout the history of Western civilization"). *Bowers* was overruled in Lawrence v. Texas, 539 U.S. 558 (2003).

80. *Lawrence*, 539 U.S. at 573 (referring to the ECtHR's decision in Dudgeon v. United Kingdom, 45 Eur. Ct. H.R. (ser. A) (1981)).

81. On the difficulties of judges' ignoring what they know in making decisions, see Guthrie, *Misjudging*, *supra* note 78; Andrew J. Wistrich, Chris Guthrie & Jeffrey J. Rachlinski, *Can Judges Ignore Inadmissible Information? The Difficulty of Deliberately Disregarding*, 153 U. PA. L. REV. 1251, 1264–65 (2005) (discussing the problem of "mental contamination" that can "operate outside of conscious thought"). For an introduction to the literature on cognitive bias and judicial error, see Chris Guthrie, Jeffrey J. Rachlinski & Andrew J. Wistrich, *Inside the Judicial Mind*, 86 CORNELL L. REV. 777 (2001).

82. For Justice Scalia's light-hearted proposal to Justice Breyer to "go ahead and indulge your curiosity" by reading foreign constitutional law, but "[j]ust don't put it in

your opinions!," see Norman Dorsen, ed., *A Conversation Between U.S. Supreme Court Justices—The Relevance of Foreign Legal Materials in U.S. Constitutional Cases: A Conversation Between Justice Antonin Scalia and Justice Stephen Breyer*, 3 INT'L J. CONST. L. 519, 534 (2005).

83. *See* David Shapiro, *In Defense of Judicial Candor*, 100 HARV. L. REV. 731 (1987).

84. *But cf.* MITCHEL DE S.-O.-L'E. LASSER, JUDICIAL DELIBERATIONS: A COMPARATIVE ANALYSIS OF JUDICIAL TRANSPARENCY AND LEGITIMACY (2004) (suggesting that the common law approach of public reason-giving in judicial opinions is only one path to legitimacy and that the French system of more cryptic reasoning in brief opinions nested in a bifurcated but institutionalized set of legal discourses that support and explain the decisions is an alternative). For discussion of "prudential silence," see Chapter 6, below.

85. H. Jefferson Powell, *Rules for Originalists*, 73 VA. L. REV. 659, 695 (1987).

86. *See* Michael Kirby, *Think Globally*, 4 GREEN BAG 2D 287, 291 (2001) (Australian High Court Justice arguing the benefit of looking to foreign decisions "to stimulate [the] mind with analogous reasoning"); *see also* Hirschl, *supra* note 44, at 129–30.

87. *See, e.g.*, Geoffrey R. Stone, *A Narrow View of the Law*, CHICAGO TRIBUNE, Feb. 6, 2007, at A17 (praising dissent and separate opinions and arguing that "[t]he tradition of free and open judicial debate historically has led the Court to better results over time").

88. *See* Jennifer Nedelsky, *Communities of Judgment and Human Rights*, 1 THEORETICAL INQ. LAW 245, 280 (2000) (describing connections between striving for impartiality of judgment and an "enlarged mentality," which may include consideration of "the common sense of mankind").

89. For example, the rapporteur of a matter before or likely to come to the French Conseil Constitutionnel may gather views from a wide variety of sources and may do so on an ex parte basis. *See* JOHN BELL, FRENCH CONSTITUTIONAL LAW 41–56 (1992).

90. *See* ABA Model Code of Judicial Conduct Canon 2, Rule 2.9 & cmt. (2007) (prohibiting ex parte communications, including with law teachers or other experts, absent notice to parties and opportunity to comment).

91. *See generally* Chris Guthrie, Jeffrey J. Rachlinski, & Andrew J. Wistrich, *Blinking on the Bench: How Judges Decide Cases*, 93 CORNELL L. REV. 1, 5 (2007) (developing a new model of judging, involving both intuition and a cultivated ability to override intuition through deliberation, because "intuition is generally more likely than deliberation to lead judges astray").

92. *See* Jennifer Nedelsky, *Communities of Judgment and Human Rights* 25 (Feb. 2, 2004) (unpublished manuscript) (noting that communities of judging help "mitigate the effect of [a judge's] own idiosyncrasies"), *quoted in* Jackson, *Constitutional Comparisons*, *supra* note 1, at 119 n.51.

93. Aharon Barak, *Comparison in Public Law*, *in* JUDICIAL RECOURSE TO FOREIGN LAW: A NEW SOURCE OF INSPIRATION? 287, 288 (Sir Basil Markesinis & Jörg Fedtke eds., 2006).

94. Gil Carlos Rodriguez Iglesias, *The Judge Confronts Himself as Judge*, *in* JUDGES IN CONTEMPORARY DEMOCRACY: AN INTERNATIONAL CONVERSATION 275, 277 (Robert Badinter & Stephen Breyer eds., 2004) (emphasis omitted).

95. Gerald L. Neuman, *The Uses of International Law in Constitutional Interpretation*, 98 AM. J. INT'L L. 82, 88 (2004).

96. Aharon Barak, *Foreword: A Judge on Judging: The Role of a Supreme Court in a Democracy*, 116 HARV. L. REV. 16, 23–24 (2002).

97. *See, e.g.*, Robert C. Post & Reva B. Siegel, *Legislative Constitutionalism and Section Five Power: Policentric Interpretation of the Family and Medical Leave Act*, 112 YALE L.J. 1943 (2003); Robert Post & Reva Siegel, *Originalism as a Political Practice: The Right's Living*

Constitution, 75 FORDHAM L. REV. 545 (2006); Reva B. Siegel, *Constitutional Culture, Social Conflict and Constitutional Change: The Case of the de facto ERA*, 94 CALIF. L. REV. 1323 (2006); Mark Tushnet, *Constitutional Hardball*, 37 J. MARSHALL L. REV. 523 (2004); *see also* Larry Kramer, *Generating Constitutional Meaning*, 94 CALIF. L. REV. 1439 (2006).

98. *Cf.* Allen Buchanan, *Human Rights and the Legitimacy of the International Order*, 14 LEGAL THEORY 39, 61–62 (2008) (discussing the need for institutions of human rights definition and enforcement to develop factfinding mechanisms and other "epistemic institutional virtues").

99. H. PATRICK GLENN, LEGAL TRADITIONS OF THE WORLD 22 (2000).

100. *See* H. Patrick Glenn, *Persuasive Authority*, 32 MCGILL L.J. 261 (1987); *see also* MARY ANN GLENDON, ABORTION AND DIVORCE IN WESTERN LAW (1987).

101. On the role of learning and reflexivity in constitutionalism and constitution-making, compare ANDREW ARATO, CIVIL SOCIETY, CONSTITUTION AND LEGITIMACY 254–55 (2000) (acknowledging the role of reflexive learning in constitutional processes but suggesting "the possibility of too much learning," because a degree of finality is necessary in constitutionalism) with ULRICH K. PREUSS, CONSTITUTIONAL REVOLUTION: THE LINK BETWEEN CONSTITUTIONALISM AND PROGRESS 115, 123–25 (1995) (arguing for "morally reflexive constitutionalism"; urging that learning and reflexivity are essential to constitutional processes and that a society that "makes itself an experiment," "open to change," improves its cognitive and moral competence to govern itself). For related discussion, see Michael C. Dorf & Charles F. Sabel, *A Constitution of Democratic Experimentalism*, 98 COLUM. L. REV. 267, 290 (1998).

102. Frank I. Michelman, *Reflection*, 82 TEX. L. REV. 1737, 1758 (2004); *see* George P. Fletcher, *Comparative Law as a Subversive Discipline*, 46 AM. J. COMP. L. 683, 695 (1998) (discussing comparative law as a "unique opportunity to generate critical, subversive self-reflections about American law"); *cf.* Paul W. Kahn, *Comparative Constitutionalism in a New Key*, 101 MICH. L. REV. 2677, 2679 (2003) (arguing that "the unnoticed in our practices may become visible in the contrast with other cultural practices of law" and "can help us to understand who we are," but "cannot . . . tell us whether we should remain what we have been").

103. *Compare, e.g.*, Australian Communist Party v. Commonwealth (1951) 83 C.L.R. 1 (Austl.) (invalidating as ultra vires the national defense power a statute banning the Communist Party), *with* Dennis v. United States, 341 U.S. 494 (1951) (upholding the Smith Act under which Communist Party leaders were prosecuted and rejecting a First Amendment challenge to the application of the statute to their activities organizing the Communist Party and advocating its doctrine).

104. Kadish, *supra* note 11, at 354; *see id.* at 354–57.

105. U.S. CONST. pmbl.; *cf.* U.S. CONST. amend. IX (enumeration of rights should not be construed to deny others); amend. XI (judicial power not to be construed to extend to certain suits against states).

106. Knight v. Florida, 528 U.S. 990, 996 (Breyer, J., dissenting from denial of certiorari) (citing Catholic Commission for Justice and Peace in Zimbabwe v. Attorney-General, [1993] 1 Zimb. L. R. 239, 240, 269 (S) (Aug. 4, 1999)); *see A Conversation Between U.S. Supreme Court Justices*, *supra* note 82, at 528 (quoting Breyer as explaining that, although he may have made a "tactical error in citing a case from Zimbabwe—not the human rights capital of the world," the cited decision was an interesting one, from "an earlier time" and by "Judge Gubbay . . . a very good judge").

107. Statutory approaches could (and do) seek to assure compliance. *See, e.g.*, 18 U.S.C. §§ 2340–2340A (codifying the Torture Convention Implementation Act of 1994). Yet with

a Constitution committed to "due process of law," and protection against such arbitrary action as "cruel and unusual" punishments, it would be surprising for the interpretation of such clauses not to be at least open to influence by those norms that international law deems so fundamental to civilized humanity as to permit international criminal prosecutions for their breach. *Cf.* David Golove, The Case for Incorporating Global Justice into the U.S. Constitution, at 50, 54–56 (unpublished paper, September 2008) (on file with author) (arguing that "a 'legitimate' or 'civilized' conduct standard" has a deep "pedigree in U.S. constitutional history" and suggesting that some, but not all, aspects of international law, including *jus cogens* principles, are among the "fundamental moral requirements of global justice" that should be incorporated); John. R. Crook, *Contemporary Practice of the United States Relating to International Law,* 102 AM. J. INT'L L. 359 (2008) (reporting comments by UN High Commissioner for Human Rights on universal jurisdiction and practice of waterboarding of U.S. detainees). On possible harms to U.S. interests from perceptions of indifference to such requirements, see *infra* text at notes 134–37.

108. *Cf.* David Held, *What Hope for the Future? Learning the Lessons of the Past,* 9 IND. J. GLOBAL LEGAL STUD. 381 (2002).

109. *Cf.* Thomas H. Lee, *The Supreme Court of the United States as Quasi-International Tribunal: Reclaiming the Court's Original and Exclusive Jurisdiction Over Treaty-Based Suits by Foreign States Against States,* 104 COLUM. L. REV. 1765, 1768–75 (2004) (arguing that the Court has exclusive jurisdiction over treaty-based claims by foreign states against U.S states).

110. *See, e.g.,* Clark v. Martinez, 543 U.S. 371 (2004); Denmore v. Hyung Joon Kim, 538 U.S. 510 (2003); Zadvydas v. Davis, 533 U.S. 678 (2001); INS v. St. Cyr, 533 U.S. 289 (2001).

111. *See* Medellín v. Texas, 128 S. Ct. 1346 (2008) (Mexico); Medellín v. Dretke, 544 U.S. 660 (2005) (Mexico); Breard v. Greene, 523 U.S. 371 (1998) (Paraguay); Federal Republic of Germany v. United States, 526 U.S. 111 (1999) (denying leave to file original bill of complaint); *see also* Torres v. Mullin, 540 U.S. 1035 (2003) (Stevens, J., respecting the denial of certiorari); *id.* at 1037 (Breyer, J., dissenting from denial of certiorari). For further discussion of cases relating to the Vienna Convention on Consular Relations, Apr. 24, 1963, 596 U.N.T.S. 261, see Chapter 6, below.

112. *See* Boumediene v. Bush, 128 S. Ct. 2229 (2008); Hamdan v. Rumsfeld, 548 U.S. 557 (2006); Rasul v. Bush, 542 U.S. 466 (2004); *see also, e.g.,* Arar v. Ashcroft, 532 F. 3d 157 (2d Cir. 2008).

113. *See, e.g.,* Brief of Amici Curiae Specialists in Israeli Military Law and Constitutional Law in Support of Petitioners at 1, Boumediene v. Bush, 128 S. Ct. 2229 (2008) (Nos. 06-1195, 06-1196) (asserting, inter alia, that "in an interdependent world threatened by transnational terrorism and linked by converging rule-of-law norms, all peoples are affected by the process the United States affords to foreign nationals who fall under its control . . . [and thus] Israel has a vital stake in assuring that the United States pursues its struggle against terrorism successfully within the bounds of the law"); Amicus Brief of Canadian Paliamentarians and Professors of Law in Support of Petitioners, Boumediene v. Bush, 128 S. Ct. 2229 (2008) (Nos. 06-1195, 06-1196) (noting that one detainee is a Canadian citizen); *see also infra* note 116; *cf.* Canada (Justice) v. Khadr, 2008 Can. Sup. Ct. LEXIS 32 ¶¶ 3, 18–25, 31 (discussing application of Canadian Charter to Canadian officials who participated in interrogating a Canadian citizen detained at Guantánamo, and (drawing inferences from U.S. Supreme Court decisions involving other detainees) in so doing violated Canada's international human rights obligations).

114. *See, e.g.,* Sosa v. Alvaraz-Machain, 542 U.S. 692 (2004); United States v. Alvarez-Machain, 504 U.S. 655 (1992).

115. The Court's rules permit amicus filings, see SUP. CT. R. 37, which might imply that the Court would at least consider filings proper under the rule. (Presumably if the Court considers briefs that make apposite arguments, it will in some way respond by taking those into account.) Although there are reasons to distinguish between parties and amici, an amicus brief duly filed under the Court's rules is presumptively entitled to some degree of consideration if only as a part of the matter properly before it.

116. *See, e.g.*, Amicus Brief of Canadian Parliamentarians and Professors of Law at 2, Boumediene v. Bush, 128 S. Ct. 2229 (2008) (Nos. 06-1195, 06-1196) ("How this Court construes the obligations of the United States in relation to the treatment and prosecution of alien detainees in an inchoate and potentially indefinite campaign against terrorism will affect how other nations understand their own, identical obligations in this campaign and in future conflicts."); Brief of Equality Now and Others as Amici Curiae in Support of Petitioners at 2, Nguyen v. INS, 533 U.S. 53 (2001) (No. 99-2071) (arguing, on behalf of amici including the Argentine Ass'n of Women Judges, the Ethiopian Women Lawyers Ass'n, the Forum for Women, Law & Development (Nepal), the International Comm'n of Jurists, the International Federation of Women Jurists, Latin American and Carribean Comm. for the Defense of Women's Rights, and Women in Law and Development in Africa, that the Court should consider international approaches to gender discrimination in citizenship in part because of how influential the U.S. Court's views will be); *see also supra* note 113. This amici traffic is not one-way. *See, e.g.*, Tysiąc v. Poland, App. No. 5410/03, Eur. Ct. H.R., ¶¶ 86–90 (Mar. 20, 2007), *available at* http://www.echr.coe.int/echr (describing arguments made by amicus the Center for Constitutional Rights); Chapter 2, above, at page 68 (noting the Italian Senate's participation in a Canadian constitutional case).

117. *Cf.* Al-Kateb v. Godwin (2004) 219 C.L.R. 562, 622 (Austl.) (Kirby, J., dissenting) (arguing that "domestic courts, when deciding cases to which international law is relevant, are exercising a form of international jurisdiction" and are speaking to the international community).

118. T. Alexander Aleinikoff, *Transnational Spaces: Norms and Legitimacy*, 33 YALE J. INT'L L. 479, 487 (2008).

119. *Cf.* RESTATEMENT (THIRD) OF THE FOREIGN RELATIONS LAW OF THE UNITED STATES §102 (1987) (describing the sources of international law, including customary law, which "results from a general and consistent practice of states followed by them from a sense of legal obligation," and rules derived from "general principles common to the major legal systems of the world").

120. Although the influence of the U.S. Court may be waning in relative terms, *see* Adam Liptak, *U.S. Court, a Longtime Beacon, Is Now Guiding Fewer Nations*, N.Y. TIMES, Sept. 18, 2008, at A1, it is still influential and is one of a fairly small number of domestic supreme courts the decisions of which are read widely abroad. *See also* note 132, *infra*.

121. *Cf.* CHRISTOPHER L. EISGRUBER, CONSTITUTIONAL SELF-GOVERNMENT 60 (2001) (arguing that having to give a public account of the reasons for a decision is a special feature of judging).

122. *See, e.g.*, Curtis A. Bradley & Jack L. Goldsmith, *Customary International Law As Federal Common Law: A Critique of the Modern Position*, 110 HARV. L. REV. 815, 838–42 (1997) (also noting move away from reliance on actual state practices, rather than official positions, in defining the content of customary international law).

123. 548 U.S. 331 (2006).

124. *See id.* at 357–59 (discussing importance in U.S. system of parties timely raising objections, even on constitutional grounds); *id.* at 350 (explaining that suppression is "not the

only means of vindicating Vienna Convention rights," which may be raised "as part of a broader challenge" to the voluntariness of statements given); *see also id.* at 360–65 (Ginsburg, J., concurring) (agreeing that neither of the defendants was entitled to relief and noting other aspects of U.S. law that enabled "full effect" to be given to the treaty rights). Mexico, whose national was one of the defendants, and other foreign governments filed amicus briefs arguing that the United States should give effect to the ICJ's treaty interpretation in order to fulfill the Consular Convention's purpose of protecting foreign nationals in unfamiliar criminal processes, and that state procedural rules should not be allowed to place the United States in breach of its international obligations. *See* Brief Amicus Curiae of the Government of the United Mexican States In Support of Moises Sanchez-Llamas, Sanchez-Llamas v. Oregon, 548 U.S. 331 (2006) (No. 04-10566); *see also* Brief for Amici Curiae Republic of Honduras and Other Foreign Sovereigns in Support of Petitioners, Sanchez-Llamas v. Oregon, 548 U.S. 331 (2006) (Nos. 04-10566, 05-51).

125. *See* Aleinikoff, *Transnational Spaces, supra* note 118, at 481 ("Although he states that the Supreme Court owes 'consideration' to the ICJ judgment, the Chief Justice acts to the contrary. He lectures the ICJ on fundamentals of the U.S. adversary system and considers not the ICJ's reasoning but rather the ways in which the ICJ is an inappropriate body for rendering an opinion on the matter before the U.S. high court."). Dean Aleinikoff praises Justice Breyer's dissenting opinion as more responsive and accommodating to the reasoning of the ICJ. *See id.* at 482; *see also Sanchez-Llamas*, 548 U.S. at 378–92 (Breyer, J., dissenting) (treating the ICJ judgment as a form of persuasive authority, having weight on the question whether the Convention "sometimes prohibit[s] a state court from applying its ordinarily procedural default rule to a Convention violation claim," and seeking through interpretation to narrow the differences between the ICJ's view of the Convention's requirements and domestic procedural default rules).

126. *See, e.g.*, T. Alexander Aleinikoff, *Constitutional Law in the Age of Balancing*, 96 Yale L.J. 943, 977 (1987) (cautioning about the impossibility of a "full inventory" of consequences that balancing analysis seems to contemplate); *cf.* Lon L. Fuller, *The Forms and Limits of Adjudication*, 92 Harv. L. Rev. 353 (1978) (cautioning that the judicial process was suited to resolving essentially two-sided, limited disputes and not to resolving "polycentric" problems with effects across varied interests).

127. For a discussion illustrating the difficulties of an approach that considers the effects of U.S. law on those in other countries, see, for example, Eric A Posner, *Boumediene and the Uncertain March of Judicial Cosmopolitanism*, 2008 Cato Sup. Ct. Rev. 23, 45.

128. The United States does not have the visible presence and impact of an uncertain new polity, the European Union or "Europe," looming over its daily existence in the way that Neal Walker describes in Europe, where "post-state constitutional polities and processes . . . come to claim . . . normative authority independent of . . . the historical state," but require "metaconstitutional justification"—a continued reflection on the legitimacy of their own decision-making leading to ongoing "negotiations" of constitutional authority and legitimacy with the established national states. Neil Walker, *The Idea of Constitutional Pluralism*, 65 Modern L. Rev. 317, 356–57 (2002).

129. For an updated critique of international law based on "realist" premises, see Jack Goldsmith & Eric Posner, The Limits of International Law (2005).

130. *See* Neuman, *Uses of International Law, supra* note 95, at 87 (suggesting that countries have a stake in foreign public law because citizens may travel and find themselves subject to the laws of foreign countries, perhaps to a greater degree than in the past).

131. For thoughtful discussion, see Paul Stephan, *A Becoming Modesty—U.S. Litigation In the Mirror of International Law*, 52 DePaul L. Rev. 627 (2002); *see also* Chapter 9, below.

132. *See* Noah Feldman, *When Judges Make Foreign Policy*, N.Y. TIMES, Sept. 28, 2008 (Magazine), at 50 (arguing that the Court should engage with transnational law to advance U.S. legal views and interests and that whatever the Court does, it is "unavoidably involved"); *cf.* Claire L'Heureux-Dubé, *The Importance of Dialogue: Globalization and the International Impact of the Rehnquist Court*, 34 TULSA L.J. 15, 37–38 (1998) (suggesting that one reason for the relative decline in influence of the U.S. Supreme Court among other countries of the world is the Court's failure to participate in transnational judicial dialogue). For analysis from an "international relations" perspective, see Ken I. Kersch, *The Supreme Court and International Relations Theory*, 69 ALB. L. REV. 771 (2006).

133. *See* Stephan, *supra* note 131, at 630 (noting the possibility that "actions of U.S. judges, rather than prompting reform elsewhere in the world, might invite hostility and retaliation"); *cf.* Banco Nacional de Cuba v. Sabbatino, 376 U.S. 398, 434–35 (1964) (questioning "the sanguine presupposition that the decisions of the courts of the world's major capital exporting country and principal exponent of the free enterprise system would be accepted as disinterested expressions of sound legal principle by those adhering to widely different ideologies"). A national court's explanation of its own jurisprudence may nonetheless be helpful to foreign readers in understanding why a country's jurisprudence is as it is.

134. Sandra Day O'Connor, Remarks at the Southern Center for International Studies 1–2 (Oct. 28, 2003), *available at* http://www.southerncenter.org/OConnor_transcript.pdf ("The impressions we create in this world are important and can leave their mark. . . . I suspect that with time, we will rely increasingly on international and foreign law in resolving . . . domestic issues. . . . [This] may not only enrich our own country's decisions; it will create that all-important good impression."); *see also* Aleinikoff, *Transnational Spaces*, *supra* note 118, at 485 (arguing that "states generally seek to be 'good citizens' . . . [with] a responsibility to the system as a whole").

135. Given the U.S. history of proselytizing its own constitutional system, there is some danger of judicial silence regarding apposite transnational legal sources being read as a manifestation of arrogance, or assumed superiority. To avoid this, Justice O'Connor can be understood to say, it would not hurt to acknowledge alternative approaches and (possibly) learn something from them.

136. *See* Dan Eggen, *Dutch Citizen Pleads Not Guilty to Terrorism Charges; Man Accused in Iraq Bombings Is First Alleged Insurgent Prosecuted in U.S. Criminal Courts*, WASH. POST, Jan. 30, 2007, at A04 (reporting on the extradition of a Dutch national charged with several crimes in the first U.S. prosecution of an alleged Iraqi insurgent). According to Eggen, the agreement resulted from two years of negotiations; it provided for the defendant being tried in a regular civilian court and that the courts of the Netherlands could "review and possibly modify the terms of any U.S. sentence once [the defendant] is returned home. . . ." The defendant's attorney is described as explaining that these terms "were necessary because the U.S. government no longer can be trusted to treat prisoners humanely." The article quotes Carl Tobias, a law professor at the University of Richmond, as saying that he had "'never heard'" of an agreement for a federal court's judgment to be "'subjected to a tribunal from another jurisdiction,'" but also stating that "'maybe the U.S. had to take what it could get from the Netherlands.'"

137. *See, e.g.*, Soering v. United Kingdom, 161 Eur. Ct. H.R. (ser. A) (1989) (refusing extradition to the United States unless Britain received assurances that the death penalty would not be imposed); John F. Burns, *Extremist Cleric in Britain Moves Closer to US Trial*, N.Y. TIMES, July 24, 2008, at A10 (reporting that suspected terrorist al-Masri is threatening to go to the European Court of Human Rights to prevent extradition to the United States

because he does not trust U.S. assurances that he will not be sentenced to death); *see also supra* note 136.

138. Finzer v. Barry, 798 F.2d 1450 (D.C. Cir. 1986) (Bork, J.) (emphasis added), *aff'd in part, rev'd in part,* Boos v. Barry, 485 U.S. 312 (1988). Judge Bork would have upheld, against a First Amendment challenge, a law prohibiting demonstrations within 500 feet of embassies, in part on the grounds that securing compliance with the law of nations was a compelling government purpose. *Id.* at 1458–62. The Supreme Court did not decide whether meeting international obligations could ever require "adjust[ment]" of First Amendment analysis, because the statute was in any event not narrowly tailored. 485 U.S. at 324. Chief Justice Rehnquist, joined by Justices White and Blackmun, dissented in part, agreeing with the Bork judgment below. *Id.* at 338–39 (Rehnquist, C.J., dissenting).

139. Boos v. Barry, 485 U.S. at 323; *cf.* Banco Nacional de Cuba v. Sabbatino, 376 U.S. 398, 437 (1964) (suggesting that "both the national interest and progress toward the goal of establishing the rule of law among nations are best served by" refusing to adjudicate the legality under international law of a foreign expropriation of property under the act of state doctrine).

140. For a fascinating account of an earlier period of contest between civil liberties and national security, see John Fabian Witt, *Crystal Eastman and the Internationalist Beginnings of American Civil Liberties,* 54 DUKE. L. J. 705 (2004).

141. *See* Mayo Moran, *Inimical to Constitutional Values: Complex Migrations of Constitutional Rights, in* The MIGRATION OF CONSTITUTIONAL IDEAS 233, 239–40, 249–51 (Sujit Choudhry ed., 2006) (arguing that it is not constitutional rights but constitutional values that exert influence on common law and private law areas, and that their arena of influence "operate[s] in the relatively open-textured processes of deliberation and justification," disaggregating the influential force and binding effect of law); Mayo Moran, *Shifting Boundaries: The Authority of International Law, in* NEW PERSPECTIVES ON THE DIVIDE BETWEEN NATIONAL AND INTERNATIONAL LAW 166–74, 179–83 (Janne Nijman & André Nollkaemper eds., 2007) (noting "the mandatory influence of certain legal values" which must be considered though they are not binding); Mayo Moran, *Authority, Influence and Persuasion: Baker, Charter Values and the Puzzle of Method, in* THE UNITY OF PUBLIC LAW 357–414 (David Dyzenhaus ed., 2004) (exploring the influence of the values of ratified but not implemented treaties in Canada and Australia).

142. *Cf.* Paul Schiff Berman, *A Pluralist Approach to International Law,* 32 YALE J. INT'L L. 301 (2007) (emphasizing the jurisgenerativity of the multiple processes of interactions by which legal norms are produced).

143. *See* MARY SARAH BILDER, THE TRANSATLANTIC CONSTITUTION: COLONIAL LEGAL CULTURE AND THE EMPIRE 186–96 (2004) (tracing continued influence of the "transatlantic legal culture" on post-independence America, including on the development of judicial review); *see also* LYNN HUNT, INVENTING HUMAN RIGHTS: A HISTORY 116–26, 160–61 (2007); Judith Resnik, *Law's Migration: American Exceptionalism, Silent Dialogues and Multiple Ports of Entry,* 115 YALE L.J. 1564 (2006); Judith Resnik, *Foreign as Domestic Affairs: Rethinking Horizontal Federalism and Foreign Affairs Preemption In Light of Translocal Internationalism,* 57 EMORY L. J. 31 (2007).

144. *See* U.S. DEPARTMENT OF DEFENSE, THE NATIONAL DEFENSE STRATEGY OF THE UNITED STATES OF AMERICA (March 2005) ("Our strength as a nation state will continue to be challenged by those who employ a strategy of the weak using international fora, judicial processes, and terrorism.").

145. For helpful discussion of constitutional pluralism focused on Europe, see Walker, *supra* note 128; *see also* Sally Engle Merry, *Legal Pluralism,* 22 LAW & SOC'Y REV. 869 (1988).

146. David Held, *Globalization: The Dangers and the Answers, in* DEBATING GLOBALIZATION at 1 (2005) (quoting Immanuel Kant).

147. *See* Jenny S. Martinez, *Towards an International Judicial System*, 56 STAN. L. REV. 429 (2003); Robert B. Ahdieh, *Between Dialogue and Decree: International Review of National Courts*, 79 N.Y.U. L. REV. 2029, 2034 (2004) (characterizing the relationship of NAFTA tribunals and domestic law as a form of "dialectical review," situated between appellate review and merely persuasive authority); Ernest A. Young, *Institutional Settlement in a Globalizing Judicial System*, 54 DUKE L.J. 1143 (2005) (urging use of doctrines of exhaustion and deference to national judgments as devices to mediate conflicts); *cf.* Paul Schiff Berman, *Towards a Cosmopolitan Vision of Conflict of Laws: Redefining Governmental Interests in a Global Era*, 153 U. PA. L. REV. 1819, 1880–81 (2005) (emphasizing the benefits of managing, rather than eliminating, "hybridity," and favoring contextual analyses over hierarchical rules, giving some weight to the independent value of enforcing foreign judgments as well as to the parties' affiliations).

148. WILLIAM TWINING, GLOBALISATION AND LEGAL THEORY 51 (2000).

149. *Id.* at 52; *see also* Gunther Teubner, *'Global Bukowina': Legal Pluralism in the World Society, in* GLOBAL LAW WITHOUT A STATE (Gunther Teubner ed., 1997).

150. Teubner, *'Global Bukowina,' supra* note 149, at 3–4. *But cf.* David Schneiderman, *Investment Rules and the New Constitutionalism*, 25 LAW & SOC. INQUIRY 757, 757–58 (2000) (arguing that Teubner has missed the degree to which states have constructed the international legal regime for commercial relations).

151. *See* PHILIP BOBBITT, THE SHIELD OF ACHILLES: WAR, PEACE AND THE COURSE OF HISTORY (2002) (arguing that in conjunction with such developments states are shifting to a conception of "market state" to facilitate favorable economic growth and individual market choices, without seeking as a government to assure the well-being of their people); Schneiderman, *supra* note 150, at 758–59 (arguing that the "new constitutionalism" may entail capture of states by transnational business interests).

152. *See* North American Free Trade Agreement, U.S.-Can.-Mex., ch. 11, Dec. 17, 1992, U.S.-Can.-Mex., 32 I.L.M. 605, 642–47 (1993) [hereinafter NAFTA]; Ahdieh, *supra* note 147, at 2101–10, 2124 (describing the influence of the United States on NAFTA's legal protections of investors); *id.* at 2124 (anticipating development of "international norms of due process" applicable in both national and international tribunals, as a result of the "intersystemic" and "dialectical" nature of Chapter 11 review); *cf.* DAVID SCHNEIDERMAN, CONSTITUTIONALIZING ECONOMIC GLOBALIZATION: INVESTMENT RULES AND DEMOCRACY'S PROMISE 46–58 (2008) (exploring U.S. influence on expropriation rules embodied in NAFTA and other investment treaties).

153. *See* Neuman, *Uses of International Law, supra* note 95, at 84.

154. *See, e.g.,* Stephen J. Schnably, *Emerging International Law Constraints on Constitutional Structure and Revision: A Preliminary Appraisal*, 62 U. MIAMI L. REV. 417 (2008).

155. *See* Neil MacCormick, *Beyond the Sovereign State*, 56 MODERN L. REV. 1, 8–9 (1993).

156. *See* Walker, *supra* note 128, at 337 (describing European legal orders as more "horizontal than vertical—heterarchical rather than hierarchical"); *cf.* Daniel Halberstam, *Constitutional Heterarchy: The Centrality of Conflict in the European Union and the United States, in* RULING THE WORLD: CONSTITUTIONALISM, INTERNATIONAL LAW AND GLOBAL GOVERNANCE (Jeffrey Dunoff & Joel Trachtman eds., Cambridge Univ. Press, forthcoming 2009), *available at* http://papers.ssrn.com/sol3/papers.cfm?abstract_id=1147769.

157. TWINING, *supra* note 148, at 228, 229 (describing Santos' argument).

158. BOAVENTURA DE SOUSA SANTOS, TOWARDS A NEW LEGAL COMMON SENSE 437–38 (1995); *see id.* at 437 ("We live in a time of porous legality . . . , multiple networks of legal orders forcing us to constant transitions and trespassing. Our legal life is constituted by an intersection of different legal orders, that is, by *interlegality*.").

159. Paul Schiff Berman, *Global Legal Pluralism*, 80 S. CAL. L. REV. 1155 (2007).

160. Aleinikoff, *Transnational Spaces*, *supra* note 118, at 485, 487–88. Others see national courts as participants in projects of constructing an international or transnational legal order in which domestic norms are generally brought into conformance with international norms. See Chapter 2, above.

161. *See, e.g.*, Christoph Engel, *Hybrid Governance Across National Jurisdictions as a Challenge to Constitutional Law* (July 2001), MPI Collective Goods Preprint No. 2001/8, *available at* http://ssrn.com/abstract=278875 or DOI: 10.2139/ssrn.278875.

162. *See* BRIAN Z. TAMANAHA, A GENERAL JURISPRUDENCE OF LAW AND SOCIETY 224–30 (2001) (discussing seven different forms of law only one of which is state law); *id.* at 128–30 (arguing that globalization weakens connections between the idea of particular societies and their particular legal systems).

163. *See* Vicki C. Jackson, *Transnational Discourse, Relational Authority and the U.S. Court: Gender Equality*, 37 LOY. L.A. L. REV. 271, 315 n.155, 318 n.161 (2003). For a related discussion of a "post-sovereign" Europe, see NEIL MACCORMICK, QUESTIONING SOVEREIGNTY: LAW, STATE AND NATION IN THE EUROPEAN COMMONWEALTH 74–75, 76–78, 102–21, 123–36 (1999).

164. *Cf.* EISGRUBER, *supra* note 121, at 57–64 (discussing judicial disinterestedness and principled public reasoning as giving judges a "special ability to represent the American people with respect to issues of moral and political principle").

165. *See* Ralf Michaels, *The Re-state-ment of Non-State Law: The State, Choice of Law, and the Challenge from Global Legal Pluralism*, 51 WAYNE L. REV. 1209, 1247–49 (2005); *see also* Eyal Benvenisti, *Reclaiming Democracy: The Strategic Uses of Foreign and International Law by National Courts*, 102 AM. J. INT'L L. 241, 242 (2008) (arguing that the practice of courts in democratic countries in referring to foreign and international law is a "reaction to the forces of globalization, which are placing increasing pressure on the different domestic branches of government to conform to global standards"). Benvenisti's work suggests that what I term "engagement" may be a form of resistance to perceived global threats to national states and their democratic constitutional orders.

166. For discussion of the influence of "scripts," and of institutional isomorphism, see Chapter 9 below. There may also be specific kinds of interactions among liberal constitutional democracies that produce beneficial effects; the "Kantian peace" among democracies is only one example. *See, e.g.*, Michael W. Doyle, *Kant, Liberal Legacies, and Foreign Affairs*, 12 PHIL. & PUB. AFF. 205 (1983); Michael W. Doyle, *Liberalism and World Politics*, 80 AM. POL. SCI. REV. 1151, 1151–63 (1986); *see also* John R. O'Neal & Bruce M. Russett, *The Kantian Peace: The Pacific Benefits of Democracy, Interdependence, and International Organizations, 1885–1992*, 52 WORLD POL. 1 (Oct. 1999). Transactions, public and private, among nationals of different countries may also be affected by whether the countries are basically committed to versions of democratic constitutionalism; if they are recognizable cognates this may promote the reliance interests and trust that are necessary for many forms of sustained relationships.

167. *See* MARK TUSHNET, THE NEW CONSTITUTIONAL ORDER (2003) (describing the "chastened" ambitions of constitutional law).

168. For discussion of legal pluralism, multiple forms of globalizations, and the complex and varying effects of globalization on law, see SANTOS, *supra* note 158, at 85–86, 89–98, 165–77, 194–311, 437–38.

169. *Cf.* PHILIP BOBBITT, TERROR AND CONSENT 242, 285–88, 484–510 (2008) (emphasizing the possibility of new alliances among national "states of consent" to respond effectively to crises, including terrorism, while protecting individual rights and the rule of law, internally and transnationally).

170. *Cf.* Teubner, "*Global Bukowina*," *supra* note 149 at 4, 5–8 (noting that human rights discourse "has become globalized and is pressing . . . against the states," addressing the fragmentation of law and predicting that "global law will grow mainly from the social peripheries, not from the political centres of nation-states").

171. *See* Scott Shane, *Global Forecast by American Intelligence Expects Al Qaeda's Appeal to Falter*, N.Y. TIMES, Nov. 21, 2008, at A14 (describing conclusions of the National Intelligence Council Report, Global Trends 2025: A Transformed World, that the United States "'will find itself as one of a number of important actors on the world stage,' playing 'a prominent role in global events,' but not a decisive one as in the past").

172. H. Patrick Glenn, *Comparative Law and Legal Practice: On Removing the Borders*, 75 TUL. L. REV. 977, 985 (2001).

173. *See, e.g.*, MARGARET E. KECK & KATHRYN SIKKINK, ACTIVISTS BEYOND BORDERS: ADVOCACY NETWORKS IN INTERNATIONAL POLITICS (1998).

174. *Cf.* Benvenisti, *supra* note 165, at 242 (exploring democracy-enhancing possibilities of judges' strategic uses of foreign and international law to balance increased executive power resulting from globalization); Martin Flaherty, *Judicial Globalization in the Service of Self-Government*, 20 ETHICS & INT'L AFFAIRS 477, 485–92 (2006) (exploring judicial use of foreign or international law to help restore separation of powers balance in light of "pro-executive" effects of international information and cooperation networks).

CHAPTER 5. ENGAGEMENT, U.S. INTERPRETIVE THEORY, AND MULTIFUNCTIONAL CONSTITUTIONS

1. *See* RANDY BARNETT, RESTORING THE LOST CONSTITUTION: THE PRESUMPTION OF LIBERTY 100, 91–117 (2004); *see also, e.g.*, ROBERT BORK, THE TEMPTING OF AMERICA 143–44 (1990); ANTONIN SCALIA, A MATTER OF INTERPRETATION: FEDERAL COURTS AND THE LAW 38 (Amy Gutmann ed., 1997); Chapter 1, text at notes 12–19, above. The discussion in this Part A is drawn from Vicki C. Jackson, *Multi-Valenced Constitutional Interpretation and Constitutional Comparisons: An Essay in Honor of Mark Tushnet*, 26 QUINNIPIAC L. REV. 599 (2008).

2. *See* Akhil Reed Amar, *Intratextualism*, 112 HARV. L. REV. 747, 788–90 (1999).

3. *See, e.g.*, 1 BRUCE ACKERMAN, WE THE PEOPLE: FOUNDATIONS 47–50 (1991); Bruce A. Ackerman, *The Storrs Lectures: Discovering the Constitution*, 93 YALE L.J. 1013 (1984); Bruce Ackerman, *Constitutional Politics/Constitutional Law*, 99 YALE L.J. 453 (1989).

4. These theories are defended on democratic and contractarian grounds, responding to the countermajoritarian difficulty by permitting majoritarian preferences embodied in law to be set aside only based on prior popular decisions, intended to bind the future on the point at issue. Originalism is also defended as necessary to constrain judges from acting on their own preferences by tying their hands, interpretively, to the original understanding of the Constitution's text. In some contexts, on some issues, historically focused textual inquiries can by themselves provide compelling constitutional answers. *See* Richard H. Fallon, Jr., *The "Rule of Law" as a Concept in Constitutional Discourse*, 97 COLUM. L. REV. 1, 37 (1997). Once the Nineteenth Amendment was ratified, for example, denying women the vote because of their sex was plainly prohibited; but such clear-cut examples of recent intent, embodied in a specific text, are the exception, not the rule, in part due to the onerous U.S. amendment process.

5. If no determinate original meaning can be found by interpretation, constitutional "construction" (as distinct from "interpretation"), to which a wider range of materials might be relevant, is viewed as acceptable by some originalists; some originalists would apply a presumption in favor of the constitutionality of democratic decisions while for others a presumption of liberty would supplement commitments to original meaning. *See generally* BARNETT, *supra* note 1, at 118–30, 151–52, 350.

6. *See* Jeffrey Goldsworthy, *Originalism in Constitutional Interpretation*, 25 FED. L. REV. 1, 20 (1997) (Austl.); *see also* Jack M. Balkin, *Abortion and Original Meaning*, 24 CONST. COMMENTARY 291 (2007); *cf.* JED RUBENFELD, FREEDOM AND TIME: A THEORY OF CONSTITUTIONAL SELF-GOVERNMENT 186–88 (2001) (arguing that intentions concerning what conduct a right applies to protect should control, but that "nonapplication" intentions—understandings of what a right would not protect (or with respect to powers, what a power would not extend to) need not be treated as controlling).

7. *See, e.g.*, David C. Gray, *Why Justice Scalia Should be a Constitutional Comparativst—Sometimes*, 59 STAN. L. REV. 1249 (2007) (arguing that the Eighth Amendment's original meaning was to prohibit those forms of punishment that are, at the moment of decision, "cruel" and that "intersubjective" inquiries including contemporary comparative law are consistent with original meaning); Mark Tushnet, *When Is Knowing Less Better Than Knowing More? Unpacking the Controversy over Supreme Court Reference to Non-U.S. Law*, 90 MINN. L. REV. 1275, 1279–80 (2006). In these respects, originalist, positivist approaches may merge with purposivist or (possibly) even with natural law traditions. For a critical evaluation, see Roger P. Alford, *Roper v. Simmons and Our Constitution in International Equipoise*, 53 UCLA L. Rev. 1, 16–21 (2005). For a broader suggestion of the relevance of foreign law to originalism, see Eric A. Posner & Cass R. Sunstein, *The Law of Foreign States*, 59 STAN. L. REV. 131, 137–38 n.34 (2006) (asserting that whenever "original understanding requires courts to measure the extent to which a law burdens some behavior (speech, religious practice, commerce, etc.), the experience of foreign states with similar rules should be relevant").

8. *See* Henry P. Monaghan, *Our Perfect Constitution*, 56 N.Y.U. L. REV. 353, 374–81 (1981) (arguing that the Constitution as law should be interpreted in accord with original intent, and taking account of stare decisis).

9. *See, e.g.*, JOHN HART ELY, DEMOCRACY AND DISTRUST: A THEORY OF JUDICIAL REVIEW (1980).

10. *See, e.g.*, BARNETT, *supra* note 1, at 254–60 (combining originalism as a method with libertarianism as a theory of justice embodied in the Constitution); RICHARD A. EPSTEIN, TAKINGS: PRIVATE PROPERTY AND THE POWER OF EMINENT DOMAIN 331 (1985).

11. *See, e.g.*, RONALD DWORKIN, TAKING RIGHTS SERIOUSLY 198–99 (1977) (expressing commitment to moral values of Kantian equal regard for each person); RONALD DWORKIN, A MATTER OF PRINCIPLE 205–13 (1985) (explaining "why liberals should care about equality," and defending a version of liberalism grounded in equality, or "equal concern and respect").

12. *See* CHRISTOPHER EISGRUBER, CONSTITUTIONAL SELF-GOVERNMENT 7, 19–20, 52–58 (2001) (envisioning courts speaking "on behalf of the American people about justice").

13. *See also* LAWRENCE G. SAGER, JUSTICE IN PLAINCLOTHES: A THEORY OF AMERICAN CONSTITUTIONAL PRACTICE 3 (2004) (arguing that the core of U.S. constitutional practice involves the "liberty-bearing provisions" of the Constitution concerned with the "legitimate demands of members of our political community" for justice); James E. Fleming, *Securing Deliberative Autonomy*, 48 STAN. L. REV. 1, 2 (1995) (arguing for theory based on "deliberative democracy" and "deliberative autonomy"). Those who are regarded as

"pragmatists" also have purposive conceptions against which to measure their pragmatic inquires. *See, e.g.*, STEPHEN BREYER, ACTIVE LIBERTY: INTERPRETING OUR DEMOCRATIC CONSTITUTION 6, 18, 116 (2005).

14. *See* AHARON BARAK, PURPOSIVE INTERPRETATION IN LAW (Sari Bashi trans., 2005). Identifying and arguing from constitutional purposes is an indispensable tool for constitutional interpretation. But it is not necessarily a sufficient account of the practice of interpretation. For one thing, there are reasonable disagreements about which values interpretive theory should prioritize, for example, as between liberty and equality; yet substantive purposive theories by themselves provide no common metric for resolving interpretive disagreement rooted in different views of constitutional purpose or of the priority of the values at stake. Further, some theories "fit" certain constitutional problems better than others; "representation reinforcement" makes sense in understanding the U.S. apportionment cases, but does not shed equivalent light on the meaning of the Double Jeopardy Clause. Specific purposive theories that work well in a comprehensive way and that "fit" sufficiently with existing law are difficult to identify; and more general purposive theories need additional doctrinal tools to reconcile the different purposes a constitution will usually entail.

15. *See* Nixon v. Shrink Missouri Government PAC, 528 U.S. 377, 402–03 (2000); BREYER, *supra* note 13. Judge Richard Posner at one time argued for resort to comparative experience as a better way of determining whether punishments are constitutionally disproportionate than resort to constitutional history. *See* Chapter 3, text at notes 64–66, above.

16. Lawrence v. Texas, 539 U.S. 558, 573, 576 (2003).

17. Printz v. United States, 521 U.S. 898, 976–78 (Breyer, J., dissenting).

18. *See* Mark Tushnet, *The United States: Eclecticism in the Service of Pragmatism, in* INTERPRETING CONSTITUTIONS: A COMPARATIVE STUDY 7 (Jeffrey Goldsworthy ed., 2006).

19. *See* David Strauss, *Common Law Constitutional Interpretation*, 63 U. CHI. L. REV. 877, 913–16 (1996); David Strauss, *Common Law, Common Ground, and Jefferson's Principle*, 112 YALE L.J. 1717, 1724, 1725–26 (2003); *see also* Ernest Young, *Rediscovering Conservatism: Burkean Political Theory and Constitutional Interpretation*, 72 N.C. L. REV. 619, 688–97 (1994).

20. *See generally* K. N. Llewellyn, *The Constitution as an Institution*, 34 COLUM L. REV. 1 (1934); *id.* at 12 ("*[I]t is only the practice which can legitimatize the words as being still part of our going Constitution.*") (italics in original).

21. *See, e.g.*, Robert C. Post & Reva B. Siegel, *Equal Protection by Law: Federal Antidiscrimination Legislation After Morrison and Kimel*, 110 YALE L.J. 441, 487–502 (2000) (describing interactions in the 1960s between citizens, state and local officials, and the three branches of the federal government in contributing to constitutional understandings of federal power to enforce civil rights); H. JEFFERSON POWELL, A COMMUNITY BUILT ON WORDS: THE CONSTITUTION IN HISTORY AND POLITICS 1–7, 205–10 (2002) (explaining why and in what respects "constitutional law is a thoroughly historical phenomenon").

22. BARAK, *supra* note 14, at 148–81.

23. *See* PHILIP BOBBITT, CONSTITUTIONAL FATE 93–119 (1982).

24. *See* Richard H. Fallon, Jr., *A Constructivist Coherence Theory of Constitutional Interpretation*, 100 HARV. L. REV. 1189 (1987); *see also* Dan Simon, *A Psychological Model of Judicial Decision Making*, 30 RUTGERS L.J. 1 (1998) (describing a "coherence bias" in judicial thinking).

25. *See* Chapter 3, text at notes 109–25, above.

26. *See* BOBBITT, CONSTITUTIONAL FATE, *supra* note 23, at 3–119, 140–41; PHILIP BOBBITT, CONSTITUTIONAL INTERPRETATION 9, 11–22 (1991).

27. *See* Fallon, *Constructivist Coherence, supra* note 24, at 1194–1208 (discussing arguments from text, intent, theory and purpose, precedent, and moral or policy values as sources of interpretation).

28. *See* Strauss, *Common Law Constitutional Interpretation, supra* note 19, at 879, 882–84, 891–92 (1996); *see also* Strauss, *Common Law, Common Ground, supra* note 19, at 1738.

29. Strauss, *Common Law Constitutional Interpretation, supra* note 19, at 894–97, 917–18; *cf.* Young, *supra* note 19, at 622, 696 (arguing for a common law constitutionalism infused with a Burkean conservatism, based on a "skepticism about the capacity of human reason to order the world around us" and drawing on "eclectic" sources, including "original understanding, . . . precedents, argu[ment] by analogy, appeal to tradition, public morality, or even abstract moral philosophy, and [concern for] policy consequences").

30. *See, e.g.,* Cass R. Sunstein, *Foreword: Leaving Things Undecided,* 110 HARV. L. REV. 6, 7–8, 16–20 (1996) (arguing for a "minimalist" approach by judges to constitutional adjudication in deference to institutional and democratic considerations by leaving space for future decision-making); William N. Eskridge, Jr., *Channeling: Identity-Based Social Movements and Public Law,* 150 U. PA. L. REV. 419 (2001) (arguing for conflict-channeling and pluralism-facilitating constitutional decisions as part of a process that constructs space for, and responds to, the constitutional and political disagreement reflected in identity-based social movements).

31. Robert Post & Reva Siegel, *Roe Rage: Democratic Constitutionalism and Backlash,* 42 HARV. C.R.-C.L. L. REV. 373, 374, 379, 382–84 (2007); *see also* Barry Friedman, *Dialogue and Judicial Review,* 91 MICH. L. REV. 577, 580–81 (1993).

32. POWELL, *supra* note 21, at 5–6.

33. McIntyre v. Ohio Elections Commission, 514 U.S. 334, 381–82 (1995) (Scalia, J., dissenting) (referring to statutes in Australia, Canada, and England in arguing to uphold a ban on anonymous campaigning); *cf.* Locke v. Davey, 540 U.S. 712, 734 (2004) (Scalia, J., dissenting) (suggesting that recent events in France revealed the not "fanciful" risks of the majority's rejection of a "free exercise" challenge).

34. Roger P. Alford, *In Search of a Theory for Constitutional Comparativism,* 52 UCLA L. REV. 639, 674–75, 708, 712 (2005). For Alford's description of "conservative" and "activist" forms of majoritarianism, see Chaper 1, text at note 21, above.

35. The Court's 1964 apportionment decisions, for example, discussed the British experience with "rotten boroughs." Wesberry v. Sanders, 376 U.S. 1, 14 (1964); Reynolds v. Sims, 377 U.S. 533, 568 n.44 (1964). *See generally* Chapter 1, above, text at notes 23–26.

36. For the quotation, see Ruth Bader Ginsburg, *An Open Discussion,* 36 CONN. L. REV. 1033, 1040 (2004); *cf.* Ganesh Sitaraman, The Use and Abuse of Foreign Law in Constitutional Interpretation (Oct. 12, 2008, draft) (identifying a range of relatively non-controversial uses), forthcoming, HARV. J. L & PUB. POL'Y, *available at* http://ssrn.com/abstract=1282177.

37. *See* Mark Tushnet, *Referring to Foreign Law in Constitutional Interpretation: An Episode in the Culture Wars,* 35 U. BALT. L. REV. 299 (2006); Hon. Peter J. Messitte, *Citing Foreign Law in U.S. Courts: Is Our Sovereignty Really at Stake?,* 35 U. BALT. L. REV. 171, 182–83 (2006) (suggesting opposition to use of foreign law in constitutional cases is of a piece with government attitudes toward the International Criminal Court or the Kyoto Accords).

38. *See* Judith Resnik, *Law as Affiliation: Foreign Law, Democratic Federalism and the Sovereigntism of the Nation-state,* 6 INT'L J. CONST. L. 33 (2008); *cf.* Michel Rosenfeld, *Principle or Ideology? A Comparativist Perspective on the U.S. Controversy over Supreme Court Citations to Foreign Authority,* Cardozo Legal Studies, Research Paper No. 213, at 23–24

(Oct. 2008), *available at* http://ssrn.com/abstract=1081854 (suggesting that controversy over the Court's use of foreign law may have been related to the relative isolation the United States was experiencing in its effort to create support for the war in Iraq in 2003, the year that *Lawrence v. Texas* was decided).

39. *See* Chapter 1, text at note 1, above.

40. John Bell, *Comparing Public Law, in* COMPARATIVE LAW IN THE 21ST CENTURY 240–41 (Andrew Harding & Ecin Orucu eds., 2002).

41. In the case law, compare *Missouri v. Holland,* 252 U.S. 416, 433–34 (1920) with *Reid v. Covert,* 354 U.S. 1, 5–19 (1957) (Black, J., for the plurality); in the scholarly literature, compare Curtis A. Bradley, *The Treaty Power and American Federalism,* 97 MICH. L. REV. 390 (1998) and *The Treaty Power and American Federalism, Part II,* 99 MICH. L. REV. 98 (2000); Nicolas Quinn Rosenkranz, *Executing the Treaty Power,* 118 HARV. L. REV. 1867 (2005) with David M. Golove, *Treaty Making and the Nation: The Historical Foundations of the Nationalist Conceptions of the Treaty Power,* 98 MICH. L. REV. 1075 (2000).

42. For differing views, see, e.g., Curtis A. Bradley, *Breard, Our Dualist Constitution and the Internationalist Conception,* 51 STAN. L. REV. 529, 539–43 (1999); Carlos Manuel Vázquez, *Laughing at Treaties,* 99 COLUM. L. REV. 2154 (1999).

43. *Compare* Medellín v. Texas, 128 S. Ct. 1346 (2008) (concluding that the President lacked authority to implement a non-self-executing ratified treaty by requiring state courts to reconsider challenges to criminal convictions or sentences) *with* Carlos Manuel Vázquez, *Breard and the Federal Power to Require Compliance with ICJ Orders of Provisional Measures,* 92 AM. J. INT'L L. 683, 686–90 (1998) (arguing that even if an ICJ order was not binding or a treaty was not self-executing, the President would have power to order compliance with ICJ orders).

44. For differing views on the status and internal domestic force of customary international law, see T. Alexander Aleinikoff, *International Law, Sovereignty and American Constitutionalism: Reflections on the Customary International Law Debate,* 98 AM. J. INT'L L. 91 (2004); Curtis A. Bradley & Jack L. Goldsmith, *Customary International Law as Federal Common Law: A Critique of the Modern Position,* 110 HARV. L. REV. 815 (1997); Louis Henkin, *The Constitution and United States Sovereignty: A Century of Chinese Exclusion and its Progeny,* 100 HARV. L. REV. 853, 867–78 (1987); Harold Hongju Koh, *Is International Law Really State Law?,* 111 HARV. L. REV. 1824 (1998); Ernest A. Young, *Sorting Out the Debate over Customary International Law,* 42 VA. J. INT'L L. 365 (2002).

45. *See* Bradley & Goldsmith, *Customary International Law as Federal Common Law, supra* note 44, at 868, 869 (arguing that customary international law should not be treated as a form of federal common law because of the threat it poses to the constitutionally prescribed process of lawmaking).

46. *See, e.g.,* Bradford R. Clark, *Constitutional Structure, Judicial Discretion and the Eighth Amendment,* 81 NOTRE DAME L. REV. 1149, 1200–02 (2006); Ernest A. Young, *Foreign Law and the Denominator Problem,* 119 HARV. L. REV. 148, 163–65 (2005); *see also* Bradley & Goldsmith, supra note 44, at 857–58; Curtis A. Bradley, Jack L. Goldsmith & David H. More, *Sosa, Customary International Law and the Continuing Relevance of Erie,* 120 HARV. L. REV. 869, 904–05 (2007); *cf.* Bradford R. Clark, *Separation of Powers as a Safeguard of Federalism,* 79 TEX. L. REV. 1321, 1323, 1438–52 (2001) (questioning the constitutionality of non-treaty agreements).

47. *See* Alford, *Constitutional Comparativism, supra* note 34, at 704–12 (suggesting that the theoretical basis for constitutional comparativism may be a commitment to converge with "universal" norms of "civilized nations," without regard to democratic preferences, or past precedent and other established rule-of-law interpretive practices).

48. Antonin Scalia, *Originalism: The Lesser Evil*, 57 U. Cin. L. Rev. 849, 861–64 (1989). (For earlier work on objections to engagement, from which some of this Part is drawn, see Vicki C. Jackson, *Transnational Discourse, Relational Authority and the U.S. Court; Gender Equality*, 37 Loyola L. A. L. Rev. 271, 325–46 (2003); *Narratives of Federalism: Of Continuities and Comparative Constitutional Experience*, 51 Duke L.J. 223, 263–71 (2001); *Transnational Challenges to Constitutional Law: Convergence, Resistance, Engagement*, 35 Fed'l L. Rev. 161 (2007) (Austral.); *Constitutional Comparisons: Convergence, Resistance, Engagement*, 119 Harv. L. Rev. 109 (2005).)

49. For a classic general treatment of formalism, see Frederick Schauer, *Formalism*, 97 Yale L. J. 509 (1988). Understanding legal materials, unlike social science materials, calls on a set of specifically legal, analytical skills; judges and lawyers may thus be better situated to evaluate comparative legal materials than they are materials from other disciplines. *Cf.* Charles Fried, *The Artificial Reason of the Law or: What Lawyers Know*, 60 Tex. L. Rev. 35 (1981) (arguing that law is a relatively autonomous discipline and that what judges are good at is doing law, using reasoning by analogy and precedent for the development of legal concepts). *But cf.* Charles Fried, *Scholars and Judges: Reason and Power*, 23 Harv. J. L. & Pub. Pol'y 807, 816–19 (2000) (arguing against "expand[ing] the canon" of sources for constitutional interpretation to consider foreign law). Although particular social and legal cultures provide an important context for the evaluation of law, see Chapter 6 below, there are cross-national questions that those trained in law will tend to ask that will be germane to understanding law's meaning and operation.

50. The underlying idea here is that of a "dualist" democracy as described by Bruce Ackerman, a bifurcated concept also captured by the terms "pouvoir constituant"—the people acting as a constituent power, constituting the terms of their polity in a constitution—and "pouvoir constitué," the power that can be exercised subject to the terms established in the constitution. *See* Ackerman, *supra* note 3, at 17–24; Vicki C. Jackson & Mark Tushnet, Comparative Constitutional Law 275 (2d ed., 2006).

51. *Compare* Al-Kateb v. Godwin (2004) 219 C.L.R. 562, 592–93 (Austl.) (McHugh, J.) (arguing that reading the constitution to conform to rules of international law would result in the judiciary impermissibly amending the constitution) *with id.* at 625 (Kirby, J.) (rejecting McHugh's claim, for if "valid, it would apply equally to other decisions . . . in which the court has given new meaning to the constitutional text and expounded new rights and duties," and noting that the constitution "provides both for formal amendment and judicial reinterpretation").

52. *See, e.g.*, Ken I. Kersch, *The New Legal Transnationalism, The Globalized Judiciary, and the Rule of Law*, 4 Wash. U. Global Stud. L. Rev. 345, 346 (2005) (arguing that the "new legal transnationalism . . . is part of an elite-driven, politically-motivated worldwide trend toward judicial governance, which is antithetical to democratic self-rule"); Roger P. Alford, *Misusing International Sources to Interpret the Constitution*, 98 Am. J. Int'l L. 57, 58–61 (2004) (raising an "international countermajoritarian difficulty"); *see also* Bijon Roy, *An Empirical Survey of Foreign Jurisprudence and International Instruments in Charter Litigation*, 62 U. Toronto Fac. L. Rev. 99, 103 (2004).

53. Sarah H. Cleveland, *Our International Constitution*, 31 Yale J. Int'l L. 1, 102 (2006); *see also* Harold Hongju Koh, *On American Exceptionalism*, 55 Stan. L. Rev. 1479, 1488–89, 1505 (2003).

54. *See* Mark Tushnet, *Transnational/Domestic Constitutional Law*, 37 Loy. L.A. L. Rev. 239, 262–64 (2003). *But cf.* Kenneth Anderson, *Book Review: Squaring the Circle? Reconciling Sovereignty and Global Governance Through Global Government Networks*, 118 Harv. L. Rev. 1255, 1273 (2005) (reviewing Anne-Marie Slaughter, A New World Order

(2004)) (suggesting that even the exchange of information about foreign law may involve "serious issues of political legitimacy").

55. See Vicki C. Jackson, *Transnational Discourse, Relational Authority and the U.S. Court: Gender Equality*, 37 Loy. L.A. L. Rev. 271, 327 (2003); *cf.* Michael C. Dorf, *Dynamic Incorporation of Foreign Law*, 157 U. Pa. L. Rev. 103, 112–13 (2008) (distinguishing *sovereignty* concerns involving irrevocable cessions of power from concerns for democratic *self-governance* arising out of even revocable delegations).

56. *But see* John O. McGinnis & Michael B. Rappaport, *Our Supermajoritarian Constitution*, 80 Tex. L. Rev. 703, 791–802 (2002).

57. *Cf.* Jed Rubenfeld, *Unilateralism and Constitutionalism*, 79 N.Y.U. L. Rev. 1971 (2004) (positing an opposition between American constitutionalism, founded in democratic will, and European constitutionalism, founded in elite reason). Giving strongly presumptive weight to the views of contemporary majorities on issues of constitutional interpretation is inconsistent with the role of independent courts in protecting individual rights; "living tree" constitutionalism does not, however, require such a presumption but insists as well on the importance of text, history, constitutional values, precedent, and practice over time.

58. Rosalind Dixon, *A Democratic Theory of Constitutional Comparison*, 56 Am. J. Comp. L. 947, 949, 960–62 (2008) (explaining premise that "in an increasingly globalized world, constitutional democracies which start with sufficient commonality in a particular constitutional area are very likely to experience a co-evolution in constitutional values"). On measures of comparability, see *id.* at 980–81 (explaining that appropriate comparators would need, inter alia, to be democratic, politically liberal countries, with a thick history of constitutionalism and social movements that generate political responses, to be able reliably to infer from foreign law whether an apparent U.S. trend is likely to be an enduring shift in constitutional understanding that the Court, in dialogue with its democratic society, should recognize).

59. *Id.* at 969, 970–71 (arguing that foreign comparisons will help identify "true, evolving traditions," distinguishing between "pure legislative inertia and ongoing democratic opposition" because "[c]ompared to state-level legislative trends within the United States, foreign constitutional trends are much less likely—in aggregate—to be subject to blockages which are systematically cross-correlated").

60. As Dixon herself notes, the United States is in important respects distinctive in its public views, *id.* at 961 n.54, in ways that may well confound efforts to distinguish between legislative inertia and public disagreement. Moreover, to the extent that inertia reflects issues having not yet become a priority within domestic political parties and legislative bodies, *see id.* at 968–69, there is some risk of short-circuiting helpful democratic and social organizing processes by relying on the outcomes of those processes in other countries as a basis for constitutional resolution of controversial issues. (On a different note, some might worry about the ex ante effects of a co-evolution doctrine in establishing incentives to seek change elsewhere in order to influence the U.S. Court. Although some norm entrepreneurs will no doubt seek to influence both other countries and international fora, *see* Chapter 1 above, their reasons for doing so are already robust. Dixon's analysis, moreover, has the benefit of focusing attention on comparators with transparent and participatory democratic processes.)

61. Some scholars have suggested that courts should more generally look to foreign or international law to facilitate dynamic sociolegal change. *See* David Fontana, *Refined Comparativism in Constitutional Law*, 49 UCLA L. Rev. 539, 594–95 (2001). Although judicial interpretation may need to be dynamic to accommodate constitutionalism with

democracy under a hard-to-amend constitution, deliberately seeking to rely on transnational law to advance sociolegal change may threaten a court's ability to retain legitimacy *within* the polity. For these reasons, the primary focus of judicial interpretation is on U.S. constitutional text, structure, concepts, and precedents, drawing on traditional sources of interpretation (to which foreign practice may be relevant, for example, in understanding the consequences of alternative interpretations).

62. *See also* Cleveland, *Our International Constitution*, supra note 53, at 115–22 (arguing that an important factor influencing the weight international law should have in constitutional interpretation is the position of the political branches in ratifying, accepting, or rejecting international commitments).

63. *See* Chapter 4, text at notes 51–57, above.

64. Youngstown Sheet & Tube Co. v. Sawyer, 343 U.S. 579, 650–52 (1952) (Jackson, J., concurring).

65. *But see* Mary Ann Glendon, *Judicial Tourism*, WALL. ST. J., Sept. 16, 2005, at A14.

66. *But cf.* Fontana, *supra* note 61, at 561–62 (suggesting that comparative law ought to be considered in constitutional interpretation in order to keep pace with the many national communities that now make up the U.S. population). Although there are hints of this possibility in *Hurtado v. California*, 110 U.S. 516, 531 (1884), this suggestion ignores the degree to which many (though not all) immigrants are seeking change. They may emigrate to escape unjust or ineffective government; indeed, reasons for migration may include a desire affirmatively to change legal regime. Moreover, looking to the laws of illiberal, nondemocratic countries from which some immigrants come bears little relation to the kind of society the United States has had and aims to build, nor to the particularities of the U.S. national experience. *See* Rex D. Glensy, *Which Countries Count?: Lawrence v. Texas and the Selection of Foreign Persuasive Authority*, 45 VA. J. INT'L L. 357, 431–32 (2005).

67. Mark Tushnet, *The Possibilities of Comparative Constitutional Law*, 108 YALE L.J. 1225, 1231–32 (1999).

68. *Cf.* United States v. Klein, 80 U.S. 128, 145–46 (1871).

69. United States v. Then, 56 F.3d 464 (2d Cir. 1995). *But cf.* Diarmuid F. O'Scannlain, *What Role Should Foreign Practice and Precedent Play in the Interpretation of Domestic Law?*, 80 NOTRE DAME L. REV. 1893, 1904–07 (2005) (suggesting that the framers' intent to develop a distinctly American constitution and hostility to foreign law manifest in early state laws prohibiting citation of British precedent should lead originalists to be "wary" of foreign law).

70. 536 U.S. 304, 322 (2002) (Rehnquist, C.J., dissenting) (brackets in original) (quoting Stanford v. Kentucky, 492 U.S. 361, 377 (1989) (plurality)).

71. Under Eighth Amendment doctrine, the "cruel and unusual punishments" clause bans not only those punishments thought barred in 1791, but those condemned by "evolving standards of decency." Trop v. Dulles, 356 U.S. 86, 101 (1958) (plurality opinion). In *Atkins*, Rehnquist suggested that "objective indicia" of those standards (statutes and decisions by sentencing juries) should be the only factors considered. 536 U.S. at 324 (Rehnquist, C.J., dissenting). *But cf.* William H. Rehnquist, *Foreword* to DEFINING THE FIELD OF COMPARATIVE CONSTITUTIONAL LAW, at vii, viii (Vicki C. Jackson & Mark Tushnet eds., 2002) (suggesting that U.S. judges should stop being "laggard in relying on comparative law decisions" in constitutional law, because "now that constitutional law is solidly grounded in so many countries, . . . it's time the U.S. courts began looking to the decisions of other constitutional courts to aid in their own deliberative process").

72. *See* The Paquete Habana, 175 U.S. 677, 700 (1900) ("International law is part of our law. . . ."); *see also* Murray v. Schooner Charming Betsy, 6 U.S. (2 Cranch) 64

(1804); Patricia M. Wald, *The Use of International Law in the American Adjudicative Process*, 27 HARV. J. L & PUB. POL'Y, 431, 433 (2004).

73. 543 U.S. 551, 576–77 (2005) (discussing United Nations Convention on the Rights of the Child, Art. 37, Nov. 20, 1989, 1577 U. N. T. S. 3, 28 I. L. M. 1448, 1468–1470 (entered into force Sept. 2, 1990) and ICCPR Art. 6(5), 999 U.N.T.S., at 175).

74. *See, e.g.*, Clark, *Constitutional Structure, Judicial Discretion and the Eighth Amendment*, *supra* note 46, at 1201–02.

75. Indeed, in an earlier portion of its opinion devoted to examining the "objective indicia" of U.S. opinion in state and federal laws and jury decisions, the Court addressed an entire paragraph to the state's argument that the Senate's 1992 reservation to the ICCPR implied the absence of a domestic consensus against the juvenile death penalty in the United States. The Court concluded that the reservation "provides only faint support" for the argument: "First, the reservation was passed in 1992; since then, five States have abandoned capital punishment for juveniles. Second, Congress considered the issue when enacting the Federal Death Penalty Act in 1994, and determined that the death penalty should not extend to juveniles." Roper v. Simmons, 543 U.S. 551, 567 (2005). The Court's treatment of the ICCPR in these two different sections of the opinion illustrates the importance of clarity in the purpose for which foreign or international law is invoked.

76. Although the term is widely associated with critique of the European Community and European Union, *see, e.g.*, J.H.H. Weiler, *The Transformation of Europe*, 100 YALE L.J. 2403 (1991); J.H.H. Weiler, *European Constitutionalism and its Discontents*, 17 NW. J. INT'L L. & BUS. 354 (1996), I use it here to refer to U.S. constitutional history.

77. *But cf.* Am. Ins. Ass'n v. Garamendi, 539 U.S. 396 (2003) (treating a state law as preempted by its conflict with the President's foreign policy powers in claims settlement).

78. Alford, *Our Constitution in International Equipoise, supra* note 7.

79. *See id.* at 22–25; *see also* Roper v. Simmons, 543 U.S. at 627 (Scalia, J., dissenting) (attacking the Court's selectivity in using foreign law).

80. *See* Chapter 6, Part A, below.

81. Cass R. Sunstein, *Constitutionalism and Secession*, 58 U. CHI. L. REV. 633, 638–39 (1991).

82. Rule of law considerations might even favor interpretive rules that assume a national preference to be in conformity with international legal obligations, though this can be achieved through nonconstitutional law. *See* infra notes 111, 130–31; *see also Murray v. Schooner Charming Betsy*, 6 U.S. (2 Cranch) at 118 ("[A]n act of Congress ought never to be construed to violate the law of nations if any other possible construction remains . . .").

83. *See* cases cited above in Introduction, note 42; *see also* The Prize Cases, 67 U.S. (2 Black) 635 (1863) (upholding presidential blockade as exercise of Commander-in-Chief power in light of international laws of war); Gibbons v. Ogden, 22 U.S. (9 Wheat.) 1, 227 (1824) (Johnson, J. concurring) (relying in part on the law of nations to conclude that the federal power to regulate interstate commerce must be exclusive). For discussion, see James H. Lengel, *The Role of International Law in the Development of Constitutional Jurisprudence in the Supreme Court: The Marshall Court and American Indians*, 43 AM. J. LEGAL HIST. 117 (1999); Martin S. Flaherty, *Judicial Globalization in the Service of Self-Government*, 20 ETHICS & INT'L AFFAIRS 477, 479–80, 493–502 (2006) (making an originalist argument for interpreting the Constitution to be consistent with international law).

84. Fried, *Scholars and Judges, supra* note 49, at 819 (arguing that judges, unlike scholars, exercise power and in so doing are bound by a limited interpretive canon); *cf.* Frederick Schauer, *Authority and Authorities*, 94 VA. L. REV. 1931, 1952–60 & n.72 (2008) (distinguishing between "authority" and "bindingness" and suggesting that some justices

who resist referring to foreign law "believe that the collective production of international opinion is essentially a questionable political process of groupthink").

85. John O. McGinnis, *Foreign to Our Constitution*, 100 Nw. U. L. Rev. 303, 305, 310–11 (2006); *see also* Richard A. Posner, *Foreword: A Political Court*, 119 Harv. L., Rev. 31, 86–88 (2005). McGinnis also criticizes reliance on foreign law because it "emerged from a structure designed to generate norms for another nation," and is embedded in a foreign system with different institutional and social ways of implementing and enforcing norms. McGinnis, *supra*, at 311–12. These objections go to comparability rather than to any logical impropriety in reference; they also ignore the "suprapositive" character of some provisions. *See* Gerald L. Neuman, *Human Rights and Constitutional Rights: Harmony and Dissonance*, 55 Stan. L. Rev. 1863, 1868 (2003).

86. *Cf.* Frederick Schauer, *The Authority of Legal Scholarship*, 139 U. Pa. L. Rev. 1003, 1005, 1014–15 (2001) (focusing on how "authority is, at its core, content-independent," but recognizing that processes used to reach a conclusion may contribute to the authority of a source); Schauer, *Authority and Authorities*, *supra* note 84, at 1940–44 (distinguishing "persuasion" from "authority" but also distinguishing "authority" from that which is "binding").

87. This claim is, I believe, distinct from Professor Schauer's treatment of "expertise-influenced selection of optional authorities," as being "more likely reliable than the selector [of such authority] herself." *See* Schauer, *Authority and Authorities*, *supra* note 84, at 1949.

88. *See, e.g.*, Joan L. Larson, *Importing Constitutional Norms from a "Wider Civilization": Lawrence and the Rehnquist Court's Use of Foreign and International Law in Domestic Constitutional Interpretation*, 65 Ohio St. L.J. 1283, 1303–26 (2004) (finding no justification for the use of foreign law in "moral fact-finding," and arguing that such use expands countermajoritarian judicial discretion); *see also* Lawrence v. Texas, 539 U.S. 558, 598 (2003) (Scalia, J., dissenting) (condemning the Court for "'impos[ing] foreign moods, fads, or fashions'" (quoting Foster v. Florida, 537 U.S. 990, 990 n.* (2002) (Thomas, J., concurring in denial of certiorari)).

89. *But cf.* Sitaraman, *supra* note 36, at 26–41 (arguing that "authoritative borrowing" and "aggregation" are problematic uses of foreign law). Sitaraman correctly notes that "authoritative" use of foreign law as binding precedent does not occur in the United States, but raises questions whether dispositive uses of aggregation, as distinct from looking at other practices for confirmation of an interpretation of one's own law, have occurred, and expresses particular concern over use of aggregation in situations in which domestic law is unclear and foreign law is clear. *See id.* at 40. But in those situations, reflecting on foreign law may be understood to help clarify for a judge how to read the ambiguous domestic sources, which is not the same as treating foreign law as dispositive. In *Roper v. Simmons*, 543 U.S. 551 (2005), the majority and Justice O'Connor each indicated that considering such transnational sources was legitimate, but reached different conclusions on the constitutional issue. *See id.* at 575, 604–05 (O'Connor, J., dissenting).

90. On prudential silence, see Chapter 6, below.

91. *See* Chapter 1, text at notes 38–39, above; *see also infra* note 97. Cherry-picking of authorities can, of course, arise among domestic sources as well.

92. *See* Simon, *A Psychological Model*, *supra* note 24, at 14 (so characterizing many legal disputes at the appellate level).

93. *Cf.* Fontana, *supra* note 61, at 559–61 (arguing that comparability is a precondition for the use of comparative constitutional law).

94. On debiasing and adjudication, see Simon, *A Psychological Model*, *supra* note 24, at 137–41; Andrew J. Wistrich, Chris Guthrie & Jeffrey J. Rachlinski, *Can Judges Ignore*

Inadmissible Information? The Difficulty of Deliberately Disregarding, 153 U. PA. L. REV. 1251 (2005). Based on the Wistrich-Guthrie-Rachlinski summary of research, forbidding judges to think about foreign law may well be counterproductive. *Cf. id.* at 1276 (describing data showing the difficulties of deliberately ignoring information, including the possibility that such instructions will backfire and result in more weight being given to the excluded material).

95. *See* H. Patrick Glenn, *Persuasive Authority*, 32 MCGILL L.J. 261, 264 (1987).

96. Jennifer Nedelsky, *Communities of Judgment and Human Rights*, 1 THEOR. INQ. L. 245 (2000) (arguing that having multiple interpretive communities in mind can provide a critical footing to help judges fulfill their task sometimes to say no to their governments by enlarging a judge's "mentality" or frame of reference).

97. *See* Devika Hovell & George Williams, *A Tale of Two Systems: Use of International Law in Constitutional Interpretation in Australia and South Africa*, 29 MELBOURNE U. L. REV. 95, 120, 126–27 (2005) (finding a "discerning acceptance, rather than a wholesale adoption" of international law by the South African Constitutional Court and identifying only one case of error in failing to consider additional sources of international law); Roy, *supra* note 52, at 103–04, 127 (finding no support for concerns about cherry-picking in the Canadian Court's use of these transnational sources). Hovell and Williams do express surprise at the South African court's failure more consistently to consider international law in its more "ad hoc" approach, but they also suggest that in many cases international law "may have had little to offer." Hovell & Williams, *supra*, at 119–20. It is interesting to note that in South Africa, concerns had also been expressed about lack of knowledge of public international law. *See id.* at 125–27 (discussing the "developing expertise" of the Court in international law); *see also* Chapter 3, note 7, above (reflecting findings that in Canadian constitutional cases, foreign or international sources were rarely if ever dispositive). For studies finding evidence of "cherry-picking" or errors in the use of foreign or international law, see sources cited in Chapter 1, note 41, above.

98. *Cf.* HERBERT A. SIMON, REASON IN HUMAN AFFAIRS 19–23 (1983) (discussing "bounded rationality").

99. *See* Strauss, *Common Law, Common Ground, supra* note 19, at 1738; *see also* Young, *Foreign Law and the Denominator Problem, supra* note 46, at 165–67.

100. *See* Chapter 4, text at notes 79–84, above.

101. *See* Cass R. Sunstein, *On Analogical Reasoning*, 106 HARV. L. REV. 741 (1993); Fontana, *supra* note 61, at 618–21.

102. Some research suggests that analogical reasoning is best utilized by those who are neither novices nor experts. *See* GARY KLEIN, SOURCES OF POWER: HOW PEOPLE MAKE DECISIONS 201–13 (1998). Query whether this research would extend to judicial decision-making and if so, whether judges skilled in analogical reasoning can benefit from considering areas of law in which they are not expert to help resolve difficult questions in areas in which they are.

103. On "situation sense" in the law of commercial relations, statutory interpretation, and judicial decision-making, see Karl N. Llewelyn, *Remarks on the Theory of Appellate Decision and the Rules or Canons About How Statutes Are To Be Construed*, 3 VAND. L. REV. 395, 397–401 (1950). *See also* KARL N. LLEWELLYN, THE COMMON LAW TRADITION 59–61, 121–57, 206–08 (1960); Karl N. Llewelyn, *The Crafts of Law Re-valued*, 15 ROCKY MTN. L. REV. 1, 2–4 (1942).

104. Llewelyn, *The Constitution as an Institution, supra* note 20, at 12, 20 n.32, 21. Llewelyn argued that constitutional interpretation should be based on the working practices of constitutionalism, on structure, function, and functioning, on the normative

ideals of the particular practice at issue, and on the need for some degree of consistency, more than on the language or specific intent of the words of the Constitution. *See id.* at 28–29, 31. Although he does not draw the connection I suggest, understanding the "ways" of the Constitution as an institution may require some of the same "situation sense" he described in other areas of law.

105. *Cf.* SIMON, *supra* note 98, at 27–28 (reporting estimates across a wide range of fields that at least ten years of practice is necessary to become "outstanding" in a field of work); KLEIN, *supra* note 102, at 31–44, 94–109 (describing how expert intuition develops through experience in recognizing patterns indicative of the dynamics of a situation and contrasting intuitive decision-making with "rational choice strategy").

106. *Cf.* Lawrence B. Solum, *A Tournament of Virtue*, 32 FLA. ST. U. L. REV. 1365, 1385 (2005).

107. Both Justice Scalia, who has vociferously opposed foreign citations, and Justice Kennedy, who has referred to foreign sources, have traveled abroad for legal/educational purposes. *See* Linda Greenhouse, *What Justices Do Off the Bench: Many Find Travel Is Broadening*, N.Y. TIMES, May 21, 1993, at B9 (noting that five justices had traveled overseas in the prior year under the sponsorship of education, nonprofit, or governmental groups—Chief Justice Rehnquist and Justices Blackmun, Kennedy, O'Connor, and Scalia).

108. Interestingly, in some countries constitutional court judges (among others) are allowed to take regular sabbaticals, which may be used to spend time abroad. *See, e.g.*, Regulations under the Judges' Remuneration and Conditions of Employment Act 47 of 2001, Government Notice (GN) R894 of 5 July 2002 as amended through 29 April 2005 (S. Afr.).

109. *See* Adarand Constructors, Inc. v. Pena, 515 U.S. 200, 240–41 (1995) (Thomas, J., concurring) (asserting that a "principle of inherent equality . . . underlies and infuses" the Constitution, and quoting from the Declaration of Independence: "We hold these truths to be self evident, that all men are created equal, that they are endowed by their Creator with certain unalienable rights, that among these are Life, Liberty and the pursuit of Happiness."); *see also* GARY JACOBSOHN, APPLE OF GOLD 3–4 (1993) (arguing that for Abraham Lincoln, the Declaration represented the goal toward which the Constitution as law was working).

110. *Cf.* Banco Nacional de Cuba v. Sabbatino, 376 U.S. 398, 437–38 (1964) (referring to what is "conducive to a peaceful international order" and concluding "that both the national interest *and progress toward the goal of establishing the rule of law among nations* are best served by maintaining intact the act of state doctrine in this realm") (emphasis added). *Sabbatino* applied the "act of state" doctrine to preclude courts from determining the validity, under international law, of Cuba's expropriation of certain properties. Although often viewed as a form of federal common law, the act of state doctrine was described by the Court as having "'constitutional' underpinnings." 376 U.S. at 423.

111. Yuval Shany, *How Supreme is the Supreme Law of the Land? Comparative Analysis of the Influence of International Human Rights Treaties Upon the Interpretation of Constitutional Texts by Domestic Courts*, 31 BROOK. J. INT'L L. 341, 349, 350–52 (2006); *see also* Flaherty, *supra* note 83, at 495 (arguing that interpreting a constitutional right in a way inconsistent with international law would "effectively act as an invitation to" some of the states to "themselves engage in a violation" and that there are originalist understandings that would support interpreting the Constitution consistent with the law of nations). Such arguments might be understood to extend the *Charming Betsy* canon of statutory interpretation to constitutional interpretation. *See supra* note 82. *But cf.* text at notes 130–31, below (suggesting that Constitution's silence on conduct required by a treaty may not be inconsistent with treaty obligation if that obligation can be otherwise fulfilled).

112. *See* Michael Kirby, *International Law—The Impact on National Constitutions*, 21 AM. U. INT'L L. REV. 327, 362 (2006) ("To the greatest extent possible, in constitutional as in other branches of the law, domestic courts should seek a reconciliation of the international and municipal legal regimes.").

113. As noted earlier, explicit constitutional texts may trump this interpretive presumption. *See, e.g.*, Matthew v. State, [2004] UKPC 33, [2005] 1 A.C. 433 (appeal taken from Trin. & Tobago) (U.K.) (concluding that a mandatory death penalty was inconsistent with sections 4 and 5 of the Constitution of Trinidad and Tobago, interpreted in light of human rights treaties to which the country was party, *id.* at ¶ 12, but nonetheless finding that section 6 of that constitution, providing that nothing in sections 4 and 5 shall invalidate an existing law, precluded holding the death penalty statute unconstitutional, *id.* at ¶¶ 17–21).

114. Constitutions specify a range of statuses for and relationships with international law (of different types) and domestic law. For discussion, see Anne Peters, *The Globalization of State Constitutions*, *in* NEW PERSPECTIVES ON THE DIVIDE BETWEEN NATIONAL AND INTERNATIONAL LAW 260–66, 294–96 (Janne Nijman & Andre Nollkaemper eds., 2007).

115. *See* Robert M. Cover, *Foreword: Nomos and Narrative*, 97 HARV. L. REV. 4 (1983) (discussing how our "nomos," or "normative universe," is situated in, constructed by, and given meaning by various narratives; "For every constitution there is an epic . . . ").

116. See Chapter 8, below, for discussion.

117. Jon Elster, *Essays: Forces and Mechanisms in the Constitution-Making Process*, 45 DUKE L.J. 364 (1995).

118. Dworkin recognizes the need for both fit and justification in achieving "law as integrity." *See* RONALD DWORKIN, LAW'S EMPIRE 94, 230–31, 410–11 (1986).

119. *Cf.* Jan-Werner Müller, *A General Theory of Constitutional Patriotism*, 6 INT'L J. CONST. L. 72, 79–80 (2008) (stating that it is through "specific debates and even disagreements about the constitution" that a constitutional culture or identity "eventually emerges"); Resnik, *supra* note 38, at 65 (arguing for U.S. courts to ground their decisions vindicating human rights in U.S. law, to facilitate a "daily connection" to one's legal obligations).

120. This is not to deny the possibility of a distinctive self-conception of a national polity as international law compliant, or even as a leader in international legal compliance, in ways that would marry the "local" with the "global" in a particular nation's self-conception. But even in countries with such a "globalist" or "cosmopolitan" self-conception, it seems likely that there will be local particularities to be attended to. *See* Chapter 8, below (discussing Canadian *Adler* decision).

121. *See* McGinnis, *Foreign to Our Constitution*, *supra* note 85, at 318 (arguing that diversity of constitutional approaches is a positive good in producing "information and experimentation").

122. Neuman, *supra* note 85, at 1866–80; *see also* Gerald L. Neuman, *Import, Export and Regional Consent in the Inter-American Court of Human Rights*, 19 EUR. J. INT'L L. 101 (2008).

123. *See* Neuman, *supra* note 85, at 1869 ("Institutional realities may therefore influence both the drafting and the later interpretation of the legal provisions that articulate these rights."). Specifically, Neuman suggests that (1) bright line rules, rather than individualized inquiries, may be adopted in order to facilitate enforcement and compliance; (2) relatively weak enforcement powers of supranational courts may contribute to their demands for national state investigations and prosecutions in order to protect fundamental rights; and (3) the margin of appreciation doctrine may reflect an institutional incapacity

to evaluate differences in local conditions relevant to the implementation of rights. *Id.* at 1869–79.

124. *See, e.g.*, Hein v. Freedom from Religion Foundation, Inc., 551 U.S. 587 (2007) (restricting taxpayer standing to challenge executive branch expenditures claimed to violate the Establishment Clause).

125. *See, e.g.*, Linda C. Fentiman, *Pursuing the Perfect Mother: Why America's Criminalization of Maternal Substance Abuse Is Not the Answer—A Comparative Legal Analysis* (draft of Feb. 1, 2009, at 123, 131–35), forthcoming, 15 MICH. J. GENDER & L. (issue 2) (2009) (discussing the significance of having elected prosecutors).

126. *See* Anne-Marie Slaughter & William Burke-White, *The Future of International Law Is Domestic (Or, the European Way of Law)*, 47 HARV. INT'L L.J. 327, 328–30 (2006).

127. Gerald L. Neuman, *The Uses of International Law in Constitutional Interpretation*, 98 AM. J. INT'L L. 82, 86 (2004); *see also* Andrew Moravcsik, *The Origins of Human Rights Regimes: Democratic Delegation in Postwar Europe*, 54 INT'L ORG. 217, 229 (2000) (arguing that established democracies are less likely to embrace binding commitments to international human rights regimes, because in so doing they "incur an increased, if modest, risk of de facto nullification of domestic laws without a corresponding increase in the expected stability of domestic democracy since the latter is already high").

128. *Cf.* Shany, *supra* note 111, at 375 ("[T]he older the constitutional instrument is, the more developed is the idiosyncratic jurisprudence relating to its interpretation"). On Shany's account, this factor (and others) might help explain, as a positive matter, why some courts might avoid adopting more presumptive (or compulsory) approaches to conforming constitutional law to international human rights obligations. Whether, on his account, the age of the constitution is a sound normative reason to depart from the principle of interpreting constitutions to accord with ratified treaty obligations, is unclear. *Cf. id.* at 403 (noting that a presumption of conformity should be applied with "caution and deference to other constitutional doctrines").

129. For discussion of a "principle of international legality," a "presumption in favour of compliance with international law," see Mattias Kumm, *The Legitimacy of International Law: A Constitutional Framework of Analysis*, 15 EUR. J. INT'L L. 907, 918–20 (2004) (arguing that the international legal system fosters cooperation, contributes to constitutional checks and balances, stabilizes liberal constitutional democracies, enhances individual freedoms and mitigates abuses arising from power asymmetries). For Kumm's account of justified grounds for departure from the international legality principle, see *infra* note 134.

130. *See* Carlos Manuel Vázquez, *The Separation of Powers as a Safeguard of Nationalism*, 83 NOTRE DAME L. REV. 1601, 1613 & n.45 (2008) ("[I]nternational law . . . generally leaves it to the domestic law of each nation to determine the status as domestic law of the nation's obligations under international law. . . . [I]nternational law is generally concerned with ends and not means.") (citing IAN BROWNLIE, STATE RESPONSIBILITY: PART I, at 241 (1983) and quoting 1 OPPENHEIM'S INTERNATIONAL LAW § 21, at 82–83 (Robert Jennings & Arthur Watts eds., 9th ed. 1992) ("'From the standpoint of international law . . . the choice between the direct reception and application of international law, or its transformation into national law by way of statute, is a matter of indifference, as is the choice between . . . legislation, common law or administrative action as the means of giving effect to international obligations.'")). On treaty abrogation, see Goldwater v. Carter, 444 U.S. 996 (1979).

131. Although the decision in *Medellín v. Texas*, 128 S. Ct. 1346 (2008), found some means of implementing the United States' international obligation under the ICJ *Avena* judgment unconstitutional, the decision left open the (unrealized) possibility of national

legislation to do so (for example, by specifically providing for federal judicial review and reconsideration of the claims).

132. *See, e.g.*, David Sloss, *Using International Law to Enhance Democracy*, 47 VA. J. INT'L L. 1 (2006) (arguing that it would better serve democratic process values for courts directly to enforce human rights treaties, like the ICCPR, rather than to interpret the Constitution to incorporate their standards, thereby foreclosing the possibility of a democratic response through ordinary legislation).

133. SEAN D. MURPHY, PRINCIPLES OF INTERNATIONAL LAW 81 (2006). Jus cogens norms, however, do not allow for derogation. *Id.* at 81–82.

134. *See* Kumm, *supra* note 129, at 908–09 (arguing that although international law is presumptively a legitimate influence on "constitutional government," the procedural fairness with which the international norm is developed, the "jurisdictional legitimacy" of its producer, and the substantive justice of the norm may affect whether it should be regarded as requiring compliance). For examples of the kind of resistance to giving international legal norms effect in domestic constitutional interpretation that Kumm's theory would support, see Kim Lane Scheppele, *Other People's Patriot Acts: Europe's Response to September 11th*, 50 LOY. L. REV. 89, 91–92 (2004) (commenting on human rights deficiencies of UN Security Council Resolution 1373); Joined Cases C-402/05 and C415/05, Kadi and Al Barakaat Int'l Found. v. Council and Comm'n, paras. 285, 333–53 (Eur. Ct. Justice, Grand Chamber) (Sept. 3, 2008), *available at* http://curia.europa.eu/jcms/jcms/j_6/home (search "C-402/05" under "case no.") (rejecting lawfulness of the European implementation of UN Security Council directive on terrorist financing as inconsistent with constitutional principles of the European Community to protect fundamental rights); *cf.* Chapter 3, above (noting national court decisions resisting implementation of the European Arrest Warrant).

135. For a detailed analysis of four approaches to coordinating domestic constitutional rights regimes with international human rights, including the difficulties that may arise when the latter is apparently fully incorporated in the former, see Neuman, *supra* note 85, at 1894–98.

136. *Compare* Legal Consequences of the Construction of a Wall in the Occupied Palestinian Territory, Advisory Opinion, 2004 I.C.J. 136 (July 9) (finding the fence in occupied territory to be unlawful under international law) *with* HCJ 2056/04, Beit Sourik Village Council v. Government of Israel, [2004] IsrLR 264 (Isr.) (finding the purpose of the fence lawful, but the location in some places required change to meet standards of proportionality); HCJ 7957/04, Marabeh v. Prime Minister of Israel (Ruling on the Fence surrounding Alfei Menashe), [2005] (2) IsrLR 106, 159–69 (Isr.) (expressing agreement with the legal norms applied by the ICJ in its Advisory Opinion but concluding that the ICJ had an inadequate factual basis before it to appreciate the bona fide security needs to which the fence was addressed).

137. *See* Chapter 2, text at note 125, above.

138. *See also* Karen Knop, *Here and There: International Law in Domestic Courts*, 32 N.Y.U. J. INT'L. L. & POL. 501, 525–31 (2000).

CHAPTER 6. ENGAGING THE TRANSNATIONAL: A CONTEXTUAL FRAMEWORK

1. *See generally* Roger P. Alford, *Four Mistakes in the Debate on "Outsourcing Authority"* 69 ALB. L. REV. 653, 667–68 (2006); *cf.* Richard A. Posner, *Foreword: A Political Court*, 119 HARV. L. REV. 31, 85–86 (2005) (expressing concern about "promiscuous" usages of foreign

sources and about the increased workload for lawyers and judges that foreign citation practice would entail).

2. On the idea of constitutional law as implementation, see RICHARD H. FALLON, JR., IMPLEMENTING THE CONSTITUTION 1–12 (2001). *See also* Walter E. Dellinger, *Of Rights and Remedies: The Constitution as a Sword*, 85 HARV. L. REV. 1532, 1532–33 (1972).

3. *See also* Sarah H. Cleveland, *Our International Constitution*, 31 YALE J. INT'L L. 1, 108 (2006) (discussing the importance of "constitutional receptiveness" in evaluating the proper role of international law in constitutional interpretation).

4. *See* District of Columbia v. Heller, 128 S. Ct. 2783 (2008) (holding that a District of Columbia law prohibiting possessions of handguns violates the Second Amendment's protection of the "right of the people to keep and bear Arms"). The Second Amendment to the U.S. Constitution was previously understood to have application only in the context of the maintenance of state militias, *see* United States v. Miller, 307 U.S. 174, 178 (1939), an interpretation revised in *Heller*. There are few, if any, fully comparable provisions in other national constitutions. *See, e.g.*, CONSTITUCIÓN DE LOS ESTADOS UNIDOS MEXICANOS [Const.], art. 10 (1917) (Mex.), *translated in* 12 CONSTITUTIONS OF THE COUNTRIES OF THE WORLD: MEXICO 9 (Rüdiger Wolfrum & Rainer Grote eds., 2008) (protecting a right to have "arms in their residences" for personal defense, except those that are specifically prohibited by law or are reserved for use by the military; bearing of arms subject to federal regulation); *see also* Constitutionmaking.org, Right to Bear Arms (May 20, 2008), http://www.constitutionmaking.org/reports.html (click on "Rights" and "Bear Arms") (reporting that a right to bear arms "has always been rare and has become even less popular over time," that only 2.18 percent of constitutions surveyed included such a right, and in 2000 only the United States, Mexico, and Guatemala had provisions in force).

5. *See* Hurtado v. California, 110 U.S. 516, 530–31 (1884) (noting European procedural approaches in holding that the grand jury requirement of the Fifth Amendment was not made applicable to the states through the Due Process Clause of the Fourteenth Amendment); *cf.* Palko v. Connecticut, 302 U.S. 319, 325–26 & n.3 (1937) (referring to European law to support decision, since overruled, that Fifth Amendment double jeopardy protection did not apply to state prosecutions because not implicit in the concept of ordered liberty).

6. *See, e.g.*, Edwards v. Aguillard, 482 U.S. 578, 596–97 (1987) (holding that a requirement that public schools teach "creationism" where evolution is taught involves a prohibited state endorsement of religion); McCollum v. Bd. of Educ., 333 U.S. 203, 212 (1948) (holding that public schools may not allow religious classes to be held in school buildings during the school day and require students whose parents so request to attend those classes). *But cf., e.g.*, Zelman v. Simmons-Harris, 536 U.S. 639 (2002) (rejecting a challenge to a public subsidy for school tuition that parents could use at any private school, including a religious one); Zorach v. Clauson, 343 U.S. 306, 315 (1952) (rejecting a challenge to a school policy allowing students to leave grounds during the school day, at their parents' request, to attend off-campus religious classes). On the degree to which the Free Exercise Clause requires state accommodation of religiously motivated practices, compare Wisconsin v. Yoder, 406 U.S. 205, 234 (1972) (holding that the state must provide an exception to the age requirements for mandatory school attendance for the Amish) with Employment Div'n v. Smith, 494 U.S. 872, 885 (1990) (asserting the constitutionality of most "generally applicable" laws, notwithstanding their effects on religious practice, and rejecting a challenge to ban on peyote).

7. *See* Alfred Stepan, *Religion, Democracy and the "Twin Tolerations," in* WORLD RELIGIONS AND DEMOCRACY 3, 6–8 (Larry Diamond et al. eds., 2005) (noting that Denmark, Iceland,

Finland, and Norway all have established churches); *see also* W. Cole Durham, Jr., *Perspectives on Religious Liberty: A Comparative Framework, in* RELIGIOUS HUMAN RIGHTS IN GLOBAL PERSPECTIVE: LEGAL PERSPECTIVES 1, 17 (Johan D. van der Vyver & John Witte, Jr., eds., 1996); U.S. State Dep't, International Religious Freedom Reports, 2001–2008, *available at* http://www.state.gov/g/drl/rls/irf/.

8. 1958 CONST. art. 1 (Fr.).

9. *See* Dominique Custos, *Secularism in French Public Schools: Back to War? The French Statute of March 15, 2004*, 54 AM. J. COMP. L. 337, 356–58 (2006) (stating that France, "which epitomizes a strict secularism of the public spheres in general, and secularism of public schools in particular, . . . simultaneously displays a very sophisticated system of public aid guaranteeing the viability . . . of private-parochial schools" and, in so doing resembles Canada and the UK more than the United States).

10. *See* DONALD P. KOMMERS, THE CONSTITUTIONAL JURISPRUDENCE OF THE FEDERAL REPUBLIC OF GERMANY 444, 484–86 (2d ed. 1997); GRUNDGESETZ (GG) [Basic Law] (F.R.G.), art 140 (incorporating by reference article 137 of the Weimar Constitution). Australia's constitution prohibits the Commonwealth from making "any law for establishing any religion," CONST. AUSTL. Art. 116, and has, according to Australian scholars, been narrowly construed. *See* Attorney-General *ex rel.* Black v. Commonwealth of Australia (1981) 33 A.L.R. 321 (holding that article 116 does not prohibit financial assistance to nongovernment, including religious, schools); *see also infra* note 13.

11. GRUNDGESETZ (GG) [Basic Law](F.R.G.) art. 7 (3), (2).

12. *See McCollum v. Bd. of Educ.*, 333 U.S. at 212. Jefferson's "wall of separation" metaphor is by no means the only relevant understanding of the Establishment Clause, *see, e.g.*, Lynch v. Donnelly, 465 U.S. 668, 673 (1984) (describing metaphor as a "useful figure of speech" but not "wholly accurate"); Philip Hamburger, *Separation and Interpretation*, 18 J. L. & POLITICS 7 (2002) (arguing that the wall of separation metaphor is inconsistent with the Constitution's text), but it is one that has attracted adherence from a number of justices over many years. *See, e.g.*, Lee v. Weisman, 505 U.S. 577, 600–01 (1992) (Blackmun, J., concurring).

13. *Cf.* Zelman v. Simmons-Harris, 536 U.S. 639, 725 (2002) (Breyer, J., dissenting) (recognizing that some foreign countries have "reconciled religious school funding and religious freedom without creating serious strife," but distinguishing the United States in view of its greater religious diversity). An amicus brief argued that empirical experience in England, the Netherlands, and Australia shows that evenhanded government funding of private religious schools was not incompatible with the purposes of the Establishment Clause. *See* Brief of Amici Curiae The Association of Christian Schools International et al. in Support of Petitioners, Zelman v. Simmons-Harris, 536 U.S. 639 (2002) (Nos. 00-1751, 00-1777, 00-1779). Special weight was placed on Australia because its constitution includes a cognate clause. *See supra* note 10. As the brief notes, the leading Australian case discusses the U.S. case law "with subtlety and nuance," Brief of Amici Curiae, *supra* at 27, suggesting the complexity of what might at first appear a more straightforward comparison. Several of the Australian judges distinguished the text of the Australian clause as "more obviously reflect[ing] a concern with the establishment of one religion as against others than the language of the First Amendment which speaks of the 'establishment of religion,' not the 'establishment of any religion.'" *Attorney-General ex rel. Black v. Commonwealth*, 33 A.L.R. at 354 (Mason, J.); *see id.* at 326–27 (Barwick, C.J.) (treating article 116 as a narrower prohibition than the First Amendment); *id.* at 386 (Wilson, J.) (noting a "divergence both in word and context," in that the Australian clause is not part of an inclusive bill of rights and constrains only the national, not the state, governments).

Some judges also argued that in 1900, when the Australian constitution was adopted, the U.S. clause was understood more narrowly, *id.* at 350–51 (Stephen, J.); *id.* at 341–44 (Gibbs, J.), or that under contemporary U.S. case law there was no absolute bar on government financial aid connected to religious educational institutions. *Id.* at 344–45 (Gibbs, J.). *But see id.* at 359–69 (Murphy, J., dissenting) (arguing that U.S. case law should be followed and condemning the statute).

14. Wilkerson v. Utah, 99 U.S. 130, 134 (1879); *see* Vicki C. Jackson, *Constitutional Comparisons: Convergence, Resistance, Engagement*, 119 HARV. L. REV. 109 (2005).

15. *See, e.g.*, Weems v. United States, 217 U.S. 349, 377 (1910) (noting that the challenged punishment "come[s] to us from a government of a different form and genius from ours"); Trop v. Dulles, 356 U.S. 86, 102 (1958) (plurality opinion); McGautha v. California, 402 U.S. 183, 204–05 (1971); Furman v. Georgia, 408 U.S. 238, 255–56 (1972) (Douglas, J., concurring); *id.* at 275, 278–79 (Brennan, J., concurring); Coker v. Georgia, 433 U.S. 584, 592 n.4, 596 n.10 (1977); Enmund v. Florida, 458 U.S. 782, 788, 796 n.22 (1982); Thompson v. Oklahoma, 487 U.S. 815, 830–31 (1988) (plurality opinion); *see also Furman*, 408 U.S. at 404 n.31 (Burger, C.J., dissenting); Robinson v. California, 370 U.S. 660, 672–74 (Douglas, J., concurring); *cf.* Ford v. Wainright, 477 U.S. 399, 409 (1986) (referring to the "natural abhorrence civilized societies feel"). In cases on the special procedural requirements for death penalty sentencing developed in the 1970s, *see, e.g.*, Lockett v. Ohio, 438 U.S. 586, 600–605 (1978) (Burger, C.J., announcing judgment of the Court) (describing dueling demands of standardization and individualization in capital sentencing law); *id.* at 620–21 (Marshall, J., concurring in the judgment), the Court was less inclined to refer to foreign practice, though a British Royal Commission Report on Capital Punishment from 1953 was noted. *See, e.g.*, Gregg v. Georgia, 428 U.S. 153, 184, n.30, 191 (1976) (Stewart, J., announcing judgment of the Court); *see also* Woodson v. North Carolina, 428 U.S. 280, 320 (1976) (Rehnquist, J., dissenting); *cf.* McGautha v. California, 402 U.S. 183, 204–06 (1971).

UN bodies and supranational courts have begun to extend procedural requirements under human right instruments to death sentencing, sometimes drawing on U.S. case law. *See, e.g.*, Thompson v. St. Vincent and the Grenadines, UN Human Rights Comm. (Views), U.N. Doc. CCPR/C/70/D/806/1998, para. 8.2 (2000) (finding a violation of ICCPR art. 6(1) in provisions for a mandatory death penalty for certain murders "without regard to the defendant's personal circumstances or the circumstances of the particular offense"); Hilaire, Constantine and Benjamin et al, 2002 Inter-Am. Ct. H.R. (ser C.) No. 94, paras. 99–108 (June 21, 2002) (concluding that Trinidad and Tobago's mandatory death penalty for murder was inconsistent with Article 4(1) and 4(2) of the American Convention); *id.* at para. 103 n.110 (noting decisions from the UNHRC (from 1990), the Indian Supreme Court (from 1980), and the South African Constitutional Court (from 1995)); *id.* at para. 105 n.111 (noting *Woodson*). *But cf.* Matthew v. State, [2004] UKPC 33, [2005] 1 A.C. 433 (2004) (appeal taken from Trin. & Tobago), discussed above in Chapter 5. Such developments, in supranational or national courts, might provide a basis for useful comparison on procedural issues, including the effects of delay in carrying out death sentences. *Compare, e.g.*, Pratt v. Attorney-General for Jamaica, [1994] 2 A.C. 1 (P.C. 1993) (appeal taken from Jam.) (indicating that a delay of more than five years was presumptively unconstitutional), *cited in* Knight v. Florida, 528 U.S. 990, 995–97 (1999) (Breyer, J., dissenting from the denial of certiorari) *with, e.g.*, Li-ann Thio, *Beyond the "Four Walls" in an Age of Transnational Judicial Conversations: Civil Liberties, Rights Theories and Constitutional Adjudication in Malaysia and Singapore*, 19 COLUM. J. ASIAN L. 428, 477–86 (2006) (discussing Singapore decisions rejecting challenges to delays in execution or mandatory death penalty). For a cautionary discussion of the aftermath of some of the decisions affecting Caribbean nations, see Laurence R. Helfer, *Overlegalizing Human Rights: International Relations Theory and the Commonwealth Caribbean Backlash Against Human Rights Regimes*, 102 COLUM. L. REV. 1832 (2002) (describing, inter alia, Jamaica's renouncing its ratification of the Optional Protocol to the ICCPR in order to comply with the time period for executions set by *Pratt* and the subsequent withdrawal, also in light of a Privy Council decision condemning mandatory death sentences, of Caribbean nations from Privy Council review); Brian D. Tittemore, *The Mandatory Death Penalty in the Commonwealth Carribean and the Inter-American Human Rights System*, 13 WM & MARY BILL RTS. J. 445 (2004).

16. Stanford v. Kentucky, 492 U.S. 361, 369 n.1 (1989) (emphasis in original) (stating that foreign practices cannot "establish the first Eighth Amendment prerequisite, that the practice is accepted among our people," though it can be relevant to determining whether a "'practice uniform among our people'" is required by the Constitution) (quoting *Thompson*, 487 U.S. at 868–69 n.4 (Scalia, J., dissenting)). Under the accepted standard of *Trop v. Dulles*, 356 U.S. 86, 101 (1958) (plurality opinion), the Cruel and Unusual Punishment Clause "draw[s] its meaning from the evolving standards of decency that mark the progress of a maturing society."

17. Atkins v. Virginia, 536 U.S. 304, 316–17 n.21 (2002) (noting worldwide disapproval of the death penalty for the mentally retarded); Roper v. Simmons, 543 U.S. 551, 575–78 (2005) (explaining how the majority's conclusion that the juvenile death penalty is constitutionally disproportionate "finds confirmation in the stark reality that the United States is the only country in the world that continues to give official sanction to the juvenile death penalty"); *see also Atkins*, 536 U.S. at 324–25 (Rehnquist, C.J., dissenting) (criticizing the Court for departing from *Stanford*'s approach on relevance of foreign law). To the extent that the effort in *Stanford* was to exclude consideration of foreign law, or to limit it to situations where a "uniform" practice existed, it was rejected in *Atkins* and *Roper*; to the extent that *Stanford* can be read as an effort to limit the role of foreign law to that of confirming conclusions to which domestic sources had led the Court, *Atkins* and *Roper* were arguably consistent with that effort.

18. On treatment of the detainees after 9/11, see, for example, Padilla v. Rumsfeld, 352 F. 3d 695, 699–702 (2d Cir. 2003) (describing the incommunicado detention, for eighteen months at that point, of a U.S. citizen arrested and held in the United States), *rev'd and remanded*, 542 U.S. 426 (2004); JOSEPH MARGULIES, GUANTÁNAMO AND THE ABUSE OF PRESIDENTIAL POWER 3–14 (2006); Owen Fiss, *The War Against Terrorism and the Rule of Law*, 26 OXFORD J. LEGAL STUD. 235, 239 (2006); Harold Hongju Koh, *Can the President Be Torturer in Chief?*, 81 IND. L.J. 1145, 1150–51 (2006) (discussing the since-withdrawn "Torture Memo").

19. U.S. CONST. art. I, § 9 ("The privilege of the Writ of Habeas Corpus shall not be suspended, unless when in Cases of Rebellion or Invasion the public Safety may require it."); *see* Zechariah Chafee, Jr., *The Most Important Human Right in the Constitution*, 32 B.U. L. REV. 143 (1952).

20. *See* GEOFFREY R. STONE, PERILOUS TIMES: FREE SPEECH IN WARTIME FROM THE SEDITION ACT OF 1798 TO THE WAR ON TERRORISM (2004) (describing political and judicial tendencies excessively to sacrifice freedom of expression in six episodes of war or heightened national security related fears); *see also* Venkat Iyer, *The Supreme Court of India*, in JUDICIAL ACTIVISM IN COMMON LAW SUPREME COURTS 121, 132 (Brice Dickson ed., 2007) (referring to the likelihood of judges being influenced "by the tumultuous events" of Indian independence in their willingness to uphold preventive detention). Professor Stone nonetheless found some cause for optimism that the U.S. Court and polity have learned from past mistakes. *See* STONE, *supra*, at 533, 537, 548–50.

21. *Cf.* Jennifer Nedelsky, *Communities of Judgment and Human Rights*, 1 THEOR. INQ. L. 245, 280–81 (2000) (suggesting that the "'common sense of mankind' can . . . serve as an aid to the imagination in difficult times[,] [w]hen one's most immediate community . . . [has] become an unreliable ground for exercising the enlarged mentality" that strives toward impartial judgment).

22. *See* Hon. Margaret H. Marshall, *"Wise Parents Do Not Hesitate to Learn from their Children": Interpreting State Constitutions in an Age of Global Jurisprudence*, 79 N.Y.U. L. REV. 1633, 1650–55 (2004) (urging U.S. courts to consider other democracies that, "under constant threat . . . have developed a . . . jurisprudence for protecting fundamental rights in times of crisis" to help develop U.S. law "to prevent systematic dehumanization in times of national crisis"); *see also* HCJ 5100/94, Public Comm. Against Torture v. Israel, (Isr. 1999) (Barak, P.), *translated in* 14 Isr. L. Rep. 567, 605 ("A democracy must sometimes fight with one hand tied behind its back," because the rule of law and protection of individual liberties "constitute important components in its understanding of security," that "strengthen its spirit and . . . allow[] it to overcome its difficulties."); Al-Kateb v. Godwin, (2004) 219 C.L.R. 562, 621 (Austl.) (Kirby, J., dissenting). Cross-national judicial engagement on such issues may be of especial value as globalization has worked to increase the power of national executives vis-à-vis their own legislatures. *See* Chapter 4, note 174 above.

23. *See* Brief Amicus Curiae of Comparative Law Scholars and Experts on the Laws of the United Kingdom and Israel in Support of Respondent, Rumsfeld v. Padilla, 542 U.S. 426 (2004) (No. 03-1027) (surveying the practices for detention of suspected terrorists in Australia, Canada, France, Germany, Spain, the UK, and Israel; also noting authoritarian governments that engaged in indefinite (and abusive) detention practices and been condemned by the United States for so doing); *see also* Stephen J. Schulhofer, *Checks and Balances in Wartime: American, British and Israeli Experiences*, 102 MICH. L. REV. 1906, 1909 (2004) (concluding that "[t]he counter-terrorism adjustments sought and accepted in other countries differ by many large orders of magnitude" from those here). Both sources suggest that the "lawless enclave" approach argued for in the United States after 9/11 went well beyond the terrorism-motivated departures from ordinary procedural norms enacted or upheld in Europe or in Israel.

24. *Compare* Hamdi v. Rumsfeld, 542 U.S. 507, 554, 573 (2004) (Scalia, J., dissenting) (drawing implications from the Treason Clause to suggest that when a citizen is accused of waging war against the country, the Constitution limits the government to criminal prosecutions in Article III courts or to suspension of habeas corpus, and accordingly that Hamdi's detention as an enemy combatant was unlawful) *with id.* at 523–24 (O'Connor, J., for the plurality) (disagreeing with Justice Scalia's reading of the Treason Clause in light of *Ex parte Quirin*, 317 U.S. 1 (1942)).

25. Pending as of this writing is a case presenting some related issues, concerning the detention, as an enemy combatant, of a legal resident alien, seized at his home in Illinois and held by the military since 2003. *See* Al-Marri v. Wright, 487 F.3d 160 (4th Cir. 2007), *vacated*, Al-Marri v. Pucciarelli, 534 F.3d 213 (4th Cir. en banc), *cert. granted*, 2008 U.S. LEXIS 8886 (U.S., Dec. 5, 2008).

26. For a comprehensive discussion, see Cleveland, *supra* note 3, at 12–101 (describing uses of international law in explicating specific international law terms, as background principles on issues of sovereignty, territory, and federalism, and in individual rights cases).

27. *See* The Prize Cases, 67 U.S. (2 Black) 635 (1863); Hamdan v. Rumsfeld, 548 U.S. 557, 593–95 & n.23 (2006); *id.* at 637 (Kennedy, J. concurring) (construing federal statutes

to incorporate law of war restrictions and holding that the President had acted unlawfully in establishing military commissions inconsistent with the international law of war); *see also* David Golove, *Military Tribunals, International Law, and the Constitution: A Franckian-Madisonian Approach*, 35 N.Y.U. J. INT'L L. & POL. 363, 365–66 (2003) (arguing that by "designating him commander in chief, the Constitution grants [the President] the power to exercise (at least some of) the belligerent rights of the United States under international law"); Ingrid Brunk Wuerth, *International Law and Constitutional Interpretation: The Commander in Chief Clause Reconsidered*, 106 MICH. L. REV. 61 (2007). *See generally* Cleveland, *supra* note 3, at 20–21; David J. Barron & Martin S. Lederman, *The Commander in Chief at The Lowest Ebb: A Constitutional History*, 121 HARV. L. REV. 941, 952–55, 994–95 (2008) (noting "deep interrelationship" between Congress's war powers and "customary international laws of war" assumed in the nation's early years, and President Lincoln's assumption that use of force was constrained by customary international law).

28. Jack M. Balkin, *Bush v. Gore and the Boundary Between Law and Politics*, 110 YALE L.J. 1407, 1444 (2001).

29. Alan Watson, *Aspects of Reception of Law*, 44 AM. J. COMP. L. 335, 335, 339–41 (1996) (noting the "chance" that Scotland decided to accept degree students from three African countries, which contributed to increased borrowing from Scottish legal authorities in the development of the law of those countries). Watson's views about the frequency of borrowings and transplants are controversial. *See, e.g.*, Pierre Legrand, *The Impossibility of "Legal Transplants,"* 4 MAASTRICHT J. EUR. & COMP. L. 111, 112–20 (1997) (arguing that Watson's focus on "rules" is too narrow, that even apparently similar rules differ in their meanings in different countries, and thus that transplants, in Watson's sense, are not possible).

30. Sujit Choudhry, *Migration as a New Metaphor in Comparative Constitutional Law, in* THE MIGRATION OF CONSTITUTIONAL IDEAS 1, 19–25 (Sujit Choudhry ed., 2006).

31. Kim Lane Scheppele, *Aspirational and Aversive Constitutionalism: The Case for Studying Cross-Constitutional Influence Through Negative Models*, 1 INT'L J. CONST. L. 296, 297 (2003); *see also* Sujit Choudhry, *The Lochner Era and Comparative Constitutionalism*, 2 INT'L J. CONST. L. 1 (2004) (describing *Lochner*'s "aversive" role in constitutional development outside the United States).

32. H. PATRICK GLENN, LEGAL TRADITIONS OF THE WORLD 30–39 (2000).

33. *Cf.* Harold Hongju Koh, *Internalization Through Socialization*, 54 DUKE L.J. 975, 980 (2005) (describing "acculturation" as incomplete persuasion or a partial form of internalization); Ryan Goodman & Derek Jinks, *How to Influence States: Socialization and International Human Rights Law*, 54 DUKE L.J. 621, 638 (2004) (discussing acculturation as "the general process of adopting the beliefs and behavioral patterns of the surrounding culture"). On what can remake issues as "open" ones, see sources cited Chapter 4, note 97, above.

34. Although judicial opinions may not be researched in the way scholarly articles are, it is generally reasonable to presume knowledge of a particular system by one of its appellate judges.

35. *See, e.g.*, Leviton v. United States, 343 U.S. 946, 948 (1952) (Frankfurter, J., mem. concerning denial of certiorari) (quoting lower court's reliance on Mark Twain story); Fla. Dep't of Health & Rehabilitative Serv. v. Fla. Nursing Home Ass'n, 450 U.S. 147, 154 nn.12, 14 (1981) (Stevens, J., concurring) (quoting from Benjamin Cardozo's scholarly work, *The Judicial Process*, and from the famed account of British Lord Chancellor Sir Thomas More's devotion to the law over political pressures, "'Yes, I'd give the Devil benefit of law . . . '").

36. *Cf.* Ran Hirschl, *The Question of Case Selection in Comparative Constitutional Law*, 53 AM. J. COMP. L. 125 (2005) (explaining differences between selecting cases for comparison because they are "most similar," "most different," "prototypical," "most difficult" or "outlier cases"). Hirschl distinguishes comparisons for purposes of self-understanding from efforts to draw causal inferences about the relationships between one phenemonon and another; he argues that more systematic attention to case selection will improve the reliability of causal, functional inferences.

37. *Cf.* Katzenbach v. Morgan, 384 U.S. 641, 654–56 (1966) (upholding legislation based on the legislature's capacity to determine what neutral requirements may pose discriminatory barriers to some voters). *But cf.* Boerne v. Flores, 521 U.S. 507, 527 (1997) (rejecting *Morgan*'s implication that Congress has a non-remedial, substantive power to interpret constitutional rights).

38. *See, e.g.*, Muller v. Oregon, 208 U.S. 412, 419 & n.1 (1908); *see also* Lochner v. New York, 198 U.S. 45, 70–72 (1905) (Harlan, J., dissenting).

39. *See, e.g.*, Lawrence v. Texas, 539 U.S. 558, 571–73 (2003) (invoking European law to rebut prior suggestion that Western civilization generally condemned homosexuality); *see also* Dred Scott v. Sandford, 60 U.S. (19 How.) 393, 534–35 (1857) (McLean, J., dissenting); *id.* at 591–92 (Curtis, J., dissenting) (invoking European law to rebut majority's claims).

40. *But cf.* Rosalind Dixon, *A Democratic Theory of Constitutional Comparison*, 56 AM. J. COMP. L. 947, 961–63, 975–76 (2008) (suggesting that recently enacted statutes, like constitutional court decisions, are likely to be preceded by the kind of serious deliberation that may be considered by domestic courts in trying to identify "co-evolution" of democratic values).

41. The terms and appointment mechanisms of some constitutional courts may conduce to their judges representing the general legal views of currently dominant parties. *See, e.g.*, VICKI C. JACKSON & MARK TUSHNET, COMPARATIVE CONSTITUTIONAL LAW 498–99 (2d ed. 2006) (describing various appointment methods).

42. *See, e.g.*, Jeremy Waldron, *The Core of the Case Against Judicial Review*, 115 YALE L.J. 1346, 1382–86 (2006) (arguing, inter alia, that legislative debate on important public issues tends to get to the moral heart of the matter more than judicial reasoning); ADRIAN VERMEULE, JUDGING UNDER UNCERTAINTY 230–88 (2006) (arguing on cost-benefit grounds that judges should "defer to legislatures on the interpretation of constitutional texts that are ambiguous, can be read at multiple levels of generality, or embody aspirational norms whose content changes over time with shifting public values"); MARK TUSHNET, TAKING THE CONSTITUTION AWAY FROM THE COURTS (1999) (arguing that on balance, judicial review does more harm than good to democracy, equality, and liberty, and that such issues should be left to democratically legitimate legislatures).

43. *But cf.* Dixon, *supra* note 40, at 975–76 (emphasizing similarity of judicial and legislative decisions insofar as they "will . . . almost always be preceded by significant deliberation . . . whether changes are adopted by judicial or legislative means," such as legislative repeal of prohibitions of sodomy). Some have suggested that a court decision, unlike a statute, cannot be taken to represent the view of its polity for purposes of determining whether there is a consensus, at least if the decision does "not purport to reflect popular sentiment." Roper v. Simmons, 543 U.S. 551, 612 n.4 (2005) (Scalia, J., dissenting). This may draw too stark a line. If a court has delegated authority to rule, it is in at least some sense authorized to "speak for" as well as "speak to" its polity; a consensus of jurists, reasoning about similar constitutional commitments, may merit consideration even if the decisions are regarded as principled judgments not closely tied to then-current majority opinion. (The Eighth Amendment requires attention both to "unusual[ness]"

and "cruel[ty]"). For arguments from foreign practice for judicial *restraint* in favor of legislative decision-making concerning abolition of the death penalty, see Furman v. Georgia, 408 U.S. 238, 404–05 & n.31 (1972) (Burger, C.J., dissenting) (emphasizing the legislative character of change on the death penalty in Canada and Great Britain); *id.* at 438 & nn.23, 24, 462 n.62 (Powell, J., dissenting) (to same effect).

44. *See* Cleveland, *supra* note 3, at 115–22 (discussing impact of acceptance or rejection by U.S. political branches on the persuasive force of international law in constitutional interpretation); *see also* Mattias Kumm, *Democratic Constitutionalism Encounters International Law: Terms of Engagement,* in THE MIGRATION OF CONSTITUTIONAL IDEAS 256, 268–73 (Sujit Choudhry ed., 2006) (arguing that the procedural legitimacy by which an international norm is formed, and the degree of participation, transparency, and accountability in that process, should inform the degree to which it should attract adherence). (For earlier discussion, from which parts of this section draw, see Vicki C. Jackson, *Constitutional Law and Transnational Comparisons: The Youngstown Decision and American Exceptionalism,* 30 HARV. J.L. & PUB. POL'Y 191 (2006)).

45. For critique of such "soft law" sources of customary international law, see Jack L. Goldsmith & Eric A. Posner, *Understanding the Resemblance Between Modern and Traditional Customary International Law,* 40 VA. J. INT'L L. 639, 640–41 (2000). *Cf.* Bruno Simma & Philip Alston, *The Sources of Human Rights Law: Custom, Jus Cogens, and General Principles,* 12 AUSTL. Y.B. INT'L L. 82, 89 (1992) (describing reliance on such soft sources as a "cultured pearl version of customary law" that operates "through proclamation, exhortation, repetition, incantation, lament").

46. *See, e.g.,* Statute of the International Court of Justice art. 59, June 26, 1945, 59 Stat. 1031 (decisions are binding only as to the parties and only as to the case).

47. *See generally* SEAN MURPHY, INTERNATIONAL LAW (2006).

48. UN Security Council resolutions, which can be binding, reflect the votes of only a small number of nations, with veto power reserved to an even smaller number. Although all parties to the UN Charter have in some sense consented to decision-making by the Security Council, the delegation of authority dilutes the connection between lawmaking in the Council and democratic self-governance, at least for those members without a seat on the Council. *See generally* Michael C. Dorf, *Dynamic Incorporation of Foreign Law,* 157 U. PA. L. REV. 103 (2008).

49. *See* Chapter 5, text at notes 111–14, 129–32 above.

50. *See* Chapter 5, text at notes 130–32 above (noting that international law is ordinarily indifferent as to how an international obligation is complied with, for example, whether by constitutional or statutory law).

51. *See* U.S. CONST. art. II, § 2 (President to make treaties with the advice and consent of the Senate); *cf.* Bruce Ackerman & David Golove, *Is NAFTA Constitutional?,* 108 HARV. L. REV. 801, 873–917 (1995) (arguing that historical developments supported the constitutionality of congressional-executive agreements as an alternative to treaties). *But cf.* Laurence H. Tribe, *Taking Text and Structure Seriously: Reflections on Free-Form Method in Constitutional Interpretation,* 108 HARV. L. REV. 1221, 1249–79 (1995) (arguing that the Treaty Clause provides the exclusive method for forming international agreements and thus arguing against the Ackerman-Golove position). I take no position here on the constitutionality of congressional-executive international agreements.

52. *See* Chapter 5, above for discussion. If the United States has not ratified a treaty but has only signed it, that act would have considerably less relevance than ratification as to the constitutional understandings of the political branches, notwithstanding any obligation under international law not to defeat the object and purpose of a signed but not

ratified treaty. *See* Vienna Convention on the Law of Treaties art. 18, *opened for signature* May 23, 1969, 1155 U.N.T.S. 331; *see also* Cleveland, *supra* note 3, at 115; *cf.* Brandon P. Denning & Michael D. Ramsey, *American Insurance Ass'n v. Garamendi and Executive Preemption in Foreign Affairs*, 46 WM. & MARY L. REV. 825 (2004) (denying that the President has any power to make law preemptive on the states based on an agreement with a foreign power, absent Senate ratification). On reservations, understandings, and declarations accompanying treaty ratification, see Chapters 7 and 8 below.

53. *See, e.g.*, Sanchez-Llamas v. Oregon, 548 U.S. 331 (2006). If the political branches have clearly rejected an international rule, it may still be considered as a form of persuasive authority (like comparative law), but without whatever added weight would come from any presumption of constitutionality, or expression of legislative views of constitutional meaning, that may accompany a ratified treaty. *See also* Cleveland, *supra* note 3, at 116–18 (suggesting that political branches' rejection of a rule of international law would bear against its persuasiveness in constitutional interpretation, but is not dispositive given the Court's independent interpretive authority). In some areas, the action of the political branches would bear directly on the requirements of constitutional doctrine. *See id.* at 117–18 (suggesting that U.S. rejection of an international prohibition on a punishment would be directly relevant to whether, under Eighth Amendment doctrine, a domestic "consensus" exists, but would leave room for consideration of the international norm in the Court's exercise of independent judgment on whether the punishment was "cruel and unusual").

54. *See* RESTATEMENT OF THE LAW (THIRD) FOREIGN RELATIONS LAW OF THE UNITED STATES § 102 cmt. d (1987) ("[I]n principle a state that indicates its dissent from a practice while the law is still in the process of development is not bound by that rule even after it matures").

55. The degree to which the legal rules of international law, as compared to domestic law, are clear and determinate is itself contested. *See* Karen Knop, *Here and There: International Law in Domestic Courts*, 32 N.Y.U. J. INT'L L. & POL. 501, 507, 515–18, 525 (2000) (contrasting "traditional" understanding of international law as either binding or not with a more "multivocal" understanding of the diverse meaning and uses of international law and noting the "blurring of international law into comparative law").

56. *See* Michael D. Ramsey, *The Empirical Dilemma of International Law*, 41 SAN DIEGO L. REV. 1243, 1247–48 (2004) [hereinafter Ramsey, *Empirical Dilemma*].

57. *See* Curtis A. Bradley & Jack L. Goldsmith, *Customary International Law as Federal Common Law: A Critique of the Modern Position*, 110 HARV. L. REV. 815, 839–40 (1997).

58. *See* Knop, *Here and There*, *supra* note 55, at 525–31; *see also* David Kennedy, *One, Two, Three, Many Legal Orders: Legal Pluralism and the Cosmopolitan Dream*, 31 N.Y.U. REV. L. & SOC. CHANGE 641, 646–54 (2007) (urging study of "comparative international law").

59. In the unusual case where customary international law develops but does not apply to a country because it has been a persistent objector, *see* MURPHY, *supra* note 47, at 81, some more comparative judgment is needed in deciding on the relevance of the international rule as a source in constitutional interpretation. Not only is comparability at issue, but concerns for the role of other branches and levels of government would bear on the persuasive value of such a source. *See supra* notes 44, 53.

60. *See* Gerald L. Neuman, *Human Rights and Constitutional Rights: Harmony and Dissonance*, 55 STAN. L. REV. 1863, 1876–78 (2003).

61. *See* Chapter 8, below (discussing Justice Breyer's dissent in Printz v. United States, 521 U.S. 898, 976 (1997)).

62. 543 U.S. 551 (2005).

63. *See* Cleveland, *supra* note 3, at 79, 113–15; *see also* MURPHY, *supra* note 47, at 330 (describing conclusion of the Inter-American Commission on Human Rights, in Beazley, Case 212.412, Inter-Am. C.H.R., Report No. 101/03 (2003), that in executing juvenile offenders the United States had "violated an international norm of jus cogens").

64. The Paquete Habana, 175 U.S. 677, 700 (1900); *see also* José A. Cabranes, *International Law by Consent of the Governed*, 42 VAL. U. L. REV. 119, 122–23 (2007) (observing that unlike foreign law, which may be a tool for interpreting the Constitution, "international law is more than an interpretive tool . . . [but] is part of the law of the United States").

65. *See supra* notes 26, 27. *See generally* Cleveland, *supra* note 3; JORDAN J. PAUST, INTERNATIONAL LAW AS LAW OF THE UNITED STATES (2d ed. 2003).

66. Sujit Choudhry, *Globalization in Search of a Justification: Toward a Theory of Comparative Constitutional Interpretation*, 74 IND. L.J. 816, 838–39 (1999) (defining genealogical relationships as "the birth of one constitutional order from another," or a relationship "like siblings who have emerged from the same parent legal system"). The proper influence of "genealogical" relationships has been contested. *Compare* Roper v. Simmons, 543 U.S. 551, 577 (2005) (asserting particular relevance of British practice in light of the Eighth Amendment's derivation from British law) *with id.* at 626–27 (Scalia, J., dissenting) (arguing that British law is irrelevant, in light of its lack of a constraining written constitution and ability to simply change, e.g., double jeopardy or jury rules, and its adherence to European human rights norms). *Roper*'s majority has the better of the argument. Examining genealogically related developments illuminates a range of plausible interpretations of a similar text adopted in a similar legal context, *see* Choudhry, *supra*, at 838–39; Dixon, *supra* note 40, at 955 (describing genealogical theory's focus on "the internal logic of particular legal principles, or the relationship between those principles and specific legal rules or standards"), and due allowance can be made for specific British departures from U.S. constitutional commitments.

67. Youngstown Sheet & Tube Co. v. Sawyer, 343 U.S. 579, 651–52 (1952) (Jackson, J., concurring).

68. Printz v. United States, 521 U.S. 898, 921 n.11 (1997); *id.* at 976–78 (Breyer, J., dissenting); *cf.* Banco Nacional de Cuba v. Sabbatino, 376 U.S. 378, 439–72 (1964) (White, J., dissenting) (discussing whether the judicial power could properly address certain issues without interfering with executive power and referring to foreign judicial decisions).

69. *See, e.g.*, ICCPR arts. 2(3)(b), 8(3)(b), 9(3)–(4), 14(1); ECHR art. 6 (requiring an "independent and impartial tribunal"); *see also, e.g.*, McGonnell v. United Kingdom, 2000-II Eur. Ct. H.R. 107 (2000) (finding the Royal Court of Guernsey to lack impartiality because the Bailiff, who served as its senior judge, also served in the government and had presided over the legislative body's adoption of the development plan at issue in the litigation); Chapter 3, above. On the international law concern for "denial of justice," see Robert B. Ahdieh, *Between Dialogue and Decree: International Review of National Courts*, 79 N.Y.U. L. REV. 2029, 2127–31 (2004) (arguing that the concept has roots in the nineteenth century and extends beyond the area of human rights to commercial and investment settings).

70. *See, e.g.*, ICCPR art. 9(1) (stating that deprivations of liberty must be pursuant to such grounds and procedures "as are established by law").

71. This is not to say that customary or treaty law might not further develop over time. *See, e.g.*, Joaquin P. Terceno, III, Note, *Burying the Truth: The Murder of Belfast Human Rights Lawyer Patrick Finucane and Britain's "Secret" Public Inquiries*, 74 FORDHAM L. REV. 3297, 3309–17 (2006) (describing arguments, including by the British Parliament's

Human Rights Committee, suggesting that an inadequately independent investigatory inquiry into a murder could violate Article 2 of the ECHR).

72. *See, e.g.*, Daniel Kaufmann & Aart Craay, *Governance Indicators: Where Are We, Where Should We Be Going?*, 23 WORLD BANK RESEARCH OBSERVER 1 (2008); International Monetary Fund, The IMF and Good Governance (Factsheet, Sept. 2008), http://www.imf.org/external/np/exr/facts/gov.htm.

73. *See, e.g.*, Stephen J. Schnably, *Emerging International Law Constraints on Constitutional Structure and Revision: A Preliminary Appraisal*, 62 U. MIAMI L. REV. 417 (2008) (describing "emerging" norms concerning separation of powers and constitutional amendment); Terceno, *Burying the Truth*, *supra* note 71.

74. Michael D. Ramsey, *International Materials and Domestic Rights: Reflections on* Atkins *and* Lawrence, 98 AM. J. INT'L L. 69, 71 (2004) [hereinafter Ramsey, *International Materials*]; *see also* Ramsey, *Empirical Dilemma*, *supra* note 56, at 1255 (noting the "gap between rhetoric and reality" in the behavior multilateral treaties condemn and the actions of signatories).

75. *Cf.* Goodman & Jinks, *How to Influence States*, *supra* note 33, at 676 ("The language used to define obligations in human rights treaties is notoriously vague compared with the language used in other legal domains."). On the role of "determinacy" on the legitimacy of international law, see THOMAS M. FRANCK, THE POWER OF LEGITIMACY AMONG NATIONS 50–90 (1990) (discussing substantive and procedural aspects of determinacy).

76. *See* Jack Goldsmith & Daryl Levinson, *Law for States: International Law, Constitutional Law, Public Law* (Oct. 2008) (unpublished draft on file with author) (discussing the "proliferation" of international law). Goldsmith and Levinson suggest that there may be comparable levels of uncertainty in domestic constitutional law and that the levels of uncertainty in international and constitutional law share more in common when compared to private law. *Id.* at 15–20. But as they recognize, the Constitution's text is treated as settling many important and operative features of the U.S. constitutional system, including the makeup of the national government; and the U.S. Supreme Court operates as a final decision-maker across a wide array of domestic constitutional issues in ways that simply do not exist at the international level. Thus, I take their point to be that the *causes* of uncertainty over contested constitutional issues bear some resemblance to the causes of uncertainty in international law, because with respect to the most contested issues there may also be a contest over the authority of any one branch of the national government to provide a final settlement.

77. *See* ANNE F. BAYEFSKY, THE U.N. HUMAN RIGHTS TREATY SYSTEM: UNIVERSALITY AT THE CROSSROADS 8 (2001) ("[I]n only 20% of individual cases disclosing a violation, have state parties been prepared to provide a remedy."); Laurence R. Helfer & Anne-Marie Slaughter, *Why States Create International Tribunals: A Response to Professors Posner and Yoo*, 93 CAL. L. REV. 899, 924 (2005) (reporting that the Inter-American Commission on Human Rights in 2003 found that "full compliance" and "partial compliance" occurred in, respectively, only 8 percent and 47 percent of disputes); Laurence R. Helfer & Anne-Marie Slaughter, *Toward a Theory of Effective Supranational Adjudication*, 107 YALE L.J. 273, 344–45 (1997) (indicating that a 1995 study found that in only 30 percent of the matters before the UN Human Rights Committee did the parties to the ICCPR exhibit a "willingness" to implement the "views" of that committee or to "offer the applicant an appropriate remedy"); *see also* Oona A. Hathaway, *Do Human Rights Treaties Make a Difference?*, 111 YALE L.J. 1935 (2002) (finding that ratification of human rights treaties is in some cases associated with worse human rights practices); Laurence R. Helfer, *Nonconsensual International Lawmaking*, 2008 U. ILL. L. REV. 71, 87 (2008) ("Compliance with human

rights treaties varies widely. . . ."). *But cf., e.g.,* Ryan Goodman & Derek Jinks, *Measuring the Effects of Human Rights Treaties,* 14 EUR. J. INT'L L. 171 (2003) (questioning Hathaway's methodology and measurements and suggesting that ratifications of human rights treaties help build a "transnational human rights culture"); Helfer & Slaughter, *Why States Create International Tribunals, supra,* at 916–20 (arguing that the effectiveness of a tribunal is not fully captured by compliance rates).

78. *But cf.* Goldsmith & Levinson, *supra* note 76, at 31–35 (suggesting that the mechanisms by which constitutional law is enforced are similar to those that account for compliance with international law, whether they be through the self-enforcing dynamics of institutional self-interest or the constructive effects of the law toward legitimacy-based or acculturated "compliance pulls"). Yet the authors recognize that "there do seem to be cases in which powerful coalitions really do act in accord with constitutional rules that cut against their immediate self-interest," *id.* at 32, and acknowledge the possibility that international law's "lack of top-down enforcement is distinctive." *Id.* at 37.

79. Harold Hongju Koh, *Transnational Legal Process,* 75 NEB. L. REV. 181 (1996). On the pull of formal legality, see Kumm, *supra* note 44, at 262–64.

80. *See* Ryan Goodman & Derek Jinks, *Toward an Institutional Theory of Sovereignty,* 55 STAN. L. REV. 1749, 1753–54, 1764–65 (2003) [hereinafter *Institutional Theory of Sovereignty*] (emphasizing what they refer to as "exogenous social forces" in organization of states).

81. *Cf. id.* at 1758 (arguing that states operate within a "world culture").

82. For a discussion of the interdependence of domestic sources in constitutional adjudication, see Richard H. Fallon, Jr., *A Constructivist Coherence Theory of Constitutional Interpretation,* 100 HARV. L. REV. 1189, 1240–43 (1987).

83. *See supra* note 77. Perhaps human rights is an area in which Professor Louis Henkin's well-known assertion—that most countries comply with most international law most of the time, LOUIS HENKIN, HOW NATIONS BEHAVE: LAW AND FOREIGN POLICY 320–21 (2d ed. 1979)—holds less true. Hathaway, *supra* note 77, at 1940 (finding, in a major quantitative study of human rights treaties, that "noncompliance with treaty obligations appears to be common").

84. *See* Walter F. Murphy, *Constitutions, Constitutionalism, and Democracy, in* CONSTITUTIONALISM AND DEMOCRACY: TRANSITIONS IN THE CONTEMPORARY WORLD 3, 8 (Douglas Greenberg et al. eds., 1993) (noting Charles Beard's criticism of the Constitution's hypocrisy); JACKSON & TUSHNET, *supra* note 41, at 229; *see also* EDWARD MCWHINNEY, CONSTITUTION-MAKING: PRINCIPLES, PROCESS, PRACTICE 8–9 (1981) (discussing the Thirteenth, Fourteenth, and Fifteenth Amendments in contrasting "law-in-books" and "law-in-action"). Even in contemporary life there may be areas where compliance with the U.S. Supreme Court's decisions is far from complete. *See* Mark Tushnet, *Conservative Constitutional Theory,* 59 TUL. L. REV. 910, 913 (1985) (asserting that the Court's "school prayer decisions are widely evaded"). For an extended comparison of international and constitutional law, see Goldsmith & Levinson, *supra* note 76.

85. Indeed, Justice Breyer's citation to a judicial decision from Zimbabwe earned criticism, perhaps in part because Zimbabwe's rule of law traditions were not strong enough to credit that judicial decisions would correspond with practice on the ground. *See* Knight v. Florida, 528 U.S. 990, 995–97 (1999) (Breyer, J., dissenting from the denial of certiorari), discussed in Chapter 4, text at note 106, above.

86. Arguments, for example, from the language of an ICCPR provision may, notwithstanding its binding character as a matter of international law, be weighed differently than arguments based on the reasoned decision of a constitutional court in a comparable democracy on a related issue of constitutional law. *Cf.* Sanchez-Lllamas v. Oregon, 548

U.S. 331, 334 & n.3 (2006) (relying on domestic practice of foreign nations concerning remedies for violation of the Vienna Convention on Consular Relations).

87. *See also* Charles Fried, *Scholars and Judges: Reason and Power*, 23 HARV. J.L. & PUB. POL'Y 807, 823 (2000) ("The prospect of the real life effect of her decision gives off the vapors which the judge inhales to nourish her prophetic utterances."); Michael Kirby, *The Road from Bangalore: The First Ten Years of the Bangalore Principles on the Domestic Application of International Human Rights Norms*, http://www.lawfoundation.net.au/resources/kirby/papers/19981226_html (click on "browse date index" under the heading "Justice Kirby's papers" and scroll to December 1998) (last visited Sept. 14, 2008) (noting skepticism about international tribunals and committees, and the generality of expression in many international human rights instruments); *cf.* Michael Kirby, *The Role of the Judge in Advancing Human Rights by Reference to International Human Rights Norms*, 62 AUSTL. L.J. 514, 523 (1988) (noting concerns for "hypocrisy and double standards" in the process of norm development in international law in which "authoritarian regimes indifferent to human rights" purport to lay down law for others in "vaguely-worded instruments"). On differences among international tribunals, see *infra* note 90. The persuasive value of nonbinding decisions of foreign or international tribunals may be enhanced, or diminished, by their specific provenance in many ways: by the reputation of the tribunal's members as expert expositors of law; by the processes followed in reaching a decision; by their record of effectiveness; and by the comparability of contexts. These factors are not wholly independent: the "reputation" of a tribunal may be related to its processes and to expected compliance with its rulings; reputation may also be indirectly dependent on comparability, since the scope of reputational inquiry (especially as to foreign courts) may well be limited by language and other sociocultural factors.

88. *See* MURPHY, *supra* note 47, at 320–23. The UNHRC receives and reviews reports from states-parties, issues "general comments" on interpretive issues, and responds to individual complaints (pursuant to an optional protocol to the ICCPR and available only as to those states that are parties to that protocol) with the Committee's "Views," generally regarded as nonbinding. That international monitoring committees or courts sit outside any particular national state might be said to enable a more distanced, impartial view of the application of the international norm; but this distance may at the same time be seen as unduly isolating the decision-maker from the overarching national context of implementation. On concerns about impartiality, see *infra* text at notes 109–11. *Cf.* Helfer & Slaughter, *Why States Create International Tribunals*, *supra* note 77 (reviewing literature and describing complex relationships between a tribunal's independence and its effectiveness; noting relationship between effectiveness and access by private complainants, lacking in the ICJ).

89. *See, e.g.*, Cleveland, *supra* note 3, at 86 (noting use of guidelines of the UN High Commissioner of Refugees, a form of "soft law," in dissenting opinions on procedural due process issues in *Demore v. Kim*, 538 U.S. 510 (2003) and *Zadvydas v. Davis*, 533 U.S. 678 (2001)).

90. There are, to be sure, many different kinds of international tribunals, *see* Helfer & Slaughter, *Why States Create International Tribunals*, *supra* note 77, at 910–28, some of which may have qualities of "seriousness" more comparable to some domestic courts. In terms of expected degrees of compliance with their decisions, the constitution-like character of the norms being enforced, and the relationships between the supranational judges and domestic legal systems, the two European supranational courts may be viewed as somewhere between domestic and international tribunals, but perhaps closer to domestic constitutional courts in rule of law systems than to an international tribunal like the ICJ or *a fortiori* an international human rights committee like the UNHRC. The ECJ in

particular is embedded in something closer to a general government, and its direct relations with national court systems through preliminary references may particularly promote compliance; the ECtHR's decisions attract considerable compliance (in part because of support from the Council of Europe) and are referred to even by courts outside Europe. On the Inter-American Court of Human Rights, see Gerald L. Neuman, *Import, Export, and Regional Consent in the Inter-American Court of Human Rights*, 19 EUR. J. INT'L L. 101, 104 (2008) (reporting that compliance with remedial orders in the Inter-American system is lower than in the European system, in part because the Inter-American Court's remedial powers are wider and have been more ambitiously, or "enthusiastic[ally] exercise[d]").

91. A recent study has found that the South African Court has made more use of comparative constitutional law than international law in deciding constitutional issues relating to defamation law, even though the Constitution *mandates* consideration of international law and merely *permits* the consideration of foreign law. *See* Devika Hovell & George Williams, *A Tale of Two Systems: Use of International Law in Constitutional Interpretation in Australia and South Africa*, 29 MELB. U. L. REV. 95, 119 (2005).

92. *See* Hathaway, *supra* note 77, at 1946.

93. *See* Fried, *supra* note 87, at 823 ("[B]ecause the judge exercises power, because her decision directly [affects] lives, she will have thought differently and perhaps more deeply, more responsibly," than scholars). Constitutional decisions are typically more constraining than decisions based on statutes, even though amendment is easier in most countries than in the United States.

94. Indeed, for these reasons the application of *international* norms, by domestic courts, to their *own* governments may also have greater force to judges sitting on other domestic courts, than do the views of (relatively more remote) international courts or monitoring committees. On the ECtHR and ECJ, see *supra* note 90, *infra* note 164.

95. *Compare* Adler v. Ontario, [1996] 3 S.C.R. 609, 642 (Can.) (rejecting a challenge, under the 1982 Canadian Charter to the discriminatory refusal to provide federal funds to, inter alia, Jewish schools, because of the historic compromise in the 1867 Constitution Act requiring state funding of certain Christian schools) *with* Waldman v. Canada, U.N. Human Rights Comm. (Views), 67th Sess., U.N. Doc. CCPR/C/67/D/694/1996 (1999) (finding a violation of the ICCPR on similar facts). The Committee's Views make vivid the divergent functions of national constitutions, on the one hand, and international human rights instruments, on the other: The Committee states that "the fact that a distinction is enshrined in the Constitution does not render it reasonable and objective. . . . [T]he distinction was made in 1867 to protect the Roman Catholics in Ontario. The material before the Committee does not show that members of the Roman Catholic community . . . are now in a disadvantaged position compared to those members of the Jewish community that wish to secure the education of their children in religious schools." *Id.* para. 10.4. The Committee was not convinced by Canada's argument that given the history of discrimination against Catholics in Canada, to remove their privileged position would give rise to claims of injustice and compensation. *See id.* paras. 8.3, 8.4, 10.4, 105. The Committee's inquiry was not about history and national narrative, but about present day equalities. This illustrates the possibly divergent roles of international law, in the area of human rights, and domestic constitutional law. It may also illustrate the divergent perspectives of an expert monitoring committee, institutionally inclined to expansive understandings of protected rights, and domestic courts, which must be concerned with implementation and workability in the context of ongoing governance.

96. 523 U.S. 371 (1998).

97. Vienna Convention on Consular Relations, Apr. 24, 1963, 596 U.N.T.S. 261.

98. 548 U.S. 331 (2006).

99. *Id.* at 343–44 & n.3.

100. Case Concerning Avena and Other Mexican Nationals (Mex. v. U.S.), 2004 I.C.J. 12 (Judgment of Mar. 31) (*Avena*).

101. *Sanchez-Llamas*, 548 U.S. at 355–56 (treating the views of the ICJ as entitled to "respectful consideration," but rejecting them, noting that the United States had since withdrawn from the ICJ jurisdiction over Consular Convention claims, and concluding that because procedural default rules could be applied to very serious constitutional claims they could equally be applied to claims under a treaty). In some contrast, the German Constitutional Court in 2006 found that even though Germany was not a party to *Avena*, its criminal courts erred in failing to take more seriously the ICJ's interpretive decision. *See* Jana Gogolin, *Avena and Sanchez Llamas Come to Germany—The German Constitutional Court Upholds Rights under the Vienna Convention on Consular Relations*, 8 GERMAN L.J. 261, 269 (2007) (explaining the court's reasoning that, German courts, though not bound by the *Avena* judgment, must consider it as a guideline because Germany, by agreeing to the Optional Protocol, agreed to the ICJ's role as interpreter of the Consular Convention). The German court overturned the criminal courts' refusal to consider a violation of the Consular Convention as a basis for excluding evidence in a criminal trial. *See* Gogolin, *supra*; Carsten Hoppe, *Implementation of LaGrand and Avena in Germany and the United States: Exploring a Transatlantic Divide in Search of a Uniform Interpretation of Consular Rights*, 18 EUR. J. INT'L L. 317 (2007). (Interestingly, the German Constitutional Court reportedly cited Justice Breyer's dissenting opinion in *Sanchez-Llamas* in reading the Consular Convention as "specific enough to be applied directly by the prosecuting authorities . . . [and] regarded as 'self-executing.'" Gogolin, *supra*, at 265.) Germany, however, had not withdrawn from the ICJ's jurisdiction; and it has a single national criminal law and code of procedure, administered by the subnational governments, *see* GRUNDGESETZ (GG) [Basic Law] art. 74(1) (F.R.G.); FLOYD FEENEY, GERMAN AND AMERICAN PROSECUTIONS: AN APROACH TO STATISTICAL COMPARISON 3 (Bureau of Justice Statistics, U.S. Department of Justice, 1998), under a "more unified court system," *id.*, so the impact of the *Avena* judgment on federalism may resonate differently. *See generally* Chapter 8, below.

102. 128 S. Ct. 1346 (2008).

103. *Id.* at 1359–60 (citations omitted). For an introduction to the large U.S. literature on whether supranational judgments should be given domestic effect, and if so on what basis, see Curtis A. Bradley, *International Delegations, the Structural Constitution, and Non-Self-Execution*, 55 STAN. L. REV. 1557 (2003); Ernest A. Young, *Institutional Settlement in a Globalizing Judicial System*, 54 Duke L.J. 1143 (2005); Mark L. Movsesian, *Judging International Judgments*, 48 VA. J. INT'L L. 65 (2007), Jenny S. Martinez, *Towards an International Judicial System*, 56 STAN. L. REV. 429 (2003). For a thoughtful evaluation of the constitutionality of delegations of adjudicatory authority to supranational bodies, including the ICJ, see generally Henry Paul Monaghan, *Article III and Supranational Judicial Review*, 107 COLUM. L. REV. 833, 844–52, 881 (2007).

104. After construing the treaties by which the dispute was submitted to the ICJ as creating no self-executing obligation to enforce the ICJ judgment, the Court considered that the President, in issuing his memorandum to the state courts, was acting *contrary* to the presumed legislative judgment reserving to Congress the authority to implement non-self-executing treaty obligations in domestic law. *Medellín*, 128 S. Ct. at 1362–65, 1368–71.

105. *See id.* at 1361 n.9 (questioning whether "respectful consideration" is owed with respect to the "binding force" of an ICJ judgment, as distinguished from the "substantive scope" of a treaty obligation).

106. Thus, the Court wrote, "There are currently 47 nations that are parties to the Optional Protocol and 171 nations that are parties to the Vienna Convention. Yet neither Medellín nor his amici have identified a single nation that treats ICJ judgments as binding in domestic courts. [footnote omitted] In determining that the Vienna Convention did not require certain relief in United States courts in *Sanchez-Llamas*, we found it pertinent that the requested relief would not be available under the treaty in any other signatory country. See 548 U.S., at 343–344 n.3. So too here the lack of any basis for supposing that any other country would treat ICJ judgments as directly enforceable as a matter of their domestic law strongly suggests that the treaty should not be so viewed in our courts." *Medellín*, 128 S. Ct. at 1363. In a footnote, the Court discussed in some detail the "contention that local Moroccan courts have referred to ICJ judgments as 'dispositive,'" and concluded that "Moroccan practice is at best inconsistent. . . ." *Id.* at 1363, n.10. For description of a 2006 German Constitutional Court decision, see *supra* note 101.

107. *See* Carlos Manuel Vázquez, *The Separation of Powers as a Safeguard of Nationalism*, 83 NOTRE DAME L. REV. 1601, 1611–24 (2008) (noting that the Court implied that the only way a treaty could be self-executing for purposes of the Supremacy Clause is if it so stated, but arguing that given the divergent constitutional systems of member nations, such a treaty would be exceedingly unlikely to be negotiated). For narrower readings of *Medellín*, see Curtis A. Bradley, *Intent, Presumptions, and Non-Self-Executing Treaties*, 102 AM. J. INT'L L. 540, 546 (2008) (arguing that *Medellín* does not stand for a presumption against self-execution); Carlos Manuel Vázquez, *Treaties as Law of the Land: The Supremacy Clause and Judicial Enforcement of Treaties*, 122 HARV. L. REV. 599, 608 (2008) (urging that while *Medellín* could be read to presume against self-execution, it can and should be read more narrowly).

108. 356 U.S. 86 (1958).

109. *See* Hoppe, *supra* note 101, at 319 (suggesting that "[p]olitical factors, such as the US stance on the death penalty," played a role in ICJ decision in predecessor to *Avena*).

110. "Sovereignty" anxiety may be increased by challenges in the international community to reservations the United States has made in ratifying human rights treaties. Finland, the Netherlands, and Sweden objected to reservations the United States made to its ratification of the Torture Convention, *see* Office of the UN High Commissioner for Human Rights, Convention against Torture and Other Cruel Inhuman or Degrading Treatment or Punishment, http://www2.ohchr.org/english/bodies/ratification/9.htm (last visited Jan. 25, 2009); Spain, Portugal, the Netherlands, Norway, Sweden, Belgium, Denmark, Finland, France, Germany, and Italy objected to one or more of the U.S. reservations to the ICCPR, *see* Office of the UN High Commissioner for Human Rights, International Covenant of Civil and Political Rights, http://www2.ohchr.org/english/bodies/ratification/4.htm (last visited Jan. 25, 2009); and the UK, Sweden, Denmark, Finland, Norway, the Netherlands, Estonia, Italy, Greece, Ireland, Spain, and Mexico are listed as objecting to U.S. reservations to the Genocide Convention, *see* Office of the UN High Commissioner for Human Rights, Convention on the Prevention and Punishment of the Crime of Genocide, http://www2.ohchr.org/english/bodies/ratification/1.htm (last visited Jan. 25, 2009).

111. *Cf.* Transcript of Argument (Oct. 10, 2007), Medellín v. Texas, 128 S. Ct. 1346 (2008) (No. 06-984), 2007 U.S. Trans. LEXIS 49, *2–3 (Chief Justice Roberts, asking whether, if the ICJ determined that officers who violated the Consular Convention should receive five-year prison sentences, the U.S. Court would have a role reviewing that determination).

112. *See* STEPHEN D. KRASNER, SOVEREIGNTY: ORGANIZED HYPOCRISY (1999).

113. *See* United States Diplomatic and Consular Staff in Tehran (United States of America v. Iran), 1980 I.C.J. 3 (Judgment of May 24) (finding, on complaint by United States, violations by Iran and obligation to make reparations). *But see* Military and Paramilitary Activities in and against Nicaragua (Nicaragua v. United States), 1984 I.C.J. 169 (Order of May 10, 1984) (granting provisional measures against the United States to cease blocking access to or laying mines in the ports of Nicaragua, notwithstanding the U.S. position that the ICJ lacked jurisdiction).

114. MURPHY, *supra* note 47, at 86; *see id.* at 78; RESTATEMENT, *supra* note 54, § 102(1)(c); *id.* § 102(2); *see also* Statute of the International Court of Justice, *supra* note 46, art. 38.

115. *See* Chapter 2, above. When the U.S. Senate consents to and the President ratifies a treaty, they may be understood at once to be making international law and domestic law; as noted, their acts may have some interpretive force with respect to the constitutionality of implementing the international obligation.

116. Questions of comparability are more associated with foreign law, but when nonbinding international law sources law are invoked, questions of comparability (in the form of claims of exceptionalism or persistent objection) may arise. *See also supra* note 59.

117. Lawrence v. Texas, 539 U.S. 558, 573, 576–77 (2003) (referring to a decision of the ECtHR). ECtHR decisions are binding on states that are parties to the case, *see* ECHR art. 46; Europe's post–World War II commitments to the protection of rights through judicial review has much in common with the United States. There are, to be sure, differences between U.S. law and society and that of European nations, but the existence of some difference does not preclude useful reflection on their approaches to human liberty and privacy. Nor have U.S. justices been blind to learning from European nations as *negative* examples. *See, e.g.*, Youngstown Sheet & Tube Co, v. Sawyer, 343 U.S. 579, 650–52 (1952) (Jackson, J., concurring). *But compare* Steven G. Calabresi & Stephanie Dotson Zimdahl, *The Supreme Court and Foreign Sources of Law: Two Hundred Years of Practice and the Juvenile Death Penalty Decision*, 47 WM. & MARY L. REV. 743, 755, 804–05 (2005) (questioning references to European law in "problematic" cases like *Reynolds v. United States*, 98 U.S. 145 (1878), described as "closely on par" with *Lawrence*) *with* Harold Hongju Koh, *International Law As Part of Our Law*, 98 AM. J. INT'L L. 43, 45 (2004) (treating *Reynolds* as involving references to legal rules "of other nations . . . with similar legal and social traditions").

118. To the extent that courts need to understand something of the relationships between law (and constitutional decisions) and the society in which that law operates, there are greater disciplinary limitations on the ability of judges to "know" and evaluate social science research than exist for them to evaluate foreign law. *See* Chapter 5, note 49 above. It is difficult enough to determine in one's own society what the effects are, and findings may well be contested; it is all the more so across national lines. More possible with considered effort is to have some knowledge of the similarities and differences in the broader sociolegal context in which another constitutional system operates. And some knowledge is probably better than the "armchair intuitions" that are likely otherwise to be deployed.

119. *See* Chapters 1, 4, 5 above (noting concern for "omitted variables" in functional analysis); *see also* Hirschl, *supra* note 36.

120. *Lawrence v. Texas*, 539 U.S. at 577.

121. *See, e.g.*, Ramsey, *International Materials*, *supra* note 74, at 73–74; *see also infra* notes 122, 160.

122. Ramsey also argues that the European court evaluated the claim in *Dudgeon* under a more stringent standard of review (whether, as provided in ECHR art 8.2, a restriction is

"necessary in a democratic society . . . for the protection of health or morals, or for the protection of the rights and freedoms of others") than the reasonableness inquiry that presumptively, he says, underlay the *Lawrence* decision. *Id.* at 74. If so, the difference in standard of review would have been worth acknowledging. What standard the Court was applying in *Lawrence*, however, remains somewhat unclear. *See* text at note 120 (noting *Lawrence's* reference to the "urgen[cy]" of government interest). Even if the question was addressed under different standards and textual language, both legal texts—the right to privacy under the European Convention and the Due Process Clause of the U.S. Constitution—had been interpreted to protect liberty in a private sphere, and thus were addressing similar topics.

123. *Cf.* James Q. Whitman, *The Neo-Romantic Turn, in* COMPARATIVE LEGAL STUDIES: TRADITIONS AND TRANSITIONS 312, 336–44 (Pierre Legrand & Roderick Munday eds., 2003) (cautioning about risks of the "new romanticism" in comparative law and suggesting the possibility for "sympathetic understanding" of foreign law even from very different cultures).

124. *See* ALAN WATSON, LEGAL TRANSPLANTS: AN APPROACH TO COMPARATIVE LAW 10–15 (2d ed 1993) (identifying among the "perils of comparative law" the risks of "superficiality," of "getting foreign law wrong," and of "arguing too easily to another system"); William P. Alford, *On the Limits of "Grand Theory" in Comparative Law*, 61 WASH. L. REV. 945, 947 (1986) ("[W]e need to approach foreign subjects with an even greater tentativeness of theoretical construct and with an even greater self-consciousness than we would subjects closer to home.").

125. David Fontana, *Refined Comparativism in Constitutional Law*, 49 UCLA L. REV. 539, 556 (1999). In contrast to the arguments made here for engagement, Professor Fontana also seems to assume that the goal of comparativism is "importing," *see id.*, rather than illuminating understandings of one's own system to find the best answer to a constitutional problem within that system.

126. See the comparative law authorities collected in Fontana, *supra* note 125, at 540 n.4.

127. *Cf.* Hathaway, *supra* note 77, at 1967 (describing her use of four different sources to measure compliance with human rights treaties: "the Center for International Development and Conflict Management at the University of Maryland, College Park, the United States Department of State Country Reports on Human Rights, Freedom House's Annual Survey of Political Rights and Civil Liberties, and the Inter-Parliamentary Union").

128. On Argentina, see Chapter 3, notes 178, 179 above. According to Freedom House's 2007 and 2008 ratings, Argentina received a "2/2" rating for political rights and civil liberties; Russia received a 6/5 rating. The United States and Britain both received a 1/1 rating in those years, as did Spain; Israel's rating was 1/ 2. *See* Freedom House's Annual Survey of Political Rights and Civil Liberties, http://www.freedomhouse.org/template.cfm?page=15&year=2006 (last visited Jan. 24, 2009).

129. Likewise helpful could be statutes in Israel or in a number of European countries that have confronted terrorism but sustained commitments to a liberal, democratic, rule of law state. *See supra* notes 22–23, 128. India is a democratic country with a long history of fighting terrorism; but its success in doing so while maintaining high general levels of political and civil rights is less clear and the particularities of its constitutional provisions on preventive detention also would require great caution in comparison. *See Freedom House's Annual Survey*, *supra* note 128 (showing India rated a "free" democratic state, but with ratings of 2/3 on political rights and civil liberties from 2002–08). *See generally*

Derek P. Jinks, *The Anatomy of an Institutionalized Emergency: Preventive Detention and Personal Liberty in India*, 22 MICH. J. INT'L L. 311 (2001) (discussing how article 22 of the Indian Constitution from the outset has explicitly authorized laws providing for relatively lengthy "preventive detention," freed from ordinary procedural constraints); Iyer, *supra* note 20, at 128 n.42. The Indian Constitution's historic background and specificity in authorizing preventive detention stand in contrast to the U.S. Constitution's protections of liberty; Indian approaches, insofar as they have been permissive of executive detentions, would need to be analyzed in this context.

130. Human Rights Act, 1998, c. 42 §§ 4(2), (6) (U K.) (authorizing courts to issue determinations that a statute is incompatible with the rights set forth but not to invalidate the statute). On the range of "weak" forms of judicial review that permit various types of legislative override or response to judicial determinations that laws conflict with constitutional instruments, see Stephen Gardbaum, *The New Commonwealth Model of Constitutionalism*, 49 AM. J. COMP. L. 707 (2001); Mark Tushnet, *Alternative Forms of Judicial Review*, 101 MICH. L. REV. 2781 (2003) (distinguishing "weak" and "strong" forms); *see also* Mark Tushnet, *Judicial Activism or Restraint in a Section 33 World*, 53 U. TORONTO L.J. 89 (2003) (suggesting that "weak-form" judicial review is unstable and is likely to become "strong-form" review over time).

131. *See supra* note 130. Whether a court that is subject to being overruled would be more, or less, inclined to uphold existing laws is debatable. *Compare* Posner, *supra* note 1, at 89–90 (suggesting that constitutional courts whose decisions can be more easily overruled by amendments will be bolder) *with* Louis Favoreu, *Constitutional Review in Europe*, *in* CONSTITUTIONALISM AND RIGHTS: THE INFLUENCE OF THE UNITED STATES CONSTITUTION ABROAD 38, 46 (Louis Henkin & Albert J. Rosenthal eds., 1990) (referring to a French scholar's observation that when a parliament can easily overrule a court's constitutional decision, the court would hesitate to find a law unconstitutional). So, too, is it debatable whether formal differences in authority will affect the frequency or nature of legislative "overrulings" of judicial declarations of invalidity.

132. *See* Dixon, *supra* note 40, at 979–93 (2008) (discussing criteria of "general" constitutional comparability); Rex D. Glensy, *Which Countries Count?: Lawrence v. Texas and the Selection of Foreign Persuasive Authority*, 45 VA. J. INT'L L. 357, 420–33 (2005) (arguing that comparisons should be limited to countries with societal similarities to the United States).

133. For helpful discussion, see BRIAN Z. TAMANAHA, A GENERAL JURISPRUDENCE OF LAW AND SOCIETY, 28–30, 32–40, 107–32 (2001) (describing and arguing against "the Mirror Thesis" of Western legal theory). *See also* WATSON, *supra* note 124, at 95–101 (arguing that law often results from transplants and includes rules not peculiarly designed for a particular society); Alan Watson, *Legal Change: Sources of Law and Legal Culture*, 131 U. PA. L. REV. 1121, 1135–36 (1983) (arguing that law may develop more or less autonomously, without a close "causal relationship" with its own society).

134. Glensy, *supra* note 132, at 421.

135. Karol Edward Soltan, *Constitutional Patriotism and Militant Moderation*, 6 INT'L J. CONST. L. 96, 99–101 (2008); *see also* Glensy, *supra* note 132, at 413, 421, 447 (discussing the tolerance and diversity of a society as factors to be considered in making comparisons).

136. Dixon, *supra* note 40, at 980–81. Dixon's focus is on comparability for purposes of "co-evolution" of public understandings, but such criteria, indicative of a society's relative freedom and openness, are also relevant to functional or consequentialist analyses.

137. *See* Cass R. Sunstein, *Against Positive Rights*, *in* WESTERN RIGHTS? POST-COMMUNIST APPLICATIONS (András Sajó, ed., 1996), *reproduced in* JACKSON & TUSHNET, *supra* note 41, at 1739–40. For example, one might view the German concept of unamendable constitutional

provisions, *see* GRUNDGESETZ (GG) [Basic Law] art. 79(3) (F.R.G), as a reaction to the damaging positivism of the Nazi era, rather than as a more general precept of constitutionalism applicable to other contexts. *Cf.* Chapter 9, note 61, below.

138. "Rights" issues may also be "federalism" issues insofar as constitutionalizing a right at the national level establishes a floor below which no constituent member may fall.

139. According to the Forum of Federations, there are 24 federal nations out of 193 countries, but these 24 federal states (listed in Chapter 7, note 32, below), include 40 percent of the world's population. *See* Forum of Federations, http://www.forumfed.org (click on "federalism by country"); *see also* CIA World Factbook 2008, Rank Order—Population, https://www.cia.gov/library/publications/the-world-factbook/rankorder/2119rank.html (last visited Jan. 24, 2009) (listing, in order, the twelve largest polities—China, India, the EU (not included in the Forum of Federations list), the United States, Indonesia, Brazil, Pakistan, Bangladesh, Nigeria, Russia, Japan, and Mexico—of which eight are federal (or in the case of the EU, quasi-federal) in character).

140. *See, e.g.*, Charkaoui v. Canada (Citizenship and Immigration), [2007] 1 S.C.R. 350 (Can.) (looking to alternative procedures available in Canada and the UK to accommodate national security concerns with the procedural due process interests of aliens accused of terrorism to have notice of and be able to contest the evidence against them); *cf.* Washington v. Glucksberg, 521 U.S. 702, 734 (1997) (noting Dutch experience with legal assisted suicide); *id. at* 785–87 (Souter, J., concurring in the judgment) (reviewing evidence on Dutch law and finding factual disputes surrounding it to support upholding the challenged state law, leaving latitude to legislatures).

141. There is an undertone in some of the literature that the United States, as a powerful and leading nation, has little to learn from others. But even with respect to military actions abroad (as to which the United States may see itself as having special or unique responsibilities, see Chapter 5 above), there may be a basis for comparative engagement, for example, on the extraterritorial force of domestic norms. *See, e.g.*, R. (on application of Al-Skeini et al.) v. Sec'y of State for Defence, [2007] UKHL 26, [2008] 1 A.C. 153 (U.K.) (opinion of Lord Rodger of Earlsferry) (analyzing limited application of the Human Rights Act (HRA) to claims by family members of Iraqis killed by British troops in Iraq; upholding HRA's application to the one of six Iraqis who died after assertedly being beaten by British troops while in custody on a British military base). To be sure there are many differences between the United States' and the UK's legal contexts, including the UK's relationship to the ECHR and ECtHR, and the statutory (unentrenched) character of the HRA, which would need to be considered in a full analysis. But it is difficult to see a country's political and economic power in the world—as contrasted with its particular constitutional system, its rule of law qualities, its size, or even its relationship with other legal systems—as clearly bearing on its aptness for comparative purposes. On extraterritorial application of the Canadian Charter, see Canada (Justice) v. Khadr, [2008] 2 S.C.R. 125 (holding that although ordinarily the Charter does not apply to extraterritorial actions by Canadian officials, the Charter did apply where those actions—interrogating a U.S-held detainee in Guantánamo—were in breach of Canada's international human rights obligations).

142. Goodman & Jinks, *Institutional Theory of Sovereignty*, *supra* note 80, at 1784.

143. *See* Chapter 4, note 133, above.

144. Günter Frankenberg, *Critical Comparisons: Re-thinking Comparative Law*, 26 HARV. INT'L L. J. 411, 414–15 (1985) (arguing for a "dialectic of learning" based on "distancing"—"an attempt to break away from firmly held beliefs and settled knowledge," and "to resist the power of prejudice and ignorance"—and "differencing," developing a "sharp sense for

diversity and heterogeneity," based on a "conscious effort to establish subjectivity, that is the impact of the self" to take account of the observer's perspective).

145. Günter Frankenberg, *Comparing Constitutions: Ideas, Ideals, and Ideology—Toward a Layered Narrative*, 4 INT'L J. CONST. L. 439, 443–47 (2006) (identifying cognitive, functionalist, and hermeneutical fallacies).

146. *See, e.g.*, Cleveland, *supra* note 3, at 108.

147. *Id.* at 113 (also emphasizing clarity of norm).

148. Kumm, *supra* note 44, at 268–74. Kumm argues that substantive concerns should play only a limited role "in assessing the legitimacy" of an international rule, to respect its character as law, but that this should not preclude the possibility of a national state ignoring international rules that are "deeply unjust or extremely costly and inefficient." *Id.* at 273. In the realm of constitutional interpretation, however, some treaty norms, apart from their substantive justness or efficiency, would be irrelevant, insofar as they address subjects remote from constitutional law. Moreover, very marked divergences between international norms and well-established constitutional meaning would diminish the former's persuasive force.

Professor Kumm also argues for a principle of jurisdictional subsidiarity, *id.* at 264–68, one that may have more application to determining the appropriate level for regulation than to the persuasive force of existing international law in constitutional interpretation. Indeed, Kumm notes that although human rights treaties do not solve collective action problems (and thus his subsidiarity principle would disfavor their legitimacy as international law), "outcome-related reasons" favor their being "elevated in a way that, say, treaties addressing international postal delivery are not" to "play a central role" in constitutional interpretation. *Id.* at 276–78.

149. *See* Cleveland, *supra* note 3, at 113, 116–22. The political branches' actions can affect the binding quality of most international norms, and thus the consequences for the United States of a breach; as noted earlier, however, treaty obligations can ordinarily be satisfied at subconstitutional levels.

150. For complications in interpreting acts of ratification, see Chapter 8, text at notes 115-23 below. Some theories of constitutional interpretation envision interaction between the Court and the political branches. *See* Chapter 5, above. On these accounts, the views of the political branches reflected in treaty ratification or international agreements could be relevant on constitutional meaning. Consistent with the independent role of the Court, as well as the significance of precedent and of multi-valenced sources in U.S. constitutional practice, they certainly could not be dispositive. *See, e.g.*, Reid v. Covert, 354 U.S. 1 (1957); *cf.* Cleveland, *supra* note 3, at 115–16 (suggesting that acceptance of international obligations may give rise to constitutionally cognizable government interests).

151. *See* Kumm, *supra* note 44, at 292.

152. *See* Scheppele, *supra* note 31.

153. Ramsey, *International Materials*, *supra* note 74, at 77–79 (arguing the importance of "Get[ting] the Facts Right"). For discussions of errors in judicial resort to international or foreign law, see Chapter 1 note 41 above; *see also* Cleveland, *supra* note 3, at 96–97 (describing errors or opportunism by U.S. Court in use of international law).

154. *See* Bowers v. Hardwick, 478 U.S. 186, 196 (1986) (Burger, C.J. concurring); Dudgeon v. United Kingdom, 45 Eur. Ct. H.R. (ser. A) (1981).

155. 536 U.S. 304 (2002).

156. Ramsey, *International Materials*, *supra* note 74, at 77–78. The brief Ramsey criticizes was filed on behalf of a group of former diplomats, including a former ambassador to China, J. Stapleton Roy. Brief of Diplomats Morton Abramowitz et al. as Amici Curiae Supporting Petitioner, McCarver v. North Carolina, 533 U.S. 975 (2001) (No. 00-8727).

China is referred to in footnote 10 of this brief in support of the assertion that if the Court were to uphold execution of the mentally retarded, "it would provide fresh anti-American diplomatic ammunition to countries who have exhibited far worse human rights records." The first sentence in the footnote states that China "regularly raises the U.S. practice of executing people with mental retardation when demarched about its own human rights practices," with no citation but presumably based on the knowledge of the amici curiae. The brief then states that, although the People's Republic of China has executed "nearly three times as many people in 1998 as the rest of the world combined (nearly 1800 people), it has reportedly banned the execution of people with mental retardation for centuries." In support it cites a student note, which, as Professor Ramsey points out, on the cited page describes how in ancient China execution of the mentally retarded was banned for centuries, but on another page indicates that contemporary statutory law expressly excludes from eligibility for the death penalty only pregnant women and minors. Ramsey assumes that the amicus brief thus had no support for its assertion. However, it is possible that Ambassador Stapleton had knowledge from his own service in China of contemporary practices—*see id.*, Interests of Amici Curiae ("Amici submit this brief as friends of the Court to advise regarding the customs of nations with which amici are familiar . . .")—and that the student note was relied on only with respect to the longevity of the ban. Moreover, contemporary reports were available (in early 2001) that only three countries were known to affirmatively permit execution of the mentally retarded—the United States, Krygyzstan, and Japan, *see, e.g.*, Human Rights Watch, Beyond Reason: The Death Penalty and Offenders with Mental Retardation (March 5, 2001), http://www.hrw.org/en/node/79056/section1 (citing reports by the UN Commission on Human Rights Special Rapporteur from 1996 and 1994 and reports from 1996 of the UN Commission on Crime Prevention and Criminal Justice). Professor Ramsey's criticism thus may not be as significant as first appears.

157. Ramsey, *International Materials, supra* note 74, at 78–79 (criticizing the EU brief cited by the Court for over-reliance on a UN study, based on inadequate samples of countries that retain death penalty, and criticizing the Court's failure to investigate actual practices in accessible jurisdictions). In *Atkins*, the Court devoted one sentence in one footnote to the weight of world opinion, 536 U.S. at 316 n.21. Although I am in sympathy with the suggestion of the importance of careful research, given two unrebutted amicus briefs and the relatively small role this factor played in the Court's opinion, the suggestion for additional independent research before accepting the two amici's representations might be seen as disproportionate, though Professor Ramsey's point emphasizes the benefits of adversarial briefing on such questions.

158. Jeffrey Rosen, *Juvenile Logic*, NEW REPUBLIC, Mar. 21, 2005, at 11, 12 (asserting that Japan is "the death-penalty country that most resembles the United States").

159. *See Roper*, 543 U.S. at 581–85 apps. B–D (state laws providing minimum ages for voting, jury service, and marriage). It does not appear that any brief in *Roper* brought Japan's situation to the Court's attention, from an examination of briefs available on Lexis and Westlaw. Raising another concern about comparability, Justice Scalia suggested that in some foreign states, which require a mandatory death sentence, exempting juveniles "may be a good idea, but it says nothing about our system," where sentencing is individualized. 543 U.S. at 623–24. Although a fair point, it does not affect the unusually specific and concrete nature of the international norm; and the majority did explain why individualized sentencing was an insufficient protection for 17-year-olds. *See id.* at 572–73.

160. The Court in *Lawrence* has been criticized for not explaining the theory by which it was selecting countries for comparison, as has an amicus brief filed in that case.

See, e.g., Ramsey, *International Materials, supra* note 74, at 72–76 & n.20 (questioning the Court's reliance on European human rights case law without discussion of laws of other countries permitting the prohibition of sodomy, and criticizing the amicus brief for referring, for example, to laws of Ecuador and Colombia without explaining the laws of other South American countries or the basis for selection). Given U.S. legal roots and the Court's interpretive practice in constitutional cases over time, the brief comparative reference to Europe seems sensible on the basis of shared commitments to political and civil rights, democracy, and the rule of law. On the possible need for additional adversarial or expert briefing, see below, text at notes 199–215.

161. *See* Ramsey, *International Materials, supra* note 74, at 76 (arguing that a "more systematic and comprehensive study is obviously required to support" a claim of universality, as in *Atkins*, than to rebut or defeat such a claim, as *Lawrence* did in using European law to rebut implicit claims of universality made in a concurrence in *Bowers*). Likewise, examples of similar foreign regulatory laws from comparable countries may be more persuasive on whether a statute is constitutionally "reasonable," than is the existence of a single foreign statute (authorizing, for example, assisted suicide) persuasive on whether a contrary domestic law is inconsistent with the liberty protected by the Due Process Clause. *See* Chapter 4, above (noting *Washington v. Glucksberg* and discussing *Muller v. Oregon* and *Jacobson v. Massachusetts*). Foreign law may be *considered* in arguments supporting or challenging a domestic law, but against the backdrop of a presumption of constitutionality, will have different persuasive value; the mere existence of a statute is not a source of reasoning, as may be found in a judicial decision, about the consistency of a particular approach with human liberty. Yet a single example, from a highly comparable respected source, may help to answer more operational doctrinal questions. *See* Chapter 2 above (discussing least restrictive alternative analysis and *Charkaoui v. Canada*).

162. *Cf.* Jeremy Waldron, *Foreign Law and the Modern Ius Gentium*, 119 HARV. L. REV. 129, 144–46 (2005) (arguing that ignoring a consensus among "civilized" or "freedom-loving" countries would, by analogy to scientific inquiry, show an "obtuseness" to the problem-solving nature of the interpretive enterprise).

163. Ramsey, *International Materials, supra* note 74, at 79–80; *cf.* Cleveland, *supra* note 3, at 97 (arguing that the Court "should make reasonable efforts to substantiate" claims that a norm embodies "a uniform international consensus," and where relevant "should acknowledge the geographic limits" of a regional consensus).

164. There are, of course, differences between the legal status and direct effect of Supreme Court decisions in the United States, under the Supremacy Clause, and the legal status and decisions of the ECtHR. On the different approaches to "reception" of the ECHR into domestic law, see A EUROPE OF RIGHTS: THE IMPACT OF THE ECHR ON NATIONAL LEGAL SYSTEMS (Helen Keller & Alec Stone Sweet eds., 2008). *See also* Chapter 1, notes 82, 83, above. Yet, as noted, ECtHR decisions are binding on the parties to the case, have had reasonably good rates of compliance, *see* Helfer & Slaughter, *Toward a Theory, supra* note 77, at 296; *cf.* James L. Cavallaro & Stephanie Erin Brewer, *Regional Human Rights Litigation in the Twenty-first Century: The Case of the Inter-American Court*, 102 AM J. INT'L L 768, 773–74 (2008) (suggesting that with expansion of parties to the ECHR compliance faces new challenges), and exercise influence on member state decisions. (Other regional or international human rights bodies vary in the degree to which their decisions are complied with or can be taken to reflect member states views or practices.)

165. Dixon, *supra* note 40, at 982–83; *see also* Ramsey, *International Materials, supra* note 74, at 72–73 n.20 (questioning why the Court in *Lawrence* cited Israel and not India).

166. Dixon, *supra* note 40, at 983–84 (suggesting that such comparisons might provide a "sense of non-recognition that would have helped clarify the importance of commitments to sexual privacy or equality in U.S. . . . constitutional culture").

167. *See* Chapter 4, note 5, above.

168. *See* Chapter 7, below (discussing *Sharifan* case).

169. Planned Parenthood of Se. Pa. v. Casey, 505 U.S. 833, 945 n.1 (1992) (Rehnquist, C.J., dissenting).

170. *See* Cheryl Saunders, *The Use and Misuse of Comparative Constitutional Law*, 13 IND. J. GLOBAL LEGAL STUD. 37, 67 (2006); Yash Ghai, *Sentinels of Liberty or Sheep in Woolf's Clothing? Judicial Politics and the Hong Kong Bill of Rights*, 60 MOD. L. REV. 459, 479 (1997); *cf.* Roper v. Simmons, 543 U.S. 551, 627 (2005) (Scalia, J., dissenting) ("To invoke alien law when it agrees with one's own thinking, and ignore it otherwise, is not reasoned decisionmaking, but sophistry.")

171. Cleveland, *supra* note 3, at 122–24.

172. *Cf.* Saunders, *supra* note 170, at 54–56 (arguing that the apparent criteria on which jurisdictions were selected for review by the Australian High Court in freedom of expression cases—that the countries be committed to democracy and liberty, that they be regarded as countries with which Australia has something in common, and that Australian courts and lawyers be relatively familiar with them—should have led the Court to consider cases from New Zealand, South Africa, and Canada, in addition to the United States and the United Kingdom, in resolving free speech questions under the Australian Constitution).

173. For example, one scholar has implied that the Indian Supreme Court derived a positive right to provide a free public education from a general constitutional "right to life," drawing on transnational principles of proportionality. DAVID BEATTY, THE ULTIMATE RULE OF LAW 137–38 (2004). The implicit suggestion is that other courts, interpreting constitutions that protect the right to life, could do so as well. But in reaching its conclusion, the Indian Court was influenced by one of the Indian Constitution's nonjusticiable "Directive Principles," specifically contemplating that the state would provide a free public education to children under the age of fourteen. *See* Unni Krishnan v. State of Andhra Pradesh, A.I.R. 1993 S.C. 2178, 2231–32. It is one thing for a court to read into the enforceable "right to life" clause the nonjusticiable principles found elsewhere in its constitution, and another to develop from the more general "right to life" so specific an entitlement. Important to any comparative evaluation of the court's decision, then, is an understanding of the complex relationships between the justiciable and nonjusticiable portions of the Indian Constitution.

174. Saunders, *supra* note 170, at 67.

175. *See also* Chapter 3, note 21, above; *cf.* Adrienne Stone & George Williams, *Freedom of Speech and Defamation: Developments in the Common Law World*, 26 MONASH U.L. REV. 362, 363 (2000) (describing how some other common law jurisdictions have been skeptical of the rule of *New York Times v. Sullivan*, 376 U.S. 254 (1964), in part because "courts in these countries have been mindful of criticisms of [the case] by American scholars").

176. R. v. Keegstra, [1990] 3 S.C.R. 697 (Can.). Although both countries have entrenched written constitutions, Canada permits some limited-duration legislative overrides of some Charter rights, a mechanism whose role bears further analysis. *See, e.g.*, Tsvi Kahana, *Legalism, Anxiety and Legislative Constitutionalism*, 31 QUEEN'S L.J. 536, 555–60 (2006) (describing sixteen uses of the Section 33 override, most in connection with Quebec legislation); Janet L. Hiebert, *New Constitutional Ideas: Can New Parliamentary Models Resist Judicial Dominance When Interpreting Rights?*, 82 TEX. L. REV. 1963, 1968

(2004) (stating that the provision's "significance is undermined by a political culture that generally assumes its illegitimacy").

177. *See, e.g.*, Mari J. Matsuda, *Public Response to Racist Speech: Considering the Victim's Story*, 87 MICH. L. REV. 2320, 2346–47 (1989) (citing Canadian lower court decisions); Richard Delgado & David H. Yun, *Pressure Valves and Bloodied Chickens: An Analysis of Paternalistic Objections to Hate Speech Regulation*, 82 CALIF. L. REV. 871, 875 (1994).

178. Mark Tushnet, *Interpreting Constitutions Comparatively: Some Cautionary Notes, with Reference to Affirmative Action*, 36 CONN. L. REV. 649, 651 (2004).

179. On the other hand, it might be argued, the United States has an extensive system of courts whose treatment of issues of national law is hierarchically organized and subject to review, ultimately by the Supreme Court, which can assure the uniform enforcement of constitutional rules. Whether the judicial power is at present organized and exercised in such a way as to fulfill this potential function is subject to dispute. For an introduction to debates over the Supreme Court's declining merits docket and discretionary certiorari jurisdiction, see SUSAN LOW BLOCH ET AL., INSIDE THE SUPREME COURT: THE INSTITUTION AND ITS PROCEDURES (2d ed. 2008).

180. *See* Chapter 5, note 125, above.

181. *Compare Keegstra*, [1990] 3 S.C.R. at 767–71 (Dickson, C. J.) (finding "rational connection" between suppression of hate speech and diminution of the harms it causes) *with id.* at 852–53, 859 (McLachlin, J., dissenting) (noting adverse consequences of hate speech laws in affording the "joy of martyrdom" to hate mongers and temporarily preventing literary works from entering the country). *See also* RONALD J. KROTOSZYNSKI, JR., THE FIRST AMENDMENT IN CROSS-CULTURAL PERSPECTIVE 55 (2006).

182. *Compare* CANADIAN CHARTER OF RIGHTS AND FREEDOMS § 27 ("This Charter shall be interpreted in a manner consistent with the preservation and enhancement of the multicultural heritage of Canadians.") *with* New York Times Co. v. Sullivan, 376 U.S. 254, 270 (1964) (making widely cited assertion that the First Amendment contemplates discourse on public issues that is "uninhibited, robust, and wide-open"). *See generally* KROTOSZYNSKI, *supra* note 181, at 55–56.

183. *See* Alford, *Four Mistakes, supra* note 1, at 674 (describing as mistaken the view that "the outcome of constitutional comparativism will be an expansion of individual liberties").

184. *See, e.g.*, Roper v. Simmons, 543 U.S. 551, 624, 627 (2005) (Scalia, J., dissenting) (describing the majority's "basic premise" that U.S. law should "conform to the laws of the rest of the world," arguing that the Court has not acted consistently on this premise in light of differences on criminal procedure, establishments of religion, and abortion, and stating that "[t]he Court should either profess its willingness to reconsider all these matters in light of the views of foreigners, or else . . . cease putting forth foreigners' views as part of the *reasoned basis* of its decisions"); Ramsey, *International Materials, supra* note 74, at 70, 76.

185. *Compare* Roger P. Alford, *Roper v. Simmons and Our Constitution in International Equipoise*, 53 UCLA L. REV. 1, 23–25 (2005) [hereinafter *International Equipoise*] (identifying areas in which the United States would need to shift its doctrine to be in "equipoise" with international standards) *with* Cleveland, *supra* note 3, at 114–15 (rejecting claims of "norm universality" with respect to abortion regulation).

186. *Roper*, 543 U.S. at 575. The epistemic value of a strong transnational consensus may call for more thoughtful consideration of whether (and if so, why) the issue of domestic constitutional law should be decided differently, but in an engagement posture such a consensus poses a question (increasingly urgent as the consensus is broader, deeper, and

more actualized) about U.S. law, rather than providing a sufficient reason to change doctrine, while offering the opportunity to examines the reasons for, and effects of, different approaches in other countries.

187. *See* Bivens v. Six Unknown Named Agents of Fed. Bur. Narcotics, 403 U.S. 388, 415 (1971) (Burger, C.J., dissenting) (stating that the exclusionary rule "is unique to American jurisprudence" and not followed in either England or Canada); Stone v. Powell, 428 U.S. 465, 499 (1976) (Burger, C.J., concurring) (suggesting that exclusion of improperly obtained evidence cannot be necessary for judicial integrity "'when no such rule is observed in other common law jurisdictions such as England and Canada, whose courts are otherwise regarded as models of judicial decorum and fairness'") (citation omitted); California v. Minjares, 443 U.S. 916, 919 (1979) (Rehnquist, J., joined by Burger, C.J., dissenting from denial of stay) (arguing for reconsideration of the exclusionary rule and asserting that the United States is the only nation with so rigid a rule). For purposes of discussion the text assumes arguendo that these characterizations remain correct.

188. *See Roper v. Simmons*, 543 U.S. at 624–25 (Scalia, J., dissenting) (discussing Mapp v. Ohio, 367 U.S. 643 (1961)); Alford, *International Equipoise*, *supra* note 185, at 23–24. On exceptions to the exclusionary rule, *see, e.g.*, Hudson v. Michigan, 547 U.S. 586 (2006); United States v. Leon, 468 U.S. 897 (1984).

189. U.S. CONST. amend. IV. *Compare, e.g.*, *Hudson*, 547 U.S. at 597–99 (discussing civil remedies now available, in deciding not to apply exclusionary rule to "knock-and-announce" violations) *with id.* at 608–11 (Breyer, J., dissenting) (arguing inadequacy of civil remedies as a deterrent). Comparative analysis would consider both the need to deter rights violations and to avoid overdeterrence (i.e., of lawful police conduct) and how U.S. practice in fact compares to jurisdictions with more discretionary rules.

190. *See, e.g.*, Dickerson v. United States, 530 U.S. 428, 443–44 (2000) (describing *Miranda* warnings as "part of our national culture" and suggesting that later decisions reduced *Miranda*'s impact on legitimate law enforcement in ways that mitigate against overruling). One would also need to consider the more general demands of stare decisis, and the justifications for departure therefrom, before making any such change in U.S. constitutional law, as well as the effects of the legal momentum of any such change on respect for the rule of law and protection of civil liberties.

191. The important role of constitutional review by an independent court in protecting individual rights would support such a hesitation. *See* Payne v. Tennessee, 501 U.S. 808, 852–53 (1991) (Marshall, J., dissenting).

192. *Cf.* SIR BASIL MARKESINIS & JÖRG FEDTKE, JUDICIAL RECOURSE TO FOREIGN LAW: A NEW SOURCE OF INSPIRATION? 5–6 (2006) (discussing foreign law as a "source of inspiration" to update or clarify national law). On "bricolage" see Mark Tushnet, *The Possibilities of Comparative Constitutional Law*, 108 YALE L.J. 1225 (1999) (exploring how functionalism and expressivism constrain the possibilities of learning through bricolage).

193. *See* Frank I. Michelman, *Reflection*, 82 TEX. L. REV. 1737 (2004) (discussing the "mirror of comparison").

194. *See* Fontana, *supra* note 125, at 563–64 (urging that trial courts consider appointing a special master under the Federal Rules of Civil Procedure or an expert witness under the Federal Rules of Evidence, to assist the court in resolving foreign law issues raised by the parties in constitutional litigation).

195. *See, e.g.*, South African Constitutional Court Website, http://www.constitutionalcourt.org.za/site/lawclerks/southafricanlawclerks.htm#foreign (describing foreign law clerk hiring); Supreme Court of Israel Website, http://elyon1.court.gov.il/eng/Clerking_opportunities/main.html (describing foreign clerkships). For a discussion of Library of

Congress researchers providing memos to federal judges on foreign or international law, see Roger Alford, *Outsourcing Research About Outsourced Authority*, Opinio Juris (Nov. 22, 2006) at http://opiniojuris.org/2006/11/22/outsourcing-research-about-outsourced-authority.

196. Practice Direction on the Citation of Authorities (Lord Chief Justice of England and Wales 2001), *available at* http://www.hmcourts-service.gov.uk/cms/814.htm; *see id.* at para.1 (explaining that "the current weight of available material causes problems both for advocates and for courts in properly limiting the nature and amount of material that is used in the preparation and argument of subsequent cases"). (This Practice Direction does not appear to extend to the Law Lords.)

197. *Id.* at para. 9.1 (emphasis added). Notably, the decisions of the ECJ and ECtHR are excluded from the special rules concerning authority from "other jurisdictions," given their unique legal status in Britain. *Id.* at para. 9.3.

198. *Cf.* Roper v. Simmons, 543 U.S. 551, 575 (2005) (finding "confirmation" of conclusions in foreign practice). The Practice Direction requires those who wish to cite foreign authority to comply with requirements for citing domestic authority: for example, that counsel state the proposition of law for which the authority is being cited and, if more than one authority for a proposition is being cited, explain why multiple citations are given. *Id.* at paras. 8.1, 9.2(i). In addition, as noted in text, counsel must also indicate "what that [foreign] authority adds that is not to be found in authority in this jurisdiction" or provide other "justification for adding to domestic authority," and must "certify that . . . no authority in this jurisdiction . . . precludes the acceptance . . . of the proposition that the foreign authority is said to establish." *Id.* at para. 9.2 (ii), (iii).

199. *See* State *ex rel.* Simmons v. Roper, 112 S.W.3d 397 (Mo. 2003).

200. *See, e.g.*, Brief of Amici Curiae the European Union and Members of the International Community in Support of Respondent, Roper v. Simmons, 543 U.S. 551 (2005) (No. 03-633), 2004 WL 1619203; Brief of Amici Curiae former U.S. Diplomats Morton Abramowitz et al. in Support of Respondent, Roper v. Simmons, 543 U.S. 551 (2005) (No. 03-633), 2004 WL 1636448; Brief for the Human Rights Comm. of the Bar of England and Wales et al. in Support of Respondent, Roper v. Simmons, 543 U.S. 551 (2005) (No. 03-633), 2004 WL 1628523.

201. *See* Sup. Ct. R. 37(3)(a). Reply briefs at the time of *Roper* were limited to twenty pages, compared to the opening brief page limit of fifty pages; presently Reply Briefs are limited to 7500 words, half the length of a petitioner or respondent's opening briefs. Sup. Ct. R. 33 (eff. Oct. 2007); Sup. Ct. R. 33 (2003).

202. This is not a complete explanation for the relative silence of the petitioner's side on the relevance of international and foreign law. The Missouri state court, applying the Supreme Court's existing precedents to conclude that the juvenile death penalty was unconstitutional, had devoted a short section in its opinion to what it called "National and International Consensus," specifically noting Article 37 of the Convention on the Rights of the Child and Amnesty International's information indicating that only two other countries in the world (Iran and the Republic of the Congo) had carried out "officially sanctioned executions of juveniles" in recent years. State *ex rel.* Simmons v. Roper, 112 S.W. 3d at 410–11; *cf.* Roper v. Simmons, 543 U.S. at 577 ("Respondent and his amici have submitted, and petitioner does not contest, that only seven countries other than the United States have executed juvenile offenders since 1990: Iran, Pakistan, Saudi Arabia, Yemen, Nigeria, the Democratic Republic of Congo, and China. Since then each of these countries has either abolished capital punishment for juveniles or made public disavowal of the practice."). Petitioner was thus on notice of the possible consideration of these materials,

and indeed, petitioner's merits brief had (briefly) attacked this part of the lower court's reasoning. Brief for the Petitioner, at 41, Roper v. Simmons, 543 U.S. 551 (2005) (No. 06-633) (noting the U.S. reservation to the prohibition on juvenile execution in ratifying the ICCPR and arguing that foreign and international sources were not relevant to establishing an American consensus). But neither of petitioner's two amici addressed foreign or international law, and petitioner's reply brief focuses primarily on claims from psychological and scientific literature about adolescent cognition, maturity, and decision-making, reflecting a presumably considered choice not to address foreign or international law issues at all. *See* Reply Brief for Petitioner, Roper v. Simmons, 543 U.S. 551 (2005) (No. 03-633). Perhaps it is understandable, as a strategic matter, if one's position is that foreign or international law is not relevant, to offer no response addressed to the fairness, completeness, or accuracy of the other side's presentation; perhaps this is particularly so where the weight of foreign and international material was so overwhelming.

203. *See, e.g., supra* note 159 (noting that there was no briefing in *Roper* of the death penalty for those regarded as juveniles in Japan).

204. *See* Brief Amici Curiae of Mary Robinson, Amnesty International U.S.A., Human Rights Watch, Interights, the Lawyers Committee for Human Rights, and Minnesota Advocates for Human Rights in Support of Petitioners, Lawrence v. Texas, 539 U.S. 558 (2003) (No. 02-102), 2003 WL 164151. A search of all amicus briefs filed on the merits in the case and available on Westlaw and Lexis found no response.

205. *See* Lawrence v. Texas, 553 U.S. 558, 598 (2003) (Scalia, J., dissenting) (accusing the majority of "ignoring . . . the many countries that have retained criminal prohibitions on sodomy"). One brief argued that international and foreign decisions reflected "an emerging global movement" viewing "same-sex sodomy laws as impermissible discrimination." Brief Amici Curiae of Mary Robinson et al, *supra* note 204, at 21, and discussed those foreign and international decisions that supported that view. *See also* Brief of the American Bar Ass'n as Amicus Curiae in Support of Petitioners, Lawrence v. Texas, 539 U.S. 558 (2003) (No. 02-102) (noting a UNHRC interpretation of ICCPR art 17 to prohibit criminalizing consensual adult sodomy in complaint against Australia); Brief of Amici Curiae Constitutional Law Professors et al. In Support of Petitioners, Lawrence v. Texas, 539 U.S. 558 (2003) (No. 02-102) (noting South African constitutional court decision). One other amicus brief argued, less cautiously, that "[c]ourts all over the world have refused to follow *Hardwick*," and suggested that the "world has moved on to a more productive deployment of the criminal sanction" and that *Hardwick* should be overruled. Brief of the CATO Institute as Amicus Curiae in Support of Petitioners, at 26–27, Lawrence v. Texas, 539 U.S. 558 (2003) (No. 02-102), 2003 WL 152338. Issue was not really joined on these claims by opposing amici. One amicus brief suggested that the "link between marriage as the union of man and woman to procreation and child rearing . . . is universal . . . " Brief Amicus Curiae of the Family Research Council, Inc., and Focus on the Family in Support of Respondent, Lawrence v. Texas, 539 U.S. 558 (2003) (No. 02-102), and another referred to a Netherlands' same-sex marriage bill to suggest the outcome of upholding the constitutional challenge in *Lawrence*. *See* Brief of Liberty Counsel as Amicus Curiae in Support of Respondent, Lawrence v. Texas, 539 U.S. 558 (2003) (No. 02-102).

206. *See* Ramsey, *International Materials*, *supra* note 74, at 69, 74–75, 76, 77–79.

207. D. C. Rules of Professional Conduct, Rule 3.3 (a)(3) (2007) (emphasis added); *see also* ABA Model Rules of Professional Conduct, Rule 3.3(a)(2) (2002) (a lawyer shall not "fail to disclose to the tribunal legal authority in the *controlling* jurisdiction known to the lawyer to be directly adverse to the position of the client and not disclosed by opposing counsel") (emphasis added).

208. Contemporary foreign law would never be controlling or dispositive and international law, whether viewed as "part of our law" or not, would rarely be dispositive, though in some cases it might be an important element of the analysis. *See supra* text at notes 26–27, 64–66.

209. *Cf.* Chapter 4, note 90, above (noting model judicial ethics rule requiring that judges give notice to the parties if they seek expert legal advice about a pending matter). Another alternative might be to give notice of and seek additional briefing on transnational legal sources if they come to seem of significance in deliberation. Even on domestic legal matters errors or omissions can occur that, with more complete briefing, could have been avoided. For example, in Kennedy v. Louisiana, 128 S. Ct. 2641 (2008) the Court's initial published opinion surveying state and federal death penalty laws for rape omitted discussing the penalty in federal military law and a 2006 statute on that subject; no party or amicus had brought the statute to the Court's attention. A petition for rehearing on this basis was rejected. Kennedy v. Louisiana, 129 S. Ct. 1 (2008).

210. The Court's librarians, for example, may have or develop expertise in international and foreign sources. Note that how the Court obtains its information may raise further questions to be resolved. *See, e.g.*, Alford, *Outsourcing Research about Outsourced Authority*, *supra* note 195 (suggesting that Library of Congress research memos for federal judges on issues of foreign law be made public). For another approach taken by some foreign constitutional courts, which may resort to international or foreign law more often in the interpretation of their relatively newer constitutional instruments, see *supra* text at note 195.

211. Saunders, *supra* text at note 170, at 70.

212. It was at a German-American legal symposium that Chief Justice William H. Rehnquist first argued that U.S. courts should begin considering foreign constitutional decisions, as foreign courts had long considered U.S. decisions. *See* William H. Rehnquist, *Constitutional Courts—Comparative Remarks, reprinted in* GERMANY AND ITS BASIC LAW: PAST, PRESENT AND FUTURE—A GERMAN-AMERICAN SYMPOSIUM 412 (Paul Kirchhof & Donald P. Kommers eds., 1993); *see also* William H. Rehnquist, *Foreword* to DEFINING THE FIELD OF COMPARATIVE CONSTITUTIONAL LAW at vii, viii (Vicki Jackson & Mark Tushnet eds., 2002) (reprinting similar remarks Rehnquist made in 1999).

213. *See* Ramsey, *Empirical Dilemma*, *supra* note 56, at 1248 ("The practice of Britain, or even Germany and France, may be relatively accessible to nonspecialists through secondary sources. The practice of highly developed non-European legal systems, such as China or the Islamic countries, may require an expertise that takes years to acquire. The practice of less formal legal systems, such as may prevail in parts of Africa and Asia, may be obscure to anyone who has not grown up with them.").

214. The South African Constitutional Court, for example, although applying a new constitution quite different in many respects from that of the United States and in a very different political and social context, has issued thoughtful decisions and developed a body of jurisprudence, in English, that may prove helpful for reflective comparison. Appropriate comparators, it should be noted, may vary from issue to issue. *See supra*a text at notes 22–23 (noting comparisons to other liberal democratic countries that have experienced significant terrorist attacks). As for determining a "transnational consensus," this will not necessarily be possible through country-by-country study, given barriers of language and knowledge, and the Court will need to rely on scholars and party and amici briefs. *See also supra* text at notes 162–63.

215. Practice Direction on the Citation of Authorities, *supra* note 196.

216. *See* Fontana, *supra* note 125, at 563–64 (suggesting that the parties and court resort to the existing Federal Rules of Civil Procedure concerning giving of notice of

issues of foreign law); FED. R. CIV. PROC. 44.1 (requiring a "party who intends to raise an issue about a foreign country's law" to "give notice" while permitting the court to consider any relevant material or source in deciding the issue, which is to be treated as one of law). It is doubtful that citation or reference to foreign law, as a deliberative aid to resolving an issue of U.S. constitutional law, would be treated as "intended to raise an issue" about the foreign law. The kinds of "issues" raised in litigation under Rule 44.1 in the lower federal courts appear to arise where the foreign law is claimed to be dispositive on some point. *See, e.g.*, Faggionato v. Lerner, 500 F. Supp. 2d 237 (S.D.N.Y. 2007) (discussing whether under French law an art dealer was a proper party to a contract for the sale of a painting); Rationis Enterprises Inc. of Panama v. Hyundai Mipo Dockyard Co. Ltd., 426 F. 3d 580 (2d Cir. 2005) (applying Korean law in a case against a Korean shipyard for losses incurred when a ship split in two during a storm); *cf.* United States v. Schultz, 333 F. 3d 393 (2d Cir. 2003) (discussing whether Egyptian antiquities were "stolen" for purposes of a federal criminal prosecution, which turned on Egyptian "patrimony" law declaring all antiquities discovered after 1983 to be property of the Egyptian government).

217. *See* Adam Liptak, *Execution of Mexican is Halted*, N.Y. TIMES, May 14, 2004, at A23 (reporting that in light of ICJ interpretations of the Consular Convention, an Oklahoma state court halted the execution of a Mexican national and the state governor commuted his death sentence to life in prison).

218. Judith Resnik, *Law's Migration: American Exceptionalism, Silent Dialogues, and Federalism's Multiple Ports of Entry*, 115 YALE L.J. 1564, 1626–56 (2006); *see* Catherine Powell, *Dialogic Federalism: Constitutional Possibilities for Incorporation of Human Rights Law in the United States*, 150 U. Pa. L. Rev. 245 (2001); *see also* Martha F. Davis, *The Spirit of Our Times: State Constitutions and International Human Rights*, 30 N.Y.U. REV. L. & SOC. CHANGE 359 (2006).

219. *See* Marshall, *supra* note 22, at 1641–43 (2004); Hon. Shirley S. Abrahamson, *All the World's a Courtroom: Judging in the New Millenium*, 26 HOFSTRA L. REV. 273, 285 (1997); *see also* Hon. Judith S. Kaye, *State Courts at the Dawn of a New Century: Common Law Courts Reading Statutes and Constitutions*, 70 N.Y.U. L. REV. 1 (1995).

220. For an introduction to a literature assessing the impact of party resources on litigation as compared to legislation, see, for example, Todd. J. Zywicki, *Gordon Tullock's Critique of the Common Law* 46–47 (Geo. Mason L. & Econ. Research Paper No. 07-13, 2007), *available at* http://papers.ssrn.com/sol3/papers.cfm?abstract_id=964781; Paul B. Stephan, *Redistributive Litigation—Judicial Innovation, Private Expectations, and the Shadow of International Law*, 88 VA. L. REV. 789, 852–58 (2002); Frank B. Cross, *The Judiciary and Public Choice*, 50 HASTINGS L.J. 355, 360–64 (1999); Thomas W. Merrill, *Does Public Choice Theory Justify Judicial Activism After All?*, 21 HARV. J.L. & PUB. POL'Y 219, 222–30 (1997); Einer R. Elhauge, *Does Interest Group Theory Justify More Intrusive Judicial Review?*, 101 YALE L.J. 31, 36–38, 67–80 (1991).

221. *See* BLOCH ET AL., *supra* note 179, at 449–94.

222. *See, e.g.*, Sterling v. Cupp, 625 P.2d 123, 131 n.21 (Ore. 1981); *see also* Jones v. Florida, 740 So. 2d 520, 524–25 (Fla. 1999); Vicki C. Jackson, *Constitutional Dialogue and Human Dignity: States and Transnational Constitutional Discourse*, 65 MONT. L. REV. 15 (2004); *see also* Chapter 9, note 72 below.

223. Resnik, *supra* note 218, at 1564.

224. *See, e.g.*, Olivier Dutheillet de Lamothe, Member, Conseil Constitutionnel (Fr.), *Constitutional Court Judges' Roundtable*, 3 INT'L J. CONST. L. 550 (2005) (discussing "spontaneous comparative constitutionalism," in which the "Conseil Constitutionnel derives its decisions, without explicitly saying so, [from] previous decisions by other constitutional

courts" and referring specifically to its decisions on abortion, the independence of university professors, and equality and different treatment); *see also* Johanne Poirier, The Use of Foreign Precedents by the Constitutional Court of Belgium (Prel. Rep. Nov. 2008) (unpublished draft on file with author) (concluding, based on interviews and access to nonpublic documents, that foreign case law is used by the Belgian court even though never cited). In 2001, for example, the pleadings before the French Conseil Constitutionnel show that the laws of several other nations concerning the time within which women could choose to have an abortion were discussed in the government's submission. *See* Observations du Government 1 (B) (2), in Decision 2001-446 DC of 27 June 2001, Voluntary Interruption of Pregnancy (Abortion) and Contraception Act, *available at* http://www.conseil-constitutionnel.fr/conseil-constitutionnel/francais/les-decisions/depuis-1958/decisions-par-date/2001/2001-446-dc/observations-du-gouvernement.41669.html.

225. *See* Wen-Chen Chang & Jiunn-Rong Yeh, The Use of Foreign Precedents by the Constitutional Court in Taiwan (Nov. 2008) (unpublished draft on file with author).

226. *Cf.* Mitchel De S.-O.-L'E. Lasser, Judicial Deliberations: A Comparative Analysis of Judicial Transparency and Legitimacy (2004) (suggesting that judgments in France are legitimated through institutional structures that constrain and inform the terse formal opinions issued).

227. *See* Stephen B. Burbank, *Alternative Career Resolution II: Changing the Tenure of Supreme Court Justices*, 154 U. Pa. L. Rev. 1511, 1527–29 (2006); Mark A. Graber, *Constructing Judicial Review*, 8 Ann. Rev. Pol. Sci. 425, 429 (2005); *see also* Gerald N. Rosenberg, *The Road Taken: Robert A. Dahl's Decision-Making in a Democracy: The Supreme Court as a National Policy Maker*, 50 Emory L.J. 613, 627–29 (2001).

228. *Cf.* Ronen Shamir, *"Landmark Cases" and the Reproduction of Legitimacy: The Case of Israel's High Court of Justice*, 24 Law & Soc. Rev. 781 (1990) (noting, critically, the legitimation effects among some foreign nations' view of Israel from decisions of the Israeli court opposing government action in the occupied territories).

229. 128 S. Ct. 2229 (2008).

230. The Court did discuss British cases, mostly before and during the founding period, but it also considered "[p]ost-1789 habeas developments in England," which, "though not bearing upon the Framers' intent, do verify their foresight." 128 S. Ct. at 2247; *see id.* at 2248 (citing a 1984 English case).

231. Amici briefs by, for example, former U.S diplomats, Amnesty International, the UN High Commissioner for Human Rights, and others discussed international and regional human rights covenants, customary international law, humanitarian law and the laws of war, comparative foreign law (including A v. Sec'y of State, [2004] UKHL 56, [2005] 2 A.C. 68 (U.K.), and the adverse international effects from denying judicial review, including encouraging other countries towards abusive detention practices. An amicus brief from Israeli legal experts suggested that Israel's experience, facing fifty years of "mortal threats to its national survival," showed that even there judicial review of military detentions was not incompatible with protecting national security (and should have been afforded the several hundred Guantánamo detainees). Brief of Amici Curiae Specialists in Israeli Military Law and Constitutional Law in Support of Petitioners at 2–3, Boumediene v. Bush, 128 S. Ct. 2229 (2008) (Nos. 06-1195, 1196); *see id.* (noting that in 2002 Israeli forces, with fewer resources than the U.S. Army, seized 7,000 "suspected enemy combatants," quickly released over 5,000, and gave the remaining 1600 access to counsel and judicial hearings "within . . . weeks"); *cf.* Hirschl, *supra* note 36, at 144–46 (describing "most difficult cases" analyses). The Boumediene petitioners' brief also discussed the Israeli situation, as did the government's response. *See* Brief for the Boumediene

Petitioners, Boumediene v. Bush, 128 S. Ct. 2296 (2008) (No. 06-1195); Brief for the Respondents, Boumediene v. Bush, 128 S. Ct. 2229 (2008) (Nos. 06-1195, 06-1196).

232. *See Boumediene,* 128 S. Ct. at 2263 ("This simply confirms the care Congress has taken throughout our Nation's history to preserve the writ and its function").

233. *Id.* at 2277. *Compare* The Council of Europe, European Court of Human Rights http://www.coe.org.rs/eng/tdoc_sr/council_of_europe/coe_institutions/?conid=18 (last visited Jan. 25, 2009) (explaining that the European Convention on Human Rights protects against "arbitrary and unlawful detention"); ICCPR art. 9 (prohibiting "arbitrary" detentions and providing that no one may be deprived of liberty except in accordance with procedures established by law).

234. 128 S. Ct. 2641 (2008).

235. *Id.* at 2650 (describing *Enmund v. Florida,* 458 U.S. 782, 788 (1982) as "looking to 'historical development of the punishment at issue, legislative judgments, international opinion, and the sentencing decisions juries have made'").

236. According to the Amicus Brief of the British Law Ass'n, Scholars, Queen's Counsel, and former Law Lords, there were twenty-eight countries that still formally retained the death penalty as a sanction for rape of a child. The brief argued that six of these states were in fact abolitionist, and that none of the other twenty-two were Western democracies. *See* Brief of Leading British Law Ass'ns et al. as Amici Curiae Supporting Petitioner at 29–31, Kennedy v. Louisiana, 128 S. Ct. 2641 (2008) (No. 07-343), 2008 WL 706791.

CHAPTER 7. ENGAGEMENT, EQUALITY, AND OLDER CONSTITUTIONS

1. *See, e.g.,* H.C.J. 6698/95, Ka'adan v. Israel Land Administration, ¶30, (Mar. 8, 2000) (Isr.) (referring to *Brown v. Board of Education,* 347 U.S. 483 (1954), in explaining why an offer of a settlement exclusively for Arab citizens of Israel is not a sufficient answer to an equality-based challenge to the denial of an Arab family's right to acquire land for a home in a Jewish settlement), *available at* http://elyon1.court.gov.il/eng/home/index.html.

2. Classifications based on race are presumptively unconstitutional and subject to "strict scrutiny"; they are valid only if justified by a "compelling" government interest and are "necessary," or "narrowly tailored," to serve that interest. *See, e.g.,* McLaughlin v. Florida, 379 U.S. 184, 196 (1964); Adarand Constructors Inc v. Pena, 515 U.S. 200, 227 (1995). Gender classifications are not as suspect, because "[p]hysical differences between men and women . . . are enduring," but valid gender classifications must be justified by an "exceedingly persuasive justification," United States v. Virginia, 518 U.S. 515, 533, 534 (1996), or by an "important governmental objective," and the means chosen must be "substantially related to the achievement of those objectives." Craig v. Boren, 429 U.S. 190, 197 (1976).

3. These two constitutional values come into particular tension around such issues as the validity of prohibitions on hate speech, *compare, e.g.,* R v. Keegstra, [1990] 3 S.C.R. 697 (Can.) (upholding criminal prohibition of "wilfully promoting" group hatred in public speech) *with* R.A.V. v. City of St. Paul, 505 U.S. 377 (1992) (invalidating criminal prohibition of speech designed to arouse resentment based, inter alia, on race or religion), or the regulation of election campaign financing and spending, *compare, e.g.,* FEC v. Wisc. Right to Life, Inc., 551 U.S. 449 (2007) (finding a law limiting corporate expenditures for an "electioneering communication" within specified periods before an election to violate the First Amendment) and Buckley v. Valeo, 424 U.S. 1 (1976) (striking down expenditure limits in elections for public office) *with* R. (Animal Defenders Int'l) v. Sec'y of State for

Culture, Media and Sport, [2008] UKHL 15, [2008] 1 A.C. 1312 (U.K) (upholding a ban on the broadcast of advertisements directed "towards any religious or political end" or by a body with a primarily political or religious objective, challenged on free speech grounds under the Human Rights Act's incorporation of the ECHR), Libman v. Att'y Gen., [1997] 3 S.C.R. 569 (Can.) (striking down restrictions on independent expenditures in referenda votes but indicating support for other regulation of expenditures in elections for public office); Bowman v. United Kingdom, 1998-I Eur. Ct. H.R. 175 (finding a British law banning independent expenditures in excess of five pounds to disproportionately interfere with freedom of expression, but leaving open the possibility that a less stringent limit would be upheld). (The discussion in the first half of this chapter, through Part B, is drawn in part from my earlier work, Vicki C. Jackson, *Holistic Interpretation, Comparative Constitutionalism and Fiss-ian Freedoms*, 58 U. MIAMI L. REV. 265 (2003); *Transnational Discourse, Relational Authority, and the U.S. Court: Gender Equality*, 37 LOY. L.A. L. REV. 271 (2003); *Holistic Constitutional Interpretation: Fitzpatrick v. Bitzer and Our Bifurcated Constitution*, 53 STAN. L. REV. 1259 (2001).)

4. Equality issues, moreover, are of concern to legal communities beyond this country, given the commitments of international human rights law and the ways in which general principles of equality law may affect treatment of foreign nationals.

5. Gary Jeffrey Jacobsohn, *The Permeability of Constitutional Borders*, 82 TEX. L. REV. 1763, 1812 (2004).

6. 529 U.S. 598 (2000).

7. 533 U.S. 53 (2001).

8. 83 U.S. 36 (1873). Other early cases also read the amendments narrowly, even with respect to racial discrimination. *See, e.g.*, The Civil Rights Cases, 109 U.S. 3, 24 (1883) (holding unconstitutional an Act of Congress prohibiting race discrimination in public inns, because the Fourteenth Amendment applied only to "state action" and refusal of public inns to serve black people was not a badge or incident of slavery for Thirteenth Amendment purposes; to hold otherwise would be "running the slavery argument into the ground"); *see also* United States v. Reece, 92 U.S. 214 (1875); United States v. Harris, 106 U.S. 629 (1882).

9. For examples of purposive interpretation of a *narrowly* drawn amendment, see, e.g., Hans v. Louisiana, 134 U.S. 1 (1890); Monaco v. Mississippi, 292 U.S. 313 (1934); Alden v. Maine, 527 U.S. 706 (1999) (all interpreting the Eleventh Amendment to stand for a general principle of state sovereign immunity with applications beyond the written text). For discussion, see John F. Manning, *The Eleventh Amendment and the Reading of Precise Constitutional Texts*, 113 YALE L.J. 1663 (2004).

10. For critical discussions, see CHARLES L. BLACK, JR., STRUCTURE AND RELATIONSHIP IN CONSTITUTIONAL LAW (1969); JOHN HART ELY, DEMOCRACY AND DISTRUST 11–41 (1980); Bruce Ackerman, *Constitutional Politics/Constitutional Law*, 99 YALE L.J. 453 (1989); Akhil Reed Amar, *Intratexualism*, 112 HARV. L. REV. 747, 800–01 (1999); Akhil Reed Amar, *Foreword: The Document and the Doctrine*, 114 HARV. L. REV. 26, 30 (2000).

11. By treating slaves (who could not vote) as "three-fifths" of a person for purposes of allocating representation in the House of Representatives, the original Constitution gave greater voting power in the House to voters in large slave-holding states. *See* U.S. CONST. art. I, § 2. Each state was afforded two senators, an essentially unamendable provision. *See id.* art.I, § 3, art. V. Equality of states as political communities was thus of an importance comparable to or perhaps even greater than principles of individual political equality. Yet the membership-by-population rule for the House (notwithstanding the racism of the "three-fifths rule") embodied the idea that voting power should be related to the numbers

of persons represented, and there are traces of equality elsewhere (such as the ban on titles of nobility, U.S. CONST. art. I, § 9) suggesting that this Constitution, relative to other political systems in the minds of the framers, was more open to the idea of human equality.

12. Under these Amendments, slavery is abolished, national citizenship based on birth in the United States is defined, states are prohibited from denying to persons the equal protection of laws or due process of law, racial discrimination in voting is outlawed, the Senate is required to be chosen by popular election, gender discrimination in voting is outlawed, some voting rights for citizens in the District of Columbia in presidential elections are provided, poll taxes (that effectively discriminate in voting based on wealth) are prohibited, and the right to vote is extended to eighteen-year-olds.

13. Missouri v. Holland, 252 U.S. 416, 434 (1920) (Holmes, J.).

14. 347 U.S. 497 (1954).

15. 347 U.S. 483 (1954).

16. The Court was explicit in tying its interpretation of the Fifth Amendment obligations of the federal government to the anti-discrimination obligations that the Fourteenth Amendment applied to the states. *See Bolling*, 347 U.S. at 498–99 ("In view of our decision that the Constitution prohibits the states from maintaining racially segregated public schools, *it would be unthinkable that the same Constitution would impose a lesser duty on the Federal Government.*") (emphasis added); *see also* AKHIL REED AMAR, THE BILL OF RIGHTS: CREATION AND RECONSTRUCTION 234–37 (1998) (noting the Fourteenth Amendment's effects in extending the Bill of Rights to the states and on shifting understandings of what those earlier constitutional texts stand for).

17. *See* MARY L. DUDZIAK, COLD WAR CIVIL RIGHTS: RACE AND THE IMAGE OF AMERICAN DEMOCRACY 14–27 (2000).

18. Baker v. Carr, 369 U.S. 186 (1962).

19. Wesberry v. Sanders, 376 U.S. 1, 5 (1964).

20. *See, e.g.*, Gray v. Sanders, 372 U.S. 368, 377, 385 (1963); *see also* Colegrove v. Green, 328 U.S. 549, 570 (1946) (Black, J., dissenting) (arguing that Section 2 of the Fourteenth Amendment reinforced an understanding of Article I, Section 2 as requiring that congressional districts should contain approximately equal populations).

21. *See Gray v. Sanders*, 372 U.S. at 376–77 & n.8, 378–381; *see also* Reynolds v. Sims, 377 U.S. 533 (1964).

22. 404 U.S. 71 (1971). On the importance of the Nineteenth Amendment for interpreting the Fourteenth Amendment, see Reva B. Siegel, *She the People: The Nineteenth Amendment, Sex Equality, Federalism, and the Family*, 115 HARV. L. REV. 947 (2002).

23. 411 U.S. 677, 680 & n.5, 682–84 (1973) (noting that the Due Process Clause prohibits unreasonable discriminations, and discussing *Reed*).

24. These and other decisions in the 1970s indicated that nineteeenth-century cases rejecting women's equality claims advanced under the Fourteenth Amendment were no longer good law and that the same principle of gender equality would constrain federal as well as state action. *See id.* at 684–85 (discussing *Bradwell v. State*, 83 U.S. 130 (1873), which had upheld a state's refusal to allow women to practice law, and the rejection of its sex-biased premises in the ratification of the Nineteenth Amendment).

25. 529 U.S. 598 (2000).

26. 514 U.S. 549 (1995).

27. *Morrison*, 529 U.S. at 607–19.

28. *Id.* at 627.

29. *Id.* at 617–18.

30. *See* Brief for Law Professors as Amicus Curiae Supporting Petitioner, United States v. Morrison, 529 U.S. 598 (2000) (Nos. 99-05, 99-29), 1999 U.S. Briefs 5, at 6–7 (referring to the "need to protect commerce from the injurious effects of an environment of violence against a 'quasi-suspect' class of persons"). I was one of the counsel on this brief.

31. For UN attention to violence against women in the same year that VAWA was enacted, see UN Econ. & Soc. Council [ECOSOC], Comm'n on Human Rights, Preliminary Report submitted by Rhadika Coomaraswamy, the Special Rapporteur on violence against women, its causes and consequences, ¶79, 85 UN Doc. E/CN.4/1995/42 (Nov. 22, 1994) (prepared in accordance with Commission on Human Rights Resolution 1994/45); Declaration on the Elimination of Violence Against Women, G.A. Res. 48/104, UN Doc. A/RES/48/104 (Feb. 23, 1994). Although international law does not itself address which level in a federal government is competent to implement international obligations, the U.S. Constitution authorizes Congress to "define and punish . . . Offenses against the Law of Nations," U.S. CONST. art. I, § 8; it authorizes the President, with the advise and consent of the Senate, to make treaties, *id.* art. II, § 2; and it authorizes Congress to enact legislation to implement treaty obligations, *see* Missouri v. Holland, 252 U.S. 416, 432 (1920) (referring to the "necessary and proper" clause of Article I, Section 8). *See generally* Carlos Manuel Vázquez, *Missouri v. Holland's Second Holding*, 73 MO. L. REV. 939, 943–53 (2008). Chapter 8 below will discuss arguments grounded in congressional power to implement international law advanced, but not discussed by the Court, in *Morrison*.

32. According to the Forum of Federations, http://www.forumfed.org/en, the following nations have federal constitutions: Argentina, Australia, Austria, Belgium, Bosnia and Herzegovina, Brazil, Canada, Comoros, Ethiopia, Germany, India, Malaysia, Mexico, Micronesia, Nigeria, Pakistan, Russia, St. Kitts & Nevis, South Africa, Spain, Switzerland, United Arab Emirates, the United States, and Venezuela. Of these, it appears that the United States, Canada, Mexico, and Australia have constitutions in force that predate World War II. Austria arguably could also be included, but its status is complicated (for example, the Austrian constitution—both that of 1920, and that restored after World War II—is made up of multiple constitutional instruments) and its jurisprudence less accessible to those who do not speak German. Argentina introduced major constitutional change in 1994, which many regard as a new constitution, but some regard as a reform of the nineteenth-century constitution. *See* Néstor Pedro Sagüés, *An Introduction and Commentary to the Reform of the Argentine National Constitution*, 28 U. MIAMI INTER-AM. L. REV. 41, 52–53 (1996) (transl. by Keith Rosenn). The Swiss adopted a new constitution in 1999, though it maintained considerable continuity with the prior, nineteenth-century constitution; Switzerland's supreme court lacks jurisdiction to review national laws for constitutionality.

33. Mexico's constitution, for example, includes, in addition to a general guarantee of gender equality added in 1974, provisions requiring special treatment of pregnant women, reflecting a distinctive conception of gender relations; it also includes an expansive and oft-amended list of national powers. *Compare* CONSTITUCIÓN POLÍTICA DE LOS ESTADOS UNIDOS MEXICANOS [Const.], art. 4 (as amended, Diario Oficial de la Federación [D.O.], 31 de Diciembre de 1974 and as amended to 2007), *translated in* 12 CONSTITUTIONS OF THE COUNTRIES OF THE WORLD: MEXICO 6 (Rüdiger Wolfrum & Rainer Grote eds., Gisbert Flanz, ed. emeritus, 2008) (stating that men and women are equal before the law and that persons have a right to control through reasonable means the number and spacing of their children) *with id.* art. 123 (providing that pregnant women should not receive heavy work, are to receive specified breaks before and after birth while receiving their full salary, and should receive special breaks while nursing their babies). As to federalism, the history of

the Mexican constitution suggests that it would have required less reliance on interpretive evolution; Article 73 of the constitution, which lists national legislative powers, is the most amended provision, having been amended fifty times since 1921 to expand national power. This pattern reflected the dominance of a single party in the national congress and the state legislatures, making it easy to secure the necessary approvals. Single party dominance lasted into the 1990s. *See* Rainer Grote, *The United Mexican States Commentary, Introductory Note*, in 12 CONSTITUTIONS OF THE COUNTRIES OF THE WORLD: MEXICO 11, 16–19, 31 (Rüdiger Wolfrum & Rainer Grote eds., Gisbert Flanz, ed. emeritus, 2008). As this source notes, "the constitutional principle of federalism was largely superseded through the increasing centralization of the power of the federal presidency" during the period of one-party rule. *Id.* at 31. Although regarded as a "free" country, Mexico is not rated as highly in the protection of civil and political liberties as the United States or Canada. *See* Freedom House, Freedom in the World, http://www.freedomhouse.org (search for 2008 and Mexico) (rated 2 and 3 on political and civil rights). Turning to Argentina, even if its 1994 constitution were regarded as an amendment of its older one, *see supra* note 32, it would present a quite different and confounding history. *See, e.g.*, Chapter 3, text at note 179, above.

34. *See* CHARTER OF RIGHTS AND FREEDOMS, CONSTITUTION ACT, 1982, pt. I (Can.); CONSTITUTION ACT, 1867 (Can.). Canada and the United States are further compared in Chapter 8 below. I note here that interpretation by the Canadian Supreme Court has played an important role in Canadian constitutional evolution, although there are various amendment procedures. *See* CONSTITUTION ACT, 1982, pt. V, §§ 38–44 (Can.).

35. Reference re Firearms Act, [1998] 219 A.R. 201 (Alta. Ct. App. 1998), *aff'd* [2000] 1 S.C.R. 783.

36. *See id.* at 224, 248, 250–51, paras. 48, 156, 167. Thus, some put the issue as whether licensing and registration for "ordinary firearms" were more like registering automobiles (and thus within provincial powers), or more like registering unusually dangerous weapons, already required by a federal statute. *Id.* at 250–51, para. 167.

37. *Reference re Firearms Act*, 219 A.R. at 221–22, para. 35; *see id.* at 284, para. 303.

38. Canada allocates specific powers to each level of government. *See* CONSTITUTION ACT, 1867, §§ 91, 92 (Can.). The "pith and substance" test looks at the essential "matter" of a statute, its "dominant or most important characteristic," as part of an analysis to help reach a conclusion as to which power (and thus, which level of government) it belongs. *See Reference re Firearms Act*, 219 A.R. at 241, 243–44 paras. 125, 134–35; *see generally* 1 PETER W. HOGG, CONSTITUTIONAL LAW OF CANADA 15.5(a), (d), (e) (5th ed. 2006, supplemented through 2007). These inquiries may invoke "colourability," the idea that a statute formally directed at one purpose is really impermissibly aimed at another purpose outside the government's authority. *See Reference re Firearms Act*, at 241–43, paras. 126–30; HOGG, *supra*, 15.5(g).

39. *Reference re Firearms Act*, 219 A.R. at 284, para. 303; *see also id.* at para. 304 (because this law will result in "increased protection of women from actual violence and the fear of violence from firearms, the gender dimension of firearms use and equality guarantees weighs in favour of classifying the impugned laws under the federal criminal law power"); *id.* at 284, para. 303 ("[W]omen tend to experience guns and gun possession differently from men. . . . Focussing almost exclusively on property rights concentrates primarily on the owners and possessors of ordinary firearms. But equally important is the perspective of those put at risk by guns. . . . [C]haracterizing the law from the latter perspective is more consistent with equality rights . . . .").

40. *Id.* at 239–40, paras. 114, 119, 120 (also noting statistical data indicating, *inter alia*, that the majority of firearms used in domestic homicides are ordinary firearms, that guns

are associated with higher homicide rates, and that 72 percent of female victims of shooting homicides were killed by ordinary firearms); *see id.* at 252, para. 169 (quoting the Minister who introduced the legislation saying that registration helps "deal with the scourge of domestic violence," and referring to statistics showing "that every six days a woman is shot to death in Canada, . . . almost always by someone she knows, almost always with a legally owned rifle or shotgun"); *id.* at 252, 259, paras. 169, 195 (noting arguments that registration of firearms would make it easier for the police to effectively enforce protective orders and for the police to take appropriate steps to protect themselves when they intervene in domestic disputes).

41. *Id.* at 221, para. 35. When the Charter was adopted in 1982, the constitutional settlement resulted in the Constitution Act, 1982, which changed the name of the British North America Act, 1867 to the Constitution Act, 1867, and amended a few provisions of the 1867 Act, but not the provisions of Sections 91 and 92 at issue in the *Reference re Firearms Act* case. *See* Hogg, *supra* note 38, § 1.3; Constitution Act, 1982, pt. VI (Can.); Constitution Act, 1867, §§ 91, 92 (Can.); *cf.* Charter of Rights and Freedoms, 1982, § 31 (Can.) ("Nothing in this Charter extends the legislative powers of any body or authority.").

42. *See supra* note 35. The majority in the court of appeals consisted of Chief Justice Fraser and Justices Berger and Hetherington, each of whom wrote separately; Justice Conrad's dissent was joined by Justice Irving. *See Reference re Firearms,* 219 A.R. at 355, para. 517 (Conrad, J., dissenting) (noting that "violence against women is always a matter of concern for any level of government, [but] it is not the issue in this Reference" because even if one of the reasons for the legislation was spousal violence, "that does not answer the question of who has the jurisdiction to legislate"). The dissent went on to suggest that the legislation itself was not drafted in such a way as to make plausible that it was "aimed specifically at the problem of spousal violence," perhaps implying that if the legislation itself (instead of regulations, discussed by Fraser, that required spousal notification on application for a license) showed an "intent to prohibit conduct with a view to preventing violence to spouses," the constitutional question would be different. *Id.*

43. *Cf.* Égale Canada, Inc. v. Canada, [2003] B.C.C.A. 251, paras. 46–50, 58–72 (Brit. Col. Ct. App.) (disagreeing with the trial court, which had concluded that the federal power over "marriage" under the Constitution Act, 1867, § 91(26) was limited to the common law definition in 1867). The court of appeals instead concluded that the meaning of the federal power over marriage was not fixed in 1867 and noted the 1982 Charter's effects on the meaning of "marriage." *Id.* at paras. 106–13. *see also* Halpern v. Canada (A.G.), [2003] 65 O. R. (3d) 161, 176 (Ont. Ct. App.). In the Canadian Supreme Court, the scope of power under Section 91(26) was progressively interpreted in light of changing conditions, based on the Canadian doctrine of the constitution as a "living tree," but without specific reference to the Charter. Reference re Same Sex Marriage, [2004] 3 S.C.R. 698, 710–11 (Can.).

44. *See, e.g.,* R. v A.M, [2008] 1 S.C.R. 569, 610 (Can.) (Binnie, J.) (citing Doe v. Renfrow, 631 F.2d 91 (7th Cir. 1980)); Hill v. Hamilton-Wentworth Reg'l Police Services Bd., [2007] 3 S.C.R. 129, 184 (Can.) (Charron, J., dissenting on the cross-appeal) (citing several lower court decisions, including Gregoire v. Biddle, 177 F.2d 579 (2d Cir., 1949)); *see also* Peter McCormick, *The Supreme Court of Canada and American Citations 1945–94: A Statistical Overview,* 8 Sup. Ct. L. Rev. (2d) 527, 541–43 (1997) (reporting that roughly 25 percent of Canadian Supreme Court's citations to U.S. law in Charter cases in the period studied were to lower federal and state court decisions). Canadian lower court opinions have been referred to by jurists in other countries, as have lower court opinions from the United States. *See, e.g.,* S. v. Coetzee, 1997 (3) SA 527 (CC) at 537 n.12 (S. Afr.) (Langa, J.) (citing California and lower federal court decisions in case involving the presumption of

innocence and reverse onus provisions); *id.* at 578 n.71 (Kentridge, AJ., dissenting in part, concurring in part) (citing case from Ontario, Can.); *id.* at 596 (O'Regan, J.) (dissenting in part) (citing case from Saskatchewan, Can.); Phillips v. Director of Public Prosecutions, 2003 (3) SA 345 (CC) at 367 n.38 (S. Afr.) (Sachs, J.) (citing Ontario decision, among others, in resolving a freedom of expression question); *see also* State v. Makwanyane, 1995 (3) SA 391 (CC) at 421 nn. 83, 84 (S. Afr.) (Chaskalson, P.) (citing lower federal and state court decisions from the United States); *id.* at 432–33 (discussing California and Massachusetts decisions in deciding on the constitutionality of the death penalty). *Cf.* Shirley S. Abrahamson & Michael J. Fisher, *All the World's a Coourtroom: Judging in the New Millenium*, 26 HOFSTRA L. REV. 273, 275 n.7 (1997) (noting Buckley v. Smith Trans., 1946 O.R. 798 and Hutchings v. Nevin, 9 O.R. (3d) 776 (1992) on an issue of tort law).

45. In a federalism case decided three years before *Morrison*, the Second Amendment was noted by only a single justice, Printz v. United States, 521 U.S. 898, 937–39 (1997) (Thomas, J., concurring), and had been previously construed to apply only in the context of the collective rights of states to organize armed militias. *See* United States v. Miller, 307 U.S. 174, 178 (1939). *But see* District of Columbia v. Heller, 128 S. Ct. 2783 (2008) (finding that the Second Amendment protects an individual right of gun ownership and possession for use at least in the home). Nonetheless, the Second Amendment's existence in the U.S. Constitution might have predisposed other members of the Court to a more skeptical attitude toward other countries' constitutional decisions concerning gun registration and licensing.

46. 379 U.S. 241, 252–53 (1964).

47. 379 U.S. 294, 299–301, 304–05 (1964).

48. Selective Draft Law Cases, 245 U.S. 366, 389 (1918). The challengers had argued that the militia clauses of Article I, Section 8 were the sole basis for conscription of persons into military service, that the circumstances described therein were not met, and that accordingly the draft was beyond federal power. *Id.* at 376.

49. *Cf.* Judith Resnik, *The Programmatic Judiciary: Lobbying, Judging, and Invalidating the Violence Against Women Act*, 74 S. CAL. L. REV. 269, 270–77 (2000) (noting that the Chief Justice had, in a nonadjudicatory capacity, opposed VAWA's civil rights remedy before it was enacted); Judith Resnik, *Reconstructing Equality: Of Justice, Justicia, and the Gender of Jurisdiction*, 14 YALE J. L. & FEMINISM 393, 402 (2002) (describing the Chief Justice's prior positions as "disturbing"). As discussed in Chapter 8, although there was amici briefing on by both sides on whether VAWA could be sustained as an implementation of the ICCPR, the Court said nothing about this issue. That it did not reinforces the conclusion that at that time, the Court was simply not open to considering other arguments to sustain the law. On the roles of "law" and "attitudes" in judicial decision-making, see SUSAN LOW BLOCH ET AL., INSIDE THE SUPREME COURT: THE INSTITUTION AND ITS PROCEDURES 46–47 (2d ed., 2008) (introducing the literature).

50. *See* Boerne v. Flores, 521 U. S. 507 (1997).

51. *See* The Civil Rights Cases, 109 U.S. 3, 17–18 (1883).

52. *See, e.g.*, The Lüth Case (7 BVerfGE 198, 1958), translated and discussed in DONALD P. KOMMERS, THE CONSTITUTIONAL JURISPRUDENCE OF THE FEDERAL REPUBLIC OF GERMANY 361–68 (2d ed. 1997) (discussing the "horizontal" effect of the constitution on the law applied in actions between private parties).

53. A related argument under international law was made. *See* Brief Amici Curiae on Behalf of International Law Scholars and Human Rights Experts in Support of Petitioners, at 5–7, United States v. Morrison, 529 U.S. 598 (2000) (Nos. 99-0005, 99-0029) (arguing that the ICCPR imposed obligations on governments to provide remedies for private

violence directed at women because of their gender). For discussion of the ICCPR argument, see Chapter 8 below.

54. *See* Washington v. Davis, 426 U.S. 229 (1976); Personnel Admr. of Massachusetts v. Feeney, 442 U.S. 256 (1979).

55. *See, e.g.*, Symes v. Canada, [1993] 4 S.C.R. 695, 754–58 (Can.) (affirming that "adverse effects discrimination is comprehended by" the Charter's antidiscrimination provision, but rejecting a challenge to the nondeductability of child care expenses as a form of gender discrimination); Case 109/88, Handels-og Kontorfunktionaerernes Forbund i Danmark v. Dansk Arbejdsgiverforening acting on behalf of Danfoss, 1989 E.C.R. 3199, paras. 18–21 (recognizing that a requirement of mobility in place of work could "disadvantage" female employees and, if not justified, might violate EU requirements of equal pay for equal work). Mark Tushnet suggests that the U.S. Court's rejection of heightened constitutional scrutiny for neutral laws or practices with "disparate impacts" based on gender or race reflects concern that "an expansive disparate impact doctrine would cast constitutional doubt on a wide range of laws," thus giving "the courts a general supervisory role over essentially *all* legislation." Mark Tushnet, *Interpreting Constitutions Comparatively: Some Cautionary Notes with Reference to Affirmative Action*, 36 CONN. L. REV. 649, 652–53 (2004); *see also Washington v. Davis*, 426 U.S. at 248. Analysis of how "disparate impact" doctrines are handled over a range of cases in other countries might shed light on the strength of these concerns.

56. 538 U.S. 721 (2003).

57. *See* Bd. of Tr. of Univ. of Ala. v. Garrett, 531 U.S. 356, 368–71 (2001); Kimel v. Fla. Bd. of Regents, 528 U.S. 62, 89–91 (2000); Fla. Prepaid Postsecondary Educ. Expense Bd. v. Coll. Sav. Bank, 527 U.S. 627, 637–41 (1999); Boerne v. Flores, 521 U.S. 507, 530–32 (1997).

58. For a description of one European system, see Arnlaug Leira, *Caring as Social Right: Cash for Child Care and Daddy Leave*, 5 SOC. POLITICS 362, 370–73 (1998) (describing Norway's adoption, in connection with a general expansion of family care benefits, of a use-it-or-lose-it "daddy leave" designed to encourage fathers to take leave). For a more recent evaluation, see Trude Lappegard, *Changing the Gender Balance in Caring: Fatherhood and the Division of Parental Leave in Norway*, 27 POPUL. RES. POL'Y REV. 139 (2008).

59. Two amicus briefs supporting those who challenged the constitutionality of the law noted that despite progressive family leave policies in several European countries, fathers in those countries were for the most part still unlikely to take leave, and thus, they argued, the remedy Congress chose was ineffective toward its goal of dispelling stereotypes. *See* Brief Amicus Curiae of Coalition for Local Sovereignty in Support of Petitioners, Nevada Dep't of Human Res. v. Hibbs, 538 U.S. 721 (2003) (No. 01-1368), at 19–21; Brief Amicus Curiae of Pacific Legal Foundation In Support of Petitioners, Nev. Dep't of Human Res. v. Hibbs, 538 U.S. 721 (2003) (No. 01-1368), at 25 ("The world Congress seems to envision—in which men and women avail themselves of family leave equally—has never existed in modern times, even in countries with so-called 'progressive' leave.").

60. *See, e.g.*, *Garrett*, 531 U.S. at 368–71; *Kimel*, 528 U.S. at 89–91. At least some in Congress considered the practice of other nations in arguing for adoption of the FMLA. *See, e.g.*, 139 CONG. REC. H379, H384 (daily ed. Feb. 3, 1993) (statement of Rep. Schroeder) ("Let us get real about that and let us realize that we do have to be both care-givers and good employees. If every other country can get it, we can get it.").

61. To the extent that there were questions whether the particular statute was sufficiently likely to avoid or prevent gender discrimination, the comparative approaches of other countries similarly committed to gender equality might have been helpful in providing

a context for deciding the "appropriateness" of Congress's judgment. But divergence among international and comparative legal authorities on whether, and to what degree, commitments to gender equality should permit or forbid "protective" or differentiated treatment of women and men in employment settings may have made resort to such materials less attractive even to proponents of the FMLA. *See, e.g.*, Leira, *supra* note 58, at 373–74 (noting disagreement over whether social rights should be based on "sameness" or "difference"); Case 184/83, Hofmann v. Barmer Ersatzkasse, 1984 E.C.R. 3047 (ECJ decision upholding paid maternity leave only for women); Convention on the Elimination of All Forms of Discrimination Against Women (CEDAW) art. 11.2 (requiring maternity leave but not referring to paternity leave and authorizing the provision of special protection at work to pregnant women, subject to scientific assessments).

62. 533 U.S. 53 (2001).

63. Nguyen was born out of wedlock in Vietnam to a U.S. citizen father and a Vietnamese citizen mother. Although from an early age he lived in Texas with and was raised by his father, a state court order of parentage, based on DNA testing, was not obtained until well after he was eighteen. *See id.* at 57.

64. 533 U.S. at 62–66.

65. *Id.* at 66–68, 71 (noting that mothers, in contrast to fathers, are inevitably present at birth). The major barrier to Nguyen's citizenship claim was that the requirements for proof of biological connection were satisfied too late; in its discussion of these requirements the Court relied particularly on the argument that the special proofs for fathers were justified by the fact that mothers had the opportunity to develop relationships because they were present at birth. *Id.* at 66–69.

66. As Justice O'Connor argued, intermediate scrutiny of gender classifications to see if they are "substantially related" to the achievement of an important government interest is intended to prevent reliance on "overbroad sex-based generalizations" or stereotypes, even when they "enjoy empirical support." *See id.*, 533 U.S. at 74–79 (O'Connor, J., dissenting). To the extent that the government had an important interest in extending citizenship only to those children born abroad to unwed U.S. citizens who had opportunities to (or did in fact) develop a parent-child bond, there were individualized, gender-neutral alternatives available to meet that interest (including proof, *after* age eighteen, that a parental bond had been established earlier). *See id.* at 84–85 (O'Connor, J., dissenting). Likewise, to the extent that the government interest was in assuring a biological connection, requiring fathers, but not mothers, to establish that link before age eighteen did not substantially advance that interest as required by intermediate scrutiny, especially in light of the availability of DNA testing. *See id.* at 80–81 (O'Connor, J. dissenting).

67. *See, e.g.*, United States v. Virginia, 518 U.S. 515 (1996); Miss. Univ. for Women v. Hogan, 458 U.S. 718 (1982); Craig v. Boren, 429 U.S. 190 (1976). The Court had last clearly upheld an overt statutory gender discrimination in the early 1980s. *See* Michael M. v. Sonoma Co. Superior Court, 450 U.S. 464 (1981) (upholding statutory rape crime defined so that it required a female victim); Rostker v. Goldberg, 453 U.S. 57 (1981) (upholding a requirement that men (but not women) register for a possible draft). In 1998, however, the same issue presented in *Nguyen* was before the Court in *Miller v. Albright*, 523 U.S. 420 (1998). The Supreme Court upheld a lower court judgment sustaining the statute; two of the six justices in the majority, however, found no standing on and thus did not address the gender discrimination issue.

68. *See* U.S. Senate Resolution of Advice and Consent to Ratification of the International Covenant on Civil and Political Rights, 138 CONG. REC. 8070, 8071 (Apr. 2, 1992) [hereinafter Senate Resolution] ("the United States declares that the provisions of Articles 1

through 27 of the Covenant are not self-executing"); S. EXEC. REP. No. 102-23, at 9, 19 (1992) (including explanation that the non-self-execution declaration is "to clarify that the Covenant will not create a private cause of action in U.S. courts"). The validity and the effect of such declarations are contested. For different perspectives, see, for example, David Sloss, *The Domestication of International Human Rights: Non-Self-Executing Declarations and Human Rights Treaties,* 24 YALE J. INT'L L. 129 (1999); Curtis A. Bradley & Jack L. Goldsmith, *Treaties, Human Rights, and Conditional Consent,* 149 U. PA. L. REV. 399, 419–22 (2000); Carlos Manuel Vázquez, *Treaties as Law of the Land: The Supremacy Clause and The Judicial Enforcement of Treaties,* 122 HARV. L. REV. 599 (2008).

69. Brief of Equality Now and Others as Amici Curiae in Support of Petitioner, at 4-14, Nguyen v. INS, 533 U.S. 53 (2001) (No. 99-2071). ICCPR art. 26 provides that "[a]ll persons are equal before the law and are entitled without any discrimination to the equal protection of the law," and requires the prohibition of discrimination on grounds "such as race, colour, sex, language, religion, political or other opinion, national or social origin, property, birth or other status." *See also id.*, art. 2. On the effect of a non-self-execution clause on a treaty's persuasive value in constitutional interpretation, see Sarah H. Cleveland, *Our International Constitution,* 31 YALE J. INT'L L. 1, 119 (2006) (arguing that non-self-execution should not "be an obstacle to consideration of the treaty in constitutional interpretation," since the treaty itself is internationally binding; urging courts to "be sensitive to" the reasons the treaty's domestic effect was limited).

70. The "understanding" is ambiguous. *Compare* Senate Resolution, *supra* note 68 (expressing the understanding that the Constitution guarantees "extensive protections against discrimination" and that the United States understands that the ICCPR permits use of "distinctions based upon race, colour, sex, language, . . . or any other status . . . when such distinctions are, at a minimum, rationally related to a legitimate governmental objective") *with* S. EXEC. REP. 102-23, at 8, 14 (explaining that this "understanding" concerns the fact that "U.S. law makes some legal distinctions, for example on the basis of age," and that the understanding is "to the effect that the United States does not regard these distinctions as inconsistent with its obligations" under the ICCPR; also quoting Administration views that the ICCPR's "very broad anti-discrimination provisions [including Article 26] . . . do not precisely comport with long-standing Supreme Court doctrine in the equal protection field").

71. *See* Cleveland, *supra* note 69, at 118–20 (arguing that "reservations, declarations and understandings" on the substantive meaning of a treaty term, unlike a non-self-executing declaration, "restrict the international obligations that the United States has undertaken," and may "reflec[t] the sense of the Senate that U.S. constitutional doctrine should inform the meaning of the treaty obligation, rather than vice versa," foreclosing arguments that the United States intended to undertake a binding legal obligation to conform with the international community's interpretation of the provision; noting, however, that the Court could still consider the "persuasive force" of international understandings that bear on a constitutional question). That the United States has thus far not ratified CEDAW (which includes a more specific provision prohibiting gender discrimination between men and women with respect to the nationality of their children, *see* CEDAW, art 9.2) might also caution against placing much (if any) interpretive weight on the Senate's ratification of the ICCPR with respect to this issue.

72. *See, e.g.*, Aumeeruddy-Cziffra v. Mauritius, UN Human Rights. Comm. (Views), 12th Sess., UN Doc. CCPR/C/12/D/35/1978 (1981) (finding a violation of the ICCPR's principle of equal treatment of the sexes in a distinction made in the availability of residency permits for male and female foreign spouses, which discriminated against female

citizens of Mauritius with foreign spouses); *see also* Karen Knop & Christine Chinkin, *Remembering Chrystal MacMillian: Women's Equality and Nationality in International Law*, 22 MICH J. INT'L L. 523, 576, 584–85 (2001) (describing the UNHRC's General Comment on Equality concerning gender difference, marriage, and nationality and the position of the International Law Association against gender distinctions in requirements for "preferential treatment" under immigration and nationality laws based on parentage).

73. *See id.* at 534–35 (including a list of countries that ratified CEDAW in the 1990s but with reservations to provisions on equality with respect to citizenship and nationality); Brief of Equality Now and Others, *supra* note 69, at 12 n.8 ("Most countries with discriminatory laws on transmission of citizenship provide for transmission of citizenship through fathers rather than mothers."); *see also* Kif Augustine-Adams, *Gendered States: A Comparative Construction of Citizenship and Nation*, 41 VA. J. INT'L L. 93 (2000); Lisa C. Stratton, *The Right to Have Rights: Gender Discrimination in Nationality Laws*, 77 MINN. L. REV. 195, 202–04 (1992) (describing discrimination against women in state nationality laws as applied to issues involving foreign spouses and capacity to pass on citizenship to children); *cf.* Equality Now, Words and Deeds: Holding Governments Accountable in the Beijing +5 Review Process (February 2007 update), http://www.equalitynow.org/english/wan/beijing10/beijing10_en.html (noting that thirty-two of fifty-three countries identified in earlier reports as having laws that discriminated based on sex had not amended or repealed those statutes, including the U.S. statute at issue in *Nguyen*); *see also* Brief of Equality Now and Others, *supra* note 69, at i. (citing the 1999 version of the Words and Deeds report, concerning forty-five countries with explicitly discriminatory laws).

74. For constitutional cases invalidating gender discriminations against mothers in their capacity to pass on citizenship to children, see Benner v. Canada (Secretary of State), [1997] 1 S.C.R. 358 (Can.); Unity Dow v. Attorney General, [1992] 103 I.L.R. 128 (Botswana), *affirming* Unity Dow v. Attorney General, Misc. No. 124/90, High Court (Laboise), *reprinted in* 13 HUM. RTS. Q. 614 (1991). An Italian Constitutional Court decision reportedly reached a similar conclusion. *See* Vicki C. Jackson, *Transnational Discourse, Relational Authority and the U.S. Court: Gender Equality*, 37 LOY. L.A. L. REV. 271, 353 n.287 (2003) (noting discussion on the Women's Human Rights Resources Web page, http://eir.library.utoronto.ca/whrr (visited Nov. 2, 2003), of Decision No. 30/1983 (Const. Ct. Italy), declaring unconstitutional a law that provided that the child of an Italian father was Italian by birth without extending the same status to the child of an Italian mother). For other cases involving gender distinctions in immigration, nationality, and citizenship laws, see, for example, Abdulaziz v. United Kingdom, 94 Eur. Ct. H.R. (ser. A), at 36–39 (1985) (striking down a gender distinction between foreign spouses entitled to remain in the country; the rule making it "easier for a man settled in the United Kingdom than for a woman so settled to obtain permission for his or her nonnational spouse to enter or remain in the country" violated ECHR article 14 and was not justified by the asserted need to maintain effective immigration control or protect the domestic labor market, even if men were more likely to be ecomically active than women); Advisory Opinion OC-4/84, Proposed Amendments to the Naturalization Provision of the Constitution of Costa Rica, 1984 Inter-Am. Ct. H.R. (ser. A) No. 4, at 111–13 (Jan. 19, 1984) (expressing the view that different treatment for foreign spouses, based on their gender, in the right to acquire Costa Rican nationality was a discrimination incompatible with Articles 17(4) and 24 of the American Convention on Human Rights); *cf.* Rattigan v. Chief Immigration Officer, 103 I.L.R. 224 (Zimb. Sup. Ct. 1994) (Gubbay, CJ.) (concluding that a policy refusing to allow foreign husbands residence and work permits violated their wives' constitutional right to freedom of movement).

75. Rasmussen v. Denmark, 87 Eur. Ct. H.R. (ser. A) at 15 (1984) (upholding a gender distinction limiting the time when fathers could institute a contest of paternity proceeding, finding Denmark's law not out of line with others in Europe and within the margin of appreciation, as there was a greater likelihood that mothers' interests were aligned with their children's and a greater likelihood of men seeking to contest paternity to avoid support and maintenance). The ECtHR, however, also took note that Denmark had already changed its law to provide equal amounts of time for mothers or fathers, in light of changed economic and social conditions, thereby perhaps implying that were the issue to arise again the outcome might differ. *Cf.* Petrovic v. Austria, App. No. 20458/92, Eur. Ct. H.R.¶¶ 38–43 (Mar. 27, 1998), *available at* http://echr.coe.int/echr (rejecting challenge to failure in 1989 to provide family allowance, available to mothers, to fathers because at that time there was no common standard in Europe and Austria's approach was within the margin of appreciation; noting that by 1990 Austria had extended the leave allowance to fathers). In some more recent cases, the ECtHR has seemed less hospitable to gender distinctions. *See* Paulík v. Slovakia, App. No. 10699/05, Eur. Ct. H. R., ¶¶ 48–59 (Oct. 10, 2006), *available at* http://www.echr.coe.int/echr (finding a violation of Articles 8 and 14 in Slovakia's law that discriminated against fathers, whose paternity had been adjudicated, in their ability to reopen proceedings after the ordinary time for paternity contests had expired, as compared with fathers whose paternity had been presumed, but not adjudicated, and mothers, who could seek the intervention of the public prosecutor to bring an action to contest paternity); *cf.* Mizzi v. Malta, App. No. 26111/02, Eur. Ct. H.R., ¶¶ 25, 57, 91, 115, 133–36 (Jan. 12, 2006) (finding a violation of Article 6 (right of to a fair judicial hearing), Article 8 (right to private and family life), and Article 14 (nondiscrimination), and distinguishing *Rasmussen* because there the father had five years to bring an action, whereas here he had much less or no time).

76. *See* Malkani v. Sec'y of Ministry of Home Affairs of Bangladesh (Bangl. Sup. Ct., High Ct. Div., Dhaka 1997) (Writ Petition No. 3192 (1992)), *as described in* Women's Human Rights Resources Web page, *supra* note 74 (visited Feb. 9, 2004) and in Asia Pacific Forum on Women, Law and Development: A Digest of Case Law on the Human Rights of Women (Christine Forster et al. eds. 2003), *available at* http://www.apwld.org/pdf/final%20cedaw%20cisco%202.pdf; *see also* Knop & Chinkin, *supra* note 72, at 534–35, 547–48 (describing the *Malkani* case and the continued inability of Bangladeshi mothers to pass on citizenship to their children).

77. *See* Sharifan v. Fed'n of Pakistan, [1998] 50 P.L.D. 59 (Lahore) (1997). The challenged law provided access to citizenship for foreign female spouses but not for foreign male spouses of Pakistani citizens.

78. At the turn of the twentieth to twenty-first centuries, Canada was reportedly accepting more immigrants per capita than any other country in the world. *See* Benajmin Dolin & Margaret Young, Canada's Immigration Program, BP-190E (Oct. 2004) (Parliamentary Information and Research Service (PIRS) of the Library of Parliament of Canada), *available at* http://www.parl.gc.ca/information/library/PRBpubs/bp190-e.htm#20txt (visited Aug. 22, 2008); Nation Master, http://www.nationmaster.com/graph/imm_new_cit_percap-immigration-new-citizenships-per-capita (showing that Canada had in the year 2000 the highest rate of immigration per capita in the world, based on new citizens). Canada has had net in-migration since as early as 1941. *See* Statistics Canada, Population and Growth Components (1851–2001 Census), *available at* http://www40.statcan.ca/l01/cst01/defdemo03.htm#2 (last visited Aug. 22, 2008).

79. Brief of Equality Now and Others, *supra* note 69, at 19, 20.

80. On Canada's constitutional system, see *supra* note 38 and Chapter 8 below. Botswana, a much smaller country of under 2 milion people, has had an uninterrupted

history of democratic rule, with regular elections since independence in 1966; it is treated as a "free" country by Freedom House, with ratings of 2/2 for political rights and civil liberties. *See* Freedom House, Freedom in the World, http://www.freedomhouse.org (search for 2008 and Botswana); *see also* VICKI C. JACKSON & MARK TUSHNET, COMPARATIVE CONSTITUTIONAL LAW 1604–05 (2d ed. 2006). Interestingly, the Solicitor General's brief in *Nguyen* argued that comparative practice in countries where the U.S. had large military presences was consistent with having distinctions in the proof requirements for unwed mothers and fathers. Brief for the Respondent, Nguyen v. INS, 533 U.S. 53 (No. 99-2071), at 17, 36, 42 (reporting that in six nations in which the United States has had large military presences and from which many claims for citizenship arose, "the father's name must appear on the child's birth certificate, or . . . the father must take some other formal act to acknowledge paternity, in order for the father's citizenship to pass to the child by descent"). The government linked this argument to concerns over statelessness. The Reply Brief disagreed that foreign sex-based laws were relevant, since statelessness concerns could be addressed in a more narrowly tailored way and did not justify treating fathers differently from mothers. Reply Brief for the Petitioner, Nguyen v. INS, 533 U.S. 53 (No. 99-2071), at 7–10.

81. *See* Unity Dow v. Attorney-General, [1992] 103 I.L.R. 128 (Botswana Ct. App.). Section 15(1) of the Botswana Constitution provided, with some qualifications, that "no law shall make any provision that is discriminatory either of itself or in its effect." *Dow,* 103 I.L.R. at 149 (Amissah, JP.). Section 15(3) stated: "In this section, the expression 'discriminatory' means affording different treatment to different persons, attributable wholly or mainly to their respective descriptions by race, tribe, place of origin, political opinions, colour or creed. . . ." *Id.* Section 15(4) went on to exclude from the application of Section (15)(1) certain laws, including "personal law[s]" relating to adoption, marriage and so forth. The government argued that the purpose of excluding gender from Section 15 was to preserve the "patrilineal" character of Botswanan society. *Id.* at 136 (Amissah, JP.), 188 (Bizos, JA.). The majority judges, although noting the "difficulty" of the question, concluded in light of Section 3 of the Constitution (guaranteeing "every person," regardless of "race, place of origin, political opinion, colour, creed or sex," the "fundamental rights and freedoms," including "life, liberty, security of the person and protection of law"), that the Constitution did prohibit the challenged gender discrimination. *Id.* at 140, 158 (Amissah, JP.). The government's argument in support of the statute rested not only on the omission of gender as a prohibited ground of discrimination in Section 15 but also on the fact that another chapter of the original constitution had explicitly provided a citizenship rule more favorable for men than for women. *See id.* at 143–44 (Amissah, JP.); *id.* at 192 (Schreiner, JA., dissenting). The latter point was described as a "very fair indication" that Section 15 was not intended to prohibit discrimination against women. *Id.* at 192 (Schreiner, JA., dissenting) (summarizing government argument). The significance of the international materials relied on looms larger in the face of domestic legal support for a contrary interpretation.

82. *See* Dow v. Attorney-General, [1992] 103 I.L.R. at 142–43, 145, 147–49, 159–63 (discussing foreign constitutional law and international human rights law). Of the five judges who sat on the court of appeals bench for this decision, at least one appears to have been a well-known foreign judge, Austin Amissah, from Ghana. *See generally* Chapter 3, above at note 160. Justice Amissah sat as a judge on the Botswana Court of Appeal for twenty years and was President of that Court from 1988–2001. Patrick Smith, *Obituary: Justice Austin Amissah,* THE INDEPENDENT, Feb. 1, 2001, *available at* http://www.independent.co.uk/news/obituaries/justice-austin-amissah-728780.html.

83. Benner v. Canada (Secretary of State), [1997] 1 S.C.R. 358, 403 (Can.).

84. *See Nguyen*, 533 U.S. at 65–67 (discussing the numbers of American military forces, mostly men, deployed abroad as well as the number of short trips Americans made abroad). *Benner* might have been distinguished on the grounds that the Canadian legislature had already accepted the risks of "citizenship by male parentage," *Nguyen*, 533 U.S. at 66, including the potentially greater numbers of children without developed connections to the citizen parent that, in the majority's view, exists when citizenship of nonmarital children born abroad passes through fathers.

85. *See also* Chapter 6, at page 185 above. Although not a citizenship case, President of the Republic v. Hugo, 1997 (4) SA 1 (CC) (S. Afr.), a decision by the South African Constitutional Court upholding the President's exercise of discretion to pardon mothers (but not fathers) of young children, employs reasoning similar to aspects of the majority's reasoning in *Nguyen*. The court relied, in part, on assumptions about the greater likelihood that mothers, rather than fathers, will have relationships of care with their children. *Id.* at 21–22 (Goldstone, J.). The dissent argued that the court erred in failing to recognize a discrimination that reinforced gendered inequalities in family and the workplace, and suggested that the court may have been unwilling to invalidate a generous gesture by its first president, Nelson Mandela. *Id.* at 31 n.80, 34, 36–37 (Kriegler, J., dissenting) (condemning the gender discrimination as a relic of patriarchy that the new constitution was meant to overcome).

86. Sharifan v. Fed'n of Pakistan, [1998] 50 P.L.D. 59 (Lahore) (1997). Pakistan has been subject to military rule for a good part of its close to sixty-year existence and its record of protection of civil and political liberties is low, notwithstanding a functioning court system. *See* Freedom House, Freedom in the World, Country Report, Pakistan (2008), http://wws.freedomhouse.org (click on Freedom in the World, year and country); CIA World Factbook, Pakistan (last updated Feb. 24, 2009), https://www.cia.gov/library/publications/the-world-factbook/geos/pk.html.

87. The challenge in *Sharifan* was based on Article 25 of the Constitution of Pakistan. See 1973 Const. Islamic Rep. of Pakistan, art. 25, *available at* http://www.pakistani.org/pakistan/constitution/part2.ch1.html ("(1) All citizens are equal before law and are entitled to equal protection of law. (2) There shall be no discrimination on the basis of sex alone. (3) Nothing in this Article shall prevent the State from making any special provision for the protection of women and children."). The Lahore court reasoned that (1) foreign spouses were not citizens and thus beyond the scope of the protections of Article 25; and (2) in any event, easier access for foreign wives could be regarded as a "special provision for the protection of women"—reading the constitution (in some tension with its first argument) to enable protection for noncitizen female spouses but not for female Pakistan *citizens* whose rights to pass on citizenship to their foreign spouses, on terms of equality with male citizens, were at issue. *Sharifan*, [1998] 50 P.L.D. at 61–63.

88. *Id.* at 62–63 (emphasizing that a "woman by virtue of her marriage acquires the domicile of her husband"). Another reason given was that granting citizenship to foreign husbands of Pakistani women would result in an uncontrollable "influx" of foreigners marrying Pakistani women to become citizens, a national concern trumping equality rights, *id.* at 63 (invoking Indian law as well). This concern has some resonance with the harm apparently envisaged by the majority in *Nguyen* of a potentially large number of children making claims of citizenship even though they are in effect "foreigners" gaining access to citizenship due to the transitory presence and sexual acts of their biological fathers in a foreign land.

89. *See id.* at 61–62 (praising the "wisdom" of legislation restricting citizenship only to married women aliens as "in keeping " with the "position of women" in private international

law and quoting Dicey to the effect that a married woman, like a minor, is a "'dependent person'"). *But cf. id.* at 63 (inviting legislative change to recognize that "women are no longer to be treated as a property of the male members of the society"). As of 2004 Pakistan was still reportedly treating male and female citizens differently with respect to the availability of Pakistani citizenship for their spouses. *See* Bureau Report, *Denial of Citizenship Questioned*, DAWN: THE INTERNET EDITION, Aug. 2, 2004, *available at* http://www.dawn.com/2004/08/02.htm (stating that an alien woman married to a Pakistani citizen is entitled to citizenship, but an alien man married to a Pakistan woman is not).

90. *See, e.g.*, Craig v. Boren, 429 U.S. 190, 197–98, 201–04 (1976) (holding invalid a differential drinking age for women and men, that the state argued was justified by higher accident rates for young men, finding the law to be rational but so overbroad that it did not substantially further the state's legitimate goal).

91. The Court also suggested that it might lack power to confer citizenship other than on the terms specified by Congress. *See Nguyen*, 533 U.S. at 71–73. On the severability of an unconstitutional requirement so as to permit the award of citizenship, compare *Case to seek revocation of the disposition of issuance of a written deportation order*, 2006 (Gyo-Tsu) No. 135, Minshū vol. 62, no. 6 (Sup. Ct. Jap., June 4, 2008) *English transl. available at* http://www.courts.go.jp/english/judgments/index.html (enter date, code and case number) (after holding unconstitutional a provision imposing added requirements for attaining citizenship on the nonmarital children of Japanese fathers, treating the portion of the statute found unconstitutional as no bar to the award of citizenship under the remaining provisions, *id.* at part 5).

92. Roper v. Simmons, 543 U.S. 551, 625–26 (2005) (Scalia, J., dissenting) (citing, inter alia, Center for Reproductive Rights, The World's Abortion Laws (June 2004), http://www.reproductiverights.org/pub_fac_abortion_laws.html). Justice Scalia's statement, as such, is supported by the cited source, but does not convey either the complexity or the great diversity in the regulation of abortion in the world, as described in detail below.

93. *Id.* at 626 (citing Christopher McCrudden, *A Part of the Main? The Physician-Assisted Suicide Cases and Comparative Law Methodology in the United States Supreme Court*, *in* LAW AT THE END OF LIFE 125, 129–30 (Carl E. Schneider ed., 2000)).

94. U.S. constitutional law has been concerned to protect against forced abortions. *See, e.g.*, Planned Parenthood of Se. Pa. v. Casey, 505 U.S. 833, 859 (1992) (O'Connor, J., Kennedy, J., Souter, J., Joint Opinion); *cf.* 8 U.S.C § 1101(a)(42) (providing that a noncitizen who has been forced to abort or threatened with forcible abortion or sterilization "shall be deemed to have been persecuted on account of political opinion . . . " and thus eligible for asylum). This is not universally state practice. *See* Louisa Lim, Cases of Forced Abortion Surface in China, NPR, *available at* http://www.npr.org/templates/story/story.php?storyId=9766870 (Morning Edition, Apr. 23, 2007) (reporting that a law passed five years earlier was supposed to prevent coerced abortions but that dozens of cases had recently occurred in one province whose birth rate was higher than official guidelines called for).

95. *See, e.g.*, Stanley K. Henshaw et al., *The Incidence of Abortion Worldwide*, 25 INT'L FAMILY PLANNING PERSPECTIVES S30 (Suppl. 1999) (concluding, based on a study of data from the mid-1990s, that "[a]bortion rates are no lower overall in areas where abortion is generally restricted by law (and where many abortions are performed under unsafe conditions) than in areas where abortion is legally permitted"); Gilda Sedgh et al., *Induced Abortion: Estimated Rates and Trends Worldwide*, 370 THE LANCET 1338, 1341–42 & tbls. 2, 3, 1343 (Oct. 13, 2007) (finding that "both the highest and lowest abortion rates were seen in regions where abortion is almost uniformly legal under a wide range of circumstances")

96. According to the Henshaw study, in the mid-1990s, Canada, with no criminal prohibitions on abortions, had a legal abortion rate of 15.5/1000; England and Wales, with a reason-based regime, 15.6/1000; the U.S., 22.9/1000; Australia, 22.2/1000; Cuba, 77.7; Slovenia, 23.2. *See* Henshaw et al., *supra* note 95, at S34. (In Germany and Spain, legal abortion rates of about 7.6 and 5.7 were reported (though for Spain based on possibly incomplete data). *Id.*)

97. *See* Joyce Arthur, Abortion Rights Coalition of Canada, The Facts on Later Abortions in Canada (June 25, 2006, updated Oct. 4, 2008), http://www.arcc-cdac.ca/action/bill_c338.html (90.1 percent of abortions in Canada are performed between weeks 5 and 12; less than .5 percent of abortions occur after week 20) (based on data produced by the Canadian Institute for Health Information from 2003 and additional survey of clinics); LifeCanada, Abortions by Gestational Age, http://www.abortionincanada.ca/stats/abortion_gestational_age.html (reporting that of the less than half of all abortions in which gestational age was determinable from 2004 government data, 31,994 (or 87 percent) were first trimester, 4,845 were second trimester, and 35 were third trimester); LifeCanada, E-News Flash, http://www.lifecanada.org/html/resources/LifeCanadasMonthlyENewsflash/March%20 17_2005.htm (Mar. 17, 2005) (reporting on government data that in 2002, 89 percent of Canadian abortions were first trimester); Guttmacher Institute, In Brief: Facts on Induced Abortion in the United States (July 2008) (reporting that 89 percent of abortions in 2004 occurred in the first twelve weeks of pregnancy), http://www.guttmacher.org/pubs/fb_induced_abortion.html); *see also* Stenberg v. Carhart, 530 U.S. 914, 923 (2000) (reporting that about 90 percent of U.S. abortions in 1996 occurred in the first twelve weeks).

98. *See* Elisabeth Rosenthal, *Legal or Not, Abortion Rates Compare*, N.Y. TIMES, Oct. 12, 2007, at A8; Sedgh et al., *supra* note 95, at 1343–44 ("Unsafe and safe abortions correspond in large part with illegal and legal abortions. . . . [U]nrestrictive abortion laws do not predict a high incidence of abortion, and by the same token, highly restrictive abortion laws are not associated with low abortion incidence. . . . [M]ost abortions in [very legally restricted] settings have high risks to a woman's life and health. . . . Legalisation of abortion can have a substantial effect on the safety of the procedure: in South Africa, the incidence of infection from abortion decreased by 52 percent after a more liberal abortion law went into effect in 1997."); *see also* World Health Organization, Unsafe Abortion: Global and Regional Estimates of the Incidence of Unsafe Abortion and Associated Mortality in 2000 at 3, 9, 16–17 (4th ed. 2004) (associating "restrictive legislation" with "high incidence of unsafe abortion"), *available at* http://www.who.int/reproductive-health/publications/unsafeabortion_2000/estimates.pdf.; Heather D. Boonstra et al., Abortion in Women's Lives 13 & Fig. 2.2 (2006) (noting that as recently as 1965, illegal abortions caused 17 percent of pregnancy related deaths, which declined after legalization), *available at* http://www.guttmacher.org/pubs/2006/05/04/AiWL.pdf.

99. A further cautionary note: Although there are a number of countries in the world that are described as generally prohibiting abortions, it has proven difficult to find constitutional decisions, translated into English, discussing these laws, or challenges to them; the discussion is necessarily limited by the available sources.

100. *Planned Parenthood v. Casey*, 505 U.S., at 945 n.1 (Rehnquist, C.J., dissenting).

101. *See* Center for Reproductive Rights, *The World's Abortion Laws–Fact Sheet* (2008), *available at* http://reproductiverights.org/en/document/world-abortion-laws-2008-fact-sheet [hereinafter CRR, *World's Abortion Laws*]. The second most restrictive category, in which abortions are available to save the woman's life or her physical health, includes thirty-five countries, with 9.6 percent of the world's population. Another twenty-three countries, representing 4.2 percent of the world population, permit abortions also

to preserve the woman's mental health. In the next category, which includes Great Britain and thirteen other countries and encompasses just over 21 percent of the world population, abortions are permitted for socioeconomic reasons as well as to save the pregnant woman's life or physical or mental health. In the fifth (and least restrictive) category, which includes the United States, abortion is available without restriction as to reason, though in most of these countries the period during which abortion is allowed without regard to reason is shorter than in the United States. For more detail, see *infra* note 120.

102. Pew Forum on Religion and Public Life, Abortion Laws Around the World, at 2 (Nov. 2006), http://www.pewforum.org/publications/reports/abortion-laws.pdf ("Due to a broad interpretation of this law, abortion is available virtually upon request in Great Britain.") [hereinafter Pew Forum, *Abortion Laws Around the World*]. The Abortion Act 1967, c. 87, § 1(1)(a),(2) (Eng.), allows abortions up to the 24th week if there is a risk of injury (greater than from continuing the pregnancy) to the "physical or mental health of the pregnant women or any existing children" and provides that in determining whether such a risk to health is present, "account may be taken of the pregnant woman's actual or reasonably foreseeable environment." It also permits, seemingly without time limit, abortions if necessary "to prevent grave permanent injury to the physical or mental health of the pregnant women" or risks to her life, or where "there is a substantial risk that if the child were born it would suffer" from seriously handicapping physical or mental abnormalities. *Id.* § 1(1) (b), (c), (d). The statute provides that "two registered medical practitioners" must have the good faith opinion that the statute's conditions are met, except in case of emergency. *Id.* § 1 (1).

103. According to a 1998 report, at that time the Australian Capital Territory permitted abortion freely and without criminal sanction (with the possible exception of very late term abortions associated with the timing of normal childbirth); the state of Victoria, by contrast, limited abortions to those necessary to avoid a serious threat to the pregnant woman's life or health. *See* Natasha Cica, Research Paper 1, 1998–99, Law and Bills Digest Group, 31 Aug. 1998, Parliament of Australia, Parliamentary Library online, *available at* http://www.aph.gov.au/library/pubs/rp/1998-99/99rp01.htm#act; *see also* Crimes (Abolition of Offence of Abortion) Act, 2002, No. 24, Austl. Cap. Terr. Laws. For more recent legislation in Victoria, see Abortion Law Reform Act, 2008, No. 58, § 4, Vict. Acts (permitting physician to perform abortions to 24 weeks). *See generally* CRR, *World's Abortion Laws, supra* note 101, at 2 (describing Australia as determining abortion law at the state level, but with a predominant approach putting the country in the second-least restrictive grouping).

104. Planned Parenthood of Se. Pa. v. Casey, 505 U.S. 833 (1992).

105. Pew Forum, *Abortion Laws Around the World, supra* note 102, at 1 (reporting as well that the cost of in-hospital abortion is covered by provincial health insurance); *see* R. v Morgentaler, [1988] 1 S.C.R. 30 (Can.).

106. CRR, *World's Abortion Laws, supra* note 101, at 2; *see also* Corene T. Kendrick, *The Illegality of Abortion in Mexico*, 39 STAN. J. INT'L L. 125 (2003). In Mexico abortion is regulated predominantly at the state level, *see* Human Rights Watch, http://hrw.org/reports/2006/mexico0306/4.htm#_Toc128490404. According to news reports, Mexico City, in April 2007, legalized abortions in the first twelve weeks, replacing a prior regime that permitted abortions only in cases of rape, fetal deformity, or threats to the pregnant woman's life. "Abortion Legalized in Mexico City", BBC Reports, Apr. 25, 2007, *available at* http://news.bbc.co.uk/2/hi/americas/6586959.stm. The vote was controversial and litigation was threatened, but the new law was reportedly upheld in August, 2008. *See* Center for Reproductive Rights, Mexican Supreme Court Upholds Mexico City Abortion Law

(Aug. 27, 2008), http://reproductiverights.org/en/press-room/mexico-supreme-court-upholds-mexico-city-abortion-law; *see also* Human Rights Watch, Mexico: Rape Victims Denied Legal Abortions (Mar. 7, 2006), http://www.hrw.org/english/docs/2006/02/23/mexico12712.htm (describing efforts to discourage pregnant rape victims from exercising the legal right they enjoy in all states to obtain an abortion); Human Rights Watch, The Second Assault: Obstructing Access to Legal Abortion after Rape in Mexico, Abortion in Mexico (Part IV) (2006), www.hrw.org/reports/2006/mexico0306/4.htm#_Toc128490404 (reporting on different studies estimating between 500,000 and 1 million abortions, legal and illegal, each year in Mexico and describing variations in approaches of the different Mexican states; also reporting that in 2002, a liberalized abortion law in one jurisdiction was challenged in the Mexican Supreme Court as unconstitutional but upheld).

107. In the United States, most regulation is at the state level, but there is at least one significant federal criminal statute, constraining "partial birth abortions," and upheld in *Gonzales v. Carhart*, 550 U.S. 124 (2007). There is considerable variation; New York State, for example, reportedly imposes no waiting periods, and provides some public funding for indigent abortions. Guttmacher Institute, State Fact Sheet, New York, http://www.guttmacher.org/pubs/sfaa/new_york.html (accessed June 23, 2008); Hope v. Perales, 83 N.Y. 2d 563, 571–72 (1994) (stating that New York "has consistently included all medically necessary abortions in its State Medicaid program"). Pennsylvania's 24-hour waiting period was upheld in *Casey*. *See* 505 U.S. at 881–87. In Canada, the federal government has legislative jurisdiction over "criminal law"; provincial attempts to restrict abortions under other powers have been largely rejected by the courts. *See, e.g.*, CBC News, "Abortion Rights: A timeline of developments," May 24, 2006, http://www.cbc.ca/news/background/abortion/ (accessed June 23, 2008); Stephen Gardbaum, *State and Comparative Law Perspectives on a Possible Post-Roe World*, 51 St. Louis L. J. 685 (2007) (noting R. v. Morgentaler, [1993] 3 S.C.R. 463). Other federal systems also show variations: In Germany, abortion is regulated at the federal level; in Australia, it is regulated at the state level, *see supra* note 103; in Brazil abortion is regulated by the national government (and is legal only where the pregnancy results from rape or incest or the pregnant woman's life is in danger), *see* Human Rights Watch, Abortion, http://www.hrw.org/en/news/2009/03/31/abortion#Brazil (Mar. 31, 2009) (translating 1940 Penal Code, arts. 124–28, as amended in 1998 (Brazil)).

108. *See generally* Jackson & Tushnet, *supra* note 80, at 110–29. In its 1993 abortion decision, following unification, the German court permitted the legislature to provide that first trimester abortions, if they follow counseling for purposes of urging continuation of the pregnancy, are not subject to criminal sanction, but emphasized that such abortions cannot be declared "lawful." *See id.* at 133–34 (excerpting Professor Gerald Neuman's summary of the decision).

109. *See* Decision 64/1991: 17 December 1991, On the Regulation of Abortion, *translated in* László Sólyom & Georg Brunner, Constitutional Judiciary in a New Democracy 178–99 (2000).

110. *See* Wojciech Sadurski, Rights Before Courts: A Study of Constitutional Courts in Postcommunist States of Central and Eastern Europe 133–34 (2005) (also describing legislation enacted in response, including a new mandatory waiting period of three days, counseling requirements, and a narrower definition of "severe crisis" for abortions in the first twelve weeks).

111. Sadurski, *supra* note 110, at 102, 134–35. Sadurski is critical of these decisions; in Poland, he explains, the Tribunal's decision ignored the very recent drafting history of the constitution revealing a clear decision *not* to include a provision specifying that the right to life was protected "from the moment of conception." *Id.* at 102.

112. *See* MARY ANN GLENDON, ABORTION AND DIVORCE IN WESTERN LAW 16–17 (1987); "France approves new abortion period," BBC News, May 31, 2001, http://news.bbc.co.uk/2/hi/europe/1360960.stm; Law No. 2001-588 of July 4, 2001, art. 2, Journal Officiel de la République Française [J.O.] [Official Gazette of France], July 7, 2001, p. 10823. Thereafter, Glendon explained, abortions are legally available only on the medical determinations of two physicians, GLENDON, *supra*, at 17; and (at least under the older law) some French women reportedly have needed to leave France to have abortions elsewhere beyond the early limit, Maggie Allyson, *The Right to Choose Abortion in France*, 47 PARLIAMENTARY AFFAIRS 222, 236 (1994) (writing at the time of the ten-week limit law, stating that 3,000–5,000 women per year traveled outside France for abortions).

113. Decision of Jan. 15, 1975, Conseil Constitutionnel, [1975] D.S. Jur. 529, *translated in* MAURO CAPPELLETTI & WILLIAM COHEN, COMPARATIVE CONSTITUTIONAL LAW 577–79 (1979). The court also indicated that the law "respects the liberty of [those] who have recourse to" it and "does not authorize any violation of the principle of respect for every human being from the very commencement of life . . . except in case of necessity and according to the conditions and limitations which it defines." *Id.*

114. Carmosina et al., Corte Costituzionale, Decision of Feb. 18, 1975, No. 27 [1975] 20 Giur. Const. 117, *translated in* CAPPELLETTI & COHEN, *supra* note 113, at 612, 613.

115. Decision of Oct. 11, 1974, Verfassungsgerichtshof, [1974] Erklaerungen des Verfassungsgerichtshofs 221 (Austria), *translated in* CAPPELLETTI & COHEN, *supra* note 113, at 615–22.

116. Tysiąc v. Poland, App. No. 5410/03, Eur. Ct. H.R., ¶¶ 74, 111 (Mar. 20, 2007), *available at* http://www.echr.coe.int/echr; Vo v. France, App No. 53924/00, Eur. Ct. H.R. [GC], ¶ 82 (July 8, 2004), *available at* http://www.echr.coe.int/echr; *see also* SADURSKI, *supra* note 110, at 132 (finding that no Central or Eastern European constitution explicitly prohibits abortion and stating that the Czech Republic's Charter of Fundamental Rights and Freedoms provides that "Human life is worthy of protection even before birth," while the Slovenian Constitution "endors[es] a 'pro-choice' position, by proclaiming the freedom 'to decide whether to bear children.'").

117. *See* CRR, *World's Abortion Laws*, *supra* note 101, at 2 (showing countries in South America in at least four different categories and countries in Africa in all five CRR categories).

118. *See* American Convention on Human Rights, art. 4, *available at* http://www.oas.org/juridico/English/treaties/b-32.html (last accessed Feb. 20, 2009) ("Every person has the right to have his life respected. This right shall be protected by law and, *in general, from the moment of conception.* No one shall be arbitrarily deprived of his life.") (emphasis added). Of the thirty-five members of the Organization of American States, twenty-five states are parties to this convention; neither the United States nor Canada have ratified, though the United States signed it in 1977; Mexico ratified with an "interpretive declaration" that "the Government of Mexico considers that the expression 'in general' does not constitute an obligation to adopt, or keep in force, legislation to protect life 'from the moment of conception,' since this matter falls within the domain reserved to the States." *See id.* at http://www.oas.org/juridico/English/sigs/b-32.html. Article 4 does not speak directly to whether abortions must be permitted or prohibited. Some actions of the Inter-American Commission on Human Rights (IACHR) have indicated that abortions must be available in certain circumstances. *See, e.g.*, IACHR Country Report, Chapter XII, Rights of Women (1999), ¶¶ 49–52, *available at* http://www.cidh.oas.org/countryrep/Colom99en/chapter-12.htm (criticizing Colombia for the unavailability of legal abortions and the contribution of this regime to maternal deaths); *see also* IACHR Report No. 21/07, Petition 161-02, Friendly

Settlement, Paulina del Carmen Ramirez Jacinto, Mexico (Mar. 9, 2007), *available at* http://www.cidh.oas.org/annualrep/2007eng/mexico161.02eng.htm (approving settlement in which Mexico agreed to new training and procedures to assure the practical availability of abortions for rape victims (which were legally authorized) and agreed to pay substantial amounts in compensation and maintenance to a rape victim, unable to obtain an abortion, for the expense of raising, housing, and educating the child, as "compatible with the object and purpose of the Convention"); *see also infra* note 130 (concerning Nicaragua).

For other regional positions on the availability of abortions, see Parliamentary Assembly, Council of Europe, Resolution 1607 para. 4 (2008), *available at* http://assembly.coe.int/Main.asp?link=/Documents/AdoptedText/ta08/ERES1607.htm (resolving that abortion should not be banned "within reasonable gestational limits" and stating that abortion bans do not result in fewer abortions but lead to clandestine abortions with increased maternal mortality or to abortion tourism with resulting social inequities); Protocol to the African Charter on Human and Peoples Rights on the Rights of Women, Article 14(2) (adopted in 2003 by the African Union and calling on member states, in order to protect the reproductive rights of women, to permit abortion where the pregnancy results from rape, assault, or incest or where continuation of the pregnancy threatens the health (mental or physical) of the pregnant woman or the life of the pregnant women or fetus), *available at* Website of the African Comm'n on Human and Peoples' Rights, http://www.achpr.org (last visited Mar. 5, 2009). As of May 2007, twenty-one of the fifty-three states in the African Union had ratified the women's rights protocol, *see id.* (click on "documents" and "status of ratifications"), and according to Equality Now, by Feb. 26, 2008, a total of twenty-three states had ratified. Equality Now Website, http://www.equalitynow.org/english/campaigns/african-protocol/african-protocol_en.html (visited May 27, 2008).

119. *See, e.g.*, Human Rights Watch, International Human Rights Law and Abortion in Latin America 4 (July 2005), http://www.hrw.org/legacy/backgrounder/wrd/wrd0106/wrd10106.pdf (reporting that at least 122 concluding observations of UN human rights monitoring committees have "addressed how abortion relates to fundamental rights," which are violated by restrictive abortion laws); *supra* note 118. For a recent decision of the UN Human Rights Committee treating the denial of an abortion under particular circumstances as a violation of ICCPR Article 7 (prohibiting torture or cruel, inhuman, or degrading treatment), see KL v. Peru, U.N. Human Rights Comm. (Views), 85th Sess., U.N. Doc. CCPR/C/85/D/1153/2003 (2005), *available at* www1.umn.edu/humanrts/undocs/1153-2003.html (finding that Peru violated ICCPR Article 7 by denying an abortion to a seventeen-year-old whose fetus had anencephaly; following the birth of the child and its death a few days later, the seventeen-year-old suffered severe depression). For commentary, see Interrights Bulletin, A Review of the International Center for the Legal Protection of Human Rights (2006), http://www.reproductiverights.org/pdf/Interights_KL_v_Peru.pdf. CEDAW's article 12.1 provides that women should have "access to health care services, including family planning." CEDAW Committee members have criticized states with severe bans on abortion for the adverse effects of such bans on women. *See infra* note 130; *see also* "Abortion Bans a 'Crime,' U.N. Officials Tell Honduras," Catholic World News, Aug. 3, 2007, *available at* http://www.cwnews.com/news/viewstory.cfm?recnum=52745; Letter, National Right to Life Committee to Members of the U.S. Senate (Feb. 1, 2007), *available at* www.nrlc.org/Federal/ForeignAid/SenateCEDAWletter020107.html (opposing U.S. ratification of CEDAW because, it says, the CEDAW Committee has pressured at least thirty-seven nations to allow greater access to abortion).

120. *See supra* note 101 (describing CRR's five categories of countries). According to CRR, *World's Abortion Laws, supra* note 101, most of the countries in the fifth, most liberal

group, have a gestational limit of twelve weeks for legal abortions "without restriction as to reasons"; however, Canada, China, N. Korea, and Vietnam reportedly have no limit fixed by statute; the U.S. and the Netherlands permit such abortions up to viability; Singapore to twenty-four weeks; and Sweden to eighteen weeks. *See infra* note 156; Termination of Pregnancy Act, 1981 (Neth.), *as summarized in* Netherlands Ministry of Foreign Affairs, FAQ Abortion in the Netherlands (2008); Termination of Pregnancy Act, Chapter 324, 1974 (as amended to 2007) (Sing.), *available at* http://statutes.agc.gov.sg/non_version/cgi-bin/cgi_retrieve.pl?actno=REVED-324. (Apart from time limits there are other substantial variations among countries.) Among countries in the CRR's fourth group (defined as those that permit abortions for specified reasons including to save the mother's life, to protect physical or mental health, and for socioeconomic reasons), the Pew Forum reports that India permits abortions up to twenty weeks, and Japan and Great Britain (which is described as having abortion "available virtually upon request," *supra* note 102) up to twenty-four weeks. Pew Forum, *Abortion Laws Around the World*, *supra* note 102, at 2, 5; *see* Medical Termination of Pregnancy Act, 1971, No. 34, § 3 (India) (requiring two medical practitioners' judgment for abortions between 12 and 20 weeks; pregnant woman's "actual or reasonably foreseeable environment" relevant in deciding whether risk to health present); *cf.* Maternal Protection Law (as amended through 1996), arts. 2(2), 14 (Jap.), *translation available in* 23 ANN. REV. POPULATION L. 292 (1996-1997) (authorizing abortions up to viability). In the CRR's third group (countries permitting abortions for mental or physical health, or in cases of rape, incest, or fetal impairment), there is at least one country (Israel), with no gestational time limit identified, Pew Forum, *Abortion Laws Around the World*, *supra* note 102, at 4; Penal Law 5737-1977 (4th ed. 2001) (Isr.), and New Zealand, with a limit of twenty weeks. *See* Crimes Act 1961, § 187A(1) (as of 2004) (N.Z.), *available at* Abortion Services in New Zealand, http://www.abortion.gen.nz/legal/crimesact.html (last visited Feb. 10, 2009) (also permitting later abortions to save the woman's life or prevent serious, permanent physical or mental injury). While the U.S. approach is among the most liberal on time limits for elective abortion, it is thus hard to characterize it as an outlier, especially given the range of practices among Western liberal democracies.

121. Other reasoned decisions by European national courts on the constitutionality of statutes regulating abortion include that of the Spanish Constitutional Court, discussed in Richard Stith, *New Constitutional and Penal Theory in Spanish Abortion Law*, 35 AM. J. COMP. L. 513, 514, 524 (1987) (describing Spanish decision as influenced by German Constitutional Court in its conclusion, in the 1980s, that while there was no fetal right to life, there was a constitutional obligation for the state to protect fetal life); Decision of Jan. 15, 1975, Conseil Constitutionnel (France), *supra* note 113 (upholding 1975 liberalized abortion law); Carmosina et al., Corte Costituzionale (Italy), Decision of Feb. 18, 1975, *supra* note 114 (holding unconstitutional the absence of a health exception); and Decision of Oct. 11, 1974, Verfassungsgerichtshof (Austria), *supra* note 115, at 234–35 (upholding law permitting elective abortion in the first three months). *See also* Stith, *supra*, at 529 n.52 (describing a Portuguese decision holding that the principle of the inviolability of human life includes "'intrauterine human life,'" although a statute permitting some abortions was upheld).

122. R. v. Morgentaler, [1988] 1 S.C.R. 30, 75–76 (Can.) (Dickson, C.J.). One concurrence would have found that regardless of the procedures, under the Canadian Charter a woman cannot ("within the limits specified in *Roe*") be compelled to carry a fetus to term against her will. *Id.* at 171 (Wilson, J.). Two other concurring justices expressed their view that under a proper and less burdensome statute it would be permissible to have a requirement

of an independent medical determination that the requested abortion met the requisite standard. *Id.* at 106 (Beetz, J., with Estey, J.). Two justices dissented, and would have upheld the statute largely on the grounds that the balance struck was within the legislature's power to determine. *See id.* at 132 (McIntyre, J., dissenting).

123. *See* Decision of Feb. 25, 1975, Bundesverfassungsgericht, [1975] 39 BverfGE 1 (E. Jann. Trans.), *reprinted in* CAPPELLETTI & COHEN, *supra* note 113, at 586, 587–88, 597. The opinion at one point states that it need not decide whether the fetus has a "subjective" right to life or is protected only by the "objective norms" of the constitution in its right to life. *See id.* at 588. However, earlier the court rejects the argument that the term "Everyone" in Article 2 of the Basic Law ("Everyone has a right to life") does not extend to prenatal life. *Id.* The court also invoked the "human dignity" clause of Article 1 of the Basic Law in support of its decision that the state had a duty to "effectively protect the developing life." *Id.* at 593; *see also* Chapter 3, above.

124. *West German Abortion Decision: A Contrast to Roe v. Wade*, trans. Robert E. Jonas & John D. Gorby, 9 JOHN MARSHALL J. PRAC. & PROC. 605, 651 (1976).

125. *See* CAPPELLETTI & COHEN, *supra* note 113, at 589; *West German Abortion Decision*, *supra* note 124, at 643.

126. *West German Abortion Decision*, *supra* note 124, at 606, 648–49; *see* CAPPELLETTI & COHEN, *supra* note 113, at 592; *see also* Gerald L. Neuman, *Casey in the Mirror: Abortion and the Right to Protection in the United States and Germany*, 43 AM. J. COMP. L. 273 (1995) (summarizing 1993 German abortion decision).

127. IR. CONST., 1937, art. 40.3(3) ¶ 1 (Amend. 8, 1983), *available at* http://www.taoiseach.gov.ie/index.asp?docID=243 ("The State acknowledges the right to life of the unborn and, with due regard to the equal right to life of the mother, guarantees in its law to respect, and, as far as practicable, by it laws to defend and vindicate that right.").

128. Att'y Gen. v. X, [1992] 1 Irish Rep. 1, 53-54 (Finlay, C.J.) (emphasis added). Chief Justice Finlay's opinion, while concluding that an abortion in the case at hand would be permissible in Ireland because of the "real and substantial" risk of suicide by the pregnant fourteen-year-old victim of rape, indicated that absent such a grave risk, abortion and travel outside of Ireland to obtain an abortion could be prohibited. *Id.* at 57–58; *see also* JACKSON & TUSHNET, *supra* note 80, at 199–200.

129. *See supra* notes 118, 119; *see also supra* note 98.

130. *See, e.g.*, Comm. on the Elimination of Discrimination Against Women, *Concluding Comments of the Committee on the Elimination of Discrimination Against Women: Nicaragua*, ¶17, UN Doc. CEDAW/C/NIC/CO/6 (Feb. 2, 2007) (expressing concern over the criminalization of therapeutic abortions, with consequent risk to women's health and life); Center for Reproductive Rights, Press statement (Dec. 10, 2008), http://reproductiverights.org/en/case/challenge-to-abortion-law-in-nicaragua-amici-supreme-court-of-nicaragua (describing pending litigation in Nicaragua Supreme Court); *see also* Jocelyn E. Getgen, *Reproductive Injustice: An Analysis of Nicaragua's Complete Abortion Ban*, 41 CORNELL INT'L L.J. 143, 156 (2008) (reporting that the Inter-American Commission on Human Rights condemned the law); Center for Reproductive Rights, Press statement (Dec. 1, 2006), http://reproductiverights.org/en/press-room/inter-american-commission-issues-landmark-statement-declaring-nicaragua%E2%80%99s-abortion-ban-je (to same effect). (These two latter sources appear to be referring to a Letter from Victor Abramovich, Rapporteur for Women's Rights & Santiago A. Canton, Executive Secretary, Inter-American Commission on Human Rights, to Norman Calderas Cardenal, Minister of Foreign Affairs, Nicaragua, Nov. 10, 2006 (expressing concern that repeal of therapeutic abortion exception would threaten women's human rights including their right to life).) It has been

reported that following the change in law, maternal mortality in Nicaragua increased by 100 percent. Lance Lattig & Angela Heimburger, *Abortion Ban Killing Women*, MIAMI HERALD, Oct. 20, 2007, at A25. At least two other Latin American countries still have laws with no explicit exceptions to bans on abortions (Chile and El Salvador). *See, e.g.*, Human Rights Watch, Abortion, http://www.hrw.org/en/news/2009/03/31/abortion#Chile (Mar. 31, 2009) (translating Chile's 1874 Penal Code arts. 342–45); Guttmacher Institute, News Release (Oct. 27, 2008), *available at* http://www.guttmacher.org/media/nr/2008/10/27/index.html (noting El Salvador's elimination, in 1998, of "all grounds for legal abortion").

131. Translation of Excerpts of Decision C-355/2006, Colombian Constitutional Court Abortion Decision of May 10, 2006, published by Women's Link Worldwide (with Foreword by Rebecca J. Cook), *available at* http://www.womenslinkworldwide.org (click on "publications," click on C-355/2006, Excerpts of the Constitutional Court's Ruling That Liberalized Abortion in Colombia) [hereinafter *Case C-355, Colombian Constitutional Court Abortion Decision*]. The statute at issue banned all abortions but provided for mitigation of punishment for pregnancies resulting from rape, sexual abuse, or forcible impregnation; the Court concluded that abortion in these (and other) circumstances could not be criminalized. *Id.* at 50–51; *see infra* note 148.

132. Tysiąc v. Poland, App. No. 5410/03, Eur. Ct. H.R., ¶¶ 121, 124, 130 (Mar. 20, 2007), *available at* https://www.echr.coe.int/echr; *see supra* note 122. The case involved medical doctors' refusal to issue certificates needed to permit an abortion, on grounds of health, to a woman at risk of blindness from continuing her pregnancy. Unable to obtain the abortion she sought, in the face of medical disagreement on how severely the pregnancy threatened her eyesight, the woman suffered a dramatic loss of vision six weeks after the caesarian delivery of the child, her third. *See id.* at ¶¶ 9, 15–16. According to the ECtHR, Polish law permitted abortions on grounds of endangerment of the life or health of the pregnant woman, or serious fetal impairment (up to the point of viability), or where the pregnancy resulted from rape (up to the twelfth week). *Id.* at ¶ 38. *But cf. id.* at ¶ 49 (reporting government estimates of a "low" number of legal abortions, but between 80,000 and 200,000 illegal abortions annually in Poland). Some Polish physicians were evidently hesitant to authorize abortion based on health, absent certainty about the health risks. *See id.* at ¶ 9 (recounting a physician's unwillingness to authorize abortion because it was not certain that the patient's retina would detach as a result of the pregnancy).

133. *See id* at ¶ 104 (noting that Polish law provided for abortions to protect health and thus "it is not the Court's task . . . to examine whether the Convention guarantees a right to have an abortion"), ¶ 118 (noting the "critical importance" of the "time factor . . . so as to limit or prevent damage to a woman's health which might be occasioned by a late abortion"); *see also id.* at ¶¶ 48–52 (summarizing "relevant non-Convention material," including reports on adverse health effects for women of operation of the Polish abortion law). (Judge Borrego Borrego, dissenting, *id.* at ¶¶ 13–15 argued that the decision was a step toward establishing a right to abortion under the ECHR).

134. *See, e.g.*, *Case C-355, Colombian Constitutional Court Abortion Decision*, *supra* note 131, at 66–69; *Tysiąc v. Poland*, at ¶ 48 (noting the UNHRC's Poland report in 1999, expressing concern that strict laws on abortion led to illegal and clandestine abortions and ensuing damage to women's health). *See generally* Rebecca J. Cook & Bernard M. Dickens, *Human Rights Dynamics of Abortion Law Reform*, 25 HUM. RTS. Q. 1 (2003); Report of the Fourth World Conference on Women: Beijing Declaration and Platform for Action, UN Doc. A/CONF. 177/20/Rev.1 (1995) paras. 11, 97, 112–14, 132, 135 (noting major public

health impacts of unsafe abortions and describing enforced pregnancy in wartime as a human rights violation); Women's Protocol to the African Charter, *supra* note 118.

135. *See, e.g.*, CENTER FOR REPRODUCTIVE RIGHTS, BODIES ON TRIAL: REPRODUCTIVE RIGHTS IN LATIN AMERICAN COURTS (2003) (describing controversies in five countries). Efforts to create international "soft law" may raise concerns about the degree of transparency, democratic participation, and deliberative consensus in its formation, as noted above in Chapter 6. *Compare* Rachel Morris, *Crusaders in Wing Tips,* LEGAL AFFAIRS, (Mar./Apr. 2006), *available at* http://www.legalaffairs.org/issues/March-April-2006/feature_morris_marapro6.msp (reporting that a set of memos from the Center for Reproductive Rights was leaked, explaining the "'stealth quality'" of its work to "establish a human right to abortion in international norms and treaties by working with UN agencies and NGOs") *with* Richard G. Wilkins & Jacob Reynolds, *International Law and the Right to Life,* 4 AVE MARIA L. REV. 123 (2006) (describing and calling for more organized "pro-life" participation in international "soft law" norm formation as well as treaty-making activities).

136. *See* LAURENCE H. TRIBE, ABORTION: THE CLASH OF ABSOLUTES 73–84 (1992) (also arguing that European systems that formally condemn but then allow abortions might appear a form of "hypocrisy" that would not fit well with the U.S. approach to law). *Cf.* Rebecca J. Cook & Susannah Howard, *Accommodating Women's Difference Under the Women's Anti-Discrimination Convention,* 56 EMORY L.J. 1039, 1062 (2007) (describing how South Africa changed its abortion regime because complex certification requirements disproportionately benefitted white women and harmed poor black women).

137. *See, e.g.*, James Bopp, Jr., *An Examination of Proposals for a Human Life Amendment, in* RESTORING THE RIGHT TO LIFE: THE HUMAN LIFE AMENDMENT (James Bopp, Jr. ed.,1984) (reprinting the National Right to Life Committee's proposed Constitutional Amendment (1981) to prohibit all abortions except those "required to prevent the death of either the pregnant woman or her unborn offspring"), all as quoted and cited in Memorandum from James Bopp, Jr. & Richard E. Coleson, To Whom It May Concern, Re: Pro-life Strategy Issues (Aug. 7, 2007) [hereinafter Bopp & Coleson Memorandum] (on file with author). A statute adopted in South Dakota would have prohibited all abortions except those necessary to prevent the pregnant woman's death; the measure was defeated by state initiative. *See* Janessa L. Bernstein, *The Underground Railroad to Reproductive Freedom: Restrictive Abortion Laws and the Resulting Backlash,* 73 BROOK. L. REV. 1463, 1466–68 (2008).

138. In order for women to "participate equally in the economic and social life of the Nation," they must be able to "control their reproductive lives." Planned Parenthood of Se. Pa. v. Casey, 505 U.S. 833, 856 (1992) ((O'Connor, J., Kennedy, J., Souter, J., Joint Opinion), *quoted in* Gonzales v. Carhart, 550 U.S. 124, 171 (2007) (Ginsburg, J., dissenting); *see also* Kenneth Karst, *Foreword—Equal Citizenship Under the Fourteenth Amendment,* 91 HARV. L. REV. 1, 57–59 (1977); Sylvia Law, *Rethinking Sex and the Constitution,* 132 U. PA. L. REV. 955, 1002 (1984); Ruth Bader Ginsburg, *Essay: Some Thoughts on Autonomy and Equality in Relation to Roe v. Wade,* 63 N.C. L. REV. 375 (1985); Reva Siegel, *Reasoning from the Body: A Historical Perspective on Abortion Regulation and Questions of Equal Protection,* 44 STAN L. REV. 261 (1992); Reva B. Siegel, *Dignity and the Politics of Protection: Abortion Restrictions under Casey/Carhart,* 117 YALE L. J. 1694 (2008).

139. 550 U.S. 124 (2007). In this case the Court upheld the constitutionality of a federal law banning "partial-birth" abortions that was enacted in 2003, after the Court's decision in *Stenberg v. Carhart,* 530 U.S. 914 (2000), striking down as unconstitutional a state law prohibiting such procedures.

140. *See Planned Parenthood v. Casey,* 505 U.S. at 878–79 (Joint Opinion) (internal citations omitted) ("reaffirm[ing] *Roe*'s holding that 'subsequent to viability, the State in

promoting its interest in the potentiality of human life may, if it chooses, regulate, and even proscribe, abortion *except where it is necessary, in appropriate medical judgment, for the preservation of the life or health of the mother*'" and holding that before viability, "[u]nnecessary health regulations that have the purpose or effect of presenting a substantial obstacle to a woman seeking an abortion impose an undue burden on the right" and are unconstitutional) (emphasis added).

141. 530 U.S. 914, 937–38, 945–46 (2000). *Stenberg* rested on two grounds: First, the statute was overbroad, its language subjecting physicians to the risk of criminal liability for a common procedure, as well as the more unusual one the state argued the law was targeted at; it thus constituted an "undue burden" on women's right to end their pregnancies. Second, the Court found, the statute was unconstitutional insofar as it failed to provide an exception from the criminal ban for use of the particular abortion method where needed for the pregnant woman's health. The federal statute sought to respond to the first constitutional problem in *Stenberg* by more specifically defining the anatomical circumstances to which the prohibition applied. *See Gonzales v. Carhart*, 550 U.S. at 150–54.

142. *See Gonzales v. Carhart*, 550 U.S. at 165–66 (describing some congressional findings, including that there was a medical consensus that the procedure was never medically necessary and was not taught in medical schools, as "factually incorrect"); *id.* at 175–76 (Ginsburg, J., dissenting) (providing details on how the procedure was taught at leading medical schools including Cornell, Columbia, Yale, and Chicago).

143. *Id.* at 166–67 ("The Act is not invalid on its face where there is uncertainty over whether the barred procedure is ever necessary to preserve a woman's health, given the availability of other abortion procedures . . . [as] safe alternatives."). Evidence before the lower courts had already identified several reasons why the banned procedure might be safer than other methods in avoiding certain health risks, including risk of infection or damage to the uterus (and subsequent infertility). *See id.* at 176–78 (Ginsburg, J., dissenting). The federal statute, moreover, provided an explicit exception from its ban on the procedure where the mother's life is in danger, an exception that accentuated the absence of an exception for health threats. *Compare* Partial-Birth Abortion Ban Act of 2003, Pub. L. 108-105, § 3, 117 Stat. 1201 (codified at 18 U.S.C. § 1531(a)) (stating that the criminal prohibition on partial birth abortions "does not apply to a partial-birth abortion that is necessary to save the life of a mother whose life is endangered by a physical disorder, physical illness, or physical injury . . . ") *with id.* § 2 ("The Congress finds . . . [that] (1) A moral, medical, and ethical consensus exists that the practice of performing a partial-birth abortion . . . is a gruesome and inhumane procedure that is never medically necessary and should be prohibited . . . [and] (2) . . . partial-birth abortion . . . is . . . unnecessary to preserve the health of the mother. . . ."). To authorize an exception for threats to the mother's life but not for threats to the mother's health arguably expresses a willingness to subordinate women's health to other concerns.

144. *See Gonzales v. Carhart*, 550 U.S. at 146 (assuming "for the purposes of this opinion," but not in so many words reaffirming, *Casey*'s holding that up to viability women must have a right to choose an abortion without facing "undue burdens" from the government); *id.* at 159 (apparently applying "rational basis" review, together with "undue burden" standard, for evaluating bars on procedures "to promote respect for [unborn] life"); *see also id.* at 159 (relying on a paternalistic rationale of anticipated maternal regret over abortion and abortion procedures to justify the ban). *Compare id.* at 171, 183–85 (Ginsburg, J., dissenting) (asserting that "for the first time since *Roe*, the Court blesses a prohibition with no exception safeguarding a woman's health" and arguing that a nonpaternalistic approach would be to require disclosure to the patient, rather than to ban the

procedure altogether for fear of subsequent regret). The statute upheld in *Gonzales v. Carhart* applies both pre- and postviability.

145. *See, e.g., supra* text at and notes 97, 102, 108, 113, 114 (describing abortion law or jurisprudence in Great Britain, France, Germany, Italy, and Canada).

146. *See supra* notes 127–28. Malta and Andorra are identified as having the most restrictive regimes among members of the Council of Europe. *See* Gisela Wurm, Access to Safe and Legal Abortion in Europe, Part III, ¶ 8 (Apr. 8, 2008), http://assembly.coe.int/Main.asp?link=/Documents/WorkingDocs/Doc08/EDOC11537.htm (accessed July 8, 2008). Andorra is a "co-principality," with a population of about 82,000 and, like Ireland, is predominantly Catholic; Malta, with a population of about 400,000, is 98 percent Catholic. CIA World Factbook, entries for Malta, and Andorra, https://www.cia.gov/library/publications/the-world-factbook (last visited Mar. 6, 2009). Retention of a complete ban in these two small and religiously homogenous polities (which are also part of a broader Europe in which travel to less restrictive countries may be possible) is not necessarily a reliable indicator of regimes compatible with liberal democracy in a larger and more heterogeneous polity like the United States. Like Ireland, Monaco, with a population of 33,000 (90 percent of which is Catholic, *see* CIA World Factbook, Monaco, *supra*), prohibits abortions except where needed to save the life of the woman. *See* Wurm, *supra*, at ¶ 8.

147. *See* Ir. Const., 1937 pmbl., *supra* note 127 ("In the name of the most Holy Trinity, from Whom is all authority and to Whom, as our final end, all actions both of men and States must be referred, We the People of Eire, humbly acknowledging all our obligations to our Divine Lord, Jesus Christ . . . ").

148. Variation exists even among predominantly Catholic countries. On Poland, see *supra* notes 132–34. In *Case C-355, Colombian Constitutional Court Abortion Decision, supra* note 131, at 51–61, a court sitting in a predominantly Catholic country (that still struggles over rule of law and democracy, *see* Freedom House, Freedom in the World, *supra* note 80 (2008 ratings for Colombia as "partly free")), held that abortions must be permitted to protect women's life and health, physical and mental; women's rights in their own bodily integrity and health, the court reasoned, could not be subordinated to the potential for human life, notwithstanding the constitutional value of that life. The court held that exceptions from an abortion ban were also required where women sought termination of pregnancies resulting from illegal conduct or in which the fetus suffers from a life threatening condition.

149. Decisions of the European courts constrained Irish efforts to criminalize advertising for abortion services in other EU countries, and the Irish constitution was subsequently amended to protect access to information about such abortions and the right to travel to obtain them. *See* Jackson & Tushnet, *supra* note 80, at 196–202; *compare* Ir. Const. 1937, art. 40.3(3) ¶ 1 (Amend. 8, 1983), *supra* note 127 (recognizing the right to life of the unborn as equal to that of the pregnant woman, and asserting a state obligation, to the extent practicable, to defend the unborn's right to life) *with id.*, art. 40.3(3) ¶¶ 2, 3 (Amends. 13, 14, 1992) (protecting the right to travel outside of Ireland for an abortion and to make information available about services lawfully available in other countries).

150. *See supra* text at and notes 121, 123–26 (referring, inter alia, to Germany and Spain). On variations, for example, between countries that recognize threats to mental health, or only threats to physical health, as a basis for legal abortion, see CRR, *World's Abortion Laws, supra* note 101, at 2.

151. *See, e.g., Casey*, 505 U.S. at 846 (reaffirming "the State's power to restrict abortions after fetal viability, *if the law contains exceptions for pregnancies which endanger the woman's life or health*") (emphasis added). Commentators disagree whether *Gonzales v. Carhart*

should be viewed as a retreat from the commitment to the protection of women's health, in light of the conflicting evidence over the congressional findings, or whether it should be viewed as simply upholding legislative regulation of a means for abortion that is not in fact necessary to avoid significant impairment of women's health.

152. GLENDON, *supra* note 112, at 19, 40 (emphasis omitted). And, she argued, "compromise legislation of the type in effect in most European countries would reflect the existing consensus in our own country." *Id.* at 58.

153. *Id.* at 53.

154. Reasons-based approaches can vary widely in how they are applied and how much they limit abortions. *See, e.g., supra* note 102 (noting that Great Britain's reasons-based regime is described as close to elective).

155. On the Nordic countries' commitments to gender equality, see, for example, Leira, *supra* note 58, at 362–78 (describing Norway's "daddy leave" provisions, authorizing parental leave for an extended period of time, some portion of which is only available for fathers and is lost if fathers do not use it); Paul Kershaw, *Carefair: Choice, Duty and the Distribution of Care,* 13 SOCIAL POLITICS 341 (2006); *see also* Nordic Council of Ministers, Nordic Countries Rank Highest in Gender Equality, http://www.norden.org/en/news-and-events/news/nordic-countries-rank-highest-in-gender-equality/?searchterm=rank%20highest%20in%20gender%20equality (summarizing World Economic Forum report on 115 countries, listing Sweden as "the best," followed by Norway, Finland, and Iceland, with Denmark listed eighth). On labor force participation, see Joachim Vogel, Three Types of European Societies (1998), *available at* http://www.nnn.se/n-model/europe3/europe3.htm (finding Nordic countries studied to have highest female participation rates in Europe); Florence Jaumette, Female Labour Force Participation, Past Trends and Main Determinants in OECD Countries (Figure 1) (showing in 2001 Iceland, Finland, Norway, and Sweden with female labor participation greater than that in the United States or the United Kingdom), *available at* http://www.emancipatieweb.nl/uploads/EK/Pe/EKPehT30hQ7JoD-zztQwLQ/LFP_-_Workshop_-_NLD.PPT.

156. In Denmark and Norway, the limit is twelve weeks, in Sweden, eighteen weeks. *See* CRR, *World's Abortion Laws, supra* note 101, at 2; abortions beyond these terms are limited to particular reasons and may require third party evaluation. *See* Pew Forum, *Abortion Laws Around the World, supra* note 102, at 3 (concerning Sweden); Law No. 350, 1973 on the Interruption of Pregnancy (as amended through Law No. 389, 1995), § 1 (Den.); Termination of Pregnancy Act, 1975, No. 50 (as amended by Law No. 5, 1978), § 2 (Nor.); Abortion Act, 1974: 595 (as amended through law No. 294, 2005), §1 (Swed.); *see also* Nat'l Inst. For Health and Welfare (Helsinki, Finland), Nordic Statistics on Induced Abortions: 2007, *available at* http://www.stakes.fi/EN/tilastot/statisticsbytopic/reproduction/nordabortions_readmore.htm.

157. *See* Mary Anne Case, *Perfectionism and Fundamentalism in the Application of the German Abortion Laws, in* CONSTITUTING EQUALITY: GENDER EQUALITY AND COMPARATIVE CONSTITUTIONAL LAW (Susan H. Williams ed., forthcoming Cambridge Univ. Press 2009); *see also* Neuman, *supra* note 126, at 286–87 (explaining court's reasoning that government payment where the woman could not pay was necessary for the counseling framework to succeed). The court also invalidated other aspects of the legislative scheme, insisting, for example, that counseled but "unevaluated" abortions could not be denoted as "lawful" and requiring that counseling be more directed toward continuation of pregnancies. *Id.* at 283–85.

158. Neuman, *supra* note 126, at 281(summarizing the court's decision). An English translation prepared by the German Constitutional Court is now available at BVerfG, 2 BvF 2/90 of 05/28/1993, http://www.bverfg.de/entscheidungen/fs19930528_2bvf000290en.html.

159. KOMMERS, *supra* note 52, at 354; *see also* Vicki C. Jackson, *Gender Equality and the Idea of a Constitution, in* CONSTITUTING EQUALITY, *supra* note 157.

160. Neuman, *supra* note 126, at 280–81.

161. Youngberg v. Romeo, 457 U.S. 307, 317 (1982).

162. DeShaney v. Winnebago Co. Dep't of Social Services, 489 U.S. 189, 195 (1989); *see also* Town of Castle Rock v. Gonzales, 545 U.S. 748, 755 (2005). *But see* Steven J. Heyman, *The First Duty of Government: Protection, Liberty and the Fourteenth Amendment,* 41 DUKE L.J. 507, 508 (1991); Robin West, *Rights, Capabilities, and the Good Society,* 69 FORDHAM L. REV. 1901 (2001).

163. On the continued importance of the difference in orientation to social obligations between European states and the United States, see George S. Katroulagos, *European "Social States" and the USA: An Ocean Apart?,* 4 EUR. CONST. L. REV. 225 (2008).

164. *But cf.* Saenz v. Roe, 526 U.S. 489 (1999).

165. GLENDON, *supra* note 112, at 39.

166. *See* Planned Parenthood of Se. Pa. v. Casey, 505 U.S. 833, 879 (1992) (O'Connor, J., Kennedy, J., Souter, J., Joint Opinion) ("We . . . reaffirm *Roe*'s holding that 'subsequent to viability, the State in promoting its interest in the potentiality of human life *may, if it chooses,* regulate, and even proscribe, abortion except where it is necessary, in appropriate medical judgment, for the preservation of the life or health of the mother.' *Roe v. Wade,* 410 U.S. at 164–165") (emphasis added).

167. *See Planned Parenthood v. Casey,* 505 U.S. at 914 (Stevens, J., concurring in part and dissenting in part) (asserting that "the interest in protecting potential life is not grounded in the Constitution," but "is, instead, an indirect interest supported by both humanitarian and pragmatic concerns").

168. On efforts by pro-life proponents in the United States to establish that a fetus is a person with a right to life, see, for example, STEPHEN M. KRASON, ABORTION: POLITICS, MORALITY AND THE CONSTITUTION: A CRITICAL STUDY OF ROE V. WADE AND DOE V. BOLTON AND A BASIS FOR CHANGE 158–73, 335–92 (1984); *cf.* ROBERT P. GEORGE & CHRISTOPHER TOLLEFSEN, EMBRYO: A DEFENSE OF HUMAN LIFE (2008). If a fetus were a "person," the Court in *Roe* said, "the fetus' right to life would then be guaranteed specifically by the [Fourteenth] Amendment," and questions would arise whether lower penalties for murder of a fetus than for other murders would be constitutionally permissible. *Roe,* 410 U.S. at 156–57 & n.54. The Court thus suggested that such existing laws might provide a baseline against which the government's position would be characterized. *Cf. DeShaney,* 489 U.S. at 195 (distinguishing between the "State *itself*" acting to deprive persons of rights, which the Constitution forbids, and the state acting affirmatively to protect against harm by others) (emphasis added). More recently the pro-life movement has reframed some of its arguments as being about protecting women, though in a paternalistic way arguably incompatible with women's choiceful autonomy. *See* Bopp & Coleson Memorandum, *supra* note 137, at 9 (recommending new laws to require women to view ultrasound pictures of the fetus before deciding on abortion, and to assure "true informed consent" and waiting periods); *see* Siegel, *Dignity and the Politics of Protection, supra* note 138 (discussing paternalism, women-protective rationales, and abortion regulation).

169. *See* GLENDON, *supra* note 112, at 2, 13–24, 112; Mary Ann Glendon, *A Beau Mentir Qui Vient de Loin: The 1988 Canadian Abortion Decision in Comparative Perspective,* 83 NW. U.L. REV. 569, 589 (1989).

170. *See Case C-355, Colombian Constitutional Court Abortion Decision, supra* note 131, at 20–25; *see also* Stith, *supra* note 121, at 537 (describing approach of the Spanish Constitutional Court as "communitarian," treating the unborn fetus as having a special constitutional status, under which it is owed some protection from abortion but not when

a particular pregnancy is not "exactable" from the pregnant woman); *supra* text at notes 123–25 (discussing German Constitutional Court opinions); *cf. Hungarian Abortion Decision*, in SÓLYOM & BRUNNER, *supra* note 109, at 190–91 (suggesting that the legislature could decide either to treat the fetus as a rights-bearing human being or to treat fetal life as requiring some degree of protection from the state even if the fetus is not regarded as a rights-bearing person).

171. *Cf.* Siegel, *Dignity and the Politics of Protection*, *supra* note 138, at 1702 (describing dignity as a "value that bridges communities" that are otherwise divided in the debate over abortion).

172. *See* EILEEN MCDONAGH, BREAKING THE ABORTION DEADLOCK: FROM CHOICE TO CONSENT 69–78 (1996); *see also* Robin West, *Liberalism and Abortion*, 87 GEO. L.J. 2117, 2127 (1999).

173. *See* Leira, *supra* note 58, at 374; Kershaw, *supra* note 155, at 342–43; Lappegard, *supra* note 58, at 140. Although some suggest that childrearing after birth can be "avoided by adoption," James Bopp Jr. & Curtis R. Cook, *Partial-Birth Abortion: The Final Frontier of Abortion Jurisprudence*, 14 ISSUES L. & MED. 3, 30 (1998), women may face great pressure to raise the children they bear, *see, e.g.*, Siegel, *Reasoning from the Body*, *supra* note 138, at 371–72 (arguing that "women who are forced to bear children" cannot "simply abandon them" for emotional, social, and moral reasons).

174. *See* Siegel, *Dignity and the Politics of Protection*, *supra* note 138, at 1796–97 (noting effectiveness of approaches including improved sex education and improved availability of contraceptives, in lowering abortion rates without strong reliance on criminal sanction).

175. These would include, for example, protection of the pregnant woman's life and physical and mental health, a pregnancy resulting from a crime, the fetus suffering from a serious disability, and socioeconomic or familial conditions that would make raising a child a hardship.

176. 539 U.S. 306 (2003) (upholding individualized assessment process that included race). In *Gratz v. Bollinger*, 539 U.S. 244 (2003), the Court struck down the University of Michigan undergraduate school's use, in a more quantitative admissions system, of an award of large number of "points" towards admission based on race.

177. *Grutter*, 539 U.S. at 357–61 (Thomas, J., dissenting). Justice Thomas argued that U.S. constitutional equality law should recognize only one compelling governmental interest that could justify the use of race by the government, for "measures the State must take to provide a bulwark against anarchy, or to prevent violence." *Id.* at 353.

178. *Cf.* Tushnet, *supra* note 55, at 654 (arguing that the U.S. Court has never held that affirmative action is required, in part because of an institutional concern for judicial capacity to design such programs).

179. *See Grutter*, 539 U.S. at 344–46 (Ginsburg, J., concurring) (noting that the Court's contemplation of an end-point for affirmative action "accords with the international understanding of the office of affirmative action," referring to CEDAW, art. 4, and to the International Convention on the Elimination of all Forms of Racial Discrimination, the latter of which the United States ratified).

180. *See, e.g.*, INDIA CONST. arts. 330, 332; CANADIAN CHARTER OF RIGHTS AND FREEDOMS, 1982, § 15(1), (2) (banning discrimination on specified grounds but providing that the ban does not preclude government acts that have as their "object the amelioration of conditions of disadvantaged individuals or groups including those that are disadvantaged because of race, national or ethnic origin, colour, religion, sex, age, or mental or physical disability"); *see also id.* § 6(4).

181. For a mustering of evidence that the Fourteenth Amendment was not originally intended to bar remedial uses of race, see, for example, Eric Schnapper, *Affirmative Action and the Legislative History of the Fourteenth Amendment*, 71 Va. L. Rev. 753, 754, 765–67, 784–85 (1985). *See also* Paul R. Baier, *Of Bakke's Balance, Gratz and Grutter: The Voice of Justice Powell*, 78 Tul. L. Rev. 1955, 1997–98 (2004).

182. *See, e.g.*, Gratz v. Bollinger, 539 U.S. 244 (2003); Grutter v. Bollinger, 539 U.S. 306 (2003); Adarand Constructors, Inc. v. Pena, 515 U.S. 200 (1995); Regents of University of California v. Bakke, 438 U.S. 265, 288–305 (1978) (Powell, J., announcing the judgment of the Court). *But cf. Gratz*, at 301–02 (Ginsburg, J., dissenting).

183. *Cf.* Ruth Bader Ginsburg & Deborah Jones Merritt, *Affirmative Action: An International Human Rights Dialogue*, 21 Cardozo L. Rev. 253, 276 (1999) (suggesting that public recognition of persistent bias against disfavored castes helps explain why numerical reservations have survived in India but not in the United States).

184. *See generally* Jackson & Tushnet, *supra* note 80, at 1227–52 (readings describing great diversity and strong but sometimes troubled democratic practices of India). *See also* Freedom House, Freedom in the World, *supra* note 80, (ratings for 2008, India) (classifying India as a "free" country but with lower ratings for protection of political and civil rights than the United States).

185. *See* Soli J. Sorabjee, *Equality in India and the United States, in* Constitutionalism and Rights 98 (Henkin & Rosenthal, eds. 1990); Granville Austin, The Indian Constitution, Cornerstone of a Nation 50 (1999 ed., first published 1966); *supra* note 180.

186. India Const., arts. 15 (prohibition of discrimination based, inter alia, on caste), 17 (abolition of untouchability).

187. *See* Jones v. Alfred H. Mayer Co., 392 U.S. 409, 439 (1968) (quoting The Civil Rights Cases, 109 U.S. 3, 20 (1883).

188. *See, e.g., Bakke*, 438 U.S. at 307–10 (Powell. J., announcing the judgment of the Court); Parents Involved in Cmty. Sch. v. Seattle Sch. Dist. No. 1, 551 U.S. 701, 731–32 (2007) (Roberts, C.J., announcing the judgment of the Court) (referring to "our rulings that remedying past societal discrimination does not justify race-conscious government action"); *The Civil Rights Cases*, 109 U.S. at 11. *But cf.* Richmond v. J. A. Croson Co., 488 U.S. 469, 504 (1989) (suggesting that states may "take remedial action when they possess evidence that their own spending practices are exacerbating a pattern of prior discrimination, [but] they must identify that discrimination, public or private, with some specificity before they may use race-conscious relief").

189. *See, e.g.*, State of Kerala v. Thomas, A.I.R. 1976 S.C. 490 (Sup. Ct. India), para. 56 (Khanna, J., minority view); *see also id.* paras. 117–20 (Beg, J., majority view).

190. *See id.* paras. 31, 44 (Ray, C. J., majority judgment); paras. 82, 87, 89–92 (Mathew, J., majority view).

191. *Compare* Marc Galanter, Competing Equalities: Law and the Backward Classes in India 1, 2–3, 73–83, 551 (1984) (describing India's "compensatory discrimination" programs as a "costly success") *with* Thomas Sowell, Preferential Policies: An International Perspective 52–69, 91–103 (1990) (finding them a costly failure, increasing resentment and backlash and detracting from principles of merit in education and the civil service); Thomas Sowell, Affirmative Action Around the World 49–51 (2004) (finding that "affirmative action in India has produced minimal benefits to those most in need of them and maximum resentments and hostility toward them [by] others," especially given extensions of affirmative measures beyond the Scheduled Castes and Tribes to other "backward classes" and local groups); *see also* Devanesan Nesiah, Discrimination with Reason? The Policy of Reservations in the United States, India and Malaysia 66–74, 304–14 (2000)

(exploring how different aspects of India's complex approach work and suggesting changes to avoid harmful effects); Clark D. Cunningham & N.R. Madhava Menon, *Correspondence: Race, Class, Caste. . . ? Rethinking Affirmative Action*, 97 MICH. L. REV. 1296, 1302–07 (1999) (suggesting that multifactored approach to defining "caste" in India, including exclusion of the "creamy layer" of disadvantaged groups, as enforced by the Indian Supreme Court, has contributed to legitimacy and public acceptance of affirmative programs).

192. Although "narrow tailoring" has been justified by the U.S. Court as necessary to avoid harm to those not benefited by the classifications, *see Grutter v. Bollinger*, 539 U.S. at 341, the use of race as an indefinite, unquantified "plus" might also be thought to diminish the effect of instantiating in the expectations of all concerned the salience of race as a category, when compared to "harder" measures involving quotas or points. *Cf., e.g.*, Clark D. Cunningham, *After Grutter Things Get Interesting! The American Debate Over Affirmative Action Is Finally Ready for Some Fresh Ideas From Abroad*, 36 CONN. L. REV. 665, 674–76 (2004) (suggesting that India's experience, inter alia, supports the distinction between a program assigning significant "points" to race and one in which race is considered as one of many aspects of an individually assessed application, tracking the Court's decisions in the 2003 Michigan cases). On the many complexities of the Indian situation, including the different levels of government involved in and the methods for determining the Scheduled Castes and Tribes, and other "backward classes," see sources cited *supra* note 191.

193. *See Grutter*, 539 U.S. at 343 (referring to the "requirement" that race-conscious programs "have a termination point," and stating: "We expect that 25 years from now, the use of racial preferences will no longer be necessary to further the interest approved today.")

194. *See* JACKSON & TUSHNET, *supra* note 80, at 1238 (describing repeated extensions, the most recent being until 2010).

195. Adarand Constructors, Inc. v. Pena, 515 U.S 200 (1995). *But cf. infra* note 198.

196. Affirmative action in the public sphere is authorized for members of the Scheduled Castes and Tribes and for members of other "backward class[es]." *See, e.g.*, INDIA CONST. arts. 15(4), (5), 16 (4), (4A) (as amended through 2007), *available at* http://lawmin.nic.in/coi/coiason29july08.pdf. *Mandatory* reservations of seats in legislatures extends to the Scheduled Castes and Tribes, but not to other "backward classes." *See, e.g., id.* art. 330 (reserved seats for members of Scheduled Castes and Tribes in House of the People); *id.* art. 332 (requiring similar reservations in the states legislatures); *id.* art. 243D (requiring reservations in panchayats for women and for members of Scheduled Castes and Tribes and authorizing legislatures to reserve seats for other backward classes).

197. State of Kerala v. N.M. Thomas, A.I.R. 1976 S.C. 490, para. 153 (Sup. Ct. India) (Krishna Iyer, J., majority view); *see id.* at para. 151 (noting that Article 46 of the Constitution's Directive Principles of State Policy singles out the Scheduled Castes and Scheduled Tribes for "special mention"); *see also* MARC GALANTER, LAW AND SOCIETY IN MODERN INDIA 259–78 (1989).

198. Members of U.S. Indian tribes also experienced long and severe forms of subordination, but their constitutional status for purpose of differential government treatment has been viewed as distinct. U.S. CONST. art I § 8; Morton v. Mancari, 417 U.S. 535 (1974) (rejecting a challenge to Indian preference in federal employment).

199. *See Bakke*, 438 U.S. at 387–96 (Marshall, J., separate opinion). In *Grutter*, the Court may have been linking forward-looking "diversity" rationales with rationales concerned with promoting equality in the face of a long history of subordination. *See Grutter*,

539 U.S. at 342–43 (noting the importance of durational limits in assuring that any "'deviation from the norm of equal treatment of all racial and ethnic groups is a temporary matter, a measure taken in the service of the goal of equality itself'") (internal citation omitted). The compelling interest accepted as justifying the Michigan program was in diversity of the student body, which the Court, in the quoted material, arguably connected to goals of *equality*. To the extent that the diversity to which racial difference contributes rests in part on the experience of discrimination, "diversity" interests overlap with interests in overcoming the effects of societal discrimination in ways not formally acknowledged by the doctrine.

200. In *Goesaert v. Cleary*, 335 U.S. 464 (1948), the Court upheld a state law prohibiting women, other than the wives or daughters of male bar owners, from working as bartenders.

CHAPTER 8. CONSTITUTIONAL PARTICULARITIES, FEDERALISM, AND THE TRANSNATIONAL

1. *See* Vicki C. Jackson, *The Early Hours of the Post–World War II Model of Constitutional Federalism: The Warren Court and the World*, *in* EARL WARREN AND THE WARREN COURT: THE LEGACY IN AMERICAN AND FOREIGN LAW 137–93 (Harry N. Scheiber ed. 2007). The original U.S. Constitution imposed a small number of explicit, judicially enforceable constraints on the actions of the state governments, for example, the prohibition on bills of attainders, or laws impairing the validity of contracts, *see* U.S. CONST. art. I, § 10, but the Bill of Rights added by amendment in 1791 was interpreted, insofar as it conferred individual rights, to constrain only the national and not the state governments. The Civil War amendments extended some individual rights against the states through the Due Process and Equal Protection Clauses of the Fourteenth Amendment, but it was not until the mid-twentieth century that the Fourteenth Amendment's due process clause was viewed as incorporating against the states most of the specific constraints of the Bill of Rights. *See, e.g.*, Twining v. New Jersey, 211 U.S. 78 (1908): Adamson v. California, 332 U.S. 46 (1947). By the mid-1960s, most of the Bill of Rights had been incorporated through the Due Process Clause to apply in full force to the states as well as the national government. *See, e.g.*, Duncan v. Louisiana, 391 U.S. 145 (1968).

2. *See* Chisholm v. Georgia, 2 U.S. 419, 456–61 (Wilson, J.) (1793) (discussing foreign law in deciding whether under the Constitution, as it then stood, a state could be sued in the Supreme Court); Worcester v. Georgia, 31 U.S. (6 Pet.) 515, 560–61 (1832) (referring to the "settled doctrine of the law of nations" concerning the capacity of a "weaker power" to associate with stronger ones while retaining rights of self-governance in concluding that Indian tribes retained right of self-governance as against the states); Gibbons v. Ogden, 22 U.S. (9 Wheat.) 1, 227 (1824) (Johnson, J., concurring) (referring to the "law of nations" in discussing federal power to regulate interstate commerce); United States v. Perkins, 163 U.S. 625, 626–28 (1896) (referring to foreign law in upholding state's power to tax property bequeathed to the United States); cases cited in the Introduction, note 42, above; *cf.* Martin v. Hunter's Lessee, 14 U.S. 304, 335 (1816) (describing how the federal "judicial power" extends to matters that "affect not only our internal policy, but our foreign relations," including "cases affecting ambassadors, other public ministers, and consuls, who are emphatically placed under the guardianship of the law of nations," and cases of admiralty jurisdiction "in the correct adjudication of which foreign nations are deeply interested").

3. *See* United States v. Allegheny Co., 322 U.S. 174, 198 (1944) (Frankfurter, J., dissenting) (asserting that federal constitutional relations in Canada were identical to those in the

United States for purposes of the tax immunity issue and citing a decision of the Supreme Court of Canada as to why the United States Supreme Court should deny the claim of the federal government); Graves v. New York *ex rel.* O'Keefe, 306 U.S. 466, 491 (1939) (Frankfurter, J., concurring) (asserting that the intergovernmental tax immunity case raised the "same legal issues" as in Australia and Canada under particular provisions of their constitutions); *see also* New York v. United States, 326 U.S. 572, 583 n.5 (1946) (Frankfurter, J., delivering the judgment of the Court).

4. 317 U.S. 111, 125–26 & n.27 (1942) (upholding a federal regulatory scheme's limit on the production of wheat for home use on family farms, and noting that three other large wheat-exporting nations—Canada, Australia, and Argentina—were federal systems and in each the national government controlled wheat regulation).

5. Printz v. United States, 521 U. S. 898, 976–77 (1997) (Breyer, J., dissenting).

6. Ex parte Chairperson of the Constitutional Assembly, In re: Certification of the Constitution of the Republic of South Africa 1996 (4) SA 744 (CC) at 862 (S.Afr.).

7. Reynolds v. Sims, 377 U.S. 533, 572–75 (1964) (describing the system of representation in the two Houses of Congress as "one conceived out of compromise and concession indispensable to the establishment of our federal republic"; asserting that "the so-called federal analogy is inapplicable as a sustaining precedent for state legislative apportionment").

8. *See* Adler v. Ontario, [1996] 3 S.C.R. 609, 640–42 (Can.).

9. *Adler*, [1996] 3 S.C.R. at 640–42 (quoting Reference re Bill 30, An Act to Amend the Education Act (Ontario), [1987] 1 S.C.R. 1148, 1173–74); *accord*, Ontario English Catholic Teachers' Ass'n v. Ontario (Attorney General), [2001] 1 S.C.R. 470, 479 (Can.) (describing Section 93 as a "'solemn pact resulting from the bargaining which made Confederation possible'") (quoting *Reference re Bill 30*, [1987] 1 S.C.R. at 1173); *see also* CANADIAN CHARTER OF RIGHTS AND FREEDOMS, 1982, § 29.

10. *See, e.g.*, Attorney-General for Ontario v. Attorney-General for the Dominion (Local Prohibition Case), [1896] A.C. 348, 360–61 (P.C.); Labatt Breweries of Canada Ltd. v. Attorney General of Canada, [1980] 1 S.C.R. 914; *see also* MacDonald v. Vapor Canada, Ltd., [1977] 2 S.C.R. 134 (1976). For helpful discussion, see generally 1 PETER W. HOGG, CONSTITUTIONAL LAW OF CANADA §§ 20.1, 20.2, 20.3 (5th ed. 2006). (Some of the argument in this chapter, especially Part A concerning historically contingent compromises and interdependent balances in federalism, is drawn from my earlier work, including Vicki C. Jackson, *Narratives of Federalism: Of Continuities and Comparative Constitutional Experience*, 51 DUKE L. J. 223 (2001) [hereinafter *Narratives of Federalism*]; *Comparative Constitutional Federalism: Its Strengths and Limits*, in LE FÉDÉRALISME DANS TOUS SES ÉTATS/ THE STATES AND MOODS OF FEDERALISM: GOVERNANCE, IDENTITY AND METHODOLOGY (Jean-François Gaudreault-DesBiens & Fabien Gélinas eds. 2005); *Comparative Constitutional Federalism and Transnational Judicial Discourse*, 2 INT'L J. CONST. L. 91 (2004) [hereinafter *Comparative Constitutional Federalism*.)

11. 521 U.S. 898 (1997).

12. *See generally* Daniel Halberstam, *Comparative Federalism and the Issue of Commandeering*, *in* THE FEDERAL VISION: LEGITIMACY AND LEVELS OF GOVERNANCE IN THE UNITED STATES AND THE EUROPEAN UNION (Robert Howse & Kalypso Nikolaides eds., 2001); Daniel Halberstam, *Of Power and Responsibility: The Political Morality of Federal Systems*, 90 VA. L. REV. 731 (2004).

13. *See* Daniel Halberstam & Roderick M. Hills, Jr., *State Autonomy in Germany and the United States*, 574 ANNALS AM. ACAD. POL. & SOC. SCI. 173, 174–76, 178–82 (2001).

14. Christopher McCrudden, *A Common Law of Human Rights? Transnational Judicial Conversations on Constitutional Rights*, 20 OXFORD J. LEGAL STUD. 499, 501 (2000). (For earlier

elaboration of the ideas in this paragraph, see Jackson, *Comparative Constitutional Federalism, supra* note 10, at 109-10; Jackson, *Narratives of Federalism, supra* note 10, at 272–73 n.207).

15. International law may be developing a norm of democratic governance. *See* Thomas M. Franck, *The Emerging Right to Democratic Governance*, 86 Am. J. Int'l L. 46 (1992); Enrique Lagos & Timothy D. Rudy, *The Third Summit of the Americas and the Thirty-First Session of the OAS General Assembly*, 96 Am. J. Int'l L. 173 (2002). International law also requires that a competent court fulfill certain functions involving criminal prosecutions, and remedies, a requirement that at least in Europe is being elaborated in case law requiring a degree of independence of courts from executive or legislative functions in order to assure the requisite impartiality. *See* Chapter 3, above; *see also* Steven J. Schnably, *Emerging International Law Constraints on Constitutional Structure and Revision: A Preliminary Appraisal*, 62 U. Miami L. Rev. 417 (2008). But the content of any emerging international norm of government organization is still quite underdeveloped, in comparison to existing human rights conventions.

16. For discussion of default rules in U.S. constitutional federalism, see, for example, Gillian Metzger, *Congress, Article IV, and Interstate Relations*, 120 Harv. L. Rev. 1468 (2007).

17. *See, e.g.*, Koen Lenaerts, *Constitutionalism and the Many Faces of Federalism*, 38 Am. J. Comp. L. 205, 206–07 (1990); Bruce Ackerman, *The Rise of World Constitutionalism*, 83 Va. L. Rev. 771 (2000).

18. *See, e.g.*, Edward L. Rubin & Malcom A. Feeley, *Federalism: Some Notes on a National Neurosis*, 41 UCLA L. Rev. 903, 942–46 (1994) (arguing that even if some U.S. states were once "unique political communities," that is no longer the case). *But cf.* Vicki C. Jackson, *Federalism and the Uses and Limits of Law: Printz and Principle?*, 111 Harv. L. Rev. 2180, 2221 (1998) (suggesting that these authors may underestimate degrees of state or regional attachment).

19. *See* Jackson, *Comparative Constitutional Federalism, supra* note 10, at 121–37.

20. This holds even in cases in which the federal features of one system are used as a model or antimodel for another, as was the case for Canada (which considered the U.S. constitutional experience in drafting its 1867 Constitution Act). The Canadian Supreme Court has been found to be much less likely to refer to foreign (U.S.) law in deciding federalism cases than in deciding Charter cases. *See* C.L. Ostberg et al., *Attitudes, Precedents and Cultural Change: Explaining the Citation of Foreign Precedents by the Supreme Court of Canada*, 34 Can. J. Pol. Sci. 377, 390 (2001).

21. *See, e.g.*, Frederick Schauer, *Free Speech and the Cultural Contingency of Constitutional Categories*, 14 Cardozo L. Rev. 865, 867 (1993) ("[F]or a large group of constitutional categories, the categories come not from linguistically determinate textual provisions but instead from cultural constructs that determine what events will be considered members of what class."); *see also* Roger P. Alford, *Free Speech and the Case for Constitutional Exceptionalism*, 106 Mich. L. Rev. 1071 (book review). Schauer suggests, for example, that differences in German and American history and culture account for the wildly different reactions in those two countries to "slippery slope" arguments for prohibiting bans on hate speech. *See* Schauer, *supra*, at 877–79.

22. There are also rights provisions that may be quite rare or nationally distinctive. *See, e.g.*, U.S. Const. amend. II (discussed in Chapter 6, note 4, above).

23. *See, e.g.*, Paolo G. Carozza, *Subsidiarity as a Structural Principle of International Human Rights Law*, 97 Am. J. Int'l L. 38 (2003); *see also* Reimer von Borries & Malte Hauschild, *Implementing the Subsidiarity Principle*, 5 Colum. J. Eur. L. 369 (1999); George A. Bermann, *Taking Subsidiarity Seriously: Federalism in the European Community and the*

United States, 94 COLUM. L. REV. 332 (1994); *cf.* Mattias Kumm, *Democratic Constitutionalism Encounters International Law: Terms of Engagement, in* THE MIGRATION OF CONSTITUTIONAL IDEAS 256, 264–68 (Sujit Choudhry ed. 2006) (discussing subsidiarity).

24. Note the possible importance of the distinction between knowledge and acknowledgment. See Chapter 6, above, discussing prudential silences.

25. *See, e.g.*, Reference re Secession of Quebec, [1998] 2 S.C.R. 217, 277–88 [hereinafter sometimes referred to as *Secession Reference*] (discussing and rejecting claim under international law for a right to secede).

26. *See, e.g.*, WILLIAM SCHABAS, INTERNATIONAL HUMAN RIGHTS LAW AND THE CANADIAN CHARTER 228–29 (2d ed. 1996); Judith Resnik, *Law's Migration: American Exceptionalism, Silent Dialogues, and Federalism's Multiple Ports of Entry*, 115 YALE L.J. 1564, 1627–52 (2006) (describing how transnational norms are sometimes incorporated by state or local actors more readily than at the national level). Consider this complex set of events in Canada, which Schabas describes. Quebec "ratified" the ICCPR in 1976. After the 1982 Charter came into effect, a Quebec statute prohibiting the use of English and requiring the use of French in signage for commercial establishments was found unlawful by the Canadian Supreme Court. *See* Ford v. Quebec [Attorney General], [1988] 2 S.C.R. 712. Quebec initially responded by enacting an "override" to preserve its French-only signage law, but after complaints were filed before the UN Human Rights Committee, Quebec amended its Charter of the French Language "to conform with the views of the Human Rights Committee." *Id.* at 228. Schabas comments: "The National Assembly could live quite comfortably, given Quebec's political climate, with legislation that literally defied a unanimous judgment of the Supreme Court of Canada. It was, however, considerably more ill at ease with the conclusions of the majority of the Human Rights Committee, and took appropriate legislative action to comply with its views." *Id.* at 228–29; *see also* Singer v. Canada, UN Human Rights Comm. (Views), 51st Sess., UN Doc. CCPR/C/51/D/455/1991 (1994) (describing the course of events in detail); Ballantyne, Davidson, McIntyre v. Canada, UN Human Rights Comm.(Views), 47th Sess., UN Doc. CCPR/C/47/D/359/1989 and 385/1989/Rev.1 (1993).

27. On Canada's distinctive mechanism for legislative override of certain Charter rights, see Ford v. Quebec (Attorney General), [1998] 2 S.C.R. 712, and Chapter 6, note 176, above. In the "notwithstanding" clause of Section 33, the Canadian Charter of Rights and Freedoms authorizes an override of Charter constraints that is temporary (expiring after five years but subject to reenactment) and is applicable only to some parts of the Charter; it is not, for example, available with respect to democratic rights (like voting) and mobility rights, nor with respect to specific minority language rights, *see* CHARTER §§ 3, 6, 23.

28. *See* sources cited above in Chapter 3, note 179.

29. *See* Chapter 1, above, at text at notes 31–32; *see also* Jonathan M. Miller, *A Typology of Legal Transplants: Using Sociology, Legal History and Argentine Examples to Explain the Transplant Process*, 51 AM. J. COMP. L. 839, 880–81 (2003).

30. Michael C. Dorf, *Dynamic Incorporation of Foreign Law*, 157 U. PA. L. REV. 103 (2008).

31. *See* Amalgamated Society of Engineers Case v. Adelaide Steamship Co. Ltd. (1920) 28 C.L.R. 129, 146 (Austl.); Bank of Toronto v. Lambe, 1887 12 A.C. 575, 587 (P.C.) (appeal taken from Can.).

32. *See generally* Bijon Roy, *An Empirical Survey of Foreign Jurisprudence and International Instruments in Charter Litigation*, 62 U.T. FAC. L. REV. 99 (2004) (analyzing the Charter cases decided by the Supreme Court of Canada, 1998–2003); Louise Arbour & Fannie LaFontaine, *Beyond Self-Congratulation: The Charter at 25*, 45 OSGOODE HALL L. J. 239 (2007);

cf. Diarmuid F. O'Scannlain, *What Role Should Foreign Practice and Precedent Play in the Interpretation of Domestic Law?*, 80 NOTRE DAME L. REV. 1893, 1895 (2005) (stating that between 1990 and 2003 the U.S. Supreme Court cited contemporary British or Canadian cases in twenty-one decisions, while the Canadian Supreme Court cited U.S. case law 230 times in 1990 alone). This tendency also appears to exist if lower court decisions are included in the comparison. A search on August 20, 2008 of LEXIS for Canadian provincial court cases, combined, yielded 213 references to the "Universal Declaration of Human Rights"; the same search of U.S. state court cases combined yielded 47. An earlier LEXIS search on Aug. 24, 2004, in "Canadian Cases," a file that consisted of "all reported and available unreported decisions" of the provincial and federal courts of Canada, including the Supreme Court, for "Universal Declaration of Human Rights," found 623 references; a LEXIS search of the most comparable U.S. file, "Federal and State Cases combined," produced 187 references. (Most of these, at least 153 of the 187, were in the federal, not the state, courts.) The differences between Canada and the United States are even more significant than these numbers suggest: the United States has by far the larger population and many more courts and judges than in Canada. According to the U.S. Census Bureau, there are about 34,000 judges in the United States. *See* http://www.census.gov/pubinfo/www/radio/pa0821.htm (visited Sept 6, 2004); by contrast, Canada has a total of about 2,500 judges, 1,000 in federally appointed courts, the remainder in section 92 provincial courts. *See* LAW, POLITICS AND THE JUDICIAL PROCESS IN CANADA 117 (F. L. Morton ed., 3d ed. 2002).

33. For examples of Canadian Supreme Court decisions on issues of constitutional law that refer to and discuss foreign or international legal materials, see, for example, R. v. Morgentaler, [1988] 1 S.C.R. 30, 46 (Dickson, C.J.); *id.* at 108, 113 (Beetz, J.) (discussing U.S., European, and German abortion-related case law in a decision striking down Canadian abortion law); R. v. Keegstra, [1990] 3 S.C.R. 697 (upholding law criminalizing certain hate speech, discussing U.S. law); Little Sisters Book & Art Emporium v. Canada (Minister of Justice), [2000] 2 S.C.R. 1120, 1258–59 (Iacobucci, J., dissenting in part) (citing West Virginia State Board of Education v. Barnette, 319 U.S. 624 (1943) on freedom of religion and conscience). For (controversial) reliance on a ratified but unimplemented international convention on other public law issues, see Baker v. Canada (Minister of Citizenship and Immigration), [1999] 2 S.C.R. 817, 829–30, 860–63 (Can.) (L'Heureux-Dubé, J.) (stating that the Convention on the Rights of the Child, though having no "direct application" in Canada, reflects "values . . . [that] may help inform the contextual approach to statutory interpretation and judicial review"). *But cf. id.* at 865–66 (Iacobucci, J., with Cory, J.) (disagreeing with L'Heureux-Dubé's giving any weight to an unimplemented Convention in interpreting domestic law, because such an international obligation has "no force or effect within the Canadian legal system" until it is incorporated through implementing legislation).

34. Health Services & Support Facilities Subsector Bargaining Ass'n v. British Columbia, [2007] 2 S.C.R. 391, 433–34; *see also, e.g.,* Suresh v. Canada (Minister of Citizenship and Immigration), [2002] 1 S.C.R. 3, 31–32; R. v. Hape, [2007] 2 S.C.R. 292, 324 (LeBel, J.) (Can.).

35. *See* Ostberg et al, *supra* note 20, at 390.

36. For illuminating discussion, see Sarah K. Harding, *Comparative Reasoning and Judicial Review*, 28 YALE J. INT'L L. 409 (2003).

37. Although it "came to be . . . axiomatic that the judiciary was the umpire to determine whether a statute enacted either by Parliament or a provincial legislature" was within its constitutional powers, Gordon Bale notes that Canada's 1867 Constitution Act did not specifically provide for such review, but provided a political mechanism, of federal

disallowance of provincial laws, that might have served as "an entirely different mechanism for regulating the division of legislative powers." GORDON BALE, CHIEF JUSTICE WILLIAM JOHNSTONE RITCHIE: RESPONSIBLE GOVERNMENT AND JUDICIAL REVIEW 97–132 (1991) (discussing debate over judicial review occasioned by the *Chandler* case in early 1870s). On the expected role of judicial review on federalism (and other issues) in the United States, see LARRY D. KRAMER, THE PEOPLE THEMSELVES: POPULAR CONSTITUTIONALISM AND JUDICIAL REVIEW (2004) (suggesting that at the time of the Framing, constitutions would have been understood to be enforced largely through political action of the people, not through judicial review, though opinions were mixed).

Different theories seek to explain the relationship(s) between federalism and judicial review. For Justice Michael Kirby, on the Australian High Court, federal systems cultivate habits of mind that are skeptical of claims in any political branch of absolute power: He writes:

> Federation cultivates the habit of mind which accompanies constitutional superintendence by the courts. Courts recognise a large measure of power in, say, the chamber of a State Parliament, to define and enforce its notion of its own privileges. But the Australian constitutional context does not accord to such a body a completely unreviewable entitlement, in law, to define and enforce its own powers. Any such powers can only be exercised in conformity with the political and judicial system which the Constitution creates.

Egan v. Willis, (1998) 195 C.L.R. 424, 490-93. For another account, see Martin Shapiro, *Some Conditions for the Success of Constitutional Courts: Lessons from the US Experience, in* CONSTITUTIONAL JUSTICE, EAST AND WEST: DEMOCRATIC LEGITIMACY AND CONSTITUTIONAL COURTS IN POST-COMMUNIST EUROPE IN A COMPARATIVE PERSPECTIVE 37, 46–59 (Wojciech Sadurski ed. 2002) (suggesting judicial review of federalism issues, where power-holders have vested stake in having a neutral umpire to settle disputes, builds institutional legitimacy to support more general review of substantive individual rights issues).

38. Note that the U.S. Articles of Confederation made special provision for Canada's joining the Union. *See* ARTICLES OF CONFEDERATION, art. XI (Nov. 15, 1777) (effective 1781).

39. Until well into the twentieth century, there were few constitutional rights enforceable by the federal courts against both levels of government in the United States. The Bill of Rights protections in criminal cases were long enforceable against the federal government, as were the due process and takings clauses; but such individual rights provisions were held not to apply to the states. Barron v. Baltimore, 32 U.S. (7 Pet.) 243 (1833). Not until after the Civil War, with the adoption of the Fourteenth Amendment, did the possibility of expanding rights protections as against the states under the federal constitution arise, and the Fourteenth Amendment was not construed to incorporate most constitutional criminal procedure rights applicable to the federal government until the 1960s. *See, e.g.*, Mapp v. Ohio, 367 U.S. 643 (1961); Gideon v. Wainright, 372 U.S. 335 (1963).

40. *See* Chapter 6, above, text at & note 107. *Compare* Medellín v. Texas, 128 S. Ct. 1346, 1364 (2008) (indicating that treaties are self-executing only "when the textual provisions indicate that the President and Senate intended for the agreement to have domestic effect") *with* U.S. CONST. art. VI (stating that "*all* Treaties . . . which shall be made . . . under the Authority of the United States, shall be the supreme Law of the Land; and the Judges in every State shall be bound thereby") (emphasis added).

41. *See* Carlos Manuel Vázquez, *The Four Doctrines of Self-Executing Treaties*, 89 AM. J. INT'L L. 695, 706 (1995).

42. *See, e.g.*, U.S. Senate Resolution of Advice and Consent to Ratification of the International Covenant on Civil and Political Rights 138 CONG REC. 8070, 8071 (1992) [hereinafter Senate Resolution] ("the United States declares that the provisions of

Articles 1 through 27 of the Covenant are not self-executing"); U.S. Senate Resolution of Advice and Consent to Ratification of the Convention Against Torture and Other Cruel, Inhuman or Degrading Treatment or Punishment, 136 CONG. REC. 36198 (1990) (declaring that Articles 1 through 16 of the Torture Convention are not self-executing); *see also infra*, text at notes 122–23; Chapter 7, text at & notes 68–71, above.

43. *See, e.g.*, Breard v. Greene, 523 U.S. 371 (1998) (per curiam); Brief for the United States as Amicus Curiae Supporting Respondent at 34–35, Medellín v. Dretke, 544 U.S. 660 (2005) (No. 04-5928) (arguing that the court of appeals properly denied petitioner the right to appeal from the district court's denial of habeas relief because the state court's procedural default ruling was not "debatably in conflict with, or an unreasonable application of" Supreme Court holdings); *see also* Medellín v. Texas, 128 S. Ct. 1346 (rejecting the president's claimed authority to require states to ignore procedural rules to give effect to an ICJ judgment).

44. 252 U.S. 416, 433–34 (1920). For revisionist views of *Missouri v. Holland* that would limit Congress's powers to legislate to implement a valid treaty, see, e.g., Nicholas Quinn Rosenkranz, *Executing the Treaty Power*, 118 HARV. L. REV. 1867, 1919–20 (2005); Curtis A. Bradley, *The Treaty Power and American Federalism*, 97 MICH. L. REV. 390, 456 (1998); for a response, see Carlos Manuel Vázquez, *Federalism and International Law: Missouri v. Holland's Second Holding*, 73 MO. L. REV. 939 (2008). Treaties (or statutes implementing them) cannot, however, authorize government conduct affirmatively prohibited by the Bill of Rights. *See* Reid v. Covert, 354 U.S. 1, 15–19 (1957) (Black, J., announcing judgment of the Court).

45. *See* 1 HOGG, *supra* note 10, at §§ 1.9, 11.2, 11.3.

46. Attorney-General for Canada v. Attorney-General for Ontario (Labour Conventions Case), [1937] A.C. 326 (P.C.) (appeal taken from Can.). The decision is regarded by many as in tension with the text of Section 132 of the Constitution Act, 1867. The Privy Council found that federal power to implement treaties, given in that section, pertained only to treaties ratified by the British Empire, and that although the Canadian federal government did now have the power to enter into treaties, the power to implement treaties depended on the other allocations of jurisdiction to the federal and provincial governments found in Sections 91 and 92 of the 1867 act.) For suggestions that the federal government may have such a power under the "peace, order, and good government" clause, and for critique of the *Labour Conventions* decision, see 1 HOGG, *supra* note 10, §11.5 (c).

47. Not until 1982 was the British North America Act, 1867, renamed the Constitution Act, 1867, when it was fully "patriated" to Canada (so that the consent of the Parliament in Westminster was no longer needed to make amendments to Canada's constitution). *See* 1 HOGG, *supra* note 10, at §§ 1.2, 1.3, 3.5(d). On the sense of rupture and autonomy in the founding period of the United States, see, for example, Federalist No. 1 (Hamilton) (suggesting that the Constitution was made by "reflection and choice," not by "accident and force"); O'Scannlain, *supra* note 32, at 1904 (noting late eighteenth or early nineteenth century statutes in New Jersey, Pennsylvania, and Kentucky forbidding citation of English precedents).

48. This is not to deny that there was an extensive, and contested, development of Canadian constitutional and political theory throughout the nineteenth century. *See, e.g.*, Sir C.P. Lucas, ed., *Lord Durham's Report (1839)* (Oxford, Clarendon Press, 1912); SAMUEL V. LASELVA, THE MORAL FOUNDATIONS OF CANADIAN FEDERALISM: PARODOXES, ACHIEVEMENTS AND TRAGEDIES OF NATIONHOOD, at xii–xiii, 31–48 (1996) (emphasizing Cartier's arguments); JANET AJZENSTAT, THE POLITICAL THOUGHT OF LORD DURHAM (1988). I am grateful to David Schneiderman for bringing these sources to my attention.

49. *See* Thomas Fleiner, *Commentary on Swiss Federalism, in* FORGING UNITY OUT OF DIVERSITY: THE APPROACHES OF EIGHT NATIONS 244 (Robert A. Goldwin et al. eds., 1985).

50. *See* U.S. CONST. art. V ("[N]o State, without its Consent, shall be deprived of its equal Suffrage in the Senate").

51. *See* CONSTITUTION ACT, 1867, § 22 (Can.) (providing that for purpose of representation in the Senate, there are four regions: Ontario, Quebec, the maritimes (consisting of Maritime Provinces, Nova Scotia, New Brunswick, and Prince Edward Island), and the Western Provinces (Manitoba, British Columbia, Saskatchewan, and Alberta). Ontario and Quebec each have twenty-four senators, as do the other two regions, subdivided, however, so that, for example, Nova Scotia has ten senators, and Prince Edward Island has four. *Id.* The section also provides for Newfoundland to have six senators and for the Yukon and the Northwest Territories to have one each.

52. In contrast to the "equal footing" doctrine, reflecting a founding decision that new U.S. states would be admitted on the same terms as the original ones (terms in fact subject to exceptions especially with respect to public land issues), *see, e.g.*, Alaska v. United States, 545 U.S. 75 (2005). Canada's 1867 Constitution Act treated different provinces differently in a number of regards. *See, e.g.*, CONSTITUTION ACT, 1867, §§ 62–65, 69, 71 (Can.) (relating to provincial constitutions and legislatures), § 133 (providing for English or French as official languages in national parliament and Quebec, with no mention of other provinces). These asymmetries were tempered in the amending formula of the Constitution Act, 1982, which Professor Cairns describes as a move toward equality in the treatment of all the provinces, *see* Alan C. Cairns, *Constitutional Change and the Three Equalities, in* RECONFIGURATIONS: CANADIAN CITIZENSHIP AND CONSTITUTIONAL CHANGE 216, 220 (1995), and which, he argues, creates serious obstacles to meeting the claims for equality made by the Francophone community vis-à-vis the "rest of Canada." *See id.* at 221–22 ("the flexibility . . . of the rest of Canada in responding to Quebec [is] severely limited by the two equalities [of citizens and provinces]"); *see also id.* at 216–17, 224–31 (discussing failure of Meech Lake accord and its clause recognizing Quebec as a "distinct society" and future prospects for such constitutional asymmetry).

53. U.S. CONST. amend. XI, overruling the effect of Chisholm v. Georgia, 2 U.S. (2 Dall.) 419 (1793); *see supra* note 2.

54. *See* Richard C. Risk, *The Puzzle of Jurisdiction*, 46 S.C. L. REV. 703, 713 (1995) (explaining that in the 1880s, even leading objections to the Supreme Court of Canada's jurisdiction over provincial matters receded in light of the Privy Council's role: "So long as this appeal existed, . . . the comprehensive appellate jurisdiction of the Supreme Court should also exist because it was at least within Canadian control").

55. For a description of the Privy Council's construction of the 1867 Act to strengthen the provinces' hand, arguably against the intent of its principal drafters to create a stronger central government than had existed under the U.S. constitution before the Civil War, see Martha Field, *The Differing Federalisms of the United States and Canada*, 55 LAW & CONTEMP. PROBS. 107 (1992). The Canadian literature suggests that perhaps too much attention has been given to the pro-centralization views of John A. MacDonald as against those of other persons of influence. *See, e.g.*, PAUL ROMNEY, MR. ATTORNEY: THE ATTORNEY GENERAL FOR ONTARIO IN COURT, CABINET AND LEGISLATURE, 1791–1899, at 241–42 (1986) (discussing Mowat); LASELVA, *supra* note 48, at 37–39 (discussing Cartier).

56. A principal source for this paragraph is LAW, POLITICS AND THE JUDICIAL PROCESS IN CANADA, *supra* note 32, Chapters 3–4. Professor Morton describes the Canadian judicial system as "unitary," *see id.* at 93, and it is certainly more so than in the United States.

57. These are courts created under authority Section 92 of the Constitution Act, 1867, consisting of small claims, criminal division, a family division and a juvenile division.

58. The section 101 courts are created and appointed by the federal government; they include the Supreme Court of Canada, which reviews decisions from the provincial courts of appeals, and the Federal Court, with both a trial and appellate division, that deals with specialized areas of federal law and certain claims against the federal government. *See* CONSTITUTION ACT, 1867, § 101 (Can.).

59. These Section 96 courts include the Court of Appeals for each Province, which may directly or indirectly review the judgments of the provincial Section 92 courts, and courts of first instance for more major criminal and civil cases. *See* CONSTITUTION ACT, 1867, § 96 (Can.)

60. LAW, POLITICS AND THE JUDICIAL PROCESS IN CANADA, *supra* note 32, at 118–19. The Constitution Act, 1867, §§ 99, 100, provides that judges of superior courts hold office during good behavior until age seventy-five, and requires the salaries of superior, district, and county courts to be fixed by Parliament, provisions that apply by terms only to the Section 96 courts. *See* LAW, POLITICS AND THE JUDICIAL PROCESS IN CANADA, *supra*, at 170–71. In 1997, the Supreme Court of Canada concluded that judicial independence was an unwritten principle embodied, but not fully captured by such written provisions (or by Charter Section II(d)) and applicable to provincial judges. Reference re Remuneration of Judges of the Provincial Court of Prince Edward Island, [1997] 3 S.C.R. 3 [hereinafter *Provincial Judges Reference*].

61. It is worth noting that the Canadian Supreme Court can review provincial court determinations of provincial law, unlike the U.S. federal courts under *Erie R.R. Co. v. Tompkins*, 304 U.S. 64 (1938), which treats each state as the authoritative expositor of its own law. *See* Field, *supra* note 55, at 113. This feature of the Canadian system, allowing, as Professor Field puts it, "federal judicial input into the meaning of provincial law," might be associated with an attitude toward law that more generally entails receptivity to "persuasive authority," including transnational sources. *See generally* H. Patrick Glenn, *Persuasive Authority*, 32 MCGILL L.J. 261 (1987) (distinguishing between idea of law as a binding response, "controlled and authorized by the State" and excluding all but that state as the source of law, on the one hand, and the idea of law as a form of "enquiry"). It may also be related to the more "unitary" character of the Canadian judicial system, under which the highest courts created by the Provinces are staffed with federally appointed judges. *See supra* note 56.

62. *See, e.g.*, CONSTITUTION ACT, 1867, § 93 (Can.). This is not to deny the possibility that provincial governments in Canada may have been more prone to xenophobic or racist impulses than the national government in some of the same ways that, at least at certain times, some areas in the United States were. *See, e.g.*, Roncarelli v. Duplessis, [1959] S.C.R. 121 (Can.) (holding that Quebec Premier violated rights of a Jehovah's Witness by arbitrarily revoking his liquor license in retaliation for furnishing bail for other Jehovah's Witnesses); Re Drummond Wren, [1945] O.R. 778 (Can.) (invalidating as violative of public policy a restrictive covenant in a deed prohibiting sale of land "to Jews or persons of objectionable nationality"); Saumur v. City of Quebec [1953] 2 S.C.R. 299 (Can.) (holding that Quebec City bylaw prohibiting distribution of pamphlets without consent of police chief could not apply to Jehovah's Witnesses); *cf.* Shelley v. Kraemer, 334 U.S. 1 (1948) (holding race-based restrictive covenants judicially unenforceable because state court would violate the Fourteenth Amendment); Westminster Sch. Dist. of Orange County v. Mendez, 161 F.2d 774 (9th Cir. 1947) (en banc) (holding unconstitutional segregation of students of "Mexican and Latin descent" in California public schools). *See generally* David Mullan, *The Role for Underlying Constitutional Principles in a Bill of Rights World*, 2004 N.Z. L. REV. 9. Nor is it to deny the persistence of issues of equality in public provincial funding of religious schools. *See infra* notes 140–42.

63. *See* Catherine Powell, *Dialogic Federalism: Constitutional Possibilities for Incorporation of Human Rights Law in the United States*, 150 U. PA. L. REV. 245, 266 (2001); David P. Stewart, *United States Ratification of the Covenant on Civil and Political Rights: The Significance of Reservations, Understandings and Declaration*, 42 DEPAUL L. REV. 1183, 1184 (1993). For helpful historical treatments of the Bricker amendment, see DUANE TANANBAUM, THE BRICKER AMENDMENT CONTROVERSY 1–48 (1988); CAROL ANDERSON, EYES OFF THE PRIZE: THE UNITED NATIONS AND THE AFRICAN AMERICAN STRUGGLE FOR HUMAN RIGHTS 44–50 (2003); Natalie Hevener Kaufman & David Whiteman, *Opposition to Human Rights Treaties in the United States Senate: The Legacy of the Bricker Amendment*, 10 HUM. RTS. Q. 309 (1988). On the original Constitution and slavery, see Chapter 7, note 11 above.

64. Louis Henkin, *U.S. Ratification of Human Rights Conventions: The Ghost of Senator Bricker*, 89 AM. J. INT'L L. 341, 348–49 (1995).

65. *But see infra* notes 140–41 (discussing challenges to Ontario's failure to provide public funding for all private religious schools).

66. The claim under international law was rejected on its merits by the Canadian Supreme Court, but it may have influenced the Court's interpretation of its own constitutional law to hold that if there were a clear vote on a clear question in favor of secession, the rest of Canada would have a duty to negotiate with Quebec, and give attention to the rule of law, democracy, federalism, and the protection of minority rights in those negotiations. *See* Reference re Secession of Quebec, [1998] 2 S.C.R. 217. For additional discussion, see below, this chapter.

67. On the Charter's relationship to the ICCPR and ICESCR, see Anne F. Bayefsky, *International Human Rights Law in Canadian Courts*, *in* INTERNATIONAL HUMAN RIGHTS LAW: THEORY AND PRACTICE 115, 125–29 (Irwin Cotler & F. Pearl Eliadis eds., 1992) (arguing that the Charter's legislative history includes many references to human rights law and that Canadian diplomats represented that the Charter was in part an implementation of Canada's international human rights obligations); Gaile McGregor, *The International Covenant on Social, Economic, and Cultural Rights: Will it Get its Day in Court?*, 28 MAN. L.J. 321, 330–31 (2002) (quoting Bayefsky at length); Arbour & LaFontaine, *supra* note 32, at 241–43; *see also* Errol P. Mendes, *Interpreting the Canadian Charter of Rights and Freedoms: Applying International and European Jurisprudence on the Law and Pracice of Fundamental Rights*, 20 ALBERTA L. REV. 383 (1982). For empirical data on transnational references in the interpretation of newer constitutional instruments, see, for example, Adam M. Smith, *Making Itself at Home: Understanding Foreign Law in Domestic Jurisprudence: The Indian Case*, 24 BERKELEY J. INT'L L. 218, 239-42 (2006); C.L. Ostberg et al., *Attitudes, Precedents and Cultural Change: Explaining the Citation of Foreign Precedents by the Supreme Court of Canada*, 34 CANADIAN J. POL. SCI. 377 (2001) (presenting findings and summarizing prior literature); Shannon Ishiyama Smithey, *A Tool, Not a Master: The Use of Foreign Case Law in Canada and South Africa*, 34 COMP. POLIT. STUDIES 1188, 1192-1200 (2001).

68. *See* David Schneiderman, *Dual(ling) Charters: The Harmonics of Rights in Canada and Quebec*, 24 OTTAWA L. REV. 235, 244–48 (1992) (describing in detail how the two Charters compare and concluding that in a number of respects the Quebec Charter is broader in its protections).

69. Daryl J. Levinson, *Empire-Building Government in Constitutional Law*, 118 HARV. L. REV. 915, 920 (2005) (arguing that the behavior of government institutions "depends upon some combination of the interests of the officials who comprise them and the constituents these officials represent" and that "[d]emocratic governments are unlikely to generate" "government officials who care about the interests of the institutions in which they are situated more than their own self-interest or the interests of the citizens

they represent"); *see id.* at 960–64 (applying the argument to courts and suggesting that "it is hard to see how the interests of judges would lead to a consistently expansionist federal judiciary").

70. Erie R.R. Co. v. Tompkins, 304 U.S. 64 (1938); Field, *supra* note 55, at 113–14 (comparing *Erie* regime with Canadian approach).

71. *See, e.g.*, Edwards v. Attorney-General for Canada, [1930] A.C. 124 (P.C. 1929) (appeal taken from Can.) (The Persons Case); Att'y-Gen. of Quebec v. Blaikie, [1979] 2 S.C.R. 1016, 1027–29 (Can.); Reference re Provincial Electoral Boundaries (Sask.), [1991] 2 S.C.R. 158, 180 (Can.); *see also* SCHABAS, *supra* note 26, at 233–34 (referring to both international human rights law, and the Canadian constitution, as "living tree[s]" that "continu[e] to evolve and develop").

72. *See, e.g.*, Reference re Secession of Quebec, [1998] 2 S.C.R. 217 (referring to unwritten constitutional principles of federalism, rule of law, democracy, and respect for minority rights as governing how to decide on claims to secede).

73. On unwritten constitutional principles and conventions, see *Secession Reference*, [1998] 2 S.C.R., at 239–40, 270; *see also Provincial Judges Reference*, [1997] 3 S.C.R. 3. *Cf.* Nixon v. Fitzgerald, 457 U.S. 731 (1982) (inferring an unwritten principle of presidential immunity from civil suit from the Constitution's structure even though the Constitution is explicit in granting immunity to members of Congress but not to the President).

74. *See* 1 HOGG, *supra* note 10, at § 2.4; *see also* ROBERT VIPOND, LIBERTY AND COMMUNITY 15-36 (1991) (describing negotiations leading to the 1867 Act).

75. *See, e.g.*, DANIEL J. ELAZAR, FEDERAL SYSTEMS OF THE WORLD 50 (2d ed. 1994); 1 HOGG, *supra* note 10, § 5.8.

76. *See* Jill Vickers, *Why Should Women Care About Federalism?*, *in* CANADA: THE STATE OF THE FEDERATION 1994, at 135, 143 (Douglas M. Brown & Janet Hiebert eds., 1995).

77. *See* 2 PETER W. HOGG, CONSTITUTIONAL LAW OF CANADA app. 3 at A-46 & n.95 (5th ed. 2006) (noting that section 35.1 was added in 1983). The Constitution Act, 1982, was enacted as Schedule B to the Canada Act, 1982 (U.K.), by which Canada's constitution was "patriated" to Canada. *See supra* note 47. Part I of the Constitution Act, 1982 is the Canadian Charter of Rights and Freedoms; Part II of the Constitution Act, 1982, concerns "Rights of the Aboriginal Peoples of Canada." *See generally* 1 HOGG, *supra* note 10, § 1.3 (discussing the Constitution Act, 1982).

78. Reference re Secession of Quebec, [1998] 2 S.C.R. 217.

79. The commitment to negotiation should not be overstated. The Canadian constitution was patriated to Canada and the Charter itself adopted in 1982 *without* the agreement of Quebec; and commitments to negotiation did not help women's First People's groups in their challenge to the national government's failure to fund their participation in the constitutional conferences of the early 1990s. *See* Native Women's Association v. Canada, [1994] 3 S.C.R. 627. Nonetheless, in comparison to the United States the Canadian constitutional traditions of negotiation are marked.

80. *See supra* note 46. As Hogg explains the decision, the implication was this: "If the statute which was required for implementation of the treaty related to a matter allocated by s. 91 to the federal Parliament, then the federal Parliament would have the power to implement the treaty. If, on the other hand, the statute which was required for the implementation of the treaty related to a matter allocated by s. 92 to the provincial Legislatures, then the provincial Legislatures would have the power to implement the treaty." 1 HOGG, *supra* note 10, § 11.5(b).

81. *Id.* at § 11.5(c).

82. *See supra* note 44 and accompanying text.

83. The province of Saskatchewan, under the leadership of Premier T.C. Douglas, adopted the first bill of rights in Canada in 1947, a year before the Universal Declaration of Human Rights. *See* Saskatchewan Bill of Rights Act, 1947, S.S. 1947, c. 35. Douglas's views were influenced, in part, by his attention to abuses in Germany and Italy in the 1930s and 1940s. *See* Ken Norman, Saskatchewan Bill of Rights, The Encyclopedia of Saskatchewan, http://esask.uregina.ca/entry/saskatchewan_bill_of_rights.html (last visited Feb. 12, 2009).

84. *See e.g.*, Roderick A. MacDonald & Jason Maclean, *Navigating the Transsystemic: No Toilets in Park*, 50 McGill L. J. 721 (2005); Roderick A. MacDonald, *Legal Bilingualism*, 42 McGill L.J. 119 (1997); Joost Blom, *Looking Ahead in Canadian Law School Education*, 33 U.B.C. L. Rev. 7 (1999).

85. See Canadian Charter of Rights and Freedoms, 1982, § 27; Schabas, *supra* note 26, at 221.

86. *Id.* at 10–14; *see supra* note 67; Hon. Claire L'Heureux-Dubé, *It Takes A Vision: The Constitutionalization of Equality in Canada*, 14 Yale J.L. & Feminism 363 (2002). On women and the Charter, see generally Alexandra Dobrowolsky, The Politics of Pragmatism: Women, Representation and Constitutionalism in Canada 44–74 (2000).

87. *See* Glenn, *supra* note 61, at 288–96; *cf.* Harding, *supra* note 36, at 414–18, 424, 439 (contrasting more "dialogic" approach in Canadian cases, a model "centered on horizontal, transnational and interdependent decision-making" with the U.S. "enforcement" model of judicial review, one "based on a preference for local, independent, and final decision-making"); Schabas, *supra* note 26, at 231 (noting that "Canadian courts may, perhaps due to their colonial origins, be more open than those of other jurisdictions to such a comparative law approach").

88. For example, after consultation (and before ratification), all ten provinces approved Canada's adoption of both the ICCPR and the ICESCR. Schabas, *supra* note 26, at 8. On the continued vitality of the *Labour Conventions* case from 1930s, see *MacDonald v. Vapor Canada Ltd.*, [1977] 2 S.C.R. 134, 167–72 (implying that *Labour Conventions* might be reconsidered, although the validity of the federal statute was rejected); Maxwell Cohen & Anne Bayefsky, *The Canadian Charter for Rights and Freedoms and Public International Law*, 61 Can. Bar. Rev. 265, 292–93 (1983). *See also* 1 Hogg, *supra* note 10, § 11.5(c) (critically examining *Labour Conventions* rule and noting that the existence of a treaty may affect how implementing legislation is characterized). *See generally* John Claydon, *The Application of International Human Rights Law by Canadian Courts*, 30 Buff. L. Rev. 727, 729–30 (1981) (noting the possibilities in Canadian law for evolution of "'judicial action toward changing international relations'" (quoting a judicial decision); *id.* at 732–33 (noting the seriousness with which Canadian lawyers and judges were taking arguments concerning international law); *cf. id.* at 750 (noting "some evidence . . . that judges of the civil law Quebec system may be doing better than their common law counterparts in handling international law issues").

89. Unlike the United States, for example, Canada ratified the ICESCR, the CEDAW, the Convention on the Rights of the Child, *see* Schabas, *supra* note 26, at 246–48, 252, 281–82, and the Rome Statute creating the International Criminal Court, *see* International Criminal Court Web site, http://www2.icc-cpi.int/Menus/ASP/states±parties (click on "C," click on "Canada"). Yet Canada may have had its own milder version of a "Bricker-esque" moment, experiencing some objections (ultimately overcome) to Canada's voting for the UDHR. *See* William A. Schabas, *Canada and the Adoption of the Universal Declaration of Human Rights*, 43 McGill L.J. 403, 420–23 (1998). According to Schabas, provincial federalism was an articulated concern and there was particular discomfort in some provinces

with the international religious freedom guarantees. *Id.* at 422, 432. *See also id.* at 418–19 (suggesting that DuPlessis, head of Quebec, opposed these rights and quoting another speaker as saying that "[t]hese . . . rights . . . exist in Christian civilizations" and not "elsewhere"); *see also* text at notes 8–9 *supra.*

90. *See, e.g., Appropriate Role of Foreign Judgments in the Interpretation of American Law: Hearing on H.R. 568 Before the Subcomm. On the Constitution of the H. Comm. On the Judiciary*, 108th Cong. 37 (2004) [hereafter *Appropriate Role of Foreign Judgments*] (Statement of Vicki C. Jackson, Professor of Law, Georgetown Law Center).

91. *See, e.g.,* Constitution Restoration Act of 2004, S. 2082, 108th Cong. § 201; American Justice for American Citizens Act, H.R. 4118, 108th Cong. § 3 (2004).

92. *See* Henkin, *supra* note 64 (discussing the "Ghost of Senator Bricker"); *see also* Vicki C. Jackson, *World Habeas Corpus*, 91 CORNELL L. REV. 303, 332–34 (2006). Resistance to understanding treaties as a form of both international and domestic law is reflected in the prohibition, in the Military Commissions Act of 2006, on reliance on the Geneva Conventions "as a source of rights," and a further prohibition on foreign or international sources of law serving as a "basis for a rule of decision" in interpreting provisions of a federal statute designed to prohibit war crimes. *See* Military Commissions Act of 2006, Pub L. No. 109-366, § 3(a)(1), 120 Stat. 2600, 2602 (2006) (codified at 10 U.S.C. § 948b(g) (2006)) ("No alien unlawful enemy combatant subject to trial by military commission under this chapter may invoke the Geneva Conventions as a source of rights."); *id.*, § 6(a)(2), 120 Stat. 2632 (codified at 18 U.S.C. § 2441 note (2006)) ("No foreign or international source of law shall supply a basis for a rule of decision in the courts of the United States in interpreting the prohibitions enumerated in [the War Crimes Act]."). Federal resistance to international norms is not necessarily shared by state or local governments, some of which, for example, have adopted resolutions in support of the CEDAW, even though the United States has not ratified it. *See* Resnik, *supra* note 26, at 1639–40; *cf.* Thomas Buergenthal, *Modern Constitutions and Human Rights Treaties*, 36 COLUM. J. TRANSNAT'L L. 211, 220–22 (1997) (arguing that the states and their courts may deem international treaties like the ICCPR directly effective).

93. 74 U.S. 700 (1869).

94. *Id.* at 725.

95. *See id.* at 720 ("Some not unimportant aid . . . in ascertaining the true sense of the Constitution, may be derived from considering what is the correct idea of a State, apart from any union or confederation with other States. . . . It describes sometimes a people or community of individuals united more or less closely in political relations, inhabiting temporarily or permanently the same country; often it denotes only the country or territorial region, inhabited by such a community; not unfrequently it is applied to the government under which the people live; at other times it represents the combined idea of people, territory, and government. . . . [I]n all these senses the primary conception is that of a people or community. . . . This is undoubtedly the fundamental idea upon which the republican institutions of our own country are established.").

96. *Id.* at 726.

97. Reference re Secession of Quebec, [1998] 2 S.C.R. 217.

98. International law treatises as early as the seventeenth century had discussed what one might conceive of as a right of secession in limited circumstances. *See* HUGO GROTIUS, DE JURE BELLIS AC PACIS LIBRI TRES [ON THE LAW OF WAR AND PEACE: THREE BOOKS] (1646), *reprinted in* 3 THE CLASSICS OF INTERNATIONAL LAW 261 (James Scott ed. & Francis W. Kelsey trans., 1995) (concluding that a part of the people may not secede from a state "unless it is evident that it cannot save itself in any other way."); EMMERICH DE VATTEL, THE LAW OF

NATIONS bk. I, §§ 263–64 (1758) (Béla Kapossy & Richard Whatmore eds. & Thomas Nugent trans., Liberty Fund 2008) (discussing power of a nation to cut off or cede some parts of its territory, saying that while nations have duty of self preservation, a nation may lawfully abandon its parts in cases of extreme necessity, and may give up a town or city to another sovereign or an enemy, and stating that the dismembered part need not accept the new sovereign if it is capable of maintaining its own liberty); *id.* bk. I, §§ 200–02 (stating that if a member part of a state is attacked, it has a duty to defend, not separate; but if it is abandoned by its sovereign, it does not have duty to remain); *see also* LEE BUCHHEIT, SECESSION: THE LEGITIMACY OF SELF-DETERMINATION 46–47 (1978) (stating that natural law theory imposes "clear qualifications" on the right of secession); ALLEN BUCHANAN, SECESSION: THE MORALITY OF POLITICAL DIVORCE FROM FORT SUMTER TO LITHUANIA AND QUEBEC 151 (1991) (concluding that there is a "moral right to secede, though a highly qualified one").

99. *Secession Reference*, [1998] 2 S.C.R. at 287. For a contrary view from within the political leadership of the Quebec separatists, see Daniel Turp, *The Recognition of Quebec's Right of Self-Determination and Its Exercise Within a Novel Body Politic*, *in* SELF-DETERMINATION: INTERNATIONAL PERSPECTIVES 277, 279–80 (Donald Clark & Robert Williamson eds., 1996) (arguing that enactment of the 1982 Constitution Act without the consent of Quebec was a breach of Quebec's rights of self-determination under international law that would support a claimed right of secession).

100. *See, e.g.*, Allen Buchanan, *Federalism Secession and the Morality of Inclusion*, 37 ARIZ. L. REV. 53, 56 (1995).

101. Being an independent state accords greater status to its leaders; there may be greater status (and financial benefits for the area) in being able to join international organizations and borrow funds as a state. The protections of human rights and a common market provided by Europe may already be contributing to devolution movements in regions in a number of countries, as the perceived costs of regional autonomy (especially in terms of economic well-being and access to markets) go down.

102. 514 U.S. 549 (1995).

103. *Id.* at 553 (quoting Gibbons v. Ogden, 22 U.S. (9 Wheat.) 1, 194–95 (1824)).

104. 529 U.S. 598, 617–18 (2000); *see Lopez*, 514 U.S. at 567–68. For a critical discussion of this focus, see Judith Resnik, *Categorical Federalism: Jurisdiction, Gender, and the Globe*, 111 YALE L.J. 619 (2001).

105. Labatt Breweries of Canada Ltd. v. Attorney General of Canada, [1980] 1 S.C.R. 914, 935 (quoting Citizens Insurance Company of Canada v. Parsons, (1881) 7 App. Cas. 96, 112); 1 HOGG, *supra* note 10, at § 20.1; *see also* Chapter 7, note 38, above.

106. 1 HOGG, *supra* note 10, at § 18.1.

107. *See* Canadian Federation of Agriculture v. Attorney-General of Quebec (*The Margarine Reference*), [1951] A.C. 179 (P.C.) (appeal taken from Can.), which Professor Hogg discusses as a leading case. 1 HOGG, *supra* note 10, § 18.2. The Privy Council affirmed the decision of the Supreme Court of Canada in *Reference re Validity of Section 5(a) of the Dairy Industry Act*, [1949] S.C.R. 1, which struck down a law criminalizing the manufacture, importation or sale of margarine. The Canadian Supreme Court had held that Parliament's power to enact criminal laws was limited to prohibitory laws with penalties that serve "a public purpose which can support it as being in relation to criminal law." *Id.* at 50. Such purposes would include, but are not limited to, "[p]ublic peace, order, security, health, [and] morality," none of which were served by the margarine ban (which was intended to protect the dairy industry). *Id.*

More recently, in R. v. Hydro-Québec, [1997] 3 S.C.R. 213, the Court divided five to four in upholding an environmental statute in which administrative regulations were enforced in part through criminal sanctions. The majority concluded that the statute's objective, protection of human health and the environment from harmful substances, was in "pith and substance" within the federal criminal law power. *See id.* at 298 (LaForest, J.). The dissent, however, distinguished between regulation and prohibition, and said the statute was "more an attempt to regulate environmental pollution than to prohibit or proscribe it. As such, [the challenged provisions] extend beyond the purview of criminal law. . . ." *Id.* at 246. The dissenters also considered the possibility that the national power over "peace, order and good government" could extend to environmental regulation, on the doctrinal theory that the provinces acting separately could not address the problem, and rejected it. *See id.* at 258–64 (Lamer, C.J., and Iacobucci, J., dissenting).

108. Reference re Firearms Act, [1998] 219 A.R. 201, 284 (Alta. Ct. App. 1998) (Fraser, C.J.).

109. *Id.* at 261. Canada was at this time a party to the CEDAW, *see* SCHABAS, *supra* note 26 at 247–48 (indicating that Canada ratified CEDAW in 1981), which thus may have been among the human rights obligations to which the opinion refers. *See also infra* note 111.

110. *Reference re Firearms Act,* [1998] 219 A.R. at 261 (noting the recommendations of the "United Nations Expert Group Meeting on Gathering Information on and Analysis of Firearm Regulation"); *id.* at 262 ("Although the Expert Group's recommendations are not binding on Canada domestically, they reflect some of the same concerns that motivated Parliament to enact the challenged laws. As such, they reinforce the public safety purpose of the laws and their connection with 'crime prevention and criminal justice'"). On "pith and substance," see Chapter 7, note 38, above, and Dale Gibson, *The Firearms Reference in the Alberta Court of Appeals,* 37 ALBERTA L. REV. 1071, 1075–77 (1999) (explaining the doctrine's role in determining the "matter" and its assignment to federal or provincial power).

111. *Id.* at 262 (citing G.A. Res 48/104, UN Doc. A/RES/48/104 (Feb. 23, 1994), 33 I.L.M. 1049). This UN Resolution repeatedly invokes CEDAW, to which Canada is a party, and states that combatting violence against women is necessary to "full implementation" of CEDAW.

112. *Reference re Firearms Act,* [1998] 219 A.R., at 262; *see id.* ("Parliament's efforts with Bill C-68 were motivated, in part, by the desire to reduce the incidence of firearms-related domestic violence. This being so, one should not ignore the international human rights context."); *see supra* notes 109, 111.

113. *See* Edwards v. Attorney General of Canada, [1930] A.C. 124, 136 (P.C.) (1929) (appeal from Canada) (The Persons Case).

114. *Cf.* R. v. Crown Zellerbach Canada Ltd., [1988] 1 S.C.R. 401, 408–09, 431–33, 436–37 (noting Canada's international obligations in upholding a federal statute regulating pollution in intraprovincial marine waters under the "national concern" branch of the "peace, order and good government" power). For Canadian cases under the 1982 Charter that refer to international or foreign law, see Chapter 3, text at and notes 114-16, above.

115. 252 U.S. 416 (1920).

116. *See, e.g.,* ICCPR art. 2(1) (state parties undertake to "respect and to ensure to all individuals. . . . the rights recognized in the present Covenant without distinction of any kind," including those based on sex); *id.* art. 3 (parties undertake to "ensure the equal right of men and women to the enjoyment of all civil and political rights" protected by the Covenant); *id.,* art. 26 ("All persons are equal before the law and are entitled without any discrimination to the equal protection of the law. In this respect, the law shall prohibit any discrimination and guarantee to all persons equal and effective protection against discrimination" on listed grounds including sex).

117. *See* Brief Amici Curiae on Behalf of International Law Scholars and Human Rights Experts in Support of Petitioners, at 4–17, United States v. Morrison, 529 U.S. 598 (2000) (Nos. 99-0005, 99-0029) (treating the Declaration on the Elimination of Violence Against Women as bearing on the interpretation of the ICCPR, in addition to the CEDAW). The amicus brief noted the ICCPR's call to "ensure the equal rights of men and women" to the civil and political rights it protected, and the ICCPR's protection of rights to life, liberty and the security of person. *See id.* (also relying on the Torture Convention). The brief also argued that the VAWA provision was supported by Congress's power under Article I, Section 8 to "define and punish . . . Offenses against the Law of Nations," and its power under the "necessary and proper" clause to give the federal courts jurisdiction to enforce customary international law, *id.* at 18–28, and further urged that Congress's Commerce Clause and Fourteenth Amendment powers should be interpreted in light of international law. *Id.* at 28–30.

118. *See* Brief of Amicus Curiae Eagle Forum Education & Legal Defense Fund in Support of Respondents, at 25–26, United States v. Morrison, 529 U.S. 598 (2000) (Nos. 99-5, 99-29); Brief of the Nat'l Ass'n of Criminal Defense Lawyers as Amicus Curiae in Support of Respondents at 4–5, 17, United States v. Morrison, 529 U.S. 598 (2000) (Nos. 99-5, 99-29). Even Senator Joseph Biden, whose amicus brief described him as the "author" of the VAWA, did not refer to treaty-implementation as a constitutional basis for legislation. *See* Brief for Senator Joseph R. Biden Jr. as Amicus Curiae in Support of Petitioners, United States v. Morrison, 529 U.S. 598 (2000) (Nos. 99-5, 99-29). On the merits, the opposing briefs did not so much take issue with the argument concerning the scope of what the ICCPR's text would support; rather, they sought to reject the premises of *Missouri v. Holland*, 252 U.S. 416 (1920) and extend *Reid v. Covert*, 354 U.S. 1 (1957), to limit the effects of treaties on federal powers under the Constitution. *See* Brief of Amicus Curiae Eagle Forum Education & Legal Defense Fund, *supra*, at 26–28 (arguing that the treaty power cannot expand federal authority over wholly domestic relations and distinguishing *Holland* as involving a subject matter only transitorily in a state); Brief of the Nat'l Ass'n of Criminal Defense Lawyers as Amicus Curiae, *supra*, at 4–5, 18–19 (relying on *Reid v. Covert* for the proposition that "the Constitution takes precedence over" international law and treaties). One brief also relied on the non-self-execution declaration and a proviso that "[n]othing in this covenant requires or authorizes legislation . . . by the United States of America prohibited by the Constitution," to argue that the ICCPR was without legal effect on this issue, and disputed other arguments from international law that had been made in support of the VAWA. *See id.* at 24–25 & n.11.

119. *See, e.g.*, Fla. Prepaid Postsecondary Educ. Exp. Bd. v. College Savings Bank, 527 U.S. 627, 642 n.7 (1999). On "reasonably conceivable" facts and rational basis review, see, for example, FCC v. Beach Communications, Inc., 508 U.S. 307, 313 (1993).

120. The U.S. Court in 1966 implied that a civil rights statute might have been upheld as an implementation of the international obligations of the United States if it were not otherwise within an enumerated federal power. *See* Katzenbach v. Morgan, 384 U.S. 641, 646 n.5 (1966) (stating that since a challenged provision of the Voting Rights Act was upheld under the Fourteenth Amendment, it was unnecessary to consider whether it could be upheld as implementing U.S. obligations under the Treaty of Paris, 1898 or the UN Charter). For a further argument that there was a treaty basis for enactment of the contested part of VAWA, see Catherine A. MacKinnon, *Disputing Male Sovereignty: On United States v. Morrison*, 114 HARV. L. REV. 135, 167–68 (2000) (noting that the United States reported VAWA to the UNHRC in its initial report under the ICCPR).

For an Australian example of reliance on a treaty to authorize federal gender equality legislation, see Aldridge v. Booth (1988) 80 A.L.R. 1, 12 (Fed'l Ct., Austl.) (upholding Australian Sex Discrimination Act of 1984's prohibition of sexual harassment as an implementation of CEDAW and thus within the federal government's "external affairs" power under Section 51 (xxix) of the Australian Constitution). (Section 3 of the Australian federal Sex Discrimination Act of 1984 specifically referred to giving effect to provisions of the CEDAW as one of its purposes. *See* Ferneley v. Boxing Authority of New South Wales (2001) 115 F.C.R. 306, 311 (Fed'l Ct., Austl.). Interestingly, *Aldridge* referred to a leading U.S. case, *Barnes v. Costle*, 561 F. 2d 983 (D.C. Cir. 1977), as well as Scottish and Canadian case law, on the question whether sex harassment should be treated as a form of sex discrimination.

121. *See* S. Exec. Rep. No. 102–23, at 4 (1992).

122. Senate Resolution, *supra* note 42, at 8070–71; *see* S. Exec. Rept. No. 102-23, at 18 (describing the "federalism" understanding as designed "to emphasize domestically that there is no intent to alter the constitutional balance of authority between the State and Federal governments"). *Cf.* Initial Report of the United States of America to the UN Human Rights Comm., CCPR/C/SR/1401 (April 17, 1995), ¶11 (U.S. representative stating that because of extensive protections in U.S. law, no special implementing legislation was being sought); *but cf. id.* at ¶29 (reporting the enactment of VAWA).

123. *Compare, e.g.*, Gerald L. Neuman, *The Global Dimension of RFRA*, 14 Const. Commentary 33, 52 (1997) (suggesting that the federalism understanding of ICCPR does not as a legal matter limit Congress's power to enact implementing legislation); M. Cherif Bassiouni, *Reflections on the Ratification of the International Covenant on Civil and Political Rights by the United States Senate*, 42 DePaul L Rev. 1169, 1180–81 (1993) (suggesting that a proviso that the "treaty at issue does not impose any duty on the United States to enact implementing legislation that may be contrary to the Constitution as interpreted by domestic law and judicial interpretations" violates the good faith obligations of treaty parties); and Louis Henkin, *U.S. Ratification of Human Rights Conventions*, 89 Am. J. Int'l L. 341, 347–48 (1995) (critically discussing reservations and non-self-executing declarations) *with, e.g.*, Curtis A. Bradley & Jack L. Goldsmith, *Treaties, Human Rights, and Conditional Consent*, 149 U. Pa. L. Rev. 399, 455–56 (2000) (defending the legality under international and constitutional law of U.S. practices of reservations, understandings and declarations in agreeing to human rights treaties, specifically including "federalism" understandings); Brad R. Roth, *Understanding the "Understanding": Federalism Constraints on Human Rights Implementation*, 47 Wayne L. Rev. 891, 901–10 (2001) (disagreeing with Neuman's analysis). For a different view of the federalism understanding of the ICCPR, see Carlos Manuel Vázquez, *Breard, Printz, and the Treaty Power*, 70 U. Colo. L. Rev. 1317, 1354–57 (1999) (suggesting that the "intended purpose of [the federalism] understanding is a matter of some uncertainty," and may require the federal government to require the states to act). On the non-self-executing declaration, see *supra* note 42. For helpful discussion of the effects of "understandings" on analysis of constitutional issues, see Sarah H. Cleveland, *Our International Constitution*, 31 Yale J. Int'l L. 1, 118–20 (2006).

124. At the end of 2003 there were 3,351 state prisoners on death row and twenty-three federal prisoners on death row in the United States. *See* Bureau of Justice Statistics, U.S. Dep't of Justice, Bulletin, Capital Punishment, 2003 at 1, 5 tbl. 4 (Nov. 2004) *available at* http://www.ojp.usdoj.gov/bjs/pub/pdf/cp03.pdf (last visited Feb. 7, 2009). According to this BJS Bulletin, thirty-eight states and the federal government authorized the death penalty at year end of 2003. *Id.* at 2. In 2003, there were sixty-five executions carried out, only one of which was a federal prisoner. In 2004, fifty-nine persons were executed in the United States, and in 2008, the number had dropped to thirty-seven. Bureau of Justice

STATISTICS, U.S. DEP'T OF JUSTICE, KEY CRIME & JUSTICE FACTS AT A GLANCE (executions), *available at* http://www.ojp.usdoj.gov/bjs/glance/tables/exetab.htm (last visited Feb. 15, 2009).

125. *See* Amnesty International, The Death Penalty in Canada: Twenty Tears of Abolition (2000), http://www.amnesty.ca/deathpenalty/canada.php (describing legislative abolition of death penalty for all but military offenses in 1976). Although public opinion polls in Canada showed support for the death penalty, an effort to reintroduce the death penalty failed in the Canadian House of Commons in 1987. *See* Jeffrey L Kirchmeier, *Another Place Beyond Here: The Death Penalty Moratorium Movement in the United States,* 73 U. COLO. L. REV. 1, 84 & n.452 (2002); Sharon A. Williams, *Extradition and the Death Penalty Exception in Canada: Resolving the Ng and Kindler Cases,* 13 LOY. L.A. INT'L. & COMP. L. REV. 799, 829 (1991); *see also* Paul C. Weiler, *Rights and Judges in a Democracy: A New Canadian Version,* 18 U. MICH. J. L. REFORM 51, 53 n.6 (1984) (indicating that the Canadian Supreme Court in the 1970s rejected a challenge to the death penalty as cruel and unusual under a statutory bill of rights, but the legislature abolished anyway).

126. *See, e.g.,* Atkins v. Virginia, 536 U.S. 304, 316 n.21 (2002) (long footnote including a one-sentence reference to the "world community" disapproving of executing mentally retarded offenders).

127. Stanford v. Kentucky, 492 U.S. 361, 369 n.1 (1989); *see also* Thompson v. Oklahoma, 487 U.S. 815, 868–69, n.4 (1988) (Scalia, J., dissenting).

128. *Atkins,* 536 U.S. at 322–35 (Rehnquist, C.J., dissenting).

129. *See* Knight v. Florida, 528 U.S. 990, 991–93 (1999) (Thomas, J., responding to Justice Breyer's dissent from denial of certiorari) (arguing that Breyer's reference to foreign law condemning long delays in carrying out death penalties only illustrates that the claim is without validity under the U.S. Constitution).

130. *See* Kennedy v. Louisiana, 128 S. Ct. 2641 (2008); Brief for Leading British Law Associations, Scholars, Queen's Counsel and Former Law Lords as Amici Curiae Supporting Petitioner, Kennedy v. Louisiana, 128 S. Ct. 2641 (2008) (No. 07-343) (discussing British and international law and arguing that as a party to the ICCPR, the United States is obligated to limit use of the death penalty to the most serious crimes).

131. *See* United States v. Burns, [2001] 1 S.C.R. 283 (Can.).

132. Coleman v. Thompson, 501 U.S. 722, 726 (1991). This statement in *Coleman v. Thompson* went more to concerns of judicial federalism and respect for state court procedural default rules, but one hears in it an echo of concerns expressed in other opinions for the weight of democratic opinion on the issue and its relationship to what can be regarded as "cruel and unusual."

133. Although the provinces have some authority to provide for punishments through prison terms for violations of statutes within provincial powers, they lack authority to provide for capital punishment. *See* Constitution Act, 1867 § 92(15) (authorizing provinces to impose "punishment by fine, penalty or imprisonment" for the purpose of enforcing otherwise valid provincial laws); 1 HOGG, *supra* note 10, § 18.13 n.180 (explaining that the language of Section 92(15) "excludes some kinds of sanctions, for example, capital punishment" and citing Laskin, Canadian Constitutional Law 851 (5th ed. 1986)).

134. Public opinion polls in Canada in 1987 (when a motion to reenact a death penalty was narrowly defeated in the Canadian House of Commons), and in 1995, indicated substantial majority support for the death penalty; a survey in 1998, following a controversy over the death sentence in Texas of a Canadian citizen, showed the public about evenly divided or only slightly favoring the death penalty. *See* Amnesty International Canada, *The Death Penalty in Canada: Twenty Years of Abolition* (last updated April 2000), *available at* http://www.amnesty.ca/deathpenalty/canada.php (visited Nov. 2, 2008). Were provincial

legislatures free to enact criminal statutes with the death penalty, it is possible that some would have provided for it.

135. Everson v. Bd. of Education, 330 U.S. 1 (1947) ("Neither [a state nor the federal government] can pass laws which aid one religion, aid all religions, or prefer one religion over another."). All agree that the Establishment Clause forbids government preferences among religions, though some argue it does not require government neutrality with respect to "religion over irreligion." Rosenberger v. Rectors & Visitors of the Univ. of Virginia, 515 U.S. 819, 855 (1995) (Thomas, J., concurring).

136. Adarand Constructors, Inc. v. Pena, 515 U.S. 200 (1995).

137. *See, e.g.* Nguyen v. INS, 533 U.S. 53, 70 (2001); United States v. Virginia, 518 U.S. 515, 532–33 (1996); Miss. Univ. for Women v. Hogan, 458 U.S. 718 (1982).

138. *See, e.g.*, Parents Involved in Cmty. Sch. v. Seattle Sch. Dist. No. 1, 551 U.S. 701, (2007) (invalidating use of students' race to balance and integrate public schools); Gratz v. Bollinger, 539 U.S. 244, 270 (2003) (invalidating use of race in undergraduate admissions through point system); *Adarand Constructors*, 515 U.S. at 227 (subjecting federal minority contracting provisions to strict scrutiny); City of Richmond v. J. A. Croson Co., 488 U.S. 469, 505–06 (1988) (invalidating City of Richmond's affirmative action program for minority contracting). In *Adarand Constructors*, 515 U.S. at 227, the Court held that all racial classifications, whether imposed by federal, state, or local entities, are subject to strict scrutiny analysis, and overruled *Metro Broadcasting, Inc. v. FCC*, 497 U.S. 547 (1990).

139. *See* United States v. Morrison, 529 U.S. 598, 617 (2000) (holding that Congress exceeded its authority under the Commerce Clause and under the Fourteenth Amendment by enacting a law that provided for a civil remedy for violent crimes against women); *cf.* City of Boerne v. Flores, 521 U.S. 507, 536 (1997) (holding that Congress exceeded its enforcement power under Section 5 of the Fourteenth Amendment in the Religious Freedom Restoration Act's provisions applicable to the states).

140. Adler v. Ontario, [1996] 3 S.C.R. 609, 643; *see* page 229, above.

141. *See* Waldman v. Canada, UN Human Rights Comm. (Views), 67th Sess., UN Doc. CCPR/C/67/D/694/1996, paras. 2.8, 6.3, 8.3, 8.4, 11–13 (1999). For discussion of *Waldman* and *Adler*, contrasting the central concerns of constitutional as compared to international human rights analyses, see Chapter 6, above, note 95.

142. *See* Chris Eisgruber & Mariah Zeisberg, *Religious Freedom in Canada and the United States*, 4 Int'l J. Const. L. 244, 256–58 (2006) (reporting on legislation enacted in 2001); but *cf.* Emily Wexler, *Privatization of Public Education: An Examination of U.S. and Canadian Policy and Trends Utilizing Vouchers that Indirectly Aid Sectarian Schools*, 12 New Eng. J. Int'l & Comp. L. 327, 360–61 (2006) (reporting that the tax credit was repealed in 2003). *See also Waldman v. Canada*, UN Hum. Rts. Comm., at Appendix paras. 1–5 (Individual Opinion by Martin Scheinin, concurring) (suggesting that there were a variety of ways in which the discrimination found there could be redressed).

143. Canadian Charter of Rights and Freedoms, 1982, § 15 (1) (equality and antidiscrimination guarantee); *id.* § 15 (2) ("Subsection (1) does not preclude any law, program or activity that has as its object the amelioration of conditions of disadvantaged individuals or groups including those that are disadvantaged because of race, national or ethnic origin, colour, religion, sex, age or mental or physical disability").

144. [2000] 1 S.C.R. 950.

145. *Lovelace*, [2000] 1 S.C.R. at 1009–10; *see also id.* at 986–88 (discussing and mostly applying the contextual approach to ameliorative purpose of Law v. Canada, [1999] 1 S.C.R. 497).

146. *See Lovelace*, [2000] 1 S.C.R. at 983–87, 998–1001. For a very recent decision treating Section 15(2) as having a more independent role, see R. v. Kapp, 2008 Can. Sup. Ct. LEXIS 50, ¶¶ 37–40 (June 27, 2008) (McLachlin, C.J. and Abella, J.) (indicating that "if the government establishes that the program falls under s. 15(2)," a Section 15(1) discrimination claim must fail).

147. *See Lovelace,* [2000] 1 S.C.R., at 991 (citing United Nations Committee on Economic, Social and Cultural Rights, Concluding Observations of the Committee on Economic, Social and Cultural Rights (Canada), E/C. 12/1/Add. 31, Dec. 4, 1998.). Canada, unlike the United States, is a party to the ICESCR, having ratified it in 1976.

148. *See* Parents Involved in Cmty. Schs. v. Seattle Sch. Dist. No. 1, 551 U.S. 701 (2007); Gratz v. Bollinger, 539 U.S. 244 (2003).

149. *See* Grutter v. Bollinger, 539 U.S. 306, 344–46 (2003) (Ginsburg, J., concurring) (noting support from two specified international covenants for an "end point" for affirmative measures but suggesting that the Court's proposed twenty-five-year period was a "hope," not a "forecast"); *see, e.g., Appropriate Role of Foreign Judgments, supra* note 90, at 2 (statement of Rep. Chabot, Subcommittee Chair) (criticizing Ginsburg's references and quoting commentator Stuart Taylor's strong critique in the *National Journal*). Justice Ginsburg reported that in 2005 she and Justice O'Connor received death threats because of their references to foreign and international law. *See* Ruth Bader Ginsburg, Associate Justice, Supreme Court of the United States, "A decent Respect to the Opinions of [Human]kind": The Value of a Comparative Perspective in Constitutional Adjudication, Address to the Constitutional Court of South Africa (Feb. 7, 2006), *available at* http://www.supremecourtus.gov/publicinfo/speeches/sp_02-07b-06.html (also describing proposed bills in Congress that would prohibit courts from referring to contemporary foreign or international law in constitutional interpretation, and noting a resolution to similar effect that as of late 2005, had eighty-three sponsors); *see also, e.g.*, Mark Rahdert, *Comparative Constitutional Advocacy*, 56 Am. U.L. Rev. 553, 574 n.110 (2007); Resnik, *supra* note 26, at 1569.

150. *See* Supreme Court Act (R.S.C. 1985, c. S-26) § 6 (Can.); Adler v. Ontario, [1996] 3 S.C.R. 609 and text at notes 8–9, 140–42, *supra.*

151. *See supra* note 51 (describing how the representation of provinces in the Canadian Senate is not "equal" and how equality is achieved on more of a regional basis). Some provinces, moreover, are declared to have unicameral, and some bicameral, legislative bodies. Constitution Act, 1867, §§ 69 (Ontario, unicameral), 71 (Quebec, bicameral). In contrast, the U.S. Constitution contains explicit guarantees of equality of suffrage for the states in the United States Senate, a provision that is essentially unamendable. U.S. Const. Art. V. The U.S. Constitution also includes provisions explicitly prohibiting favoritism, for example, of one state's ports over others. U.S. Const. art. I, § 9. No distinctions are made as among the states in the nature of their internal organization in the U.S. Constitution.

152. When and how territories were admitted as states may, however, have depended in part on concerns about their ethnic or racial composition. *See* Eric Biber, *The Price of Admission: Causes, Effects, and Patterns of Conditions Imposed on States Entering the Union,* 46 Am. J. Legal Hist. 119, 171–72 (2004) (discussing Hawaii); *see also* Christina Duffy Burnett, *"They say I am not an American . . .": The Noncitizen National and the Law of American Empire,* 48 Va. J. Int'l L. 659, 675–76 (2008) (noting expressions of concern about race in evaluating whether territories acquired from Spain and Mexico could become states); Christina Duffy Burnett, *Untied States: American Expansion and Territorial Deannexation,* 72 U. Chi. L. Rev. 797, 812, 879 (2005) (noting evidence of the significance of race in discourses and decisions relating to distinctions between territories and states);

cf. Gary Lawson & Guy Seidman, The Constitution of Empire 108–10 (2004) (discussing racial and ethnic concerns about Hawaii's status as a territory).

153. *See* Chapter 7 above (discussing *Heart of Atlanta Motel v. United States,* 379 U.S. 241 (1964) and *Katzenbach v. McClung,* 379 U.S. 294 (1964)).

154. Charles L. Black, Jr., Structure and Relationship in Constitutional Law (1969).

155. *See, e.g.,* Ex parte Virginia, 100 U.S. 339, 358–59 (1879) (Field, J., dissenting) (predicting the demise of the federal system from the majority's decision to uphold the constitutionality of a federal criminal statute applied to convict a state court judge of failing to call any but white persons to serve as jurors and arguing that "nothing . . . could have a greater tendency to destroy the independence and autonomy of the States" than to uphold Congress's "exercise [of] coercive authority over judicial officers of the States in the discharge of their duties under State laws," a doctrine that would lead toward consolidation of a "similar coercive authority over governors and legislators of the States"); Champion v. Ames (The Lottery Cases), 188 U.S. 321, 371 (1903) (Fuller, C.J., dissenting) (arguing that the majority decision upholding a federal statute regulating interstate commerce in lottery tickets would mean that "[a]n invitation to dine, or to take a drive, or a note of introduction, all become articles of commerce under the ruling in this case. . . . It is a long step in the direction of wiping out all traces of state lines . . . "); Garcia v. San Antonio Metropolitan Transit Agency, 469 U.S. 528, 567 n.12 (1985) (Powell, J., dissenting) (accusing the Court of abdicating its responsibility to enforce federalism limits on Congress). (Much of this and the next paragraph is drawn from Jackson, *Narratives of Federalism, supra* note 10, 275–77.)

156. *See, e.g.,* Paul Bernd Spahn & Wolfgang Föttinger, *Germany, in* Fiscal Federalism in Theory and Practice 228–30 (Teresa Ter-Minassian ed., 1997) (describing the circumscribed authority of Länder governments in Germany over taxation); *see also* Clifford Larsen, *States Federal, Financial, Sovereign and Social. A Critical Inquiry into an Alternative to American Financial Federalism,* 47 Am. J. Comp. L. 429, 438 (1999) (describing German constitutional requirements for transfers of tax revenues to poorer regions from richer ones).

157. Rubin & Feeley, *supra* note 18, at 907–09.

158. *See* Vicki C. Jackson & Mark Tushnet, Comparative Constitutional Law 526 (2d ed. 2006); Donald P. Kommers, The Constituitional Jurisprudence of the Federal Republic of Germany 31 (2d ed. 1997); Halberstam, *Of Power and Responsibility, supra* note 12, at 750–54 (describing central government's emergency takeover of power in Prussia, Prussia's legal challenge to that effort in the Staatsgerichtshof, the subsequent rise to full power of the Nazis and their elimination of federalism); *see also* Arnold Brecht, Federalism and Regionalism in Germany: The Division of Prussia 117–23 (1945); *cf., e.g.,* Gordon M. Hahn, *Putin's "Federal Revolution:" The Administrative and Judicial Reform of Russian Federalism,* 10 E. Eur. Const. Rev. 60, 64 (2001) (describing Russian President Putin's procuring enactment of a law authorizing removal from office of a governor of a republic who fails within six moths to address constitutional violations). In the United States, a vibrant federal system is now grappling with the constitutional status of state and local involvement in immigration law and policy, with some local governments resisting federal immigration policies or requests to aid in their execution, and other state and local governments enthusiastically applying or extending federal policies or pursuing their own. For a flavor of the debate, see Cristina M. Rodriguez, *The Significance of the Local in Immigration Regulation,* 106 Mich. L. Rev. 567 (2008); Clare Huntington, *The Constitutional Dimension of Immigration Federalism,* 61 Vand. L. Rev. 787 (2008); Peter H. Schuck, *Taking Immigration Federalism Seriously,* 2007 U. Chi. Legal F. 57; Orde F. Kittrie, *Federalism,*

Deportation, and Crime Victims Afraid to Call the Police, 91 IOWA L. REV. 1449 (2006); Michael J. Wishnie, *State and Local Police Enforcement of Immigration Laws,* 6 U. PA. J. CONST. L. 1084 (2004); Hiroshi Motomura, *Federalism, International Human Rights, and Immigration Exceptionalism,* 70 U. COLO. L. REV. 1361 (1999); Peter J. Spiro, *Learning to Live with Immigration Federalism,* 29 CONN. L. REV. 1627 (1997).

159. In the United States, the smallest seventeen states (whose thirty-four votes in the Senate can block passage of a proposed amendment) represent 7.4 percent of the total U.S. population, while the smallest thirteen states (just over one-fourth of the states, three-fourths of which must approve an amendment) contain only 4.4 percent of the total population, and their failure to ratify can also block amendment. *See* U.S. CENSUS BUREAU, ANNUAL ESTIMATES OF THE POPULATION OF THE UNITED STATES, REGINS, STATES AND PUERTO RICO: April 1, 2000 TO JULY 1, 2007 (NST-EST2007-01) (2007), *available at* http://www.census.gov/popest/states/tables/NST-EST2007-01.xls (last visited Oct. 14, 2008).

The German Basic Law can be amended by a law passed by two-thirds of the Members of the Bundestag (the popularly elected house) and two-thirds of the votes of the Bundesrat (which represents the Länder governments). GRUNDGESETZ (GG) [Basic Law] art. 79 (F.R.G.). The votes of the Länder in the Bundesrat are not determined on the basis of equality that prevails in the United States Senate, but bear some, though not exact, relation to the population size of the Land. *See* GRUNDGESETZ (GG) [Basic Law] art. 51 (F.R.G.) (each Land has at least three votes; Länder with population over two million get four; over six million get five; and with over seven million get six). Altogether there are sixty-nine votes in the Bundesrat. Bundesrat Distribution of Votes, *available at* http://www.bundesrat.de/cln_099/nn_10946/EN/organisation-en/stimmenverteilung-en/stimmenverteilung-en-node.html?__nnn=true (last visited Oct. 26, 2008). Together the seven smallest Länder have twenty-four votes in the Bundesrat, *id.*, which is the amount needed to block an amendment, *see* GRUNDGESETZ (GG) [Basic Law] art. 79 (F.R.G.). These seven Länder include 15.0 percent of the German population, *Bundesrat Distribution of Votes, supra,* more than two and three times the percentage of the population in the United States that can block amendments (in the Senate and in the state legislatures, respectively).

Under Canada's Constitution Act, 1982, different procedures for amendment apply to different kinds of changes; with respect to some changes particularly affecting the provinces, the consent of an affected province is required. *Compare* CONSTITUTION ACT, 1982, pt. V, § 43 (Can.) (stating that no amendment that applies to less than all provinces, including alteration of their boundaries or use of English or French languages, can be made without authorization of the legislature of each affected province), *with* U.S. CONST. art. IV, § 3 (formation of a new state from parts of or through joinder of existing states requires the consent of the affected states' legislatures), and *id.* Art. V ("No state, without its consent, shall be deprived of its equal Suffrage in the Senate."). The default rule in Canada is that amendments require a resolution in the national parliament, approved by at least two-thirds of the provinces with at least one-half the population, CONSTITUTION ACT, 1982, pt. V, § 38(1) (Can.); 1 HOGG, *supra* note 10, § 4.3(a). *Compare* U.S. CONST. art. V (requiring the approval of three-fourths of the states). For an analysis of the disproportionalities in Congress resulting from the allocation of equal voting power to each state in the Senate, and of the difficulties of using the constitutional amendment process to redress the problem, see generally Lynn Baker, *Federalism: The Argument from Article V,* 13 GA. ST. U. L. REV. 923 (1997); Lynn Baker & Samuel H. Dinkin, *The Senate: An Institution Whose Time Has Gone?,* 13 J.L. & POL. 21 (1997).

160. *See* Peter H. Schuck, *Citizenship in Federal Systems,* 48 AM. J. COMP. L. 195, 211 (2000) (describing four different ways in which federations originate).

161. *See, e.g.*, Lynn A. Baker & Ernest A. Young, *Federalism and the Double Standard of Judicial Review*, 51 DUKE L. J. 75, 153–54 (2001).

CHAPTER 9. CONSTITUTIONS AS MEDIATING INSTITUTIONS, TRANSNATIONAL CONSTITUTIONAL VALUES, AND ENGAGEMENT IN TWENTY-FIRST CENTURY CONSTITUTIONAL INTERPRETATION

1. Examples of such conflicts that have or may come before the courts include the application of constitutional norms prohibiting, permitting, or requiring the suppression of hate speech, *see, e.g.*, Yahoo v. La Ligue Contre Le Racisme et L'Antisemitisme, 433 F.3d 1199 (9th Cir. 2006) (en banc), or permitting or prohibiting the award of damages for defamation. *See, e.g.*, Ehrenfeld v. Mahfouz, 9 N.Y. 3d 501, 881 N.E. 2d 830 (2007); Ehrenfeld v. Mahfouz, 518 F. 3d 102 (2d Cir. 2008); Bachchan v. India Abroad Publications, Inc., 585 N.Y.S.2d 661 (N.Y. App. Div. 1992); *see also, e.g.*, the proposed Free Speech Protection Act of 2009, S. 449, 111 Cong. §3 (2009) (proposing to give U.S. "persons" who are defendants in libel actions brought in foreign countries a right to sue in the United States to bar enforcement of foreign judgments and obtain other injunctive relief where the First Amendment would prevent an award of damages in the United States and to obtain damages for losses or harm caused by the foreign litigation); N.Y.C.P.L.R. § 5304(b)(8) (as amended 2008) (stating that a foreign defamation judgment need not be recognized as valid in New York unless "the defamation law applied in the foreign court's adjudication provided at least as much protection for freedom of speech and press in that case as would be provided by both the United States and New York constitutions").

2. CHARLES L. BLACK, JR., THE PEOPLE AND THE COURT (1960). I thank Henry Monaghan for a helpful conversation on this point.

3. *See, e.g.*, Ronen Shamir, *"Landmark Cases" and the Reproduction of Legitimacy: The Case of Israel's High Court of Justice*, 24 LAW & SOC'Y REV. 781 (1990).

4. *See* Edward T. Swaine, *Negotiating Federalism: State Bargaining and the Dormant Treaty Power*, 49 DUKE L.J. 1127, 1198–1201 (2000); *see also* JACK N. RAKOVE, ORIGINAL MEANINGS 26–28 (1996).

5. *See* SEAN D. MURPHY, PRINCIPLES OF INTERNATIONAL LAW 33 (2006) (explaining that on the "declaratory" theory of state recognition in international law, once a state has met the conditions for statehood, it "is *ipso facto* a state," while on the "constitutive" theory a new state is only constituted when "other states decide that such conditions have been met"). Professor Murphy observes that "[w]hile the declaratory theory is probably more widely subscribed to, in reality a new entity can only achieve many of the benefits of statehood (e.g., access to international organizations) when other states agree to accord it such benefits." *Id. See also* J.L. BRIERLY, THE LAW OF NATIONS 138–39 (6th ed. 1963); JAMES CRAWFORD, THE CREATION OF STATES IN INTERNATIONAL LAW 16–25 (1979).

6. Duncan Kelly, *Revisiting the Rights of Man: Georg Jellinek on Rights and the State*, 22 LAW & HIST. REV. 493, 525 (2004), *quoting in part*, David Armitage, *The Declaration of Independence and International Law*, 59 WM. & MARY Q. 39 (2002). Some scholars have downplayed the significance of the Declaration for current debates over the role of transnational law in constitutional interpretation, arguing that "the declaration was written to shape the opinions of mankind; it did not contemplate being influenced by them." Eugene Kontorovich, *Disrespecting the Opinions of Mankind: International Law in Constitutional Interpretation*, 8 GREEN BAG 2d 261, 265 (2005). Influence, however, is a two-way street, especially for relatively weak and newly forming states, as the quite incipient national state of the United States was at this time. The Declaration itself showed the intellectual

influences of transnational thought (most notably by John Locke, but others, including Jean Jacques Rousseau) and appealed to it. Had foreign nations—including France—reacted negatively and refused to extend assistance, those who signed the Declaration and fought with them might well have been influenced in how they framed their claims in order to gain foreign support.

7. *Cf.* EMMERICH DE VATTEL, THE LAW OF NATIONS (Joseph Chitty ed., 1883) (orig. 1758) §§ 4, 26, 27 (defining a state's constitution as that "fundamental regulation that determines the manner in which the public authority is to be executed" and describing as a sovereign state a nation that "govern[s] itself by its own authority and laws"); BARRY E. CARTER ET AL, INTERNATIONAL LAW 453–54 (5th ed. 2007) (quoting P.K. Menon's discussion of the role of "popular support," in the sense of "apparent acquiescence" to the government, in the law of recognition).

8. *See, e.g.*, CONSTITUCIÓN (Spain) pmbl. (referring to the "sovereignty" of Spain).

9. RESTATEMENT (THIRD) OF FOREIGN RELATIONS LAW OF THE UNITED STATES § 201 cmt. e. (1987).

10. This does not mean that a constitution itself necessarily incorporates international law, but that it provides for which levels of governments, and by what procedures, the country makes or implements international obligations.

11. *See* Convention on Rights and Duties of States (Montevideo Convention), Dec. 26, 1933, 165 L.N.T.S. 19, 25 (art. 1) (1933); RESTATEMENT (THIRD) OF FOREIGN RELATIONS LAW, *supra* note 9, § 201; *id.* cmt. e.

12. *See, e.g.*, U.S. CONST. art. I, § 8 (limits on circumstances in which state militias may be called into federal service), § 10 (no state to maintain ships of war in peace time without consent of Congress); FED'L CONST.OF THE SWISS CONFED'N, 18 April 1999, arts. 58(3), 60 (as amended effective 2008), *English translation available at* http://www.admin.ch/ch/e/rs/101/index.html (providing that deployment of the army is for the Confederation and reflecting amendments repealing earlier provisions authorizing cantonal forces and appointment of officers (for earlier versions, see 17 CONSTITUTIONS OF THE COUNTRIES OF THE WORLD: SWITZERLAND 179–80 (Gisbert H. Flanz ed., 1999)); GRUNDGESETZ (GG) [Basic Law] arts. 35.2, 35.3, 87a(2) (F.R.G.) (prohibiting the federal Armed Forces from activities other than defense, except as specifically authorized by law; authorizing federal forces to provide assistance to *Land* police if aid is requested in event of a natural disaster or accident; and authorizing the deployment of federal forces without request to assist the *Land* police in responding to disasters or accidents that affect more than one *Länder*). The German Constitutional Court relied in part on these provisions of the Basic Law in 2006 to hold unconstitutional the Aviation Security Act provisions authorizing federal forces to shoot down hijacked passenger aircraft. *See, e.g.*, Judgment of the First Senate of 15 February 2006, BVerfG, 1 BvR 357/05 vom 15.2.2006, Absatz-Nr. (1–154), ¶¶ 90, 103 (concluding that the Aviation Act "cannot be reconciled with the . . . constitutional law relating to the armed forces" because the authorization in art. 35.2 to assist a *Land* "does not permit an operational mission of the armed forces with specifically military weapons" of the type called for in shooting down aircraft), *English translation available* through the German Constitutional Court Website, at http://www.bverfg.de/entscheidungen/rs20060215_1bvr035705en.html.

13. *See, e.g.*, U.S. CONST. pmbl. ("We the People"); 1958 CONST., pmbl. (Fr.) ("The French people solemnly proclaim . . . the principle of national sovereignty . . ."); CONST. ETHIOPIA, pmbl.(1994) ("We the Nations, Nationalities and Peoples of Ethiopia . . ."), *available at* http://www.ethiopar.net (last visited Feb. 18, 2009); *id.* art. 2 (defining the territory of Ethiopia). *See also* Chapter 1, text at notes 6–8, above.

14. *See* Vienna Convention on the Law of Treaties, art. 46, May 23, 1969, 1155 U.N.T.S. 331 (permitting a state to invoke a "manifest" violation of its own "internal law of fundamental importance" to vitiate apparent ratification of a treaty by a member of its government); Stephen J. Schnably, *Emerging International Law Constraints on Constitutional Structure and Revision: A Preliminary Appraisal*, 62 U. MIAMI L. REV. 417, 433–36 (2008).

15. There are debates over whether, assuming a state is recognized to exist, particular governments of the state also should be "recognized," and whether, in deciding on recognition, other countries ought to consider only if the government in question exercises effective control, or ought also to consider such criteria as whether the government violates international "standards of self-determination, human rights or nonaggression." LORI DAMROSCH ET AL., INTERNATIONAL LAW: CASES AND MATERIALS 297–99 (4th ed. 2001); *see also* RESTATEMENT (THIRD) OF FOREIGN RELATIONS LAW, *supra* note 9, at § 203(2) ("A state has an obligation not to recognize . . . a regime as the government of another state if its control has been effected by the threat or use of armed force in violation of the United Nations Charter."); *id.*, Reporters' Notes 1 (noting that U.S. "policy has varied as to whether recognition should be withheld from a regime that has obtained power" unconstitutionally); DAMROSCH, ET AL, *supra*, at 298 (noting a new British policy that it would no longer "recognize" governments but would "decide the nature of our dealings with regimes which come to power unconstitutionally in light of our assessment of whether they are able" to exercise effective control over the territory of the state concerned). The point here is that the unconstitutionality, within domestic law, of a change in government may at least raise a question of recognition, even if it is by no means determinative. *See id.* at 298–99; *see also* STEFAN TALMON, RECOGNITION OF GOVERNMENTS IN INTERNATIONAL LAW WITH PARTICULAR REFERENCE TO GOVERNMENTS IN EXILE 10–14 (1999); M.J. Peterson, *Recognition of Governments Should Not Be Abolished*, 77 AM. J. INT'L L. 31 (1983); *cf.* Robert D. Sloane, *The Changing Face of Recognition in International Law: A Case Study of Tibet*, 16 EMORY INT'L L. REV. 107, 123 (2002) (discussing tacit approaches to recognition, notwithstanding the "Estrada" doctrine that excludes inquiry into internal affairs for purposes of recognition of governments).

16. *See* MURPHY, *supra* note 5, at 37 (noting that "[t]he reaction to . . . military coups . . . has not been uniform"). Thus, when General Musharraf overthrew the elected government of Prime Minister Sharif in Pakistan in 1999, the United States called for a return to civilian rule but without calling for outside military action to restore the prior government. *See* "World, South Asia, Clinton Urges Return to Civilian Rule", BBC News, Oct. 14, 1999, http://news.bbc.co.uk/2/hi/south_asia/473507.stm (quoting State Department spokesperson James Rubin as stating that "[t]he spirit and the letter of the [Pakistan] constitution should be respected"). A number of other countries also condemned the action as unconstitutional, and at least one, Nigeria, reportedly broke off relations. *Id.* By contrast, after elected President Aristide of Haiti was overthrown by military coup in 1991, a UN Security Council Resolution three years later authorized military intervention by a multinational force to restore the elected government to power. S.C. Res. 940, UN Doc. S/RES/940 (July 31, 1994).

17. *See* MURPHY, *supra* note 5, at 37.

18. 31 I.L.M. 1486 (1992); *see* MURPHY, *supra* note 5, at 34.

19. MURPHY, *supra* note 5, at 34.

20. *See* DAMROSCH ET AL., *supra* note 15, at 260; *see also* Declaration on Yugoslavia, 31 I.L.M. 1485 (1992).

21. *See* Organization of American States, Inter-American Democratic Charter, arts. 19, 20, Sept. 11, 2001, 40 I.L.M. 1289.

22. Resolution Concerning Southern Rhodesia, S.C. Res. 217 (November 20, 1965), *excerpted in* DAMROSCH, ET AL., *supra* note 15, at 265–66; *see* Domingo E. Acevedo, *The Haitian Crisis and the OAS Response: A Test of Effectiveness in Protecting Democracy, in* ENFORCING RESTRAINT: COLLECTIVE INTERVENTION IN INTERNAL CONFLICTS 119 (Lori Fisler Damrosch ed., 1993).

23. Thomas M. Franck, *The Emerging Right to Democratic Self-Governance,* 86 AM. J. INT'L L. 46 (1992).

24. *See* Reference re Secession of Quebec, [1998] 2 S.C.R. 217, 289 (Can.) ("[O]ne of the legal norms which may be recognized by states in granting or withholding recognition of emergent states is the legitimacy of the process by which the de facto secession is, or was, being pursued. The process of recognition, once considered to be an exercise of pure sovereign discretion, has come to be associated with legal norms").

25. *Id.* at 274–75, 288–89 (emphasis added).

26. For more on the possible development of an international legal norm requiring compliance with domestic constitutions as part of the rule of law, see Schnably, *supra* note 14 (describing international interventions in moments of domestic constitutional conflict). For example, Professor Schnably describes how, in response to a claim by the President of Nicaragua that efforts by the national legislature to limit presidential powers were impermissible, the Central American Court of Justice found that certain ostensibly ratified amendments violated the constitution because they would effect a change to a parliamentary system that required compliance with the procedures for wholesale ("total") constitutional revision. *Id.* at 467–70. The Nicaraguan Supreme Court, however, denied the jurisdiction of the Central American Court, concluding that it was unconstitutional, with the "practical effect" of Nicaragua's having "'two constitutions: one approved by the executive; and the other approved by the legislature.'. . ." *Id.* at 470 (internal citation omitted). *See also id.* at 474–76 (describing how international actors condemned as unconstitutional under the Togo Constitution the accession of the son of the President to that office and condemned further action by Togo to amend its constitution to allow the son to take office in a formally lawful manner). Such assertions embody a claimed interest by members of the international community in a nation's compliance with its own constitution, as well as an implicit claim of capacity to interpret that constitution more appropriately than internal bodies. *See also id.* at 478–85.

27. *Cf., e.g.,* Laurence R. Helfer, *Nonconsensual International Lawmaking,* 2008 U. ILL. L. REV. 71, 110–11 (noting the "powerful nations" effects in securing compliance with UN Security Council's antiterrorism resolutions that weaker states may disagree with). *But cf.* Craig Whitlock, *Terrorism Financing Blacklists at Risk: Global System Faces Multiple Challenges,* WASH. POST, Nov. 2, 2008, at A1 (suggesting that UN requirements for blacklisting terrorist organizations were threatened by recent court decisions in Europe finding that the directive violated fundamental due process rights of those on the list).

28. *Cf.* Gerald L. Neuman, *Human Rights and Constitutional Rights: Harmony and Dissonance,* 55 STAN. L. REV. 1863, 1873–80 (2003) (discussing how even parallel provisions relating to "supranational" human rights in national constitutions and international agreements may diverge due to differences in the positive commitments or institutional mechanisms for their enforcement).

29. *See* UN Charter arts. 2 (4), 51 ("All Members shall refrain in their international relations from the threat or use of force against the territorial integrity or political independence of any state. . . .," while preserving rights of self-defense); KENPO [Constitution], art. 9 (Japan) (renouncing war and any right of belligerency and prohibiting maintenance of a military with offensive capacity for war). This provision is a controversial one, with

periodic attempts at revision; and it has been interpreted to permit the development of a military force for defensive purposes. But it is not the only modern constitutional provision that addresses and seeks to limit government action that would promote war. *See, e.g.*, GRUNDGESETZ (GG) [Basic Law], art. 26 (F.R.G.) (banning acts that tend to disturb peaceful relations with other nations, including preparations for aggressive war, and banning manufacture of weapons of war without federal permission); *see also* U.S.CONST., art. I, § 8 (no standing armies). *Cf. supra* note 12.

30. *See* Lori Fisler Damrosch, *Constitutional Control over War Powers: A Common Core of Accountability in Democratic Societies?*, 50 U. MIAMIL. REV. 181 (1995) (discussing possible tendency of democracies to require legislative deliberation and authorization before commitment to war).

31. *See, e.g.*, Didier Maus, *The Influence of Contemporary International Law on the Exercise of Constituent Power, in* NATIONAL CONSTITUTIONS IN THE ERA OF INTEGRATION 45, 47–49 (Antero Jyränki ed., 1999); Antero Jyränki, *Transferring Powers of a Nation-State to International Organizations: The Doctrine of Sovereignty Revisited, in* NATIONAL CONSTITUTIONS IN THE ERA OF INTEGRATION, *supra*, at 61, 71–72; *see also* Hjalte Rasmussen, *Denmark's Maastricht Ratification Case: The Constitutional Dimension, in* NATIONAL CONSTITUTIONS IN THE ERA OF INTEGRATION, *supra*, at 87 (discussing a pending case challenging the constitutionality of Denmark's ratification of the Treaty). For critical discussion of the German Constitutional Court's Maastricht decision, see Joseph Weiler, *Does Europe Need a Constitution? Demos, Telos and the German Maastricht Decision*, 1 EUR. L.J. 219 (1995) (analyzing tensions between the court's emphasis on safeguarding the democratic character of Germany by exercising its own competence to determine the limits of EU authority, on the one hand, and its acceptance of the Treaty, given the democratic deficits of the EU, on the other).

32. *See* 1958 CONST. art. 66-1 (Fr.) (inserted by Constitutional Act No. 2007-239 of Feb. 23, 2007), *translated in* 7 CONSTITUTIONS OF THE COUNTRIES OF THE WORLD: FRANCE 33 (Rüdiger Wolfrum & Rainer Grote eds., 2008) ("No one shall be sentenced to death."); Office of the United Nations High Commissioner for Human Rights, Second Optional Protocol to the International Covenant on Civil and Political Rights, aiming at the abolition of the death penalty (New York, Dec. 15, 1989), *available at* http://www2.ohchr.org/english/bodies/ratification/12.htm (listing France as having acceded to ICCPR Optional Protocol 2 on Oct. 2, 2007); Council of Europe, Protocol No. 13 to the Convention for the Protection of Human Rights and Fundamental Freedoms, concerning the abolition of the death penalty in all circumstances, CETS No. 187 (listing France as having ratified Optional Protocol 13 on Oct. 10, 2007), *available at* http://conventions.coe.int/Treaty/Commun/ChercheSig.asp?NT=187&CM=8&DF=10/31/2008&CL=ENG.

33. *See* Helfer, *supra* note 27, at 102 (describing the EU's Generalized System of Preferences, offering reduced tariffs to developing countries that must, however, ratify some twenty-seven governance, human rights, and environmental agreements).

34. Rome Statute of the International Criminal Court, art. 17(1)(a), *opened for signature* July 17, 1998, 2187 U.N.T.S. 3, *available at* http://www.icc-cpi.int. *See* Allison Marston Danner, *Enhancing the Legitimacy and Accountability of Prosecutorial Discretion at the International Criminal Court*, 97 AM. J. INT'L L. 510, 517, 522 (2003); *cf.* Christine Chinkin, *Monism and Dualism, in* NEW PERSPECTIVES ON THE DIVIDE BETWEEN NATIONAL AND INTERNATIONAL LAW, 134, 138–39 (Janne Nijman & André Nollkaemper eds., 2007) (noting the range of relationships that now exist between different international and national legal institutions, including doctrines of exhaustion of national remedies, doctrines of complementarity, superiority of international over national law, and "fictions" to allow the internal incorporation of international norms).

35. *See* Steve Charnovitz, *Rethinking WTO Trade Sanctions*, 95 AM. J. INT'L L. 792, 794 (2001); Laurence R. Helfer & Anne-Marie Slaughter, *Why States Create International Tribunals: A Response to Professors Posner and Yoo*, 93 CALIF. L. REV. 899, 919–22 (2005). On the relationships between the WTO, international economic law more generally, and domestic constitutions, see THE POLITICAL ECONOMY OF INTERNATIONAL TRADE LAW (Daniel L.M. Kennedy & James D. Southwick eds., 2002); NATIONAL CONSTITUTIONS AND INTERNATIONAL ECONOMIC LAW (Meinhard Hilf & Ernst-Ulrich Petersmann eds., 1993). For an argument that WTO adjudication enhances democracy within member states by limiting private business groups' domestic "rent–seeking" activity, see John O. McGinnis & Mark L. Movsesian, *The World Trade Constitution*, 114 HARV. L. REV. 511 (2000). On the possible effects of accession to the WTO the development of independent courts in China, see Chapter 3, note 180, above.

36. *Cf.* Colin Scott, *Regulating Constitutions, in* REGULATING LAW, at 240 (Christine Parker et al. eds., 2004) (noting that international organizations, including the Council of Europe and the European Union, as well as OECD, UN and World Bank, have "used their various levers and monitoring capacities to regulate some aspects of national constitutional regimes").

37. *See, e.g.*, CONST. ARG. art. 75 (22); GRUNDGESETZ (GG) [Basic Law], art. 25 (F.R.G.) ("general rules" of international law as integral part of federal law).

38. *See, e.g.*, Samantha Besson, *Sovereignty in Conflict* (European Integration Online Papers No. 8, 2004), *available at* http://ssrn.com/abstract=594942 (rejecting effort to establish hierarchy by which conflicts between supranational and national law are resolved in Europe and arguing for mutual processes of justification and interpretation); Giuseppe Martinico, *Complexity and Cultural Sources of Law in the EU Context: From the Multilevel Constitutionalism to Constitutional Synallagma*, 8 GERMAN L.J. No. 3 (2007), http://www.germanlawjournal.com/article.php?id=802; Paul Craig, *Unreasonableness and Proportionality in UK Law, in* THE PRINCIPLE OF PROPORTIONALITY IN THE LAWS OF EUROPE 85 (Evelyn Ellis ed., 1999) (discussing "Wednesbury" review and the possibility that the proportionality standard could alter or replace its "unreasonableness" standard of review).

39. For an approving view, see Anne Peters, *The Globalization of State Constitutions, in* NEW PERSPECTIVES ON THE DIVIDE BETWEEN NATIONAL AND INTERNATIONAL LAW, *supra* note 34, at 251. For a more skeptical view of the same phenomenon, see Melissa A. Waters, *Creeping Monism: The Judicial Trend Toward Interpretive Incorporation of Human Rights Treaties*, 107 COLUM. L. REV. 628, 694–705 (2007).

40. Ernest A. Young, *Institutional Settlement in a Globalizing Judicial System*, 54 DUKE L.J. 1143, 1232–36 (2005) ("shared law"); *cf.* Mayo Moran, *Inimical to Constitutional Values: Complex Migrations of Constitutional Rights, in* THE MIGRATION OF CONSTITUTIONAL IDEAS 233, 233–35 (Sujit Choudhry ed., 2006) (discussing the ways in which "constitutional values" migrate and influence other systems, for example, of private law); David S. Law, *Generic Constitutional Law*, 89 MINN. L. REV. 652, 687–99 (2005) (discussing "generic constitutional analysis").

41. On the role of values and their persuasive influence on the justification of legal interpretation in domestic law, as compared with the idea of "binding" clear rules within particular domains of controlling authority, see Mayo Moran, *Shifting Boundaries: The Authority of International Law, in* NEW PERSPECTIVES ON THE DIVIDE BETWEEN NATIONAL AND INTERNATIONAL LAW, *supra* note 34, at 163, 166 (arguing for a "different conception of authority" than one bounded by spatial categories, one involving the "mandatory influence of certain legal values" that places "primacy not on the selection of rules but rather on the distinctive nature of legal deliberation and justification").

42. Thus, for example, the secession of Eritrea from Ethiopia and the separation of Ireland from Great Britain each followed years of civil war or physical resistance; Eritrea held a UN-supervised referendum and voted in favor of independence; Ireland and Britain eventually negotiated a new status for the Republic Ireland. On Eritrea, see EYASSU GAYIM, THE ERITREAN QUESTION: THE CONFLICT BETWEEN THE RIGHT OF SELF-DETERMINATION AND THE INTERESTS OF STATES 469–94, 612–34 (1993); Bereket Habte Selassie, *Self-Determination in Principle and Practice: the Ethiopian-Eritrean Experience*, 29 COLUM. HUM. RTS. L. REV. 91, 112–20 (1997); Minasse Haile, *Legality of Secessions: The Case of Eritrea*, 8 EMORY INT'L L. REV. 479, 484–88 (1994). On Ireland, see JOSEPH M. CURRAN, THE BIRTH OF THE IRISH FREE STATE, 1921–1923, at 11–61 (1980); James J. Friedberg, *Ambiguity, Sovereignty, and Identity in Ireland: Peace and Transition*, 20 OHIO ST. J. ON DISP. RESOL. 113, 124–28 (2005); Ronald A. Christaldi, *The Shamrock and the Crown; A Historic Analysis of the Framework Document and Prospects for Peace in Ireland*, 5 J. TRANSNAT'L L. & POL'Y 123, 146–52 (1995). That secessionary movements were resolved by force does not mean that they were not accompanied by ideologies of self-determination. *See, e.g.*, Susanna Mancini, *Rethinking the Boundaries of Democratic Secession: Liberalism Nationalism and the Right of Minorities to Self-determination*, 6 INT'L J. CONST. L. 553, 575–76 (2008) (noting constitutional theory of an abrogable compact accompanying secession of southern states in U.S. Civil War).

43. On the role of international law in territorial disputes, see Steven R. Ratner, *Land Feuds and Their Solutions: Finding International Law Beyond the Tribunal Chamber*, 100 AM. J. INT'L L. 808 (2006). For evidence of contemporary trends requiring adoption of constitutions for future self-government as part of an internationally supervised effort to bring hostilities to an end, see, e.g., the Dayton Accords, Annex 4 (Constitution of Bosnia and Herzegovina) (drafted in English by U.S. State Department lawyers); JANE STROMSETH ET AL., CAN MIGHT MAKE RIGHTS? 92 (2006); *see generally* Christine Bell, *Peace Agreements: Their Nature and Legal Status*, 100 AM J. INT'L L. 373 (2006) (discussing constitutions as tools of peacemaking). For a view of the U.S. Constitution as a "peace pact," designed to avoid war and a drift toward multiple federations, see DAVID HENDRICKSON, PEACE PACT: THE LOST WORLD OF THE AMERICAN FOUNDING 257-60 (2003) (suggesting that the "Constitution stood at a juncture between the worlds of constitutionalism and diplomacy"); *see also* Akhil Reed Amar, *Some New World Lessons for the Old World*, 58 U. CHI. L. REV. 483, 485–97 (1991) (describing geostrategic approach of the U.S. Constitution).

44. *See* Reference re Secession of Quebec, [1998] 2 S.C.R. 217, 285–86, 287; Thomas M. Franck et al., *The Territorial Integrity of Quebec in the Event of the Attainment of Sovereignty, Report prepared for Québec's Ministère des relations internationales*, para. 1.17 (William Boulet trans. 1992), *available at* http://english.republiquelibre.org/Territorial_integrity_of_Quebec_in_the_event_of_the_attainment_of_sovereignty (rejecting the "erroneous assumption that the right to self-determination is the equivalent of, or at least implies, the right to independence"); Christopher J. Borgen, *Kosovo's Declaration of Independence: Self-Determination, Secession and Recognition*, ASIL Insights, Feb. 29, 2008, http://www.asil.org/insights080229.cfm.

45. *See* Vicki C. Jackson, *Comparative Constitutional Federalism and Transnational Judicial Discourse*. 2 INT'L J. CONST. L. 91, 127, 134 n.182 (2004); Mancini, *supra* note 42, at 575, 578, 580, 582–83.

46. CONST. [FORMER] USSR, art. 72 (1977). *See* Jackson, *supra* note 45, at 125.

47. *See* CONST. ETHIOPIA art. 39 (1994).

48. For plebiscitary, self-determination theorists, see, e.g., Daniel Philpott, *Self-Determination in Practice, in* NATIONAL SELF-DETERMINATION AND SECESSION, 79 (Margaret Moore ed., 1998); Will Kymlicka, *Federalism and Secession: At Home and Abroad*, 13 CAN. J. L.

& JURIS. 207 (2000); Harry Beran, *A Democratic Theory of Political Self-Determination for a New World Order*, *in* THEORIES OF SECESSION 32 (Percy B. Lehning ed., 1998); Kai Nielsen, *Secession: The Case of Quebec*, 10 J. APPLIED PHIL. 29 (1993). For more restrictive ("just cause") theories of secession as a remedy where, for example, historic wrongs are not redressable within the existing state, see Allen Buchanan, *Federalism, Secession, and the Morality of Inclusion*, 37 ARIZ. L. REV. 53 (1995). And for an emphasis on whether a particular group has a claim to a specific *territory* due to historic injustice, see Lea Brilmayer, *Secession and Self Determination: A Territorial Interpretation*, 16 YALE J. INT'L L. 177 (1991); *see also* Lea Brilmayer, *Secession and Self-Determination: One Decade Later*, 25 YALE J. INT'L L. 283 (2000).

49. CASS R. SUNSTEIN, DESIGNING DEMOCRACY: WHAT CONSTITUTIONS DO 95–114 (2001); *see* Jackson, *supra* note 45, at 120; Donald L. Horowitz, *Self-Determination: Politics, Philosophy, and Law*, *in* NATIONAL SELF-DETERMINATION AND SECESSION 181, 182 (Margaret Moore, ed., 1998). *But cf.* Mancini, *supra* note 42 (arguing that constitutionalizing secession rights may, notwithstanding their risks, induce useful cooperation within an existing polity).

50. *See* Vivien Hart, *Democratic Constitution Making* (U.S. Inst. Of Peace, Special Rep. 107, July 2003), *available at* http://www.usip.org/resources/democratic-constitution-making; *cf.* Franck, *The Emerging Right to Democratic Governance*, *supra* note 23.

51. *See* Agreement Reached in the Multi-party Negotiations, Apr. 10, 1998, 37 I.L.M. 751.

52. *See generally* Bell, *supra* note 43, at 377–79, 398–99.

53. In Ireland the state's agreement is reflected in a constitutional amendment, approved by referendum the same day that the people of Northern Ireland voted in favor of the Belfast (or "Good Friday") Agreement by referendum. In Britain the Agreement led to a statute, regarded by a number of the law lords as constitutional in character. *See* Robinson v. Sec'y of State for N. Ir., [2002] U.K.H.L. 32, paras. 25, 33 (Lord Hoffman); *id.* at para 11 (Lord Bingham).

54. Agreement Reached in the Multi-party Negotiations, Apr. 10, 1998, *supra* note 51, Constitutional Issues, para. 1, at 752, For the British statutory implementation, see Northern Ireland Act 1998, ch. 47, § 1 & Sched. 1 (providing that if in the future it appears that a majority in Northern Ireland favor union with Ireland, the Secretary of State shall hold a voting poll for the purposes of a majority expressing their wish either to join Ireland or remain part of the UK; such polls are not to be held more often than every seven years).

55. *See* Ratner, *supra* note 43, at 810 (describing the two principal methods of resolving territorial disputes in international law—either by showing lawful receipt of the territory from a prior sovereign, or "[i]n the absence of such proof . . . the guiding principle remains that set . . . in the *Island of Palmas* case, that 'continuous and peaceful display of the functions of State within a given region is a constituent element of territorial sovereignty'") (citing Island of Palmas (Neth./U.S.), 2 REP. INT'L ARB. AWARDS 829, 840 (1928)).

56. Reliance on majoritarian voting rules in contested areas may create incentives for population migrations, as scholars think may have occurred in the area involved in the *Western Sahara* case. *See* Ratner, *supra* note 43, at 820. It is for such reasons that many international law scholars have vigorously opposed recognition of a right to secede based simply on rights of self-determination.

57. *See* Neil Walker, *The Idea of Constitutional Pluralism*, 65 MODERN L. REV. 317, 355 (2002) (describing the Good Friday Agreement as one of "a new legal genus in which traditional 'international' relations between states develop in new 'constitutional' ways"). International reliance on voting to determine boundaries has predecessors, including the plebiscites held in the wake of World War I to determine boundary lines for divided

population pockets, and extends to quite recent UN-supervised activities, for example, the plebiscite on independence held in 1999 in East Timor. On the post–World War I plebiscites, *see* KAREN KNOP, DIVERSITY AND SELF-DETERMINATION IN INTERNATIONAL LAW 281–309 (2002); *see also* HURST HANNUM, AUTONOMY, SOVEREIGNTY, AND SELF-DETERMINATION: THE ACCOMMODATION OF CONFLICTING RIGHTS 27–33 (rev. ed. 1996) (suggesting a very limited role for plebiscites in the post–World War I map drawing). On East Timor, *see* CIA, The World Factbook, Timor-Leste, *available at* https://www.cia.gov/library/publications/the-world-factbook (search for Timor-Leste) (last visited Jan. 24, 2009); *see also* STROMSETH ET AL., *supra* note 43 at 33, 278.

58. Jiunn-Rong Yeh & Wen-Chen Chang, *From Origin to Delta: Changing Landscape of Modern Constitutionalism* (Bepress Legal Series, Working Paper 1815, Oct. 6, 2006), *available at* http://law.bepress.com/expresso/eps/1815. In the late 1940s, Allied occupying forces in West Germany supervised the process of drafting and adopting the new Basic Law after World War II, and the United States played a more aggressive role in the formation of the postwar constitution of Japan. On Germany, see JOHN FORD GOLAY, THE FOUNDING OF THE FEDERAL REPUBLIC OF GERMANY (1958); PETER H. MERKL, THE ORIGIN OF THE WEST GERMAN REPUBLIC (1963); Inga Markovitz, *Constitution Making After National Catastrophes: Germany in 1949 and 1990*, 49 WM & MARY L. REV. 1307, 1308–09 (2008); on Japan, see RAY A. MOORE & DONALD L. ROBINSON, PARTNERS FOR DEMOCRACY: CRAFTING THE NEW JAPANESE STATE UNDER MACARTHUR (2002); KOSEKI SHŌICHI, THE BIRTH OF JAPAN'S POSTWAR CONSTITUTION (Ray A. Moore ed. and trans., 1997); LAWRENCE W. BEER & JOHN M. MAKI, FROM IMPERIAL MYTH TO DEMOCRACY: JAPAN'S TWO CONSTITUTIONS, 1889–2002 (2002); THEODORE MCNELLY, THE ORIGINS OF JAPAN'S DEMOCRATIC CONSTITUTION (2000). Earlier in the twentieth century, the Platt Amendment required concessions in the new constitution of Cuba. *See* Christina Duffy Burnett, The Legalist Origins of an Extralegal Space: The Platt Amendment, Guantanamo and International Law in the Americas (unpublished manuscript Fall 2008 on file with author); Kal Raustiala, *The Geography of Justice*, 73 FORDHAM L. REV. 2501, 2535–37 (2005). (For earlier work from which some of this draws, see Vicki C. Jackson, *What's in a Name? Reflections on Timing, Naming, and Constitution–Making*, 49 WM. & MARY L. REV. 1249 (2008)).

59. *See* RUTI G. TEITEL, TRANSITIONAL JUSTICE (2000).

60. *See, e.g.*, HEINZ KLUG, CONSTITUTING DEMOCRACY: LAW GLOBALISM AND SOUTH AFRICA'S POLITICAL RECONSTRUCTION 4–5, 55, 74–85, 137 (2000) (emphasizing the role of local actors in drawing on and reinterpreting "legal forms . . . from a variety of jurisdictions to suit their own locally-defined ends" and charting the course by which the ANC came to endorse judicially enforced constitutional rights).

61. *Cf.* S. AFR. CONST. 1996 § 167(4)(d) (authorizing constituitional court review of the constitutionality of amendments); Matatiele Municipality v. President of the Republic, 2006 (5) SA 47 (CC) (finding unconstitutional part of the 12th amendment, on procedural grounds). Whether (or on what basis) the court may review the *substantive* constitutionality of amendments is unclear. For skeptical evaluations of use of a "basic structure" doctrine, as in India, or of drawing on the Interim Constitution's thirty-four principles for such purposes, see IAIN CURRIE & JOHAN DE WAAL, THE NEW CONSTITUTIONAL & ADMINISTRATIVE LAW 182–83 & nn.281, 282 (2001); Steven Budlender, *Substantive Constraints on Legislative Authority, in* CONSTITUTIONAL LAW OF SOUTH AFRICA § 17.3(g) (Stu Woolman et al. eds., 2d ed. 2008).

62. *See* STROMSETH ET AL., *supra* note 43, at 96–97, 104–05 (describing constitutional process in East Timor, Iraq, and Afghanistan).

63. *See* Russell A. Miller, *Self-Determination in International Law and the Demise of Democracy?*, 41 COLUM. J. TRANSNAT'L L. 601 (2003); *cf.* AMY CHUA, WORLD ON FIRE: HOW EXPORTING FREE MARKET DEMOCRACY BREEDS ETHNIC HATRED AND GLOBAL INSTABILITY (2003) (arguing that the combination of increased democracy and free markets in developing

countries contributes to ethnic conflict, as the tools of democracy are wielded against economically successful but unpopular minority ethnic groups).

64. For provisions in the constitutions of Bosnia-Herzegovina and Kosovo requiring international members of their respective constitutional courts, see Chapter 2, note 79, above. For more on international supervision in such areas, *see, e.g.*, STROMSETH ET AL., *supra* note 43 at 111–17; Ralph Wilde, *From Bosnia to Kosovo and East Timor: The Changing Role of the United Nations in the Administration of Territory*, 6 ILSA J. INT'L & COMP. L. 467, 469–71 (1999); Matthias Ruffert, *The Administration of Kosovo and East-Timor by the International Community*, 50 INT'L & COMP. L.Q. 613 (2001); *see also* Jackson, *supra* note 58, at 1295–98. The South African Constitutional Court functioned as a check on the final constitution as well as an interpreter of its provisions. *See* S.AFR. (Interim) CONST. 1993 § 71(2) (providing for judicial review of the final constitution for its compliance with the thirty-four constitutional principles agreed to by the multiparty negotiators).

65. *See* Agreement Reached in the Multi-party Negotiations, Apr. 10, 1998, *supra* note 51, Strand One, §§ 1, 15, Strand Two, §§ 1, 5 (ii); Northern Ireland Act 1998, ch. 47, § 16 (3) (Eng.). The Agreement specified that the North-South Ministerial Council's existence was dependent on the Assembly for Northern Ireland, another unusual form of relationship between a part of one national state (UK) and another national state. *Id.*, Strand Two, §§ 2, 7. The Council is to choose at least six areas from a longer list including agriculture, education, transport, health, and tourism for their work. *See id.* Strand Two, § 9 & Annex.

66. *Id.* at Strand Three, §§ 1, 2, 5, 7. The Agreement also established a new British-Irish Intergovernmental Conference. *Id.* at Strand Three (British-Irish Intergovernmental Conference).

67. Medellín v. Texas, 128 S. Ct. 1346 (2008) (holding unconstitutional the President's effort to require the State of Texas to provide the procedural review called for by the ICJ judgment in *Avena*).

68. *See* Christina Duffy Burnett, Untied *States: American Expansion and Territorial Deannexation*, 72 U. CHI. L. REV. 797, 797, 802 (2005) (discussing the *Insular Cases*, such as Downes v. Bidwell, 182 U.S. 244 (1901), as recognizing the possibility of a temporary annexation of territory that would not preclude later divestiture, or possibly even secession). *Cf.* Texas v. White, 74 U.S. 700, 725–26 (1869) (concluding that states had no unilateral rights to secede and that Texas accordingly had never left the Union, but leaving open the possibility of secession with the consent of other states).

69. Although the federal government has been criticized for failing to provide for binding referenda in Puerto Rico, there is as yet little secessionary pressure there, at least based on results of locally sponsored referenda. *See, e.g.*, Burnett, *supra* note 68, at 873 (describing election results in several referenda and in candidate elections, with independence party or position never polling above five percent).

70. *See, e.g.*, Amer. Ins. Ass'n v. Garamendi, 539 U.S. 396 (2003) (invalidating California's statutory effort to force insurance companies doing business in the state to disclose insurance policies issued in Europe before and during World War II that might belong to Holocaust victims' heirs); Crosby v. Nat'l Foreign Trade Council, 530 U.S. 363 (2000) (invalidating Massachusetts's efforts to discourage businesses from dealing with Burma if they want to do business with the state of Massachusetts).

71. *See* Judith Resnik, *Foreign as Domestic Affairs: Rethinking Horizontal Federalism and Foreign Affairs Preemption in Light of Translocal Internationalism*, 57 EMORY L.J. 31 (2007) (noting that as "of 2004, forty-four cities, eighteen counties, and sixteen states have passed or considered legislation relating to CEDAW," as a result of lobbying efforts by a coalition of 190 NGOs); Judith Resnik, *The Internationalism of American Federalism: Missouri and Holland*, 73 MO. L. REV. 1105, 1122–23 (2008).

72. *See, e.g.*, State v. Wilder, 748 A.2d 444, 449 n.6 (Me. 2000) (reversing parent's conviction for assaulting child, discussing British and ECtHR approaches and concluding that Maine law allows parents to administer moderate, reasonable punishment, even though several European countries ban corporal punishment of children); Moore v. Ganim, 660 A.2d 742, 771, 780–82 (Conn. 1995) (Peters, J., concurring) (noting the UDHR and the ICESCR in discussing state constitutional right to minimal subsistence); Arroyo v. Rattan Specialities, Inc., 117 P.R. Dec. 35, 59 n.15 (1986) (citing a German case on polygraphy, Judgment of Bundesgerichtshof (I. Strafsenat), Feb. 16, 1954, 5 Entscheidungen des Bundesgerichtshofes in Strafsachen 332); Sterling v. Cupp, 625 P.2d 123, 131 n.21 (Or. 1981) (Linde, J.) (referring to human dignity and the UDHR, ICCPR, and ECHR in interpreting state constitutional protection of prisoners against "unnecessary rigor" of confinement). *See generally* Vicki C. Jackson, *Constitutional Dialogue and Human Dignity: States and Transnational Constitutional Discourse*, 65 MONT. L. REV. 15 (2004).

73. *See, e.g.*, Peter J. Spiro, *The States and International Human Rights*, 66 FORDHAM L. REV. 567, 583–86 (1997) (describing the "rising international profile of subnational governments"); Peter J. Spiro, *New Players on the International Stage*, 2 HOFSTRA L. & POL'Y SYMP. 19, 30–32 (1997); *infra* note 79 (concerning Belgium); *cf.* Chapter 7, note 44, above (noting citations of subnational courts by foreign high courts).

74. U.S. Term Limits, Inc. v. Thornton, 514 U.S. 779, 838 (Kennedy, J., concurring).

75. *See, e.g.*, Arthur Gunlicks, *German Federalism Reform: Part One*, 8 GERMAN L. J. 111, 116–27 (2007), http://www.germanlawjournal.com/article.php?id=792.

76. On federalism, secession and state breakup, compare, e.g., Will Kymlicka, *Federalism and Secession: At Home and Abroad*, 13 CAN. J.L. & JURISP. 207 (2000) (suggesting that if federal systems permit political pursuit of secession, secession is less likely to occur), with Jackson, *supra* note 45, at 116 & n.106, 118 & n.113 (noting arguments that allowing votes within existing subnational units in favor of secession will discourage adoption of federal form). On "shared sovereignty," see *infra* note 78.

77. *See, e.g.*, Reference re Secession of Quebec, [1998] 2 S.C.R. 217 (Can.) (discussing obligation of the rest of Canada to negotiate in the event of a decided majority vote in Quebec clearly in favor of secession); Agreement Reached in the Multi-party Negotiations, Apr. 10, 1998, *supra* note 51, Constitutional Issues, para. 1, para. 2, Annex A, § 1, Schedule 1 (providing for a referendum on whether Northern Ireland should become part of the Republic of Ireland in the event that public opinion in the future appears to favor such a change); CONSTITUTION OF SAINT KITTS AND NEVIS (1983), §§ 113, 115 (providing for secession of Nevis by a two-thirds vote of the assembly and at a subsequent referendum); Draft Treaty for Establishing a Constitution of Europe, June 18, 2003, art. 59 (procedures for withdrawal).

78. *See* Stephen D. Krasner, *The Case for Shared Sovereignty*, 16 J. DEMOCRACY 69 (2005).

79. *See* COORDINATED CONST. KINGDOM OF BELGIUM arts. 127, 128, 167 (1994, as amended through Feb. 2, 2005), *translated in* 2 CONSTITUTIONS OF THE COUNTRIES OF THE WORLD: BELGIUM 29–30, 42 (Rüdiger Wolfrum & Rainer Grote eds., 2005); TREATISE ON BELGIAN CONSTITUTIONAL LAW 248 (André Alen ed., 1992); Alexander Murphy, *Belgium's Regional Divergence: Along the Road to Federation*, *in* FEDERALISM: THE MULTIETHNIC CHALLENGE 73, 87-88 (Graham Smith ed., 1995); Richard Cullen, *Adaptive Federalism in Belgium*, 13 U. NEW SOUTH WALES L. J. 346, 354 (1990).

80. For suggestions along these lines, see, e.g., Spiro, *The States and International Human Rights*, *supra* note 73 (proposing that subnational entities at level of U.S. states become parties to international human rights conventions); Peter J. Spiro, *Disaggregating U.S. Interests in International Law*, 67 LAW & CONTEMP. PROBS. 195, 211 (2004) (discussing

significance of subnational actors in international regimes); Eyal Benvenisti, *Domestic Politics and International Resources: What Role for International Law?*, *in* THE ROLE OF LAW IN INTERNATIONAL POLITICS 109, 114, 125–27 (Michael Beyers ed., 2000) (arguing that international law should "recognize that governments are agents of only a part of the communities they purport to represent at the international negotiating table," provide incentives for national governments to more fully internalize the costs of international agreements for all domestic communities in order to enhance prospects for long-term international cooperation, and recognize subnational cross-border agreements). *See also* Spiro, *Disaggregating U.S. Interests*, *supra*, at 204–10 (noting increased role of nonstate generators of norms, including NGOs, social movements and business corporations).

81. *See supra* notes 40, 41; *see also* Walker, *supra* note 57, at 344 (noting linkage of constitutionalism to a "series of core governance values—such as democracy, accountability, equality, the separation of powers, the rule of law and fundamental rights" and suggesting that "a plausible claim to constitutional status[] must at least be seen to take these values seriously") (emphasis omitted).

82. *See* Freedom House, Freedom in the World Country Ratings, 1972 to 2007, http://www.freedomhouse.org/uploads/FIWAllScores.xls. Mongolia, rated as "free" since 1991–92, in 2008 had scores of 2/ 2 on these scales.

83. TOM GINSBURG, JUDICIAL REVIEW IN NEW DEMOCRACIES: CONSTITUTIONAL COURTS IN ASIAN CASES 189 (2003).

84. *Id.* at 188–90 (also noting legal arguments concerning symbolic presidencies in Israel and Italy); *see also* Tom Ginsburg & Gombosuren Ganzorig, *When Courts and Politics Collide: Mongolia's Constitutional Crisis*, 14 COLUM J. ASIAN L. 309, 312–13 (2001) (describing argument that Mongolian democratic practice "had already established the parliamentary character of the political system" and that "[u]nlike the U.S. system, where there is a separation between party leadership and electoral candidates, Mongolian democratic practice after 1990 had required that party leaders stand as candidates").

85. GINSBURG, *supra* note 83, at 191 (quoting Mongolian constitutional text); *see id.* at 165, 187–88, 190–92. Ginsburg also concludes that the effect of the decision was deleterious, weakening the parliament, empowering the executive, and creating difficult governance tensions. *Id.* at 191–95.

86. *Id.* at 196–97.

87. *Id.* at 197. The president had vetoed the law on constitutional grounds (arguing that broader consultation by the parliament should have occurred), but his veto was overridden, which led to an appeal to the constitutional court. *Id.*

88. *Id.* at 197–98. After this the court, with a full bench, went forward to reconsider the amendment, and ruled again that it was unconstitutional, albeit on procedural grounds. In response, the political bodies reenacted the constitutional amendment, avoiding the procedural defects, in an action eventually upheld by the court. After several years, in 2001 the court withdrew from its efforts to prevent members of parliament from serving in the government. *Id.* at 199–200, 159.

89. *See* VICKI C. JACKSON & MARK TUSHNET, COMPARATIVE CONSTITUTIONAL LAW 779–80 (2d ed. 2006) (noting that members of Parliament serve in the UK cabinet); *cf., e.g.*, Wen-Chen Chang, *Interpretative Politics: Judicial Avenue in Constitutional Transformation*, *in* DIE ROLLE DER VERFASSUNGSRECHTSWISSENSHAFT IM DEMOKRATISCHEN VERFASSUNGSSTAAT: ZWEITES DEUTSCH-TAIWANESISCHES KOLLOQUIUM, VOM 26, BIS. 28 SEPTEMBER 2002 IN TAIPEH (Christian Starck ed., 2004) (describing decision by the Grand Justices Council of the Judicial Yuan of Taiwan (ROC), in 1995 that the Premier of the Executive Yuan had to offer his resignation to the President after new *parliamentary* elections as contemplated by the original

text, notwithstanding a 1994 revision making the president directly elected); GINSBURG, *supra* note 83, at 152–53 (describing a 1996 decision in Taiwan indicating that the premier need not resign at each new *presidential* term but that the premier's concurrently holding the position of vice-president was not in full conformity with the purpose of having the distinct constitutional offices); U.S. CONST. art. I, § 3 (making vice-president the president of the Senate, with a tie-breaking vote).

90. For introductions to the debates, including whether (and if so, why) presidential systems are more associated with instability than parliamentary ones, see Juan J. Linz, *Presidential or Parliamentary Democracy: Does It Make A Difference?*, *in* 1 THE FAILURE OF PRESIDENTIAL DEMOCRACY 3 (Juan J. Linz & Arturo Valenzuela eds., 1994); JOSÉ ANTONIO CHEIBUB, PRESIDENTIALISM, PARLIAMENTARISM, AND DEMOCRACY (2007); GIOVANNI SARTORI, COMPARATIVE CONSTITUTIONAL ENGINEERING: AN INQUIRY INTO STRUCTURES, INCENTIVES AND OUTCOMES 153 (1994) and Bruce Ackerman, *The New Separation of Powers*, 113 HARV. L. REV. 633 (2000).

91. *See* Schnably, *supra* note 14, at 460. *See also* Chapter 6, notes 71–73, above.

92. For example, Professor Schnably reports, the U.S. State Department accused the Nicaraguan Supreme Court of "ignoring the constitutional principle of separation of powers" in its decisions in connection with disputes over actions by the legislative assembly to limit the powers and immunities of the executive branch. Schnably, *supra* note 14, at 473. *See also id.* at 476–78 (discussing international condemnation of a constitutional amendment in Togo designed to regularize a presidential succession); *see generally supra* note 26.

93. A concurring opinion in Bush v. Gore, 531 U.S. 98, 111–22 (2000) (Rehnquist, C.J., concurring), disagreed with the Florida court's interpretation of its own law, but did so based on appeal to the normatively superior law of the U.S. Constitution and what the concurrence found was its allocation of decisional authority to state legislatures. Identifying a normatively superior standard for the substantive structures of constitutionalism in the transnational setting is a greater challenge. Moreover, although understandings of domestic law may benefit from the perspectives of outsiders, interpretation of domestic constitutions by international authorities lacks whatever democratic legitimacy attaches to the decision of a domestic court. Situations may arise where, due to civil war, deep polarization among groups, or other comparable conditions, internal actors are so lacking in trust or legitimacy among important segments that independent external actors are necessary. But the democratic legitimacy of domestically constituted (appointed or elected) organs of government will ordinarily be superior. (This discussion assumes that both domestic and transnational actors are engaged in good-faith interpretation; interventions in Togo and Nicaragua, described by Professor Schnably, *see supra* notes 26, 92, may have been less about law, or constitutionalism, and far more about the underlying politics and distributions of power. Yet the language of law that was used cannot, as a matter of principle, necessarily be cabined to the more particular political settings.)

94. Jan-Werner Müller, *A General Theory of Constitutional Patriotism*, 6 INT'L J. CONST. L. 72, 87 (2008); *see also id.* at 88 ("These particular institutions . . . have meaning for us by virtue of our attachment—and our involvement in the shared history of supporting, criticizing, and revising them."); Judith Resnik, *Law as Affiliation: "Foreign" Law, Democratic Federalism, and the Sovereigntism of the Nation-State*, 6 INT'L J. CONST. L. 33 (2008).

95. *See generally* Karol Edward Soltan, *Constitutional Patriotism and Militant Moderation*, 6 INT'L J. CONST. L. 96 (2008).

96. *See generally* Moran, *Shifting Boundaries*, *supra* note 41, at 165–67, 184 (emphasizing how "discrete rules may generate larger values" that have influence as nonbinding authority).

97. *Compare* Starrs v. Ruxton, [2000] J.C. 208 (H.C.J.) (Scot. 1999) (invalidating temporary, one-year appointments of judges as incompatible with judicial independence secured by the ECHR) *with* Evans v. Stephens, 387 F.3d 1220 (4th Cir. 2004) (en banc), *cert. denied*, 544 U.S. 942 (2005) (rejecting challenges to "recess" (i.e., temporary) appointments of judges to Article III courts, found to be explicitly permitted by the U.S. Constitution).

98. *See* McGonnell v. United Kingdom, 2000-II Eur. Ct. H.R. 107, 123–24 (finding that participation of an official (called the Bailiff) as a judge on a court, where that official also performed nonjudicial executive functions (including involvement with adoption of the development plan relevant to the dispute), was inconsistent with the requirement of an "independent and impartial tribunal" under ECHR art. 6).

99. *See* Reference re Remuneration of Judges of the Provincial Courts of Prince Edward Island, [1997] 3 S.C.R. 3, 63–64 (Can.) (holding that the principle of judicial independence is "at root an unwritten constitutional principle, in the sense that it is exterior to the particular sections of the Constitution Acts" which refer to the principle in particular settings); *id.* at 158–59 (concluding that although the principle of judicial independence does not preclude diminution of judicial salaries in times of economic exigency, it requires establishment of commissions, to meet at periodic intervals and recommend salary adjustments for provincial judges and that legislatures, though not bound to accept those recommendations, must give rational reasons for departures). *See also* Provincial Court Judges' Assn. of New Brunswick v. New Brunswick (Minister of Justice), [2005] 2 S.C.R. 286 (Can.) (reviewing several disputes over provincial legislatures' departures from recommendations of judicial salary commissions).

100. *See* Helfer, *supra* note 27, at 103.

101. *See* Michael C. Dorf, *Dynamic Incorporation of Foreign Law*, 157 U. PA. L. REV. 103, 115–24 (2008).

102. *See* MARGARET E. KECK & KATHRYN SIKKINK, ACTIVISTS BEYOND BORDERS: ADVOCACY NETWORKS IN INTERNATIONAL POLITICS 39–58 (1998); *see also* Judith Resnik, *Sisterhood, Slavery, and Sovereignty: Trasnational Antislavery Work and Women's Rights Movements in the United States During the Twentieth Century, in* WOMEN'S RIGHTS ANDTRANSATLANTIC ANTISLAVERY IN THE ERA OF EMANCIPATION 19 (Kathryn Kish Sklar & James Brewer Stewart eds., 2007).

103. *See* Judith Resnik, *Law's Migration: American Exceptionalism, Silent Dialogues and Federalism's Multiple Ports of Entry*, 115 YALE L.J. 1564, 1584–91 (2006).

104. If constitutional amendment is more readily available, then the pressure on interpretation is less, and the choice to promote change by interpretation may be correspondingly less legitimate. With the possible spread of "new commonwealth" modes of what Mark Tushnet calls "weak" judicial review, constitutional change might be more likely to occur through amendment, though perhaps under the shadow of interpretation. *See* Stephen Gardbaum, *The New Commonwealth Model of Constitutionalism*, 49 AM. J. COMP. L. 707, 755, 744–48 (2001); Mark Tushnet, *Alternative Forms of Judicial Review*, 101 MICH. L. REV. 2781 (2003) (discussing "weak" forms of judicial review). *But cf. id.* at 2792–95 (suggesting that weak form review is likely over time to behave like stronger form review).

105. By referring to constitutions as "institutions," I mean to invoke not only the text and case decisions, but also the practices, values, and decisions of those who "work it" in courts and in other parts of the government. *See generally* Karl Llewelyn, *The Constitution as an Institution*, 34 COLUM. L. REV. 1 (1934). The "institution" of the U.S. Constitution thus refers both to the courts (and especially the Supreme Court, as the organ of U.S. government that is its most prominent interpreter) and to the "normative, cognitive, and regulative environments" in which the Constitution operates, including the "rules or shared beliefs" that

surround it and are claimed to emerge from its operation or interpretation. *See* Ryan Goodman & Derek Jinks, *Toward an Institutional Theory of Sovereignty*, 55 STAN. L. REV. 1749, 1756, 1781 (2003).

106. Harold Hongju Koh, *Review Essay: Why Do Nations Obey International Law?*, 106 YALE L.J. 2599, 2602 (1997).

107. *See* Goodman & Jinks, *supra* note 105, at 1781. Their key argument for the impact of global culture is what they describe as the "decoupling" of function and structure, together with substantial "isomorphism" of state organization. *Id.* at 1759–64.

108. *Id.* at 1786.

109. Anne-Marie Slaughter & William Burke-White, *The Future of International Law Is Domestic (or, The European Way of Law)*, 47 HARV. INT'L L.J. 327, 330–31, 346, 348 (2006).

110. *Id.* at 339–40.

111. FRANCIS FUKUYAMA, STATE BUILDING: GOVERNANCE AND WORLD ORDER IN THE 21ST CENTURY 92–93 (2004).

112. PHILIP BOBBITT, TERROR AND CONSENT: THE WARS FOR THE TWENTY-FIRST CENTURY (2008).

113. Goodman & Jinks, *supra* note 105, at 1784.

114. *See also* Harold Hongju Koh, *On American Exceptionalism*, 55 STAN. L. REV. 1479, 1483, 1487 (2003) (criticizing U.S. "double standards" approach to international law and arguing that "by opposing the global rules, the United States can end up undermining the legitimacy of the rules themselves, not just modifying them to suit America's purposes").

115. *See* Chapter 4, note 136, above (describing this incident). For other examples of an attitude of heightened suspicion in European countries concerning perceived U.S. departures from established international standards, see, e.g., Ahmed and Aswat v. United Kingdom, App. No. 24027/07, Eur. Ct. H.R. (1998) *summary available at* http://www.echr.coe.int/Eng/InformationNotes/INFONOTE_No__99.htm (granting requests of defendants found by UK courts to be extraditable to the United States for "interim measures," indicating that they should not be extradited until the court has given due consideration to the case, in which the defendants claimed they were at risk of being designated enemy combatants and held without due process); Al Moayad v. Germany, App 35865/03, 44 Eur. H.R. Rep. SE22 (2007), para. 69 (noting that Germany sent a representative to the criminal trial of a defendant extradited to the United States from Germany to monitor that U.S. assurances "that the applicant will not be transferred to one of the detention facilities outside the United States of America in respect of which interrogation methods at variance with the standards of Article 3 have been reported" would be fulfilled); *see also* Tracy Wilkinson, *Warrants for 3 CIA Officers Issued in Imam's Abduction*, L.A. TIMES, July 6, 2006, at A4 (reporting on Italian efforts to criminally prosecute CIA officers for allegedly abducting someone in Italy and sending him to Egypt to be tortured). Arrest warrants charging more than a dozen CIA operatives with kidnapping and battery have reportedly also been issued in Germany in connection with the alleged kidnapping of a German citizen of Lebanese descent in Macedonia and his being sent to Afghanistan, where he was allegedly beaten and interrogated for five months. Jeffrey Fleishman, *Germany Seeks Arrest of U.S. Agents*, L.A.TIMES, Feb. 1, 2007, at A10.

116. The possibility of "mimicry" (or of reciprocal attitudes contemptuous of either international law or the benefits of considering others approaches) thus may reinforce the degree of interest each system has in showing some measure of respect for transnational sources of law. *See also* Paul J. DiMaggio & Walter W. Powell, *The Iron Cage Revisited: Institutional Isomorphism and Collective Rationality in Organizational Fields*, *in* THE NEW

INSTITUTIONALISM IN ORGANIZATIONAL ANALYSIS 63 (Paul J. DiMaggio & Walter W. Powell eds., 1991).

117. T. Alexander Aleinikoff, *Transnational Spaces: Norms and Legitimacy*, 33 YALE J. INT'L L. 479, 488 (2008) (emphasis added).

118. *Cf.* Alan Watson, *Legal Change: Sources of Law and Legal Culture*, 131 U. PA. L. REV. 1121, 1146–47 (1983) (suggesting, critically, that patterns of legal borrowing are influenced by habits of regard for particular foreign legal systems rather than search for "best rule").

119. *See, e.g.*, Laurence R. Helfer & Anne-Marie Slaughter, *Toward a Theory of Effective Supranational Adjudication*,107 YALE L.J. 273, 335–36 (1997); KAREN ALTER, ESTABLISHING THE SUPREMACY OF EUROPEAN LAW: THE MAKING OF AN INTERNATIONAL RULE OF LAW IN EUROPE 41–49 (2001) (noting incentives especially for lower-level national courts to invoke ECJ jurisdiction).

120. For a sampling of the growing literature on jurisdictional coordination, deference, comity, and/or hierarchy involving issues before both national courts and supranational tribunals, see, e.g., Ernest A. Young, *Toward a Framework Statute for Supranational Adjudication*, 57 EMORY L.J. 93 (2007); Paul Schiff Berman, *Global Legal Pluralism*, 80 S. CAL. L. REV. 1155 (2007); Mark L. Movsesian, *Judging International Judgments*, 48 VA. J. INT'L L. 65 (2007); Robert B. Ahdieh, *Between Dialogue and Decree: International Review of National Courts*, 79 N.Y.U. L. REV. 2029 (2004); Jenny S. Martinez, *Towards an International Legal System*, 56 STAN. L. REV. 429 (2003); *see also* Chapter 4, note 147, above.

121. *See, e.g.*, Yahoo! Inc. v. La Ligue Contre Le Racisme et L'Antisemitisme, 169 F. Supp. 2d 1181 (N.D. Cal. 2001) (prohibiting enforcement of French court judgment because enforcing the foreign judgment would threaten First Amendment values). On appeal, the original panel decision of the Ninth Circuit, 379 F.3d 1120 (9th Cir., Aug. 23, 2004) (reversing, due to lack of personal jurisdiction over the defendants), was vacated and the case reheard en banc, 399 F.3d 1010 (2005). The en banc court issued a per curiam opinion directing the district court to dismiss without prejudice the complaint. 433 F.3d 1199 (9th Cir. 2006). The majority and several dissenters disagreed over whether the French court's interim orders were plainly unconstitutional under U.S. law. *Compare id.* at 1220–22 (Fletcher, J.) (questioning conclusion that the French court's order was on its face inconsistent with the First Amendment, especially given uncertainty as to its territorial reach) *with id.* at 1247–53 (Fisher, J., dissenting in part, concurring in part) (explaining why the French order is inconsistent with U.S. Constitution).

122. An array of approaches have been suggested to anticipated future conflicts between U.S. and foreign law touching on First Amendment interests affected by potential liabilities for Internet communications. *See, e.g.*, Gregory S. Cooper, *A Tangled Web We Weave: Enforcing International Speech Restrictions in an Online World*, 8 U. PITT. J. TECH. L. & POL'Y 2, 3 (2007) (arguing for a combination "effects" and purposeful targeting test to determine when states may subject Internet communication to their own regulatory laws); *Developments in the Law—The Law of Media*, 120 HARV. L. REV. 990, 1031–43 (2007) (Part V, Internet Jurisdiction: A Comparative Analysis) (arguing that substantive divergences will likely prevent interjurisdictional agreement on a conflicts of law regime, and that a technological fix is most likely). *See also* Mark D. Rosen, *Exporting the Constitution*, 53 EMORY L.J. 171 (2004) (arguing that categorical refusal to enforce foreign judgments, which would not be constitutional if issued here, is an inappropriate effort to export the U.S. Constitution); *but see supra* note 1 (describing recent legislation and legislative proposals).

123. *See, e.g.*, Sanchez-Llamas v. Oregon, 548 U.S. 331, 344 & n.3 (2006) (discussing foreign public law on whether other countries would apply an exclusionary rule to preclude

evidentiary use of statements taken absent compliance with article 36 of the Vienna Convention on Consular Relations).

124. For a possible illustration, *see* the helpful discussion of the *Loewen* case, arising under the NAFTA Chapter 11 procedures, in Ahdieh, *supra* note 120, at 2036–44.

125. For discussion of extraterritorial prescriptive jurisdiction, *see, e.g.*, Anthony J. Colangelo, *Constitutional Limits on Extraterritorial Jurisdiction: Terrorism and the Intersection of National and International Law*, 48 HARV. INT'L L.J. 121, 127–30 (2007); *see also* Rosen, *supra* note 122. International law, for example, recognizes jurisdiction by citizenship (active nationality), *see also* RESTATEMENT (THIRD) OF FOREIGN RELATIONS LAW, *supra* note 9, at § 402(2); but in the future, will citizenship alone remain a viable basis on which to regulate conduct anywhere in the world? Will the reciprocal interests of other nations (or, conceivably, a transnational right to travel) be brought to bear on this question in more complex ways?

126. *See, e.g.*, Judith Resnik et al., *Ratifying Kyoto at the Local Level: Sovereigntism, Federalism, and Translocal Organizations of Government Actors (TOGAs)*, 50 ARIZ. L. REV. 709, 719–20 (2008) (discussing translocal government organizations and cross-boundary agreements); Carole Silver, *The Case of the Foreign Lawyer: Internationalizing the U.S. Legal Profession*, 25 FORDHAM INT'L L.J. 1039 (2004); *see also* ANNE-MARIE SLAUGHTER, A NEW WORLD ORDER 131–215 (2004) (discussing networks of officials working together across national boundary lines).

127. *See* Mohamed v. President of the Republic of South Africa, 2001 (3) SA 893 (CC) (S. Afr.). The South African Constitutional Court found that the cooperation by South African officials with the removal of a Tanzanian, accused of participating in bombing U.S. embassies in Africa, violated the South African constitution, in part, because the alien was not given the opportunity to request that his deportation to the United States be conditioned on an agreement not to seek the death penalty, as one of his codefendants had successfully done. *See id.* at 914–15, 917. In rejecting the South African government's argument that because the defendant had already been removed there was nothing for it to rule on, the court noted that it wanted the trial court in New York to be aware of its conclusions concerning the illegality of the removal. *See id.*, at 922 (noting that defense counsel and the government disagreed on the relevance of the court's findings to the New York proceedings, but that it should be left to the U.S. trial court judge to decide). After declarations of unconstitutionality and invalidity over the removal of Mohamed, the South African court concluded its judgment as follows: "The Director of this Court is authorised and directed to cause the full text of this judgment to be drawn to the attention of and . . . delivered to the Director or equivalent administrative head of the Federal Court for the Southern District of New York as a matter of urgency." *Id.*, at 924. This occurred, and the judgment went to Judge Sand. Donald J. McNeil, Jr., *The Terror Verdict: The Reverberations: South Africa Regrets Its Role in a Defendant's Extradition*, N.Y. TIMES, May 31, 2001, at B4.

On defense counsel's motion, Judge Sand refused to rule out the death penalty as a matter of U.S. law, but held that the defense "may present to the jury, as a mitigating factor, the fact that the Constitutional Court has ruled that had the proper procedures been followed by South African authorities, Mohamed's delivery to United States officials would have been conditioned on an assurance that he would not be eligible for the death penalty." United States v. Bin Laden, 156 F. Supp. 2d 359, 362 (S.D.N.Y. 2001). Pursuant to the District Court's ruling, counsel for Mohamed argued the South African judgment to the New York jury considering whether or not to recommend a death sentence, urging the unfairness of sentencing the defendant to death when a codefendant, who had been extradited *with* assurances that no death penalty would be imposed, could not be. Lecture by Hon. Richard Goldstone, Georgetown University Law Center, Jan. 10, 2008; Benjamin Weiser, *Argument on Death Penalty for 2nd Convicted Terrorist*, N.Y. TIMES, June 20, 2001, at B2. The jury did not unanimously recommend the death penalty; eleven of twelve jurors found that others of similar culpability were not being sentenced to death (a mitigating factor), and Mohamed was sentenced to life in prison. *See* William Schabas, *Indirect Abolition: Capital Punishment's Role in Extradition Law and Practice*, 25 LOY. L.A. INT'L & COMP. L. REV. 581, 600–01 (2003).

128. David S. Law, *Generic Constitutional Law*, 89 MINN. L. REV. 652 (2005).

129. Jeremy Waldron, *Foreign Law and the Modern Ius Gentium*, 119 HARV. L. REV. 129 (2005); Jeremy Waldron, The Storrs Lectures: "'Partly Laws Common to All Mankind': Foreign Law in American Courts," Yale Law School (Sept. 10–12, 2007), *available at* http://www.law.yale.edu/news/5408.htm (available in writing in part at http://iilj.org/courses/2008iiljcolloqium.asp).

130. *See* Michael C. Dorf & Charles F. Sabel, *A Constitution of Democratic Experimentalism*, 98 COLUM. L. REV. 267, 288–89 (1998).

131. *See, e.g.*, YASMIN NUHOĞLU SOYSAL, LIMITS OF CITIZENSHIP: MIGRANTS AND POSTNATIONAL MEMBERSHIP IN EUROPE (1994); *cf.* JÜRGEN HABERMAS, THE INCLUSION OF THE OTHER: STUDIES IN POLITICAL THEORY 107, 226 (2000) (arguing for the idea of constitutional patriotism, of universal legal values embedded in historically specific cultures, in a postnational society).

132. Anna Yeatman, *The Idea of the Constitutional State and Global Society*, 8 LAW TEXT CULTURE 83, 83–84 (2004).

133. For normative defenses of national states, see Martti Koskenniemi, *The Future of Statehood*, 32 HARV. INT'L L.J. 397 (1991) (arguing that in the face of persistent diversity and disagreement, national states are the best method to assure that modernism's authoritarianism does not overwhelm its liberalism); Vicki C. Jackson, *Citizenships, Federalisms and Gender, in* MIGRATIONS AND MOBILITIES: CITIZENSHIPS, BORDERS AND GENDER 439 (Seyla Benhabib & Judith Resnik eds., 2009) (arguing that the territorially based government of national states provides a useful space for public participation at some remove from familial and ascriptive group identities, a space rooted "in a shared geography of everyday life," that links legal equality commitments and their implementing mechanisms "to the particularized communities of identity that human beings seem to need"); *cf.* Weiler, *supra* note 31, at 247 (describing "territoriality" as an "elemental bonding agent"). *But cf.* JEAN-MARIE GUÉHENNO, THE END OF THE NATION-STATE 111–12 (Victoria Elliott trans. 1995) (suggesting that nation-states "are no more" in a world of networks and diffusions of power).

134. SLAUGHTER, *supra* note 126, at 243 (suggesting that the U.S. Court "might well try to argue for the US approach as compared to less speech protective doctrines applied in other countries. . .").

135. *Id.* at 247 (discussing principle of "legitimate difference").

136. Mayo Moran has been a particularly astute observer of related phenomena, arguing that cases such as *Baker v. Canada (Minister of Citizenship and Immigration)*, [1999] 2 SCR 817 (Can.) and *Minister of State for Immigration & Ethnic Affairs v. Teoh* (1995) 183 C.L.R. 273 (Austl.), should be understood as ones in which international law is without binding force, but has mandatory effect in the sense that it must be considered. *See* Mayo Moran, *Authority, Influence and Persuasion: Baker, Charter Values and the Puzzle of Method*, in THE UNITY OF PUBLIC LAW 389-414 (David Dyzenhaus ed., 2004) (focusing on ratified but not yet implemented or domestically incorporated conventions in Canada and Australia). She has observed a similar development of what she has termed "influential authority" in

constitutional adjudication's effects on 'private law' issues within a single system, as well as across national boundaries. Mayo Moran, *Inimical to Constitutional Values, supra* note 41, at 233–34, 236–40, 253–54. *Cf.* Walker, *supra* note 57, at 339 (referring to the "relational" dimension "between constitutional units"). In a posture of deliberative engagement, clear international law or a strong transnational consensus could be considered and might prompt interpretive self-reflection; in more relational postures, courts would feel an obligation to consider and to explain their responses, especially if a court reaches a different conclusion.

137. *See* Chapter 6, above.

138. Notwithstanding the fragility of distinctions between "norms" and "information," *see* Chapter 3, note 82 above, the distinction captures something important about how law is experienced as a constraint by many judges and lawyers. And postures of "resistance" or indifference to transnational ideas will not, in fact, insulate "law" from those ideas. Legal ideas—like ideas more generally—travel in many ways other than through conscious borrowings. *Cf.* William Ewald, *The Jurisprudential Approach to Comparative Law: A Field Guide to "Rats,"* 46 AM. J. COMP. L. 701 (1998) (arguing for a comparative study of law that focuses on the "ideas at work" in a foreign legal system, as an alternative approach to viewing legal texts as relatively autonomous, or to viewing law as entirely contextualized within a particular society).

139. A posture of relational engagement may be less inclined to see, even metaphorically, the norms of a national constitution as entirely "closed." *See* Chapter 3, above, text at notes 81–82.

140. Slaughter & Burke-White, *supra* note 109, at 128–29.

141. *See* S.C. Res. 1373, UN Doc. S/RES/1373 (Sept. 28, 2001). *Cf.* Frank Hoffmeister, *International Decision: Bosphorus Hava Yollari Turizm ve Ticaret Anomin Sirket v. Ireland,* 100 AM. J. INT'L L. 442, 447 (2006) (Daniel Bodanksy, ed.) (describing the ECtHR as "develop[ing] a new theory of justifying interferences in human rights—one based on the need to comply with obligations arising out of an international act").

142. Andreas L. Paulus, *The Emergence of the International Community and the Divide Between International and Domestic Law, in* NEW PERSPECTIVES ON THE DIVIDE BETWEEN NATIONAL AND INTERNATIONAL LAW, *supra* note 34, at 230; *see also* Kim Lane Scheppele, *Other People's Patriot Acts: Europe's Response to September 11,* 50 LOY. L. REV. 89, 91–93 (2004); *cf.* Mary Robinson, *Shaping Globalization: The Role of Human Rights,* 19 AM. U. INT'L L. REV. 1, 12 (2003) (noting "repressive new laws and detention practices" in a number of countries, "all broadly justified by the new international war on terrorism").

143. *See* Joined Cases C-402/05 and C-415/05, Kadi and Al Barakaat Int'l Found. v. Council and Comm'n, paras. 281–85, 333–53 (Eur. Ct. Justice, Grand Chamber) (Sept. 3, 2008), *available at* http://curia.europa.eu/en/transitpage.htm (select "Case Law," then select "Search form," then enter "C-402/05) (holding invalid certain regulations adopted by the Council to implement UN Security Council Resolutions because individuals' rights to be heard and to effective judicial review were not respected). The Court indicated that the individuals whose assets were frozen were not entitled to prior notice or opportunity to contest the freeze order, but were entitled to such an opportunity "within a reasonable period" afterward. *Id.* paras. 341–52. The Court stayed its order for three months to allow the Council to revise its approach while the freeze order remained in effect. *Id.* paras. 373–76. For helpful analysis of the opinion, see Daniel Halberstam & Eric Stein, *The United Nations, the European Union and the King of Sweden: Economic Sanctions and Individual Rights in a Plural World Order* (Working Paper, Dec. 2008), forthcoming, 46 COMMON MARKET L. REV. (2009), *available at* http://papers.ssrn.com/sol3/papers.

cfm?abstract_id=1312082. *Cf.* Mattias Kumm, *Democratic Constitutionalism Encounters International Law: Terms of Engagement, in* THE MIGRATION OF CONSTITUTIONAL IDEAS 256, 282–91 (Sujit Choudhry ed. 2006) (discussing domestic review of international legal decisions so as to "[p]reclud[e] the migration of unconstitutional ideas," in context of decisions by ECJ and ECtHR in the "Bosphorus" case, concerning Ireland's impoundment of a plane under European regulations designed to implement a UN Security Council Resolution); Hoffmeister, *supra* note 141.

144. *See, e.g.*, Peter Drahos & John Braithwaite, *Intellectual Property, Corporate Strategy, Globalisation: TRIPS in Context*, 20 WIS. INT'L L.J. 451 (2002); A. Samuel Oddi, *TRIPS—Natural Rights and a "Polite Form of Economic Imperialism,"* 29 VAND. J. TRANSNAT'L L. 415, 459–60 (1996); Susan K. Sell, *Trade Issues and HIV/AIDS*, 17 EMORY INT'L L. REV. 933, 934–35 (2003).

145. *Cf.* BALAKRISHNAN RAJAGOPAL, INTERNATIONAL LAW FROM BELOW: DEVELOPMENT, SOCIAL MOVEMENTS AND THIRD WORLD RESISTANCE (2003) (exploring how social movements have both resisted and sought to influence international law); Boaventura de Sousa Santos & César A. Rodríguez-Garavito, *Law, Politics and the Subaltern in Counter-Hegemonic Globalization, in* LAW AND GLOBALIZATION FROM BELOW: TOWARDS A COSMOPOLITAN LEGALITY 14–15, 20 (Boaventura de Sousa Santos & César A. Rodríguez-Garavito eds., 2005) (arguing that most of the world's population needs "a different type of cosmopolitanism," a counter-hegemonic cosmopolitanism that will work toward the "reconstruction of human rights," especially through increased emphasis on socioeconomic and collective rights). For a thoughtful treatment of how legal concepts vary in the degree to which they can "travel," see William Twining, *Have Concepts, Will Travel: Analytical Jurisprudence in a Global Context*, 1 INT'L J. LAW IN CONTEXT 5, 35 (2005) (quoting Clifford Geertz's concern about "'mistak[ing] convergence of vocabularies for convergence of views'").

146. *See* David Kennedy, *The International Human Rights Movement: Part of the Problem?*, 15 HARV. HUM. RTS. J. 99, 118–19 (2002) (describing concerns that human rights regimes do "More To Produce and Excuse Violations than To Prevent" them and that "human rights has become a standard part of the justification for the external use of force by the state against other states and individuals").

147. *Cf.* Slaughter & Burke-White, *supra* note 109, at 129 (discussing domestic checks and balances as a factor to consider in distinguishing those national states whose internal structures will be likely to "further international legal objectives" from those that will not); SLAUGHTER, *supra* note 126, at 254–56 (arguing that disaggregation of the state enables "government institutions of the same type in different systems, national and international . . . [to] check each other . . .: [n]ational courts can resist the excessive assertion of supranational judicial power; supranational courts can review the performance of national courts").

148. McCulloch v. Maryland, 17 U.S. (4 Wheat.) 316, 415 (1819).

TABLE OF CASES

INDEX